A Political History
of the Bible in America

A Political History
of the Bible in America

PAUL D. HANSON

WESTMINSTER
JOHN KNOX PRESS
LOUISVILLE · KENTUCKY

© 2015 Paul D. Hanson

First edition
Published by Westminster John Knox Press
Louisville, Kentucky

15 16 17 18 19 20 21 22 23 24—10 9 8 7 6 5 4 3 2 1

Book design by Sharon Adams
Cover design by Allison Taylor
Cover photo ©iStock.com/TokenPhoto

Library of Congress Cataloging-in-Publication Data

Hanson, Paul D.
  A political history of the Bible in America / Paul D. Hanson.
    pages cm
  ISBN 978-0-664-26039-2 (alk. paper)
1. United States--Church history. 2. Bible and politics--United States. 3. Politics in the Bible. 4. Christianity and politics--United States. I. Title.
  BR515.H36 2015
  220.0973--dc23

                                                                    2015002917

Most Westminster John Knox Press books are available at special quantity discounts when purchased in bulk by corporations, organizations, and special-interest groups. For more information, please e-mail SpecialSales@wjkbooks.com.

To My Grandchildren:

Lilja

Gabriel

Nicholas

Winslow

Christopher

Joshua

Andrew

Contents

Preface

Politics is virtually synonymous with controversy, and religion frequently sparks discord both within a given faith community, between religious bodies, and among the nonreligious. Combine religion and politics, and a climate arises that can degenerate into rancor and conflict.

Yet the practice of infusing public discourse with teachings drawn from personal belief is deeply ensconced in the American consciousness. The contributions of religiously inspired movements to social reform and courageous leaders who awaken the conscience of the nation in the crusade for universal justice and equal rights and opportunities for all are often pivotal in the life of the nation. But when religious beliefs inflame partisan passions leading to conflict, remonstrance is understandable. From secular as well as religious segments of society, the call arises to keep faith out of politics, either because its effects on public debate are deemed to be toxic or because faith is understood as an individual's personal relationship with God that becomes tainted when mixed with politics.

Two strategies aim to preserve a place for religion in the public forum. Advocates of civil religion present a genial concept of religiosity that is sufficiently broad to embrace adherents of all faiths. Reacting against the alleged doctrinal vagueness and tepidity of "liberal religion," the second strategy asserts a bold, uncompromising version of faith that denounces attempts at accommodation. This politically assertive strategy in turn is shaped in service of two distinct theologies: one growing out of a politically reenergized wing of Evangelical Christianity, the other embracing a communitarian strand of reformed theology.

From this religio-political landscape arises the contours of our task. That task is impelled by two convictions that stand together in a tensive relationship that can either kindle the flames of cultural warfare or inspire initiatives dedicated to reawakening commitment to global justice, economic equality, and healing of an endangered environment. On one side is the mandate to incorporate the moral resources of all communities of conscience in a manner that does not set as a condition for full engagement a reduction of their convictions and beliefs to the lowest common denominator of civil religion but enables them to contribute wholeheartedly from the specificity and purity of their traditions. On the other side is the cultivation of civility in public debate leading to a vision of the common good and enlisting the public resources required for its fulfillment. A study capable of preserving this tensive relationship will inevitably require an approach that is respectful of the core beliefs of all participating communities and compatible with religious pluralism within the framework of the First Amendment. The question becomes, how do we reach the goal of the cultural blending of moral passion with inclusive civility?

Such blending is a complex matter. As is clear from the inconsistent nature of Supreme Court decisions bearing on religion and public policy, no paradigm exists that is capable of settling disputes once and for all, be it derived from the Constitution or from the history of judicial pronouncements. As for arguments invoking scriptural warrants, the picture is even more bewildering with opposing sides on issues like abortion and gay marriage citing Bible verses in endless conflict that discredits religion in the minds of many thoughtful citizens. Arising from this culturally and religiously complex phenomenon is an agenda that determines the structure of this book.

In the prologue we present a style of political discourse that is both intimately communitarian and broadly inclusive. It is predicated on the notion that personal and public attitudes and actions arise under the identity-shaping influence of stories. When stories are dominated by bigotry and violence, the influence they exercise is deleterious, whereas stories of healing and liberation contribute to the shaping of virtue and good-hearted civility. When the latter stories are shared, the moral capital of the host society is enriched.

In part 1 we apply the metaphor of story to the unfolding of the Epic that shapes American identity. What we discover is a legacy mixing instances of moral progress with impenitent failures in a nation seeking to define itself in relation to its own people, other nations, and the natural environment. Politically the picture is open-ended, as leaders and their constituencies devise different institutional structures in response to a changing world. Yet that picture is neither arbitrary nor capricious; indeed, over the course of four centuries it has been customary for American political and religious leaders to ascribe to Providence the growth and prosperity of the nation. Sadly, however, the full potential of religion to cultivate a society and world order in which the benefits of freedom and opportunity are placed within the reach of all has been trammeled by notions of imperial privilege, exceptionalism, manifest destiny, and discrimination. To gain a solid footing for understanding the mixed legacy of American political history, it is necessary to turn to the more ancient Epic from which the leaders of our nation, from colonial times to the present, and for better or for worse, derived justification for their actions. That Epic is the Bible.

Part 2 traces the millennium-long growth of that Epic with attention to the manner in which religious beliefs were translated into political institutions within the context of an ever-changing world. Given the common tendency for interpreters of the Bible to manipulate Scripture into the service of their personal political ideologies, a method is called for that will allow the ancient texts to speak in their own voices. That method is commonly called historical criticism, inasmuch as it is intended to clarify as accurately as possible the original meaning of a text, its author and audience, its original and subsequent settings. As a tool, it is neutral as regards theological or philosophical convictions, and hence it can facilitate the research of theists, atheists, and secularists, thereby providing a hospitable discursive common ground for adherents of diverse worldviews.

Subsequent to shared historical reconstruction, however, a choice presents itself. The path of interpretation pursued in this book goes beyond neutrality by identifying with the testimony of the Bible that God acts redemptively within the concrete events of human experience and enlists mortals like ourselves as witnesses to the meaning and goal of history and creation. For Christians, Jesus of Nazareth does not represent an exception to this historicist perspective, but serves as the paragon of God's presence in the midst of human experience. This explains the fullness of our treatment of the words and acts of the historical Jesus as well as the story of Jesus Christ in the four Gospels.

Paragon, however, implies neither exclusivity nor supersession. Rather the unity of Scripture is secured by a theme that is woven from beginning to end in the canon and generously weaves into its fabric many extracanonical writings as well. That theme we call the Bible's "theocratic principle," which is the political iteration of the First Commandment. While testimony to God's presence in the everyday lives of ordinary people is foundational to an authentic political interpretation of the Bible, a clear understanding of God as the universal sovereign constitutes its heart. For from that understanding alone arises the standard against which human governments can be held accountable: Given that God's sovereignty alone is ultimate, all mundane regimes are penultimate at best, and that only to the degree that they mediate the qualities of God's reign in the domain of the provisional structures of human government. To ascribe any higher status to the institutions of this world constitutes idolatry.

Application of the theocratic principle to the successive stages of biblical history leads to a significant discovery: No single authoritative biblical model of government can be found. Rather six distinct models are found arising in response to the ever-changing world in which the community of faith lived and to which it was forced to adjust. No clearer evidence could be given in support of the thesis that politics is a phenomenon that unfolds in the realm of the provisional and the ephemeral. It follows that persons of faith must live as sojourners whose true allegiance is reserved for God alone. And it is that identity that provides the foundation for authentic, albeit restrained, patriotism.

In the postscript we translate the insights gleaned from our exploration of the open-ended nature of stories and the dynamic character of the American and biblical Epic into a theo-political hermeneutic or, in plain English, a theory for applying biblical politics to the challenging issues of the contemporary world. Because those verities present themselves not as timeless abstractions but as applications to the concrete circumstances of human history of what inspired prophets and sages came to understand to be the nature of God's reign, theo-political interpretation is not a mechanical exercise. An ancient Scripture must be allowed to speak to a contemporary situation in its own voice, and this is possible only when careful attention is paid to the contemporary applicability of a given text.

Essential to the task of theo-political interpretation is preservation of the beliefs and values of each participating party or community within a climate of respect and civility that defends the right of open expression as robustly for others as for oneself. Such nonpolarizing public discourse is possible only to the extent that deeply held convictions are placed in the service of projects and policies fostering the common good.

Before turning to the task at hand, it is only fitting that I acknowledge the crucial role played in the shaping of my own story by two dear friends and colleagues: S. Dean McBride and Patrick D. Miller. Owing to the influence of these two Presbyterians, a Lutheran was able to appreciate the profound significance of theocracy in the Bible and the sublime beauty in the psalmist's praise of God. To a younger scholar, Tim Castner, I owe a huge debt of gratitude for his careful research on the role played by the Bible in American history. I consider it my good fortune to have benefited from the editorial skills of Bridgett Green and Julie Tonini at Westminster John Knox Press. A solid start to the process of organizing my thoughts on the Bible and politics in written form was provided by the year I spent as a Henry Luce III Fellow at the Center of Theological Inquiry in Princeton, New Jersey. Finally, I express heartfelt appreciation to my wife, Cynthia, whose loving patience and encouragement enabled me to complete this study.

Notwithstanding the contributions of scholars in many fields, faults remain, for which I take full responsibility. But the burden that imparts is lifted by my confidence that future generations will continue to tell identity-shaping stories. To seven of those storytellers I dedicate this book.

Prologue

Story, Identity, and Making Sense of the Bible

I can only answer the question, "What am I to do?" if I can answer the prior question, "Of what story or stories do I find myself a part?"
—Alasdair MacIntyre[1]

ENABLING STORIES

At the end of an archaeological season, it is a pleasant sight to ascend the photography tower and look back over a freshly dug section of the *tel*: A checkerboard of five-meter squares separated by walls, called balks, consisting of one meter of soil that has been left undisturbed. In the soft light of the sinking sun, the one-meter balks stand out, revealing through their hues of tan and red and gray the layers of civilization that have been uncovered in the past months of digging. Records have been kept of the findings discovered in each square, and the evidence from those excavated areas survives only in the notebooks of the field supervisors and in buckets of carefully numbered shards.

From a material point of view, archaeology is a destructive science. What has taken millennia to deposit can be removed in a season. Therein lies the importance of the meter-wide balks that remain: A trace of history is left for future generations to revisit in the ongoing task of recovering the past.

---

1. Alasdair MacIntyre, *After Virtue: A Study in Moral Theory* (Notre Dame, IN: University of Notre Dame Press, 1981), 250.

1

Looking closely, the observer detects colored tags attached to the balks at what appear to be random intervals. But they are not arbitrarily placed, for they mark significant strata in the long sequence of humanity's mute deposit. A gray layer flecked with black chunks of charred wood is interpreted as evidence of Thutmose III's destructive invasion of Canaan. A reddish layer is tagged as belonging to an early stage of the Iron Age on the basis of a distinctive pottery type interpreted by the expedition director as evidence of newcomers in Canaan whom Pharaoh Heremhab had named "the people Israel." In this manner, pieces of evidence are assembled that shed light on the development of civilization and offer glimpses into our shared identity as human beings.

The "stratigraphy" preserving traces of our past is also found closer to home than a Middle Eastern archaeological site. We grow up surrounded by stories in both written and oral form, some describing our ancestral roots in terms of religious traditions, some drawing on our nation's Epic, some retelling personal experiences. Such stories play an important role in the way we live and the choices we make, for the values and aspirations that guide us generally take less the form of abstract principles than of inclinations and intuitions rooted in our sense of origins.[2] By *sense* of origins, we imply something quite distinct from an objective newsreel account. What we retain and what guides us are not an exhaustive documentary, but a personal narrative with a plotline defining us as heirs to a distinct legacy. This is to say that we understand our essential being in historical terms, defined by philosophy as *historical ontology* and by ethnography in terms of myth/epic and ritual. Highlighted, like the colored tags in the balk, are episodes that retain for us a special significance in shaping our understanding of who we are and what purpose guides our lives into the future. We call such special memories *paradigms*.

As I look to my own past, I recall vividly the following episode that, in its blending of tradition and personal experience, imprinted itself on my consciousness in such a way as to assume paradigmatic force in shaping my sensibilities. When I was nine I received my first weapon, an air rifle. Brimming with manly pride, I entered the forest behind my home; spotting movement in a tree, I took aim and fired. Much to my surprise a bird fell to the ground, a very colorful bird that turned out to be a downy woodpecker. Not knowing whether to be proud or ashamed, I carried it home. My father chanced to meet me as I entered the yard. A conversation ensued that amid parental reprimand and juvenile sobbing became etched into my memory and helped shape my attitude toward nature for the rest of my life. To be sure, my heart had already been prepared for such a lesson by Sunday school Bible stories like Noah's ark brimming with beautiful creatures. Future experiences amplified the lesson taught by my father's

---

2. In many traditional cultures, storytellers are venerated for the role they play in keeping alive the values of a tribe that are embedded in their stories. Martin Nkafu Nkemnkia expresses this point succinctly: "[Storytellers] are the memory of the people, because they preserve the values of the tribe in the absence of any written form" (*African Vitalogy: A Step Forward in African Thinking* [Nairobi, Kenya: Paulines Publications, 1999], 157).

reaction to my kill, like my study of Native American tradition in college that added Chief Seattle's letter to Congress to my personal canon and powerfully reinforced my respect for all forms of life and my abhorrence of wanton slaughter. Later still, I embraced as a model the delicate balance achieved by medieval Benedictine monasteries between human needs and the dignity of all other forms of life.

Page by page our life stories unfold. From them we derive a sense of direction, ethical values, and in fortunate cases generosity of spirit and contentment with life. For many, an important dimension in the life story is religious in nature.

A number of years ago, a handful of students and I invited to lunch a professor of psychology to discuss his research on the roots of human happiness. One student asked, "Aside from the genes we inherit, please name the source of happiness that most clearly emerged from your study." "Religion," my colleague replied. Something deep inside of me nodded assent, for I have long experienced weekly celebration of the Eucharist as the wellspring of a profound sense of peace and joy. That is understandable, given the fact that that simple meal was as much a staple in my childhood home as my mother's scrumptious Sunday dinner that followed.

Similarly, the fact that prayer has been a central part of my life surely has roots in my childhood experience of witnessing my father on his knees at his bedside as I passed (due to the peculiar floor plan of our modest home) through his bedroom to mine. Add to that the example of my mother, ahead of her time with her peripatetic version of "meals on wheels" for all in town who were ill and a kitchen well known to the hoboes who traveled the rail line through our mining town as a reliable source of Swedish meatballs and scalloped potatoes. Thus it was that religion, most of it embodied and unself-conscious, opened my eyes to the presence of meaning, even transcendent meaning, in all that surrounded me.

But what about the strains and pains caused by facets of one's tradition that seem inadequate in the search for an understanding of life's experiences? The intertwining of the warp of tradition and the weft of personal experience is not always genial. Knots appear. Threads fray and snap. In such cases, does one find it necessary to cast off what has been received like a tattered garment? Not necessarily, especially if one is heir to a tradition capable of transforming challenges into opportunities for growth.

Recently I began a seminar on genealogy in the Bible with an exercise in which each student presented a brief oral account of his or her life story, with attention both to events that had special importance in shaping personal identity (*paradigms*) and to the narrative thread that unified diverse life experiences into a sense of identity and purpose (*epic*). Since the setting was a divinity school, it is not surprising that religious roots were repeatedly mentioned, though there was wide variation in the nature of the relationship between student and tradition. One young woman, raised within an Irish Catholic family, had been drawn to the feminist orientation of a Unitarian Universalist congregation. A Methodist, after being shaken by several traumatic experiences during college, found in Greek Orthodoxy a home that addressed her deepest spiritual and emotional needs. A middle-aged man, descendant from a long line of Presbyterian ministers, was receiving instruction in Reformed Judaism. A young man raised within an Amish community was exploring a decidedly Epicurean lifestyle. Other cases were characterized by a greater degree of continuity. A woman of Armenian descent described a childhood of growing up in a close-knit Eastern Orthodox community that still served her and her own family well, even though she had adopted a more critical stance vis-à-vis all institutions. A student with a history of depression had found in his family's Adventist congregation a safe and supportive spiritual home that helped him develop the confidence that he could recover from recurring dark periods of self-doubt and despair.

Walking home from class, I recalled my own pilgrimage within the Lutheran Church, one characterized by change, not only in my own religious understanding, but in some of the policies of my denomination as well. But throughout, even when introduction to a historical-critical approach to study of the Bible led me as a freshman in college into a dark period of doubt, my tradition provided sufficient constancy at the core, combined with elasticity on the margins, for me to ask questions, to test assumptions, and to grow in faith and understanding.[3]

When strains and tensions do arise in one's relation to tradition, dreams can be swift to respond. At a midpoint in career and family life, I found myself in a dream at work in my basement wood shop, where I observed cement flaking off of a section of the fieldstone wall. As I scraped off more and more mortar and began removing the granite stones, a large glass patio door appeared. Just outside of it grew a lush tropical garden, lavishly arrayed in orchids and cyclamens. Directly beyond my private Eden lay a field covered with sparkling snow, with antique farm implements protruding through the white blanket. Just as I positioned myself to slide open the door to begin exploring, I recognized that I was gazing over the backyard of my childhood home and into the face of my recently deceased mother, as she peered through the window of our little red garage and, with a sternness I had never before seen on her loving face, lipped the urgent message, "It is time for church!"

Though some religious communities construe tradition as a rigid edifice guarding occupants from the world outside and accordingly repudiate the challenges of the wider culture, my experience was more flexible. In my life there has always been time for church. But the biblical-confessional congregation of

---

3. As if I were in need of a reminder that not all who are raised within a religious tradition respond to intellectual challenges to their faith in the way I did, I recently read a blog about Todd Stiefel, an ex-Catholic and currently the generous financial supporter of a nationwide atheist movement, in which he is quoted describing his response to encounter with a historical-critical approach to the Bible in a course at Duke University: "Wait a second, is what I believe in really the truth or is it really the accumulation of myths bundled in a package? That was the end of my faith right there." "The money man behind atheism's activism," http://religion.blogs.cnn.com/2013/03/23/the-money-man-behind-atheisms-activism/

which I am a lifelong member has welcomed dialogue with other perspectives and has not shied away from social challenges.

My spiritual growth can be compared to the dwelling in which Cynthia and I raised our children and continue to live. After taking occupancy as a young couple, we converted its Victorian single-family configuration into a 1970s-style commune for ourselves and two other young couples. As our family grew, walls were moved, an addition was built, and a fence was placed around the yard. What remained constant were roof, walls, and hearth providing safety and warmth against the rain and cold. Continuity and change similarly have characterized my religious home, for it has fostered a living faith, compassionate ethical principles, and examples of virtue that have provided direction throughout my life, but never in such a way as to stultify the benefit of encounters with alternative perspectives on life.

Flexibility capable of accommodating change becomes particularly important in the encounter with cultures or religions differing from one's own. Some religious groups respond defensively, either by avoiding contact with "the other" or permitting contact strictly on unilaterally determined conditions. Why people erect walls of defense is understandable: To be genuinely open to an understanding of life that differs from one's own can be threatening, especially to one who is less than secure in one's own spiritual home. But walls diminish rather than enhance understanding, while border crossings can lead to remarkable enrichment of the stories that guide and shape us.

Consider this family experience. Our family was in the midst of a sabbatical year in southern Germany when the question arose: Should we take our three young children to Dachau? Not irrelevant to the question is the fact that Cynthia and I are heirs to a religious tradition rich in cultural and intellectual achievement, but disgraced by the complicity of the *Deutsche Kirche* during the Third Reich that culminated in the Holocaust. After considerable heart searching, we boarded a train to face the dark side of a tradition whose founder, Martin Luther, had authored alongside brilliant theological writings vitriolic diatribes against Jews and Turks.

The Dachau visit was traumatic beyond anything we could have imagined. Most deeply affected was eight-year-old Mark, whose innocent mind grasped what few adults can comprehend, that Evil can grow into monstrous proportions, defying limits we normally attribute to individual humans. We began to doubt our parental wisdom: Had we not elevated moral rigor above simple loving care of our children?

Then a miracle unfolded. A stranger crossed over a border to join us on the picnic blanket where we were trying in vain to comfort our distraught son. Though Sid Feldman's manner was informal, he possessed the rare gift of a *hacham* (wise teacher). "What did you folks do this afternoon?" "How could Hitler do that to those good people?" Mark sobbed. "Because he was a very sick man . . ." and the message with which Mr. Feldman continued in a language comprehensible to children was essentially this: "Hate is a terrible and scary thing. It hurts good people. But there is something very beautiful and far stronger in the world than hate. It is love."

We learned that it was love that each year brought this man from Hartford, Connecticut, to Dachau, to the very prison that had etched the number tattooed on his arm. His message was as simple as it was profound: "Love is more powerful than all the hatred in the world."

In the months that followed, in which Mark awoke from nightmares screaming that Hitler was pursuing him, it was Sid Feldman's words that were most effective in calming his soul. Long after the terror had gone, the childhood family experience of border crossing imprinted indelibly onto Mark's life story a lesson regarding what it is to be authentically human. As for my own story, I remember that the *shalom* with which this wonderful man bade farewell embraced in an exquisite moment all the stories of bondage and freedom and the ultimate triumph of universal love that I as a Christian have received from his people's Scripture.

FRIGHTENING STORIES

Thus far we have been reflecting on the interplay of personal experiences and inherited tradition as a basically positive phenomenon, not without tensions to be sure, but in balance leading to a sense of self within the larger world that equips one for the new challenges that life is sure to bring. Sadly, though, memory can also become the repository of an inner turmoil that obstructs efforts to find happiness and meaning. Many people are crippled by intimations of dread rooted in experiences of violence at the hands of those responsible for their safety. Particularly pernicious is the experience of abuse within one's own household, for if one cannot depend on protection from cruelty and shame within one's home, on what basis can a foundation of trust be built for other relationships? Commonly the deposit of inner chaos left by domestic abuse gives rise to depression and suicidal tendencies as well as the perpetuation of abuse in succeeding generations.

A *Boston Globe* report on domestic violence described the plight of eighteen-year-old Tammy Jo, a victim of abuse at the hands of her mother's boyfriend since the age of eleven: "Rarely leaving her father's one-bedroom apartment, she chain-smokes cigarettes that engulf her in a haze of smoke symbolizing her inner confusion. 'I guess I need help,' she says. 'I'm all stressed out. They say I'm depressed. I don't know what's going to happen to me.'" The probation officer assigned to Tammy Jo's case observes that her plight is endemic to the poverty-stricken sections of rural and small-town Massachusetts: "The chaos is a diversion from the boredom, from the feeling of uselessness and powerlessness in these communities. These people live life really on the cuff. They go from emotion to emotion. For them to maintain any kind of purpose in their lives, they truly need this chaos."[4]

4. Ellen O'Brien and David Armstrong, "Rape, child abuse, neglect," *The Boston Globe*, March 10, 1997, A6.

The downward spiral that traps people whose chaotic past vitiates hope for the future and a sense of direction in life is like a black hole ever sucking in new victims. Abuse breeds abuse and consumes victims and perpetrators alike. Caregivers working with such people are often plagued with the fear that they are dealing with insuperable odds and have arrived on the scene too late to help.

The disintegration of the sanctity and safety of the home and the breakdown of personal self-respect and purpose rapidly spread their cancerous effects into the larger society. School safety is jeopardized by rifle-bearing pupils. Adolescents developmentally at a stage for watching cartoons and building with Legos enter streets prepared to kill, lest they themselves fall victim to rival-gang assaults. Humans cannot thrive in the absence of a story, and lacking the positive kind of story that fosters self-worth, love of learning, and the patient pursuit of vocational goals, an alternative story marked by self-destructive habits and violence is likely to grow, ensconced in the motto of Nick Romano in the 1950s novel *Death at an Early Age*: "Live fast, die young, and have a good looking corpse," a motto that has modulated into an even more lethal version in contemporary rap glorifying cop killing as a prelude to getting one's own brains blown out.

The young authors of these sinister stories are not acting on their own but are participants in a wider loop. Their tutors and editors come from many segments of society: parents more committed to professional careers than nurturance of their children; politicians ranking reelection ahead of bipartisan strategies for accessible health care, equal vocational opportunity, and quality education; leaders in the advertising and entertainment industries flouting moral principles in promoting their products; and financiers showing no shame in their public display of greed and profligate luxury.[5]

Unfortunately, forgetfulness is one characteristic with which prosperous Americans seem richly endowed, forgetfulness that economic bubbles burst, inequality in the distribution of wealth is self-propelling, the ensuing social unrest spawns violence, and a chain is forged that historically has led to the decline and fall of proud empires. Also forgotten is the sobering fact that the plotline tracking the fate of a nation arises from an anthology in which the stories of all of its citizens are brought together, from those suffering deprivation in inner-city slums to those living in gated communities protected from angry fellow citizens by private police. The failure of our society to clarify its public values and to set priorities for improving the quality of life of *all* citizens is threatening to split the American epic down the middle, with one half trumpeting the smug theme, *We've worked hard and deserve our wealth and bear no*

5. An impassioned plea for moral awakening: "I think that we have lived for a very, very long time in a beautiful country, in a beautiful life, and it's made us quite lazy—certainly to the extent that we can barely remember that we are at war—because we don't have to give *anything* up, at any moment in our life. We have no seeming responsibility to a larger whole. This book is a call to that responsibility, a call at least to consider it, because the father is saying to his thrice-blessed sons, 'You have a responsibility to the world. You can't have received so much, and be willing to only follow your own heart's desire.' I think that's really endemic to our country right now, and it's something that I am very obsessed with" (From "A Conversation with Ann Patchett," one of several postscripts included in her novel *Run* [New York: HarperCollins Publishers, 2007], 9).

responsibility to others (or as Elizabeth Warren formulated it in her 2012 Democratic convention speech, "I've got mine, the rest of you are on your own"[6]), the other half sizzling with a countertheme, *Playing by the rules is futile when the rules are rotten, so we write our own rules to get our share.*

MISSING PAGES AND THE MENTORING ROLE OF SOCIETY

Life stories, besides containing positive and negative pages, sometimes include blank pages or pages missing entirely due to disruptions in the normal course of things or tragic events. Not uncommonly we read the story of an individual, separated since infancy or early childhood from a parent due to adoption or war, embarking on a search for a lost past. More is at play than an exercise in genealogical research, for something deep down feels an attachment to the missing person. Until the lost one is found, an aspect of one's identity remains enshrouded in obscurity. Blank and missing pages thus underscore the key role played by story in the human endeavor of identity formation and discovery of direction and meaning in life. The pages that are missing from the plotline of many individuals place upon the wider community a particularly solemn responsibility.

Social environment is a factor in moral development that is ignored at great peril. Since the quality of a society depends on the quality of its citizens, and at the same time environment affects human development, we are viewing a circular process. Complicating the picture is the debate among psychologists regarding the relation between nurture and nature. Rather than becoming mired in what is likely an insoluble conundrum, it is wise to acknowledge the irreducible mystery that is an essential part of every person. Do we not observe cases in which individuals rise above impoverishment and suffering to build lives filled with dignity and purpose? At the same time, common sense leads us to conclude regarding the interrelation between a good society and good citizens that one cannot exist without the other. Therefore, it should be accepted as a moral mandate that every civilized society create for all of its citizens (and especially its most vulnerable members) a stable and supportive environment conducive to fulfillment of life's full potential.

This in turn makes it the moral duty of every citizen to commit to the public task of ending inequality, discrimination, and unequal opportunity, which— sadly in the case of the United States—continue to spread in the very face of an accelerating concentration of wealth within 1 percent of the population. For far too long a land of promise has shirked its responsibility to foster an environment

---

6. "Transcript: Elizabeth Warren's Convention Speech," ABCNEWS.com, last modified September 5, 2012. http://abcnews.go.com/Politics/OTUS/transcript-elizabeth-warrens-democratic-convention-speech/story?id=17164726&singlePage=true. Compare the economic philosophy of Ayn Rand as seen through her protagonist John Galt in works such as *Atlas Shrugged* (New York: Plume, 1999).

in which each citizen has a fair chance to compose a life-affirming story. But this returns the discussion to the perennial circle: such an environment can be constituted only by a citizenry equipped with the requisite virtues to comprehend the severity of, and then take incisive action against, hunger, racism, classism, prejudice, and global conflict. But how in a religiously and ideologically diverse society that is respectful of liberty and religious freedom can such virtues be defined and cultivated?

FAMILY AND COMMUNITY AS THE PRIMAL TUTORS IN PERSONAL INTEGRITY AND PUBLIC VIRTUE

The launchpad for the cultivation of integrity and virtue is the individual's *primary* environment, namely, home and community, for there is written the introductory chapter that sets the direction for all that follows. This is a conclusion that has taken shape over the course of my forty-five years of teaching. Repeatedly my puzzling over the contrast between students who view the future with courage, hope, and generosity and those who labor under the burden of prejudice and insecurity that shrinks vocational plans to a competitive zero-sum contest aimed at wealth accumulation has led me back to the phenomenon of story. Aside from the genes we inherit at birth, what seems most determinative of happiness and fulfillment is the quality of the love and nurturance experienced in the seventeen years leading to high-school graduation. From my vantage point as a college professor, healthy students arrive with positive scripts. In conversations they speak fondly of relatives, teachers, religious leaders, and, above all, parents and guardians who have contributed to a robust sense of personal integrity and respect for others. By fostering in a child a vivid sense of his or her membership in a community of nurturance and purpose, by cultivating a home environment in which ample room is provided for reflection on childhood experiences as they unfold, and by providing a healthy balance between affirmation and moral expectations, parents and other involved adults function as tutors and editors in the important process of each child's writing a life story. With steadfast, loving cultivation, that story provides the foundation for a life filled with integrity, compassion, and moral principles. And one by one, citizens are trained in a life philosophy that can renew the moral vitality of a society.[7]

---

7. The strong influence of family experience on childhood development is supported by recent research. Bruce Feiler writes: "The single most important thing you can do for your family may be the simplest of all: develop a strong family narrative." He summarizes the findings of two psychologists, Sara Duke and Robyn Fivush: "The more children knew about their family's history, the stronger their sense of control over their lives, the higher their self-esteem and the more successfully they believed their families functioned" ("The Stories that Bind Us," *New York Times*, March 17, 2013, Sunday Styles, p. 10).

STORIES WRIT LARGE: GROUP IDENTITY

The line between individual identity and collective identity is fluid, for personal stories provide the threads that are woven into the narratives that craft a sense of honor and destiny for groups of people, whether defined by nationality, race, or religion.[8] The importance of a group's story is especially vital in the case of people with a past scarred by injustices and cruelties. "We don't know who we are apart from a history of oppression," wrote Debra Dickerson.[9] She described how groups of African Americans in the Chicago area assembled memorabilia of their parents' Mississippi homes in the effort to recover their sense of history. Alex Haley's book *Roots: The Saga of an American Family* and the television series that followed struck a deep chord in the American consciousness because African Americans as well as their lighter-skinned neighbors recognized in its chapters a poignant illustration of the importance of a communal account of origins. Especially within the ethnic diversity of American society, a sense of a people's past becomes an important part of its identity.

As other groups celebrate their festivals and customs, it is essential for the development of an individual's positive self-image to be able to display in story and enactment what it is that makes one's own group unique. Like the nautical chart spread out beside the captain at the helm of a ship, a sense of ethnic origins guides a community through a wide spectrum of ways of being human. Identity rooted in history becomes especially important when a group is assailed by the public display of negative images that can tear into the sense of pride and self-worth.

In the history of the United States, black churches (and more recently mosques) have contributed powerfully to the restoration of a sense of history to a people torn violently from their places of origin and then subjected to the dehumanizing effects of institutions (e.g., slavery followed by Jim Crow) designed to obliterate awareness of rooted identity. As James Cone has shown,[10] Negro spirituals blended biblical motifs with lived experiences in a way that fomented resistance to the twisted worldview of slave masters and built up a vision of the day when slaves could cast off their chains and be free at last.

The potential for reform that resides in tradition is illustrated profoundly by the life of Martin Luther King Jr. In one leader's career the biblical office of prophet was charged with a fresh formulation of the biblical themes of justice, compassion, and liberty, with the result that a movement that had languished since the evisceration of the Sixteenth Amendment by Jim Crow legislation was

---

8. Story is intended here in the broad sense of an account fulfilling an etiological function. As for specific genres, it may take the form of extended genealogy, historical narrative, epic, or myth.

9. Greg Jaffe, "Chicago Club Helps Blacks Reclaim their Southern Past," *Wall Street Journal*, March 12, 1997, A1.

10. James Cone, *The Spirituals and the Blues: An Interpretation* (New York; Seabury Press, 1972).

put back on a track with unstoppable force.[11] But reform is not a one-time event; it must be renewed in every generation.

Sadly, the miscreants of complacency, greed, and moral impoverishment staunched hopes for a just society in the decades following MLK's assassination. In a nation lacking the civic resolve to sustain a united offensive against economic injustice, a broken urban school system, inadequate health services for the poor, and a penal system more effective in criminalization than in rehabilitation,[12] frustration grew. The Occupy Wall Street movement provided a channel for the peaceful expression of dissatisfaction with the status quo. But unless business leaders begin to self-regulate on the basis of transparent ethical norms and members of Congress rediscover a productive bipartisan way to meet their constituents' demands to take action on the huge problems facing the nation, those dedicated to peaceful demonstrations could be sidelined by those disposed to violence. As in tragic moments of the past, the nation's story could turn ugly.

To the facile optimists and their prophets of weal who argue that the lessons of the past are sufficient to prevent the nation from falling into another major crisis, moral realists must point to the precipitous fall of Germany in the 1920s and '30s. Deep divisions over foreign policy combined with economic volatility handed to unscrupulous leaders the opportunity to produce a revised version of the nation's story that scorned all respect for historical fact, censored criticism, and punished dissent. National pride and the illusion of racial superiority trumped moral principles in promoting a policy of hatred, exclusion, and the resolution of domestic and international problems through military force. Leaders, disdainful of any aim besides the ultimate victory of their Fascist ideology, played on the wounded national pride that resulted from defeat in World War I and the perceived injustices of the Versailles Treaty to indoctrinate a whole generation of youth in the superiority of their race and the threat to purity posed by the mentally impaired, Roma, and Jews.

To be forgotten at great peril is the fragile nature of the stories to which nations appeal for identity, patriotism, and group pride. While national legends and epics can play an important humanizing role, it is sadly the case that tradition can be degraded to serve the goals of tyrants and demagogues. In the case of Nazi Germany, an Aryanized gospel wedded to a Teutonic myth of motherland produced a story promoting a nationalistic idolatry that in one crushing blow abolished the ethical standards of the Hebrew prophets, the reconciling gospel of Jesus Christ, and the whole span of moral philosophy from Plato and Aristotle to Kant and Hegel. Once the theocratic principle of the sole sovereignty of God was supplanted by idolatrous allegiance to the Fuehrer, and love of neighbor by unqualified devotion to the Aryan race, the moral restraints of law—whether construed in terms of natural law, civil law, or biblical tradition—evaporated. No longer was the

11. Cf. Taylor Branch, *Parting the Waters: America in the King Years 1954–63* (New York: Simon & Schuster, 1988).

12. A poignant description of our failed prison system can be found in Michelle Alexander, *The New Jim Crow: Mass Incarceration in the Age of Colorblindness* (New York: The New Press, 2012).

intrinsic dignity of every human being taught to the young. Gone was the goal of harmony among all the nations as an inference drawn from the notion of universal human rights. The pursuit of international understanding through negotiation yielded to a policy of world conquest. The execution of those who dared oppose the crimes of the regime demonstrates the moral abyss into which a nation can plunge, once it replaces a national conscience imbued with universally recognized moral principles with values predicated on the divinization of native land. The lesson taught by history is clear: a nation's story may enjoy monumental intellectual formulation in philosophy and theology as well as magisterial expression in art, but once hubris defeats modesty and racial supremacy extinguishes a deep respect for all cultures, calamity lurks in the gathering darkness. To our understanding of story a sobering dimension is thus added: stories stand in need of constant surveillance and critique, provided in the case of individuals by candid family members and friends and in the case of nations by a free press and the freedom of religious bodies to send their prophets to the citadels of economic, political, and military authority to speak truth to power.

Rather than learning from history, however, humans frequently choose to *repeat* history. In the decades following World War II the hatchet-style division of the spoils among the Allies and the subsequent growth of the Soviet Union into a nuclear world power again cast a dark cloud over the family of nations. Yet in less than a half century and with unexpected rapidity, the crumbling of Soviet control over eastern Europe culminating in the collapse of the Berlin Wall led to jubilation over the passing of the most recent example of nationalist idolatry and police-state control.

Though the restoration of liberty and the opportunity to rebuild democratic structures in the countries formerly under the repressive control of the Soviet Union awakened hope for a new era of world peace, that hope once again was short-lived. With the resurgence of ideological conflict and racial cleansing in Serbia, Bosnia, Rwanda, Zaire, the Sudan, Mali, and Syria, it has become clear that the assault on human rights has not ended, but merely morphed into a pernicious regional guise. Tragically, the tutoring of each new generation of youth in ethnic and religious intolerance and the practice of settling grievances through violence rather than arbitration has continued unabated into the opening decades of the third millennium. As a result, the global catastrophe that was averted with the thawing of the cold war is being stealthfully accomplished by starvation, HIV/AIDS, and regional conflict.

THE AMBIGUOUS NATURE OF STORIES AND THEIR ACTORS

To this point we have discussed positive stories and negative stories, which could suggest a world unambiguously divided between good and bad, light and darkness, the evil and the righteous. Such a Manichean worldview is often favored by national leaders seeking to consolidate citizen support. It has the twin advantages of imbuing complex situations with the appearance of moral clarity and of portraying homeland as the divinely appointed agent of world order. But it is no friend of the techniques of arbitration and reconciliation that moral philosophers have long recognized as the most dependable guidelines to conflict resolution.

Individuals and their leaders alike are reluctant to acknowledge that human affairs are generally marked by moral ambiguity. After all, most individuals fit the mold of neither Mother Teresa nor Adolf Hitler, but rather Malcolm X or Richard Nixon, even as most nations resemble neither Augustine's City of God nor Idi Amin's Uganda, but rather Japan or the United States. What is more, people often disagree in their evaluation of individuals and nations. The reason for disagreement is clear: we scrutinize and assess not from a neutral perspective, but on the basis of specific moral presuppositions. Such presuppositions are an essential part of the conceptual worlds within which persons and groups live, for they provide grounding for their identity-shaping stories. The alternative to morally constructed competing worldviews is anomie, a chaotic universe in which ethical discourse becomes impossible, due to the fact that the contestants are unable to identify the standards of right and wrong that shape each other's judgments. Acknowledging the importance of moral presuppositions, however, does not solve the problem posed by diversity, but rather places it in sharper focus. At this point we shall turn to a historical retrospect intended to provide an adequate framework for examining the challenges contemporary societies face as they struggle to integrate into purposeful dialogue ideologically and religiously diverse constituencies, each seeking to preserve and be guided by its particular traditions and practices.

HOW WE GOT HERE: A HISTORICAL RETROSPECT

Most early societies developed their stories on the basis of a higher degree of group solidarity than is characteristic of modern societies. Moral discernment in the case of the former was quite straightforward: does an action conform to the group's definition of the good and the right? In contemporary life that simpler world of moral evaluation can be observed in pockets of traditionalism referred to as affinity groups, that is, circles of people holding certain values and standards in common. It is also preserved in regimented professions like the military.

Consider a hypothetical episode in which a military council is evaluating the record of a soldier who has been recommended for a citation of bravery. Let us imagine that the criteriology of all of the officers is shaped by an Aristotelian understanding of their profession, and from that perspective they ask, "Has this individual exhibited the courage, high spirits, and loyalty of an excellent soldier?" The process moves smoothly to a decision. Or consider a church's political action committee evaluating, on the basis of a shared Calvinist model of civic virtue, the record of a mayor seeking reelection: "Has our mayor remained true to his election promises by funding programs for improving the quality of our schools, increasing the safety of our neighborhoods, and encouraging job creation in the private sector?" In both cases the homogeneous framework within which each group conducts its evaluation imputes a clear definition of goals as well as the virtues requisite for reaching those goals. The resulting process of discernment is quite straightforward.

These days, however, such homogeneity of purpose is uncommon beyond such pockets of the like-minded. More typical is a college seminar where diversity rather than commonality of perspective prevails. Feminist voices are heard taking issue with traditional Roman Catholic positions, Buddhist insights challenge Western theistic presuppositions, and atheists deny the need for a transcendent basis for ethical behavior. Rather than drawing the conclusion that such diversity necessarily leads to impasse, picture the possibility that the ensuing discussion proves to be beneficial to all participants, demonstrating that civil discussion is possible in a pluralistic setting. Possible, but not inevitable, for discord rather than engagement would have ensued, were it not for preliminary agreement on basic rules such as commitment to finding common ground and willingness to compromise. The effectiveness of such civil discourse has been demonstrated on a larger scale in the approach to regional and international conflict resolution developed and effectively applied by Roger Fisher.[13]

Theories explaining the basis upon which productive dialogue can be carried on in a religiously diverse society include John Rawls's neo-Kantian theory of "overlapping consensus"[14] and Jeffrey Stout's more pragmatic understanding of productive goal-oriented strategy and action.[15] To this important issue we shall return in the epilogue. At this point it is sufficient to be open to the possibility of productive public discourse within a pluralistic society and even to the suggestion that discourse can be chastened and enriched by the questions and challenges posed to one another by participants comfortable with explaining their particular points of view while listening attentively to the arguments emerging from other traditions.[16] To be sure, that ideal is easiest to visualize for those who already have experienced the deep satisfaction that arises from transcending differences to reach goals in which all parties benefit and no one leaves the table with a sense of having been marginalized.

13. With notable success, this approach to arbitration has been developed by Roger Fisher, author of *Getting to Yes: Negotiating Agreement without Giving In* (New York: Houghton Mifflin, 1981).

14. John Rawls, *A Theory of Justice* (Cambridge, MA: Belknap Press of Harvard University Press, 1971).

15. Jeffrey Stout, *Democracy and Tradition* (Princeton, NJ: Princeton University Press, 1994).

16. Cameroonian philosopher Martin Nkafu Nkemnkia describes the discovery of "making oneself one with the other persons of different cultures" in terms of a "resurrection." "[I]nstead of losing oneself and one's own culture, the meeting with different cultures becomes an enrichment, thus inaugurating in us a new way of seeing the world, God, ourselves, our neighbour and a whole new field of vital values" (*African Vitalogy*, 13).

To be productive, however, the vision of building trust dedicated to the common good must not be confined to an elite coterie of thinkers, aloof from the messiness of everyday life. There seems to be abundant evidence to suggest that, more than in earlier epochs, the contemporary world resembles Babel with its cacophony of voices promoting religious and ideological perspectives in such disparate language as to seem incongruous. This is not to say that sharp differences in belief and practice were unknown in earlier times. But forceful instruments of control were available for identifying and banishing "heretics" and promoting uniformity.

A common past strategy for taming the centrifugal effects of religious and philosophical discord was enforcement of "orthodoxy" through ecclesial bull or royal decree. Another was the emergence of a particular philosophical school to preeminence, such as the "reign" of Platonic thought from St. Augustine (354–430) to the early Middle Ages and the widespread influence of Aristotle and philosophy in the era of Averroës (1126–98), Maimonides (1135–1204), and Thomas Aquinas (1225–74).

The rancorous debates between nominalists and realists that followed, however, foreshadowed a tectonic shift in the political and intellectual organization of the Western world. The independence of scholarly inquiry that arose with the Renaissance, the erosion of central ecclesial authority and an emphasis on the freedom of the individual in matters of belief fomented by the Reformation, and the accompanying rise of independent princedoms and nation-states marked the end of hegemonic authority as the basis for cultural cohesion. The repercussions were vast and devastating, with the Copernican Revolution in science and the Thirty Years' War (1618–48) in politics serving as examples. A broken and divided world cried out for a new paradigm for reconstituting order.

The Enlightenment rose up to provide that new paradigm. Negatively, it indicted religion and its appeal to divine revelation as a capricious source of sectarian divisions, tension, and war. Positively, it announced a new instrument capable of banishing the contentious rival truth claims of religion and equipping humans with a tool capable of leading to genuine knowledge in the realms of science and philosophy, namely, reason. In the place of clerics, philosophers were to be the ones trained in clarifying universally valid moral principles and guiding leaders in applying them to matters of governance.

Like headstrong intellectual programs before it, the Enlightenment project soon revealed fractures in its basic claims. Having displaced the ancestral God and his earthly representatives, the high priests of the newly liberated humanity, the philosophers, could not agree on a definition of the universal good. Immanuel Kant (1724–1804) explained why: the road to the Truth involved something more complicated than simply refining the learned instruments of investigation. An epistemological conundrum had to be faced: rather than *discovering* order, the philosopher was guided by internal structures of reason that *imposed* order on what was being observed.

The consequent history of post-Enlightenment thought is the history of the collapse of the ambitious project to build a universal consensus based on human reason. The nineteenth-century Danish philosopher theologian Søren Kierkegaard (1813–55) marks an important turning point. While repudiating rational philosophy's attempt to establish a universal basis for truth, he argued passionately for giving wholehearted assent to an unabashedly Christian morality, based not on the alleged "proof" of reason, but as an affirmation of a human faced with the either/or decision between a self-centered aesthetic lifestyle and a Christ-centered (authentic) moral way of living.[17]

A final step into the conundrum that has imprinted the moral and political philosophy of the modern period was taken by the German philosopher Friedrich Nietzsche (1844–1900). While concurring with Kierkegaard's dethronement of reason as a path to a purported universal understanding of the right and the good, he pressed toward moral anarchy by repudiating the privileged status that had been accorded traditional Christian morality and promoting the will to power as the paradigm of the future. Within the subjectivist framework of post-Enlightenment philosophy, there was in Nietzsche's view no defensible basis for privileging the love ethic of Christ over other options. The human race, emancipated from the bonds of tradition and left to its human resources, was therefore to follow the leadership of the quintessential human being, one transcending conventional human society and through his self-accorded authority empowered to impose on his weaker, less willful mortals a code of law generated by his superior consciousness. In Nietzsche's transmutation of conventional values, traditional Judeo-Christian virtues were subject to particular ridicule on the grounds that they were patterned after the docility of a submissive Christ rather than the assertive might of the Superman (*Übermensch*).

For our study, the significance of Nietzsche lies less in the specific program he promoted than in the conceptual world he introduced. Morality in that world was cut off from history and detached from collective human experience. Norms were to be dictated arbitrarily by the Übermensch without regard for obligations preceding or transcending the individual. Though no individual Übermensch was able to reign for long, a less tangible but more tenacious tyrant than Hitler or Stalin emerged on a stage denuded of moral direction. Denied recourse to the concept of universal norms and without the value and purpose imbuing a living culture's traditions and practices, an ethical open market was created with rivals such as utilitarianism, voluntarism, Marxism, empiricism, pragmatism, and fundamentalisms of different sorts, all contending for the loyalty of adherents. The winner was the contestant most in sync with liberated, "unencumbered" humanity, namely, emotivism.[18]

17. Søren Kierkegaard, *Either Or*, trans. David F. Swenson and Lillian Marvin Swenson (Princeton, NJ: Princeton University Press, 1971).

18. Poignantly, Michael Sandel has characterized the individual living in a world circumscribed by self-interest as the "unencumbered self" (*Democracy's Discontent: America in Search of a Public Philosophy* [Cambridge, MA: Harvard University Press, 1996], 12).

In a society in which emotivism has triumphed, the source of moral truth no longer resides in traditions, practices, and institutions, but in the subjective consciousness of the individual.[19] If that consciousness has not been trained in virtue within the context of a clear definition of social values and commitment to a public notion of the common good (Aristotle's *telos*), it is only as reliable as the whirling compasses of unfettered human hearts. John Rawls, to be sure, sought to restore rational order to the search for a reliable moral foundation for contemporary society. But Alasdair MacIntyre has argued persuasively that Rawls's neo-Kantian attempt to restore a shared sense of justice by appeal to the perspective glimpsed from under "the veil of ignorance" and benefiting from an "overleaping consensus" was deficient, inasmuch as it perpetuated the error of the Enlightenment by not recognizing that neutral ground and objectivity are not available to humans.[20] To be comprehensible and generative of a viable society, values and moral principles need to be embedded in that society's traditions and practices.

So is the future to be conceded to emotivism? This question is one that must be taken very seriously by anyone concerned with the confusion that characterizes contemporary ethical thought, for the roots of emotivism run deeply in the culture. It did not triumph as the philosophy of choice by happenstance. Rather, it represents the most congenial philosophy for denizens of a new age who are enthralled with the immediate gratifications of a materialistic lifestyle, who celebrate emancipation from traditional duties and restraints, and who pursue personal advancement unhampered by concerns for social reform and global equality. Moreover, it would be inaccurate to view the ascendancy of emotivism as marking the end of the role played by stories in the formation of identity. What it does mean is that stories are narrowed down to private affairs within the lives of individuals and the affinity groups to which they belong. Storytelling in the traditional epic sense of the etiology of an entire state or nation becomes an endangered genre. Serious consequences follow. The effort to identify the commonalities constitutive of group identity and purpose wane, inasmuch as individual and affinity group stories promote a myopic vision of the world. Rather than building bridges, they erect walls, and the casualty is the sense of neighborliness fostered by the traditional belief that "no man is an island." In the world of "unencumbered" individualists, if an inner-city child enters adulthood with a learning disability caused by exposure to lead paint or a young man on the other side of the tracks falls victim to gang violence, citizens (or should we call them "inmates") neither hear the bell toll nor are they moved to action, for without the sense of solidarity provided by a *shared* story, we feel no personal diminution through the loss of anonymous others, or in the case of humans on the other side of the globe, through the loss of anonymous millions!

---

19. MacIntyre, *After Virtue.*
20. Rawls, *A Theory of Justice.*

Emotivism then does not promote lively public dialogue but promotes an antisocial climate in which individuals become so enthralled with schemes for personal gain that they become blinded to the commonweal. In such a climate CEOs of corporations prioritize lucrative contracts above the interests of laborers and consumers on a scale that astonishes even their counterparts in the other industrial nations. And in ever-increasing numbers voters are losing confidence in the representatives they elect and whose salaries they pay in anticipation of efficient, bipartisan service dedicated to the common good. The reason for their cynicism is clear. In response to daunting fiscal, social, and international threats, they witness ideological gridlock, campaign-motivated rhetoric, and petty-mindedness tarnishing the stature of the nation's highest office holders.

In spite of the enormous popularity of emotivism, however, its continued grip on society should not be regarded as a foregone conclusion. Clear voices can be heard in defense of the traditional American republican virtues of public-spiritedness and a value system that transcends individual self-interest.[21] These voices look with cautious hope to the future on the basis of lessons, both positive and negative, from the past. They stress the importance of story as a source of identity and purpose for both individual and the wider society. But they also recognize a formidable challenge facing those dedicated to a communal approach to creating a good society for *every* individual and enlisting *all* citizens in contributing toward that goal. The challenge arises from the phenomenon that most emphatically distinguishes modern societies from earlier ones, namely, proliferating religious and philosophical *diversity*.[22]

Diversity on the visceral level of the beliefs and values that define us and structure our lives can generate deep-seated anxiety. Two common responses are withdrawal into self-validating enclaves and its polar twin, an aggressive campaign to impose one's own philosophical/religious position on others. Far more difficult is engagement in a process in which commitment to unprejudiced inclusivity draws citizens into developing a mode of civic discourse and political action in which all voices are heard.

Right at the point where the goal of enlisting the whole range of viewpoints into civil discourse seems within reach, however, another threat to political discourse and action arises. What makes its challenge the most difficult of all is the fact that its proponents come from the ranks of the most tolerant, public-minded members of the society. We are referring to a discursive etiquette that,

---

21. Sandel, *Democracy's Discontent*, 12.

22. Alasdair MacIntyre has reminded us that in the modern world public discourse is fraught with difficulty. He points out that once cut off from community and ascribed solely to the individual, the language of virtue and morality lapses into incoherency. And with the accompanying loss of a public sense of human purpose (Aristotle's *telos*), the disparate constituencies making up the society go their separate ways resulting in "incompatibility" and "incommensurability." Traditional terms like liberty, freedom, and rights, to be sure, continue to be used, but for different groups they have widely divergent meanings derived from the incompatible moral worldviews within which they have been shaped and the parochial stories and practices in which they are embodied (MacIntyre, *After Virtue*, 125).

for fear of conflict and with commitment to goodwill among all citizens, strives to find a middle ground by bracketing out of public debate the deepest moral insights drawn by faith communities from their respective sacred writings and traditions.[23] The dreary end products of such polite debate are often anemic lowest-common-denominator strategies and policies lacking the passion and vitality capable of lifting a community's sights to a higher moral plane.

Withdrawal into the safety of affinity enclaves, aggressive attempts to impose one's own values and policies on others, and tepid discursive etiquette: are these the only options available to a nation struggling with gargantuan domestic and international problems?

A WAY FORWARD

In invoking the metaphor of story, we have begun to build the case for an understanding of political process that reclaims the historical dimension of nationhood and the essential role of memory in fostering a vibrant and just society while at the same time taking into full account the modern phenomenon of diversity. When national identity is understood in terms of historical ontology rather than abstract theory, the question of who we are as a people invokes the historical question, where do we come from and what are the narratives and practices that shape our sense of shared goals? When those questions evoke memories of flights from bondage to freedom and an inheritance of copious streams and fecund fields, a sense of pride infuses the national consciousness. But when deeper scrutiny discloses the expropriation of those streams and fields from their native owners, the role of memory in defining national identity tempers national pride with self-critique.

To be sure, many citizens, desirous of an ebullient picture of the past, cultivate a national story that resembles fable more than fact. Patriotism becomes the pretense for bowdlerizing the textbooks teaching American history to the next generation. To pledge allegiance to the flag takes on the aura of worship that categorically erases any sense of regret or need for redress. But as we have learned from Nazi Germany, history teaches a severe lesson: if a sanitized version of the nation's story becomes official, lies trump hard truths, sanctimoniousness excludes all sense of remorse, and a climate is created in the nation's citadels of power for combative politics and belligerent foreign policy. A potentially deadly disease invades the heart of the land.

Though less pernicious than the demagogical hijacking of Scripture, another dubious interpretive practice is widespread in the United States. It involves consulting the Bible as one would a recipe book or a repair manual in search of clear answers to complex questions that deserve not facile directives but careful

---

23. Richard Rorty, *The Ethics of Citizenship: Liberal Democracy and Religious Convictions* (Waco, TX: Baylor University Press, 2008).

analysis drawing on the profound moral insights of Scripture. Flat-footed proof-texting errs by failing to recognize the subjective aspect of all interpretation. The way forward must be one that courageously and patiently seeks to honor traditions by hearing them in their own voices and then patiently and diligently strives for answers benefiting from the contributions of all participants in a diverse society.

THE STRUCTURE OF OUR STUDY

Moving forward in the case of this study has as its goal the formulation of a theo-political hermeneutic capable of channeling the cacophony of religious beliefs and moral principles that reside in contemporary society into a rich and productive public dialogue. But before we embark on that theological task, our historicist perspective calls for two historically oriented investigations to provide essential background. Both will reflect the concrete cultural location of the author, one his US citizenship, the other his biblically based religious orientation.

In part 1, we shall trace chapters of a story that over the course of several centuries has fashioned the heart of US identity and, in new chapters that continue to be written, unfolds further its open-ended plot. Because of the resiliently religious character of the American people from colonial times to the present, we shall be attentive to the role that biblical tradition has played in shaping the national story. That that role was considerable is understandable in light of a shared quality: the nation's history and biblical history are both filled with identity-building stories, stories depicting origins, adjustments to new experiences, enrichment through encounters with the alien and the unexpected, and above all, a sense of purpose that asserts the need to make sense of the whole. In the case of ancient Israel, this implied the triumph of epic over myth;[24] in the case of the United States, it implied a dynamic notion of risk taking and growth into newness over a static model of eternal order.

The legacy uncovered in part 1 will be a checkered one, ranging from rank exploitation of biblical texts on behalf of national self-interest to instances of exemplary charity and self-sacrifice that bring to light the nation's potential for promoting equality, justice, and well-being both at home and abroad. But the most ominous discovery to surface will be the arbitrariness characterizing most applications of the Bible to political issues. Repeatedly one detects neither concern for the meaning intrinsic to the scriptural texts in their own setting nor sensitivity to the delicate balance between religion and state established by the First Amendment.

---

24. Cf. Frank Moore Cross, *Canaanite Myth and Hebrew Epic: Essays in the History of the Religion of Israel* (Cambridge, MA: Harvard University Press, 1973).

Part 2 in turn will present a detailed study of politics in the Bible, beginning with tribal judges and moving on to kings, priests, prophets, governors, and seers. Framed by the challenges and crises discussed in the survey of American history, its purpose is that of securing a reliable biblical-historical foundation for the constructive task that follows in the epilogue of formulating a theo-political hermeneutic defining guidelines for the application of scriptural tradition to contemporary issues.

For the sake of clarity, we shall now give a more detailed description of the pivotal position held by part 2 within the overall structure of our study. Alexander Pope penned an apt caption for that section: "A little learning is a dangerous thing; Drink deep, or taste not the Pierian spring." For as noted above, our survey of the relation of Bible and politics in US history unveiled flagrant arbitrariness in the use/abuse of Scripture from colonial times to the present. In the case of a source with such latent power in a highly religious country, "a little learning" is not only dangerous; it is potentially lethal to many defenseless people at home and abroad. Serious learning is urgently called for to liberate the Bible from the control of opportunists and the unscrupulous and to place it in the hands of the meek and the poor and those who seek to restore the dignity and rights of all. Fair-minded people of all persuasions can unite in respecting the Bible as a classical source to be studied for the insights it can provide and to opposing the self-serving exercise of treating Scripture as a mirror to be peered into for the comfort of "discovering" in its pages one's own ideological views and prejudices!

Specifically regarding the political exploitation of the Bible, one discovery that emerges from a rigorous historical method is that the Bible does not formulate one monolithic, timeless political model ready to be cut out and pasted as a template for contemporary policy, but six distinct models, each the product of a community applying its central beliefs and values to the changing circumstances of its own time and place. Grasping and being tutored by the dynamic that enabled biblical communities to apply core beliefs and moral principles to the challenges raised by the concrete issues with which they contended emerges as the responsible alternative to the mechanistic practice of imposing subjectively formulated (though purportedly inerrant!) "biblical" truths on the vastly different world of modernity.

The dynamic, historically adaptable character of the Bible that emerges from disciplined research places a solemn responsibility on anyone seeking to present the relevance of Scripture for contemporary politics in a manner both sensitive to the Bible's historical richness and comprehensible to the modern reader. While attention to historical context and original meaning and function of biblical texts provides a necessary restraint on the temptation to exploit the Bible for ideological purposes, it runs the risk of overwhelming the reader interested in the contemporary political relevance of Scripture with an unfathomable welter of details. While arguing that the Bible is not a timeless manual providing ready-made answers to every contemporary issue, it would be a serious blunder to give the impression that it is a *compendium rerum* accessible exclusively to archaeologists and antiquarians. What is accordingly called for is an approach capable of re-presenting in terms comprehensible to modern readers the biblical dynamic of fidelity to core beliefs and principles as the basis for applying the Bible to an ever-changing society and world.

Once again we are reminded of the relevance of the lessons we derived from our exploration of the identity-generating function of story for a historical approach to the politics of the Bible. Ancient Scriptures, our nation's history, and our contemporary personal and political existence constitute the threads from which we weave a sense of meaning and purpose. Attentiveness to those threads reveals the common ground shared between our ancestors, ourselves, and our progeny. The resulting generation-transcending experience fosters a sense of indebtedness to the stories passed on to us for our consciousness of selfhood and community-belonging in the present and of confidence that we are preserving for and handing on to our descendants a story that they will continue to compose.

This sense of *in medias res* given to us by the metaphor of life as story saves us from the imprisonment of fossilization (we are slaves of our past) and predeterminism (we have no influence on the future). The past that nourishes us and the future we bequeath to the next generation are dynamic in nature, creating a sense of reality that is open though not aimless, affected by events already recorded though not stuck in them. While providing us with a sense of identity and purpose, our story is not exclusive or parochial, but open and hospitable to all who are willing to contribute from the richness of their stories to the common human task of building a just and peaceable world.

This last point invites us to extend the metaphor in the direction of our goal of reclaiming the Bible for political edification: Storytellers share a very large tent. Among those accepting the invitation to participate are Aristotelians seeking to guide their society (*polis*) on the basis of a shared vision of the common good (*telos*). Joining them are those pious lovers of *torah* who perform daily acts of kindness (*miṣwôt*) because their inner being is fashioned by the *Seder* tale of an ancient act of divine mercy. Hans-Georg Gadamer's disciples join the show, with their sense of the *fusion* of ancient and modern horizons,[25] as do the students of Alasdair MacIntyre with their embrace of narratives pregnant with present-day meaning.[26] The guest list goes on, because if your invitation welcomes all who love stories and are willing to share theirs and hear others, walls are converted into bridges and dimly burning wicks turn into torches illuminating the pathway from the events that built community consciousness in antiquity to the groundbreaking experiences of our own forebears as they struggled to build

---

25. "Fusion of horizons" is a concept developed by Hans-Georg Gadamer in *Truth and Method* (New York: Seabury Press, 1975), 269, 302.
26. MacIntyre, *After Virtue*, 212, 216.

a nation and finally on down to our own involvement in the vital issues of contemporary existence.

Once we as public-minded citizens have grasped the ongoing, open-ended nature of our individual and communal identities with the aid of the metaphor of story, the contribution of the two diachronic studies constituting parts 1 and 2 to our overarching topic of the Bible and politics becomes evident: biblical history, enriched by many religious and cultural traditions, flows into and is intertwined with our nation's epic, both for better and for worse. To ignore that history is to cut ourselves off from our roots and to deny the ancestral experiences that forged our individual and collective identity. Expressed in terms of historical ontology, our neglect or forgetfulness of the diachronic dimension of life is tantamount to the refutation of our authenticity and essential being, a refutation that readily leads to uprootedness and alienation.

History in the vast arc of its unfolding over the centuries and millennia is the most reliable tutor available from which to learn from our ancestors the mistakes they made as well as the things they got right. For believers of all types, as well as for historically sensitive secularists and atheists in a richly diverse society, ancient scriptural legacies (including non-Judeo-Christian traditions), as they flow into a nation's history and finally into the lives of families and individuals, can be treasured as generative chapters enriching our own sense of identity and location within the larger scheme of things.

Having secured in parts 1 and 2 the historical foundation for our theo-political task, we shall broach in the epilogue the question of the contemporary message of the Bible, keenly mindful of the dynamic phenomenon of story that furnishes the lens through which we can grasp the nature and abiding significance of both national and biblical history. Indeed, the essential lineaments of our theo-political hermeneutic should arise organically from the two historical surveys. What we shall propose is a manner of public moral discourse that invites full participation by members of all religious and philosophical groups in a robust style of engagement enriched by full expression of the deepest moral insights of each, rather than a tepid exchange of ecumenical platitudes. The universal harmony envisioned by rationalism will be eschewed in favor of the inevitable messiness of genuine debate among adherents of distinct systems of belief and morals that resists meltdown into a single mold. Deeply rooted convictions will not be checked at the door like so many colorful umbrellas, for the invitation will stipulate for open conversation respectful of the distinctiveness of each group and appreciative of the fact that values are not the products of dispassionate rational deliberations, but rather are expressions of the identities shaped by specific narrative traditions and practices. In terms introduced earlier in this chapter, beliefs, ethical principles, and the identities they shape are the products of the particular historical ontology and distinctive paradigms embedded in a given community's story.

In the public forum that we envision, fear of conflict arising from divergent perspectives is not the driving factor, but rather the appeal of substantive moral inquiry that benefits from the mix of insights found where participants grant to others the same right of expression that they enjoy themselves. The challenge is of such complexity as to be eschewed by those who persist in pursuit of an imaginary neutral ground productive of universal principles, as well as by those dedicated to the triumph of their purported *superior* systems of belief and morals over all other *inferior* systems and wont to withdraw bitterly from public engagement when denied that triumph.

The more difficult path of discourse predicated on diversity represents in itself a rigorous moral test, since participation must extend beyond persons viewing all religious/philosophical differences from a relativistic perspective. To have any social traction, the path into the future must include those who hold a deep commitment to the truthfulness of their beliefs, values, and moral principles, while at the same time acknowledging that since no human is omniscient, enrichment from other perspectives is beneficial. Add to this the pragmatic consideration that the path of inclusive participation is the only peaceable way forward for a diverse society and one has laid the foundation for a promising model of productive public discourse. If we succeed in our investigation, we shall have demonstrated that an important aspect of that discourse revolves around the politics of the Bible.

PART 1

A Historical Retrospective
on the Relation between the Bible
and Politics in the United States

Introduction

The relationship between religious organizations and government developed over the course of US history in a way that set it apart from Great Britain and the Continent. Drawing on the lessons of the leaders of the thirteen colonies who preceded them, as well as on the political writings of French and English philosophers, the founders, though frequently differing over the specific inferences they drew from their religious and philosophical views, were able to agree upon the principle that, whatever the individual states decided for themselves, the nation as a whole was to eschew the notion of an established church. As for the citizens, their freedom to choose a particular religion or no religion was to be protected from congressional interference. Under the protective canopy of the two religion clauses of the First Amendment, older denominations as well as native-born movements developed within a climate of free expression and intense competition.

As the new nation developed, many citizens as well as their political leaders drew inspiration from the Bible and sought with varied success to achieve a more just, righteous, and compassionate society. Reformers across the generations inspired by biblical ideals sought a wide range of reformist goals. Temperance advocates sought to protect families and children from the scourge of alcoholism.

At the same time a coalition of northern Evangelicals petitioned Congress to protect the Cherokee from being expelled from their ancestral lands. Scriptural ideals of equality and liberation for the oppressed inspired Frederick Douglass, Theodore Dwight Weld, Theodore Parker, and the Grimké sisters to organize to abolish the sin of slavery from the land. During the Progressive Era a range of religious leaders sought to improve conditions for immigrants in the inner cities and to restrain the excessive power of emerging business oligopolies. As the twentieth century progressed and the United States assumed a more prominent role in world affairs, biblical ideals shaped both Woodrow Wilson in his quest for a war to end all wars and a just and lasting peace and later generations of pacifists who opposed American intervention in wars ranging from Vietnam to Iraq. Most notably in the last several generations, religiously inspired imagery and reform strategies were central to the nonviolent civil rights movement led by Martin Luther King Jr. and helped to build bridges between people of goodwill from all races and walks of life.

Yet this sketch of the positive legacies of religion in American life tells only one side of a much more complicated story, wherein Americans all too frequently failed to live up to their highest political and religious ideals. Significantly, the ideal of religious freedom remained an elusive one for many. Though the religious climate in the new land spawned numerous sectarian innovations, the yearning of many nonconformist groups to reach the status of full participation in American society was thwarted by encounters with intolerance and violence that contradicted the notion of equality under the law. Such was the case in the century and a half before the Revolutionary War, and such was the case in the era that followed. Separatists like Roger Williams and dissenters like Anne Hutchinson, who questioned the political and religious authority of the Puritan leaders of the Massachusetts Bay Colony, fled to Rhode Island after being banished from their communities. Quakers who defiantly returned after being expelled were executed in Boston. Men and women accused of witchcraft were tried and sentenced to execution in Salem, Ipswich, and Andover. As the grinding wheels of intolerance rolled into the first century of the new nation, Mormons, in the face of lethal persecution, fled westward on a route taking them from New York to Ohio, Illinois, and Missouri before they finally found sanctuary in the wide-open spaces of the mountainous West.

As for Native peoples, they were progressively displaced from their land through intimidation by colonial leaders, tricked into shoddy land-purchase agreements, and massacred mercilessly in reprisal for their attempts to reclaim their tribal territories. As the growing young nation pressed inexorably toward the Pacific in response to its growing population, their pleas for redress usually fell upon deaf ears. Even in the few cases where their claims were brought to trial and resulted in a favorable decision, victory in court was no guarantee of justice at home.[1] The same pattern of injustice has reached down to modern times, as demonstrated by the state of Oregon's denial of unemployment compensation to Native American employees Galen Black and Alfred Smith on the basis of their participation in tribal religious ceremonies that included the sacramental use of peyote.[2]

Given the all too frequent instances of glaring contradictions between the constitutional ideal and the persistence of discrimination against religious minorities, it is important to cultivate public awareness of our First Amendment tradition and its strengths and vulnerabilities, a goal greatly enriched by a historical perspective. In the following eight chapters, therefore, our objective is to examine the relationship between religion and politics in US history and to identify the theo-political models that were adopted and developed to shape that relationship.

1. Though the court sided with the Cherokee in *Worcester v. Georgia* (1832), both the state and federal authorities (including President Andrew Jackson, whose policy was articulated in the Indian Removal Act that he signed into law in 1830) ignored John Marshall's ruling.

2. "Oregon Peyote Law Leaves 1983 Defendant Unvindicated," *New York Times*, July 9, 1991, A14.

Chapter 1

The Theocratic Model
of the Puritans

The unique political thought of the Puritans cannot be understood without an awareness of the historical and cultural context in which it developed. During the persecutions of English Protestants that occurred under the Catholic Queen Mary (1553–58), many refugees sought asylum on the Continent. Due to the tumult of religious wars that engulfed the German states in which the Lutheran Church had taken root, most of those refugees were drawn to the more peaceful havens of Amsterdam, Geneva, and neighboring Calvinist cities. This twist of history had a lasting effect on the nature of the Christian political theory that many of the reform-minded Puritans brought back with them when the restoration of Protestant rule under Elizabeth I (1558–1603) allowed them to return to their homeland.

Once resettled in England, the Puritans set themselves to the task of preparing the New Israel for the imminent return of Christ. The Puritan divines searched the Bible for direction, being guided by a hermeneutic that sought signs not of the universal body of Christ transcending all political boundaries, in the style of Luther and Calvin, but of the reform of the English nation by God's redemptive work. Granted, the obstacles that stood in the way of reform were formidable, given their perception of corruption infecting a church with papist

31

leanings and kings (James I [1603–25] and Charles I [1625–49]) not hesitating to exploit the theo-political doctrine of the divine right of kings for blatantly self-serving purposes. The Puritans viewed themselves as God's agents in carrying on the holy struggle that would inaugurate the new era of righteousness and peace.

The polity that guided the activities of the Puritans blended the theocratic ideals of Geneva with an apocalyptic fervor fired by their expectation that Christ's return was imminent. They proclaimed that the nation was being summoned to submit to God's rule as revealed in the biblical commandments and to embody the purity of life that would prepare the land for Christ's triumphal return.

As seems inevitable throughout human history in the case of apocalyptically motivated political movements, the program of reform brought back by the Puritans from Geneva ended in failure. Leaders of both the church and the state, fearing that England would become consumed by the kind of religious wars that had swept over the Continent, united in repudiating their positions as extreme.[1] During the reign of James I and on into the first half of Charles I's reign, the tide flowed in the direction of reaffirming the power-sharing arrangement between monarchy, church, and parliament that left the Puritans without a base from which to create the New Israel, at least in the motherland. Increasingly they became an alienated group, and were it not for their fervent faith, they may have withdrawn altogether from politics into the solace of otherworldly sectarianism.

Deftly, though, they introduced into their vision of God's plans for an earthly habitation a significant alteration: "As sure as God is God, God is going from England," proclaimed Thomas Hooker in 1633 in his sermon "The Danger of Desertion," as he embarked from England to sail with his followers (including Anne Hutchinson) to Holland and then on to a land of promise on the other side of the Atlantic.[2] Depictions of an apocalyptic denouement remained central in his sermons and in the sermons of other Puritan divines like John Cotton; but now, instead of the motherland being the object of God's redemptive activity, England had become the satanic obstacle that God would have to remove to prepare for the establishment of the New Israel in the fresh soil of America. As John Winthrop expressed it, the new settlements would "raise a Bulworke against the kingdome of Ante-Christ . . . [and provide] a refuge for many whome he meanes

---

1.The brief triumph of the Puritan movement under the leadership of Oliver Cromwell culminating in the Commonwealth of 1653–58 is not directly relevant to our discussion of the roots of Puritanism in New England, inasmuch as it occurred roughly two decades after the emigrations that led to the founding of Plymouth Plantation (1620) and the Massachusetts Bay colony (1629). Though the Commonwealth preserved many of the religious aims of the earlier Puritans, it enacted a Shakespearean-style conflict between two formidable characters, Cromwell with his charisma and formidable military prowess and Charles I with his arrogant flaunting of power and disdain for the complaints of parliamentarians, religious dissidents, and commoners alike.

2.Thomas Hooker, *The Danger of Desertion* (1641, 1657), reprinted in Karen Ordahl Kupperman, ed., *Major Problems in American Colonial History* (Boston: Houghton Mifflin Co., 1993), 90–91.

to saue out of the general calamity" that was coming to the churches in Europe. Finally, Winthrop believed the whole enterprise to be "a worke of God for the good of his Church . . . which he hat reveled to his prophetts."[3]

In 1630, aboard the *Arbella*, Winthrop wrote "A Modell of Christian Charity." In this oft-quoted thesis, he described the principles upon which the new society would be built. His work is a consistent attempt to translate the teachings of the Bible into a political model. The "city upon a hill" was to be a covenant community, living in faithfulness to the laws of God revealed in the Bible, and opposing every vice and evil that would seduce the hearts of the people and lead to the same punishments that were about to visit the apostates of England. The political model he described is theocratic in nature, and there is little reason to doubt that Calvin's Geneva hovers over the experiment as a source of inspiration. By interpreting the Bible typologically, the leaders of the early New England settlements were able to identify their bridgehead on the American continent with biblical Israel's entry into Canaan. For example, William Bradford, the founder of Plymouth Colony, adapted Moses' words to the Israelites recorded in Deuteronomy 26 to the Pilgrims: "May not and ought not the children of these fathers rightly say: Our fathers were Englishmen which came over this great ocean, and were ready to perish in this wilderness; but they cried unto the Lord, and he heard their voices, and looked on their adversities."[4]

The theoretical foundation of the relationship between church and state in early New England can best be explored by a close examination of the Cambridge Platform, which was composed in 1648. The seventeenth chapter seeks to delineate the responsibilities and limits on both sides of the divide. Churches have rights that are unique to themselves and do not, for example, need the permission of the state in order to meet. The church and the state should be mutually supporting communities within the larger society. The ministers should counsel obedience to the magistrates, just as the magistrates should aid and support the church. Yet there are clear limits to this relationship. The magistrates, for example, have no authority to compel church membership or

---

3. *Winthrop Papers,* II, 1623–1630 (Boston: Massachusetts Historical Society, 1931), 138–40; cited in *A Documentary History of Religion in America to the Civil War,* ed. Edwin S. Gaustad (Grand Rapids: Eerdmans, 1990), 105.

4. William Bradford, *Of Plymouth Plantation, 1620–1647* (New York: McGraw Hill, 1981), 71. Biblical scholars use the term "typology" for this kind of application of Scripture to a contemporary situation. The biblical theme of exodus remains to the present day a very popular one for typological interpretations, even as it has enjoyed an honored place in the long history of biblical interpretation, having been adopted and applied by an anonymous prophet of the exile heard in Isaiah 40, by the Essenes of the Dead Sea Scrolls, by John the Baptist according to Matt. 3:3, and by liberation theologians and other reform-minded prophetic crusaders throughout history. Here for comparison is the passage from Deut. 26:5–8 that Bradford was paraphrasing: "You shall make this response before the LORD your God: 'A wandering Aramean was my ancestor; he went down into Egypt and lived there as an alien, few in number, and there he became a great nation, mighty and populous. When the Egyptians treated us harshly and afflicted us, by imposing hard labor on us, we cried to the LORD, the God of our ancestors; the LORD heard our voice and saw our affliction, our toil, and our oppression. The LORD brought us out of Egypt with a mighty hand and an outstretched arm, with a terrifying display of power, and with signs and wonders.'"

participation in the ritual of communion. The platform expresses this separation in the following terms: "As it is unlawful for church-officers to meddle with the sword of the magistrate, so it is unlawful for the magistrate to meddle with the work proper to church-officers." Yet this separation seems profoundly limited to a contemporary sensibility. Magistrates were specifically authorized to punish "idolatry, blasphemy, heresy, venting corrupt and pernicious opinions, that destroy the foundation, open contempt of the Word preached, profanation of the Lords day, disturbing the peaceable administration and exercise of the worship and holy things of God." Finally, the magistrates were even given authority to intervene in churches that were deemed "schismatical," out of communion with other churches, or acting "incorrigibly or obstinately." These strictures were composed in an atmosphere where only church members in good standing were eligible for the franchise, and ministers were specifically barred from holding political office.

The Puritans thus saw church and state as separate institutions with separate leadership, but mutually reinforcing and supporting. Instead of a wall of separation dividing the two, church and state would provide two of the three pillars, the third being the family, for the growth of a godly commonwealth.[5] Parents publicly testifying to their conversion and manifesting saintly behavior, children raised in obedience to biblical laws and gaining admission to communion through an account of their own experience of rebirth, magistrates ruling in conformity with orthodox Calvinism, admonished and supported by a patriotic body of clergy: such was the harmonious whole envisioned by the first and second generations of the Puritans as the commonwealth willed by God and attainable through the diligence and commitment of its citizens.

Though the ideal envisioned by the first Puritans was thus theocratic in nature, the communities to which they gave birth soon began to evolve in a different direction. As George Armstrong Kelly explains the distinction, "the Calvinist regimes in Massachusetts and Connecticut were not 'theocratic' but secular: the ecclesiastical and civil governments were not coterminous, although 'saints' were presumed to possess indispensable qualities of leadership."[6] A theocratic state is based upon the principle that the religious laws received through tradition determine both the religious norms and the political structures in a seamless unity. But among the early settlers were many who understood the political implications of the Bible in ways that differed from the theocratic views of Puritans like John Cotton and Thomas Hooker.

Though disagreeing among themselves on matters of polity and belief, business leaders with mercantile interests, farmers and small business owners with responsibilities that often clashed with Sabbath laws, and religious dissidents

5. *A Platform of Church Governance . . .* (Cambridge, MA: Samuel Green, 1649) Evans Collection of Early American Imprints, 5938, 10 in the Archive Americana produced by the American Antiquarian Society, 25, 27–29.

6. George Armstrong Kelly, *Politics and Religious Consciousness in America* (New Brunswick, NJ: Transaction Publishers, 2004), 27.

guided by their own interpretations of Scripture and their perception of the promptings of the Holy Spirit found common cause on one front: their opposition to the theocratic tenets of the Puritan leaders. But the consequences of their opposition varied: those buttressed by sufficient political influence and economic leverage were tolerated and ultimately influenced change in the web of relations between religion and politics in Massachusetts; those made vulnerable by accidents of gender or station in life were ostracized or executed; those falling betwixt those two categories either managed to escape or were banished.[7]

7. The trial of Anne Hutchinson occurred in 1638, after which she managed to escape to Rhode Island and then Pelham, New York. In 1692 and 1693, nineteen men and women charged with practicing witchcraft in Salem and surrounding towns were sentenced to death by hanging, an act of brutality supported by the Puritan divine Cotton Mather.

Chapter 2

The Challenge of the
Prophetic-Dialectical Model

EARLY EXPRESSIONS OF DISSENT

Roger Williams, because of his courageous defense of freedom of conscience and the accessibility of the individual to God's revelation in Scripture, is remembered by history as the most notable of the fugitives from the rigid Calvinism of the Puritans of New England. With his life story and that of prophetic figures like Anne Hutchinson, who found sanctuary in the colony that he founded, we find the fitting segue to a theo-political model that has exercised a profound influence on the relation of religion and politics on the American continent, what we designate as the prophetic-dialectical model. Within the prophetic-dialectical model, religiously and morally motivated leaders arise who speak the perspective of God into a contemporary situation to challenge the hubris or injustice of the government.

The challenges Williams faced after his banishment from Massachusetts in 1636 were formidable. In 1643 his trip to England to obtain a charter for his new colony encountered a complicated political situation in which King Charles I and Parliament were locked in a contentious struggle for power. Moreover, the Puritan leaders of Massachusetts persisted in their harassment of their dissident divine both by plotting to thwart his diplomatic efforts in England and by conducting hostile forays into his newly founded settlements along the Narragansett Bay. And although his acquisition of land from the Indians took the form of treaties rather than hostile dispossession, relations with the Natives remained tense, finally exploding in 1675 in the bloodbath of King Philip's War.

The issues that led to Williams's dismissal from his pastoral duties in Salem, Massachusetts, and subsequent banishment from the colony of John Winthrop are reflected in the principles of government that he established in his new settlement in Providence. In opposition to the exclusivist theocratic notions of the Puritans, he reached back to a universalizing strand of Reformation teaching in proclaiming that Christ had transcended the boundaries separating nations and peoples. His defiance of the severe laws that the Puritans insisted were dictated by Scripture was based on his understanding of the law of love introduced by Jesus Christ, a law that had laid the foundation for a very different notion of the relation between human and divine government.

In his thinking it was not human obedience to God but human imperiousness that gave birth to the notion that God had elected one people as his new Israel, had endowed its clergy with a definitive understanding of both the religious and political implications of Scripture, and had empowered its magistrates with the authority to enforce conformity to Puritan polity. In arguing for freedom of conscience Williams wrote, "God requireth not a uniformity of religion to be enacted and enforced in any civil state; which enforced uniformity sooner or later is the greatest occasion of civil war, ravishing of conscience, persecution of Christ Jesus in his servants, and of the hypocrisy and destruction of millions of souls."[1] Religious tolerance consequently became one of the central hallmarks of the charter of the Rhode Island colony.

Rhode Island became the sanctuary for separatists and dissenters such as Anne Hutchinson, William Coddington, and John Clarke. The fruits of its policy of tolerance were dramatic: the first Baptist church was organized in 1639, followed by the founding of the Truro Synagogue in 1658 and the first Free Black Church, also in 1658.

In the initial years of the fledgling colony, amicable relations with the Native population were maintained, in large part due to the fact that treaties were based on purchase rather than the tactics of intimidation and dispossession commonly practiced in Massachusetts and Connecticut.[2] Unfortunately, the tragic war that

---

1. Roger Williams, "A Plea for Religious Liberty," an excerpt from *The Bloody Tenent of Persecution* (1644), cited in *Daily Life in American History through Primary Documents*, ed. Randall M. Miller et al. (Westport, CT: Greenwood, 2011), 263.

2. Though instances of intimidation and dispossession of Native land were common in the history of the Puritan colonies, one must also take note of countertrends such as the inclusion of both "English and Indian youths" in the 1650 charter of Harvard College and the humane treatment of the Native population that characterized John Eliot's missionary endeavors. While Eliot's policy can be understood historically as the extension of his Reformed theology to a new situation, it is interesting to note that the Indians were not "savages" lacking their own considered perspective on the situation: only a minority of them were willing to adopt Christianity as a condition for entering into

broke out in 1675 between the Indians and the settlers and led to the deaths of hundreds of colonists and thousands of Natives spilled over from bordering colonies into the colony that had begun propitiously as a model of harmony between diverse ethnic and religious groups. Rhode Island thus became implicated in the legacy of mistreatment of Native Americans that remains one of this country's deepest moral stigmata.

Its policy of religious tolerance notwithstanding, the Rhode Island of Williams and Coddington did not extend the benefits of a civilized society in equal measure to all of its citizens. One of the effects of its loose sense of cultural cohesion was a greater gap between rich and poor than was able to develop in Massachusetts or Connecticut. The wealth of many of the prominent families of Rhode Island was enhanced in particular by a thriving slave trade. It is therefore fortunate that when a later generation of leaders sat down to define the principles and goals of the nascent republic, they adopted neither Rhode Island's nor Virginia's nor any other colony's charter as template, but drew discriminately from diverse sources, both native and foreign. In that process, however, there is no gainsaying the fact that the founding documents of the United States owe much to the principle of religious toleration that Roger Williams placed at the heart of his colony's charter.

Though the studies of a past generation of scholars focused disproportionately on the relations between clergy, magistrates, and citizens in Puritan New England, it is now clear that the range of approaches to matters of "church and state" was very wide from the beginning of the colonization of the North American continent. Like much of New England, New Amsterdam had an established Reformed Church, yet the emphasis of the Dutch West India Company was on financial gain, and the great diversity of early settlers allowed a variety of religious bodies, including an early Jewish community, to flourish. After the arrival of the English and the renaming of the colony New York, the Dutch ministers continued to maintain an elite status based on the patronage of the royal governors. In time, however, their influence waned under the pressure of out-migration to upstate New York and New Jersey, as well as an increasingly assertive Anglican Church. Soon royal governors such as Lord Cornbury strengthened control over Anglican and Dutch churches, asserting the right to appoint ministers, while the churches acquiesced in civilian control, as they

---

the safety of the "praying towns" established by the missionaries and traders. Sachems like Metacom (alias King Philip) came to view the proselytizing of Indians as one aspect of the colonial strategy of conquest that was threatening their Native nations. The Native American revolt in the 1670s was but the beginning of a chain of uprisings, including the Deerfield massacre in 1703 and the periodic attacks on settlements like Stockbridge during Jonathan Edwards's tenure as that town's pastor. To borrow a term that has become fashionable in our own period in history, what was unfolding was a serious "clash of civilizations," one in which the Indians witnessed with a mixture of growing wrath and despair the inexorable conquest of their land by the colonists. See Neal Salisbury, "Red Puritans: The 'Praying Indians' of Massachusetts Bay Colony and John Eliot," *William and Mary Quarterly* 31, no. 1 (Jan. 1974): 27–54, and John Demos, *The Unredeemed Captive: A Family Story from Early America* (New York: Vintage, 1995).

sought to resolve religious differences through the civilian courts.[3] Despite the occasional controversies between church and state, religious diversity continued to flourish in New York, with tolerance extended to most Protestant sects, but specifically denied to Catholics through a measure that barred Catholic priests from even entering the colony. Similarly, New Jersey developed with broad religious tolerance extended to all Protestant groups.

Pennsylvania, founded by the Quaker William Penn in the early 1680s, sought to create a new government founded upon the principles of religious toleration and civil liberty. While Pennsylvania has been justly celebrated for its broad economic opportunity and benevolent attitude toward local Native American tribes, it was not immune from the types of church-state conflicts that beset the other colonies. There was frequent tension between the Quaker leaders in Pennsylvania and the already-established settlements in the lower counties that later broke away to form Delaware.

The potential for difficult relations between church and state is perhaps best revealed in the Keithian schism of the early 1690s. George Keith sought a series of reforms in Quaker beliefs that would have placed a greater emphasis on biblically based doctrine and decreased the importance of the "inner light." In 1691 he was charged with heresy by the Quaker meeting, but he refused to be silenced. His movement was interpreted as a threat against both the civil and religious standing order, and the magistrates responded by having the printers of his tracts arrested, their presses destroyed, and his followers arrested and fined. Ultimately separate platforms were set up at opposite ends of the Quaker meetinghouse in Philadelphia, which the rival groups attacked with axes in the midst of the service. While it is difficult to separate the religious elements of Keith's protest from the political components, it is clear that the Quaker elites were comfortable using the combined powers of church and state to stifle dissent. It is also evident that both sides acted with a paucity of Christian charity.

Later the Quaker leaders of Pennsylvania denied Anglicans the right to petition the government for a redress of grievances. Gary Nash has argued that such conflicts and the great difficulty leaders had in preserving order in Pennsylvania stemmed from both the Quaker tradition of resistance to established authorities and the inability of the state effectively to eliminate dissenters in the name of the preservation of societal and religious cohesion, a tactic that was common in Massachusetts. Indeed Penn himself argued that there was a strong connection between church and state when he said that government "was a part of religion itself, a thing sacred in its institution and end." It is perhaps no surprise then that the Quaker Party in Pennsylvania has been identified as the first modern political party.[4]

3. Randall Balmer, *A Perfect Babel of Confusion: Dutch Religion and English Culture in the Middle Colonies* (New York: Oxford University Press, 2002), passim.

4. See Gary B. Nash, *Quakers and Politics: Pennsylvania 1681–1726* (Princeton, NJ: Princeton University Press, 1968), 178–80 and passim. The Penn quotation is on p. 338. Cf. Jon Butler, *New World Faiths: Religion in Colonial America* (New York: Oxford University Press, 2007), 82.

Maryland provides another interesting case study of religious developments in the colonies. While it was originally founded by George Calvert as a proprietary colony to provide a haven for Catholics, it attracted far more Protestant settlers than Catholics. Inundated by Anglicans from Virginia and Puritans from New England, Maryland was forced to enact a strict policy of toleration, as seen in the Maryland Toleration Act of 1649, which guaranteed freedom of worship for all Trinitarian Christians. In time, however, an Anglican majority emerged, the Toleration Act was repealed, and the Church of England was established and supported through tax dollars.

Thus religious freedom and toleration were cited as a desideratum in Rhode Island and the middle colonies. Nevertheless the religious policies of the mother country stipulating the exclusion of Catholics from full citizenship and from high office were extended to the New World. Furthermore, the ideals of religious liberty were rarely achieved, as the church frequently sought the assistance of the government to support its aims and vice versa. Remarkable, though, was the result that emerged from the crosscurrents of the eighteenth century: the British government's active role in promoting Anglicanism, together with the rise of Evangelical religion stemming from the Great Awakening, put strains on the religious accommodations of each of the colonies, contributed to the final break with Great Britain, and influenced the *new order* of church-state relations culminating in the First Amendment to the Constitution.

THE OLD AND THE NEW IN THE THOUGHT
OF JONATHAN EDWARDS

The *old order*, however, with its Puritan aristocratic ideal of a pious and God-fearing populace living under the strict twin leadership of orthodox divines and powerful magistrates, was not to yield without a final heroic restoration effort. Key to that effort was Jonathan Edwards (1703–58). Paradoxically, his defense of classical Puritan ideals was integrated into a deep appreciation of newly emerging philosophical ideas with such deftness as to lay the foundation for an authentic New-World contribution to political theology. Though many of his ideas regarding the relation of church and state proved to be increasingly out of step with religious and cultural trends of his times, his writings continue to be valued, not only as a witness to a critical period in the development of an American national identity, but also as an enduring source of contemporary philosophical and theo-political reflection.

When in 1727 Edwards was ordained as assistant pastor of the Northampton church of his grandfather, Solomon Stoddard, the winds of change that had begun to erode the theocratic ideals of the Winthrops, Cottons, and Mathers were gathering force as increasing numbers of savants, within the church and outside, came under the spell of Deist theologians, Cambridge Neoplatonists, and adherents of the Scottish Enlightenment. Submission to the authority of

Scripture and unswerving fealty to orthodox Calvinism were being challenged by the new arbiter of truth, human reason. Belief in a God who suspended the laws of nature in the form of miracles and who divided humanity into those predestined to be united with Christ for eternity and those who were to suffer eternal punishment in hell elicited diverse forms of reaction. Benign was the reaction of the Arminians, who insisted on a role for the free will of humans to accept or reject God's forgiving and regenerating mercy. More aggressive was the reaction of those who rejected the central tenets of Christian orthodoxy in favor of a worldview built up empirically from human observation and rational thought.[5]

As Edwards, after the death of Solomon Stoddard, was making the transition from assistant to senior pastor, he was confronted with a third challenge to orthodox Calvinism, one that by growing within the heart of the Reformed community itself was more threatening to the hegemonic Puritan ideal than the "heretical" views of Arminianism and Deism. Within the context of growing secularism and in response to a decline in church membership, related to the requirement of public testimony to a conversion experience as a precondition for both participation in the sacrament of communion and full franchised citizenship within the community, his grandfather Stoddard, from the prestigious base of the Northampton parish, assumed leadership in promoting the policy of the "half-way covenant," that is, a more lenient criterion for membership that allowed children of members in good standing to receive communion. Communion thus came to be regarded as allied to the sermon and catechesis in promoting conversion, rather than as an emblem of rebirth.

In a move that created no small amount of inner turmoil, Edwards embarked on a mission aimed at reversing the modernizing movement of his grandfather and restoring orthodox Calvinism, first within his community, then within New England, and finally within the entire world! His reform-driven campaign bears resemblance to the offensive of his seventeenth-century English Puritan forebears in their struggle against what they regarded as grave threats to church and nation posed by king, parliament, and church hierarchy, threats in the form of heresy, lax morals, corruption, and papism. It was a campaign that led to his articulation of a political theology that defended the central tenets of orthodox Calvinism while combining those tenets with the apocalyptic/millennialist theme of the imminent second coming of Christ. While the combination of theocratic polity with millennialist yearnings had already been tested in early seventeenth-century England, where converting the land to true faith was regarded as the preparatory step necessary for the triumphal return and eternal reign of Christ, the new element in Edwards's understanding of church, New England community, and world was this: God's chosen method of achieving that preparation was through an awakening beginning in Northampton, spreading into neighboring

5. Among the radical revisionists was John Taylor, to the refutation of whose writings Edwards devoted considerable energy.

colonies, reaching back across the Atlantic to Scotland and England, and ultimately encompassing the entire world. This daring theological vision was to exercise profound influence on future generations, sowing the seeds for a style of evangelizing that would profoundly shape nineteenth-century Protestantism, firmly establish chiliastic speculation as a central part of American Christianity, and abet disputes between two approaches to church polity designated as Old Lights and New Lights.[6]

Edwards tackled the disputes threatening to fracture the colonies with intellectual rigor and an emotional and physical intensity that frequently sent his fragile mind and body into deep crisis. Paramount in his mind was the theopolitical question of identity: was the church to be the communion of saints called out from the defilement of the world (e.g., the position of the Baptists), or was the church to be coextensive with the civic community (à la Solomon Stoddard)? At issue was the classic struggle between two concepts: sectarian Christianity and cultural Christianity. Edwards's strategy arose out of the situation in the first third of the eighteenth century: the authoritativeness of the traditional three-pillared structure of community, namely, church-state-family, was eroding, especially among the increasing number of landless, listless unmarried men in their twenties. Too orthodox to adopt the half-way covenant compromise, and too elitist to abandon the ideal of a community obedient to its magistrates and divines, Edwards developed an approach that was not free from inner contradictions, a renewal of strictly orthodox Calvinism through the means of revivals—many of them conducted by itinerant preachers—that became the hallmark of the First Awakening. In his thinking, the intransigent conflict between the ideals of "pure called-out congregations" and "theocratic commonwealth" would be resolved once the Awakening had reached its goal of converting all members of the community, that is to say, church and state would be coterminous, and the commonwealth would be the pure called-out congregation writ large. Edwards believed it was God's purpose that the glorious awakening would not stop until it had brought the entire world into its embrace, thus preparing for Christ's return. In his thinking, John Winthrop's "city on a hill" was on the cusp of becoming the New Jerusalem of the book of Revelation! Millennialist exuberance reverberates in the following words that he penned in 1743: "'Tis not unlikely that this work of God's Spirit, that is so extraordinary and wonderful, is the dawning, or at least a prelude, of that glorious work of God, so often foretold in Scripture, which in the progress and issue of it, shall renew the world of mankind. . . . [W]e can't reasonably think otherwise, than

6. More recent scholars such as Thomas Kidd have divided views on the Great Awakening into three perspectives: antirevivalists, moderate evangelicals, and radical evangelicals. Most past analysis focused on the antirevivalists as the Old Lights and the moderate evangelicals as New Lights. See, for example, Thomas S. Kidd, *The Great Awakening: The Roots of Evangelical Christianity in Colonial America* (New Haven, CT: Yale University Press, 2007), xiv.

that the beginning of the great work of God must be near. . . . And there are many things that make it probable that this work will begin in America."[7]

From the pulpit Edwards described the day in which Satan would be defeated and "all the inhabitants of this new discovered world shall be brought over into the kingdom of Christ, as well as all the other ends of the earth."[8] That such a positive assessment of the eschatological role of the New Israel and the importance of his own ministry in preparing for the end times was for him not the product of fanciful enthusiasm but the product of careful interpretation of Scripture is indicated by his application of the prophetic promises of Isaiah 60 to eighteenth-century America: "[W]hat is now seen in America, especially in New England, may prove the dawn of that glorious day: and the very uncommon and wonderful circumstances and events of this work, seem to me strongly to argue that God intends it as the beginning or forerunner of something vastly great."[9]

Edwards's eschatologically infused revivalism was not unanimously affirmed by his coreligionists, whether at home or abroad. Opposition to what was regarded as the destabilizing emotionalism of the awakeners was formidable in New England and became a major factor in the widening gulf between representatives of the Old Light, such as Charles Chauncy, and the New Light and more radical Evangelicals, many of whom (e.g., James Davenport) were far more extreme than Edwards in their abandonment of reason-accompanied interpretation of Scripture and respect for tradition, in favor of a passionate assault on ecclesial authority and traditional doctrine. A solemn word of caution from abroad was expressed in typical English litotes by the highly respected hymn writer, Isaac Watts: "I think his reasonings about America want force."[10]

The disputes that were growing increasingly heated not only between Old Lights and New Lights, but also among different representatives of the New Lights, were often rooted in different understandings of the relation of Scripture to tradition and reason. How are we to understand Edwards's own hermeneutic, which by his own testimony revolved around a reasonable exposition of Scripture guided by Reformed theology? The difference between his approach and the radical pneumatic tendencies of the controversial James Davenport is enormous, but it is also important to recognize the distinction between his approach to biblical interpretation and that of the more moderate Anglican evangelist George Whitefield, with whom he in other respects cooperated wholeheartedly. Marsden describes the contrast thus:

---

7. Jonathan Edwards, *Some Thoughts Concerning the Present Revival of Religion in New England* (Boston [1743]), in Jonathan Edwards, *The Great Awakening*, vol. 4 of *The Works of Jonathan Edwards*, ed. C. C. Goen (New Haven, CT: Yale University Press, 1972), 4:291.

8. Jonathan Edwards, *Sermon 24*, in *A History of the Work of Redemption*, in *The Works of Jonathan Edwards* (New Haven, CT: Yale University Press, 1989), 9:435.

9. Edwards, *Some Thoughts*, in *Works*, 4:291–95.

10. Ibid., 4:353–58, quoted in George M. Marsden, *Jonathan Edwards: A Life* (New Haven, CT: Yale University Press, 2003), 556n25.

Whitefield and many of his fellow awakeners were following what they took to be direct leadings from God's Spirit. They would, after intense prayer about a decision, become convinced that God was directly telling them what they should do. Edwards believed such "impressions" were often the products of the imagination. . . . He strongly favored prayerful spiritual intensity accompanied by wonderful images of God's grace. . . . But for Edwards these ecstatic experiences had to be disciplined by the rational mind, informed by Scripture.[11]

Having recognized in Edward's hermeneutic the critical function exercised by Scripture and reason in holding in check inward promptings blithely identified with the will of God, one may be puzzled by his robust theo-political assumptions regarding the role of America in God's universal plan of redemption. It behooves us to apply the safeguards Edwards raised against the subjective absolutism of the spiritualists to the conclusions he himself drew from the Bible in relation to the historical events of his time. The picture that emerges is mixed, for on the one hand his hermeneutic is predicated on a dynamic historicism and a deep respect for the role of reason. On the other hand, his perspective is conditioned by his strong-willed defense of an aging orthodoxy and a theocratic legacy that privileges one particular civilization over others.

The time-conditioned nature of Edwards's theology is starkly visible in the notes he kept recording events—both past and contemporary—in which he saw evidence of the providential direction of history toward the eschaton. He was particularly fascinated by reports filtering down from Canada regarding the attack of the New England regiments against the French fortress in Louisburg in 1745. What had been anticipated as an easy conquest turned into a bitter struggle. When the confident prediction of George Whitefield that God would intervene on the side of the desperate Protestant allies appeared to have been fulfilled in a stunning victory, Edwards described the event as not only a crucial setback for Satan and his Catholic allies but evidence of the unfolding of God's mighty works in the history of his people.

While the combination of millennialist fervor and anti-Catholic vitriol is offensive to modern sensibilities, it is important to recognize that Edwards, as a child of his times, was adding his voice to a view that was practically universal among Protestant church leaders of that time. Even Charles Chauncy, one of the most outspoken critics of what many of the Boston Old Light leaders regarded as emotional excesses in Edwards's revival-style preaching, joined in the exuberant trumpeting of the Louisburg triumph: "I scarce know of a conquest, since the days of Joshua and the Judges wherein the finger of God is more visible."[12] Critics of this patriotic nationalism, like Benjamin Franklin, who debunked the identification of God with the military campaigns of Protestant Christendom,

11. Marsden, *Jonathan Edwards*, 212.
12. Charles Chauncy, *Marvellous Things Done by the Right Hand and Holy Arm of God in Getting Him the Victory* (Boston, 1745), 12.

tended to come from the ranks of those whose critique of Christianity reached to its central tenets.

The initial success of the Great Awakening experienced by Edwards and reported by him to his friends both in New England and abroad was of the kind that corroborated his blending of provincial patriotism and millennialist enthusiasm. But over the course of Edwards's life, the spirit of awakening ebbed and flowed; during times when the tide was subsiding and conversions dwindled in number, crisis in confidence and soul-searching became the bitter spiritual diet that Edwards was forced to digest. Ever resourceful, however, he managed to emerge from such travail with new energy by entering into new alliances and experimenting with new strategies. Foremost among new alliances was the close spiritual and professional bond he established with the Anglican evangelist George Whitefield, who after tours in Georgia and other southern provinces accepted Edwards's invitation to come to Northampton in 1740.

In the arena of new strategies for awakening spiritual backsliders, however, Edwards was capable of serious misjudgments. In an effort to restore the traditional authoritarian structures of Puritanism in Northampton in 1742, he summoned the community to enter into a solemn covenant by pledging to conform their lives to the strict standards of orthodox Calvinism. George Marsden describes the less than successful outcome of that initiative: "[I]t was like asking a town of the 1740's to become like a Puritan village of the 1640's. . . . Edwards was impaled on the horns of a dilemma inherited from the tradition. Puritanism and its Reformed-pietist successors constantly vacillated between whether they were rebuilding Christendom by making towns and eventually nations into virtually Christian societies, or whether they were advocating a pure, called-out church."[13]

Never one to abandon his vision of a church universal conforming to his understanding of Calvinist orthodoxy, however, Edwards directed his attention beyond the ups and downs of his own parish in two directions.

Firstly, he rekindled his vision of the transatlantic scope of the revival movement in a new initiative he called a concert of prayer. The notion of the extension of the Northampton awakening to the ends of the earth breathed into his flagging spirits a renewed enthusiasm, "till the awakening reaches those that are in the highest stations, and till whole nations be awakened, and there be at length an accession of many of the chief nations to the church of God."[14]

Secondly, after being dismissed from his Northampton parish and moving westward to Stockbridge, he articulated, both in word and in action, his understanding of the place intended for the Native Americans in God's redemptive

---

13. Marsden, *Jonathan Edwards*, 350.

14. Jonathan Edwards, "An humble attempt to promote explicit agreement and visible union of God's people in extraordinary prayer for the revival of religion and the advancement of Christ's Kingdom on earth, pursuant to Scripture-promises and prophecies concerning the last time" (Boston: Daniel Henchman, 1747), Evans Collection of Early American Imprints, 5938, 10 in the Archive Americana produced by the American Antiquarian Society.

plan. It again combines theological insights that continue to enrich contemporary theo-political discourse with elements that can strike the contemporary person of conscience as inadequate. But this is the kind of ambivalent picture that is to be expected in examining the thoughts—however profound—of a past figure from one's own historical vantage point. For example, he held the culture of the Indians in such low regard as to believe their Native tongues were inadequate as a vehicle of the gospel message. Accordingly, the schools he helped set up for educating the Natives were conducted solely in English. This is not far from the pedagogy of the previous generation's praying towns, where missionaries such as John Eliot often failed to distinguish between Christian discipleship and training in English cultural norms.

Defending Edwards against the charge of colonialist condescension vis-à-vis the Native cultures by appeal to his particular location in time would be much simpler, were it not for the trenchant critique of one of that generation's foremost missionaries to the Indians, Gideon Hawley:

> I won't go among the Indians in the character of a Christian missionary, except I can go upon Christian principles. . . . But why do I talk of *Christian* zeal in this case 'tis a *political* affair. . . . Mr. Edwards . . . has blind notions about things and no wonder seeing he knows nothing but by hearsay and the half has never been told him. If he would endeavor to excite me to engage in my mission and use only the motives which are suggested in Christianity I should like it better. Mr. Edwards is a very good man but capable of being biased.[15]

Marsden offers this interpretation of Hawley's critique: "Working from a Constantinian perspective, [Edwards] never questioned the premise that God used Christian empires to bring his message to uncivilized peoples."[16] Here one can note that Edwards cited Constantine's conquest of the Roman Empire as one of the propitious dates on his millennial calendar. Edwards, it seems, was drawn to strong leaders capable of ordering unruly populations on the basis of authoritative structures of governance, which of course is a profile bearing striking resemblance to himself.

Marsden, while meticulous in chronicling the monumental achievements of a theologian whom he clearly holds in high regard, nevertheless upholds the responsibility of the historian by recognizing Edwards's shortcomings and their roots. Rather than exonerating Edwards, he points to his participation in the zeitgeist of his time, to his social location in the aristocratic elite of eighteenth-century New England, and to his authoritarian style of leadership. Specifically with regard to Edwards's simultaneous defense of Indian rights and denigration of their Native customs, Marsden notes that "almost all the British interest in the Indians was with the ultimate aim of displacing them. Many of the less

15. Gideon Hawley, *Journal*, Congregational Library, Boston, February 12 and 17, 1757, cited in Marsden, *Jonathan Edwards*, 588n28.
16. Marsden, *Jonathan Edwards*, 409.

religious British and Americans acknowledged that explicitly. Others, such as Edwards, who wed the political to the religious, were in Hawley's view naïve if they thought that the Gospel was not undermined when it was used for military recruitment."[17]

In evaluating Edwards's contribution to the history of the relationship of biblical faith to politics in America, it is necessary to recognize his pivotal location in that history. He is situated at a critical threshold, with a tidal wave of theological and philosophical change cascading over the Atlantic toward a loose confederation of colonies in search of a new notion of self-rule. Unwilling to abandon all features of the old, both intrigued and skeptical regarding daring new intellectual explorations in Continental and British universities, Edwards found himself contending at home with leaders considering themselves authorized by a divine mandate to uphold the old order as well as heady innovators announcing the recentering of reality from an otiose god to a resurgent rational human race capable of taking charge of its destiny. Edwards responded by simultaneously assuming the role of guardian of what is of enduring value in the old order and prophetic herald of the new world aborning.

Though it is difficult to capture the complexity of a savant like Jonathan Edwards in a single figure, it may be fitting to compare him with the wise scribe of Matthew 13:52, for he proved to be a master of the art of bringing "out of his treasure what is new and what is old." While the challenges of his time cried out for the high degree of originality that he brought to his understanding of Puritan-Calvinist tradition, his abiding appreciation of the old order was unwavering. The dialectical balance that he was able to maintain was propitious, for his generation was not lacking in enthusiasts for a form of homocentric modernity ready to jettison classic religious principles such as the sole sovereignty of God and the grounding of human dignity, equality, liberty, and inalienable rights in an eternal order vouched safe by a Creator infinitely transcending in stature and authority any human order or agency. It may not be rash to see in the work and thought of Jonathan Edwards an adumbration of the neo-orthodox movement inaugurated a century and a half later by another Calvinist, Karl Barth.

THE PROPHETIC-DIALECTICAL MODEL TAKES ROOT

The balancing of the ultimate standard of divine government and the pragmatic necessity of human government sought and in part achieved by Jonathan Edwards constitutes the heart of the prophetic-dialectical model. Its longevity is remarkable, with roots reaching back to ancient Israel and a tenacity to outlive theocracies, oligarchies, and monarchies, as well as tyrannies and dictatorships. Like the phoenix rising out of the primordial darkness or Ariel whispering defiantly from the ashes of enemy conquest, the prophetic dialectic has throughout

17. Ibid., 426.

history provided the platform for reconstituting civil order after the collapse of powerful earthly regimes. Any inquiry hoping to explain this tenacity must grapple with the paradox of a theo-politics that strips every form of human government of ultimate authority and yet devotes itself unstintingly to the vitality of human government through programs of reform modeled after its understanding of the nature of divine rule. On the basis of this model, religious communities, while not confusing earthly governments with the city of God, nevertheless are able to recognize the important role they can play in fostering the growth of a healthy society.

Central to this role is the Aristotelian task of tutoring citizens in the virtues that are the sine qua non of civil order. In the case of colonial New England, the chief agent in that tutoring task was construed in terms of a "learned ministry" trained to nurture within the general populace those essential virtues and to foster the strength of character requisite to the task of speaking out against the abuse of human rule in the form of tyranny or injustice. Ezra Stiles, while serving as pastor of the Second Congregational Church in Newport, Rhode Island, gave clear expression to the prophetic-dialectic perspective in 1772: "I am a Friend to American Liberty . . . [but] we have another Department, being called to an Office and Work, which may be successfully pursued . . . under every species of Civil Tyranny or Liberty. We cannot become the Dupes of Politicians with Alliances, Concessions and Connections dangerous to evangelical Truth and spiritual Liberty."[18]

Another courageous representative of the prophetic-dialectic perspective who repudiated attempts to equate nation with divine rule was Samuel Hopkins, a student, close friend, and biographer of Jonathan Edwards. The basis for Hopkins's rejection of facile scriptural arguments for morally offensive acts by and practices within the young nation was what in contemporary scholarship would be recognized as a hermeneutic sensitive to the historical dimension of the biblical texts.

The transfer of meaning from the ancient account of God's election of Israel to a doctrine of American exceptionalism could be accomplished, according to Hopkins, only by ignoring a rudimentary fact, that historical Israel and historical colonial America were two distinct entities. He made his point succinctly and with passion in his scathing attack on those who defended slavery by appeal to the biblical laws granting Israel permission to enslave the Canaanites: "the distinction [i.e., distinctiveness] [of Israel] is . . . at an end, and all nations are put upon a level; and Christ . . . has taught us to look on all nations as our neighbors and brethren." Hopkins's stand appears even more courageous in light of the fact that it was published in 1776, the very year that Americans were boldly declaring their independence from British "slavery" while simultaneously insisting on

18. Mark A. Noll, *America's God: From Jonathan Edwards to Abraham Lincoln* (New York: Oxford University Press, 2002), 134n68.

preserving as their own "property" enslaved Africans.[19] When we turn in later chapters to analyze the politics of the Bible, we shall discover that Hopkins was reiterating a phenomenon that lies at the heart of biblical religion, namely, the dynamic of change in response to new historical circumstances. Specifically with regard to slave holding and release, there are three distinct iterations legislating slavery in the Bible, each manifesting a heightened degree of humaneness.[20] Though writing nearly a century before slavery was abolished in the United States, Hopkins was prophetic in condemning the kind of *a*historical interpretation that facilitated the abuse of Scripture in his time—abuse that, alas, continues in relation to the moral issues of our own day.

By including attentiveness to the historical context of biblical texts and to the presence of diversity and development in biblical traditions, he gave an early hint at a historical-critical understanding of Scripture that held promise of aiding religious leaders and politicians alike in developing guidelines for a responsible correlation of Bible and politics. But the insights of Hopkins, Stiles, and Edwards were ahead of their time, soon to be swept aside by a surging wave of patriotism that lifted up the notion of divine election to new heights of popularity and reinforced a legacy of privilege that has plagued the nation ever since.

This was true of the feverish years leading up to war with Britain, but sadly, even after an otherwise propitious period in US history, the period that produced the Constitution and Bill of Rights, that legacy reasserted itself and expanded its reach over the course of the nineteenth century. Notwithstanding the fact that it represented an utter contradiction to their concept of inalienable rights, the founders were driven by the expediency of political compromise to bracket slavery from their thinking. The consequence of not heeding Hopkins's cry in the wilderness was a century of turmoil and bloodshed. Before we turn to the struggles of that century, however, we have yet to examine the final quarter of the eighteenth century, a period giving shape to two more theo-political models.

19. Mark A. Noll, Nathan O. Hatch, Geroge M. Mardsen, *The Search for Christian America* (Colorado Springs, CO: Helmers & Howard, 1989), 24. In this warning, Hopkins was anticipated by a Hebrew critic of nationalistic exceptionalism: "Are you not like the Ethiopians to me, O people of Israel? says the LORD. Did I not bring Israel up from the land of Egypt, and the Philistines from Caphtor and the Arameans from Kir?" (Amos 9:7). This repudiation of allegiance to homeland stands in stark contrast to the position reflected in William Bradford's identification of the Puritans with the ancient Israelites cited above.

20. Exod. 21:2–11; Deut. 15:12–18; Lev. 25:39–55.

Chapter 3

The Revolutionary Period and the Lure of the Apocalyptic Model

As has been so tragically common in human history, the frenzy of war over-whelmed the subtlety of thought that had encouraged the beginnings of a critical reading of the Bible and a dialectical understanding of the relation of faith to civic duty. Threatened with extinction was the civility that recognized the inevitability of moral ambiguity in political process and that accordingly embraced both self-criticism and openness to the challenges of opposing points of view. Rather than developing further the distinction between the kingdom of God and the regimes of this world, a generation of patriotic preachers arose that uncritically translated the evangelical passion for spiritual purity into a nationalistic passion for defeat of the English. When conflicts with England arose over economic and political matters such as taxation and representation, the pragmatics of political compromise were denounced as pacts with the devil that were below the dignity of a Christian statesman. King George III was identified with the antichrist and the members of parliament with Satan's hosts. God's plan for the emerging republic was equated with God's plan for humanity. Robert Smith, a Presbyterian, in 1781 declared that "the cause of America is the cause of Christ."[1]

1. Robert Smith, "The Obligations of the Confederate States of North America to Praise God" (Philadelphia: Francis Bailey, 1782), Evans Collection of Early American Imprints 17722, 33.

The apocalyptic politics that in seventeenth-century England had convinced many that Christ was soon to arrive to transform their isles into the New Israel was translated to a transatlantic setting that was even more hospitable to evangelical zealotry. In the New World a war was being fomented through which God could accomplish the new creation.[2] In such a time, disobedience to God's call to war was depicted as a despicable fusion of blasphemy and lack of patriotism. War preparations were thus abetted from the pulpit with a millennial fervor that left no gray areas, but portrayed the contestants as strictly divided between children of light and children of darkness. When Ethan Allen and his troops took Fort Ticonderoga, he proclaimed the victory "in the name of the Great Jehovah and the Continental Congress."[3] In 1784 the New England Baptist Association issued this millennial proclamation: "Nor is it at all improbable that America is reserved in the mind of Jehovah to be the grand theatre on which the divine Redeemer will accomplish glorious things. . . . If we observe the signs of the times, we shall find reason to think he is on his way."[4]

Thus there began to emerge a nationalistic reading of biblical religion that in the next two centuries captivated the thinking of many leaders, clergy and politicians alike, with notable exceptions to be sure, especially among Anglicans. It is perhaps unfair, however, to berate ordinary citizens striving to be both faithful and patriotic, for they belonged to a generation taught to respect its leaders, most especially its religious leaders. As David Ramsey has written, "The clergy of New England were a numerous, learned, and respectable body, who had a great ascendancy over the minds of their hearers. They connected religion and patriotism, and in their sermons and prayers, represented the cause of America as the cause of Heaven."[5]

The blurring of the line between religion and national destiny that became characteristic of what George Armstrong Kelly has called "patriotic provincialism" was to become something of a style in American politics. While becoming well established in the popular practice of the nation, however, it did not become the legal position, thanks to the caution and distrust of unbridled sectarianism of those who wrote the founding documents. We turn to the history of the origins of those documents, for they continue today to place restraints upon abuses that arise from a fuzzy, albeit often piously motivated, fusing of religion and politics.

---

2. Commonly drawn were typologies such as George Washington=Moses and Ethan Allen=Joshua.

3. Michael A. Bellesiles, *Revolutionary Outlaws: Ethan Allen and the Struggle for Independence on the Early American Frontier* (Charlottesville: University Press of Virginia, 1993), 118. Ethan Allen's synergistic formulation echoes Gideon's battle cry as he routed the Midianites, "For YHWH and for Gideon" (Judg. 7:18).

4. Minutes of the Warren Association, at their meeting, in Middleboro, Sept. 7 and 8, 1784 (Boston: 1784), in Evans Collection of Early American Imprints 18869, 7. Compare President Reagan's comment to Tom Dine quoted on p. 108.

5. David Ramsey, *History of the United States from their First Settlement as English Colonies in 1607, to the Year 1808, or the Thirty-Third Year of the Sovereignty and Independence* (Philadelphia: M. Carey, 1816), 2:17.

Chapter 4

Church and State
in the Founding Documents

Though, as noted earlier, millennial interpretations of biblical faith proclaimed with fiery passion from the Christian pulpits in the period leading up to the Revolution played an important role in molding the popular attitude toward the bearing of religion on the struggles against England, there was also present another tradition, which contributed substantively and lastingly to the shape of the emerging nation and served as a counterbalance of immense importance to the excesses of the religious zealots. This was the political philosophy of the Whig party, a philosophy that in many cases merged with political principles that the Puritans had drawn from their understanding of the Bible, while at the same time remaining surprisingly free from direct reference to biblical religion.

The roots of Whig thinking lay rather in the writings of Hume and Locke and in the British common-law tradition of liberties serving as a defense against the abuse of centralized power. It founded rights on nature rather than on the Bible and sought enlightenment more through the tools of reason than through divine revelation. Whereas the Puritans John Winthrop, John Cotton, Thomas Hooker, and their successors founded society on the basis of covenant as an extension of God's election of Israel as the chosen people, the Whigs appealed to the concept of social contract.[1]

On the face of it, the difference did not appear great. Both traditions fostered distrust of the abuse of power, whether by monarch, parliament, or established church. Both thereby contributed to a growing resistance to British authority, to the demand for parliamentary concessions and reforms, to the defense of inalienable rights, and finally to the call to a war of independence. Both were capable of describing the struggle in the absolute terms of good and evil that diminished the likelihood of compromise.

The two traditions, Puritan and Whig, thus were interrelated in various ways, and the connections went beyond overlap on principles and involved more than common roots in some distant classical and biblical heritage. The connections were often made in the lives of individuals who, like Goethe's Faust, experienced the cohabitation of two souls in their breasts. Clearly there was no rigid separation in people's minds between the Puritan and Whig traditions; instead they were melded and meshed together, making it next to impossible for the modern scholar to parse out the disparate sources of ideas. One example of the overlapping of categories can be seen in James Madison, who drew upon the biblical Christianity of his Calvinist teacher at Princeton, John Witherspoon, but from the same savant was able to imbibe the liberal philosophy of the Scottish Enlightenment philosopher David Hume.

Madison's life also reveals another source of the emerging political philosophy that would shape the founding documents, namely, a kind of pragmatism born of experience and refined by careful reflection. Thus Madison, deeply religious in his youth, also was greatly influenced by Enlightenment philosophy. While it is extremely difficult to pin down Madison's religious views, he distrusted those classmates at Princeton that embraced enthusiastic religion, but whose lives fell short of the ideal. He was also profoundly influenced by a series of Anglican persecutions of Baptists that swept Virginia during the early 1770s. Madison's disgust at this persecution inspired him to try to introduce the Pennsylvania model of religious liberty in Virginia. Eventually combining his efforts with his close political collaborator Jefferson, Madison became a staunch opponent of the establishment of a state church.[2]

The influence of Thomas Hobbes and John Locke is easily detected in Madison's thought, especially in his sober anthropology regarding the human in the natural state as a warring animal, his fear of the corruption accompanying the concentration of power within a society, and his awareness of the need for an

1. See especially Bernard Bailyn, *The Ideological Origins of the American Revolution* (Cambridge, MA: Harvard University Press, 1992), 22–54, and Gordon Wood, *The Creation of the American Republic* (New York: W. W. Norton & Co., 1969), 3–45, for two classic expositions of the Whig tradition.
2. Steven Walman, *Founding Faith: Providence, Politics, and the Birth of Religious Freedom in America* (New York: Random House, 2009), 96–106.

agreement among the citizens over the kind of government to which they were willing to submit. But here too the political philosophy of the Whigs combined easily with biblically based Puritan pessimism regarding Homo sapiens as expressed succinctly by the prophet Jeremiah: "The heart is devious above all else; it is perverse—who can understand it?" (Jer. 17:9). Madison would have found no need to choose between Whig and biblical anthropology when he denounced religious factionalism fanned by the "impulse of passion, or of interest, adverse to the rights of other citizens, or to the permanent and aggregate interests of the community," a frightening state rooted "in the nature of man."[3] At the same time Madison's trust in human reason and the possibilities of building a new national government with scarce a reference to God or explicitly scriptural principles demonstrates that he had drunk deeply from the well of Enlightenment optimism.

There is a further reason why the dichotomy between biblical Puritans and Whigs should not be overdrawn. Unlike persons in other biblical-political movements simultaneously developing on the North American continent, the Puritans did not set biblical revelation in opposition to reason. They promoted education and brought into their libraries the writings of the Cambridge Platonists, as well as Pascal, Newton, Fénelon, and Locke. They were fond of the classics, as the libraries of divines like John Harvard revealed.[4] The Puritan legacy in our early history thus made a positive contribution to the unique symbiosis that emerged for relating faith and reason, namely, biblical Christianity and rational philosophy. Not to be forgotten as well is the influence of spiritualism, with its openness to natural theology, on seventeenth-century English theology. To be sure, the integration of those two traditions was much more thorough in the case of Madison than in the case of the free-thinking Benjamin Franklin or even more emphatically the skeptic Thomas Paine, who in his embrace of Enlightenment and Deist thought rejected much of Christianity.

Eclipsed by the developments leading toward the drafting of the Declaration of Independence and the Constitution were the eschatological interpretations of political history, whether of the popular variety of the New England clergy or of the more subtle Augustinian variety of Jonathan Edwards. While biblical

3. James Madison, "Federalist No. 10," The Library of Congress, accessed December 20, 2014, http://thomas.loc.gov/home/histdox/fed_10.html.
4. Samuel Eliot Morison, *Harvard College in the Seventeenth Century*, vol. 1 (Cambridge, MA: Harvard University Press, 1936), 194–95. There were works by Thomas Aquinas, Luther, Calvin, Plutarch, Homer, and many others (Josiah Quincy, *The History of Harvard University*, vol. 1, 1840, 10–11). Despite the 1764 fire, there were earlier records of many of these books. A catalogue of John Harvard's books was compiled by Alfred C. Potter (1867–1940) in 1920 and published by the then Colonial Society of Massachusetts (*Publications*, vol. 21, 190–230). Reprinted copies of the catalogues are also held at the Harvard University Archives and the Houghton Library. In November 1938, the *Harvard Alumni Bulletin* published an article by Henry J. Cadbury, "What Happened to John Harvard's Books?" (vol. 41, 241–48).

eschatology was not a preponderant dimension in the thinking of the founders, they at times pursued a secular millennialism arising from their belief that they were building a new order of the ages. They were little troubled by the disparity between the city of God and the human state they were building. This is not to deny that they were acutely aware that the unruly proclivities of humans presented a challenge. But the rationalist tilt of their thinking gave them hope that with proper leadership humans could be tamed and even civilized. They seemed confident that what they were building could succeed, if it was founded upon and preserved the principles of truth and justice that were built into nature and were in harmony with "nature's God." In this respect they were bona fide children of the Enlightenment.

At the same time they were deathly afraid that the common people lacked adequate "civic virtue" to make the republican experiment work. Their desire to have the churches promote virtue will be discussed in more detail below. At this juncture, however, the point we wish to emphasize is this: the personal faith and acquaintance with the Bible of many of the founders notwithstanding, the climate in the chambers of the Constitutional Convention, in which they sweated over their drafts and proposals, was predominantly the climate of the English Enlightenment and its theological offspring, Deism.

Preliminarily it may be well to reflect on the implications of the ascendancy of reason at this critical crossroads in United States history for the question of the relation between religion and politics. It is not unreasonable to surmise that the victory of Evangelical exclusivism would have had deleterious consequences for church and state alike, whereas the incorporation of the Enlightenment/Deist perspective into the Constitution was largely salutary. Worth pondering is the question, what might have been the historical consequences for the nation if at this period it had been endowed with a constitution that enforced a nationalistic sectarianism identifying God's cause with that of the Republic, that condemned all who opposed that identification as evil, that equated the structures and laws of the land with biblical law, that conferred upon certified clergy the authority to interpret the Constitution, that obliterated distinctions between church and state, and that awaited the imminent return of Christ in wrath to rectify any deviation from a founding document believed to be the direct product of divine command? In other words, what would have been the course of US history if a theocratic model of government had prevailed?

The criterion of reason followed by the founders, while not without defects (e.g., the contradictions posed by slavery), produced structures of relationships between the branches of government and between government and religion that have proven very suitable for a nation moving with every passing decade toward greater religious, ethnic, and cultural diversity. Distrust of the claim of any mortal to possess certainty created checks and balances and a resulting dynamic of political adaptation and reform. The God of Christianity was not ensconced in the Constitution as patron of the chosen nation. In the Deist thought of Jefferson and Franklin, there was no room for certainty that a personal deity existed whose job it was to show special favor to one country over all others.[5] Where international conflict or domestic problems arose, solutions had to be found by the application of the principles of sound reason, guided by the wisdom and lessons of the past. The Lockean/biblical anthropology of more orthodox Christians like Madison and Witherspoon enabled them to lend their support to the drafting of a nonevangelical Constitution, to which the First Amendment was soon added to make explicit the proscription of the "establishment of religion," that is, the denunciation of any religious body's claim to be entitled to dictate federal political policy. The result was a secular structure of federal government that has tended to serve both religion and government well. The assumptions of the founders at the federal level subsequently spread through a combination of state constitutional amendments, federal constitutional amendments, and Supreme Court decisions to cover all levels of government within the United States.[6]

But this is only half of the picture. The First Amendment balanced the proscription of the establishment of religion with the protection of the "free exercise thereof." On the basis of this clause the churches and, and, in later years, other religious assemblies were accorded a solid foundation for their life within the larger society. Taken together, the establishment and the free-exercise clauses balance interaction within the larger culture. Congress is barred from either establishing religion or interfering with its exercise, while religious institutions are left free to make their own contributions to public and personal life. This delegation of distinct responsibilities, when carried out respectfully and harmoniously, contributes to the vitality of both sides, which vitality in turn enhances the common weal. Without the protection of government, the freedom of religious bodies would be in jeopardy. Without the contribution to moral education and personal virtue of the churches, government would be weakened. Mutual respect, in the thinking of the founders, was to characterize these separate but interacting bodies within society.

Embedded in this dialectic of separation and mutual engagement was a public duty assigned to religion. This duty, while implicit in the documents themselves, was spelled out in the personal letters, essays, and speeches of the founders in terms of the virtues of individual citizens, though it was later ascribed also to religious institutions such as churches and synagogues. Benjamin Franklin wrote, "History will . . . afford frequent Opportunities of showing the Necessity of a Publick Religion, from its Usefulness to the Publick; the Advantage of a Religious Character among Private Persons; the Mischiefs of Superstition, etc. and the Excellency of the CHRISTIAN RELIGION above all others ancient

---

5. Jefferson's Deist worldview is reflected by his deletion of all supernatural elements from his translation of the Gospels (*Life and morals of Jesus of Nazareth*, 1819). Franklin's understanding of Jesus is reflected in his admonition to emulate Jesus and Socrates (Benjamin Franklin, *The Autobiography of Benjamin Franklin* [Boston: MacMillan & Co., 1921], 80).

6. Some states maintained their established churches well into the nineteenth century. Connecticut ended taxpayer support for religion in 1818, Maine in 1820, and Massachusetts in 1833.

or modern."[7] In his farewell address, George Washington said, "Whatever may be conceded to the influence of refined education on minds of peculiar structure, reason and experience both forbid us to expect that National Morality can prevail in exclusion of religious principle."[8] Even Thomas Jefferson, in his first inaugural address in 1801, maintained, "The liberties of a nation [cannot] be thought secure when we have removed their only firm basis, a conviction in the minds of the people that their liberties are a gift of God."[9]

While the founders were emphatic in their insistence that governmental deference with respect to any specific sectarian belief contradicted the principles of the republic, they were simultaneously consistent in respecting the indispensable role of religion in cultivating a morally dependable populace. The roots of their thinking on this matter actually were closely tied to those that influenced their advocacy of the separation of church and state, namely, the sober anthropology of Hobbes, Hume, Locke, and other eighteenth-century philosophers. In 1748 Montesquieu wrote, "He who has no religion at all is that terrible animal who can only feel his freedom when he is destroying and devouring."[10] A democratic republic could not depend on instinctively virtuous citizens for its well-being.[11] Religion carried the responsibility of tutoring and civilizing a very unruly species! Its positive attitude toward religion stands in marked contrast to the atheism and bitter animosity toward religious institutions generated by the French and Russian Revolutions. As Mark Noll has argued, the compatibility of liberal republican thought and traditional Christianity marks an important difference between American and European political developments.[12]

Two other details fill out the picture: First, the Constitution specifically bars all religious tests for office holding. Although many of the state constitutions possessed such tests, the refusal of the founders to incorporate them demonstrates the intentional nonsectarian nature of the document. It is noteworthy that some of the opponents to the Constitution focused specifically on the proscription of religious tests in their criticism of the new document. This is a minority position that has refused to be silenced to the present day.

Second, it is important to recognize a very pragmatic dimension in the debate over that relation of church and state. In the minds of leading theorists like Jefferson and Madison, creation of an effective and enduring structure of governance was not possible without neutralizing the potentially explosive religious issue. By preventing religious tests for public office and carefully balancing the

---

7. James A. Reichley, *Religion in American Public Life* (Washington, DC: Brookings Institution, 1985), 101n119.

8. Ibid., 103.

9. Thomas Jefferson, First Inaugural Address, The Avalon Project, last updated 2008, http://avalon.law.yale.edu/19th_century/jefinau1.asp.

10. Baron De Montesquieu, *The Spirit of Laws* (New York: Cosimo Classics, 2011), 28.

11. It is interesting to note that the need for the contribution of religious communities to public virtue arose more out of a sober assessment of human nature than out of evangelical enthusiasm.

12. Mark Noll, *America's God: From Jonathan Edwards to Abraham Lincoln* (Oxford: Oxford University Press, 2002), 87–88.

First Amendment's nonestablishment and free-exercise clauses, they managed to garner support both from those who wanted to guarantee a separation between the federal government and the churches and those who feared that the new government might threaten their state establishments.[13]

Of course, no constitutional document is effective without judicial reaffirmation, but here too our system has weathered the tests of time. Christopher Mooney has documented how the history of Supreme Court decisions relating to the First Amendment quite consistently has preserved a congenial attitude of government toward religious bodies.[14] This civility has not always been reciprocated. Shocked by growing federal power and the application of federal principles upon state and local governments, some zealous Christian groups have collided with the First Amendment tradition, not as victims of government suppression, but as activists demanding that the government give legal status to explicitly Christian principles, with the resulting infringement upon the rights of citizens holding other religious beliefs or none at all.

With the First Amendment, the founders contributed a dialectical relationship that must be respected by everyone dedicated to strengthening the moral foundation of our country. It defines the rules of the game more fairly than many religious groups define them, by eliminating special pleading and special privilege from the public domain. Equal respect is to be accorded all participants; all viewpoints civilly presented are to be welcomed, including those rooted in religious and philosophical convictions. Through mutually respectful civil discussion, common goals are then identified and pursued within an atmosphere of noncoercive persuasion and the free exchange of ideas. Specifically among those whose political views are informed by religious beliefs, there should be cultivated a manner of empathetic discourse that promotes rather than impedes interreligious understanding within a diverse society.

When we call to mind the high-pitched religious rhetoric of contemporary politicians and the hardball ideological sales talk of many of their religious counterparts, we have a right to ask, what happened to the careful formula created by the founders? The nature of the relationship between religion and politics in contemporary life resembles instead the patriotic provincialism of the eighteenth-century preachers promoting the war against England.

The explanation lies at least in part in the nineteenth century, a century in which churches and other religious bodies often failed to meet the challenge handed to them. The formula created by the founders moved almost as far as possible in the direction of clarifying the legal structure for the interrelationship between religion and politics. But it did not and could not prescribe a particular political theology or a specific hermeneutic to guide religious communities in

13. John F. Wilson, "Religion, Government, and Power in the New American Nation," in Mark A. Noll and Luke E. Harlow, eds., *Religion and American Politics: From the Colonial Period to the Present*, 2nd ed. (New York: Oxford University Press, 2007), 83–84.

14. Christopher F. Mooney, *Boundaries Dimly Perceived: Law, Religion, Education, and the Common Good* (South Bend, IN: University of Notre Dame Press, 1990).

their task of relating their Scriptures to their duties within the republic. That task fell to the religious communities themselves and demanded at least as much wisdom for clarifying their role in society as was mustered by the framers of the founding documents.[15]

Unfortunately, Protestant denominations, as they entered the nineteenth century, tended to drop the challenge, reverting instead to the familiar habits of moving reflexively from biblical text to political action and identifying the sovereign of the universe as the patron of the New Israel. This habit amounted to an abdication of the church's responsibility, in relation both to its own integrity and to its place within the larger culture. Without the guidance of a political theology capable of denouncing nationalistic idolatry and safeguarding the role of faith communities as prophetic critics and moral guardians, those communities only too easily were co-opted by the imperializing trends that were emerging in the young nation. In the free religious marketplace of the young republic many northern Protestants cooperated through voluntary societies to try to encourage and at times even to impose moral reform within the nation, while at the same time doctrinal disputes threatened to turn the churches into warring camps. Throughout the struggles and strife of the nineteenth century, the privileged position that no longer was legally conferred upon the Protestant majority was partially reclaimed through the cultivation of a rather vague but widely embracing "civil religion." Furthermore, the emerging market economy encouraged many ministers uncritically to accept the worldview advocated by Adam Smith, which often undermined efforts to promote the common good and pushed biblical and other ethical questions to the side.[16] Though lacking a legitimate "marriage certificate," the ancient wedding of religion and politics was thus granted a de facto extension.

15. How religious communities can develop a means of relating their traditional values to public issues will be the theme addressed in the epilogue of this book.

16. Stewart Davenport, Interview with Ken Myers, Mars Hill Audio Journal, no. 95, Charlottesville, VA, January/February 2009.

Chapter 5

The Church-State Partnership
of the Antebellum Years

The nineteenth century was the century that created the notion of Christian America. It was the century in which figures as dissimilar as Abraham Lincoln and Andrew Carnegie were celebrated as models of Christianity, and denominations vied with one another in their demonstrations of patriotism. It was the century in which John L. O'Sullivan of the *New York Morning News* coined the phrase "manifest destiny" to describe the nation's new assertive self-confidence. On Independence Day 1837, John Quincy Adams captured the essence of the creed of the emerging nation cult: "Is it not that, in the chain of human events, the birthday of the nation is indissolubly linked with the birthday of the Savior? That it forms a leading event in the progress of the Gospel dispensation? Is it not that the Declaration of Independence first organized the social compact on the foundation of the Redeemer's mission upon the earth?"[1]

1. John Quincy Adams, An Oration Delivered before the Inhabitants of the Town Of Newbury at Their Request on the Sixty-Fourth Anniversary of the Declaration of Independence (Newburyport, 1837), last accessed via Google Books, September 15, 2008, 5–6. http://books.google.com/books?id=5h1CAAAAIAAJ&printsec=frontcover&dq=an+oration+delivered+before+the+inhabitants+of+the+town+of+Newburyport#PPA5,M1.

For John Quincy Adams and many other religious voices of the mid-nineteenth century, however, the transformation of America into the New Israel represented more than a flirtation with national idolatry; it included a call to perfect the nation and purge it of its corporate and national sins. Later in the same address Adams clarified that his reverence for the Declaration was based on the fact that it issued a clarion call for "Freedom to the slave! Liberty to the captives! Redemption! Redemption forever to the race of man from the yoke of oppression!"[2] A sobering truth thus began to find proponents: the identification of America with the purposes of God would only be true to the degree that the new nation carried out God's purposes through the abolition of slavery.

But the churches in general remained staunch promoters of unity within the fractious nation through the application of religion as an effective cultural glue. Lyman Beecher issued the call for clergy who would help the nation develop "institutions of homogeneous influence" that would cultivate "a sameness of views, and feelings, and interests, which would lay the foundation of our empire upon a rock."[3] In so doing they would build upon a foundation provided not by humans but by God: "Our own republic in its Constitution and laws is of heavenly origin. It was not borrowed from Greece or Rome, but from the Bible."[4] But like Adams, Beecher insisted on the redemption and reformation of American society as he pursued a wide range of reform agendas, from abolishing dueling to promoting temperance and rescuing young women from promiscuity, prostitution, and other forms of sexual exploitation.

The work of reformers such as Lyman Beecher can only be understood in the context of the massive Evangelical Awakenings that coursed through the United States in the early nineteenth century, dramatically changing the religious, political, social, and cultural composition of the nation. The so-called Second Great Awakening briefly shook the institution of slavery in the South, spawned significant reform movements in the North, and created a dominant Protestant and Evangelical culture that both sought the status of an established church and frequently acted as if it achieved that despite the constitutional barriers in place. The different varieties of Evangelicalism that developed in the North and South led to greatly different assessments of slavery and contributed to the nation's deep political and cultural schism that ultimately exploded into the Civil War.

The Second Great Awakening had its roots in the growth of Evangelical religion during the eighteenth century. Emphasizing a direct and personal connection with God's Spirit and reveling in charismatic preaching and experiences,

2. Ibid., 54.
3. Quoted in Martin E. Marty, *Protestantism in the United States: Righteous Empire* (New York: Scribner's, 1986), 232.
4. Lyman Beecher, *Works* (Boston: J. P. Jewett, 1852), 1:189.

Evangelicalism had a strong appeal to socially marginal groups, including the rural poor, women, and, increasingly, both free and enslaved African Americans.

The Cane Ridge Revival in Kentucky in 1801, which marked the beginning of the Awakening, exemplified many of these patterns. Rural Kentuckians came for several days to hear a series of revival preachers, experience the immediacy of the Holy Spirit, and break the tedium of their daily lives. Episcopalians and other elites were shocked by what were perceived as the excesses associated with the event. Strange phenomenon such as "barkings," "jerkings," and fainting in the "Spirit" were surely signs of disordered personalities and lives, they averred. The influence that charismatic ministers had over impressionable young women and the attractiveness of the developing camp meetings for purveyors of liquor and other vices caused traditionalists to fear the collapse of an ordered and moral society. When some early Baptists and Methodists began to allow such seemingly outrageous innovations as female exhorters, enslaved preachers, and racially integrated churches, it became clear to many that the country was spiraling down into the pits of hell.

Yet for the converts themselves, the revival provided a new sense of meaning and spiritual importance that transcended boundaries of class, gender, and race and challenged the hegemony of the Southern planters. While the more radical elements of the Awakening in the South were ultimately crushed by a resurgence of planter culture and white supremacy, the South had been transformed by the rapid growth of Methodist and Baptist churches that continue to influence the United States culturally and politically to the present day. In the wake of the Awakening arose a form of Evangelicalism that emphasized personal salvation and holiness, eschewed efforts to reform society, and maintained significant blinders in the areas of race and gender.

The Second Great Awakening in the North appeared later in the 1820s and 1830s and is primarily associated with the work of evangelists and moral reformers like Charles Grandison Finney and Lyman Beecher. Finney's influence was so great that it has led some historians of religion to argue that the 1830s should be more properly named the Age of Finney than the Age of Jackson.[5] Revivalists such as Finney rejected the strict Calvinism of the Puritan fathers and believed that people could actively participate in their own salvation. Finney adopted the Arminian theology of the Wesleys and the Methodists, as well as many of their techniques, including the "anxious seat," lengthy public prayer, and female exhorters. In his lectures on the revival of religion, Finney even implied that revivals and conversion could be brought about through the organization, planning, and work of the revivalists and did not depend solely on the Spirit and will of God. Additionally, the northern Evangelicals were strongly postmillennialist, which meant that they believed Christ would return only after the world had been perfected, leading to the thousand-year reign of peace. As the Northern

5. Mark A. Noll, *America's God: From Jonathan Edwards to Abraham Lincoln* (New York: Oxford University Press, 2002),176.

Evangelical churches grew, they provided shock troops for the Whig and later the Republican parties, as they attempted to build their benevolent empire and reshape the society into the image of the kingdom of God on earth.

The Second Great Awakening served as both a catalyst and an accelerant for a broad range of reform movements that swept the North during the antebellum years. Whether attempting to save the Cherokees from the expansive nationalism of Andrew Jackson and the cupidity of Georgians, blocking the delivery of mail on Sunday (which had provided a convenient end-around for liquor stores to remain open on the Sabbath), saving prostitutes from denigration, distributing Bibles, launching the Sunday school movement, supporting temperance or prohibition, reforming criminals, or promoting more humane treatment of the insane, there were few social ills that Evangelicals did not believe could be solved by the proper combination of prayer, organization, adequate financing, and if necessary, government coercion.

This "benevolent empire" combined the efforts of Congregationalists, Presbyterians, some Methodists, and many other Northern Protestants. These common reform efforts helped to mute theological differences as Evangelicals worked together to promote "Godly living" throughout the land. At the height of the Second Great Awakening, during the Finney revivals in upstate New York (soon to be known as the "burnt-over district"), Evangelical reformers coalesced into a key constituency of the Whig party in the North.[6]

While Horace Bushnell represented the opposite end of the Protestant spectrum in the mid-nineteenth century as he promoted a more romantic view of religion and sought to modify many of the harsh edges of Calvinist orthodoxy, nevertheless he shared the assumption of his theological opponents regarding America's status as a chosen nation. In one address he pulled out all stops as he trumpeted his strident postmillennialism: "The wilderness shall bud and blossom as the rose before us; and we will not cease, till a Christian nation throws up its temples of worship on every hill and plain; till knowledge, virtue, and religion, blending their dignity and their healthful power, have filled our great country with a manly and happy race of people, and the bonds of a complete Christian commonwealth are seen to span the continent."[7]

This was not a mere announcement; it was a battle cry. For there were challenges to Bushnell's "manly and happy race," among them immigrants bringing alien forms of faith and indigenous peoples proud of their own traditions and resistant to the missionaries' invitations to adopt the white man's customs, costumes, and religious beliefs. Indeed, the assurance of many American Protestants

6. See, for example, Robert P. Swieringa, "Ethnoreligious Political Behavior in the Mid-Nineteenth Century: Voting, Values, Cultures," in Mark A. Noll and Luke E. Harlow, eds., *Religion in American Politics: From the Colonial Period to the Present*, 2nd ed. (New York: Oxford University Press, 2007), 145–68.

7. Horace Bushnell, *Barbarism the First Danger: A Discourse for Home Missions* (New York: American Home Missionary Society, 1847), 32.

of their own moral, religious, ethnic, and national superiority blinded them to the many ways in which they substituted self-righteousness for godliness and forgot about the more subtle spiritual gifts of kindness, patience, gentleness, and humility.

These faults, combined with a resurgent nativism, spawned a whole series of abuses throughout antebellum America. The ease with which Christians could countenance the orderly theft and extortion of Native land holdings is one of the most conspicuous examples. Riots that destroyed a Catholic convent in Boston and public school textbooks that defamed Catholics and the Irish gave expression to the fears of nativists as well as to their unwillingness to accept divergent cultural forms of Christianity. The willingness of public school administrators to beat Catholics who refused to recite the Protestant translation of the Ten Commandments vividly illustrates the bitter fruits of nativist attitudes.[8]

Perhaps no sin ranks in magnitude or horror with the suffering, dehumanizing humiliation, and bloodshed of black Americans. The question of the effects of guilt on human destiny has been pondered over the ages by sensitive sages including Jeremiah (Jer. 17:7), Ezekiel (Ezek. 36:26), and Henrik Ibsen. If one cardinal lesson can be extrapolated from the ponderings of such savants, it is this: the downward spiral of moral turpitude cannot be arrested without radical redress, named variously in religious history as atonement, repentance, and rebirth.

Understandably, the authors of the textbooks responsible for teaching new generations of US citizens the nature of their national heritage are reluctant to dip into the darkest colors found on the palette of their historical knowledge, especially on the level of primary school curricula. Although considerable progress has been made in the past several decades to cultivate critical thinking within our classrooms, especially through inclusion of primary sources dealing with broken treaties and the slave trade,[9] a more concerted effort is needed if the nation is to confront with candor the stark fact that a national epic containing in chapter one the obliteration of its antecedent civilizations and in chapter two the denial of full humanity to all of its inhabitants has infected its being on a level so fundamental as to require soul-searching scrutiny and radical redress.

The first half of the nineteenth century was thus increasingly torn between two perspectives. On the one hand was a diverse coalition consisting of dyed-in-the-wool racists, businessmen habituated to the economic benefits of slavery,

8. John T. McGreevy, *Catholicism and American Freedom* (New York: W. W. Norton & Co., 2003), 7–8.

9. In the value of bringing original source material into the classroom, perhaps no better example can be found in the nineteenth century than *The Columbian Orator,* an anthology of writings addressing social issues published by a series of progressive editors, beginning with Caleb Bingham in 1797 and carried on in 1998 by David W. Blight. See *The Columbian Orator,* ed. Caleb Bingham and David W. Blight (New York: New York University Press, 1998).

politicians reluctant to introduce conflict into their states and electoral districts, and religious leaders perpetuating the poisonous hermeneutic of white supremacy. On the other hand was a growing abolition movement spearheaded by courageous black crusaders backed by reform-minded political progressives and persons of faith discovering in Scripture a call to struggle for justice and equality for all citizens. Caught in between was the vast majority, a citizenry trapped in the jaws of ignorance and apathy. Though crying out to the deafness of a moral wilderness, the admonitions and warnings of the nineteenth century's prophets could not be silenced. The greatest among them were Frederick Douglass and Abraham Lincoln.

The contradictions and ironies that had become lodged in the heart of the nation could not have found a more propitious alignment of time, setting, and mouthpiece than on July 5, 1852, in Rochester, New York, with Frederick Douglass's speech "What to the Slave Is the 4th of July?":

> What, to the American slave, is your 4th of July? I answer: a day that reveals to him, more than all other days in the year, the gross injustice and cruelty to which he is the constant victim. To him, your celebration is a sham; your boasted liberty, an unholy license. . . . [Y]our prayers and hymns, your sermons and thanksgivings, with all your religious parade, and solemnity, are, to him, mere bombast, fraud, deception, impiety, and hypocrisy—a thin veil to cover up crimes which would disgrace a nation of savages. . . . You boast of your love of liberty, your superior civilization, and your pure Christianity, while the whole political power of the nation . . . is solemnly pledged to support and perpetuate the enslavement of three millions of your countrymen. . . . You can bare your bosom to the storm of British artillery to throw off a three-penny tax on tea; and yet wring the last hard-earned farthing from the grasp of the black laborers of your country. You profess to believe "that, of one blood, God made all nations of men to dwell on the face of all the earth" [Acts 17:26], and hath commanded all men, everywhere, to love one another; yet you notoriously hate (and glory in your hatred) all men whose skins are not colored like your own. . . . The existence of slavery in this country brands your republicanism as a sham, your humanity as a base pretense, and your Christianity as a lie.[10]

Alongside all of the crass proof-texting of his time, devoted to giving biblical support to unjust, bigoted, and imperialistic causes, Douglass's indictment thundered forth with the poignancy of classical biblical jeremiads like Isaiah 58 and Jeremiah 7. It presented an anatomy of the sick soul of Christian America with the precision of a neurosurgeon. It uncovered the contradiction at the heart of "the most Christian" of the industrialized nations by listing the qualities of which its leaders loved to boast, then tersely naming the *lie* undermining the boasting, and finally unveiling the transmutation of virtue into vice that ensued:

---

10. David W. Blight, ed., *Narrative of the Life of Frederick Douglass, An American Slave, Written by Himself, with Related Documents* (Boston: Bedford St. Martins, 2003), 158–59, 166–67.

Boasted Virtues	The Lie	Transmutation
Celebration	Enslavement of three million Americans	Sham
Liberty	Ditto	Unholy license
Greatness	Ditto	Vanity
Rejoicing	Ditto	Heartlessness
Equality	Ditto	Injustice
Prayers	Ditto	Deception
Hymns	Ditto	Bombast
Sermons	Ditto	Deception
Thanksgiving	Ditto	Impiety
Worship	Ditto	Hypocrisy
Purity	Ditto	Fraud
Scripture	Ditto	Veil over crimes
Love	Ditto	Hate
Humanity	Ditto	Base pretense
Christianity	Ditto	A lie

James Russell Lowell, writing just prior to the Civil War, provides insight into the device utilized by a Christian people to pervert biblical faith into an instrument of injustice and repression, its distortion of the Gospel into a personal guide to salvation of the soul, simultaneously freeing the wealthy oppressor from a sense of guilt and enabling the church to feel that its obligations were fulfilled by preaching heavenly salvation without concern for social injustice and human suffering on earth. That device he illustrated with stinging irony by reference to members of the American Tract Society, who remained unmoved by the plight of black slaves, "provided only they could save the soul of Sambo alive by presenting him a pamphlet, which he could not read."[11]

The domestication of prophetic Christianity that came to characterize much of the nineteenth-century church in the United States was due in no small part to the thickness of its defenses. Gratitude for the security and bounty enjoyed by the privileged members of the society was expressed through patriotic support of God's "chosen nation." Wealth was deemed proof of divine blessing and poverty evidence of sloth. The "purity" of the gospel was safeguarded through evangelism, rather than through involvement in the messiness of politics and economics. As highlighted by Lowell's reference to "tract-evangelism," the poor were promised assurance of eternal salvation as a source of patient endurance,

11. Quoted in Marty, *Protestantism*, 89.

rather than assisted in their struggle to change social and institutional structures that were implicated in the misery of their day-to-day lives. With remarkable self-confidence this Christianity propagated Sunday schools, campaigns against drunkenness, street evangelism, and Sabbath reform. In the realm of combating private sins, its accomplishments were considerable. But these accomplishments were not matched by commensurate efforts directed toward injustices that were built into the infrastructure of public institutions like schools and the judiciary, private enterprise, and the assemblies that were often the most segregated of all, the churches.

Within this climate the challenge handed on to the nineteenth century from the generation of the founders could scarcely be met, the challenge for religious America to develop a political theology capable of clarifying its responsibility within the society and making its contribution to the ongoing process of forging a good society available to all citizens. The failure was in no small part due to a deficient understanding of biblical theology, and more specifically of the bearing of biblical texts on contemporary realities. In a word, an adequate theo-political hermeneutic had not been developed. Consequently, application of the Bible remained reflexive and undisciplined, thus largely unchastened by moral principles and interpretive guidelines that could enable the faithful to distinguish between proper use and self-serving abuse of Scripture.

The dominant hermeneutical paradigm throughout the nineteenth century was based on the commonsense realism stemming from the writings of Francis Bacon. Using this approach, Americans believed that ordinary people could easily read, understand, and apply the Bible in all situations. Unfortunately, this hermeneutic provided no reliable way for believers to expose their own prejudices about race, politics, and economics to the testimony of a scriptural tradition that often ran against the grain of prevailing cultural values.[12] The result was a battlefield of words paralleling the battlefield of weapons that threatened to sunder the fragile Union at mid-century. In the one case, men in gray fired their cannons to kill kinsmen clad in blue; in the other, proponents of slavery hurled biblical texts against abolitionists, only to receive in turn volleys of verses drawn from the same book. Slavery, moreover, was only one of the issues provoking citizens to engage one another in passionate verbal combat, for there was no issue—political, economic, or international—that did not elicit recourse to Scripture by opposing sides.[13]

The shape of the moral legacy that the nineteenth century would pass on to the twentieth was not determined alone by the religiously minded. On the other side of the public dialogue there were both political leaders who adhered to and exploited the myth of manifest destiny to further their personal and partisan

12. Brooks E. Holifield, *Theology in America: Christian Thought from the Age of the Puritans to the Civil War* (New Haven, CT: Yale University Press, 2003), 174–78.

13. See Willard M. Swartley, *Slavery, Sabbath, War, and Women: Case Issues in Biblical Interpretation* (Scottdale, PA: Herald Press, 1983); Noll, *America's God*, 396–400; see also Noll, *The Civil War as a Theological Crisis* (Raleigh: University of North Carolina Press, 2006).

interests and others who found in biblical tradition a perspective transcending the parochial and self-serving. As was earlier the case with James Madison, Abraham Lincoln's deep pondering on questions of moral ambiguity in national crises like the Civil War was enriched by serious study of the Bible and by a level of ethical reflection that was rare even among the theologians of his time. Urged by a group of clergy to make a clear statement concerning God's alliance with the Union cause, he shocked them with the reply, "In the present civil war, it is quite possible that God's purpose is something different from the purpose of either party." He went on to urge Christians in both the North and the South to desist from efforts to prove that God was on their side and instead redouble their efforts to conform *their* lives to *God's* will.

Lincoln's prophetic discernment and ability to distance himself from the hyperpatriotism of the North during the Civil War rose to classic expression in his Second Inaugural Address, delivered on March 4, 1865. While Union soldiers and clergy were repeating the exegetical excesses of their Revolutionary forerunners in interpreting the current war as the final fulfillment of God's eschatological purposes, Lincoln's assessment was much more sober. In questioning whether God gave "to both North and South, this terrible war, as the woe due to those by whom the offence [slavery] came," he identified the complicity of both regions of the country in the sin of slavery. In refusing to pass personal judgment on the religion of the South he demonstrated a humility that understood how easily humans could be led astray and how desperately dependent all mortals are on God's mercy. In Lincoln's tragic awareness of the duration and cost of the war, we see his acceptance that "the judgments of the Lord are true and righteous altogether." Finally, in the closing section beginning "With malice toward none; with charity for all . . ." we see a profound summary of the Christian gospel, calling for self-denying love and prayer for one's enemies. The call to care for the veterans, widows, and orphans profoundly echoes the assertion in James 1:27 that the only pure religion is "to care for orphans and widows in their distress." The final call to "achieve a just, and lasting peace" echoes not the shallow nationalistic triumphalism of many popular nineteenth-century preachers, but rather the eschatological vision of Israel's prophets of the peaceable kingdom at the end of days that God alone could inaugurate.[14]

One is led to ask, why were many of the preachers and religious thinkers of that period less capable of probing the more profound dimensions of the relationship between religion and politics than an autodidactic lay thinker like Lincoln? Were they hobbled by an uncritical biblical theology that encouraged them to clothe political policies and actions with the cloak of biblical certainty? Was Lincoln's capacity to move beyond reflexive proof-texting and exploitation of the Bible for the sake of political expedience enhanced by the fact that he, a denominational nonadherent with a deep interest in the Bible, was not subjected

---

14. Abraham Lincoln, Second Inaugural Address, in *This Fiery Trial: The Speeches and Writings of Abraham Lincoln*, ed. William E. Gienapp (New York: Oxford University Press, 2002), 220–21.

to the certainties of churchly postmillennialism and the popular hermeneutic that furnished facile biblical warrants for every social issue? Was more room available to Lincoln to probe the critical moral questions of his time in light of a Bible that itself was the home of moral struggle amid human ambiguity? What changes in attitude, polity, and theology might have enabled the churches of that era to regain the measure of freedom necessary to pursue their prophetic role within society with courage and integrity? These questions, far from being limited to past history, continue to lurk within and divide religious and political activists down to the present day.[15]

Before proceeding to the postbellum period, an additional episode deserves highlighting. As the Civil War raged on, a number of concerned citizens concluded that part of the reason for the turmoil of the war was the inadequately sacred nature of the Constitution. They decided to push for a constitutional amendment that would announce the explicitly Christian nature of the American experiment and in so doing nullify the separation of church and state that had been established by the founders. The amended preamble to the Constitution would have read:

> We the people of the United States, humbly acknowledging Almighty God as the source of all authority and power in civil government, the Lord Jesus Christ as the Ruler among the nations, His revealed will as the supreme law of the land, in order to constitute a Christian government and, in order to form a more perfect union, establish justice, insure domestic tranquility, provide for the common defense, promote the general welfare, and secure the inalienable rights and the blessings of liberty, and the pursuit of happiness to ourselves, our posterity, and all the people, do ordain and establish this Constitution for the United States of America.

The proposal failed to get a clear endorsement from Abraham Lincoln and ultimately languished in Congress for about ten years without getting a favorable nod from the House Judiciary Committee. However, it revealed the determination among some Christians to bolster their control over the political apparatus, a move that inevitably would have led to relegating to an inferior status members of minority religious groups and those identifying themselves as nonreligious.[16] Subsequent history has proven that the defeat of what was basically a theocratic initiative did not extinguish the crusade of zealous evangelicals to (re)claim the country for Christianity, for it was a cause nourished by the confluence of several social forces, including apprehension among traditionally conservative circles that their preeminence in American life was being challenged by growing immigrant communities, alarm over the increase of vice and crime in rapidly growing

---

15. Mark Noll suggests that Lincoln's brilliant mind coupled with a tragic personal life contributed to his deeper understanding. But he also suggests that Herman Melville and Emily Dickinson shared his insights and that Lincoln never escaped the view of America as divinely chosen. See *America's God*, 426–38.

16. See William R. Hutchinson, *Religious Pluralism in America: The Contentious History of a Founding Ideal* (New Haven, CT: Yale University Press, 2003), 78–83, quote at 79.

urban centers, and new scientific ideas that many felt challenged the very core of the biblical message. As intellectual questions and social problems proliferated over the next half century, Protestant churches, in the effort to preserve their Evangelical heritage, would be forced to come to terms with the growth and flowering of religious diversity and pluralism and to strive to develop a theo-political hermeneutic adequate for the times.

But they were hard pressed to raise up leaders capable of addressing funda-mental questions such as these: How should religious communities respond to the rapidly growing cities and industrial landscapes of the United States and the corresponding decline of small-town community life? What role should indi-viduals and groups seeking to live true to biblically informed moral principles play in response to the increasingly aggressive posture being taken by the United States Navy in Central and South America, Asia and Africa? How should they react to new scientific discoveries and religious ideas that seemed to call into question many traditional Christian beliefs? Finally, how were they to adjust to a political and cultural world where the traditional influence of Evangelical Christianity was not only questioned but often openly defied?

Chapter 6

The Gilded Age
*The Gospel of Wealth
and the Social Gospel*

The quest to establish a hegemonic Protestant Christian America was exhibition number one among the numerous expressions of national hubris and idolatry that emerged in the so-called Gilded Age. It was allied with two other quests: the move to sanctify money making as the ideal Christian good, and the intermingling of the economic goal of building an American Empire and the religious goal of spreading the kingdom of God to all corners of the earth.

Notwithstanding the protests of some courageous reformers, the defense of private property, the accumulation of wealth, and unbridled industrial progress became notions widely identified with Christianity. Those falling outside of the sphere of benefits of this system, such as Irish and Italian Roman Catholics, were stigmatized as morally lax, requiring not economic assistance and enhanced access to high-quality education and health care, but repentance leading to the salvation of their souls.

This "Gospel according to Mammon" had been "canonized" already in 1835 in an election-day sermon delivered by Episcopal bishop Jonathan Mayhew Wainwright, who would later preside over the funeral of America's wealthiest citizen, John Jacob Astor, a man remembered for his shrewd business tactics and emphatically not for his generosity:

> The unequal distribution of wealth we believe to be not only an unalterable consequence of the nature of man, and the state of being in which he is placed, but also the only system by which his happiness and improvement can be promoted in this state of being. We do not deny that there are some evils attending it, and that in some countries it has been fostered by artificial and injurious regulations until it has become oppressive and unreasonable. The principle itself is fundamentally true and just, but it may be, and often has been, pushed to such an extreme as to be detrimental to the best interests of society. . . . Once touch the rights of property, let it be felt that men are imperiled and harassed in their efforts to obtain it, that its possession is insecure and that portions of it may be taken by unequal taxation, and you immediately stop enterprise, . . . the progress of knowledge . . . and also of virtue—and then where is the happiness of such a community?[1]

As vast fortunes were being amassed by elite monopolies during the Gilded Age, the defense of inequality and the God-given responsibility of the rich to order the lives of the working class were welded into a campaign against the organization of labor into unions and the improvement of conditions in the workplace. George F. Baer, the president of Reading Railroad and the chief owners' spokesman in the anthracite coal strike of 1902, gave expression to a creed that wedded an appeal to Christianity with blatant social Darwinism: "The rights and interests of the laboring man will be protected and cared for— not by the labor agitators, but by the Christian men to whom God in His infinite wisdom has given the control of the property interests of the country. . . . Pray earnestly that the right may triumph, always remember that the Lord God Omnipotent still reigns, and that His reign is one of law and order, and not of violence and crime."[2]

Many of the nation's leading political and religious leaders endorsed this audacious proclamation. But not all members of the new superwealthy class agreed. In his *Gospel of Wealth,* Andrew Carnegie emphasized the obligation of the rich to contribute back to society what they had gained from the labor of the many in a form of philanthropy that would open up the doors of self-improvement and economic advancement. The Carnegie libraries that remain landmarks in many cities are cardinal examples of his philosophy. In a manner anticipating contemporary debates, he advocated for a graduated system of estate taxes that would end the accumulation of enormous wealth by a small percentage of the population. Remarkably, the warrants to which he appealed in constructing the socioeconomic ideas in *Gospel of Wealth* were the same ones to which champions of the entitlements of the wealthy like Wainwright and Baer appealed, the Bible and Christian teaching!

---

1. Jonathan Mayhew Wainwright, *Inequality of Individual Wealth the Ordinance of Providence and Essential to Civilization: A Sermon Preached before His Excellency John Davis, Governor* (Boston: Dutton and Wentworth, 1835), 35f.

2. Cited in David M. Kennedy and Thomas A. Bailey, *The American Spirit,* vol. 2, *Since 1865,* 10th ed. (Boston: Houghton Mifflin, 2002), 209.

Disagreement among wealthy entrepreneurs reflected the sharp division that also was emerging among religious leaders. While many pulpits were amplifying a robust defense of wealth, a growing number of Protestant and Catholic leaders were developing a theology of social salvation that culminated in the so-called social gospel movement. Although leaders of the social gospel often brought with them the assumptions of their age about Anglo-Saxon supremacy, traditional ideas about women, and the need for the lower classes to adopt Victorian notions of morality, they nevertheless imagined a reinvigorated church in which the pressing social issues of the day would be addressed.

In 1876 Washington Gladden became the first effective spokesperson of the social gospel by giving support to labor unions and articulating the idea that Christianity was not simply about individual conversions, but required churches to apply the lessons of the gospel to the broader socioeconomic challenges facing the country. Gladden later formulated his ideas in the 1886 book *Applied Christianity*: "We must make men believe that Christianity has a right to rule this kingdom of industry, as well as all the other kingdoms of this world . . . that ways must be found of incorporating good-will as a regulative principle, as an integral element into the very structure of industrial society."[3]

While some might accuse Gladden of inappropriately trying to impose religious values upon a secular government and society, a criticism that has some merit, his more important point was that the moral lessons of Christianity mandated a check on the prevailing unlimited pursuit of individual gain and the concomitant abuse of employees. The Christianization of the social order would thus protect the weak, the vulnerable, and the marginalized and ensure them a place in a truly just society. Gladden's ethic is clearly expressed in his well-known hymn, "O Master, let me walk with thee in lowly paths of service free." Here the emphasis is placed on service to others from a posture of humility, eschewing efforts to seize political power to impose change upon the outsider.

A significant chapter in the emerging vision of the social gospel is found in Josiah Strong's classic work *Our Country*, written in 1885. Best remembered today for its jingoistic nationalism and confident expressions of Anglo-Saxon superiority, the book also included a trenchant critique of the failure of churches adequately to address the growing challenges of American life in the late nineteenth century. Especially disturbing in his judgment was the widening chasm between rich and poor, to which the wealthy were responding with smugness and the impoverished with growing anger and despair.

In understanding *Our Country* and its arguments, it is important to remember that the book was written as a fund-raising piece for the American Home Missionary Society. By the nature of its genre it tended to exaggerate the magnitude of the threats to "Christian America," so as to avoid alienating its audience

---

3. Washington Gladden, *Applied Christianity: Moral Aspects of Social Questions* (Boston: Houghton, Mifflin & Co., 1886), 37, cited in Christopher H. Evans, *The Kingdom Is Always but Coming: A Life of Walter Rauschenbusch* (Grand Rapids: Eerdmans, 2004), 54.

by questioning their cultural or nationalistic assumptions and rather focusing its prophetic critique on the lack among Christians of charitable contributions, the cardinal virtue it sought to inspire. Accordingly, Strong uncritically conflated the expansion of American power and business with the spread of the gospel, a view succinctly expressed in the following quotation: "The World is to be Christianized and civilized. . . . And what is the process of civilizing but *the creating of more and higher wants?* Commerce follows the missionary."[4] Furthermore, Strong is both a reflection of and spokesperson for the view that America is God's chosen nation to prosper and then redeem the world. His arguments are frequently supported by appeals to demographics, the social sciences, evolutionary theory, and American political traditions. Only in his final call for generosity does he reference Scripture, and then quite frequently. While keeping these caveats in mind, there is still much we can discern from the book about how this important Congregational leader understood the intersection between faith, duty, and politics.

The central portion of *Our Country* is an exploration of the major perils facing the United States in the late nineteenth century, perils that, if not adequately addressed, could lead to permanent damage to the American way of life and the growing kingdom of God. These perils include the following: a high rate of immigration, which, while bringing some benefits, degrades morals and tears at bonds of community; the Roman Catholic Church, which, according to Strong, inculcates absolute obedience to the pope instead of developing the independence of thought crucial for a democracy; assaults on the public school system, designed either to set up a separate educational system for Catholics or dilute the teaching of Christian morality in public institutions; the Church of Latter-day Saints, which promotes the absolute power of the leader of the church and polygamy, an egregious threat to the traditional family; intemperance, which does irreparable harm to families and creates a liquor industry that endangers free institutions of government in the major cities; socialism, which threatens to undermine the constituted political and economic order by lending support to anarchists and undermining the necessity of hard work; and urbanization, which tends to concentrate areas of vice and create communities less susceptible to the leavening effects of the gospel. While all of these concerns were typical of the attitudes and prejudices of the middle class in Gilded-Age America, the inclusion of an additional area of criticism reveals Strong's affinity to the social gospel. For Strong, the growing wealth of the country, and especially its increasing concentration among the richest Americans, was a threat to the whole social order. Indeed "mammonism" was turning legitimate trade into gambling, "corrupting popular morals," blocking reform, "corrupting the ballot-box," increasing the power and influence of large corporations, and threatening to overturn higher virtues with a gross materialism.[5] Such wealth might, according

4. Josiah Strong, *Our Country* (Cambridge: Belknap Press of Harvard University Press, 1963), 26.
5. Ibid., 162–64.

to Strong, decay the very center of American civilization. The solution to this crisis was not a radical redistribution of wealth through taxation or a socialist revolution. Indeed, we have already noted his strong endorsement of the spread of American commerce throughout the world. Rather, what he propounded was the voluntary support of a massive home missions program within the country, in order to enable the churches and social services to meet social needs and ensure the triumph of Protestant Christianity. When the church began to teach that all property is owned by God and humans are merely the stewards of its use, Strong believed his vision would be achieved. The wealthy and the business owners would then voluntarily redistribute their resources, deal with their employees justly, and pursue integrity in business instead of narrow self-interest or squeezing the greatest profit out of each trade. While Strong's aspirations are praiseworthy, an additional sixscore years has not revealed a significant trend toward his hope, nor is it at all clear that workers would be satisfied to rely on the generosity of their employers as their only security.[6]

While there is much to lament in Strong's jingoistic nationalism, racism, anti-Catholicism, and uncritical acceptance of the exploitation of the earth, he also pointed the way toward using Christian principles and charity as an antidote to the growing class stratification and endemic poverty and exploitation of late nineteenth-century cities. For that reason he can be viewed as a voice in the wilderness preparing the way for the greatest exponent of the creation of a godly social order during a time of rapid industrial change, namely, Walter Rauschenbusch.

Although often stuck in traditional ideas of middle-class morality and gender roles, Rauschenbusch developed a powerful and fresh critique of the "social crisis" in American Christianity and sought to reapply the teachings of the Hebrew prophets to create a just social system reflecting the ideals of the kingdom of heaven. His vision for social justice was laid out most clearly in a book written in 1907, *Christianity and the Social Crisis*. Beginning with an examination of the history and theology of ancient Israel, he identified an abiding concern for the poor and the notion of a communal ownership of property. As Rauschenbusch expressed it, "The manhood of the poor was more sacred than the property of the rich."[7] As Jewish religious thought evolved during the time of the exile, concern for the poor and a just society remained. As the prophets developed the idea of the "day of Jehovah," it meant in part "punishment for the wicked. . . . the rescue of the weak . . . [and] moral justice rather than economic prosperity."[8] This emphasis on social regeneration and the kingdom of God was expanded in the Gospels and the early church, only to be crushed as the distinctive thought of the Hebrews merged with the greater individualism of the Hellenistic world and finally the empire building of Constantine blunted the revolutionary edge of the

6. Ibid., 248–52.
7. Walter Rauschenbusch, *Christianity and the Social Crisis* (Louisville, KY: Westminster/John Knox Press, 1991), 21.
8. Ibid., 34.

church.[9] Through his work Rauschenbusch, while never questioning the need for individual salvation, sought to recover the notion of the kingdom of God and to translate its ideals into the social and economic structures of this world.

After building the historical case for refashioning the social order on the basis of the teachings of the prophets and Jesus, Rauschenbusch turned his sights on those institutions that he felt were degrading the common life during his time. The first of these was competitive capitalism. As he saw it, "competitive commerce exalts selfishness to the dignity of a moral principle."[10] In words that seem eerily prescient today, he described the life of the stock or mercantile exchange as a form of gambling in which speculation had replaced honest work and the few are able to profit immensely from the toiling of the many. Once great wealth is thus acquired, it corrupts the rich with "vicious luxury" that allows ostentation and greed to trickle down to the lower classes, but never the resources that would allow for a fairer distribution of profits.

Rauschenbusch also expressed special concern that the declension of morals leads to an erosion of family life as women are forced into the workplace, marriage is delayed, and parents choose to reduce the size of their families out of economic necessity. While some may disagree with his conservative social outlook, clearly there is a great deal of psychological and sociological evidence that healthy family relationships help to promote healthy children and the broader health of society. For Rauschenbusch, the social crisis was acute, and unless American society found a way to restrain greed, redistribute the wealth, and strengthen the family, it would face irreversible decay and decline. He concluded one chapter, "It is either a revival of social religion or the deluge."[11]

While Rauschenbusch was an acute observer of the challenges facing American life and issued the traditional prophetic call to social justice, his proposed solutions were not as compelling. He called upon churches to establish kindergartens, playgrounds, children's centers, and educational facilities, but doubted that the churches had an adequate financial or volunteer base to carry out the work on a necessary scale. He wished to see wealth redistributed more equitably, but aside from Henry George's single tax and the benevolence of the wealthy, he proposed no workable scheme to carry that out. While recognizing that the greatest contribution that individuals could make to social reconstruction "is the contribution of a regenerated personality, of a will which sets justice above policy and profit, and of an intellect emancipated from falsehood," he failed to generate a revival equal to the task of serving as vanguard for his social revolution.[12] He

9. For contemporary divergent explorations of the impact of Constantine's reign on the development of Christian theo-political thought and institutions, see James Carroll, *Constantine's Sword: The Church and the Jews; A History* (Boston: Houghton Mifflin, 2001) and Peter J. Leithart, *Defending Constantine: The Twilight of an Empire and the Dawn of Christendom* (Downers Grove, IL: IVP Academic, 2010).

10. Rauschenbusch, *Christianity*, 265.

11. Ibid., 286.

12. Ibid., 351.

urged the Christianization of commerce and the choosing of the commonweal over self-interest.

To this end he advocated a renewal and expansion of the Christian doctrine of stewardship, through which all of an individual's resources would be made available for the purposes of God. He especially urged the adoption of socialist and even communistic principles: "The question is now, how quickly Christian thought will realize that individualism is coming to be an inadequate and antiquated form of social organization which must give place to a higher form of communistic organization, and how thoroughly it will comprehend that this new communism will afford a far nobler social basis for the spiritual temple of Christianity."[13]

One must keep in mind that *Christianity and the Social Crisis* was written in the early twentieth century, before the Communist revolution had laid waste to the Orthodox churches of Russia and long before Mao's Cultural Revolution decimated a significant portion of China. Nevertheless, from the perspective of the early twenty-first century, his vision seems naive. At the same time, must not one remain open to the idea that if the majority of professed Christians in the United States heeded the admonition of Paul in his letter to the church at Philippi to "look not to your own interests, but to the interests of others," we as a society would be much closer to achieving the ideals of the kingdom of God than we are today?[14]

The writings of both Rauschenbusch and Strong provide us with a valuable lens to consider the connections between Christian missions and belief and the expanding imperial aspirations of the United States, with the deeper involvement in world affairs that inevitably followed. Josiah Strong became firmly associated with a muscular and aggressive expansion of American power understood as an aspect of the kingdom of God. In 1893 he wrote, "In this era mankind is to come more and more under Anglo-Saxon influence, and Anglo-Saxon civilization is more favorable than any other to the spread of those principles whose universal triumph is necessary to that perfection of the race to which it is destined; the entire realization of which will be the kingdom of heaven fully come to earth."[15] While such interpretations of Scripture and history through white supremacist and culturally chauvinistic lenses during this time period were tragically common, even Strong himself came to realize their excesses. As Richard Gamble has noted, in 1900 Strong was aware of the overweening importance of a global consciousness: "Local, and even national, interests must be sacrificed, if need be, to universal interests."[16]

---

13. Ibid., 396–97.

14. Phil. 2:4.

15. Josiah Strong, *The New Era: Or the Coming Kingdom* (New York: Baker & Taylor, 1893), 80.

16. Dorotha R. Muller, "Josiah Strong and American Nationalism: A Reevalution," *Journal of American History* 53, no. 2 (1966): 490–92, 495, 501, cited in Richard M. Gamble, *The War for Righteousness: Progressive Christianity, The Great War, and the Rise of the Messianic Nation* (Wilmington, DE: ISI Books, 2003), 73.

Rauschenbusch shared Strong's early enthusiasm for American imperial adventures, but became decidedly more irenic in the aftermath of the Spanish-American War, especially as World War I approached. During the Spanish-American War he asserted his belief in a divine mission propelling American participation in the world; yet he felt that America's mission could be fulfilled only through a dependence upon God's help and light.[17] Eventually he abandoned jingoism and came to question both American militarism and imperialism. Such questioning is evident in a prayer from his 1910 collection, *Prayers of the Social Awakening*:

> Grant to the rulers of nations faith in the possibility of peace through justice, and grant to the common people a new and stern enthusiasm for the cause of peace. Bless our soldiers and sailors for their swift obedience and their willingness to answer to the call of duty, but inspire them none the less with a hatred of war, and may they never for love of private glory or advancement provoke its coming. May our young men still rejoice to die for their country with the valor of their fathers, but teach our age nobler methods of matching our strength and more effective ways of giving our life for the flag.[18]

Possessing deep cultural roots in Germany, where he both had received his education and later spent a considerable amount of time, Rauschenbusch was relatively immune from the demonization of the "enemy" and the self-righteousness of many American clergy during World War I. Nevertheless, his pacifism and evenhanded treatment of the situation caused him to be deeply distrusted by Americans who believed he was blinded by his German ancestry. This limited the extent to which his prophetic witness could become the catalyst both for a repudiation of the nationalistic idolatry that had developed over the course of the previous century and for a genuine reform of economic structures capable of securing equal opportunity for all Americans. The American dream was still out of the reach of large segments of the population, including Catholic immigrants, former slaves, factory workers, and Native Americans. The doctrine of laissez-faire capitalism continued to be defended by many religious leaders as in harmony with the Christian gospel.

Middle-class Christians in general were cajoled into complicity with the accumulation of wealth by an elite entrepreneurial oligarchy and the global ventures of an emerging world power. How were they cajoled? Firstly, by the material benefits following in their wake; secondly, by the fear of being stigmatized as "unpatriotic" in a land that equated stinting allegiance to the flag with blasphemy against the heavenly Father; thirdly, by the persistent narrowing of the Christian message into a personalism that numbed the sensitivity of Christians to the social implications of the gospel and the biblical principle of divine justice that was blind to distinctions between members of the human family. Though the

17. Evans, *The Kingdom*, 139.
18. Ibid., 217.

reforms initiated by the defenders of the social gospel and their pious nineteenth-century forerunners are not to be belittled, the voting public increasingly came to view the political options available to the country and the world as radical socialism (seen as the forerunner to virulent Communism) and capitalism in the tradition of Adam Smith. When construed in this polarized manner, it was inevitable that capitalism prevailed as the patriotic option of choice.

The anemic social position that prevailed in many churches was tied to the domestication of Christianity. Those who felt most at ease listening to sermons on Sunday were those sharing in the benefits of full citizenship. Those marching in God's favored army toward their eternal destiny did not have time to worry about the nameless masses who fulfilled their earthly destiny as menial instruments of God's chosen, for example, recent immigrants, indigenous peoples, the producers and purveyors of commodities and goods from foreign lands, and former slaves who had fallen victim to deplorable working conditions and crushing debts owed to company-owned stores.[19] In the increasing tension between labor and management, representatives of the church commonly aligned themselves with those who were opposed to labor organizers protesting against low wages, long hours, and deplorable conditions in factories and mines. The increase of poverty, especially in America's cities, while evoking prophetic warnings from reformers like Rauschenbusch and Strong, failed to ignite a nationwide soul-searching and reexamination of priorities within Protestant denominations, where appeals to personal generosity, intercession for the poor, and contributions to world missions seemed to fulfill what Christ demanded of his followers.

Part of the reason for this blindness can be found in the growing popularity of the premillennialist interpretations of the Bible that were being promulgated by John Nelson Darby (1800–82) and William Kelly (1821–1906) and were infiltrating the beliefs and values not only of newer denominations like the Seventh-day Adventists, Jehovah's Witnesses, and Disciples of Christ, but of mainline churches as well. It is not hard to understand that motivation for involvement in the difficult task of challenging wage structures and working conditions in factories, shoddy primary and secondary school systems, and inadequate health services for the poor was debilitated by a gospel primarily focused on another world. If the tainted structures of this world were soon to be eradicated by divine judgment and replaced by the millennial reign of Christ, spiritual preparation, including patience in suffering and want, that would qualify one for that glorious future was all that really counted in life.

Though more apparent from the perspective of the historian than that of those living at the time, the fin de siècle was a time marked by two construals of the relation of Christianity to society locked into a collision course that would persist into the tumultuous events of the twentieth century. On the one side was

---

19. For a shockingly revealing account of the debt slavery of former slaves in the South, see Douglas H. Blackmon, *Slavery by Another Name: The Enslavement of Black Americans from the Civil War to World War II* (New York: Anchor Books, 2009).

a cultural understanding of Christendom emphasizing introspection, personalistic piety, nationalism, and otherworldly visions of salvation. On the other was the social gospel movement with its reformulation of prophetic faith in terms of justice, compassion, and international peace. The latter kept alive the possibility of limiting the deleterious effects of individualistic and nationalistic understandings of biblical religion that had emerged over the course of the nineteenth century and was represented within a broad range of churches, from Evangelical and Pentecostal groups construing the future in postmillennialist rather than premillennialist terms to liberal churches within the Reformed tradition as they cultivated an understanding of the Bible that did not set eschatological hopes and this-worldly reforms in opposition to each other.

Also indebted to initiatives with roots in the nineteenth century were movements not confined by denominational boundaries, such as Hull House in Chicago, founded by Jane Addams, to which one can compare the civil rights movement of the 1960s led by Martin Luther King Jr. That a significant segment of the population remained receptive to the social dimensions of the gospel was manifested by the enormous popularity of Charles Sheldon's bestseller *In His Steps,* published in 1896, which through the medium of fiction envisioned the contagious power of compassionate justice in reforming urban blight into the beauty of shared humanity.

While the accomplishments of the social gospel movement were significant, the impact of its witness in its own time and the full potential of the legacy it left for future generations were weakened due to its vulnerability to the seductive power of an emerging popular zeitgeist. Increasingly liberal Christianity came under the influence of the heady optimism of the broader culture. Though its historical-critical hermeneutic enabled it to refute a narrow focus on otherworldly spiritual salvation and to devote energy to redemption of conditions here on earth, the concept of ineluctable progress and the perfectibility of human society set the stage for many progressive and liberal congregations to accommodate to the comforts and benefits of civil religion.

While in a broad cultural sense the lines between liberals and conservatives thus grew less distinct, on a fundamental moral level the struggle between Mammon and his uncritical, worshipful minions and the prophetic gadflies of the God of universal compassion and justice persisted into and across the new century. As we look back to that era from the perspective of a new millennium, it seems clear that Bishop Wainwright's celebration of the sanctity of wealth had not lost its appeal among "Christian" entrepreneurs in Chile, El Salvador, Guatemala, and Brazil, even as Frederick Douglass's tradition of prophetic denunciation of racial discrimination and injustice continued to result in the persecution and martyrdom of a courageous breed of clergy and laity dedicated to the plight of the poor. When one penetrates beneath the rhetoric of both patriotic Christianity and reform politics, one thus becomes aware that the legacy handed down by the nineteenth century to the twentieth was one containing flickers of hope amid ominous darkening clouds for which people of faith were ill prepared to cope.

Chapter 7

Twentieth-Century Challenges

On our journey through the stages of the history of the relationship between biblical religion and politics in the United States, we are struck by the disparity between the sobriety with which church-state relations were addressed at the end of the eighteenth century and the ascendancy of an imperialist Christian nationalism in the nineteenth. For anyone expecting of the twentieth century a return to the sobriety of the founders, a speech delivered in 1900 by Senator Albert Beveridge in support of US military intervention in the Philippine Revolution issues an early warning:

> God has not been preparing the English-speaking and Teutonic peoples for a thousand years for nothing but vain and idle self-contemplation and self-admiration. No. He made us master organizers of the world to establish system where chaos reigned. He has given us the spirit of progress to overwhelm the forces of reaction throughout the earth. He has made us adept in government that we may administer government among savage and senile peoples. Were it not for such a force as this the world would relapse into barbarism and night. And of all our race He has marked the American people as His chosen nation to finally lead in the redemption of the world.[1]

1. Robert C. Byrd, ed., *The Senate 1789–1989: Classic Speeches 1830–1993* (Washington, DC: US Government Printing Office, 1994), 514.

At the turn of the century the mainline churches faced a rapidly changing society and world without the benefit of a carefully reflected political theology, social ethics, or biblical hermeneutic. The First Amendment steadfastly preserved the basic framework for church-state relations, but the nineteenth century had contributed little to produce a positive definition of the role of religious institutions within that framework. While revivalism followed the route of abdication, the facile liberalism of many denominations modulated into uncritical support of the emerging American imperialism and laissez-faire capitalism. Even as waves of new immigrants were transforming the demographic configuration of the country, the traditional white Protestant churches retained their self-image as guardians of the culture. Their ability to develop a genuinely inclusive political theology was hampered by the degree to which they were held captive by the "myth of America," which portrayed a nation founded on godly principles by Christian heroes, sanctified by churches infusing the nation with righteousness, and commissioned by God as an agency for Christianizing the world in preparation for God's reign. There was little room for humility in this self-image and scant moral capital to enable succeeding generations to deal honestly with the inner contradictions lodged in the heart of the national soul. The racism and self-righteousness inherent in the notion of manifest destiny cultivated instead the habit of denial and the pathology of moral paralysis.

Denial and moral paralysis carried serious consequences, given the grave threats that the new century held in store. These threats called not for cowardice and retreat, but for courageous self-scrutiny of the sort that could deal openly with the denial of equal rights to women, the ravaging effects of Jim Crow laws persisting a century after the Civil War, the bitter disputes that were splitting the nation's religious institutions, and the injustices that were being perpetrated by the economic system. In this system robber barons were free to amass immense fortunes through exploitation of natural and human resources at the cost of an increasingly toxic environment and sprawling urban poverty breeding hopelessness, crime, and despair. The emphasis of revivalism on personal salvation, while marshaling enormous energy and resources, too often jettisoned the moral armament requisite to opposing the schemes of unscrupulous financiers and industrialists to shelter the sphere of business and economics from rigorous scrutiny. The headstrong belief in progress by liberal branches of the church diluted their testimony against inequality and injustice.

Thrust into the ambivalent legacy of the past century were menacing new challenges to public well-being and international accord, in the form of two world wars, dozens of regional conflicts, economic depression, and a dramatic rise in secularism, materialism, and individualism. To this volatile domestic and world situation were added the strains of religious pluralism, as other world faiths and indigenous religions entered the culture. As the century advanced, tensions grew within almost all of the religious communities as minorities and women began to give voice to their disquiet, leading to the formation of movements around the issues of feminism, black power, and liberation theology.

The era of the First World War provided a chilling example of the ways in which postmillennial faith in the inevitability of human progress, coupled with an immanentist view of God and an identification of America as a messianic nation, could muzzle the prophetic critique of nationalistic idolatry. Up to this point in the nation's history, Americans had proudly viewed themselves as playing a special role in God's divine plan. With the growth of America's overseas empire in the late nineteenth century, this tendency both deepened and expanded. In contradistinction to present-day trends, it was then the progressive voices among the clergy who were the standard bearers of this movement. One example of the overheated rhetoric of the time came from the dean of Yale Divinity School, Charles Reynolds Brown, who asked, "May we not believe, that this country, strong and brave, generous and hopeful, is called of God to be in its own way a Messianic nation [so that the rest of the world] may be blessed?"[2] Agents of the Committee of Public Information as well as leading proponents of the social gospel such as Lyman Abbott referred to World War I as a crusade nobler than its antecedents in the Middle Ages.

As Richard Gamble has persuasively argued, such absolutist understandings of the conflict and identification of the cause of America with the cause of Christ influenced some ministers to support unlimited objectives, even praying for the war to continue so that the work of redemption would reach fulfillment, despite the staggering increase in the death toll. These ministers

> failed to see their own role in perpetuating the Great War as a total war, a deadly conflict for abstract and unlimited objectives, a war for righteousness that could never be won. Their millennialist, idealist pacifism had led them into unlimited, uncompromising war. Once they ascribed to America the work of the Redeemer, to Germany the work of the Adversary, and to warfare the work of Calvary, the mentality of total war followed inescapably.[3]

Such beliefs in the far-reaching benefits of the war continued into the postwar peacemaking process. Many philanthropists, such as Andrew Carnegie and John D. Rockefeller, as well as prominent progressive ministers, fully supported Woodrow Wilson's plans for a new world order based upon the formation of a League of Nations. They believed that the only way to prevent a recurrence of war was through an international structure under which the aspirations of individual states would be made subordinate to the broader global community. While there was much to admire in their idealism, a number of factors prevented their vision from being realized. First, they were overly optimistic in their assessment that the world would cooperate in an impartial and just way to put down aggression. Second, they were blinded by views of their own cultural and racial superiority from seeing and respecting the aspirations for

---

2. Richard M. Gamble, *The War for Righteousness: Progressive Christianity, The Great War, and the Rise of the Messianic Nation* (Wilmington, DE: ISI Books, 2003), 159.
   3. Ibid., 175–76.

self-determination kindled by Wilson's Fourteen Points among less powerful cultural and racial groups. Thirdly, because Wilson so believed that the work of building the League of Nations was assigned to him by God, he refused to support any compromise with Republican opponents at home. Finally, Wilson's deteriorating health, waning popularity in the United States, and maladroit handling of opposing viewpoints hastened the collapse of his world vision.

The 1920s introduced an ominous rift within American Christianity. On the one hand the messianic liberalism of Wilson and many social gospel progressives proved itself to be incapable of coping with the combination of deep disillusionment and compensatory hedonism that emerged out of World War I. Meanwhile, the emerging fundamentalist movement clung ever more tightly to an increasingly ossified set of dogmas, often devoid of both the spirit of love and a sense of the dynamism inherent in an understanding of the Bible as the living Word of God. In other quarters the resurgent Ku Klux Klan attempted to dress up their doctrines of hatred and exclusion with the garb of Christianity.

Witnessing what he perceived to be humanity's descent into a spiritual and political void, the Swiss theologian Karl Barth sought to formulate a biblically based neo-orthodoxy capable of recapturing crucial Augustinian insights that had been lost in the heady days of the utopian modernism that preceded the Great War. In effect, he set out to refute the dreamy illusions of well-intentioned liberal theologians and return to the sober realism of the Bible and classical Christian theology, according to which humans, seeking through their agency to establish social justice and world peace, were doomed. One and only one path to peace and justice was available, the one opened up to humanity when God extended his grace to a fallen humanity in the life, death, and resurrection of his Son.

In the final year of World War I, Karl Barth shocked the world of liberal theology and philosophy with his commentary on the Epistle to the Romans. In his reinvigoration of orthodoxy, Barth boldly declared, "The Gospel is not a religious message to inform mankind of their divinity or to tell them how they may become divine. The Gospel proclaims a God utterly distinct from men. Salvation comes to them from Him, because they are, as men, incapable of knowing Him, and because they have no right to claim anything from Him."[4] Rejecting an overly immanentalist conception of God, Barth instead urged his readers to accept their inferior and created status, in other words, to reject the original lie of the serpent, believing that they could become like God. Further, Barth argued against those modern theologians who denied the reality of the curse and the fall: "The whole burden of sin and the whole curse of death still press heavily upon us. We must be under no illusion: the reality of our present existence continues as it is!"[5]

4. Karl Barth, *The Epistle to the Romans*, trans. E. C. Hoskyns (New York: Oxford University Press, 1968), 28.
5. Ibid., 38.

Nevertheless, Barth's counsel was not one of despair, for he held fast to the classic theocratic principle of Scripture contrasting the depths of human fallenness with the supreme otherness of God and proclaiming that the grace of God alone is able to redeem the world. However, given the opportunity to reflect upon developments in the United States in the subsequent decade, he likely would have seen little with which to be encouraged.

Indeed, the swells of heady nationalistic religion continued to bathe the sandy beaches of "Christian" America. January 17, 1920, marked the culmination of one of the longest sought goals of American Christians, the implementation of a constitutional amendment enacting prohibition as the law of the land. Since at least the 1830s a broad group of reformers pushed first for temperance (moderation in the consumption of alcoholic beverages, or switching from distilled spirits to beer or wine) and then ultimately for outright prohibition. Workingmen's groups such as the Washingtonians were joined by evangelists of the Second Great Awakening like Lyman Beecher and Charles Grandison Finney. By 1851 the mayor of Portland, Maine, had shepherded through the legislature a law banning alcohol from his state, though it would remain in place for less than a decade. But the movement could not be stopped, for its heart was found among women seeking to protect themselves, their homes, their children, and their husbands from the ravages of drink. Figures as diverse as Susan B. Anthony, Elizabeth Cady Stanton, Frances Willard, and Carrie Nation joined forces to purge the country of the evils of drink.

For members of the Woman's Christian Temperance Union such as Willard, fighting for women's suffrage was a necessary corollary goal to prohibition, because only with the right to vote could women protect themselves from the scourge of alcohol. Yet as the movement expanded and the focus switched to complete prohibition, the tactics shifted as well. Now they would not use just moral suasion to convince people to become teetotalers; they would seek to seize the levers of power to impose their moral vision on the rest of the country through the power of the state.

The prohibition movement offers an example of an alliance comprised of diverse individuals and groups dedicated to a shared goal. For example, a former chemistry teacher named Mary Hunt worked tirelessly through the WCTU and other organizations to ensure that "Scientific Temperance Instruction" became mandatory in every state. Congressional legislation provided the warrant to spread the new curriculum to schools in federal territories and military academies. Hunt's influence was extended over textbook companies as well, with her personal stamp of approval appearing on as many as half the textbooks in the country. Much of her material, however, fit the description of propaganda rather than a balanced account of the health consequences of alcohol.[6]

6. Daniel Okrent, *Last Call: The Rise and Fall of Prohibition* (New York: Scribner, 2010), 20–22.

Soon, under the leadership of Howard Hyde Russell and later Wayne Wheeler, the Anti-Saloon League eclipsed the WCTU as the predominant pro- hibitionist group in the nation. By keeping its focus on the sole issue of prohi- bition and using existing church networks to mobilize supporters, Russell was able to convince about 10 percent of registered voters to be single-issue voters. The unusual parity existing at that time between the two major parties allowed him to provide the necessary swing voters to whichever candidate most strongly embraced prohibition and to punish politicians who did not hew to his litmus tests. The movement's political clout was proven in Ohio in the early twentieth century when the popular incumbent, Republican governor Myron Herrick, was defeated for reelection after weakening a state local-option bill designed to allow individual communities to ban alcohol.[7]

Prohibition supporters were not averse to appealing to voters' baser instincts and some of the worse prejudices of the era to make sure their candidates were successful. Frances Willard frequently engaged in nativist language defining the saloon and the consumption of alcohol as un-American. Southern politi- cians such as John Newton Tillman of Arkansas and Hoke Smith of Georgia played upon the racial and sexual fears of white southerners to suggest that white women would be safer from black men if the latter were barred from access to alcohol. On the other side, the Anheuser Busch Corporation fought to preserve the right to vote for black men in the South so that they could more easily block prohibitionist candidates.[8] Leading northern progressives succumbed to similar invective as leaders such as Theodore Roosevelt fought against the influ- ence of Democratic Irish saloonkeepers in politics. Even the passage of progres- sive legislation such as worker's compensation laws became an opportunity to expand prohibition. If employers were to be held liable for the accidents of their employees, then they were justified to fire employees who drank alcohol.[9]

In the end it was a combination of factors and unique circumstances that pushed the Eighteenth Amendment toward passage in Congress and eventual ratification by the states. The earlier passage of the Sixteenth Amendment legal- izing the income tax, coupled with dramatically higher tax rates during World War I, eliminated much of the need for the revenue that had been produced by taxes on liquor. Prior to Prohibition such taxes had been the federal govern- ment's second largest source of income, second only to the tariff. The synergy with the proposed women's rights movement also aided prohibition as the two movements became linked in people's minds, and they often traded activists. Clumsy efforts by the alcohol industry to resist prohibition ended up backfiring, with the result that the testimonies their representatives gave at congressional hearings had the ironic effect of adding to the groundswell of support for pro- hibition. Timing was also crucial for several reasons, foremost among them the

7. Ibid., 39–40.
8. Ibid., 42–43.
9. Ibid., 47, 51.

determination of the Anti-Saloon League to get the amendment approved before 1920, when the decennial census was to show substantial growth in the nation's cities, with a majority of Americans living in urban areas for the first time in the history of the country. By moving quickly they avoided the redistricting that would have diminished their power in the House of Representatives.

Furthermore, the coincidence of the Prohibition movement with World War I provided added fervor to outlaw an industry that was seen as foreign, German, and even anti-American. The Busch family owned millions of dollars of German war bonds (purchased before we entered the war) and even spent time in Germany during the war, caring for wounded German soldiers. In this atmosphere voting for Prohibition seemed patriotic. The success of the Anti-Saloon League in electing dry candidates in 1916 provided the necessary boost to get the Eighteenth Amendment through the House of Representatives by late 1917. Malapportionment in the legislatures of many states, giving disproportionate power to rural areas, eased the passage through state legislatures, even in states with demonstrable wet majorities.

Yet passage of the amendment proved much easier than its enforcement. While the amendment did succeed in dramatically decreasing alcohol consumption, it was unable to eliminate drinking in the country. Probably the largest factor that contributed to the collapse of Prohibition was the simple inability to enforce the law. There was only one border patrol agent for every six miles of border. Smuggling from Canada and Mexico was widespread; speakeasies proliferated in cities, with law enforcement often looking the other way. Various stills and homebrew options provided another avenue for the production and consumption of ardent spirits. The growing influence of urban areas, boasting over 50 percent of the nation's population, a substantial proportion of them immigrants, contributed to the erosion of support for the amendment. In the long run this most "Christian" of all constitutional amendments contributed to discrediting the idea of legislating morality and undermining many of the high-minded moral goals its ardent supporters had sought.

In the mix of religious currents crisscrossing the 1920s religious landscape, the most disturbing is probably the powerful rise of the Second Ku Klux Klan. The dedication ceremony held in 1915 on Stone Mountain in Georgia was replete with the requisite burning cross and a Bible opened to Romans 12.[10] One wonders what part of the chapter they had in mind, inasmuch as the concluding section contains verses that fly in the face of the purposes of the Klan: "Do not repay anyone evil for evil, but take thought for what is noble in the sight of all. If it is possible, so far as it depends on you, live peaceably with all. Beloved, never avenge yourselves, but leave room for the wrath of God. . . . Do not be overcome by evil, but overcome evil with good" (Rom. 12:17–19, 21).

---

10. Nancy MacLean, *Behind the Mask of Chivalry: The Making of the Second Ku Klux Klan* (New York: Oxford University Press, 1994), 5.

In a detailed community study of the Klan in Athens, Georgia, Nancy MacLean drew attention to the affinity between local Protestant churches and the Klan. In her judgment, an especially significant sign of the close relationship between Evangelicals and the Klan was the overlap between membership in middle-class and working-class churches and Klan affiliation. Correspondingly, she found significantly less overlap in more elite or liberal denominations.[11] A similar statistical correlation, however, exists for the socioeconomic profile, raising the possibility that the affinity may be based more on socioeconomic factors than specifically religious ones. It is still worth noting that MacLean was able to identify at least ten area ministers who were Klan members, a phenomenon abetted by the policy of free membership for ministers.[12] All things considered, the conclusion she drew remains plausible, namely, that clerical support was crucial for the Klan, constituting perhaps the most important factor lending legitimacy to and facilitating the Klan's successes.[13]

The close alignment between the Klan and fundamentalist religion was also noted by MacLean. As she argued, "the Klan advocated fundamentalism as a parallel, all-encompassing explanation and prescription for the social order . . . backed by the authority of the Almighty." Thus the Klan was able to use the church to help determine power relationships between competing groups.[14] They also used the opportunity to repeat claims about the biblical basis of the Constitution, and insist on the need to promote spiritual revival to preserve their Christian way of life. They joined with fundamentalists in battling against alcohol, evolution, and religious liberalism. Likewise their attempts to maintain "traditional" values were linked to purity campaigns and efforts to preserve the power of men within families in a decade in which many conventions of family life and personal relationships were rapidly changing.[15]

Most appalling was the willingness of some Klan members to use the burning cross, biblical language, and even the alleged example of Jesus to justify their reign of lynching and terror against blacks. While MacLean rightly drew attention to the affinity of this rhetoric with the "muscular Christianity" popular around this time period, clearly there was something darker at work in the attempted use of biblical warrants to support white supremacy and violence.[16]

Perhaps the key factor linking Klan members with the emerging fundamentalist movement was the fear that societal change was leaving them and their value system behind. The early twentieth century saw the vast expansion of public education and especially the rise of high schools in the South. As previously isolated communities came into increasing contact with a rapidly modernizing world, inevitable tensions rose to the surface. Nowhere was this more evident

11. Ibid., 8.
12. Ibid., 10.
13. Ibid., 15.
14. Ibid., 91.
15. Ibid., 98–99.
16. Ibid., 160–61.

than in Dayton, Tennessee, during the Scopes Trial (1925). As Edward Larson has convincingly argued, much more was at stake in Dayton than simply a debate between evolution and creationism. A rising fundamentalist movement coupled with a populist-majoritarian backlash sought to preserve traditional doctrines, in the face of a slow assault from the "acids of modernity." The rising influence of scientific secularism, converging with an emergent rights consciousness promoted by the nascent American Civil Liberties Union, brought pressure upon the courts to safeguard academic freedom and prevent parents or state legislatures from interfering with the advance of science.[17]

From the perspective of history, it is easy to see much to disapprove of in both sides of the ensuing trial. Darrow's full-bore assault upon religious belief, coupled with defense of a blatantly racist and eugenicist textbook, did little to promote civil discourse or cultural understanding. Meanwhile the prosecution's use of unabashedly fundamentalist prayers during the trial, coupled with its dogmatic defense of a strictly literalist interpretation of Scripture and an unwillingness to engage openly with the findings of science, only further exacerbated an already tense situation. In response to this disappointing chapter in dialogue between science and religion, contemporary scientists and theologians such as Francis Collins, Kenneth Miller, and Alister McGrath have articulated a promising alternative, namely, that interdisciplinary conversations are both possible and fruitful for science, theology, and public discourse, when conducted in a respectful civil spirit and dedicated to common social goals.

As the Scopes trial and the recrudescence of the Klan revealed, American religion was becoming increasingly contentious and fractured in the early twentieth century. Swelling populations of immigrant groups, including large numbers of Catholics, Eastern Orthodox, and Jews, dramatically increased the diversity of religious life and belief in the United States. Meanwhile, growing splits between modernist and fundamentalist wings of the major denominations crippled the ability of the mainline churches to speak with a unified voice. Such diversity necessarily adds to the complexity of a historical retrospective such as ours. Trying to follow all of the threads of development would make it increasingly unwieldy and diffuse. Simply following a few themes invites criticism of oversimplification or, worse, ignoring the contributions and nuances of diverse groups. While acknowledging that risk, the nature of this analysis requires a selective treatment of representative themes.

One voice seeking to apply the Word of God in fresh and distinctive ways to the challenges of the time was that of Reinhold Niebuhr. Niebuhr is best known in scholarly circles for being a "celebrity theologian" in the early years of the cold war, when he helped provide the theological justification for the policy of containment and served as a spiritual mentor for key diplomats and policy makers. But his public voice emerged during the crises of the Great

17. See Edward J. Larson, *Summer for the Gods: The Scopes Trial and America's Continuing Debate over Science and Religion* (New York: Basic Books, 1997), 11–83.

Depression. Niebuhr viewed himself as an exponent of true radical Christianity, which he saw emerging when "loyalty to the 'kingdom of God,' the vision of a pure and unconditioned justice and love, creates dissatisfaction with the imperfect love and justice of any given economic and political order." Since this ideal can never be fully realized in human society, we must expect to live always "under the tension and the criticism of the Kingdom of God."[18] Niebuhr's self-understanding of his role as a public theologian places him squarely within the tradition of the prophetic-dialectical model pioneered in biblical times by Amos and Jeremiah and rejuvenated in US history by Jonathan Edwards and Frederick Douglass.

Niebuhr began to address public challenges as the pastor of Bethel Evangelical Church in Detroit in the 1920s, where he stood against the KKK and challenged the paternalism of Henry Ford, especially his unwillingness to allow workers to pursue their aspirations through labor unions. Within this context he furthered the work of an earlier generation of social gospel ministers and activists. However, it was only after a move to New York City and Union Theological Seminary that he gained access to a sufficiently broad and diverse audience to address the challenges of Depression-era America.[19]

In 1932 Niebuhr released his seminal work, *Moral Man and Immoral Society*. The work represented a personal declaration of independence from the progressive liberalism associated with John Dewey's philosophy and affirmation instead of the somber Barthian theme of the fallenness of humanity. Niebuhr was particularly critical of the hypocrisy of business leaders whose laissez-faire philosophy and accompanying declaration of prerogatives as owners and employers left no room for governmental interference, except to defend them from even the gentlest regulation on behalf of public safety or workers' rights. In the face of such entrenched power Niebuhr went so far as to defend limited support of revolutionary violence, if it would promote greater justice. As Niebuhr summarized his views, illusions were necessary for progress, but acting upon those illusions entailed risks:

> The most important of these illusions is that the collective life of mankind can achieve perfect justice. It is a very valuable illusion for the moment; for justice cannot be approximated if the hope of its perfect realization does not generate a sublime madness in the soul. Nothing but such madness will do battle with malignant power and "spiritual wickedness in high places." The illusion is dangerous because it encourages terrible fanaticisms. It must therefore be brought under the control of reason. One can only hope that reason will not destroy it before its work is done.[20]

18. Reinhold Niebuhr, "The Creed of Modern Christian Socialists," *Radical Religion* 3, no. 2 (Spring 1938): 13, 18.

19. Richard Wightman Fox, "Niebuhr, Reinhold," accessed November 14, 2009, http://www.anb.org/articles/08/08–01094.html; *American National Biography Online*, Feb. 2000.

20. Reinhold Niebuhr, *Moral Man and Immoral Society: A Study in Ethics and Politics* (New York: Scribner's, 1946), 277.

Moral Man and Immoral Society represented Niebuhr in his most radical guise. As the perilous decade of the 1930s unfolded, and as he observed both the progress made possible through incremental reform and the dangers of conservative reaction, he moved away from radical activism and toward the more accommodationist strategy of supporting the policies of the Roosevelt administration.

Niebuhr's subsequent career reveals some of the core tensions at the heart of the prophetic-dialectical approach to politics and the perduring question of the degree to which the prophet was obliged to accommodate to existing political and socioeconomic realities. What is clear is that the unequivocal spiritual solution of apocalyptic visionaries and premillennialist preachers was an option excluded by his sober biblical anthropology and down-to-earth realism.

How does one balance a clear vision of a just society with the need to compromise in a pluralist society? Also, how much oversimplification is necessary to goad others to political action, especially if that oversimplification dulls or even drowns out needed prophetic critiques of one's own country? Niebuhr's growing endorsement of Roosevelt's New Deal and abandonment of his longtime goal for a vibrant Socialist or Farmer/Labor party reveals his own concession that there was insufficient public support for a genuinely radical transformation of American society. In 1936 that endorsement of Roosevelt remained qualified, as evident in his observation that the nation "has chosen a messiah rather than a political leader, committed to a specific political program; and unfortunately the messiah is more renowned for his artistic juggling than for robust resolution."[21]

The growing power of Republicans and conservative Southern Democrats, coupled with the outbreak of World War II in Europe, pushed Niebuhr in 1939 to endorse Roosevelt for an unprecedented third term: "Twilight is falling on the whole western world. Let us not permit the forces of social injustice to win a victory here."[22] The rising threat of Nazism in Europe, especially following the capitulation of most of western Europe in the spring of 1940, led Niebuhr to break all remaining ties with the Socialist Party—which still embraced neutrality—and launch a campaign to enter the war. As he editorialized in *The Nation*, "If Hitler is defeated in the end it will be because the crisis has awakened in us the will to preserve a civilization in which justice and freedom are realities, and given us the knowledge that ambiguous methods are required for the ambiguities of history."[23]

This final statement embracing "ambiguous methods" as a result of historical ambiguities became the highlight of his approach to foreign policy and how it could be sold to the American people. Excessive concern about the failures of American society might blind us to the need to fight against much greater evils, whether they were represented in the 1940s by Hitler's Germany or after the war by Stalin's Soviet Union. This theme was developed more fully in his 1944 book

---

21. Reinhold Niebuhr, "The National Election" *Radical Religion* 2, no. 1 (1936): 3.
22. Reinhold Niebuhr, "The Coming Presidential Election," *Radical Religion* 4, no. 4 (1939): 3–4.
23. Reinhold Niebuhr, "An End to Illusions," *The Nation* 150 (June 29, 1940): 778–79.

The Children of Light and the Children of Darkness. By seeing the United States in particular and pragmatic democracy in general as the "children of light," he rallied people for the defense of democratic values.

Over the next decade Niebuhr gained a position of considerable influence among liberal foreign-policy leaders in the United States. He was now firmly ensconced in the Democratic camp. His effective rhetoric and willingness to employ emotionally powerful oversimplifications helped to sell the basic premises of containment to the American people. Yet Niebuhr's growing association with the foreign-policy establishment also represented a dulling of the prophetic perspective that he had valued so dearly in earlier years. By focusing his attention on the evils arising in the Soviet regime, he failed to maintain a critical perspective on American attitudes and actions in the early years of the cold war. Perhaps seduced by his proximity to the powerful and influential, he did not want to attack the men that enhanced his own prestige. His oversimplifications abetted a growing national smugness regarding the righteousness of America's cause. But his ability to respond and adjust to historical change remained intact even in his later years, when he made another tactical turn and resumed his earlier role as prophetic critic of American policy, this time in relation to deepening US involvement in the Vietnam conflict.[24]

Other voices that sought to bring a Christian social conscience to the challenges of the 1930s were Dorothy Day and her occasional collaborator Peter Maurin. Maurin was a French Catholic who lived in sympathy with the poor and homeless and helped form Maryfarm, a rural outpost of the Catholic Worker movement. Day herself abandoned the Episcopalianism of her youth and became sympathetic with popular front groups during her college years. After a troubled early life that included multiple marriages, she converted to Catholicism in 1927 and was left by her husband to become a single mother. In May of 1933, with the Depression in full grip and many Catholics listening to the right-wing radio show of Father Charles Coughlin, Day and Maurin began distributing their newspaper, the *Catholic Worker.*

The paper articulated a powerful new social vision and inspired many Catholics to embrace voluntary poverty and form houses of hospitality for the poor. The *Catholic Worker* also included sympathetic coverage of the labor movement and discussions of the important artistic, literary, and intellectual trends of the day. While the Catholic Worker movement did not always live up to its ideals (as Martin Marty has argued), it did provide a powerful alternative to Communist atheism, bourgeois complacency, and the failure of political, religious, and intellectual leaders to respond effectively to a growing national crisis.[25]

Reinhold Niebuhr's emerging neo-orthodox realism and Dorothy Day's Catholic Worker movement were not the only new religious ideas being

24. Richard W. Fox, *Reinhold Niebuhr: A Biography* (Ithaca, NY: Cornell University Press, 1985), 264–65.
25. See Martin E. Marty, *Modern American Religion*, vol. 2, *The Noise of Conflict, 1919–1941* (Chicago: University of Chicago Press, 1991), 334–37.

spawned during the cultural and economic ferment of the Great Depression. New voices on the right pushed both the boundaries of Christian orthodoxy and the tolerance of many Americans, including the Roosevelt administration, for right-wing rhetoric. William Dudley Pelley merged some traditional Christian ideas with theosophy and astrology as he sought to promote himself and his own particular vision for American life. Publishing a magazine called *Liberation*, founding a college to study "Christian economics," and forming legions of "silver shirts," reminiscent of European paramilitary groups but without the mass following, Pelley clamored for popular attention and utilized increasingly anti-Semitic rhetoric. The major effect of his unsuccessful bid for the presidency in 1936 was the encouragement of marginal extremist groups.

Gerald Winrod was more orthodox and fundamentalist in his Christian belief, but similarly enthralled by right-wing solutions to the challenges of the Depression. Like Pelley, his foray into elective politics was abortive, as he failed to win the Kansas primary for senator. Nevertheless, he did reveal many characteristics of the later Christian right in politics, including an effort to see world events through the lens of biblical prophecy, a consistent anti-Catholicism, and a propensity to interpret politics through a conspiratorial lens. Both Pelley and Winrod were attacked in the courts by the Roosevelt administration for fomenting discontent in the armed services during World War II, which simultaneously deadened their influence and threatened freedom of speech and the press. In his study *The Old Christian Right*, which examines the lives of Pelley, Winrod, and Gerald L. K. Smith, Leo Ribuffo argues that the Roosevelt administration's "brown scare" against native fascists, with the assistance of many liberals and leftists, helped pave the way for the postwar "red scare" that has become associated with Joseph McCarthy.[26]

The most influential agitator of the Depression years was Gerald L. K. Smith. A powerful orator and a Disciples of Christ minister, he yoked his career to that of the populist demagogue Huey Long in Louisiana. After Long's assassination Smith failed to take over leadership of the Long organization, but he sought to build alliances with other agitators of the decade, including radio priest Charles Coughlin and Francis Townsend, who sought a guaranteed income for all seniors over the age of sixty. While efforts to build a Union Party collapsed after Roosevelt's landslide reelection in 1936, Smith continued to have a voice in politics, inveighing against liberal and Jewish conspiracies, causing some to regard him "the dean of American anti-Semitism."[27]

The 1930s thus saw a continuation of the trend toward radical Christian nationalism, previewed in the 1920s with the reemergence of the Ku Klux Klan. It was a trend driven by a convergence of social and economic changes that many

26. Leo P. Ribuffo, *The Old Christian Right* (Philadelphia: Temple University Press, 1983), 183, 237–49. See also Sidney E. Ahlstrom, *A Religious History of the American People* (New Haven, CT: Yale University Press, 2004), 926–29, for his coverage of right-wing religion during the Great Depression.

27. See Ribuffo, *Christian Right*, 177.

conservative Christians found highly disturbing, including demographic shifts, the collapse of Prohibition, and the economic dislocations of the decade. Refuge was sought in a politics of smear and nostalgia. The marketing of religion for political purposes was not limited to the right; many mainstream politicians of the 1930s utilized religious and biblical language to sell their programs to the American people.

Franklin Roosevelt's speeches were often replete with biblical allusions and metaphors, as he sought to tap into the nation's civil religion and build support for his political programs. In his first inaugural address he referred to the day as a "national consecration." Quoting Proverbs 29:18, he accused the business and financial leaders of the country of lacking vision and insisted that "when there is no vision the people perish." Repeatedly he referred to financial leaders as "money changers" and claimed that they had "fled from their high seats in the temple of our civilization," consciously echoing the Gospel account of Jesus attacking the money changers on the temple grounds in Jerusalem. He closed that speech with a prayer: "[W]e humbly ask the blessing of God. May he protect each and every one of us. May he guide me in the days to come."[28]

On October 31, 1936, in Madison Square Garden, in what was perhaps his most heated campaign address, FDR not only welcomed the hatred of business elites and promised to master them; he articulated a biblical vision for social justice. He claimed that the government must remain "on the same side of the street with the Good Samaritan," alluding to one of Jesus' most famous parables. Later in the speech he encouraged Americans to maintain their "altars of faith . . . that maintain all that is best in us and all that is best in our nation." Finally, he urged the country to follow the counsel of the prophet Micah (6:8) by working and sacrificing for one another: "What doth the Lord require of thee—but to do justly, to love mercy and to walk humbly with thy God."[29]

Such language continued as Franklin Roosevelt and the country made the transition from Depression to World War II. He continued the Wilsonian tactic of melding religious iconography with patriotic imagery to promote the war and sell victory bonds.[30] He even seized upon the nation's war effort as an opportunity to redefine the nation's social compact by declaring a new Economic Bill of Rights, which included the right of every American to a job, sufficient income for recreation, possession of a decent home, adequate medical care, protection from the economic and other perils of old age, and access to a good education. By focusing on how we as a nation treated the least among us, FDR sought to expand a biblically based vision for economic justice.[31] But his appeal to biblical warrants went beyond support for badly needed social and economic reforms,

28. Richard Polenberg, ed., *The Era of Franklin D. Roosevelt 1933–1945: A Brief History with Documents* (Boston: Bedford St. Martins, 2000), 40–44.
29. Ibid., 53–57.
30. Ibid., 189.
31. Ibid., 226–27.

and a balanced picture of this great leader must also describe the more controversial dimensions of his application of religion to politics.

As the United States geared up for entry into World War II, it experienced a resurgence of the themes linking America with providential destiny that had become so powerful in previous conflicts, especially the Revolutionary War, the Civil War, and World War I. What is more, World War II soon seized a special place in the moral imagination of Americans, leading to the growth of a saga in which the providentially guided nation reluctantly responded to a call to combat after an unprovoked and barbaric attack on its unsuspecting navy. After selfless heroism, courage, sacrifice, ingenuity, and prayer, this godly agent was able to defeat two of the most evil empires in world history. However, as David Kennedy and other historians have rightly shown, America's memory of its Good War does not always square with the historical record. For most of the 1930s the nation tried to ignore the threat posed by Hitler's Nazi regime in Europe, despite the attempts of theologians like Reinhold Niebuhr, James Luther Adams, and Dietrich Bonhoeffer to raise people's awareness. Though Roosevelt himself initially complied with the isolationist mood of the nation, he did assert his leadership in 1937 by calling for a quarantine on rogue regimes and agreeing to fight an undeclared naval war against Hitler prior to the Japanese surprise attack on Pearl Harbor in 1941.

While Pearl Harbor has been ensconced in the annals of American history as a paradigmatic example of justification for war, scant attention has been given to the ways in which more skillful diplomacy might have defused the crisis. We emphasize our sacrifice, but do not pay adequate heed to the sacrifice of the Soviet Union, which lost close to forty times as many soldiers as the United States. We praise the genius of our scientists but are often still unwilling to look deep within our own soul at the horror of atomic weapons, which we alone have unleashed upon the world in combat.[32]

During the earliest phase of the combat of World War II, Roosevelt justly and presciently condemned the bombings of civilian populations by the Soviet Union.

> The ruthless bombing from the air of civilians in unfortified centers of population during the course of hostilities which have raged in various quarters of the earth during the past few years, which has resulted in the maiming and in the death of thousands of defenseless men, women and children, has sickened the hearts of every civilized man and woman, and has profoundly shocked the conscience of humanity.
>
> If resort is had to this form of inhuman barbarism during the period of the tragic conflagration with which the world is now confronted, hundreds

32. See David M. Kennedy, *Freedom from Fear: The American People in Depression and War, 1929–1945* (New York: Oxford University Press, 1999), 855–56.

of thousands of innocent human beings who are not even remotely participating in hostilities, will lose their lives.[33]

While the dogs of war were teaching the American people and their combatants to hate their enemies and repay hostility with daunting force, Roosevelt
authorized research into building atomic weapons and oversaw firebombing
campaigns that decimated civilian populations in Germany and Japan. Furthermore, scholars have documented the rampant anti-Semitism within the State
Department during World War II and the delays in processing entry visas for
Jewish refugees, which prevented many of them from leaving in time to escape
the gas chambers. American unwillingness to alter our strict quotas for immigrants or provide succor for the Jews on the SS *St. Louis* have caused some to
indict the United States for its complicity in the Holocaust.

At the same time Roosevelt took only the most halting steps, and then under
extreme pressure, to limit our own system of racial apartheid at home. Hatred
of the Japanese was ubiquitous after Pearl Harbor, with children's cartoons such
as *Popeye* even depicting the supposedly inferior racial traits and tricky character
of Japanese soldiers and citizens. Historian John Dower has detailed the ways
in which the war in the Pacific became a race war, and even former secretary of
defense Robert McNamara has raised the question of whether or not we were
acting as war criminals in the final years of the conflict. The internment of Japanese Americans under Executive Order 9016 was merely another manifestation
of the larger trend. In time, however, Christian voices did speak up prophetically
against the internment policy. Christians in Seattle and San Francisco provided
meals and lobbied for more just treatment of Japanese Americans, and many
leading Christian periodicals such as *Christian Century* and *Christianity and Crisis* spoke up against internment.[34]

The emergence of the cold war in the aftermath of World War II both confirmed and strengthened the American tendency to see itself as the "chosen
nation" whose religiosity and special relationship with God would allow it to
spread peace, democracy, and capitalism to the rest of the world. The speeches
of American presidents of the era were replete with this type of rhetoric. Harry
Truman in 1948 argued, "We must always make spiritual values our main line
of defense. . . . Freedom of religion as well as the freedom and security of nations
is seriously threatened by anti-religious forces. . . . It is, therefore, necessary that

33. John T. Woolley and Gerhard Peters, *The American Presidency Project* [online]. Santa Barbara, CA. Available at http://www.presidency.ucsb.edu/ws/?pid=15845.

34. See Martin E. Marty, *Modern American Religion*, vol. 3, *Under God, Indivisible, 1941–1960*
(Chicago: University of Chicago Press, 1996), 82–83. Also Martin Gilbert, *Auschwitz and the Allies*
(New York: Henry Holt & Co., 1981); *The Fog of War: Eleven Lessons from the Life of Robert S.
McNamara*, directed by Errol Morris (Sony Pictures Classics, 2003); John W. Dower, *War without
Mercy: Race and Power in the Pacific War* (New York: Pantheon, 1987); Richard Rhodes, *The Mak-
ing of the Atomic Bomb* (New York: Touchstone, 1986), "America and the Holocaust" (*The American
Experience*, PBS, 2005).

all loyal American citizens join together to stem the tide of these evil forces by girding ourselves with the sword of faith and the armor of truth."[35]

In the theo-politics of Harry Truman, religion became a necessary instrument of foreign policy. Promoting religion at home was regarded as a first line of defense for freedom and security overseas.

Four years later Dwight Eisenhower made a similar point: "What is our battle against communism if it is not a fight between anti-God and a belief in the Almighty? Communists know this. They have to eliminate God from their system. When God comes in, communism has to go."[36] Such descriptions of events were also common in preachers across the ideological and doctrinal spectrum, with the left-leaning Reinhold Niebuhr describing the Soviet Union as "demonic" and the mainstream Evangelical Billy Graham remarking at his 1949 Los Angeles crusade that the Soviet Union was "against God, against Christ, against the Bible, and against all religion."[37] In each of these formulations the cold war was construed not so much as a geopolitical, economic, or ideological struggle as a war of religion, threatening to let loose all of the excesses lurking in the Pandora's box of holy war.[38] Joseph McCarthy used very similar language to motivate his anticommunist crusade and attack on liberalism in the early 1950s. Central to his shrill rhetoric was the Marxist categorization of religion as the "opiate of the masses."

There is no denying the viciousness and brutality that inhered in Soviet attitudes, policies, and actions toward religion. Accompanying the bloody conflicts of the Russian civil war was a massive and coordinated assault by the Communist Party upon the Russian Orthodox Church, which had long been a mainstay of support for the tsar. Similarly, Soviet education and propaganda worked hard to eliminate vestiges of religion from Russian life, even going so far as to have Yuri Gagarin declare that he did not see God when he traveled in the heavens following his first successful flight as a cosmonaut orbiting the earth. On the American side of the cold war, the consequences included the religious revival of the Eisenhower era, effects on the ecumenical movement, increased tolerance of non-Protestant faiths, and a more explicit iteration of civil religion. Within the hotbed of the cold war, however, the facile association between the United States as the power of goodness aligned with the forces of God quickly led to excesses and examples of moral blindness.

35. *New York Times*, March 13, 1948, cited in T. Jeremy Gunn, *Spiritual Weapons: The Cold War and the Forging of an American National Religion* (Westport, CT: Praeger, 2009), 52.

36. Quoted in William Inboden, *Religion and American Foreign Policy, 1945–1960: The Soul of Containment* (New York: Cambridge University Press, 2008), 259.

37. Quoted in Marty, *Modern American Religion*, 3:127, 152.

38. Dianne Kirby in particular has developed this approach to understanding the cold war. See Dianne Kirby, "The Cold War, the Hegemony of the United States, and the Golden Age of Christian Democracy," in Hugh McLeod, ed., *The Cambridge History of Christianity*, vol. 9, *World Christianities c. 1914–c. 2000* (New York: Cambridge University Press, 2006), 285.

As cold war fears and the specter of the atomic bomb swept over the United States, prominent religious leaders, media moguls, and politicians urged the American people to return to more traditional forms of religion. Billy Graham's 1949 crusade in Los Angeles, in which he proclaimed grave warnings against the dangers of godless Communism, caught the attention of William Randolph Hearst. The influential publisher urged his editors to "puff Graham," with the result that Graham's Evangelicalism received an establishment "stamp of approval." As noted previously, both Truman and Eisenhower urged Americans to find strength in their religious traditions for the stand against Communism. Eisenhower was belatedly baptized prior to his inauguration and, through his example of regular church attendance, gave iconic expression to the blending of religion and patriotism.

The personal exemplification of patriotic piety was accompanied by more formal efforts to reaffirm the religious nature of the country. In 1953 Congress voted to make "In God We Trust" the national motto and to have it stamped on the national coinage. In 1954 the pledge of allegiance was amended to include the line "under God." These changes took place in a context within which the strong support of associating the country with traditional Protestantism was weakening. Will Herberg's 1955 book *Protestant, Catholic, Jew* began to articulate the idea of a Judeo-Christian culture in which shared basic beliefs were more important in public than specific doctrinal differences. A similar approach was emphasized by Eisenhower in his oft-quoted remark, "Our government makes no sense unless it is founded in a deeply felt religious faith—and I don't care what it is." While some have criticized Eisenhower for his vacuous sense of religiosity, William Inboden correctly points out that Eisenhower was in fact promoting America as a religious nation in the face of atheistic Communism, while being much more inclusive about the type of religion that could play this role than many of his predecessors.[39] With this renewed emphasis on religion, church attendance surged to the highest levels in all of American history.

While religion strongly shaped the perception of events of American policy makers, it was also seen as an effective way to sell foreign policy decisions to the American people. Harry Truman's lightning-fast recognition of Israel after it declared its independence is seen as being highly influenced by his traditional reading of Old Testament narratives of the land of Israel belonging to the Jewish people. Truman even sidestepped long-standing American concerns about Catholicism to cooperate with the Vatican in an undercover campaign to undermine the Communist Party in elections in Italy.

Furthermore, by the early Eisenhower administration, the United States exhibited a much more aggressive approach to foreign policy, and religious themes were often cited to justify interventions on foreign soil. While the 1953 coup in Iran overthrowing the democratically elected regime of Mohammad

---

39. Inboden, *Religion and American Foreign Policy*, 259.

Mossadegh was motivated primarily by economic and geopolitical concerns, the Eisenhower administration deftly co-opted religious leaders and organizations to support later efforts at regime change. In 1954 the CIA engineered a coup d'état against the popularly elected government of Jacobo Arbenz in Guatemala. Arbenz's crime had been his support of a land-reform proposal that would have stripped land from the United Fruit Company. Secretary of State and former Presbyterian lay leader John Foster Dulles had done legal work for the United Fruit Company. His brother, Allen, was then serving as CIA director and simultaneously sat on the board of the United Fruit Company. With their own economic interests dovetailing with a purported national security concern, the Dulles brothers quickly went to work. The CIA assisted the Honduran Catholic Church to produce and distribute a pastoral letter that declared, "Our struggle against Communism must be . . . a crusade of prayer and sacrifice . . . and a total rejection of Communist propaganda—for the love of God and Guatemala."[40] While the CIA and the Catholic Church were ultimately successful at removing Arbenz, the end result of the coup was forty years of instability and human rights abuses, far from the reign of justice and widespread economic opportunity that both the US government and the Catholic Church claimed to represent.

Similarly US policy in Vietnam was significantly shaped by specifically religious concerns. Since the Catholic Church had already proven to be a reliable partner of the United States in fighting Communism in Italy, Guatemala, and at home, the American government turned to the Catholic Ngo Dinh Diem to lead South Vietnam in the aftermath of the Geneva Accords. Diem's candidacy was urged by the Catholic leader Francis Cardinal Spellman, and his primary qualifications appeared to be his Catholicism and the fact that he had spent time in the United States. Portrayed as a Vietnamese Joan of Arc, Diem was given substantial support by the US government. He even benefited from a major propaganda coup in the United States when he put his support behind the reception of over one million refugees of alleged religious persecution from North Vietnam. Despite this fact, close observers quickly recognized his incompetence and complete inability to work with the Buddhist majority in Vietnam.

Furthermore, as Catholicism was often viewed by the people as a foreign religion associated with the French colonial regime, US efforts to prop him up in power contributed to the Vietnamese perception that the new foreign presence on their soil was installing itself as the next colonial regime. By the time the Kennedy administration gave up on Diem in late 1963, the damage had already been done by his political incompetence and extreme alienation of the Buddhist population. Once again an oversimplified religious solution to a

---

40. Quoted in T. Jeremy Gunn, *Weapons*, 144.

complex geopolitical problem ended up exacerbating an already tense situation and undermining possibilities for building a just society.[41]

One of the most significant changes in church-state relations over the past century has come through changing Supreme Court interpretations of the Constitution. Historically, the court's jurisprudence has expanded rights and recognition to non-Christian religion, seeking to make the public square open to people of faith, without favoring one religious tradition over another. But the record of the courts in the past several decades has been marked by controversy. Many decisions, especially those handed down in the 1960s, marked a major shift from previous practice and threatened public displays of religiosity at the state and local level. Many religious believers have interpreted efforts to raise the wall of separation as threatening their religious freedom and attacking cherished traditions. As a result, the role of the Supreme Court in adjudicating religious questions and the role of religion in American public life remains one of the most contested fronts in the ongoing culture wars.

Prior to the 1920s the First Amendment's clauses were interpreted only as limiting the power of the federal government. As the opening phrase of the amendment worded it, "Congress shall make no law . . ." Individual state constitutions typically had language defining the separation of church and state as well as the religious freedoms of their citizens. As discussed previously, all states had formally disestablished their churches and ended taxpayer funding of ministers' salaries by 1833. In the 1925 free-speech case, *Gitlow v. New York*, the Supreme Court began the process of selectively incorporating the First Amendment into the Fourteenth Amendment. The Reconstruction Era amendment had been primarily designed to protect the rights of former slaves from encroachments by state and local governments. The Fourteenth Amendment reads, "No state shall make or enforce any law which shall abridge the privileges or immunities of citizens of the United States; nor shall any state deprive any person of life, liberty, or property, without due process of law; nor deny to any person within its jurisdiction the equal protection of the laws." In *Gitlow* the Court ruled that free speech was one of the "privileges or immunities of citizens" that could not be limited by the states.

In 1940 with *Cantwell v. Connecticut* the Court began applying this logic to the religious clauses of the First Amendment by specifically stating that state legislatures could neither limit the free exercise of religion nor establish religion. This ruling was expanded seven years later in *Everson v. Board of Education*, which attempted to spell out much more specifically what the First Amendment prohibited. Even more significantly it effectively introduced a clause from Jefferson's letter to the Danbury Baptists into the case law governing the interpretation of the Constitution by declaring that "[i]n the words of Jefferson, the clause against establishment of religion by law was intended to erect 'a wall of separation between Church and State.'" Whether the building of such a wall

---

41. See particularly Gunn, *Weapons*, 155–96.

was indeed the intention of the founders remains highly contested; nevertheless, it is clear that these decisions ushered in a vastly different landscape for public religion in the United States.

Another set of decisions during World War II profoundly expanded the rights of religious dissidents to practice their religious beliefs and dissent from patriotic exercises that they saw as limiting their religious freedom. The cases involved the widely derogated sect of Jehovah's Witnesses. Starting in the mid-1930s, Watchtower Society president J. Rutherford began to teach that the salute to the flag—which at the time included a literal salute similar to the Nazi *Sieg Heil*—amounted to idolatry, forcing religious believers to worship the flag and the nation it represented, thereby violating the commandments against idolatry and worshiping other gods. As Witness children began to apply this teaching in the classroom, they suffered social ostracism and were quickly disciplined by school authorities. The cases worked their way up through the courts until in 1940 the Supreme Court ruled in *Minersville School District v. Gobitis* that the state's interest in promoting national unity and patriotism overrode Witnesses' rights not to be compelled to violate their religious beliefs.

In the aftermath of the decision Jehovah's Witnesses were harassed and subjected to violence, and many of their places of worship were burned down. Aggravated assaults on Witnesses were further sparked by the rise in nationalistic fervor in the years approaching World War II. Some of the worst attacks on property occurred in Maine and Wyoming, and over three hundred cities experienced some form of discrimination against Witnesses. In part shocked by the violence that they had helped to precipitate, the Supreme Court revisited the issue three years later in *West Virginia v. Barnette*. While the new decision rested primarily on the free speech rights of religious minorities, it clearly stated that students could not be compelled to participate in civic activities that conflicted with their religious beliefs. This set the stage for a series of later decisions that clarified this issue and expanded the rights of religious minorities to be free from government coercion.

An additional set of important decisions regarding the establishment clause of the First Amendment came in the early 1960s during the tenure of Earl Warren as chief justice. In the 1962 case *Engel v. Vitale*, the court struck down a New York State law that required students to recite a prayer composed by the state Board of Regents. The prayer as composed was broadly written, nonsectarian, and relatively benign: "Almighty God, we acknowledge our dependence upon Thee, and we beg Thy blessings upon us, our parents, our teachers and our country. Amen." Yet, regardless of the specific language of the prayer and the ubiquitous nature of school prayers prior to this time period, the plaintiffs raised an important question: should government at any level compel students to participate in a religious activity or prayer? The justices answered in the negative and in a series of subsequent decisions banned prayer—even when voluntary and led by students—at graduations and football games. For many traditional believers this was a sign that the government no longer respected them and was attempting to drive traditional religion from the school in favor of secular humanism.

The next year's decision, *Abington County Township v. Schempp,* expanded upon *Vitale* by proscribing devotional Bible reading in the school, but protecting the ability to study the Bible in literature or history classes. Later decisions barring the teaching of creationism and then creation science only compounded the impression that conservative Christians were being driven from the public schools and losing control of local institutions that they were required to support through their tax dollars, even if they were not compelled to send their children to them. Many responded by sending their children to a growing number of private Christian schools or, later, entering the burgeoning homeschooling movement. These important court decisions helped to strengthen the principle of nonestablishment of religion and to protect the rights of religious minorities.

At the same time they contributed to the perception of many religious individuals who adhered to traditional Christian values that they were not welcome in the public schools, and as they left, those schools experienced an evisceration of their ability to serve as a melting pot where American children of all backgrounds could interact and thereby become active participants in the cultivation of the public values of their society.

This brief survey of major twentieth-century court decisions regarding freedom of religion and the role of religion in public life should give pause to culture warriors on both sides of the ideological divide. Secularists should recognize the ways in which these decisions have marginalized people who previously were closer to the center of American life. Undermining traditions that have been maintained for generations is never an easy process and will often be met with firm resistance. Certainly some accommodation to the wishes of local majorities has a long history in the federalist structure of the United States. At the same time the United States has become significantly more ethnically and religiously diverse since its founding. Especially since the passage of the Immigration Reform Act of 1965, the number of Americans practicing Buddhism, Hinduism, and Islam has surged. In order to maintain the nonestablishment clause of the First Amendment and resist the temptation to promote religious belief with the power of the state, Christians need to be wary of infringing on the rights of religious minorities. They would do well to remember the temptation of Jesus in the wilderness in which he refused the offer of temporal power, and instead chose to promote his kingdom through self-sacrificing acts of love and service.

Recently Harvard Law School professor Noah Feldman has suggested one possible way out of the present impasse by allowing traditional believers more public space for the exercise of their religious speech and display of religious symbols in exchange for stricter separation in other areas, especially government funding of religious groups.[42] While the specific details of his proposal are open

---

42. See Noah Feldman, *Divided by God: America's Church State Problem—And What We Should Do About It* (New York: Farrar, Straus & Giroux, 2005), 237–38.

to debate, the suggestion that a middle ground be found captures the spirit of the role of open discussion and compromise that is both essential to a democratic republic and threatened by the recent increased polarization of ideological blocs in the nation's legislative bodies, resulting in rising acrimony and crippling gridlock. What is more, history offers precedents for the legitimacy of alternatives to absolutist tactics and their bitter fruits of culture wars and international conflict—such as the tactics of accommodation practiced by Ezra, adaptation by Hillel, and Christian realism by Reinhold Niebuhr—and happy will be the day when living members of Congress will become candidates for this Hall of Civic High-Mindedness.

No public movement in recent history has better displayed both the potential for a constructive religious voice in social reform and its perils than the modern movement for African American civil rights. The black church was not the place where many knowledgeable observers would have looked for comprehensive social change. During the first half of the twentieth century, communists were more likely than Southern black churches to crusade for civil rights, and many Southern ministers were dependent for their social position and financial support on prominent whites. Indeed, Barbara Savage has argued that "[t]he emergence in the late 1950s of a Southern civil rights movement with churches, church people, and church culture at its center was a powerful and startling departure. . . . The movement is best thought of not as an inevitable triumph or a moment of religious revival, but simply as a miracle."[43]

In the aftermath of World War II the confluence of several developments created a climate for change. Persons returned from military service with a new sense of empowerment, political identity, and purpose. Fundamental transformations were taking place in the Southern economy that opened the door to fresh leadership. A new liberalism was arising with increased focus on individual and civil rights. Propitiously and in step with the progressive social climate of the time, the Supreme Court took moves that lent crucial moral, ideological, and constitutional support to the civil rights movement, moves that were accompanied by increasingly bold actions by several presidential administrations that in turn were followed by sweeping legislative initiatives. Some of the religious themes that were brought into play have been so thoroughly absorbed into the narrative of the civil rights movement that visions originally promulgated by the Hebrew prophets came to be attributed to Martin Luther King Jr. One example is the "reattribution" of the words of Amos 5:24 to King on the civil rights memorial in Montgomery, Alabama.

A quick survey of the civil rights movement reveals how central religious voices were to the movement. Martin Luther King Jr. was of course a Baptist minister, and he named his organization the Southern Christian Leadership Conference. In one of his most famous statements, *The Letter from a Birmingham Jail*,

---

43. Barbara Dianne Savage, *Your Spirits Walk beside Us: The Politics of Black Religion* (Cambridge: The Belknap Press of Harvard University Press, 2008), 2.

he unself-consciously compared himself to both the Hebrew prophets and the apostle Paul as he sought to "carry the gospel of freedom." Earlier in his career he had even adopted the strategy of writing in the style of a Pauline epistle in seeking to reach the conscience of America. Later in his famous "I've Been to the Mountaintop" address, he explicitly compared himself to Moses, as he preached a message of hope on the eve of his assassination. David Chappell has argued that such use of prophetic religion was central to the eventual success of the civil rights movement.[44] It should be added that King's own career prominently featured his ability to blend New Testament themes and motifs from the Hebrew prophets with the American democratic tradition, especially as set forth in the Declaration of Independence, the Constitution and its amendments, and amplified by the abolitionist movement and Abraham Lincoln's Gettysburg Address.

While the Student Nonviolent Coordinating Committee became radicalized as the 1960s proceeded, its founding document also revealed the centrality of Christian theology and eschatology to its philosophy. In part it read, "Nonviolence, as it grows from the Judeo-Christian tradition, seeks a social order of justice permeated by love. . . . Through nonviolence, courage displaces fear. Love transcends hate. Acceptance dissipates prejudice; hope ends despair. Faith reconciles doubt. Peace dominates war. Mutual regards cancel enmity. Justice for all overthrows injustice. The redemptive community supersedes immoral social systems."[45]

The program of the March on Washington for Jobs and Freedom in August of 1963 also reveals the centrality of clergy to the movement; speakers besides Dr. King included the archbishop of Washington, Patrick O'Boyle; Dr. Eugene Carson Blake of the Presbyterian Church; Rabbis Uri Miller and Joachim Prinz (a Holocaust survivor); and Mathew Ahmann, the executive director of the National Catholic Conference for Interracial Justice.[46]

Freedom songs that were so central to building community and courage in the civil rights movement also display the importance of religious themes, steeped as they were in the African American spiritual tradition. Lyrics such as "Oh Freedom, Oh Freedom, Before I'll be a slave I'll be buried in my grave, and be home with my Lord and be free, and be free"[47] helped build determination and reinforced the belief that African Americans would ultimately gain their freedom, whether in this life or the next. At other times traditional spirituals and even children's songs such as "This Little Light of Mine" were reworked to challenge the power and fearmongering of Alabama governor George Wallace

44. David L. Chappell, *A Stone of Hope: Prophetic Religion and the Death of Jim Crow* (Chapel Hill, NC: University of North Carolina Press, 2004).

45. "Student Nonviolent Coordinating Committee (SNCC) Founded (April)," *Civil Rights Movement Veterans*, accessed April 28, 2015, http://www.crmvet.org/tim/timhis60.htm#1960sncc.

46. "March on Washington" (Program), 08/28/1963; Bayard Rustin Papers; John F. Kennedy Library; National Archives and Records Administration, accessed July 27, 2011, http://www.ourdocuments.gov/doc_large_image.php?flash=true&doc=96.

47. See Lea VanderVelde, *Redemption Songs: Suing for Freedom before Dred Scott* (New York: Oxford University Press, 2014).

and Jim Clark, the sheriff of Dallas County, Alabama. Even more radical phases of the civil rights movements were cloaked in religious language and ideology taken from sources as diverse as liberation theology among Catholics and the Islam of Malcolm X.

The role of religion during the time of the civil rights movement was checkered with dissent alongside widespread support. Many religious leaders either ignored the crusade for equality or actively resisted it. King's *Letter from a Birmingham Jail* was directed to white pastors in the community who had labeled him an outside agitator and asked him to leave. Jerry Falwell refused to get involved in civil rights, purportedly because of the traditional Baptist aversion to politics. Yet it should be noted that aversion quickly changed to political activism in the late 1970s when the opportunity arose to wed his conservative theology to a compatibly conservative political movement.

Jane Dailey has pointed out that a "theology of segregation" was central to the resistance to the civil rights movement and as much a part of traditional American religion as the prophetic inclusionist strand represented by King. She also notes the ways that fears about interracial dating, sex, and marriage were used to rally opponents of civil rights, frequently with appeal to scriptural warrants.[48]

Other scholars, such as Randall Balmer, have made the observation that resistance to integration, especially at Bob Jones University, played a major role in mobilizing the religious right.[49] David Chappell, in the meantime, pointed out that Southern ministers often used their influence to dispel resistance to *Brown v. Board of Education,* frequently setting "pulpit against pew" and opening a rift between the more liberal politics of the clergy and the conservative leanings of their congregations.[50] In the weeks prior to *Brown* the Southern Presbyterian Church had approved a statement which read, "Enforced segregation of the races is discrimination which is out of harmony with Christian theology and ethics."[51] With these words a denomination born in defense of the institution of slavery took a historical movement into a new future.

In 1965, one year after the passage of the Civil Rights Act of 1964 and in the immediate aftermath of passage of the Voting Rights Act of 1965, the Southern Baptist Convention made a similarly groundbreaking move by passing a resolution that rededicated its members to a ministry of reconciliation among all people, claimed the equality of all persons in the face of God, and pledged "to provide positive leadership in our communities, seeking through conciliation and understanding to obtain peaceful compliance with laws assuring equal rights for all. We further pledge ourselves to go beyond these laws in the practice

---

48. Jane Dailey, "Sex, Segregation, and the Sacred after *Brown,*" *Journal of American History* 91, no. 1 (June 2004): 119–44.

49. Randall Balmer, *The Making of Evangelicalism: From Revivalism to Politics and Beyond* (Waco, TX: Baylor University Press, 2010), 64–66.

50. Chappell, *A Stone of Hope,* 131–52.

51. Quoted in *Rhetoric, Religion, and the Civil Rights Movement: 1954–1965,* ed. David Houck and David Dixon (Waco, TX: Baylor University Press 2006), 273.

of Christian love." The resolution was not passed without controversy, as some wanted also to condemn nonviolent civil disobedience as a means of bringing about change.[52]

By the late 1960s, then, many religious groups that had initially resisted integration, including many Evangelicals and fundamentalists, had publicly repented of their past beliefs and dedicated themselves to a colorblind gospel and a colorblind society. This insistence on colorblindness, however, was accompanied by resistance to proactive measures to counteract the legacy of past injustices, such as affirmative action. In the meantime, other groups took inspiration from the success of the African American freedom struggle, and soon parallel movements developed among Hispanics, Native Americans, Asian Americans, the elderly, the disabled, and, most significantly, women. Before long, the barriers that had stood in the way of full participation in churches across much of the political spectrum began to erode.

The atmosphere of the time was increasingly charged with foment on many levels. Young people began questioning their government, especially about its policies in Vietnam. Traditional familial values were challenged, as a hip generation started experimenting with drug use and a variety of alternative lifestyles. Such rapid societal and cultural change inevitably provoked a backlash tapping into older streams of both conservative and fundamentalist thought that had lain percolating below the surface of American society, waiting for the appropriate moment and a strong enough incentive to reemerge.

The conservative movement that was symbolized by the rise of Ronald Reagan to the presidency in 1980 had its roots in the reaction to FDR's New Deal. Conservative activists, never having reconciled themselves to the greatly expanded power of the federal government, formed a series of networks and organizations to promote their views. Lyndon Johnson's expansion of the social safety net through the creation of Medicare and Medicaid further enraged conservatives. Prominent political and religious leaders climbed over the "wall of separation" and spoke with one voice. As early as the late 1940s Ronald Reagan and Billy Graham had warned of the dangers of rising bureaucracy and the loss of individual freedom. Central to their fear was the belief that as the state usurped the role of providing social services it would crowd the church out of its traditional role and lure believers into a false sense of complacency.

Once the state had taken over one part of the church's mission, what would stop it from taking over others? Scholars such as Darren Dochuk, Lisa McGirr, and Bethany Moreton have amply documented how a collection of ministers, successful entrepreneurs, and citizen activists built private primary and secondary schools, colleges, political networks, and think tanks to promote the values and structures of the free enterprise system, namely, small government, right-to-work laws, conservative institutes and lobbying organizations, as well as a

52. "Resolution on Human Relations," accessed March 11, 2015, http://www.sbc.net/resolutions/amResolution.asp?ID=887.

vigorous place for faith in the public sector. These groups gained significant political power in the Sun Belt, an area stretching from the states of the old Confederacy through the Southwest to southern California.

During the 1950s and 1960s, influenced by changing public convictions and a desire to appeal to a broader cross-section of the American population, such groups shed many but not all of their more extreme racist and anti-Semitic views. Expressing growing frustration with the moderate Republicanism of the Eisenhower years and the resurgent liberalism of Kennedy and Johnson, they mobilized to support the candidacy of Barry Goldwater in 1964. Barely chastened by their humiliating defeat in that presidential election, southern California conservatives attached themselves to the 1966 gubernatorial candidacy of Ronald Reagan, who campaigned as a moderate and pragmatic conservative who could get things done in Sacramento. While advancing the conservative agenda, in many ways he also separated himself from the more radical fringes of the conservative movement by publicly distancing himself from the John Birch Society and even signing a bill to liberalize abortion. Nevertheless, by attaching himself symbolically to many of the goals of conservative Christians and forcefully reacting to radicalism on the left, symbolized by growing unrest and rioting on the campuses of the University of California, Reagan earned the undying admiration of "suburban warriors" who before long would set their sights on elevating Reagan to the White House.[53]

In many ways the 1970s marked the coming of age of the religious right in American politics. An enigmatic role was played in the political ascent of conservative/Evangelical Christianity by the candidacy and then one-term presidency of Jimmy Carter, the first outwardly "born again" candidate to campaign for the White House. Carter won significant enthusiasm from the Evangelical community, garnering about 40 percent of their vote. To many, the opportunity to get a Southern Baptist into the White House signaled the dawn of a new age. However, the initial euphoria was short-lived. Carter's strict insistence on the separation of church and state, perceived alliance with liberals on hot-button issues such as abortion, and inability to handle effectively the significant economic and foreign policy challenges of his presidency caused many Evangelicals to grow disenchanted and to seek political salvation within the ranks of the Republican Party. Furthermore, many Evangelicals who had previously eschewed all political activity were mobilized by the likes of Jerry Falwell, whose Moral Majority, established in 1979, vigorously advanced in the public arena a platform of reclaiming traditional values combined with conservative economic and social policies. Nowhere was the new theo-political alignment displayed more clearly than at the 1980 Moral Majority conference, where Ronald Reagan

53. See Darren Dochuk, *From Bible Belt to Sunbelt: Plain-Folk Religion, Grassroots Politics, and the Rise of Evangelical Conservatism* (New York: W. W. Norton, 2012); Lisa McGirr, *Suburban Warriors: The Origins of the New American Right* (Princeton, NJ: Princeton University Press, 2002); Bethany Moreton, *To Serve God and Walmart* (Cambridge: Harvard University Press, 2010).

famously acknowledged the inability of the group to endorse him but declared that he endorsed them. Effectively, the endorsement was bilateral and charged with enormous political significance.

Ronald Reagan's popularity as a president was enormous, an accomplishment attributable in no small part to his ability to tap into the groundswell of Evangelical Christianity of his time. The spontaneity and enthusiasm with which he drew upon Scripture in support of his political positions provides ample opportunities for those interested in the topic of the Bible and politics to analyze the understanding of scriptural authority that guided his use (or abuse) of the Bible.

In one concise statement he expressed his overall view toward scriptural authority: "[The Bible contains] all the answers to all the problems that face us today."[54] Toward the end of his second term in the presidency, he applied his robust hermeneutic to a specific issue in a conversation with an Israeli lobbyist named Tom Dine: "You know, I turn back to your Old Testament and the signs foretelling Armageddon, and I find myself wondering if—if we're the generation that's going to see that come about. I don't know if you've noted any of these prophecies lately, but believe me, they certainly describe the times we're going through."[55]

What was the source of President Reagan's understanding of biblical prophecy and its bearing on the decisions he had to make as commander-in-chief of the most advanced nuclear power in the world? Against the background of what is known of his relationship to conservative Evangelical Christianity in his later years, it seems possible that his biblical views were shaped by Hal Lindsey, whose success in selling millions of copies of books like *The Late Great Planet Earth* gives him a prominent place in the "hall of fame" of a brand of apocalyptic charlatanry that is alien to classical Christianity and is shaped not by rigorous biblical scholarship but by lurid phantasy.

Lindsey, like Herbert Armstrong before him,[56] found it necessary to change the date he had initially assigned to the end of the world, since 1982 passed without the occurrence of his announced rapture. But he has persisted in offering a detailed account of the countdown to the great assize by identifying the European Common Market as the Antichrist, Russia as Gog of Magog, and China as the horde of 200,000 that will attack Israel and initiate the final battle of Armageddon. Is this cheap sensationalism the kind of biblical understanding we expect of our presidents? If one accepts Lindsey's concept of the ultimate trip (his mod term for the rapture as disclosing the meaning and goal of history), that is, if one believes that God's final plan for history is the fiery destruction of the mass of humanity, as the chosen gaze on from their vantage point in the clouds, one wonders what effect such disdain for creation will have on policy

54. Gaston Espinoza, ed., *Religion and the American Presidency: From George Washington to George W. Bush* (New York: Columbia University Press, 2009), 384.

55. Quoted in Paul S. Boyer, *When Time Shall Be No More: Prophecy Belief in Modern American Culture* (Cambridge: Belknap Press of Harvard University Press, 1994), 142.

56. See Herbert W. Armstrong, *1975 in Prophecy* (Edmond, OK: Ambassador College, 1956).

decisions relating to non-Western nations, world hunger, and environmental degradation?[57] Only by following the habits of the proverbial ostrich can citizens exempt from critical scrutiny the religious views of their political leaders and the political ideologies of their spiritual leaders.[58]

While the Yale-educated Episcopalian George H. W. Bush comes from a social and religious background vastly different than Ronald Reagan's, critics concerned with the relation of faith to politics have taken note of some his theo-political pronouncements. Of particular interest for our study is the manner in which he drew upon the Bible in dealing with the events leading up to the Gulf War in 1991. In early January of that year the President was in the midst of discussing with his advisors alternative responses to Saddam Hussein's invasion of Kuwait. His dilemma was complicated by the fact that as his evolving strategy was moving toward an incisive military initiative, his Episcopal bishop, Edmund Browning,[59] was giving public expression to his opposition to US military action against Iraq. It is against that background that one must inquire into the significance of Bush's invitation to evangelist Billy Graham to be an overnight guest at the White House on the very eve of the January 15 ultimatum he had placed before Saddam Hussein for the removal of Iraqi troops from the invaded territory.

How were religious themes related to military strategy in that conversation? What were the reasons behind his rejecting his own bishop's morally and religiously based critical position in favor of the patriotic evangelist's? Was he seeking guidance from biblical faith with a prayerful openness to that faith's informing and even raising questions regarding his own views, or was his turning to the counsel of the evangelist an instance of a political leader welcoming a religious warrant for a policy he had already embraced? In terms of electoral politics, was he falling to the temptation of enlisting religion as a political tool in the effort to gain popular support for a policy that had the potential of becoming

57. The potential of debased religious views to initiate violence is gruesomely illustrated by the anti-Islamic film *Innocence of Muslims*, whose mocking of the prophet Muhammad became the catalyst for deadly protests in Libya, Egypt, Iraq, and other Islamic nations. And the violence has spread to France, Belgium and England. http://news.nationalpost.com/2012/09/13/convicted-criminal-revealed-as-filmmaker-behind-anti-islam-youtube-clip-that-incited-deadly-riots.

58. Presidential historian Michael Beschloss gives the following account of Reagan's apocalyptic politics: "In the Oval Office, he terrified a South Korean leader by jovially warning that the Apocalypse was near. After that, aides convinced the President to keep such views to himself—at least in the presence of foreigners. But in private, Reagan insisted that 'signs and events' showed the imminence of Armageddon, such as 'wars fought to no conclusion' and 'earthquakes, storms, volcanic eruptions.' When the Apocalypse came, there would be armies invading the Holy Land, and a plague in which 'the eyes are burned from the head.' Reagan's longtime consultant Stuart Spencer told him, 'That's kind of scary to be talking about.' The President replied, 'Yeah, but it's going to happen'" (Michael Beschloss, *Presidential Courage: Brave Leaders and How They Changed America, 1789–1989* [New York: Simon & Schuster, 2007], 285–86).

59. Herbert S. Parmet, *George Bush: The Life of a Lone Star Yankee* (New York: Scribner, 1997), 476. One might compare this to the 1960 presidential campaign, in which Kennedy, in response to allegations he would take orders from Rome, felt he had to say, essentially, "As president I will not take too seriously what my church says."

a serious liability in an election year, an additional liability he could ill afford at a time when support was eroding among a growing number of conservative Republicans and leaders of the religious right, who were questioning whether he was too liberal to remain their standard bearer? If so, he adheres to a very old tradition, for as we shall discover in part 2, the Bible cites many instances of political expediency and opportunism enticing leaders to banish religious counselors who raise questions regarding their policies, while turning instead to priests and prophets who demonstrate their loyalty by invoking the name of the Lord in support of their patrons' positions.[60]

While examining the tactics of political leaders, the concomitant answerability of religious leaders must not be overlooked. So how did Billy Graham view his role? Was he relating to the commander-in-chief as priest, prophet, or seer? Upon what biblical warrants was he drawing? What was the nature of his hermeneutic? Did he formulate his counsel in terms of religious certainties? Was he prepared to deal with complex international dilemmas imbued with moral ambiguities? Did he appeal to biblical proof texts, or did he take the more complex route of scrutinizing contemporary issues under a lens constituted by core biblical principles (e.g., the theocratic principle upholding the sovereignty of God over *all* nations) and guided by a carefully reflected hermeneutic?

To these questions we shall return. But first we shall describe a sequel to the January 1991 incident, since light is shed on the nature of the relationship between the president and his religious advisors (both the sidelined bishop and the ensconced evangelist) by remarks made by Bush approximately a year after the "line drawn in the sand." In an address to a conservative-Evangelical group, the National Religious Broadcasters, given on January 26, 1992, the former president cited the teachings of Jesus Christ as the moral force behind the Persian Gulf War. He went on to commend the televangelists for their support of his war effort: "I want to thank you for helping America, as Christ ordained, to be a light unto the world."[61] How does that statement stand up to critical scrutiny from a biblical theological perspective? Has Christ ordained the United States to be a light to the world? If so, how is this country to fulfill that charge? In what way was the Gulf War a clear instance of obedience to Christ's will? Without deciding on the question of whether the Gulf War was justified politically, one must raise serious questions about the legitimacy of Bush's invoking the name of Christ as a warrant for this particular military decision of the commander-in-chief of the most powerful nation in the world. In light of the religious rhetoric and biblical themes employed by our political leaders, we cannot dodge the question of whether a critical, deliberately reflected understanding of the relation of scriptural traditions to contemporary events informs their thought, or whether we are faced with a more arbitrary process vulnerable to misuse. This

---

60. First Kings 22; Amos 7; Jer. 23 and 28. See especially Jer. 38:4.
61. Andrew Rosenthal, "In a Speech, President Returns to Religious Themes," *New York Times*, January 28, 1992, A17.

question takes on added poignancy in light of the leitmotif of "manifest destiny" that we have traced through much of US history.

For twelve years the offensive in enlisting biblical themes in support of national policy seemed to reside in the Republican Party. Not only did its standard bearers occupy the White House; it also was hospitable to the increasing political assertiveness of the religious right. Bolstering this pattern is the demographic fact that secular voters are preponderantly Democratic, as are the majority of Jews. The Democratic Party has tended to exercise extreme caution in relation to scriptural texts and sectarian themes.

Yet the decade-long monopoly was about to be broken in the 1992 Democratic convention by a candidate for president capable of enlisting religion while avoiding the negative reaction within a wide swath of Democrats that had debilitated Jimmy Carter. In his acceptance speech Governor William Jefferson Clinton deftly drew upon the Bible and highlighted the biblical concept of covenant as a rubric for the political program he was announcing. Christian theologian Harvey Cox responded with praise: "I very much welcome the decision on the part of the Democrats to no longer cede this whole rich realm of conversation and debate to the right-wing Republicans."[62] In the initiatives of his first term in office aimed at issues like universal health insurance and the alleviation of poverty, the Southern Baptist president, assisted by his Methodist wife, seemed to touch the deep religious convictions of many citizens. In Clinton's second term, however, even before the shroud of the Monica Lewinski affair descended on the Oval Office, religious themes became muted, in part it would seem due to the President's strategic effort to build a moderate bipartisan coalition. But the echoes of Southern Evangelical religion were by no means obliterated. Likely they contributed to the ability of Clinton to bounce back from numerous setbacks and the relentless pursuit of political enemies, for he was appealing to a stream of tradition that runs deeply in the American populace.

---

62. Renee Loth, "Democrats Use Old-Time Religion," *The Boston Globe,* July 26, 1992, National/Foreign Section, 1.

Chapter 8

The Twenty-First Century's Perilous Debut

In the campaign leading to the November 2000 presidential election, the Republican Party was able to exploit Clinton's personal missteps by presenting itself as the defender of traditional values, that is, family, personal morality, sanctity of life (antiabortion), and marriage as an institution between a man and a woman. Buttressing its traditional platform was its appeal to religious conservatives, a factor that secured Bush's victory over Al Gore in a close and contested election.

Throughout George W. Bush's two-term presidency, the religious right remained a staunch ally, and the president proved to be willing and able to articulate not only his ethical principles, but also the source of those principles in his religious faith. In his second inaugural address, on January 20, 2005, he identified that source in terms that ring true with many Americans: "From the day of our Founding, we have proclaimed that every man and woman on this earth has rights, and dignity, and matchless value, because they bear the image of the Maker of Heaven and earth." He went on to emphasize the tie between public and private spheres, while simultaneously giving voice to his religious inclusiveness: "Self-government relies, in the end, on the governing of the self. That edifice of character is built in families, supported by communities with standards, and sustained in our national life by the truths of Sinai, the

Sermon on the Mount, the words of the Koran, and the varied faiths of our people." While emphasizing the importance of national security, intensified by the shocking terrorist attack on the twin towers of the World Trade Center, and his policy of supporting "the growth of democratic movements and institutions in every nation and culture," he located the source of his confidence in "the eventual triumph of freedom," not in the nation's special status, but in the God who "moves and chooses as He wills."[1]

The ever-rising number of casualties and waning public support of the Second Iraq War became a plague on the Republican Party as it mounted its campaign to retain the White House after Bush's second term. Another liability was the tendency of John McCain's running mate Sarah Palin to project a weak professional image. The primary factor behind the decisive Democratic victory, however, was the vision of a fresh start projected by Barack Obama to a nation perceiving itself to be stuck in failed policies, both at home and abroad.

On the domestic front, Obama's most concerted effort was dedicated to health-care reform. Debate continues as to whether that focus led to unjustifiable neglect of other important issues, though the adeptness with which he responded to the "fallout" from the financial crisis of 2008 to some extent blunts that criticism. In regard to the question of the role of religious beliefs in his political goals, President Obama has given expression to views that reflect a level of theological sophistication not witnessed in the White House since Jimmy Carter's presidency. His ability to navigate the hazardous crosscurrents of religion and politics was put to the test early on by a crisis that could have doomed his candidacy for the Democratic presidential nomination, the issue of his relationship to the Reverend Jeremiah Wright. In a deft move combining discretion with incisiveness, he paid respects to his former pastor while announcing his decision to leave his congregation due to their divergent views on the United States.

Once in office, the proverbial honeymoon period eluded the new president, in spite of the robust electoral mandate he had received. Opposition to his health plan and proposed immigration reform, combined with promotion of policies of limited government, fiscal restraint, and a particular theo-political interpretation of the Constitution, constituted the agenda of the Tea Party movement, led by Michele Bachmann. This movement, rapidly growing from the grass roots of religiously and politically conservative districts, in the 2010 midterm election led to congressional victories that transferred majority control of the House of Representatives to the Republican Party. Though the caucus it organized within Congress soon languished, the confrontational style it introduced into political debate has set a mood in Washington that has proven to be difficult to overcome.[2]

1. "President Bush's Second Inaugural Address," NPR, January 20, 2005, http://www.npr.org/templates/story/story.php?storyId=4460172.

2. Ideological conflict between political parties is, of course, a natural part of the American way. It is interesting to note that the current themes of the right wing of the Republican Party closely

As the platforms of the major parties for the 2012 quadrennial election began to take shape, the lines were drawn with a clarity promising to generate lively debate and to offer voters a real choice. What is more, it proved to be a year in which religious dimensions of the debate were prominently displayed.

Noteworthy is the fact that the Mormonism of Republican nominee Mitt Romney proved to be a nonissue. Released from the burden of explaining the compatibility of Mormonism with the office of President, he was able to project the image of a supporter of conservative Christian values by hiring the prominent Evangelical public relations consultant Mark DeMoss as a senior advisor. This team of like-minded conservatives had already played effectively during Romney's years as governor of Massachusetts. During the 2012 campaign it again found expression in the link forged between conservative economics and morally charged issues like entitlement programs and health plans.

Early in his campaign Romney's central theme emerged, namely, the inseparability of a strong economy and a strong national defense and the purported job-generating dynamism they provided for improving the lives of the poor and vulnerable at home and abroad. In an address at the 113th gathering of the Veterans of Foreign Wars, he blamed Obama's policies for an anemic recovery from "the deepest recession in seventy years," resulting in a serious weakening of US military superiority around the world. What he put forth instead were the changes to social welfare programs contained in the budget proposed by Representative Paul Ryan, the Republican vice presidential candidate, and passed by the House of Representatives in March 2012, changes designed to yield savings that could be redirected to strengthening the military.

In elaborating on his foreign policy, Romney used concepts echoing the strident rhetoric of the nineteenth century: "This century must be an American Century." More specifically: "I am not ashamed of American power. I take pride that throughout our history our power has brought justice where there was tyranny, peace where there was conflict, and hope where there was affliction and despair."[3]

The responses of religious leaders revealed the depth of divisions in religious America. Not surprisingly, Billy Graham and his son Franklin cast their support behind Romney, citing his commitment to religious principles, support of Israel, protection of the sanctity of life, and defense of marriage as between a man and a woman. Given the Roman Catholic Church's antiabortion stance, as well as its policy on marriage, the sharp refutation of the Ryan budget issued by the US Conference of Catholic Bishops caught many Republicans by surprise.

---

resemble earlier Republican campaigns, e.g., against FDR's New Deal and Lyndon Johnson's Medicare/Medicaid programs. Like the script guiding the replay of political strategy in the second decade of the twenty-first century, it derives its clout from the religious right/right wing Republican coalition introduced already in the 1940s by Billy Graham and Ronald Reagan, with its warnings against burgeoning bureaucracy and the diminution of individual freedoms. What is new, however, is the shrillness with which the Tea Party promoted its radical ideology.

3. "At the Intersection of Faith and Culture," *Beliefnet*, last accessed October 25, 2012, http://blog.beliefnet.com/attheintersctionofffaithandculture/201209.

But it reflected the willingness of Roman Catholic leaders to tread the difficult path of discernment in applying prophetic principles: "A just spending bill cannot rely on disproportionate cuts in essential services to the poor and vulnerable persons; it requires shared sacrifice by all."[4] Thus exposed was a major divide separating Catholic politicians like John Boehner and Paul Ryan from the bishops of their church, a phenomenon echoing tensions between pulpit and pew at many points in US history.

In the meantime, citizens interested in possible religious roots of President Obama's firm positions on education, welfare, abortion, gay marriage, and US foreign relations were treated to an unusually personal testimony to the role of his Christian faith on both his personal life and his public service that he submitted to the Circle of Protection: "There have been many times over the past four years when I have fallen on my knees asking God for guidance, not just in my personal life and my Christian walk, but in the life of this nation." Whereas in a parallel statement Mitt Romney addressed protection of the poor and vulnerable in terms of reducing the federal debt and restoring the economy so as to create jobs (with a passing reference to cooperating with faith-based organizations), Obama was specific in his defense of programs he regarded as vital: "We can pay down our debt in a balanced and responsible way, but we cannot balance the budget on the backs of the most vulnerable. And certainly can't ask the poor, the sick, or those with disabilities to sacrifice even more, or ask the middle-class to pay more, just so we can offer massive new tax cuts to those who've been blessed the most. It's not just bad economics, it's morally wrong. It's not in line with our values, and it's not who we are as a people."[5] Naturally it is possible to take the cynic's position and characterize his words as opportunistic posturing. Noteworthy, however, is his balancing reason and faith ("bad economics/morally wrong") and his grounding political advocacy in the identity-fostering power of a nation's story ("who we are as a people").

By the time of the Democratic and Republican national conventions, the lines dividing the parties were clearly drawn, which is an important aspect of democratic process. In general both political and religious leaders freely related faith to politics as they combined high-spirited campaign rhetoric with civil restraint. This was exhibited with verve at the Democratic convention by the nun Sister Simone Campbell and the professor-turned-politician Elizabeth Warren, the former buttressing her critique of Paul Ryan's budget with reference to the assessment of the American bishops ("failed a basic moral test, because it would harm families living in poverty"), the latter tracing her defense of progressive socioeconomic policies to her years as a Methodist Sunday school teacher and to the guidance of one of her favorite biblical verses, Matthew 25:40 ("Just

---

4. Jonathan Weisman, "Catholic Bishops Protest House Budget," *New York Times*, April 18, 2012; http://thecaucus.blogs.nytimes.com/2012/04/18.

5. "Elections," *Circle of Protection*, last accessed September 15, 2012, www.circleofprotection. us/elections/2012/09/12.

as you did it to one of the least of these who are members of my family, you did it to me").

If in fact the vibrancy of the democratic process was manifest in the distinctly different, clearly formulated party platforms, and if in fact candidates felt free to draw on norms (including religious beliefs) that supported their positions, what explains the years of legislative gridlock that followed?

If asked to choose one word for the paralysis that afflicted the mechanisms of government in 2013 and 2014, it would be "absolutism," defined as a certainty of the truthfulness of one's own position that categorically falsifies opposing views. The worldview inhabited by absolutists is one in which in every area of human inquiry (1) there is but one truth and (2) that truth is accessible exclusively to the protagonist group.

Contrary to popular opinion (especially among liberals), no political party or movement has a monopoly on the absolutist point of view. What imbues it with such power within American politics, however, is the habitual self-confident idealism that is rooted so firmly in US history and continues to influence our manner of framing public issues. Magnifying the capacity of absolutist idealism to undermine constructive democratic process is its propensity for "fueling" both its allies and the opposing side. For example, from the *political* right comes the argument that the prospects of world peace are being undermined by a fiscally driven weakening of US military power. The absolutist tone of this argument is then amplified by the *religious* right as it clothes global tensions with the apocalyptic/dualistic trappings of the final battle between good (us) and evil (them).

This in turn energizes the *political* left to enter the fray with its own certainty: Addressing world tensions with military might not only exacerbates international discord; it depletes the resources (such as diplomacy, economic development, and humanitarian relief) that are our surest means of promoting global peace. The absolutist tilt of this argument is augmented by support from the *religious* left: not only strategically, but seen from the vantage point of faith, the right way is the path of feeding the world's hungry; helping young economies develop their natural resources; reforming immigration law; and combating Ebola, malaria, and AIDS among those who are, in Jesus' words, "the least of these."

This much is clear: as movements and parties stake out their positions in absolutist terms, the aim readily becomes destroying the position of the opposition—whether by political maneuvers like the filibuster, character assassination, gerrymandering electoral districts, or manipulation of polls and economic statistics—rather than engaging in rigorous debate committed to finding common ground. There is also widespread public opinion that gridlock is debilitating and that reasoned civil debate must be recovered in the halls of Congress and in the nation as a whole. What remains unclear is this: how in a predominantly idealistic/religious society can First Amendment rights be preserved, while simultaneously avoiding the combative tactics endemic to absolutism? To frame the question in terms at home in a study of religion and politics, can individuals and parties hold firm to religious beliefs and moral values they believe to be true, while at the same time being committed to productive public discourse and open, democratic process in a highly diverse society? Clearly both sides would do well to heed the admonition of Martin Luther as summarized by historian Carter Lindberg:

> To Luther the identification of any political program, regardless of its intrinsic merit, with the will of God subverts both politics and the gospel. The political process is subverted because the claim to absolute righteousness precludes the ambiguity present in all social life as well as the art of compromise necessary in social relations. Group and national self-righteousness lead people to see political opponents as followers of the devil, that is the "ungodly" who have no right to live. The gospel is subverted when identified with a political program because then all citizens are forced to conform to a religious norm, and salvation is made dependent upon a particular political affiliation and program, a political form of good works.[6]

We conclude part 1 having discovered in US history encouraging examples of effective, religiously and philosophically informed public debate, alongside instances of all that can go morally awry in an open society, for example, abuse of power, gloating national idolatry, merciless neglect of vulnerable groups, and opportunistic manipulation of scriptural sources. In a more systematic way, we shall return to the riddle of the Bible and politics in our contemporary world in the epilogue concluding this study, but not before conducting a thorough investigation of politics in the Bible itself, an investigation that will lead to insights and lessons that are essential ingredients for blazing a trail beyond abuse and gridlock to substantive dialogue enriched by the diverse religious and ethical resources present in our modern nation and world.

6. Carter Lindberg, *The European Reformations*, 2nd ed. (Malden, MA: Wiley Blackwell, 2010), 159.

PART 2
Politics in the Bible

Chapter 9

Defining a Suitable Interpretive Method

For the sake of structural clarity, the chapters of part 2 are ordered chronologically. Our aim, however, is not to write a history of Israel and the early church in the conventional sense. Rather, we intend to study the interaction between realms that in modern terms are designated as religion and politics, and the effect that interaction had on the policies and institutions of the communities that produced the writings of the Hebrew Bible and the New Testament.

Because treating religion as a discrete realm of human experience did not arise until the Enlightenment, one could question the legitimacy of studying the interplay between spheres that virtually were inseparable in antiquity. The justification is this: phenomena that we associate with religion and phenomena understood in modern times as politics did act upon one another in antiquity, whether in conflict or alliance. For example, prophets did repudiate the abuse of power by kings, and sages did draw on moral principles in describing the traits of a just ruler.

Accompanying any study of religion and politics in antiquity, however, must be this cautionary note: in dealing with a world temporally and cognitively far removed from one's own, it is essential that an approach be taken that is suitable for the task. Modern historical study has been enriched by multiple methods of study, each of which opens up valuable avenues of inquiry. Our approach accordingly will be eclectic, drawing on the social sciences, philosophy, theology, and literary studies. Moreover, a comparative dimension will be visible at all stages, since biblical history did not occur in a cultural vacuum. Already in the stage of Israel's emerging consciousness as a distinct people, which is the focus of the present chapter, roots in the customs and traditions of earlier cultures are discernible. In subsequent stages, influences from neighboring nations will be seen to play a significant role in reshaping religious and political institutions. At the same time, however, cross-cultural comparisons will bring to light ways in which distinctive perspectives emerged, perspectives that will be of particular interest to anyone raising the question of the relevance of the Bible for contemporary social and political issues, a question to which we shall devote particular attention in our epilogue.

Among such perspectives is a historical orientation, developed over the course of biblical times, that diverged from the mythopoeic construal of reality characteristic of the thought world of Israel's powerful imperial neighbors. Though it would be an oversimplification to make this contrast absolute, careful study will uncover qualitative differences between institutions understood in terms of immutable divine prototypes and institutions understood as developing in response to changing historical circumstances. Royal myth in Egypt, Canaan, and Mesopotamia emphasized immutability and permanence; in Israel, life in relation to a deity encountered in the events of this world fostered the growth of an epic, that is to say, a national story whose plotline included both a beginning and a purposeful movement into an open future.[1] Rather than being frozen into eternally binding forms, the institutions and practices nurtured by that Epic were responsive to changing historical circumstances, though fragments of myth continued to find expression in the hymnody of the temple and royal court as well as in postexilic prophecy and apocalyptic.

The Epic-historical perspective that threads its way through biblical history is of great importance for our analysis, for once our survey of religion and politics in the Bible is complete, we shall bring to the question of contemporary relevance neither a rigid template nor an exhaustive rule book, but a plotline still reaching for a conclusion and a story inviting each new generation to participate through interpretation and adaptation to new situations.

Since this study is itself an affirmative reply to the invitation, it is important to clarify that our response does not take the shape of a freestyle exercise such as arbitrary proof-texting or random eisegesis, but rather resembles an orderly relay, for the story we continue to elaborate is one with threads already woven into our own communal and individual identities.[2] That is to say, the biblical

---

1. Within the biblical worldview, "open future" is not a future determined by whimsy or blind fate, but one unfolding within the reciprocity of divine purpose and divinely accorded human freedom.

2. Allan Bloom identified the Bible along with the Greek and Roman classics as the preeminent sources of Western democracy (*The Closing of the American Mind: How Higher Education Has Failed Democracy and Impoverished the Souls of Today's Students* [New York: Simon & Schuster, 1987], 180).

worldview intersects with our own perceptions of the world in many ways, and whether the intersections are characterized by harmony or discord, the biblical themes and values that are a part of our cultural heritage invite a response. Such is the nature of a world understood in terms of a historical ontology.

For the dialogue between our present and the past that contributed to the formation of our individual and communal perspectives and identity to be genuine, the method of study we follow must enable the texts to be heard in their own voice, as alien as that may sometimes seem to our modern sensibilities. Above we mentioned how diverse disciplines of research enrich our study of antiquity. The method that integrates those disciplines into a comprehensive approach to recovering the testimonies of the ancient biblical world is called the historical-critical method. It is designed to recover what was being conveyed by the original authors of biblical texts to their audiences within the concreteness of their place in time and space. This objective to be sure is an ideal that is beset by a host of obstacles, such as errors that have been introduced over the long course of textual transmission, an imperfect understanding of the original languages and the history of their host cultures, the ideological perspectives of the ancient writers, and, above all, the subjectivity that inevitably influences the conclusions drawn by contemporary interpreters. While conceding that no method is capable of achieving pure objectivity, we shall present our case for the historical-critical method being the preferred choice among what we can identify as the three major options available to modern readers.

Lessons learned from our survey of the treatment of the Bible in US history chasten our search for a reliable method of biblical interpretation. We found instances when political and religious individuals and movements "got it right" by employing scriptural themes of evenhanded justice, mercy to the oppressed, and peaceful coexistence with other nations. Too often, however, we witnessed biblical texts and motifs being pressed into the service of goals blatantly self-serving in nature or abusive of the rights of others. For example, some political actors in the antebellum period and beyond lifted to virtual canonical status a version of US history that grossly distorted the past and degraded historiography into the servile position of buttressing inhumane institutions such as slavery and unjust practices like expropriation of the land of indigenous peoples, not to mention imperialistic international policies violating the sovereignty of other nations.

Though appeal to a nation's epic in defense of specific political doctrines (e.g., "the original intent of the founders") already entails risks, the potential for abuse increases exponentially when appeal is made to the Bible itself, for here the authority invoked transcends the status of revered forebears by appealing to none less than the *heavenly Father!* In the face of such a highly hazardous phenomenon, the interpreter must take care to cultivate a mind-set adapted to the delicacy of the undertaking. Ears must be trained to filter out the din of blustering talk-show hosts so as to hear the "voice in the wilderness" of prophets endeavoring to speak truth to power; mental faculties must be sharpened for the demanding task of discernment; and the heart must be opened to the Spirit's testimony to the compassionate justice that constitutes the core of all authentic moral deliberation. The resulting insights will take the form of neither thunderous commands aimed at trumping opposing points of view nor apodictic formulations on every contemporary topic, predicated on a purported certainty of access to the very mind of God. The habits that will be cultivated instead are awe before a Holy One at once elusive and present with his creatures and humility within a caring community inclusive of viewpoints differing from and therefore capable of enriching one's own.

Mind-set and habits dwell within the inscrutable depths of the human soul. While they represent the essential starting point of interpretation theory, attention must also be paid to the nuts and bolts of the interpretive process. This leads then to our description of the historical-critical method in contrast to its two major alternatives.

OPTION 1: REJECTIONISM

Of the three interpretive options,[3] the *rejectionist option* is amenable to the most succinct description due to its categorical nature: in relation to contemporary political or ethical problems, it ascribes to the Bible no relevance, validity, or authority beyond that potentially inherent in any literary corpus. In the case of adherents who are motivated by a combative form of atheism, this attitude toward the Bible goes beyond rejection to scorn and condemnation.[4] But rejectionists can also present a more pragmatic position, stating that introduction of scriptural arguments or warrants into public discussion inhibits fruitful discussion, given the intrinsic incompatibility of the diverse religious and philosophical perspectives found in most modern societies.[5] The discomfort introduced into the thinking of serious students of the Bible by option 1 is minor compared to the distress experienced by coreligionists peering at one another from opposite sides of the border separating options 2 and 3. Both embrace the Bible as

---

3. The difficulty inherent in any attempt to organize interpretive methods into a neat taxonomy is illustrated by a type of sectarianism that in practice aligns itself with the rejectionists while holding inerrantist beliefs sooner associated with fundamentalism. The apparent paradox is resolved when one observes that it is precisely its "high" view of Scripture that leads to the refusal to be exposed to the corrosive effects of the profane world of politics and economists. The role of Scripture thus is defined in terms of nurturing the spiritual life of the individual within the community of born-again Christians. In part 1 we noted that this apolitical position was typical within fundamentalist circles until the latter half of the twentieth century, when the evangelical politics of Robertson and Falwell led to the recruitment of many—although not all—conservative Christians to political activism within the Republican Party.

4. For example, Richard Dawkins, who indicts belief in God for the major calamities that have afflicted and continue to afflict humanity, includes in his denunciation the scriptural source of the theistic worldview.

5. Cf. Richard Rorty, "Religion as Conversation-Stopper," in *Philosophy and Social Hope* (New York: Penguin, 1999), 168–74.

their story. Both trace their essential identity to the chapters of Hebrew Scripture and the New Testament.[6] Both look to the Bible for guidance amid the challenges and threats that are a part of the daily life of religious individuals and communities. Given such apparent commonality amid the global tumult of clashing ideologies, it seems reasonable to expect mutually enriching discussions regarding the relevance and meaning of Scripture for modern life. What ensues instead is bitter conflict into which the Bible is drawn as a weapon to refute the positions of the opposing side. In what has been named "the battle for the Bible,"[7] the vitriol with which intrafaith arguments are charged commonly exceeds that found between believers and their atheistic interlocutors. Sadly for the health and vitality of the nation, that vitriol spills its poisonous effects into the arena of civic debate and political process, leading to a climate conducive to "culture wars."[8]

It would be rash to jump to the conclusion that those divided from one another by disputes over biblical interpretation are all zealous combatants dedicated to the defeat of their opponents. Many conscientious, fair-minded believers, both liberal and conservative, view with sadness a social landscape in which a spirit of ecumenical cooperation could have a positive impact on crises like urban decay and world hunger, where they witness instead passion and energy dissipated in internecine religious warfare.

The centuries-long history of denominational conflict that we traced in part 1, not to mention the tragic history of religious wars reaching back to medieval and ancient times, cautions against facile prescriptions for a solution (and the invitation to forswear your position and embrace mine is no solution!). However, another avenue does merit attention. It identifies the root cause of much of the acrimony that hamstrings interreligious debate, namely, inadequate understanding of the opposing side's method of interpretation and the presuppositions upon which it is based. Therefore the first step in an effort to reclaim constructive biblically based public discussion is an "anatomy" of the method of interpretation employed by each party. For clarity of discussion, we shall consolidate a wide spectrum of interpretive strategies into two general categories, our options 2 and 3.

Every bona fide method of interpretation consists of two interrelated dimensions. Dimension one is the method's *comprehensive perspective*; dimension two is the *theory of interpretation* that facilitates an understanding of texts in a manner consistent with the comprehensive perspective (by definition our option 1,

---

6. It is a central tenet of my Christian faith that those loyal to the tenets of Judaism are essential partners in the project in which I am engaged, to identify guidelines for a proper understanding of the meaning of Scripture for contemporary life. Only my inability to include that hermeneutic dimension in my already dauntingly wide endeavor has led to my focusing primarily on the politics of the Christian canon and its relation to contemporary life.

7. Harold Lindsell, *The Battle for the Bible* (Grand Rapids: Zondervan Publishing House, 1976).

8. See James Davison Hunter, *Culture Wars: The Struggle to Define America* (New York: Basic Books, 1991).

rejectionism, includes the former dimension, but not the latter).[9] We shall give a brief description of these two dimensions as they are understood by their adherents.[10] This should shed light on the reasons diametrically opposing conclusions are often drawn from the same Scripture. It will also situate within the context of contemporary biblical studies the historical-critical approach that guides our investigation of the political models that developed over the course of more than a millennium in the communities that produced the Bible.

OPTION 2: FUNDAMENTALISM

Comprehensive Perspective

On the basis of a *literalist* comprehensive perspective, God is viewed as the creator of a natural and social order that from the beginning of human history to its culmination is fixed. Example: God created a complete heavens and earth in six days, and purported evidence (such as fossils) cited in defense of an evolutionary process extending over millions of years is bogus.

Theory of Scriptural Interpretation

Being verbally inspired by God, the Bible is *inerrant*. Example: God revealed to Moses laws that are eternally valid and binding; for example, sexual intimacy is to be the exclusive domain of heterosexual couples, and those deviating from that law are liable for punishment.

OPTION 3: INCARNATIONAL HERMENEUTICS

Comprehensive Perspective

As understood from an incarnational comprehensive perspective, revelation is mediated through the testimony of members of the covenant community who experience the presence of God in the events of their world and in their lives.[11] Example: The experience of God's delivering the children of Israel from slavery in Egypt imprinted itself indelibly on the conscience of the early Hebrews, and through the retelling of the national Epic of which it became a part, it shaped and reshaped their laws and institutions in response to ever-changing

9. In John Rawls's terminology, the term equivalent to "comprehensive perspective" would be "comprehensive dogma" (Rawls, *A Theory of Justice* [Cambridge, MA: Belknap Press of Harvard University Press, 1971], 13, 175). In the scholarly literature, the technical term for "theory of interpretation" is "hermeneutic."

10. Options 1, 2, and 3 are what sociologists of knowledge call ideal types. Defining and distinguishing between them is not an analytic exercise, but a heuristic aid to ordering discussion of a complex subject.

11. See Paul D. Hanson, *Dynamic Transcendence* (Philadelphia: Fortress Press, 1978).

circumstances. That dynamic process is illustrated by comparison of the following two passages. In Exodus 21:2–11, a distinction is drawn between male slaves who are set free in the seventh year and female slaves who are not. In the slave law in Deuteronomy 15:12–17, which belongs to a legal corpus originating several centuries later than Exodus 20–23, the gender distinction is replaced by an emphatic inclusion of women slaves in the year of release.

Theory of Scriptural Interpretation

Viewed in terms of *covenantal testimony*, the laws and institutions contained in the Bible are interpreted within the ongoing relationship of God and people, with attention to change over time as circumstances call for new responses and theological and moral understanding deepens. From this perspective, verbal inerrancy is found to lack a biblical basis and can be understood as retrogression to the prebiblical static worldview endemic to myth. What is therefore called for is a historical approach, which in a comprehensive manner seeks to grasp the meaning of the biblical writings within their original contexts; that meaning then becomes the basis for theological reflection within later generations of the faith community on the bearing of the entire Bible to the issues of their times.

What effect might we expect our comparison of options 2 and 3 to have on our discussion of politics in the Bible? First, it seems reasonable that the reader be given a clear idea of the comprehensive perspective and theory of interpretation that guides my own biblical research. Secondly, it should shed light on the major discrepancies found in the conclusions different interpreters reach in spite of their studying the same Scripture. While only the foolhardy could expect of our brief foray into hermeneutical theory a major opening in the wall separating the various scholarly communities, I personally believe that an explicit accounting of presuppositions and theories is the most propitious move that can be taken by those seeking to promote constructive dialogue as an alternative to culture war and unending battles over what the Bible says to those inhabiting a threatened planet.

Chapter 10

Charismatic Rule

Israel's First Polity

THE NATURE OF THE SOURCES

As we turn to study politics in the Bible, our starting point is the critical juncture where clan members of diverse origins began to develop a distinctive sense of a communal identity and religious consciousness that distinguished them from neighbors with whom they otherwise held much (linguistically, sociologically, and religiously) in common.[1] Before examining the textual sources available for this period for the light they shed on the politics of earliest Israel, however, we need to address the nature of those sources and the problems they raise for the interpreter.

Even more than in the case of subsequent periods, we are limited to the testimony of texts that served purposes vastly different from providing modern historians with the information needed for their research. We can illustrate the problem by reference to two categories of textual material that shall be central to our study of Israel's first polity.

1. Cf., Karel van der Toorn, *Family Religion in Babylonia, Syria and Israel* (Leiden: E. J. Brill, 1996); and more recently David J. Schloen, *The House of the Father as Fact and Symbol: Patrimonialism in Ugarit and the Ancient Near East* (Winona Lake, IN: Eisenbrauns, 2001).

Important though enigmatic are archaic poems and poetic fragments embedded in the narratives of Exodus and Judges. They are parts of the Epic through which early Israel's storytellers recounted events explaining the community's origins in terms of divine initiative. While falling short of the modern historian's standards for reliability, they contain important clues regarding the manner in which early Israel understood the religious dimension of the events that gave rise to the nation as a political entity.

The second group of materials is more historiographical in nature, consisting of narratives extending from Deuteronomy through 2 Kings referred to by scholars as the Deuteronomistic History. Methodologically, the problem presented by these texts is the same one confronting the reader of any historical work, namely, distinguishing between the underlying facts and the interpretive interventions of the author. Naturally, when dealing with ancient writings the difficulty of differentiating between authorial *Tendenz* and historical data is intensified due to the dearth of alternative sources serving as controls. However, the input provided by archaeological discoveries (inscriptions as well as nonliterary artifacts) and anthropological analysis can fill in gaps left by the biblical texts themselves.

THE COVENANTAL FRAMEWORK OF GOD'S SOVEREIGNTY: THEOCRACY

In the pages that follow, we shall show how careful study of biblical texts, combined with consideration of the relevant extrabiblical evidence, can paint a plausible picture of the origins of political thought in the Bible. We shall find that during the reign of Ramesses II a group of Hebrews that would later constitute the core of the early Israelite community found itself swept up in a series of events that defied human explanation. Harsh servitude imposed by a powerful pharaoh claiming divine status was broken and replaced by rebirth as a liberated community led by a God who disclosed his name as YHWH. From that point forward, devotion to any being other than YHWH was to be deemed idolatrous. Though centuries of growth in theological discernment would pass before the primal confession of sole allegiance to YHWH would be formulated in terms resembling what in modern parlance would be called monotheism, the cornerstone of biblical faith had been laid: Israel's life as a community depended on one relationship alone, the covenant relationship with the incomparable God whose commitment to the dignity of all creation was demonstrated in the realm of human experience through the liberation of slaves.

In that covenant resided the definition of authentic government and the norms that distinguished between legitimate and counterfeit polity. From this emerged a bold political conclusion: To be true to the story, Israel was to be constituted as a theocracy, founded and ruled by the only ultimate sovereign, who revealed himself to those responding to his call as YHWH.

Due to the fact that in modern parlance theocracy has come to be associated with jihadist regimes and the political philosophy of Christian fundamentalism, we need to clarify at the outset that our understanding of the term is the classical one, defined already by Josephus in his *Antiquities* and elaborated on by Benedict Spinoza in chapter 17 of *A Theologico-Political Treatise*: the rule of the entire cosmos by the only one who is sovereign and deserving of worship and obedience. No political principle is more foundational to biblical thought than this one, for its discovery by slaves experiencing the defeat of the "divine" pharaoh and his retinue of gods by the incomparable God YHWH established the norms for all future biblical thought on matters of governance and polity.

From their growing understanding of the nature of YHWH they inferred the institutions and laws that were to regulate their lives as individuals and as a nation. Specifically regarding forms of government and those who governed, one criterion alone provided the basis for evaluation, namely, the degree to which earthly regimes and their leaders conformed to the rule of the sovereign of the universe, as the quality of that rule and the attributes of the sovereign one came to be known in the events of their ongoing life as a covenant people.

In this chapter, then, it will be our task to trace the origins and delineate the tenets of Israel's theocratic understanding of politics. We shall describe the nation's implementation of its theocratic understanding in covenant and Torah, and document how its theory of governance came to expression in laws and institutional structures safeguarding the sole sovereignty of God from usurpation by tyrants and perversion through corrupt commandments and abusive policies. While noting the courage and tenacity with which many of the leaders of early Israel sought to embody the theocratic principle in the apparatus of civil rule, we shall note the persistence throughout the premonarchical period of countertendencies, varying from the lure of despotic monarchy to institutional tyranny to popular anarchy, all sharing the fatal flaw of refuting the only form of rule that was able to preserve the health and vitality of the nation: ultimate allegiance to the only true sovereign.

Our chapter on Israel's first polity, charismatic rule organized as theocracy, will end on a tragic note. The combined forces militating against the efforts of those following in the Mosaic covenant/Torah tradition succeeded in undermining the rudimentary structures of theocratic rule that had begun to take shape under the leadership of charismatic "judges" from Joshua to Samuel. What they could not obliterate, however, was the theological foundation of a political ideal affirming the sole rule of the sovereign of the universe, for by the end of the period of the judges that foundation had been ensconced in an Epic reciting the source of Israel's identity in YHWH's merciful acts and in a covenant formulary and Torah that defined the life of a people committed exclusively to one sovereign. In subsequent periods different forms of government would come and go, their successes and failures arising from the precarious and often failed task of preserving ultimate allegiance to God while constructing political structures that were viable within a changing world.

The next step in our study brings us to textual fragments deposited in the Bible and material traces left in the foothills of Canaan, as we seek to understand what it was about the two hundred years before kings ruled over Israel that birthed and then brought to maturity a theo-political philosophy that provided the key to a millennium of political experimentation followed by centuries of scholarly debate reaching down to the present day.

EVIDENCE OF POLITICAL ORIGINS IN BIBLICAL AND RELATED SOURCES

The task of reconstructing the political structure of earliest Israel involves sifting through biblical stories that have undergone a centuries-long process of editing and retelling, relating those stories to the knowledge we can gain of the history and sociopolitical realia of the Early Iron Age from inscriptions and material remains unearthed by archaeologists, and judiciously applying suitable methods of study such as demography and comparative anthropology. It is fortunate that the past several decades have witnessed considerable interest in this period, resulting in studies that enable us to present a credible picture of Israel's first experiments with self-government.[2]

No political entity arises in a vacuum. In the case of early Israel, the political-cultural environment within which the Hebrews gradually emerged as a distinct people can be reconstructed—albeit imperfectly—on the basis of a critical reading of biblical sources in light of fragmentary epigraphic and mute archaeological finds. As reflected in the Amarna letters,[3] Canaan, the land that would become home to the Hebrews, was ruled in the fourteenth century BCE by the local rulers of small city-states. These city-states were vassals of the Egyptian royal house, which, through the conquests of the warrior-kings of the Eighteenth Dynasty, Thutmose III, Amenophis II, and Amenophis III, had established hegemony over the area.

Archaeological discoveries at urban centers like Gezer, Hazor, and Megiddo reveal a consistent city plan. Dominated by an acropolis with monumental-sized palaces and temples, the surrounding neighborhoods consisted of humble dwellings densely packed together and often spilling over into areas beyond the massive fortifications that offered protection from the warfare that was a recurrent part of life in the Late Bronze Age. While some of the luxury of the ruling elite extended to a small client class benefiting from payments for services rendered in the military, in commerce, and in other departments of the royal bureaucracy, the masses were consigned to subsistence living, due to the impoverishment

---

2. See Norman K. Gottwald, *The Tribes of YHWH* (Maryknoll, NY: Orbis Books, 1979) and Baruch Halpern, *The Emergence of Israel in Canaan* (Atlanta: Scholars Press, 1983).

3. Egyptian royal archives from the reigns of Amenophis III and Amenophis IV (who adopted a name honoring his new god, Akhenaten); the designation "Amarna letters" derives fror their discovery site of Tel el-Amarna (ancient Akhetaten, the site of Akhenaten's new capital).

through the heavy taxation imposed by local rulers, who in turn lived under the unrelenting pressure to produce the tribute imposed by the Egyptian overlord. A relatively small proportion of the poor in the land of Canaan lived as a servant class within the urban centers; the majority lived in the countryside as peasant farmers and pastoralists. Of these, a significant number maintained commercial ties with neighboring cities by producing the foodstuffs and derivative products upon which the urban populations depended. Over them economic control was exercised by means of an onerous tax system through which king and clients grew wealthy by retaining a large percentage of the annual agricultural yield.

The boundary between village and rural peasants on the one hand and city dwellers on the other remained porous, a demographic pattern that social scientists call a "dimorphic society."[4] Sometimes peasants and pastoralists, lured by the perceived benefits of the urban economy, became absorbed into one of the city-states. In other cases, however, especially in villages located in hillside areas quite removed, and hence largely insulated, from the economic monopoly of the crown, an ideology of independence or even outright defiance developed.

Within such settings, a system of authority and social control developed that contrasted sharply with the centralized authority of the throne. Dispersed through a social structure within which the extended family was the basic unit, authority resided in the heads of households, to whom members looked for leadership in matters of domestic dispute and for regulation of the intervillage exchange of commodities. These heads in turn assembled from time to time in councils to resolve larger issues, such as border disputes and intertribal conflicts.

To the above general socioanthropological picture specific detail has been added, thanks to the above-mentioned Amarna letters.[5] In several of those letters reference is made to restless bands of people designated as 'apiru who inhabit the central hill country of Palestine. This appellative denotes not an ethnic affiliation or nationality, but rather an amorphous group characterized by a lifestyle resistant to assimilation to the dominant culture of the city-states. One of the Amarna letters revealingly defines an 'apiru as one who declares to his king, "You are no longer my king."[6] While this definition implies stubborn refusal to submit to the authority of one of the petty kings installed by the Egyptians, it is clear that individual 'apiru leaders did not hesitate, when opportunity presented itself, to gain territory for themselves. In the area around Shechem, for example, an 'apiru leader named Labayu was able to build up a small dominion in a manner adumbrating the later emergence of tribal Israel.

Because of the defiance toward authority that characterized the 'apiru and their propensity to engage in marauding and other disruptive activities, they were commonly denounced by the local petty kings in their groveling pledges of fidelity and obsequious appeals for aid to the Egyptian monarch. From the

---

4. Michael M. Rowton, "Dimorphic Structure and the Problem of the 'Apiru-'Ibrim," *Journal of Near Eastern Studies* 35 (1976): 13–20.

5. See note 3.

6. See Moshe Greenberg, *The Hab/piru* (New Haven, CT: American Oriental Society, 1955).

perspective of the royal palace, regardless of whether it was the *big* house of the pharaohs in Thebes and Akhetaten or the lesser palace of the Canaanite petty dynasts, troublemakers who refused integration into the city-state system were manifestations of chaos, and were to be taken quite as seriously as foreign invaders like the Hatti or natural calamities like drought or pestilence. For if their influence were to spread widely throughout a restive population, it could threaten the political and economic stability of the entire Canaanite region. This explains the inclusion in some of the Amarna letters of reports of military measures taken against them by local armies and appeals made by some of the local rulers for supplementary troops from Egypt to help repulse the renegades.

In a culture in which separation of political and religious realms in the modern sense was unknown, it was inevitable that the Canaanite kings depended for security not only on their military forces, but also on the elaborate myths ritually celebrated in the temples they erected for their gods like Baal and ʿAnat. The most complete documentation of the mythology of Canaan comes from the fourteenth-century-BCE archives of Ugarit, a royal capital lying north of Canaan proper but belonging to the same eastern Mediterranean cultural/religious horizon. These texts reveal the intimate relationship between king and deity commonly referred to as sacral kingship. The king, through all stages of life, was exalted above the lot of mere mortals. At birth he was suckled by a goddess and at death elevated to divine status. His lofty station in life was part of a divine plan, for through him were channeled the benefits of the gods upon which human society depended. In turn the subjects owed the king unqualified fidelity. His word was authoritative, thereby circumscribing the jurisdiction of clan and family heads and the effect of local laws and customs.

Translated into economic terms, this meant that the king controlled the trade and commerce of the land. For the peasant farmer or pastoralist to question the taxes in grain or livestock that he was required to pay to the royal stewards was to question the basis upon which both natural and political order were founded. Traces of the lavish palace compound unearthed at Ugarit, which cast its shadow over the Spartan dwellings of the rest of the population, bear testimony to the exalted position enjoyed by the king and to the rigid social stratification that divided royalty and nobility from peasantry and commoner.

Unfortunately, the nature of the evidence found in the Bible, in Egyptian inscriptions, and in the ancient ruins unearthed by archaeologists offers neither an exact chronology nor a precise historical account of the rise of the people Israel in Canaan. The convergence of diverse kinds of evidence, however, makes it probable that the pharaoh of the exodus was Ramesses II (1279–1212), and that the emergence of a loose confederacy called Israel began toward the end of the thirteenth century and extended on into the twelfth. Around 1209 BCE the Egyptian pharaoh Merneptah erected a monument to commemorate a successful military campaign into Canaan. Consistent with a convention in hieroglyphic writing, a determinative in front of each of the vanquished political entities indicated whether they belonged to the category of city-state, land, or people. Accordingly, the choice of terminology in the clause "the *people* Israel is laid waste and his seed is not" indicates that the Israel Merneptah encountered was not yet an established state in the fashion of the city-states he mentions, namely, Ashkelon, Gezer, and Yano'am; nor was it equivalent politically to the "land" Canaan. Rather, Israel belonged to the category of a loosely organized collectivity, that is, a *people*.

On the basis of epigraphic evidence it is difficult to be more specific about the nature and organizational structure of this "people Israel." It is useful to note, however, that this first mention of Israel outside of the Bible came from a time of considerable ferment in Canaan. The two great empires that had contended for this area for several centuries were on the threshold of serious decline; this created a political vacuum that was to be filled in part by a dozen or so states differing in structure from the city-states that were the norm in Canaan throughout the Late Bronze Age. Whereas the latter had been territorially defined, the new states were organized along lines that reflected tribal origins. This is apparent in the two onomastic types into which their names fall, namely, "house of PN [personal name]" (e.g., *bit 'Adini, bit Shilani*) and "sons of PN" (e.g., *bene 'Ammon, bene Yisrae'el*). These name types indicate that the new states derived their cohesiveness and identity from a sense of shared kinship. Once Israel had emerged as a political entity, it often found itself contending with some of these states that like it had tribal roots, especially the Ammonites, Moabites, and Edomites.

All things considered, conditions were propitious for the birth and growth of smaller, clan-based states. Much of the strength of the local Canaanite city-states had been dissipated by incessant internecine conflict. Egyptian hegemony in the region had been weakened both by the internal instability that characterized the Amarna Age and by the increasing pressure being exerted from the north (present-day Turkey) by the Hittites. This is not to say that either the Egyptians or their Canaanite allies were willing to abdicate control. It simply meant that they had to concentrate on their primary economic and strategic assets, namely, regulation of the important trade routes that crossed the area and control over agricultural and other commodities.

Within this already volatile situation, a menacing new threat arose to challenge the viability of the embryonic small states. This threat originated in the west, which was unusual in a world accustomed to enemy forays coming from Mesopotamia. Except for trade contacts between the Minoans, Egyptians, and Canaanites reaching back to the Middle and Late Bronze Ages, few bridges had been built between the Aegean cultures and the Levant. That changed in the Early Iron Age as the result of the collapse of the Mycenaean hegemony in the Greek mainland and islands and the subsequent migration eastward of marauders seeking new homelands.

Collectively referred to by scholars as the Sea Peoples, these marauders consisted of different tribes, one of them being the *peleset*, known from the Bible as Philistines. The Sea Peoples advanced into the Levant with daunting force, leading to the devastation of the once-mighty empires of Hatti and Ugarit and the near collapse of the Nineteenth Dynasty in Egypt. As for the Israelite tribes, they first witnessed the settlement of the Philistines along the eastern shore of the Mediterranean and subsequently found themselves struggling for survival as the well-organized foreign invaders parlayed their chariotry, advanced weaponry, and monopoly of iron production and fabrication into an enormous strategic advantage over the loosely structured Israelite militia.

Although the Philistine offensive from the west created a threat to the entire region reaching from the Nile to the Orontes, a counterbalancing force had already begun emerging out of the political ferment of the Canaanite heartland. Accompanying the above-mentioned weakening of Egyptian control over the Canaanite city-states and the infighting among the local tyrant-kings was a move by indigenous elements like the 'apiru and kindred groups entering Canaan from the outside to secure a foothold in the sparsely populated hillside regions lying outside the control of the faltering city-states. By the time these groups were forced to confront the armies of the Philistines, they had already experienced a sufficiently long period of development to forge a sense of collective identity distinct from the one inculcated by the indigenous urban culture. The end result would be a defiant sense of ancestral and tribal identity capable of challenging the control of the fortified urban centers of the Canaanites and contending with the aggressive armies of the Philistines.

Specifically regarding the encounter between the Israelites and the indigenous Canaanite population, the pattern of conquest given by the biblical narrative may seem sufficiently straightforward as to suggest that recourse to epigraphic and mute archaeological evidence would be unnecessary. Did not Joshua lead the Israelites as armed warriors into the land of Canaan, resulting in victories over one city-state after the other until the entire territory from Dan to Beer-sheba was under their control? Closer scrutiny of the biblical text, however, suggests that the depiction of a blitzkrieg conquest of the land is a summary statement reflecting a final outcome that came no earlier than the time of King David. Corroborating this interpretation is the fact that the first chapter of the book of Judges depicts a different pattern, namely, a partial settlement of the land by separate tribes who were obliged to live alongside the ancient Canaanite city-states that maintained control over the fertile plains and valleys. The new arrivals had to content themselves with the regions that had been home to pastoral groups for centuries, namely, the hill regions lying beyond the sphere of economic control of the city-states.

This general picture of settlement in the hill country has been nicely corroborated by archaeological excavations and surveys. At the end of the thirteenth century the hitherto sparsely populated hills reaching from Hebron northward to the area around Shechem experienced nearly a fourfold increase in population. What is also clear is that the new settlers situated themselves in small villages, the number of which increased from 23 to 114.[7] Careful excavation at

---

7. Lawrence E. Stager, "Highland Village Life in Palestine Some Three Thousand Years Ago," *The Oriental Institute News and Notes* 69 (March 1981), 1.

sites like Raddana and Mesash has given a clear picture of the layout of the newly proliferating villages, a layout that stands in stark contrast to the city plans of the large urban sites that for over a century enjoyed the exclusive attention of archaeologists.

Absent from these villages were the large public buildings like temples, palaces, and administrative centers, which, strategically situated upon the acropolis of the typical urban capital, symbolized the absolute authority of crown over common citizenry within the rigidly stratified Canaanite culture. Absent as well were the massive fortifications that enclosed cities like Gezer and Megiddo. Replicated throughout the small unwalled villages were houses consisting of two to four rooms situated around an open courtyard. Several of these buildings in turn were clustered together around a larger common courtyard. This village plan has been convincingly correlated by scholars with the kinship-based character of the newcomers appearing in the Canaanite countryside at the turn from the Bronze to the Iron Age.

It also comports with the picture given within the Bible of early Israelite society, the smallest unit of which was the nuclear family, consisting of the warrior-aged male adult (*geber*), his wife, and children. While each nuclear family would have occupied one of the small houses, the larger compound tied together houses sufficient in number for the extended family (*bēt 'āb*). Presiding over the extended family was the paterfamilias (*'āb*), the senior male member, who typically was the grandfather. In addition to the sons of that elder and their wives and children, the family compound could contain (economic resources permitting) rooms for servants and even a resident priest.[8] Finally, included in the compound was an area into which livestock would be corralled for protection during the night.[9]

In the nesting fashion of Russian dolls, a cluster of extended families in turn constituted a clan (*mišpāḥā*). Heading the clan was the head of household recognized by the others as most worthy of representing them in the next level of organization, the tribe. At that point, the bounds of the village had been transcended, as had the bonds of blood lineage in any strict sense. As is known from modern tribal societies, kinship on the tribal level is largely a fiction, in effect an extension of the source of identity on the family level to the tribal level, where it still provides a sense of solidarity. Finally, the outer limit of the kinship model of society is reached on the level of the league or confederacy of tribes. Even at that widest extension, however, the nomenclature of the family persists, as seen, for example, in the two name types mentioned above that were carried by the

8. Cf. Judg. 18:1–4.

9. The basic contours of the Iron Age compound can still be seen in traditional villages in many parts of the world, e.g., the Masai Bomas of the Ngorongoro Conservation Area in northern Tanzania. It is also possible to recognize vestiges of traditional vertical models of polity in the postcolonial states of sub-Saharan Africa (see Patrick Chabal and Jean-Pascal Daloz, *Africa Works: Disorder as Political Instrument* [Bloomington and Indianapolis: Indiana University Press, 1999]).

new peoples appearing toward the end of the thirteenth century in the Levant, for example, the House of Adini, the Sons of Ammon, and the Sons of Israel.

Coming upon the stage of history right at the point of decline of the city-state culture of Canaan, the newly emergent village culture posed a serious threat to the older hegemony. On the basis of his findings as the excavator of the Benjaminite sites of 'Ai and Rudanna, Joseph Callaway explained that "the village was an economic entity within itself, independent of other villages and, for the most part, not subject to any market or trade system."[10]

From the perspective of economics, politics, and religion, therefore, village culture introduced a serious alternative to the city-state system. Whereas the latter was territorially defined and strictly regulated by a bureaucracy controlled by the royal house, village culture was defined by kinship alliances within which the individual units enjoyed a high degree of autonomy. Whereas the urban centers were dependent on complex systems of political treaties and trade agreements, the villages were largely self-sufficient. While this contrast between two distinct types of civic organization—one horizontal and the other vertical—does not paint the portrait of the specific entity Israel, it does provide a valuable backdrop against which certain details within the biblical narrative can be projected. The result is a plausible reconstruction of the people of YHWH in the premonarchy period. To the task of such a reconstruction we now turn.

CHARISMATIC RULE IN EARLY ISRAEL AS PORTRAYED IN POEMS AND NARRATIVES

When subjected to close scrutiny, certain narrative and poetic sections of the book of Judges point to features that seem to have been constitutive of Israel's first form of governance, rule by charismatic leaders responding to the ultimate theocratic rule of YHWH. They are features, moreover, that comport with what we should expect to find in a polity arising within the kind of village and clan-based society described above. In it leadership arose from the organization of the individual family and family-writ-large on the levels of clan and tribe. In local matters such as economic arrangements, interfamily disputes, and small-scale defense, decisions were made in the gathering "in the gates" of the family heads, constituted as a council of elders (neśî' îm). In the case of intervillage matters, a similar gathering—now on a higher level consisting of representatives of each of the villages concerned—would settle differences and enter into mutual agreements. Such normal functioning of the clan system had a decidedly centrifugal bias, with focus held steadily on the independence of the separate units, that is, the extended families under the leadership of their respective "fathers."

---

10. Joseph A. Callaway, "The Settlement in Canaan: The Period of the Judges," in *Ancient Israel: A Short History from Abraham to the Roman Destruction of the Temple*, ed. Hershel Shanks (Washington, DC: Biblical Archaeology Society, 1988), 79.

Historians over the centuries, however, would not have referred to a collective entity called Israel if there had not been instances in which the tribes suspended—albeit temporarily and on the basis of strictly delineated circumstances—their stubborn preference for autonomy. Two situations in particular summoned the generally freedom-loving smaller units to acts of tribal solidarity: (1) the mustering of a militia in response to enemy attack on one or more of the tribal territories, and (2) the periodic cultic assembly of the scattered clans in renewal of their covenant with YHWH and recital of the Epic tracing the origins of that covenant to the saving acts of God. On a fundamental level, these two instances of movement toward the center are intertwined, inasmuch as they both attest to the theocratic core of ancient Israel's sense of a shared identity, expressed in the one instance in holy war, in the other in holy worship.

Those two circumstances then, the one intermittent and the other routine, revealed the defining numinous center of ancient Israel's first political system, *charismatic rule* serving to mediate YHWH's sovereignty within the framework of a theocratic notion of government. We now can enrich our understanding of that center by examining more closely specific biblical texts. The first two, though bearing marks of a long process of interpretation and redaction, are characterized by a sufficiently high degree of verisimilitude as to suggest that they preserve essential characteristics of the early confederacy. The third text is a poem with archaic features reflecting the way in which Israel's charismatic leaders organized loosely affiliated clans into a unified body capable of translating YHWH's lordship into a specific strategic action.

The world of Gideon according to Judges 6–8 is one that is in both religious and political flux. Politically, we see evidence of tensions arising as different clans began to confederate and lay claims to the limited amount of arable land not controlled by the urban centers and their vassal kings. As the drama opens in Judges 6, the Israelites are in a situation threatening their very survival in the land:[11]

> The hand of Midian prevailed over Israel; and because of Midian the Israelites provided for themselves hiding places in the mountains, caves and strongholds. For whenever the Israelites put in seed, the Midianites and the Amalekites and the people of the East would come up against them. They would encamp against them and destroy the produce of the land. (Judg. 6:2–4)

Within the context of this crisis, Gideon is introduced in terms of the "nesting" structure typical of kinship societies: He is a "mighty warrior," that is, an adult male of fighting age whose father Joash is the patriarch of a family (*bēt 'āb*) of the Abiezrite clan, which clan in turn was a member of the tribe of Manasseh

---

11. The editorial hand of the Deuteronomistic Historian is seen in the framework of the Gideon story: "The Israelites did what was evil in the sight of the LORD"; the Lord punishes them by giving "them into the hand of Midian seven years"; "the Israelites cried to the LORD"; and the Lord commissions Gideon to "deliver Israel from the hand of Midian" (Judg. 6:1, 7, 14).

(Judg. 6:11, 15). Gideon does not enjoy the professional status of a commissioned military officer responsible for defense of his people. Within the tribal milieu of which he is a part, he is eligible—but in a formal sense no more or less eligible than any other adult male of fighting age—by virtue of his being a "mighty warrior." The process leading to his being chosen as the one to muster the militia is not routine, but charismatic: "Then the LORD turned to him and said, 'Go in this might of yours and deliver Israel'" (Judg. 6:14).

Specific details lend credibility to the general picture this narrative gives of the political organization of premonarchy Israel. The symmetry of a mature, well-organized twelve-tribe league, in which each tribe has precisely defined borders, is absent from the account. Only five tribes participate in the battle, and altercations among the tribes ensue immediately after the main battle has been won. The religious situation is also unstable: Gideon's father maintains a shrine dedicated to the Canaanite divine pair Baal and Asherah. As a pious devotee of his ancestral gods, he has given his son a Baal name, Jerubbaal, an embarrassment to which later tradents responded by rechristening him Gideon ("the Destroyer").

Then the religiously ambiguous situation thickens further: The religious zealot who had earlier destroyed his father's Baal altar uses the booty gained in war to build an idol that the Israelites then worship. Totally absent from the story are the characteristics of the centralized cult and regulated priestly hierarchy that became normative in later biblical writings. True to the village-based socioanthropological model discernible in the archaeological findings from the Early Iron Age in this region, management of political, economic, and cultic affairs is a distinctly local matter dictated by the needs of the extended families and little influenced by centralized institutions like the ones that later would regulate the institutions and practices of Israelite society.

The central theme of the story, the united military response to a threat to one village's security, reveals relevant details about the clan structure of early Israel. The defense effort is led by an ordinary male of fighting age whose authority derives from divine charisma ("the spirit of the LORD took possession of Gideon" [Judg. 6:34]). In his person he combines features later divided among the specialized offices of king, priest, and prophet. Professional standing armies are nowhere in evidence; instead, a militia from the clans is mustered. The battle is construed in terms of sacral warfare, with resort to omens and under a cry ("a sword for the LORD and for Gideon" [Judg. 7:20]) that highlights the mediation of divine power through a chosen human agent. Troop size is held to a minimum to assure that divine participation in battle is recognized as the source of victory. Finally, the tactics used by the militia descending from hills against the enemy in the plains fit the category of guerrilla warfare.

A final question arises out of the Gideon story: in what way does it anticipate the model of governance that would succeed charismatic rule, namely, monarchy? A prima facie reading of the story has led many interpreters to the conclusion that it belongs to a tradition categorically opposed to kingship. Gideon is portrayed as one who demonstrates in battle precisely the qualities normally associated with an effective king, namely, humility before God combined with prowess and courage in battle and skill in military strategy. The grateful recipients of his deliverance from the enemy are quick to recognize his qualifications and extend to him the invitation to establish over them dynastic rule ("Rule over us, you and your son and your grandson also" [Judg. 8:22]). Gideon not only declines but also poignantly expresses his reason: "the LORD will rule over you" (Judg. 8:23). Is this not a categorical rejection of monarchy in favor of a form of rule more suitable for a people recognizing YHWH as sole sovereign (i.e., a polity true to the theocratic principle)?

A deeper look has introduced serious questions regarding the antikingship interpretation of the Gideon story.[12] First to be recognized is a small but important detail. We already have taken note of the motif of reduction of troop size as a means of downplaying the role of human agency and emphasizing the central importance of divine initiative. But how does one reconcile this with Gideon's war cry, "a sword for the LORD *and for Gideon*" (Judg. 7:20; cf. v. 18; italics added)? One's suspicion grows when this phrase is viewed against the background of the dream interpretation immediately preceding in verse 14: "This is no other than the sword of Gideon son of Joash, a man of Israel; into his hand God has given Midian and all the army."

To the ostensibly pious phrase in 8:23, "I will not rule over you, . . . the LORD will rule over you," Dennis Olson juxtaposes several vexing details: "Gideon has been acting more and more like an independent and improper king. He took the law into his own hands in a personal and violent vendetta (8:13–17). He accumulated gold (8:24–26), a sign of a bad king according to the law in Deuteronomy 17:17. He crafted an ephod (i.e., an idol) to which 'all Israel prostituted themselves' (8:27), obviously in egregious violation of Israel's First Commandment tradition. Finally, Gideon had many wives and seventy sons (8:30), a clear mark of a kingship like the nations (cf. Deut. 17:17)."[13]

As if the reader's "hermeneutic of suspicion" had been offered insufficient evidence to be aroused, the story goes on to relate in 8:31: "His concubine who was in Shechem also bore him a son, and he named him Abimelech." This son devoted his energies to fulfill the dynastic implications of his name, "My Father Is King," by ruthlessly slaying his seventy rival brothers. But the momentary victory proved to be pyrrhic, with the self-proclaimed king shortly thereafter suffering a disgraceful demise under the superior might of a woman (Judg. 9:53).

The story of Gideon reflects a complex history, and the debate among scholars whether it propounds a protheocracy/antimonarchy bias or the opposite bogs down in ambiguities inherent in the text itself. Perhaps the clearest historical-political lesson to be gained is this: the Gideon narrative reflects a struggle

---

12. See Dennis T. Olson, "Buber, Kingship, and the Book of Judges: A Study of Judges 6–9 and 17–21," in *David and Zion: Biblical Studies in Honor of J. J. M. Roberts*, ed. Bernard Batto and Kathyn Roberts (Winona Lake, IN: Eisenbrauns, 2004), 199–218.

13. Ibid., 210–11.

that plagued the Yahwistic community from the beginning, as it sought to implement structures of governance capable of handling difficult domestic and international problems, at the same time as remaining steadfast in its acknowledgment of YHWH as its only ultimate authority. That struggle would not end with Gideon and Abimelech, but would extend with force into the period of the monarchy.

With regard specifically to the final redaction of the book of Judges, however, a pattern does seem evident of a propitious beginning under early judges who served as mediators of divine deliverance (Othniel, Ehud, and Deborah), followed by "a gradual but progressive religious, social and military decline during the time of judges."[14] Within that pattern, the Gideon story, replete as it is with internal tension, was pivotal, leading to the description of the reckless exploits of Abimelech and Jephthah, followed by the chaos resulting from Samson's vain heroic excesses, and finally the internecine chaos and dissemination of the Benjaminites with which the book ends. Within this structure, the final verse of the book of Judges exquisitely captures the precariousness of the transitional point between charismatic leadership and monarchy: "In those days there was no king in Israel; all the people did what was right in their own eyes" (Judg. 21:25).[15]

Chapters 17 and 18 of the book of Judges contain another story that, while replete with legendary and etiological elements, again contains details reflective of conditions in the period before kings reigned in Israel (Judg. 17:6; 18:1). Pictured is the *bēt 'āb* of a man named Micah, in the territory of Ephraim. His household had accumulated sufficient wealth to erect and support a domestic ancestral shrine, replete with a central idol flanked by other cult objects and served by a private priest. The shrine's sacral function of bringing prosperity in return for patronage was restricted to this one household (Judg. 17:3; 18:24). However, the destiny of that household was shaken through encounter with a tribe that was migrating through Ephraim in search of a new territorial holding. Recognizing the benefits of Micah's shrine, the wandering Danites exercised their superior power to purloin his cult objects along with the attending Levitical priest, which they then took with them to their new central city of Laish, which they renamed Dan.

Reflected in the Micah story is a time predating centralized leadership in both political and religious spheres.[16] It is important to note that the installation of a priest is a local affair involving a contract between an affluent head of household and a suitable candidate. After Micah's priest is kidnapped, though the level of cultic leadership moves up two steps to the tribal level, it is still geographically circumscribed and offers no hint of an integrated hierocratic structure. Furthermore, any sign of a normative regulation of the divinity and the iconography of the cult is absent. Reflected in this narrative, therefore, is a pattern of scattered

14. Ibid., 208.
15. The hand of the final redactor is also visible in 17:6; 18:1; and 19:1.
16. Reference to the priest as a Levite gives the appearance of a later addition from the time when one clan came to enjoy special prerogatives in the domain of the sacred.

tribal units with borders lacking clear definition, units that are at most loosely confederated into what the Merneptah inscription named "the people of Israel."

Of signal importance among texts shedding light on the clan structure of emergent Israel is Judges 5, an archaic poem whose earliest parts may reach back as far as the twelfth century BCE. The clans are portrayed as settled in diverse locations from the hills of Ephraim to the northern highlands to the Mediterranean coast. In the instances where economic activities are ascribed to specific tribes, they are ones congruous with their particular ecological settings, for example, grain farming, small-scale cattle herding, and seafaring. Insofar as one can speak of a unifying political structure, one must describe it in terms of a very loose confederacy. This confederacy is identified in verse 11 simply as the people of YHWH, a designation reminiscent of the onomastic classification found in the Merneptah monument, "the people Israel," while at the same time highlighting the key role played by religion in the identity of this people. It is also noteworthy that the twelve-tribe structure that became normative at a later stage of development is not yet in evidence, for only ten tribes are mentioned. According to the poem, the tribes are driven to cooperative action by a threat to their security, but even in the case of enemy assault, only six respond to the muster, while four choose to remain home.

The threat is not trifling, for it is poised to destroy the modus operandi of this struggling clan-based society. The lines of trade between villages that facilitate an exchange of basic commodities have been disrupted (5:6). The response to this threat conforms to the pattern expected of a loose confederation of tribes. The individual tribes send volunteers to form a militia. The numerical and technological superiority of the enemy is to be offset by the cunning associated with guerrilla warfare and, above all, by the presence of the deity YHWH, who fittingly appears in the role of a Divine Warrior leading heavenly hosts (5:20). The poem identifies his home base (5:5) as Sinai in the south which is recognized as an archaic feature when one recalls that a cult center in that location likely dates to the Mosaic era.

Who are the enemies threatening the existence of these autonomy-loving clans? No less formidable a threat than "the kings of Canaan" (5:19), that is, the local dynasts who rule as vassals of the Egyptian pharaoh, a political arrangement we have already seen to be well documented by the fourteenth-century Amarna correspondence. The general historical situation begins to emerge from the clues given by the poem. The clans have settled in their respective ecological niches and formed a treaty arrangement with neighboring groups on the basis of a shared village-based and YHWH-centered oppositional ideology. After the clans' settlement in villages and the development of a network of intervillage trade routes, the Canaanite kings, viewing the growing village populations as a threat to their hegemony, initiate a military offensive against them. The relative peace that has enabled the development of the villages attested to by the archaeological surveys mentioned above has been disrupted. Crushing defeat and reenslavement can be averted only by a courageous military counteroffensive.

A close reading of Judges 5 is repaid with considerable information about the nature of the strategic alliance formed by scattered peasant farmers and villagers in times of crisis. The response to the threat is not uniform. Those joining the muster are the ones, centering in the central hill country and led by Ephraim, that are most immediately threatened by the Canaanite offensive. While the twelve-tribe organization visible in the archaic poem in Genesis 49 has not yet evolved, the essential ingredients of such a league are inchoately present. True, only six tribes send troops, while four are reprimanded for attending to their parochial affairs.

But the curse hurled at the inhabitants of Meroz "because they did not come to the help of the LORD, to the help of the LORD against the mighty" (5:23) indicates that the religious sanctions to which those pledging fealty to YHWH bound themselves are deemed to be in force, for such curses make sense only when based on credible covenantal warrants. The drama of battle also assumes the covenant between YHWH and the tribes, for it unfolds in terms consistent with the obligations with which the divine partner has bound himself to vassals who remain faithful to their side of the agreement.

Therefore, what from a military standpoint would seem implausible happens. Pitted against the professional armies of Canaanite kings equipped with the latest technology (horse-drawn chariots) was the ragtag militia of the clans consisting of peasant foot soldiers lacking the regimentation of urban cultures. Men and women alike have been recruited to participate in the voluntary army. Leadership is determined by evidence of divine empowerment (charisma). The stratagem used by the female judge Deborah and her crafty compatriot, the tent-dwelling Jael, the wife of a foreigner, is decidedly irregular in nature. The syntax of the poem reveals how even topography is used to offset the military advantage of the Canaanites: both verbs and prepositions reflect movement from the hillside villages down to the fortified city of Taanach: "down to the gates marched the people of the LORD" (5:11); "marched down . . . against the mighty" (5:13); "into the valley" (5:15).

Verse by verse the details of the poem in Judges 5 describe a battle fought from a theocratic perspective. Human participation is by no means excluded. As a group, those "who offered themselves willingly among the people" are commended, the tribes that respond with willingness of heart are blessed, and the courageous acts of Deborah, "a mother in Israel" (5:7), Barak her commander, and Jael, "of tent-dwelling women most blessed" (5:24), are praised. But humans do not enter the battlefield alone. Ultimately the leader of the campaign is "YHWH, the God of Israel" (5:5). The one who had created a people by delivering them from slavery under Pharaoh has returned to combat against a new generation of tyrant kings seeking their reenslavement. Mythic images are enlisted to depict the transcendent dimension of early Israel's theocratic worldview: "The stars fought from heaven. . . . The torrent Kishon swept them away" (5:20, 21).

More was at stake than a historical skirmish. The moral order YHWH had begun to establish within his covenant community was under threat, and the repercussions were cosmic in scope: "the earth trembled, and the heavens poured. . . . The mountains quaked before the LORD" (5:4, 5). Thanks to the compassionate justice of the God of Israel, the life-and-death conflict was decided in favor of "[the LORD's] peasantry in Israel" (5:11). Demythologized, the report would have read thus: Hebrew peasants of the Canaanite hill country have escaped reenslavement by local feudal lords seeking to revive the ideology of special privilege imported from pharaonic Egypt. But from Israel's theocratic perspective, the battle and its outcome were determined by the sovereign of all nations (5:20–23).

A glance back to the archaic poem in Exodus 15 opens a window on how an earlier generation of Hebrews had faced the same daunting superiority of royal cavalry and chariotry as did Deborah. Behind the catastrophe that broke the might of the Pharaoh's pursuing armies, the fleeing slaves had recognized the hand of their God YHWH. To him they ascribed steadfast love and incomparable power. The Song of Deborah indicates that her generation had not forgotten the faithfulness to slaves and peasants that revealed God's essential nature. The epithet ascribed to YHWH in Judges 5:5, "the One of Sinai," likely stems from one of the pilgrimage sites to which members of the various clans gathered to celebrate their common story.

Throughout the league (premonarchy) period, pilgrimages to similar sites, including Gilgal, Shechem, and Shiloh, provided opportunity for the scattered tribes to recite their Epic, which recounted the beneficent acts of their God, to recommit themselves to that God in worship and obedience to divine commandments, and thereby to deepen their sense of a common identity. At such sites their identity-fashioning story was recited, transmitted to future generations, and augmented on the basis of new manifestations of God's merciful acts on their behalf. Thus it was that a nation's epic took root and flourished.

Scholars such as George Mendenhall and Norman Gottwald plausibly aver that among the growing numbers of those swearing fealty to YHWH were inhabitants of the land of Canaan, like indigenous farmers and herders, who were drawn to the story of the God who took the side of the politically vulnerable and empowered them to resist the oppressive rule of Egyptian-sponsored tyrant kings. Though the transmission history leading up to the final form of the Deuteronomistic History is complex and multilayered, the motif of growth through assimilation described in narratives like the story of the clever Gibeonites in Joshua 9 likely preserves in the community's collective memory an authentic early phenomenon. Joshua 24 in turn gives a credible picture of the covenantal ritual that inducted new adherents into the growing confederation. A vivid example of ethnic and social inclusiveness within the peasant class is reflected in Judges 5, where the heroine Jael, of the "tent-dwelling women," is identified as the wife of a foreigner, "Heber the Kenite" (5:24).

Running throughout these otherwise diverse stories is thus a common theme. The focal point and the source of cohesion of this growing grassroots movement is YHWH, a deity offering an alternative to the royal cult of the urban centers and the pyramidal political and socioeconomic structures to which that cult gave sacral warrant. Steadily, it would seem, the fledgling YHWH community attracted the attention of a diverse array of peoples, united by a shared background of oppression and moved by a newborn sense of liberation and personal dignity to extend hospitality to all who identified with their story. It seems clear that the early epic was generous in extending an invitation to anyone seeking to escape bondage and to find a pathway to freedom.

The poetry and prose narratives from the book of Judges that we have examined comport nicely with the social-anthropological pattern visible in the archaeological evidence described earlier. We see the early Israelites organized as clans, holding themselves at arm's length from the Canaanite city-states and eschewing the centralization and bureaucracy typical of urban culture, occasionally finding it necessary to bracket their autonomy in mustering volunteers to defend against rival tribal groups or the professional armies of Canaanite kings, but then in periods of normalcy reengaging in their separate day-to-day activities. The clear contrast between urban centralization and village autonomy, however, also directs our attention back to the theme of unity that runs as a steady current through the stories of the otherwise freedom-loving clans. What countervailing tendency induced them to gather regularly around a common ritual and to muster at least a partially united front when faced by outside aggression? What dynamic was present among them that led to the greater unity represented by a twelve-tribe league and a centralized priesthood?

Both the song celebrating the defeat of Pharaoh in Exodus 15 and the one commemorating victory over the Canaanite coalition in Judges 5 identify the source of an emerging sense of religious unity and political solidarity. Exodus 15 describes in detail the stunning victory achieved by YHWH and affirms the bond between this God and Israel: "YHWH is my strength . . . my salvation. . . my God. . . . In your steadfast love you led the people whom you redeemed" (Exod. 15:2, 13). Judges 5:11 designates those who marched down to the gates of the Canaanite city as "the people of YHWH." Though scattered in pockets over a wide area, pursuing diverse economic activities with a high degree of independence of each other, organized under local family leaders, and worshiping in scattered local sanctuaries, the clansfolk of Israel nevertheless affirmed a sense of unity that survived myriad challenges, from both internal tensions and external threats.

The source of that sense of unity was the encounter at a time of deepest need with YHWH, a God unique among the gods, in that he identified not with the powerful of the world, but the weak, the vulnerable, the despised and neglected, that is, those at the very bottom of the culturally dominant socioeconomic ladder, the Hebrew slaves. Fittingly, having experienced his deliverance from their bondage, the liberated slaves gratefully identified themselves as "the people of YHWH."

Deriving a sense of identity from an understanding of the nature of the nation's chief deity, or in more general terms, from its concept of the heavenly realm, was not unique to Israel. What lends distinctiveness and cohesiveness to any civic entity is a comprehensive account of origins, and in the ancient world in which Israel developed as a nation, origins were traced to the activities of the gods as recounted in myth.[17] In Egypt (and similarly in the empires of Mesopotamia), the structures of the divine realm provided a template for structures in the mundane realm of humans.[18] Of key importance in that heavenly template was justification of the divine status of the king. Correspondingly, it assigned to the populace discrete functions contributing to the prosperity and stability of the ruling dynasty. Immutably and in keeping with the purported nature of the universe, humans were divided into classes. The laws and institutions that grew out of this mythopoeic worldview were viewed as essential to maintaining both the natural and the social order.

The stories in Exodus and Numbers of the children of Israel murmuring in the wilderness and longing to go back to the fleshpots of Egypt, together with the tales of discord and internecine conflict in the book of Judges, offer a glimpse of the magnitude of the challenge facing a loosely organized community as it struggled to construct laws and institutions capable of providing security from outside threats as well as internal cohesion. One option was to borrow from the time-tested myths and institutions of its powerful neighbors. To a degree, that option was exercised, as evidenced by the mythic motifs often appearing in early hymns (e.g., Ps. 29) and by the case laws comprising the greater part of the earliest legal corpus (Exod. 21–23).

However, such lines of continuity do not hide a more significant fact. From earliest times, the people of Israel looked for direction not to the *timeless realm of the gods* that served to order neighboring cultures. Rather, they drew their sense of peoplehood from the account of what God had done *in the mundane world* on their behalf. As a result, their account of origins took shape not as a timeless myth, but as an unfolding epic. The effect on religion and politics was revolutionary. Rejected as bogus religion was the claim of the pharaoh and the "divine kings" of other nations that their exalted status was established for all time in heaven. Rejected as bogus politics was the claim that special royal and sacerdotal entitlements sustained by the division of society into classes of slave and free were of divine origin.

Out of their story of origins arose an audacious religious claim, namely, that there was in the vast universe solely one being worthy of worship, the heavenly king YHWH. Drawn from that king's gracious championship of slaves was an accompanying political claim. Every human, by virtue of being created in the *image of God*, was endowed with intrinsic worth and entitled to inalienable rights of freedom, land and its usufruct, and equal protection under the law.

---

17. See Henri Frankfort et al., *Before Philosophy* (New York: Penguin Books, 1974).

18. In *Enuma Elish,* the cosmogonic myth of ancient Babylon, the heaven/earth typology was stated succinctly. The patron deity Marduk was ordered to "make a likeness on earth of what he has wrought in heaven" (Tablet VI, 113, in *Ancient Near Eastern Texts Relating to the Old Testament,* ed. James B Pritchard, 3rd ed. [Princeton, NJ: Princeton University Press, 1969], 69).

Biblical historian Baruch Halpern has formulated the heart of the Hebrew revolution succinctly: "Israelites had exchanged an Egyptian for a divine suzerain."[19] With that exchange, the theo-political notion of theocracy was born in Israel: Throughout the entire cosmos there existed but one being with ultimate, universal sovereignty and authority, whose name was revealed to Israel as YHWH.

GOD'S THEOCRATIC RULE EXPRESSED COVENANTALLY IN EPIC AND TORAH

As political prototypes, myth and epic both embody reciprocity, in myth between deity and king, in epic between deity and people. In myth the reciprocity is lapidary, as illustrated by sculptures depicting the deity embracing the pharaoh in an intimacy suggesting metaphysical inseparability. In epic the reciprocity is historical and relational: "You shall be my people, and I will be your God."

The effects of Israel's embracing epic in place of myth as the primary source of its identity were far-reaching. Within the context of its annual festivals, early hymns like Exodus 15 provided the seeds for an epic that grew with Israel's ongoing experience of YHWH's presence in its history.[20] With the growth of the story of the God who rescued the oppressed and drew them into a covenant relationship came an ever-deeper understanding of God's nature and the implications of God's nature for the conduct expected of members of the community called by his name. That YHWH was a God of justice and compassion placed a distinct stamp on Israel's understanding of government, expressed especially in the theme of special care for the vulnerable and the poor. How could a people conceived in an act of merciful deliverance from slavery in turn impoverish and enslave others without contradicting their selfhood and nullifying their birthright? Freedom, equality, and human rights thus were inscribed onto the heart of every Israelite and elaborated in Torah, understood as the "charter" of a covenant people.

Studying the laws and institutions that arose in early Israel within the context of covenant serves as a safeguard against the modern inclination to limit one's approach to secular criteria. Indeed, any approach to biblical politics that does not begin with Israel's unconditional and exclusive pledge of fidelity to YHWH misses the vitality constituting the core of a people that understood its norms and institutions in theocratic terms. From that fidelity arose its identity as a people called to a teleological purpose and committed unconditionally to obeying God's commandments above all human considerations. In Israel's view, purpose, as inferred from the drama unfolding in its Epic, entailed agency in

---

19. Halpern, *Emergence*, 172.

20. Johannes Petersen's suggestion that Exodus 1–15 took shape as a Passover legend is plausible (*Israel: Its Life and Culture*, vol. 4 [London: Oxford University Press, 1953], 728–37). Joshua 24:1–28 provides a vivid portrait of the part recital of the Epic played in the covenant renewal festivals of early Israel.

God's plan for universal *shalom.* Obedience was understood as an expression of gratitude to the divine benefactor and the desire to conform in all areas of life to God's nature. The philosophy of ancient Israel accordingly entails a historical ontology centered on an intrinsic religious dimension reaching back to the earliest events that the biblical texts allow us to glimpse. To deny either the religious dimension of Israel's self-understanding or the historical dimension of its identity-shaping story is to miss the principal sources of political reflection and policy throughout the span of biblical history.

The "people Israel" that emerged in the period of the judges is thus one that combined ancient clan notions of autonomy with new religious experiences of a kin god YHWH, who intervened on behalf of a subjugated people and guided them toward liberty and a deep sense of self-worth and self-transcending purpose. The clans constituting that people were permitted to pursue their individual livelihoods and defend their freedoms from outside interference, so long as they gave expression to their allegiance to one divine authority under two clearly defined conditions: at annual religious festivals and in cases of threat by outside aggressors. In religious festivals, they developed their Epic as an identity-sustaining story of life as a people led by YHWH. In holy war, they defended themselves from any threat that sought to take that identity from them. Additionally, in their laws and institutions, they sought to conform themselves to the nature of their redeemer as they had experienced him in the flux of a precarious existence, first as a band of slaves and then as a small and oft-threatened emerging nation.

It is vitally important to recognize the nature of the relationship between early Israel's Epic and the laws that gave expression to its understanding of covenant and gave shape to its political institutions. The Bible in its final canonical form describes Torah as commandments Moses received from YHWH on Mount Sinai. The profound theological message this narrative theme conveys is overlooked at the cost of missing the heart of Israel's understanding of its origins as a nation. Not luck, not accident, certainly not its own cleverness or strength, but divine love expressed in saving acts accounts for all that it is (in contrast to a dismal past) and all that it is called to become (not only for its own sake, but for the sake of all the nations of the earth). An etiology like this mandates a twin response, enactment of the theocratic principle in grateful worship and obedience embodying the attributes of the divine Lover.

The epithet "divine Lover" may strike the reader as an imposition of modern sentimentality on the "stern" God of the Bible; in fact it reclaims one of the central attributes Israel ascribed to the God who chose to enter into covenant with a formerly enslaved people.[21] The indissoluble connection between the loving

21. William L. Moran has demonstrated on the basis of ancient epigraphic evidence that "love of vassal for suzerain" was a normal part of political treaty nomenclature ("The Ancient Near Eastern Background of the Love of God in Deuteronomy," in *The Most Magic Word: Essays on Babylonian and Biblical Literature,* ed. Ron Hendel [Washington, DC: Catholic Biblical Association of America, 2002], 170–81).

divine initiative ensconced in the Epic and the requisite human response of worship and obedience became a permanent part of biblical tradition, as exemplified in the classic formulation of Deuteronomy 7:7–11:

> It was not because you were more numerous than any other people that the LORD set his heart on you and chose you—for you were the fewest of all peoples. It was because the LORD loved you and kept the oath that he swore to your ancestors, that the LORD has brought you out with a mighty hand, and redeemed you from the house of slavery, from the hand of Pharaoh king of Egypt. Know therefore that the LORD your God is God, the faithful God who maintains covenant loyalty with those who love him and keep his commandments, to a thousand generations, and who repays in their own person those who reject him. He does not delay but repays in their own person those who reject him. Therefore, observe diligently the commandment—the statutes, and the ordinances—that I am commanding you today.

Within the context of the covenant inaugurated by God with a people God has redeemed and embraced in loving faithfulness, law is not an onerous obligation imposed on a body politic. It is, rather, an invitation to the human partners of the covenant to reciprocate in the only manner befitting an intimate relationship, loving obedience. Thus arose the profound legal theory intrinsic to Israel's theocratic understanding of civil order. Laws are protective measures growing out of God's antecedent acts of loving-kindness and inviting the beneficiaries of God's grace to affirm their essential nature by patterning their behavior after God's.

This dynamic understanding of the etiology of biblical law does not imply that Israel's laws and customs were unique in all respects in relation to neighboring cultures. The debate whether or not Israel—and hence, biblical religion—is unique is overly simplistic.[22] As self-evidently as no individual is "self-made" and utterly unique, neither was an ancient nation like Israel. Even from a confessional perspective, it is apparent that when the ancient Hebrews gave testimony to God's gracious acts in songs of praise and Epic narrative, they did so using the idioms of the northwest Semitic dialect of the eastern Mediterranean and drawing on images for God native to the Canaanite cultural horizon of which they were a part. Similarly, in the earliest stages of formulating the norms that were to guide the social practices and moral behavior of the community, they drew from the dominant culture of the time case laws regulating reparations and punishments for violations against property and person.

In pursuing the politics of early Israel, what we seek to grasp, therefore, is not uniqueness, but rather an understanding of the essential character of the "people Israel" that was formed under the tutelage of its divine deliverer and that gave rise to laws and institutions reflecting origins in God's loving-kindness. The fact

---

22. Paul D. Hanson, "War das Alte Israel einmalig?" in *Jahrbuch für Biblische Theologie 7* (Neukirchen-Vluyn: Neukirchener Verlag, 1992), 3–20.

that the specific components constituting that character were culturally diverse underlines the historical ontology undergirding Israel's theology.

We shall now move from general phenomenology to concrete examples, first focusing on the earliest corpus of law in the Hebrew Bible and then tracing the dynamic development of Torah through reinterpretation and adaptation to new situations in which YHWH was experienced as a sovereign steadfastly committed to justice and mercy.

While not lacking traces of redacting, at its core Exodus 20:22–23:19 (the "Book of the Covenant" referred to in Exod. 24:7) is the earliest collection of laws found in the Hebrew Bible.[23] Evidencing the antiquity of those laws are the allusion to archaic practices such as determination of guilt on the basis of an ordeal before the gods (Exod. 22:8 [v. 7 in Heb.]) and the absence of any reference to the king or the institution of monarchy. Also noteworthy is the juxtaposition of two types of law, case (or casuistic) laws and Yahwistic (or apodictic) laws. The case laws—which reflect common-law conventions known best from the Code of Hammurabi and can be traced all the way back to the Sumerian city-states of the third millennium—provided precedents upon which legal decisions could be rendered.[24] Their structure, by mandating different levels of severity in punishment, depending on the class to which defendant and victim belonged, reflects a strictly stratified society. Yahwistic laws in contrast state apodictically the behavior expected of the people of Israel by the God with whom they are covenanted, with no distinctions as to rank or status. In them we see clear evidence of roots in the historical experiences of Israel celebrated in the Epic and of their ultimate origin in the nature of the God revealed in those experiences. For our purposes the significance of the case laws resides in their testimony to early Israel's openness to borrowing from the legal conventions of its neighbors.

Our closer attention now turns to the Yahwistic laws and the window they open to the process through which a young nation—while not opposed to borrowing—inferred from its Epic specific laws deemed appropriate for a people seeking to conform its life to the nature of its divine redeemer.

"You shall not oppress a resident alien; you know the heart of an alien, for you were aliens in the land of Egypt" (Exod. 23:9). With remarkable concision, this Yahwistic commandment illuminates the moral philosophy of ancient Israel. Humane treatment of an outsider is not experienced as a burdensome obligation or an abstract option, but as the spontaneous expression of the loving nature that has been created within you by the God who, when you were an alien, gave *you* a home. For members of the covenant community the experience of being homeless is written upon heart, as is the experience of being rescued

23. See Paul D. Hanson, "The Theological Significance of Contradiction in the Book of the Covenant," in *Canon and Authority*, ed. G. W. Coats and B. O. Long (Philadelphia: Fortress Press, 1977), 110–29.

24. See David P. Wright, *Inventing God's Law: How the Covenant Code of the Bible Revised the Laws of Hammurabi* (Oxford: Oxford University Press, 2009).

by a loving benefactor. Homelessness and rescue are not abstract categories, but lived experiences that constitute the opening chapter of a personal story. To show kindness to the alien in your midst accordingly gives expression to the identity that constitutes your essential being ("heart," Heb. *nepeš*).

Two other Yahwistic laws accompany the one concerning treatment of aliens and add important substance to our understanding of ancient Israel's moral universe. In them YHWH identifies himself as the personal source of Israel's ethical principles. In Exodus 22:21–23 (22–24 in English versions), God commands that there be no abuse of the most vulnerable members among God's people, that is, widows and orphans. Motivation for obedience is grounded in God himself: God will not remain silent if anyone among God's people abuses a widow or orphan and thereby contradicts the moral consciousness that God has planted in his or her heart through God's saving acts. God thereby not only requires consistency of moral behavior from Israel. God also demonstrates God's own steadfastness to the covenant God has established. For how could the One who responded in mercy to the cry of Hebrew slaves suffering abuse under Egyptian taskmasters be deaf to the cries of widows and orphans victimized by members of their own community? God's wrath is thus revealed to be an essential aspect of the moral integrity of the created order.

The law in Exodus 22:25–27 (Heb. vv. 24–26) addresses a major source of impoverishment and misery among the peasant class, namely, inability to pay back loans incurred in purchasing basic essentials such as clothing, food, and seed for the next season's planting. Contrary to the ubiquitous practice of usury at the time, those covenanted with YHWH were neither to burden debtors with interest nor to hold essential goods as collateral, because the same God who showed his compassion to the Hebrew slaves when they cried to him out of their bondage in Egypt would again act decisively on behalf of those made destitute by their heartless compatriots. In the motivation class of this law, as in the one discussed in the previous paragraph, the inseparable bond between Israel's Epic and the laws that arose inferentially from it is clearly depicted by the repetition of the motif of the victims crying to God out of their misery (Exod. 3:7 > Exod. 22:23 and 22:27 [cf. Exod. 6:5]).

These three laws from the Book of the Covenant give clear expression to early Israel's *dynamic* understanding of its relationship with God and the moral theory that it implied. It was a relationship created on the basis of God's beneficent acts, acts including deliverance from political slavery and the gift of a land as a refuge from reenslavement. As already observed, those acts were recorded in the form of an Epic, Israel's story of the events through which God made known to his people God's nature and the moral qualities that were to be inferred from that nature. According to this understanding, Israel's laws were to embody God's attributes and give expression in all areas of human life to the moral principles that were constitutive of the identity of God's people.

Application of the adjective "dynamic" to Israel's understanding of the covenant relationship points to the two dimensions defining its perimeters. In the first place, it is a dependable relationship characterized by a teleological consistency reflecting the steadfast commitment of God to a plan for creation and for God's people's role in that plan. Secondly, it is a living relationship in which the eternal God re-presents himself in the ever-changing circumstances of human history. The resulting worldview thus combines continuity and change. In the case of early Israel's formulation of legal norms, the covenant fidelity of God as source of compassionate justice is unchanging, but the way in which God's faithfulness comes to expression in human laws and institutions adapts, in keeping with the covenant community's new experiences within a changing world and its consequent growth in understanding.

THE LIVING CHARACTER OF EPIC AND TORAH

God's living relationship with his people did not cease with the exodus, nor did it cease with their occupation of the land and organization into a loosely structured confederation. Indeed, within the vast historical horizon of the Bible, God's involvement in the affairs of Israel would continue until God's plan for creation and Israel's role in that plan had been brought to completion in "a new heaven and a new earth."[25] In keeping with that historical view, Israel's story of its relationship with God grew, and with each new chapter came both the opportunity for a deeper knowledge of its God and the danger of regression due to sin. We now turn to a brief consideration of the effect this historical perspective had on the development of *torah* in the Bible.

In cultures deriving their laws and institutions from the primordial sphere of myth, what law codes prescribed was generally an unchanging structure for human society. In the case of ancient Egypt, the pharaoh embodied the law of the land; in effect, his word *was* the law. The Hebrews broke with the concepts of an immutable heavenly prototype and its patron deity, by following the God who led them out of the "eternal" order of slavery into an open future as a free people. The opening up of the future to new chapters in God's ongoing presence brought with it the opportunity for deeper insight into God's nature and will. Consequently *torah*, in harmony with the Epic, came to be conceived as a reality as living and dynamic in nature as was God's relationship with God's people.

A comprehensive account of the unfolding of Israel's Torah through its biblical stages (Book of the Covenant > Deuteronomy > Holiness Code >Leviticus) would require several separate volumes, with many more following to extend the study through the Mishnah, Talmud, and medieval commentaries. Here it must suffice to offer two examples of how the process of inferring law from Epic evidenced in the Book of the Covenant continued on into later formulations and applications of *torah* in the Hebrew Bible.

25. Rev. 21:1; cf. Isa. 65:17.

As described above, one of the Yahwistic laws in the Book of the Covenant proscribed usury and the accompanying practice of taking a piece of property in pledge (i.e., as collateral), in that case, the debtor's mantle (Exod. 22:25–27 [vv. 24–26 in Heb.]). The motive clause substantiating that law appealed directly to God's compassion, known to members of the Jewish community through their familiarity with their Epic. To understand the potential for such a law to spark further ethical reflection, it may be helpful to recall the phrase used by Paul Ricoeur in reference to symbols, namely, "surplus of meaning." By exposing the practice of usury to the compassion of the God revealed in the exodus, the "garment taken in pledge" functioned metonymously to depict the precariousness of those living within a subsistence economy.[26] Thus a single law, though citing a concrete situation, invited augmentation. The invitation was taken up in Deuteronomy, where the taking of a *millstone* in pledge was proscribed as equivalent to taking a *life* in pledge (Deut. 24:6).

The result is striking. The reader in effect is placed in the presence of a mother who draws each day a portion of maíze from her meager larder, which she then grinds between her millstones into flour for the family's corn mush dinner. But what happens if she—whose pecuniary state already has been indicated by the desperate move of securing a loan against an implement indispensible to her household's viability—does not have her millstone returned to her? An ominous conclusion is written indelibly into the story: She slides inexorably into deeper and deeper debt, leading either to slavery or to death (or likely both), for the lender has taken not just an object in pledge, but her very *life.*

With such a cruel act, the nation's Epic has been blatantly violated. An alarming crisis is at hand, demanding response from anyone who understands his or her origin in God's mercy and experiences Torah not as an artifact, but as the presence of God's living will among them.[27]

Understood thus, *living* Torah resembles the ripples emanating from a stone thrown into a glassy lake, for the dreaded image of the pledge did not come to rest with the books of Exodus and Deuteronomy. It continued to disturb the moral guardians of the Jewish community. The prophet Amos cries out, "[T]hey lay themselves down beside every altar on garments taken in pledge" (Amos 2:8). Eliphaz describes his revulsion at the wickedness of the one who has "exacted pledges from your family for no reason, and stripped the naked of their clothing" (Job 22:6). The sage adds this counsel: "Do not be one of those who give pledges, who become surety for debts. If you have nothing with which to pay, why should your bed be taken from under you?" (Prov. 22:26–27). Heartless are we as readers, heirs to the biblical Epic and its moral mandates, if we do

26. The Bible contains ample evidence to suggest that subsistence living would have described the economic circumstances of the majority of the population both early and late in the biblical times (Samuel L. Adams, *Social and Economic Life in Second Temple Judea* (Louisville, KY: Westminster John Knox Press, 2014).

27. Zechariah's flying scroll wins the contest for the most awesome image of living Torah in the entire Bible (Zech. 5:1–4).

not recognize the relevance of purloined millstones and confiscated garments, extending to the homeless person bundled in his coat on a freezing sidewalk past whom we blithely walk.

Our second example of living epic and Torah relates to Exodus 21:1–11, which, in contrast to the previous example, belongs not to the category of Yahwistic law, but rather to the conventional form of ancient Near Eastern law referred to as case law. It legislates conditions pertaining to the redemption of slaves. As would be expected in laws of this type, it does not include a motive clause appealing to Israel's Epic and the attributes of that Epic's god, YHWH.

The sensitive reader may react with a sense of moral indignation to this law's stipulations. Given its unequal treatment of male and female slaves, how could this law stand up under the scrutiny of the evenhanded justice implied by Israel's Epic, in which a merciful God delivered, without discrimination, slaves of both genders? A brief examination of the process of reinterpretation through which the law of release passed subsequent to the Book of the Covenant produces a bold answer. Such scrutiny in fact created a tension between the lofty standards inherent in the Epic and the discrimination embodied in this law, a tension that the community seeking to embody the attributes of its Deliverer could not ignore.

The following quotations depict the tension between the Epic, epitomized in the preamble introducing Exodus 20–23, and the two cases concerning the redemption of slaves:

Preamble	"I am the LORD your God, who brought you out of the land of Egypt, out of the house of slavery." (Exodus 20:2)
Case One	"When you buy a male Hebrew slave, he shall serve six years, but in the seventh he shall go out a free person, without debt." (Exodus 21:2)
Case Two	"When a man sells his daughter as a slave, she shall not go out as the male slaves do." (Exodus 21:7)

The discrimination between treatment of males and females and the tension this creates with the central theme of the Epic is clear.

Deuteronomy, generally dated several centuries later than the Book of the Covenant, eliminates the gender-based distinction: "If a member of your community, *whether a Hebrew man or a Hebrew woman*, is sold to you and works for you six years, in the seventh year you shall set that person free" (Deut. 15:12, italics added). In addition, the freed slave, male (5:13–14) or female (5:17b), shall not be sent forth empty-handed, but shall be liberally provisioned. With these emendations, a law emerges that is more in harmony with the story of the Deliverer of male *and* female slaves from Egypt than the differentiated provision for release in Exodus 21.[28]

---

28. Another vivid example of Deuteronomic elaboration on the themes of earlier law is found in Deut. 24:10–15. First, the command to return the garment taken in pledge "by sunset" is reinforced with a double motive clause, "so that your neighbor may sleep in the cloak and bless you; and it

But the tension has not been eliminated entirely. What justification is there for holding slaves at all in the community called to bear testimony in the world to God's mercy? Leviticus 25, from a time somewhat later than the Deuteronomic law of release, replies incisively and with explicit reference to the central theme of the Epic: "[The people of Israel] are my servants, whom I brought out of the land of Egypt; they shall not be sold as slaves are sold" (Lev. 25:42). With poignant clarity, the transformative effect of the Epic on the formulation of Torah comes to expression, resulting in a further step toward resolving the tension between the two.

Even after this important step, however, tension still remains: "It is from the nations around you that you may acquire male and female slaves. You may also acquire them from among the aliens residing with you" (Lev. 25:44–45).[29] While the declaration that foreigners are fair game to replenish the slave labor force depleted by the prohibition of enslaving Hebrews strikes one as morally offensive, the further inclusion of "the aliens residing with you" opens an even deeper ethical conundrum. Already in Israel's earliest code of law, the Book of the Covenant, we found this law: "You shall not oppress a resident alien; you know the heart of an alien, for you were aliens in the land of Egypt" (Exod. 23:9). Whereas the first half of the law in Leviticus illustrates dramatically the *progressive* dimension of the biblical moral universe, the second half reintroduces tension between the Epic and Torah. Even in Leviticus 25, the birthplace of the revolutionary concept of the jubilee, the tutoring of a people called to be witnesses to God's universal justice and mercy remains unfinished, their understanding of God's will remains partial, and their task of being God's agents of compassionate justice remains unfinished.

We turn now from cases of reinterpretation of Torah to an example of the moral influence Israel's Epic exercised on the realm of economics, specifically, the rules regulating ownership and transfer of land. It was customary in the ancient Near East for land to be treated like any other commodity. As such, the wealthy were able to leverage market forces to their advantage, with the impoverishment, disenfranchisement, and debt slavery of the poor a common consequence. In addition to laws addressing the deleterious effects of practices like usury and the holding of property as collateral, the commitment to impartial justice and equality that arose within Israel's Epic came to expression in an alternative *system* of land tenure. Designated by the Hebrew term naḥălā (translated as "inheritance" or "patrimony"), this system granted to each extended family (bēt ʾāb) an apportionment of land sufficient to its need, which was to remain in

---

will be to your credit before the LORD your God." This is followed by the injunction to pay "poor and needy laborers, whether other Israelites or aliens who reside in your land . . . their wages daily before sunset," reinforced again by a double (human/divine) motive clause, "because they are poor and their livelihood depends on them; otherwise they might cry to the LORD against you and you would incur guilt."

29. Discriminatory treatment of the foreigner in the practice of charging interest on loans is also found in Deuteronomy: "On loans to a foreigner you may charge interest, but on loans to another Israelite you may not charge interest" (Deut. 23:20).

its possession in perpetuity. It is not difficult to recognize the socioanthropological background to this concept: the resistance of members of clans and villagers to the oppressive economic instruments of Iron Age urban culture described above. To this historical catalyst the guardians of Torah tradition added a theological warrant, the authority of the deliverer and patron of commoners, peasants, and slaves: the God of Israel.[30]

Though both the system of naḥălā and the antiusury laws succumbed during the monarchy to the conventional ancient Near Eastern economic practices of seizing land through debt slavery and eminent domain,[31] they could never be eradicated from the moral consciousness of God's people, for they had become an integral part of their story (Epic), their ethical principles (Torah), and their sense of communal identity (covenant).

As a community living in a covenant relationship with a God active in history, Israel was a sojourning community, striving to live faithfully and obediently by constructing institutions and social structures that embodied God's justice and compassion, but repeatedly falling short. Concepts such as story, communal identity, and ontological self-understanding thus do not eliminate paradoxes and tensions. The haunting existential question of the prophet persists: "O LORD of hosts, how long . . . ?" (Zech. 1:12). That question, however, far from discrediting the biblical worldview, frees it from the kind of bondage into which many modern interpreters unwittingly bind it and with which many cultural despisers mistakenly define it, the bondage of otherworldly timelessness.

Timelessness belongs to the realm of myth, not to the world of the biblical Epic. Immutability describes the character of imperial law, not the living Torah of Israel's God. Because the living Torah and its proactive God are experienced in the messiness of real life, the historical applications of God's rule to the realm of politics are not eternally fixed, but adapting and developing within the covenantal relationship between the living God and flesh-and-blood people. Of all forms of governance, theocracy alone unequivocally describes the terms capable of sustaining such a relationship and the fragile balance between God's ultimate sovereignty and the penultimate human institutions that it implies.

As already may be evident from our frequent references, Deuteronomy captures like no other biblical book the dynamic nature of God-covenant-Torah and the concomitant theocratic political ideal. Twice above we have used passages from Deuteronomy as specific examples of reinterpretation of Torah in response to moral inferences drawn from YHWH's acts as depicted in the Epic. We have also noted examples where tension remained between specific laws and the compassionate acts of YHWH. But it is not only the eye of the critical scholar that detects points of tension and instances of updating earlier tradition.

A sense of the *contemporary* significance of the Torah comes to expression in the words of the Deuteronomists themselves, for example, in the introduction

---

30. Lev. 25:23; Deut. 19:14; cf. Num. 27:1–11.
31. Isa. 5:8; 1 Kgs. 21.

to the Ten Commandments: "The LORD our God made a covenant with us at Horeb. Not with our ancestors did the LORD make this covenant, but with us, who are all of us here alive today" (Deut. 5:2–3).[32] The terms of the Horeb covenant are then spelled out in the following twenty-three chapters. But in chapter 29, another covenant is introduced, the Moab covenant, which applies the covenant mediated by Moses to a *new* generation. S. Dean McBride pinpoints the differences between the two covenants in terms of geographical, temporal, and political distance:

> the geographical distance between Horeb, where in wilderness isolation Israel first became God's people, and Moab, where its history as a territorial state, surrounded by other nations, is about to begin; the temporal distance, between ancestral generations to whom divine promises were made and the present generation for whom those promises could become actuality; and, perhaps greatest of all, the political distance between a fledgling community of liberated slaves and an institutionally structured society, responsible for the maintenance of civil order, economic well-being, and human rights for all of its citizens.[33]

What comes plainly into view is the keen historical sense of the authors of Deuteronomy. Their aim goes deeper than adding glosses to previous laws. They are engaged in keeping Torah relevant to the changing circumstances in which Israel finds itself, such as the move from Horeb to Moab. Even more significant than response to change on the level of the narrative is the substantive reshaping of the body of Torah in Deuteronomy 12:2–26:15, into what S. Dean McBride, citing Josephus, has aptly named Moses' "divinely authorized and comprehensive 'polity' or 'national constitution.'"[34] The fact that this constitution (in Josephus's terminology *politeia*) is constructed in the form of a theocracy may at first blush appear to be backward looking, inasmuch as it has long been recognized by biblical historians that Deuteronomy was written during the monarchy, which is to say, in a period postdating the confederation of tribes with which many identify theocratic rule. A more careful reading, however, indicates that the Deuteronomic strategy is profoundly *forward* looking. It presents theocratic polity as restricted to no single phase of Israelite history, but rather as codifying the *core* of Israel's understanding of what it means to be a historical entity called into a covenant relationship with God, regardless of the specific form of human government under which it was living at any given time.

From a Deuteronomic point of view, covenant consists of two aspects: first, the inaugural acts recited in the Epic, through which God preveniently revealed himself to the Israelites and called them into existence as a people, and second,

---

32. See Gerhard von Rad, *Deuteronomy, a Commentary* (Philadelphia: Westminster Press, 1966), 55.

33. S. Dean McBride, "Polity of the Covenant Community," *Interpretation* 41, no. 3 (July 1987): 236.

34. Ibid., 229.

"treaty-stipulations"[35] and "statutory rulings"[36] that set forth the civic order implied by the Epic. Formulated in political terms, we can state that Deuteronomy sets forth the exclusive sovereignty of God as the essential foundation of government and then follows with the terms of implementation of that central principle through structures and policies safeguarding God's rule from all forms of distortion and idolatrous abuse. We now turn to texts that flesh out the Deuteronomic notion of theocracy.

The classic formulation of the saving acts of God that inaugurated the covenant is the historical credo in Deuteronomy 26:1–11.[37] The fact that the setting in which it is recited is worship is significant, since it draws attention to the indispensable role of worship in shaping the community's religious identity and molding its moral consciousness.

Drawn inferentially from God's saving acts are rules defining how Israel was to express its gratitude to God in a life conforming to God's justice and mercy (Deut. 12–26). Together, divine initiative and human response in reverent obedience created the framework of reciprocity that was integral to the covenant and the starting point for reflection on political theory in the Bible.

The covenantal pattern of divine initiative and human response appears several times in the introductory chapters of Deuteronomy. For example, in 4:32–38 God's acts of creation, election of the ancestors, redemption of slaves from Egypt, and gift of a homeland constitute the historical foundation of the covenant. Upon that foundation are constructed the stipulations, beginning with the core commandment that serves as the keystone for the theocratic principle, "So acknowledge . . . the LORD is God . . . there is no other" (4:39), and followed by "his statutes and his commandments." The passage ends with a promise, "so that you may long remain in the land that the LORD your God is giving you for all time" (4:40).

In Deuteronomy 6:20–25 the covenantal pattern of Epic and stipulations creates an envelope structure, with children inquiring as to the meaning of "the decrees and the statutes and the ordinances" (6:20), followed by a succinct account of the Epic (6:21–23), and concluded with divine commandment and implied promise, "to observe all these statutes . . . for our lasting good" (6:24–25).

Chapter 11 serves as a final example of the pattern of Epic recital establishing the foundation of the covenant, followed by stipulations drawn inferentially from the Epic. As in chapter 6, the pattern is expressed in the literary structure of an envelope. Verse 1 opens with the central commandment, "You shall love the LORD your God," and alludes to the other stipulations of the Torah. Then verses 2–7 recapitulate "every great deed that YHWH did." Verses 8–32 return

---

35. ʿēdôt
36. ḥuqqîm wĕmišpāṭîm
37. Gerhard von Rad, *Das formgeschictliche Problem des Hexateuchs* (Stuttgart: Kohlhammer, 1938).

to admonishing the people to keep the "entire commandment," followed by "so that" and enumeration of the consequences of obedience and disobedience.

The inseparability of history teleologically perceived and morality inferentially drawn from the experiences of the faith community explains why growth of the Epic was accompanied by development of the Torah. New experiences of God's presence in its history fostered ongoing reflection on the implications of God's acts and the divine attributes manifested in those acts for all aspects of life. What did not change in the process was the sole sovereignty of God, and it was that quintessential fact of its existence and identity as a people that established the theocratic character of its polity.

The First Commandment principle was not rigid, however, but adaptable— not as a pragmatic concession, but as an inference from principle. For if there was only one ultimate sovereign, then there was only one authoritative order. Since no earthly regime could claim to be that order, all models of government were relativized to the status of derivative and penultimate. To claim to be more constituted an idolatrous distortion of the theocratic principle, by erasing the distinction between divine and human authority.[38] On the other hand, to do less than strive to pattern political and social structures as closely as possible after God's righteous standard was to be irresponsible to the sovereign and unfaithful to the terms of the covenant. It is on the basis of this theo-political understanding that the Deuteronomists formulated their "charter for a constitutional theocracy."[39]

The criteria inherent in this charter for constructing the instruments of government were far-reaching. To grasp the distinctive nature of those criteria, it may be helpful to recall the mythic basis of rule in ancient Egypt. There the picture of an eternal celestial order provided the template for human government. Political stability was predicated on symmetry between structures in heaven and structures on earth, a symmetry manifested by the identification of the pharaoh with his divine patron (e.g., Horus).[40] The priestly guardians of social order discharged their duty by enforcing the divine order incarnated in the pharaoh in all spheres of public life. In contrast, the Deuteronomic picture of reality was predicated not on identity, but on a fundamental distinction between the ultimate order of God's reign and the provisional order of all human regimes. But into this distinction was built a paradox: while it was as impossible for human government to replicate heaven on earth as it was for the king to become a god, YHWH's universal rule was to be the sole standard against which Israel's political, social, and economic institutions were to be judged.

---

38. In Kierkegaard's words, "the infinite qualitative distinction" (Søren Kierkegaard, *Training in Christianity*, trans. W. Lowrie [Princeton, NJ: Princeton University Press, 1944], 139).

39. McBride, "Polity," 24.

40. Representations of the intimacy/identification between Egyptain kings and deities can be found in James B. Pritchard, *The Ancient Near East in Pictures Relating to the Old Testament* (Princeton, NJ: Princeton University Press, 1969), e.g., 377 and 422.

But how did the norms of divine justice and mercy that define God's rule become known to humans, if not through the celestial knowledge of priests specially trained to read the holy symbols (hieroglyphs)? The Deuteronomists were careful to explain that knowledge of the principles of compassionate justice was within the grasp of humans, due to divine grace. Rather than remaining aloof in heavenly splendor, Israel's God set himself apart from the gods of other nations by manifesting himself to God's people in word and deed within the context of their historical existence:

> For what other great nation has a god so near to it as the LORD our God is whenever we call to him? And what other great nation has statutes and ordinances as just as this entire law that I am setting before you today? (Deut. 4:7–8)

> Surely, this commandment that I am commanding you today is not too hard for you, nor is it too far away. . . . No, the word is very near to you; it is in your mouth and in your heart for you to observe. (Deut. 30:11, 14)

The paradox of transcendence safeguarded by holiness and presence vouchsafed by divine grace is inherent in the covenant. It is from the resulting relational vitality of the covenant that Deuteronomy derives the stipulations inherent in theocratic polity, of which we shall consider two, the role of human mediators and the centrality of egalitarian justice.

HUMAN MEDIATORS AND EGALITARIAN JUSTICE IN THEOCRATIC POLITY

Human mediators play a critical role within a theocracy, for they provide the covenantal link through which God's sovereign rule becomes effectual within the human community. In a world in which theocracy is a living concept, both in the idolatrous form of regimes exploiting a claim to divine authority for self-serving objectives (a danger alive in fundamentalisms of all kinds) and in the magnanimous struggles of reform movements for impartial justice, the question of mediation continues to raise deep theological, moral, and political questions. A particular nation or party may claim to rule by divine mandate; but given the fact that, in the human domain, divine rule of necessity is exercised through human agents, the questions of legitimacy, proper exercise of authority, and abuse of power remain critical.

In Deuteronomy, careful attention is paid to these questions in the form of a description of the qualifications requisite for each of the major offices. Foundational throughout is the guiding principle of God's ultimate sovereignty. Even as a given regime is legitimate only to the degree that it faithfully serves God's universal rule, so each officeholder is legitimate only to the degree that he or she exercises derivative authority under the strict terms and limits of the ultimate authority of God. Careful adherence to this stipulation is of utmost importance, for its violation inevitably leads theocratic leaders into misappropriation of authority and self-aggrandizing idolatry.

The principle of God's ultimate sovereignty comes to clear expression in the "law of kingship" in Deuteronomy 17:14–20. Though this law will accompany us into the next chapter, on monarchy, it also serves to clarify the safeguards against the distortion of theocracy that are built into Deuteronomic law. Proscribed are the amassing of military power, acquisition of a large harem, and the accumulation of excessive wealth. While such practices are elemental aspects of absolute kingship, they eviscerate the heart of Israel's covenant in both of its aspects: the central covenantal principle of only one absolute sovereign is repudiated, and the equality of all citizens under God is destroyed, when one human is exempt from censure and exalted to a privileged status.

Purging monarchy of elements alien to Israel's founding experiences and hostile to its undivided devotion to YHWH creates room for a king of God's own choosing and drawn from the citizenry. Undistracted by the seductive embellishments of royal privilege, this king will lead the people through his example of godly fear and obedience:

> When he has taken the throne of his kingdom, he shall have a copy of this law written for him in the presence of the levitical priests. It shall remain with him and he shall read in it all the days of his life, so that he may learn to fear the LORD his God, diligently observing all the words of this law and these statutes, neither exalting himself above other members of the community nor turning aside from the commandment, either to the right or to the left, so that he and his descendants may reign long over his kingdom in Israel. (Deut. 17:18–20)

The king serving within the terms of the constitutional theocracy was, in sum, a faithful servant chosen by God from among his people to lead them unpretentiously and reverently before God and in obedience to God's will. But an important question follows: what office is responsible for mediating and interpreting the law, which a leader (whether king or judge) in solidarity with all the people was to follow? Moses was of course the model mediator of the Torah, and after his death Joshua inherited his mantle. But what of the subsequent generations envisioned by the Deuteronomists? What about the instances in which specific judges like Abimelech and Jephthah overreached the terms of their charismatic calling and cases where kings like Solomon, Ahab, and Manasseh *mis*ruled Israel by exalting themselves above their subjects and breaking the commandments? Who would there be in the land to renew God's word and hold kings and subjects to account?

These serious questions were addressed in Deuteronomy 18: "I will raise up for them a prophet like you from among their own people; I will put my words in the mouth of the prophet, who shall speak to them everything that I command" (18:18). Through the office of *prophet* the Torah would be defended against lapsing into desuetude and exploitation by opportunistic rulers. God would continue to speak with authority, and true to the strict conditions of the covenant, "[a]nyone who does not heed the words that the prophet shall speak in my name, I [YHWH] myself will hold accountable" (18:19).

Even as the Deuteronomists were conscious of the possibility of kings abusing their office, they were also aware of the precarious nature of human mediation of divine words. First they warn against pagan forms of divination (18:9–14), then denounce false prophets arising within Israel itself (18:19–22). Interesting to note is the historical sense visible in the Deuteronomist's warnings. In the case of the law of kingship, the abuses cited mirror the high-handed court style of Solomon. In the case of prophecy, history again was a reliable tutor, for it reminded them of the abominations of Mesha, king of Moab, as well as the false oracles spoken by some of Israel's own prophets.

Also included in their statutes concerning the forms of office compatible with a constitutional theocracy were laws pertaining to the duties of priests, judges, appellate courts, and warriors. In each case, offices and institutions were shaped by the overarching principle of God's rule over Israel.

Rather than extending to these other offices the discussion regarding mediation, we turn to the theme that captures the heart of Deuteronomic polity more than any other, namely, egalitarian justice as the expression of true worship. Its importance stems from both its historical roots and its eschatological orientation. It is rooted in the community's memory of God's saving actions on their behalf, and it anticipates the time when all God's people would be obedient to the commandments.

The roots of the moral code forming the heart of the theocratic charter are beautifully described in Deuteronomy 10:17–21:

> For the LORD your God is God of gods and Lord of lords, the great God, mighty and awesome, who is not partial and takes no bribe, who executes justice for the orphan and the widow, and who loves the strangers, providing them food and clothing. You shall also love the stranger, for you were strangers in the land of Egypt. You shall fear the LORD your God; him alone you shall worship; to him you shall hold fast, and by his name you shall swear. He is your praise; he is your God, who has done for you these great and awesome things that your own eyes have seen.

In discussing Israel's earliest formulation of Torah, the Book of the Covenant in Exodus 21–23, we noted how the motive clauses concluding several Yahwistic laws traced to God's saving acts the behavior expected of Israelites toward foreigners, widows, and orphans. In the above passage, the source is traced back one step further, to the God of gods himself, "who is not partial and takes no bribe, who executes justice for the orphan and the widow, and who loves strangers, providing them food and clothing." To be sure, God in the Bible does many other things as well, but in focusing specifically on God's impartiality and God's loving care for the most vulnerable members of the human family, *egalitarian ethics* becomes the living heart of the theocratic charter. The God who loves strangers becomes your inspiration to do likewise. Thus on the deepest level, love of neighbor reaches back to its source: "You shall fear the LORD your God, him alone you shall worship; to him you shall hold fast" (Deut. 10:20). The fabric of human relations, assailed by selfishness and sin, finds the promise of healing in God's lavish love.

The living Torah, whose roots are traced to the very heart of God, also reaches toward the day of fulfillment. It is not surprising that the most magnificent formulation of fulfillment of the covenant promise is found in Jeremiah, the prophetic book with the strongest ties to Deuteronomy:

> The days are surely coming, says the LORD, when I will make a new covenant with the house of Israel and the house of Judah. It will not be like the covenant that I made with their ancestors when I took them by the hand to bring them out of the land of Egypt—a covenant that they broke. . . . But this is the covenant that I will make with the house of Israel after those days, says the LORD: I will put my law within them, and I will write it on their hearts; and I will be their God, and they shall be my people. (Jer. 31:31–33)

Later in our study, we shall see how, even when more regressive policies and institutions were imposed on the nation, the theocratic ideals ensconced in the Epic could not be extinguished, but were reformulated poetically in classics like Psalm 103 and the Song of Moses (Deut. 32:1–43), in elaborations on the motifs of Sabbath and jubilee (Isa. 56:1–7 and 61:1–3) and in prophetic visions of the return of a faithful Israel to God and the restoration of the blessings of the covenant (Jer. 31:1–14). Even kings, who by dint of their lineage and office were disposed to replace egalitarian structures with elitist prerogatives, were obliged to accommodate to grassroots reform movements or experience the censure of citizens and their prophetic advocates empowered by the theocratic conviction that their ultimate allegiance was exclusively to one sovereign.

THE THEOCRATIC PRINCIPLE AND CHARISMATIC RULE

The concept of theocracy that arose in early Israel bears the marks of a political initiative shaped by powerful new experiences, experiences through which a diverse body of peasants and outcasts were introduced to the sovereign of all creation. From that introduction arose a powerful lesson that placed an indelible stamp on a community's view of politics and government: only one leader was deserving of *ultimate* allegiance, namely, the God who had delivered them from the bondage of earthly tyrants and called them into existence as a nation. Pragmatically speaking, human leadership of some sort was necessary, but it would have to be shaped in such a way that the supremacy of the divine leader was not placed in jeopardy.

Leadership, therefore, would be construed in a provisional manner, its lineaments inevitably influenced by historical situation and zeitgeist. The brief description of the judge Jephthah that introduces his tragic story illustrates this point with stark clarity: "Now Jephthah the Gileadite, the son of a prostitute, was a mighty warrior" (Judg. 11:1). The fact that he was of disreputable pedigree and had been denied inheritance in his father's house did not annul the quality Israel's current crisis required; whatever his background, he was a mighty warrior manifesting divine charisma that equipped him to serve as YHWH's agent in delivering endangered Israel. From this rough-hewn starting point began a long political process of defining the qualities of leadership implied by the theocratic principle of God's sole sovereignty, qualities never abstracted from the concrete situation at hand.

The specific form of leadership arising from tribal Israel's embryonic theocratic perspective was charismatic leadership, and it preserved with elemental clarity the concept of a people led by its deity. To be acceptable to a community founded on theocratic principles, the limited, mediating status of leadership would have to be manifest. Such an ideology understandably proved to be very resistant to the dynastic principle of succession that is inherent in monarchy, since dynastic succession conforms to biological determinacy rather than to divine intent.

Against the background of the theocratic understanding of divine rulership, it is easy to understand the fluidity with which descriptions of battle move from valorization of human figures (Judg. 5:7, 24) to description of direct divine involvement (Judg. 5:20, 23). Also intrinsic to the theocratic worldview, whether early (Judg. 5:4–5, 9) or late (the Dead Sea sectarian work *War between the Sons of Light and the Sons of Darkness*), is the belief that the participation of humans in war was limited to assisting the Divine Warrior and his heavenly hosts. From this followed the law of continence for warriors both in the ancient Hebrew law and at Qumran, for those who fought in the presence of angels had to maintain the purity of their heavenly cocombatants.

Congruous with the ad hoc nature of a charismatically empowered militia is the lack of formal structures of rank or division of function into rigid specializations. The volunteers responding to the call to war are farmers, herders, traders, and they include both women and men. Priestly leadership is not monopolized by an elite guild, but is quite open to anyone demonstrating the requisite skills and charisma. Lacking centralized authority, leaders cannot coerce the clans into the field of battle, but they must depend on the persuasion of the shared divine Spirit and the curses stipulated by the covenant. The picture that emerges, both regarding the spontaneity of the divine Spirit and the lack of the "routinization" typical of more developed forms of governance, resembles what Max Weber called "charismatic" leadership.[41]

---

41. Max Weber, *Ancient Judaism*, trans. H. H. Gerth and D. Martindale (London: Collier Macmillan, 1967), 17–19, 294.

It is on the basis of that resemblance that we have designated Israel's first polity as charismatic rule, recognizing it to be a model of governance shaped by early Israel's foundational theocratic principle, namely, that ultimately Israel could acknowledge but one ruler and that the legitimacy of those who mediated divine sovereignty through human offices and institutions derived exclusively from divine appointment and faithful adherence to the will of God.

It was perhaps inevitable that a certain degree of routinization emerged as the tribes struggled to preserve their identity amid competing claims to both their territory and their national autonomy. The transition to more permanent, fixed structures did not wait for the institution of kingship, as if on the day that Saul was enthroned, Israel suddenly moved from the freedom of the Spirit to the rigidity of centralized rule. Granted, Gideon is reported to have refused the offer of kingship, purportedly in deference to YHWH's sole claim, but at the same time the eventual desire of the people for a permanent form of human rule is anticipated by growing restiveness and dissatisfaction with the character and accomplishments of those officiating as charismatic leaders.

What happens when a charismatic leader's mustering of the tribes fails to safeguard the security and autonomy of the tribes? Who is to be held responsible for the climate of anarchy when tribes begin to battle against one another? Who deals with the issue of alleged misconduct of priests and their heirs or the sons of the presiding judge? The pithy refrain placed by the redactors of the league traditions in the middle and at the end of their account of premonarchic Israel captures the ambiguity of the ad hoc structures of charismatic rule: "In those days there was no king in Israel; all the people did what was right in their own eyes" (Judg. 17:6; 21:25). While constituting good news at times when the free and equally-available-to-all Spirit is maintaining harmony among the clans, the same characterization becomes ominous in times of discord such as is described in the last three chapters of the book of Judges.

The tendency among some biblical scholars (e.g., George Mendenhall and Norman Gottwald) to describe the league and the monarchy as diametrical opposites and to attach a positive value judgment to the former and a negative to the latter both oversimplifies the biblical evidence and paves the way for a misappropriation of their scholarly arguments by those seeking to draw inferences for contemporary debates. On the eve of the Israelite monarchy, a considerable degree of centralization already had developed within both the priesthood and the office of judge. The hereditary principle seemed to have emerged in both. In the case of the priesthood, the Levites had established authoritative claims, and Eli's sons, before they sullied their family image, seemed positioned to inherit the office of their father (1 Sam. 2:12). First Samuel 8:1–3 indicates that Samuel's sons similarly were set to succeed their father. Against this background, it seems prudent to view the introduction of kingship as the culmination of a longer process of centralization and diversification of roles in a society that was moving toward greater complexity and being forced by hostile encounters with other cultures to develop a suitable political apparatus and military capability.

Indeed, it was the encounter with the highly centralized and sophisticated military might of the Philistines that provided the specific catalyst for change.

On the other side of the divide between the league and the monarchy, one also encounters transition rather than a sharp break. Saul and David were both designated for office after the manner of the earlier charismatic leaders, and both continued to utilize the services of a voluntary militia, though David moved increasingly toward a professional army as well as other institutions associated with monarchy. It is also important to note that the view propounded by G. Ernest Wright that David and Solomon supplanted the basic structure of clan organization when they rationalized the tribal territories into twelve districts, each capable of providing the required revenue for one month of the year, has been called into question by Lawrence E. Stager on the basis of eighth-century receipts for wine deliveries to the royal warehouses made by clans in the area of Samaria.[42] It has become clear that the dimorphic model that sheds light on the nature of the clans of the earlier confederacy continued to some extent to shape the political and economic structures of villages in the monarchy period. Clearly, the supersessionist model popular in earlier scholarly literature must be abandoned in favor of a more nuanced picture of transition.

From the political complexity that characterized both the waning hours of Israel's first polity and the early years of monarchy arises a warning to anyone interested in the bearing of biblical politics on the modern world: rather than idealize one form of governance over another, one must follow the more difficult path of evaluating each form of government that arose in Israel against the foundational theocratic principle of the sole sovereignty of God and the ensuing mandate of suitable mediation. What we have discovered in our examination of charismatic rule will recur as we move on to the other models of governance that were to emerge over the course of biblical history. No model proved to be perfect. Rather, each served as the stage upon which flesh-and-blood rulers and their subjects struggled with the challenge of acknowledging one sovereign while simultaneously mediating divine purpose within the ambiguities of human institutions.

THE PLACE OF CHARISMATIC RULE WITHIN THE LARGER PICTURE OF POLITICAL MODELS IN THE BIBLE

In a break with the mythopoetically based political ideologies of the ancient Near East, early Israel came to discern the origins of political institutions and social structures within the context of human history, rather than in the timeless realm of the gods. The resulting historiographic perspective was not a thin view of events filtering out all traces of transcendence, mystery, and the miraculous,

---

42. Lawrence E. Stager, "The Patrimonial Kingdom of Solomon," in *Symbiosis, Symbolism, and the Power of the Past*, ed. W. G. Dever and S. Gitin (Winona Lake, IN: Eisenbrauns, 2003), 68.

but one from which reverent observers recognized a pattern of divine intentionality. What is more, the deity thus revealed was not an impersonal force, but one manifesting the qualities of a beneficent redeemer, qualities such as compassion, evenhanded justice, and faithfulness to those responding to his initiative.[43] Specifically in the experience of deliverance from slavery to freedom that we call the exodus, early Israel witnessed quintessentially the qualities of the God by whom it felt drawn into a life-giving and community-building covenant.

Accompanying this historical understanding of the relation of the divine realm to human existence was a radically new understanding of the process by which political institutions were built and codes of moral conduct were constructed. Leadership did not come down from heaven in the form of divine kingship. Economic structures and laws were not lapidary transcriptions of an otherworldly template. What we find instead is a community developing structures of governance and ethical norms patterned after the mercy and evenhanded justice of the deity who saved them from bondage. The laws that ordered their life as a nation were translations into historical realities of the divine attributes to which they owed their very existence. YHWH was a God showing compassion to the outcasts of the earth and evenhanded justice to the oppressed, and from the story of his beneficent acts they were to draw the qualities that were to shape their communal identity, social values, and institutions.

The resulting process for constructing political institutions was inferential in nature; that is, Israel as the people of YHWH was to be a people embodying YHWH's justice and compassion in all aspects of its existence. Its laws were to be consistent with the mercy and righteousness of the One who brought it from slavery to freedom. Its social and economic structures were to embody the attributes of the loving Father who showed equal favor to all of his children. The structure of governance by which its political existence was to be ordered was to amplify the *ultimate* allegiance it reserved exclusively for the sovereign One. This means that it was to take its place within the family of nations as a theocracy, a theocracy, that is, in the ultimate sense of a people acknowledging only one ultimate authority. Penultimately, the institutional structures through which *divine* rule would be mediated in any given period were to be congruous with prevailing cultural realities and historical circumstances.

Earliest Israel's forging the theocratic principle into charismatic rule can be seen as a fitting mediation of God's sovereign rule, inasmuch as it was both sociologically congruent with the tribal origins of the Hebrews and politically sensitive to their visceral opposition to the unbridled power of despotic kings. But does it follow that earliest Israel should serve politically as a model for all future ages? Conceivably one could elicit support for this position by referring to Jeremiah's rather idealistic reference to Israel's youth (Jer. 2:1–8) and to the faithfulness of the Rechabites (Jer. 35:12–17). But the flaw inherent in the

---

43. The depiction of Boaz, redeemer of Ruth, can help the modern reader conceptualize the social reality from which the picture of YHWH as divine redeemer arises.

golden-age hermeneutic is fatal. It conflates the provisional structure of charismatic rule with the foundational biblical principle of theocracy, that is, God's ultimate sovereign rule. The former is one of many models of mediation found in the Bible; the latter is the standard against which all such models are judged.

This distinction is one that will accompany us into the next chapter and through all of the subsequent chapters of part 2, for it is inherent in a worldview at the center of which is a God encountered within the ambiguities of human existence. While God's rule is enduring through all ages, the legal, political, and economic structures arising within Israel's covenant relationship with God were not immutable, but responsive to the changing circumstances of history. Thus an understanding of tradition developed in which "the former things" did not contain the final word, but provided the basis from which the new could arise.

Key to this worldview was memory, for memory of God's saving acts in the past fostered growth of an account of origins in the form of a national Epic, an account that, due to its historical and hence unfinished nature, maintained an openness to things to come. Such is the nature of a historical understanding of being (ontology) or, in plain language, of identity understood in terms of story.

The next chapter will explore a dramatic example of the effects of the influence of early Israel's theo-political tradition of theocracy and the inevitability of change that is intrinsic to the biblical understanding of divine-presence-in-the-messy-stuff-of-human-existence. Charismatic rule as a political model was forced to yield to a polity capable of dealing with a radically changed historical situation, namely, the political model of monarchy. Due to the codification of the theocratic principle in the Epic and the Torah, monarchy would be refashioned into a form that broke in fundamental ways with the royal ideology of the dominant empires of the ancient world. Thus it is that in the next chapter and those that follow we will find tradition construed as continuity and change persisting in its dynamic process of growth, proving that biblical politics is an agile phenomenon that will never lie quietly in the coffins into which the dogmatically minded seek to place it.

Manifesting the sensitivity to the dynamic of continuity and change on the part of the ancient tradents of Scripture is the location they chose for one of the most exquisite formulations of the political ideal of theocracy: at the vortex of the struggle between the passing regime of Israel's last judge, Samuel, and the rule of the first one to be anointed as a king, Saul son of Kish. Witness the shimmering power of the Song of Hannah in 1 Samuel 2:

> The bows of the mighty are broken,
>   but the feeble gird on strength.
> Those who were full have hired themselves out for bread,
>   but those who were hungry are fat with spoil.
> The barren has borne seven,
>   but she who has many children is forlorn.
> The LORD kills and brings to life;
>   he brings down to Sheol and raises up.

The LORD makes poor and makes rich;
   he brings low, he also exalts.
He raises up the poor from the dust;
   he lifts the needy from the ash heap,
to make them sit with princes
   and inherit a seat of honor.

                            (1 Sam. 2:4–8a)

As a revered monument to the discovery of a radically new way to structure a society, the Song of Hannah has stood tall through the ages, frequently assailed by "the mighty" as they schemed to reintegrate "the feeble" into their self-aggrandizing initiatives, but defiantly offering inspiration and empowerment to those remembering the God who "raises up the poor from the dust." So it stood with its proclamation of liberty throughout the era of the kings of Judah and Israel. Thus it was to stand and continue to bear witness to the God of the poor and needy during another era of foreign domination, its message once again proclaimed by a brave handmaiden of the Lord (Luke 1:46–55).

Chapter 11

Monarchy

"Like the Other Nations"

THE PRESSURES OF A RAPIDLY CHANGING WORLD

The reconstruction presented in this chapter should not be confused with a widely accepted understanding of Israel's second form of governance, monarchy, that presents this clear dichotomy: while the charismatic rule of the judges gave authentic political expression to Mosaic religion, monarchy was an alien importation, the noxious by-product of Israel's being lured away from her true religious nature into the alien polity of pagan neighbors.

The appeal inherent in this romantic, nostalgic interpretation is undeniable and is reflected even in biblical passages like Jeremiah 2 and Hosea 11, where the early relationship between YHWH and his people is painted in hues bespeaking innocence, intimacy, and trust. While historical scrutiny mandates a more nuanced interpretation, deconstruction of a romance must not be carried so far as to obscure the grain of truth it contains: From Israel's earliest encounters with the deliverer God YHWH, the young nation inferred a theo-political principle that defined its essential character for all time: the principle of theocracy declaring that Israel was to acknowledge the ultimate authority of only one ruler, YHWH. However, beyond the preservation of that principle—narratively in an

Epic and politically in a covenant formulary—Israel in the time of charismatic leaders struggled with mixed results to implement God's rule within mundane structures capable of mediating rather than distorting divine rule.

What we take with us from the previous chapter, then, is not a portrait of the Bible's ideal and eternally normative concept of human government, but a bold inference drawn from a life-changing experience that birthed a principle guiding all future biblically based political reflection: the universe is ruled not by the pharaoh and his divine sponsors, but by a God whose nature is disclosed historically in the merciful deliverance of slaves and whose temporal rule is mediated by a people responding in worshipful gratitude by embodying God's compassionate justice in their structures of governance.

Against this background the period of monarchy comes to be understood not as a fall from dreaming innocence, but as a second step in Israel's ongoing task of crafting a mode of community befitting a people whose ultimate government is God's universal rule. This step would be taken in a changing world presenting new challenges in the swirl of which one governing reality alone would remain constant: God's comprehensive sovereignty. Because of the sovereign's choice to draw humans as covenanted partners in the implementation of divine rule in human society, however, Israel would enter the new chapter of her history equipped with neither a timeless political handbook nor a definitive institutional blueprint. Rather, she would be invited to renew her singular commitment to God and to express her loyalty politically through the ongoing task of patterning laws and judicial structures after God's justice and mercy, cultivating economic structures that safeguard the well-being of vulnerable members of society, and implementing political policies capable of safeguarding God's rule from the desecration and idolatry of imposters and tyrants.

In essence, then, our treatment of monarchy will be guided by the same interrogation as the one that is followed in our previous discussion of charismatic rule and will be continued later as we trace the long path through yet other forms of governance. The lead question will not be whether monarchy categorically was a suitable form of government in Iron Age Israel, but in what ways and during which periods it adhered to or violated the central Yahwistic imperative of compliance with the universal rule of one true sovereign. The evidence that will carry weight will be drawn primarily from sources found in the Bible itself, a procedure entailing no small challenge, given the complexity of the composition history of the Bible. The methodology we shall follow will continue to be the one described above (chap. 9).

Regarding biblical sources relevant to the study of the kings of Israel, paramount importance is to be ascribed to the Deuteronomistic History (DH). While in its canonical form stemming from the time of Josiah's reign (the latter half of the seventh century BCE), DH encompasses seven books (Deuteronomy through 2 Kings, the book of Ruth being a later addition). Close literary analysis has uncovered signs of a complex history of compilation and redaction that includes incorporation of the Deuteronomic Law (Dtr) as an introduction with hymnic and narrative sources serving as integral parts of a final composition unified around the twin themes of divine anointment of David as king and the choice of Jerusalem as home for the nation's central sanctuary.

Our use of DH necessitates distinguishing between two dimensions, namely, materials deemed reliable as sources for historical reconstruction and themes revealing the historiographic and theo-political perspectives of both the Deuteronomistic Historians and the authors of the sources upon which they draw. Though distinguishing between them is more an art than a science, the fact that both dimensions, each in its own way, contributes to our investigation of politics in the Bible leaves us with no option other than proceeding in full knowledge that fellow scholars will not hesitate to subject to rigorous scrutiny what inevitably remain tentative conclusions.

THE SITUATION CIRCA 1000 BCE

Intermittently over the course of some two hundred years leading up to the first millennium BCE, Israelite peasants were compelled to leave flocks, vineyards, and fields to muster in defense of the threatened territory of a member clan. As we discovered in the preceding chapter, this informal arrangement worked relatively well. A member of the clan, indistinguishable from the others except perhaps for a reputation of uncommon strength and courage, would rise to the occasion, lead the volunteers against the invaders, and reestablish conditions conducive for the resumption of normal activities such as dry farming on the mountain terraces and trade of commodities between sister villages. Some of the more spectacular victories, such as the one accomplished against the daunting force of Canaanite royal chariotry (Judg. 5), were preserved in hymnic-epic form. Normally, however, the invaders faced by the volunteers of the league were not the professional armies of kings, but either seminomadic bands, like the Amalekites sweeping down to raid the fields of their more settled neighbors, or members of leagues similar to Israel's, like the Ammonites attacking from their east Jordanian settlements. The biblical narrative reports battles with such adversaries in the form of prose narratives embellished by legendary elements.

Each victory during the premonarchic period served to validate the political structure and religious ideology of the Israelite confederation. To YHWH alone was ascribed kingship, and to YHWH were sung hymns of praise for his intervention as Divine Warrior to deliver his people from the threat of enemies. Indeed, many archaic biblical texts can best be situated in the league sanctuaries, where the clans gathered to affirm their common identity as a people created and sustained by YHWH the Warrior (Exod. 15:3; cf. Num. 10:35–36; Deut. 33:2; Judg. 5:4–5). The texts also leave no doubt that the Divine Warrior expected the wholehearted participation of the able-bodied in the field of battle (Judg. 5:9, 23) and the unwavering loyalty of the entire community to his sovereignty. To that end, YHWH raised up charismatic warriors in times of crisis to save the "people of YHWH" from annihilation. The final editors of Judges 2–16 schematized the stories about judges available to them according to a theological pattern: a charismatic leader led the people in defeating their enemy/they enjoyed a period of peace/they broke faith with their divine sovereign by worshiping other deities/they fell prey to another enemy/the chastened people cried out to YHWH, who raised up another charismatic leader. Their pattern serves well as a précis of Israel's first polity and its mixed theo-political legacy.

The Israelites living on the eve of the transformation from a charismatic to a monarchic regime (ca. 1000 BCE) likely would not have been aware of being poised on the threshold of epoch-making change. Since the time of Deborah and Gideon, accommodations gradually had been made that nudged the governance of the land toward a higher degree of centralization and role differentiation. A priestly class, the Levites, had become established, and both the presiding judge and the high priest had managed to establish right of succession for their offspring. But life was still ordered primarily along the lines of family and clans, and threats to the security of any tribe continued to be answered by the mustering of the volunteer army.

It would be fallacious indeed to assume that charismatic rule as an expression of theocracy functioned without problems. Traces of defection from YHWH worship to the local Canaanite deities are scattered throughout the narratives. For example, to Gideon's father is attributed both an altar dedicated to Baal and his son's pagan name Jerubbaal ("Baal contends"). When one recalls that the primary unifying factor among the Hebrew clans was allegiance to the YHWH cult, it becomes clear that adherence to Canaanite cult practices inevitably raised the specter of political defection and collapse of shared identity; that is, it represented nothing less than a frontal assault on the theocratic principle that defined Israel as a people.

Moreover, by placing stories of brutal intertribal conflict at the end of the book of Judges, the editors suggested that the centrifugal forces that were present within the loose confederation of freedom-loving tribes were threatening to unravel any remaining semblance of unity, thereby calling into question the adequacy of charismatic rule as a mediating instrument of divine rule. For the reader who missed that point, those editors inserted in the final chapters as a leitmotif the phrase, "In those days there was no king in Israel" (Judg. 17:6; 18:1; 19:1; 21:25), with the following apodosis added in envelope fashion in 17:6 and then in the verse that concludes the book of Judges, "all the people did what was right in their own eyes" (21:25). Israel's experiment with charismatic rule as a viable instrument for mediating divine sovereignty was ending with a drift toward anarchy!

ISRAEL BECOMES A MONARCHY

The unraveling of the unity earlier forged in response to military crises could not have come at a less opportune moment in history. Samuel had the ill fortune of holding the office of judgeship at a time when the entire eastern Mediterranean was reeling under the impact of a new political force, fugitives from the crumbling Mycenaean civilization of the Peloponnesus and the Aegean islands. These marauders were led by a professionally trained and well-equipped soldiery. The cohort that settled on the coast adjacent to Israelite territory, the Philistines, organized themselves as a federation of five city-states, each under a tyrant-king. Then they set out to expand their territory. With their backs to the Mediterranean Sea, there was only one point on the compass toward which they could direct their aggrandizing initiatives. Thus began the war between the Philistines and Israel.

From the beginning the Philistines proved to be in possession of more advanced military technology and tactics than their adversaries. The Israelites fought in the old style with their volunteer army, but regardless of their cries to heaven, they were no match against professional armies organized under tyrant kings. This sad contrast is reflected in an archaic source incorporated by the Deuteronomic Historians, the so-called ark narrative.[1] As narrated in 1 Samuel 4, the Israelites, after a catastrophic initial engagement, brought into battle the most potent weapon within their arsenal, the ark of the covenant, that is, the palladium representing the throne upon which their Divine Warrior YHWH was invisibly enthroned. It was a sign of the desperateness of the situation that the nation swearing fealty to one sovereign increased the stakes to the ultimate. The contest would be one between the respective deities of the contending sides—from Israel's perspective, between true God and imposter. The test of the viability of the institutions of the league under vastly changed circumstances was at hand as YHWH encountered the Philistine god Dagon.

The outcome of the battle was calamitous. Not only were the Israelites defeated in a second great slaughter, but also the ark of the covenant was taken hostage and placed in the temple of Dagon. The narrative reporting these events in 1 Samuel 4 is loaded with ominous signs. Eli, the priest of the central sanctuary in Shiloh, died upon hearing the news of the ark's capture and the death in battle of his two sons. The same grave tidings, when heard by the pregnant wife of one of those sons, induced the birth of an infant whom she ominously named Ichabod, meaning, "The glory has departed [from Israel]."

The story of the life of the godly last judge of the league concludes on a brighter note with the aging leader regaining the lost territory of Israel. As for the ark of Israel's God, it proved to be an unwilling and vexatious hostage. Wherever it was lodged in the Philistine pentapolis, it wreaked havoc. Finally, the Philistines returned it to Israel, replete with guilt offerings to placate the wrath of YHWH. The colorful ark narrative comes to a conclusion with the holy object coming to rest at Kiriath-jearim, after which, according to 1 Samuel 7:2, "a long time passed, some twenty years." Israel's history at that point appears to be left hanging in a state of suspension.

1. See Patrick D. Miller Jr. and J. J. M. Roberts, *The Hand of the Lord: A Reassessment of the "Ark Narrative" of 1 Samuel* (Baltimore: Johns Hopkins University Press, 1977).

The plot takes a significant turn with the opening of 1 Samuel 8. The judge is old, his sons have succeeded him, but they "did not follow in his ways." Strains and stresses have begun to appear that jeopardize not only the confederacy but also the theocratic principle of God's sovereign reign over the Hebrew nation. The affiliated clans have narrowly escaped extermination under the assault of a military threat that their rather primitive political organization was ill equipped to repulse. To be sure, moves had been underway for some time to provide a steadier, more centralized leadership. Both the priestly office and that of judge had evolved into a hereditary structure. But military defense still relied on voluntary contributions from the clans for both personnel and materiel. To make matters worse, the new generation poised to inherit the offices of judgeship and priesthood was besmirched by charges of corruption.

The succeeding episode practically writes itself. The elders representing the clans have convened their council and brought this request to Samuel: "Appoint for us . . . a king to govern us, like other nations" (1 Sam. 8:5). One can guess their reasoning: With hereditary succession already in place but qualified to such an extent as to exclude its chief benefits, why not take the final step to civil maturity? They would continue to be organized under a paterfamilias, with the only difference being the more centralized manner of his organizing the military and the economy. By adopting monarchy, Israel would join the family of nations as a full-fledged member. Its ruler would become endowed with exceptional attributes and the authority befitting his office.

It is not difficult to understand Samuel's demurral. The prestige of his family, within a culture placing great value on family reputation, was at stake; but beneath issues of clan custom lurks the deeper religious principle of theocracy and unrivaled divine authority. To be sure, the solidarity of the clans was tied to a traditional patriarchal structure of organization. But from earliest times, the ability of the freedom-loving clans to overcome natural centrifugal tendencies by mustering behind a common cause was grounded in a pantribal acknowledgment of one *divine* patriarch. Therefore a critical theological question undergirded the political ferment: Would giving up the polity of the tribal confederacy threaten the authority of Israel's supernal divine King, thereby undercutting Israel's distinct values and beliefs and finally nullifying the common identity that was the foundation of her national viability? Samuel's self-pity thus yields to a divine word that meets this deeper question: "they have not rejected you, but they have rejected me from being king over them" (v. 7). In the narrative of 1 Samuel 8, in which Kyle McCarter has correctly detected the concerns of the prophetic circles that preserved and shaped the traditions of the transition period, the central theocratic principle of early Israel was revisited: kingship in Israel ultimately and rightfully could be invested in one figure alone, YHWH.

A critical question thus arose for the people of Israel. What would the introduction of monarchy as the official form of government entail for the religious and cultural values of the nation? Clearly, in light of the ubiquity of claims to divinity among the kings of the empires of that time, it entailed the danger of an alien notion encroaching upon the central religious belief of the people of Israel, the belief that there could be only one absolute authority in the land. Would that authority be compromised by a mortal claiming by dint of office to enjoy a relation with the deity categorically different from that of his subjects?

Samuel was instructed to give a divine warning concerning the system of governance demanded by the people. He detailed for them the *mišpaṭ hammelek*, the royal ordinance that the king would enforce (1 Sam. 8:11–17). Contained therein were regulations intrinsic to a centralized regime with a professional standing army and a bureaucracy in charge of administering the diverse aspects of government. They fall under the two basic categories of taxation and conscription. For the added security and convenience of having a central bureaucracy performing tasks that under the theocratic league had fallen upon the citizens themselves, the people had to be prepared to give up basic rights and freedoms. Their response to Samuel's warning was emphatic and to the point: "we are determined to have a king over us, so that we also may be like other nations, and that our king may govern us and go out before us and fight our battles" (1 Sam. 8:19–20).

The trade-off probably seemed reasonable, amounting to a political quid pro quo. Yet an ominous chord is struck at the end of the list of regulations in the royal ordinance: "And in that day you will cry out because of your king, whom you have chosen for yourselves; but the LORD will not answer you in that day" (8:18). This can be recognized as a warning reflecting the prophetic conviction that adoption of the seemingly attractive innovation of monarchy would be fraught with danger. The sentence contains a clear allusion to the religious Epic of the people of YHWH, for both in the narrative in Exodus (Exod. 2:23; 3:7; cf. 6:5) and in later recitations of the Epic themes (Deut. 26:6–7; 1 Sam. 12:8–10; cf. Judg. 6:7–10; 10:10–16), the people cry out from their oppression, and YHWH hears their cry and responds in mercy. Israel's very identity as a people was predicated on the direct access that the people had to their God. The political move to kingship would place in jeopardy this essential relationship. The immediacy of contact between the God YHWH and his "people Israel" would be supplanted by an indirect connection, due to the interjection of kingship. While the charismatic judge was an ordinary citizen raised from the ranks of the people to address a crisis and then permitted to revert to the routine of everyday life once the situation returned to normal, the king was viewed as belonging to a category distinct from average humanity.

Clearly the terms of mediation that had evolved in the era of the judges were undergoing a categorical transformation. Under the influence of the widespread ancient Near Eastern ideology of absolute kingship, kings in Israel would be enticed to claim a special relationship to God and a royal covenant that introduced exceptions to the Mosaic covenant that bound *every* Israelite, *including* the king, to strict conditions set down by YHWH. They would preside over the cultic apparatus and its priestly personnel and, in violation of the authority reserved for God alone, shield their authority from public scrutiny and reproof.

Having transgressed the threshold of transparency, Israel's kings could find it expedient to move in the direction of claiming the divine attributes that neighboring cultures such as that of Egypt attributed to their kings.[2] In following standard international protocol, they might well enter into trade arrangements and conclude military treaties that would be sealed with royal marriages that entailed the introduction of the foreign gods of the new princesses into the Israelite cult. The basic Israelite view that every citizen, including the nation's leaders, was equal in status under their divine suzerain could quickly vanish under the shadow of a king elevated above his subjects and given privileges and immunities enjoyed by no other human. Forms of mediation safeguarding God's exclusive sovereignty could fall prey to an idolatrous misappropriation of divine appointment. Samuel, anticipating the long line of prophets to follow, refused to allow the theocratic principle to be sacrificed on the altar of expediency without remonstration: "you shall be his slaves," he bluntly announced (1 Sam. 8:17).

With the ensuing institution and implementation of kingship, Israel evolved from a political standpoint in the direction of civil maturity. No longer were religion and state indivisible. No longer did military crises evoke the sense of the Divine Warrior's epiphany and the empowerment of one of the ordinary citizens to lead the nation with one will against the enemy. The people now had a king to oversee a rational ordering of the nation's resources, including the military resources of a standing army ready to answer the threats of enemy attack.

If this were the end of the matter, Israel very well may have become like the nations also in another respect, namely, by leaving behind only the traces typically uncovered by historians of other ancient cultures, such as fragments of royal annals imbedded in Hellenistic histories and the material remains unearthed by archaeologists. However, by the time of the transition to monarchy, Israel's collective memory had already been so deeply imprinted by distinctly indigenous motifs as to resist simple blending into the cultural horizon of ancient Near Eastern culture. A national Epic had begun to develop the characteristics of a sacred story with themes that could not be silenced, even under the pressure of tectonic shifts in the balance of imperial powers in the Levant.

A pivotal aspect of Samuel's role as depicted in the Samuel narrative was his advocacy on behalf of the Epic-grounded historical identity of Israel at the juncture between charismatic rule and monarchy. In contrast to the situation in a culture like ancient Sumer, kingship could not simply descend from heaven and be imposed as a timeless template on a submissive population. Treated as a historical institution, the product of human actors, it would be obliged to accommodate itself to Israel's historical ontology and work itself into the life of this people amid the tensions between hallowed traditions and new circumstances.

Those tensions left a distinct mark on the biblical narrative itself, enabling literary critics to identify three original accounts of Saul's ascension to kingship,

---

2. The Egyptian pharaoh was seen as the incarnation of the god Horus, the son of Osiris.

accounts intertwined by later editors, but distinguishable on the basis of their respective attitudes toward kingship. One account (1 Sam. 8; 10:17–27; 12) portrays kingship in a negative light. The other two valorize Saul as a leader chosen according to divine purpose (1 Sam. 9:1–10:16; 13:5–15 and 1 Sam. 11; 13:1–4, 16–23; 14). The tensions thus embedded in the biblical narrative underscore the fact that biblical politics is not exempt from the sociopolitical dynamics typically found within nation-states in times of crisis and transition.

In essence, the introduction of kingship returned Israel to its fundamental political question: could the theocratic principle of God's sole sovereignty be safeguarded by the reshaping of monarchy in such a way that the king did not usurp authority reserved for Israel's divine king? Stated positively, to what standards and limitations would a faithful king be bound? In the delicate task of defining the proper mediating role of the king and his officials, what influence would Israel's Epic have, especially with its description of the God who delivered slaves and who, in gathering them into peoplehood, presided over them as king, in order both to safeguard them from reenslavement and to restrain the self-aggrandizing initiatives of their leaders to enhance personal power through the exploitation and enslavement of others? Finally, was there, within the religious legacy bequeathed by early Yahwistic tradition, moral capital sufficient for the reshaping of monarchy into a structure of governance that was simultaneously politically viable and uncompromising in devotion to Israel's only true sovereign?

The prophetic source the Deuteronomists drew upon for this stage of their history portrays Samuel as the wise arbiter between the values of the ancestral Epic and Torah and the emerging structures of the new form of government (1 Sam. 12:19–25). The ruler who has succeeded him as chief political authority has been acclaimed king. The charismatic regime of Israel's judges has passed. But has this rendered the notion of no-king-but-YHWH passé? The people, chastened by strategic setbacks, come to Samuel and confess that their demanding a king was an act of sin. Samuel, while not denying that in this, as in almost everything else they have done, they have sinned, insists that a more fundamental principle is at stake:

> [D]o not turn aside from following YHWH, but serve YHWH with all your heart. . . . For YHWH will not cast away his people, for his great name's sake, because it has pleased YHWH to make you a people for himself. Moreover as for me, far be it from me that I should sin against YHWH by ceasing to pray for you; and I will instruct you in the good and the right way. Only fear YHWH, and serve him faithfully with all your heart; for consider what great things he has done for you. But if you still do wickedly, you shall be swept away, both you and your king. (1 Sam. 12:20–25)

Samuel's role in this passage reflects the prophetic perspective of the tradents who shaped the source used by the Deuteronomists. As with prescience and perspicuity he formulates an innovative political theology for the new era, he presages the wisdom and courage of the succession of faithful prophets who in future centuries would hold up leaders and their policies to the stringent standards of YHWH's universal rule. His theo-political strategy presumes human participation in the realm of politics. But it does not concede the fundamental biblical conviction that any regime other than God's sovereign rule is the product of human imperfection and in need of persistent, vigilant critique. From a modern political-scientific perspective, this may seem unnecessarily negative. But when understood historically, it proffers what is arguably the most profound truth that biblical theology contributes to political theory: *every human regime, however noble its objectives, is the construction of imperfect mortals,* or, stated in stark theological terms, is a product of sin. Especially when seduced into the snare of exceptionalism or succumbing to the hubris of nationalistic idolatry, the most advanced of all nations become capable of inflicting great harm.

One of the most important functions of religion in relation to government thus comes to expression more poignantly in the age of Samuel than at any earlier time in the history of human thought: authentic, unco-opted religion exposes every human institution to the judgment of an authority that transcends all human authorities. Out of this arises a critical function that no regime can be trusted to exercise upon itself, namely, the function of viewing government sub specie aeternitatis, thereby relativizing its authority and issuing a clear warning against the deification of land and people. Stated positively, it subsumes human government under the more comprehensive moral universe of divine government. In so doing, it faithfully discharges its solemn responsibility of reaffirming the theocratic foundation of political theory in the Bible.

Denying human government the right to claim absolute authority over citizens does not undermine the civic loyalty upon which social cohesiveness depends. Samuel is cast not only as prophetic guardian, but also as paragon of the true patriot: he will not cease to pray for the people, but will instruct them "in the good and the right way" (1 Sam. 12:23). He will bear witness to the integrity that forms the heart of a healthy nation. And he argues that the only way to avoid nationalistic idolatry and to maintain the sense of the good and the right is the way of fearing the only One who is entitled to ultimate devotion. For him worship, in the comprehensive sense of correctly identifying one's ultimate loyalty, secures the foundation for true citizenship.

Let us summarize the lessons taught by the Samuel narrative. A viable nation is one that recognizes its imperfections; restricts the authority of state and the loyalty required of citizens to penultimate concerns; honors as a fundamental right of all citizens freedom of conscience based on moral and spiritual convictions; and respects the role of religion, both to point to the only one with a legitimate claim to ultimate devotion and to repudiate as idolatrous those laying claim to unqualified allegiance as a prerogative of office.

The metamorphosis to monarchy did not happen all at once. We have already noted incremental moves toward greater centralization in the late league period. Gradual transition continued under Saul and David, with no indication of a sharp break with the past. In compliance with the theocratic principle, Israel's first two kings sought guidance for their actions by consulting the divine King. Neither secured royal control over the cult by building a temple, which in ancient Near Eastern cultures was the institution that provided the ritual basis for the divine rights of kings. To be sure, the winds of change were visible. Saul's ruthless attack on the priests of Nob can be read as part of the tendency of the new centralized institution to limit, control, or remove competing loci of distributed power (1 Sam. 22). And David, according to 2 Samuel 7, harbored the desire to build a temple and was dissuaded only by the prophetic word of Nathan, suggesting that the tradition of prophetic critique had taken root already during David's reign. In general, though, the basic structures of the league remained in force. It is significant, for example, that neither Saul nor David came to office through dynastic succession. In both cases appointment of the king followed the old league pattern of selection of a strong warrior manifesting evidence (*charismata*) of divine favor.

In the realm of military defense, lines of continuity are also evident. The Israelite campaign against the Ammonites in 1 Samuel 11 follows the battle plan of the league militia in every detail. Saul by all appearances is a new Gideon. He hears of the crisis as he works in the field, the spirit of God falls upon him, he cuts up and sends pieces of a yoke of oxen to the tribes as a signal to muster, after which the responding volunteers go on to defeat the enemy. The pattern conforms closely to the model of charismatic rule, save for the conclusion, in which a grateful populace proceeds to make "Saul king before YHWH in Gilgal" (1 Sam. 11:15).

The significance of that initiative to be sure is not trivial. For the first time, there are *two* kings in Israel. *How* the divine and human kings would negotiate their relationship became and was to remain a critical religious issue throughout the period of the monarchy.

On one side of the new delicate balance of power lay the deeply rooted theocratic principle that Israel could have only one king, the divine king YHWH. Though born of the Epic tradition of premonarchic Israel, this principle was not obliterated by the new political structures of the monarchy, but continued to be cultivated among a significant segment of the populace, whose identity continued to be shaped by family and clan. The resistance of the prophetic movement to what were regarded as the excesses of monarchy likely found support among those who continued to identify with the traditional clan alliances. It is therefore noteworthy that archaeological discoveries have produced impressive evidence of the persistence of clan identity during the period of Israelite monarchy.

What is now evident is that village and urban social systems were not mutually exclusive entities in monarchic Israel, but coexisted and continued to interact on many levels. For example, individual citizens identified themselves by their clan names at the same time that they paid homage to their king. This dual identity left its mark in eighth-century ostraca from the Samarian highlands recording the taxes-in-kind (wine and olive oil) paid by clan leaders to the crown. Clearly their local jurisdictions had not been nullified by the centralized structures of the monarchy.[3]

The other side of the balance of power was also formidable. Here lay the influence of the ancient Near Eastern tradition of absolute monarchy, buttressed by an elaborate myth-and-temple-ritual system that dramatized the intimate connection between patron deity and ruling king and drew a parallel between the patron god's ordering of the cosmos and the human monarch's managing the god's terrestrial estate. Essential to this ideology was an understanding of royal power not only as absolute but as guaranteed and enforced by the patron god of the state. Conflict between the two competing concepts of government, one nurtured among the clans and the other in the urban centers, was inevitable.

THE NATURE OF ISRAELITE MONARCHY

The form of monarchy introduced by Saul and shaped by David can be classified as limited monarchy. If caution is taken not to impose modern connotations on the word, it is also possible to speak of constitutional monarchy.

Limited or constitutional monarchy was the product of a pragmatic political compromise. Both Saul and David were recipients of divine charisma, evidenced by success in the field of battle. Alongside that indication of divine designation, enthronement required a second act, the consent of the people. The resulting kingship was contractual, with both king and people binding themselves to obligations.[4] The voice of the clans was not silenced in the monarchy, at least not in its fledgling stage.

In our discussion of this important juncture in Israel's history it may be helpful to recall the analogy drawn in part 1 between personal biography and the histories of nations. As in the story of a healthy individual, so too in the case of Israel's story, the legacy of the past could neither be denied nor uncritically imitated, but needed to be adapted to new circumstances that called for change. Internal pressures like population growth, conflict between the tribes arising from competing interests, developments in the direction of greater economic complexity and professional specialization, combined with external pressures like foreign aggression, international trade, and treaty arrangements, abetted at this time in Israel's history the need for a more centralized, complex organization of the nation's human capital and natural resources.

But rash change that obliterated well-established traditions and values, ignored the social and institutional structures of the clans, and repudiated the ancestral Epic could lead only to intolerable social dislocations and a threat to the sense of a shared identity that is essential to cohesion within a diverse

3. Lawrence E. Stager, "The Patrimonial Kingdom of Solomon," in *Symbiosis, Symbolism, and the Power of the Past*, ed. W. G. Dever and S. Gitin (Winona Lake, IN: Eisenbrauns, 2003), 63–74.

4. See Baruch Halpern, *The Constitution of the Monarchy in Israel* (Chico, CA: Scholars Press, 1987).

society. Thus those faithful to their ancestral faith, throughout the series of transitions—from charismatic league theocracy to united monarchy to divided monarchy to exilic community to priestly theocratic commonwealth—preserved the kinship-based notion from their earliest history that the entire nation was an extended family, descended from the twelve sons of the patriarch Jacob/Israel and living within a covenant with its only true king. According to this view, kingship had not descended "whole cloth" from heaven, but arose and developed in Israelite history as one in an ongoing series of events, each of which had to be integrated into the Epic of Israel as a "people of YHWH." How successfully the integration was accomplished would have major bearing on the outcome of the new institution of monarchy. Thus unfolded a challenge that was to accompany the nation throughout the four-century history of kingship in Israel.

CONSTITUTIONAL MONARCHY CODIFIED: DEUTERONOMY 17:14–20

For the religious leaders who codified the laws in the book of Deuteronomy, the shape taken by kingship in Israel was a matter too important to leave to chance. As with every other institution in the society, kingship had to conform to the terms of the covenant that bound YHWH and Israel as God and nation. Those terms were rooted in values that had become established in Israel long before the introduction of kingship, values that constituted the heart of Mosaic religion.

Deuteronomy17:14–20 accordingly set down the conditions that had to be met by Israel's kings if kingship was to pass the test as a form of mediation of divine rule that preserved the unqualified sovereignty of YHWH: the king must be a member of the community, and he must not acquire many wives or amass great wealth. In other words, all that would distract the king from devotion to YHWH was to be eschewed. Such prohibitions, however, merely served as preamble to a positive formulation of the key principle upon which all else depended: his attention was to remain focused on his fealty to *his* king and that king's will as recorded in the Torah, "so that he may learn to fear the LORD his God, diligently observing all the words of this law and these statutes, neither exalting himself above other members of the community nor turning aside from the commandment" (vv. 19–20). "Fear the LORD . . . observing all the words of this law": coming to expression in this couplet is the same theologoumenon as the one formulated in 1 Samuel 12, at the heart of which is commitment to God's sovereignty expressing itself in obedience to the Torah.

Noteworthy as well is the conjoining of the king's obedience to divine law and his solidarity with all members of the community, since it contradicts one of the cardinal features of ancient Near Eastern kingship, the sharp class distinction between monarch and common citizens, a distinction drawing its warrant from the mythic theme of the divine origins of kingship. Though adopting kingship "like other nations" (1 Sam. 8:5, 20), Israel was to set clearly before its kings the strict conditions implicit in the demand for ultimate and uncompromising devotion to the divine king, coupled with the acknowledgment of the equality before God of kings and their subjects.

The integration of the office of kingship into the covenantal value system of early Israel did not strip the king of the authority requisite for maintaining order in the nation. An indigenous principle of authority had developed and become well established among the clans during their two hundred years of confederation. Within the extended family (bēt ʾāb) the paterfamilias exercised authority over nuclear family members and all other adherents, including servants, in-laws, and religious functionaries. This authority was extended to the clan leader in his rule over the larger family of the village. The authority then reached further to the tribal head. As Lawrence Stager has pointed out, the further superimposition of the king over this entire nested system of authority fit quite naturally into the earlier clan-based social system.[5] In effect, at each level, the household simply grew in extent. The model of authority, however, remained constant on all levels, namely, authority exercised over members of one's household. This familial model reached its ultimate extension when applied to Israel's God and to the bēt YHWH, the house of YHWH, a term designating in a literal sense the temple in Jerusalem but metaphorically also applying to the people of Israel, for the temple was the seat of the deity's rule over the nation.

The potential source of tension between the clan-based model of society and the institution of kingship was the one identified clearly by the law of the king in Deuteronomy 17. According to the polity of the clans, the king, though situated as "father" of the largest in the series of nested households, nevertheless remained one citizen among his fellow citizens, with no distinction in status from anyone else in standing under the ultimate authority of the final head of household, YHWH. If the king encroached upon the sovereignty of this divine paterfamilias, by insulating himself from the laws binding on all citizens and by setting up his word and command as final and exempt from critique based on the traditional Yahwistic laws, the theocratic principle of the entire familial social structure was threatened, and the religious system that was intimately tied to that system was violated. In such cases, appeal had to be made to the legal sanctions that had existed since the beginning of the league, namely, those associated with the Mosaic covenant. But in an era when an alternate legal system, appealing to its special covenant and under the authority of the king, had been superimposed upon the older one, what recourse was available to those believing that the king and officials of the royal court had veered away from legitimate mediation of divine authority and thereby broken the original covenant made by God with his people?

---

5. Stager, oral communication.

THE PROPHETS: GUARDIANS OF THE
CONSTITUTIONAL RESTRAINTS ON MONARCHY

While the tribal system was still in force, judicial proceedings functioned as an integral part of kinship structure, with family heads handling local matters and the presiding judge handling intertribal conflicts (1 Sam. 7:15–17). With the introduction of kingship a serious question arose: who now would defend the traditional rights and freedoms of the people? No doubt, local disputes continued to be handled by the family heads. But who could function as public defender in cases involving encroachment on the rights of common citizens by opportunistic entrepreneurs, corrupt nobility, dishonest judges, and self-serving kings? The need was met by the genesis of a new office, that of prophet. Unlike kings, but in the manner of the earlier judges, prophets were designated not by hereditary entitlement or the acclaim of an assembly of citizens, but by charismatic (that is, divine) commission. The prophets therefore resisted co-option and assimilation into the new bureaucratic institution. Their charisma remained distinctly unroutinized. In all essential respects, they preserve a critical lifeline between the period of charismatic rule and the monarchy.

Given their traditional theocratic perspective, the prophets frequently found themselves in conflict with kings, many of whom did not welcome challenges to their authority based on appeal to an authority transcending their own. The "institution" of which the prophets pictured themselves a part was the universal, sovereign assembly of the heavenly king. This assembly they served as messengers, relaying its decrees to designated recipients: sometimes kings, foreign or native; sometimes fellow citizens, noble or peasant. Furthermore, they pictured themselves as deputies of the divine assembly when it gathered to try cases arising out of covenant violations. The trial proceeding (Heb. *rîb*) to which they summoned self-aggrandizing kings, corrupt entrepreneurs, decadent nobility, and dishonest judges revolved around carefully drafted indictments and sentences based on traditional Mosaic covenant and law (e.g., Hos. 4:1–3; Amos 2:6–16; Mic. 3:9–12).

True to that tradition, and in defiant opposition to the social and economic stratification that developed over the course of the monarchy, the prophets insisted on the equality of all persons before the divine judge, whether they were king or subject, nobility or commoner, rich or poor, native or resident alien. The prophets also utilized other conventions at home in the court of law: the testimony of witnesses (Mic. 6:1–2), disputations (Isa. 40:12–31), admonitions (Amos 5:14–15; Hos. 14:1–3), and warnings (Jer. 13:15–17). To be sure, they freely drew from other realms of discourse as well, utilizing, for example, parables (Isa. 5:1–7), laments (Amos 5:1–2), and wisdom sayings (Isa. 1:3).

The issue in contention between kings and prophets was thus the issue of realms of legitimate authority. The prophets generally did not dispute the right of the king to administer the civil matters of the nation on the basis of royal decree. In seeking to preserve the religious identity of the nation that had been established in the league period, however, they insisted that in his executive orders, policy making, and conduct of domestic and international affairs the king not violate the central values of early Yahwism, derived from the national Epic and codified in Mosaic law, but rather respect the theocratic principle of YHWH's ultimate authority, by upholding the moral principles of the covenant and exemplifying true worship in his personal life.

Therefore, like every other citizen, the king was required to eschew worship of other gods, to respect the patrimony of every extended family, to act justly in economic transactions, to honor the dignity and rights of the poor, and in general, as stated in the summary formulation of the Deuteronomic law of the king, "to fear the LORD his God, diligently observing all the words of this law and these statutes, neither exalting himself above other members of the community nor turning aside from the commandment" (Deut. 17:19–20). In addition, as occupant of the highest civil office in the land, he was to uphold political and legal structures safeguarding the rights of all citizens and to establish sufficient protection of the weak from exploitation by the powerful and the wealthy.

When kings failed to conform to these traditional norms, the prophets responded incisively by indicting them. Conflict was inevitable, since as noted, the court to which they summoned kings or any other citizen that disobeyed the Torah was distinct from the courts subsidized by kings as part of the civil and criminal court system of the land. We might therefore imagine that the kings of Israel viewed the prophets in a manner comparable to the way a US president or other high official views the investigation of a special prosecutor. It is clear that they were feared: "Have you found me, O my enemy?" (1 Kgs. 21:20) were the words that came to the lips of King Ahab when confronted by Elijah at the place of the king's crime against the hapless citizen Naboth. The prophetic concept of a judicial system independent of the royal chancellery provided the framework for the systematic evaluation of kings of both Judah and Israel in the Deuteronomistic History.

In chapter 12 and following, we shall look in greater detail at the political model cultivated by the prophets built upon the theocratic concept of divine governance, impartial justice, and a dialectical understanding of the interplay between religion and politics. At this juncture, however, we turn to trace the stages of development of Israelite monarchy beyond the inaugural period of Saul and David.

SOLOMON'S INNOVATIONS
IN THE DIRECTION OF ABSOLUTE MONARCHY

While during the reigns of Saul and David reorganization of the government proceeded slowly and with considerable deference to the values held sacred by the clans, the pace of change accelerated under Solomon. This is not surprising, given the fact that he was the first king installed by dynastic succession, after having been imbued since childhood with the ethos of the royal court.

A critical reading of a narrative source utilized by the Deuteronomists reveals a problem endemic to the system of dynastic succession that became a plague upon the house of David (2 Sam. 9–10 and 1 Kgs. 1–2): sons began to maneuver against one another, leading to full-scale court intrigue. Immediately upon the death of his father, Solomon secured his claim to the throne with ruthless force, liquidating rivals and their supporters. And he made peace with the ancient empire of the Nile through a marriage alliance with a daughter of the reigning Egyptian pharaoh.

On the basis of a court document preserved in 1 Kings 1–6, it is apparent that Solomon, building on the modest steps taken by David (2 Sam. 8:15–18), initiated a major reorganization of the administration of the kingdom, establishing a bureaucracy led by two secretaries, a recorder, a commander of the army, an official called the "king's friend," another in charge of the palace, and one head of forced labor. Of the two high priests he inherited from David, he retained only the one that had been loyal to him in his contentious battle for the throne. Additionally, he appointed a high official to oversee twelve subordinates, each in charge of one of the districts into which Solomon subdivided the land (1 Kgs. 4:7–19). From each of these districts came one month's provisions for the royal court.

Finally, Solomon completed the overhaul of the governance of the land by building a temple for the central cult. This act had a greater impact on the society than any other, for it placed the religious establishment under the watchful eye of the crown. While a royal temple was an essential fixture in the kingdoms surrounding Israel at that time, its introduction into a culture that had insisted on the right of access of every citizen to the cult shrine and that, as we observed above, placed the king, no less than every other citizen, under the theocratic authority of the *heavenly* king, inevitably led to intracommunity tensions that at times escalated into bloody conflict.

In spite of extensive structural and conceptual innovations, the monarchy that Solomon had shaped was theoretically capable of remaining in conformity with the constitutional limits on mediation imposed by the Epic tradition of early Yahwism, if only the king submitted to the ultimate authority of God and remained obedient to the Mosaic covenant and Torah. But could he and his successors uphold this theocratic limitation on royal authority, once they grew accustomed to the title that in the neighboring lands connoted privileged status, special entitlement, and the blending of royal and divine authority?

In the plotline covering the history of kingship in Israel in 1 Samuel through 2 Kings, a distinct change is detectable as one moves from the reign of David to that of Solomon. Available to the Deuteronomistic Historians were two important sources for the Davidic period, the history of David's rise (1 Sam. 16–2 Sam. 5) and the succession narrative (2 Sam. 9–20; 1 Kgs. 1–2). Commentators have long noted the verisimilitude that characterizes both of these sources. David is presented in a realistic light as an able warrior capable of heroism and deep religious devotion as well as cowardly, lustful self-indulgence. The spokespersons of the indigenous religious traditions, the prophets, are on hand in the narrative to confront David when he strays from the conditions for mediation intrinsic to the theocratic principle of constitutional monarchy, by opening his style of rule to aspects of absolute kingship.

In contrast, for the Solomonic reign, the sources available to the Deuteronomistic Historians were apparently of a different nature. The sober realism of the Davidic narrative yields to legends valorizing a figure who is larger than life, godlike in wisdom, and shielded from close scrutiny by the nimbus of royal splendor. Prophetic gadflies are entirely absent from the storyline covering King Solomon. Yet the negative impact of Solomon's policies on the cherished values and traditions of the people was evident to the vigilant historians, both from a decline in the national security and economic stability of the large empire David had conquered and Solomon had consolidated (1 Kgs. 9:11; 11:14–25) and especially from the tumultuous, schismatic events that broke out immediately after Solomon's death. Lacking the kinds of realistic stories that they had for David, they structured their narrative to portray Solomon's descent from godly glory to worldly vice as an aspect of aging; that is, after a promising start he degenerated into a dirty old man: "For when Solomon was old, his wives turned away his heart after other gods; and his heart was not true to the LORD his God" (1 Kgs. 11:4).

For modern historians, this manner of accounting for the turmoil of the late Solomonic reign seems schematic and contrived. But this judgment should not lead to overlooking the insightfulness of the historiographic theme developed by the Deuteronomists in their interpretation of the Solomonic and post-Solomonic periods. The challenge facing these historians was to explain the sundering of the kingdom right at the point where Israel seemed to emerge from the status of a petty vassal state to that of a significant player in international relations. They avoided what could have provided a simple solution, namely, attributing the fall to a deus ex machina triggered by royal hubris, a device common in later Greek tragedy but known already to biblical writers (e.g., Isa. 14:12–20; Ezek. 28). The explanation they offered was more subtle, involving a rigorous scrutiny of the social, political, and religious tensions that characterized the period.

Historiographic intent is particularly evident in their accounts in 1 Kings 11:26–12:20 of the revolt fomented by Solomon's chief of forced labor, Jeroboam, and the brutish response of Solomon's son Rehoboam to the reasonable petition of the clan leaders for a return to the terms of the limited, constitutional monarchy and a legitimate structure of mediating God's absolute sovereignty to the temporal realm of civic order. Apparently basing their attempt to negotiate with Rehoboam on the assumption that their traditions could be reconciled with monarchy, the clan leaders announced their willingness to obey the new king, if only he would respect their civil rights.

In the minds of the Deuteronomistic Historians, there was a deep moral reason for the political chaos that had broken out. The king had tipped the scale dangerously in the direction of absolute monarchy by asserting prerogatives that rightfully belonged only to God. The law of the king in Deuteronomy 17 had articulated very clearly the conditions that would allow the king and his descendants to "reign long over his kingdom in Israel," conditions having to do with eschewing wealth, pride, and power, and remaining faithful, in solidarity with the entire populace, to the Torah. According to the Deuteronomists, Solomon and his son Rehoboam had set kingship in Israel on a path away from such limited, constitutional monarchy in the direction of the absolute monarchies of Egypt and Mesopotamia.

In order better to understand the strains that developed within Israel between the concept of limited, constitutional monarchy and the ideology of absolute monarchy that prevailed in the eastern Mediterranean of that time, we shall now turn to a description of the salient features of the latter, citing evidence of its influence on political thought within the Bible, and pointing to the ways in which it differed from the theocratic principle propounded by Samuel in 1 Samuel 8 and 12 and by the law of the king in Deuteronomy 17. Though considerable variation is found among the eastern Mediterranean monarchies that existed during the time of Solomon and the later kings of Israel, for the sake of simplicity we must be satisfied with sketching the major characteristics shared across the broad cultural horizon from the Nile to the Tigris.

ABSOLUTE MONARCHY IN THE ANCIENT NEAR EAST

From the start it is essential to recognize the source of ancient Near Eastern kingship in a mythopoeic view of reality. Everything that had substantive value in a civilized society derived that value from the realm of the gods, which realm served as the archetype for the social structures and public institutions built by humans.[6] Royal authority was rooted in the unique and exclusive relationship that the king enjoyed with his (or, rarely, her) sponsoring god. This can be understood variously in terms of the king being an incarnation of that deity (e.g., the Egyptian pharaoh's identification with Horus) or in terms of the king being adopted by the patron deity (a notion characteristic of Mesopotamian royal ideology).

The literary genre utilized more than any other by Israel's imperial neighbors to anchor the ideology of absolute monarchy in the eternal verities of the gods was the combat myth, according to which the warrior god vanquished chaos (construed as an unruly being leading malevolent hosts), (re)established cosmic order, and as a reward for his heroic deeds was given authority over the other gods.[7] The human realm, as the source of food offerings for the gods, was placed under the rule of the earthly king, who was construed as proxy of the victorious

---

6. The classic study of the mythopoeic perspective of the ancient empires of the Near East remains Henri Frankfurt et al., *Before Philosophy* (New York: Penguin Books, 1974).

7. Patrick D. Miller Jr. and Richard J. Clifford, SJ, "The Roots of Apocalypticism in Near Eastern Myth," in *The Encyclopedia of Apocalypticism*, vol. 1 (New York: Continuum, 1998), 3–38.

god. In imitation of the divine king's celestial rule, the king's commission was to maintain law and order within the borders of his terrestrial realm. The king, in effect, presided over the earthly estate of his patron god.

This position entitled him to privileges enjoyed by no other human. But his responsibilities vis-à-vis his god were daunting. These included defense of the land against the threats of enemy attack, cultivation of harvest and commerce sufficient for the support of the human population, preservation of social stability through the promulgation of law and administration of an effective court system, and above all, maintenance of the temple as the earthly home of the patron deity, central treasury of the nation-state, and storehouse for the obligatory offerings.

To fulfill his sacred duties, the king imposed his will on the land with iron-clad authority. In the actual politics of Egypt, Babylon, and Assyria, priestly families could challenge the authority of kings, coups could lead to the overthrow of royal houses, and empires could fall to foreign conquest. But in the ideal construal of kingship, the king ruled by divine election, his heirs reigned after him in an eternal dynastic succession, and his authority over all matters of state were as uncontestable as the patron deity's rule over the hosts of heaven.

The starting point for understanding the difference between absolute kingship in the major empires of the ancient Near East and the limited, constitutional variety in Israel, must be clear recognition of the fact that kingship arose in Israel against the background not of the above described mythopoeic understanding of reality, but of an Epic worldview.[8] Though the god YHWH was construed no less than his counterparts in neighboring cultures as a warrior god marching forth from his holy sanctuary to vanquish chaos and establish cosmic order,[9] the meeting point of this god and his human followers was not in the first instance the myth-ritual of the temple, but rather specific mundane locations like the Reed Sea and the Jezreel Plain, where through acts of deliverance he demonstrated his commitment to the well-being of the people of Israel, for which in turn he demanded their fealty.

The kings Saul and David, like the heroes of the period of the judges, were leaders called from the ranks of their fellow citizens to defend the land from enemy attack. Their authority derived not from a special divine nature, or a privileged relation to the heavenly realm, but from their obedient response to the divine king who had established Israel in the land by defeating the former Egyptian overlord and ordering the new nation under a covenantal system that was to be applied evenhandedly to all citizens.

True to the primus inter pares understanding of leadership, the elders as representatives of the people participated in selection of the first kings of Israel. To the divine election evidenced in the charismatic qualities of the leader the people

8. Frank Moore Cross, *Canaanite Myth and Hebrew Epic: Essays in the History of the Religion of Israel* (Cambridge, MA: Harvard University Press, 1973).

9. E.g., Deut. 33:2; Judg. 5:4–5; Hab. 3:3–6.

added their consent: "And all the people shouted, 'Long live the king!'" (1 Sam. 10:24). The "constitutional" nature of the monarchy was solemnized in writing: "Samuel told the people the rights and duties of the kingship; and he wrote them in a book and laid it up before the LORD" (10:25).

From the above it is clear that a fundamental conceptual difference existed between the limited form of kingship that arose within Israel's Epic understanding of origins and the absolute form of kingship based upon a mythopoeic worldview found in neighboring cultures. In Israel, the origins of kingship were traced to historical developments and the king's status was ontologically no different than that of any other citizen. His rule was understood functionally as a responsibility conferred upon him by God with the consent of the people and regulated by the terms of the covenant, its duration determined not in terms of the timeless "verities" of myth, but conditionally based on obedience to the Torah, "so that he and his descendants may reign long over his kingdom in Israel" (Deut. 17:20). Consonant with the conditions for implementation inherent in the theocratic principle, the king was not exempt from the traditional laws and institutions that had developed during the period of the league. His authority was viewed as dependent upon and derivative of his conformity to the will of God and the laws and community structures extrapolated from Israel's Epic.

In marked contrast, the myth-ritual view of kingship prevailing in the kingdoms extending from the Tigris and Euphrates to the Nile was expressed succinctly in the opening line of the *Sumerian King List:* "When kingship descended from heaven . . ."[10] This transhistorical origin of kingship was reiterated in the prologue to the Code of Hammurabi, which described the simultaneity of Marduk's election to divine kingship and Hammurabi's election to terrestrial kingship as king of Babylon. In the *Enuma Elish,* the theogony/cosmogony that enjoyed canonical status in the New Year's festival (*akitu*) of ancient Babylon, a detailed account is given of the drama in heaven that provided the myth-ritual basis for both heavenly kingship and its mundane counterpart. The central theme of that drama was the divine warrior Marduk's defeat of Tiamat and her hosts of chaos.

Inextricably tied to kingship was the institution of the temple. Here too origin was traced to the realm of the gods. In the *Enuma Elish* and the analogous mythic cycle from the Levant, the Baal myth from the Late Bronze Age kingdom of Ugarit, the victory of the warrior god was followed by construction of his house (i.e., the temple). The Babylonian myth, moreover, makes explicit in Tablet VI the archetypal relation between the heavenly temple and its earthly counterpart, for Marduk was expected to "make a likeness on earth of what he has wrought in heaven."

The economic implications of temple building come out clearly in the stipulation that the temple was to be the source of the food offerings for the gods and

10. Thorkild Jacobsen, *The Sumerian King List,* Assyriological Studies #11 (Chicago: University of Chicago Press, 1939).

goddesses (VII 117). Implied in this stipulation was the economic structure of the kingdom. The king was responsible for ordering the affairs of the land in such a manner as to maintain the regular offerings of the temple: "Without fail let them support their gods!" The implications of the temple being conceived of as the storehouse of the gods reached far beyond the temple precincts. *All* aspects of national policy were ordered on the basis of the mythopoeic concept of nation as an estate of the gods. Domestic stability, national security, and economic prosperity on earth were essential aspects of maintaining the stability of the universe. King and temple therefore occupied a place on earth charged with a dimension of importance categorically different from any other agents or institutions.

Against this brief description of the ideology of kingship and temple in the ancient Near East, we can grasp the significance of the struggle that erupted in Israel over matters that in neighboring cultures were taken for granted. David deemed it proper that, once he had defeated his enemies, he should build a temple for his patron God, YHWH. His plan met with prophetic opposition when Nathan reported that it was the custom of Israel's God ever since the exodus not to live in a permanent dwelling but in a movable tent-sanctuary.

The tent was clearly emblematic of the ideals of clans in contrast to the temple ideology of city-states and empires. As the clans valued autonomy and freedom of movement, so too they preserved the tradition of a deity who had demonstrated freedom of movement in accompanying them in their escape from slavery, sojourn in the wilderness between Egypt and Canaan, and entry into their new homeland. Even after their settlement on farms and in villages, they understood their ancestral deity to be unwilling to dwell in the kind of temple structure otherwise normative in neighboring monarchies. No doubt, the temple edifice represented too blatant a symbol of the control of the king over deity to please clansfolk who remained vigilant in safeguarding their autonomy and who by nature were suspicious of the self-aggrandizing tendencies of urban-based monarchies.

Since temple building was such an intrinsic part of kingship ideology throughout the ancient Near East, it was no doubt inevitable that Israel's kings finally would fall in line with the normative pattern. Solomon was the natural agent of change in this direction, having grown up in the Jerusalem royal court, having inherited the throne through dynastic succession, and having placed considerable distance between himself and the traditions of the league by drawing on Egyptian and Phoenician models to construct a native royal bureaucracy.

Reflected in the historical narrative of Solomon's reign are flashpoints of tension between the crown and the older customs and values intrinsic to Israel's Epic. Not only did Solomon strain the economic and human resources of the land to complete the temple; he situated himself at the center of the cult by assuming the priestly functions of offering the dedicatory prayers (1 Kgs. 8:22–53) and sacrifices (1 Kgs. 8:62–66).

In other ways as well he is pictured as one who repudiated traditional values. When faced with foreclosure on collateral he had provided to cover loans secured from Hiram the king of Tyre to finance his extensive building projects, he elected to turn over territory belonging to some of the northern tribes, clearly in blatant violation of the tradition of the sacred patrimony, that is, the inalienable nature of the territorial claims of the clans (1 Kgs. 9:10–14). Furthermore, in order to deploy the huge work force necessary to complete his ambitious building program, he implemented a practice widely utilized in Egypt and other absolute monarchies but loathed by the clans of Israel, the corveè or forced labor brigade (1 Kgs. 9:15–22). The blow to tribal pride inflicted by such patent violations of cherished civil rights becomes clear when Jeroboam, who by royal appointment had been commissioned overseer of "forced labor of the house of Joseph" (1 Kgs. 11:26–28), rebelled against his king and led the northern tribes out of the Davidic monarchy. The cry that accompanied their secession from the union testified to the breaking point to which Rehoboam, Solomon's son, had forced the conflict between traditional values and the realpolitik of the absolute monarchy:

> When all Israel saw that the king would not listen to them, the people
> answered the king,
> "What share do we have in David?
>   We have no inheritance in the son of Jesse.
> To your tents, O Israel!
>   Look now to your own house, O David."
> So Israel went away to their tents. (1 Kgs. 12:16)

THE LOCUTION OF ROYAL IDEOLOGY IN TEMPLE RITUAL

The ancient Near Eastern temple, given its character as the official sanctuary of the empire, was the natural setting for the celebration of royal power and authority and their legitimization in divine decree. A number of the compositions in the canonical book of Psalms reflect the hymnody sung in the Jerusalem temple in celebration of the twin reigns of Israel's celestial and terrestrial kings.

Psalm 29, which is patterned after a Ugaritic (i.e., Canaanite) hymn from the fourteenth century BCE, documents early Israel's use of imagery from the combat myth upon which most ancient Near Eastern monarchs based their claims to divinity. According to this mythologoumenon, the stability of the monarchy depended on the success of the patron deity in establishing control over chaos, symbolized by the unruly force of Yam (Sea). True to that mythic pattern, YHWH is praised in verse 3 for his assault on the ancient watery foe. The connection of the psalm to the temple is indicated in verse 9. The mastery of the deity over the threat of chaos is depicted as it had been for two millennia in the kingdoms of the Near East, by the image of YHWH "enthroned over the flood" (v. 10). The result was the security of YHWH's kingdom, upon which in turn rested the stability of its earthly counterpart, the kingdom whose capital was located in Jerusalem.

Psalm 89 is another hymn that sheds valuable light on the ascendant political model of kingship in Israel and the ideology that underlay it. It is easy to picture the setting of this psalm in the temple, for true to the mythological view of the temple as the earthly replica of the heavenly abode of the patron deity and the king as the deputized caretaker of the estate of his god, this psalm celebrates the eternal bond connecting kingship in heaven and the kingship of the house of David. Its orientation differs from the narrative perspective of 1 Samuel. Whereas the latter traced the rise of Davidic kingship to events in Israel's history, Psalm 89 provides an etiology of Israel's monarchy by depicting the events in heaven that established kingship on earth. The political-philosophical implications of this difference are enormous.

In the narrative account in 1 Samuel, the introduction of kingship was explained with reference to historical circumstances and human decisions. This does not exclude perception of divine involvement, but in keeping with Israel's ancient Epic tradition, the Divine was viewed as present within the stuff of human experience. Psalm 89, by contrast, traces the origins of the Davidic monarchy to primordial events that occurred *in illo tempore* in the realm of the gods. Not history, but creation provides the frame of reference for understanding this unique institution. The rules that govern the monarch are thus not the contingent rules that apply to other humans, but are rather comparable to the eternal laws that regulate the heavenly bodies.

Whether in heaven or on earth, rule involved contending powers, for threatening the order and harmony that constituted the central purpose of kingship was the persistent specter of chaos. At the center of the mythic drama explaining cosmic and mundane kingship, therefore, lay deadly conflict between two primordial principals, the warrior god who acted to defend the order of the universe and the chaotic antagonist who sought to return reality to the inertia of precreation formlessness.[11]

Because the roots of Israel's royal ideology lay in an ancient mythologoumenon reaching back to the third- and second-millennium dynasties of Sumer, Babylonia, Assyria, and Ugarit, the language of Psalm 89 is incomprehensible without awareness of the background mythology. The following lines describe the deadly conflict and the creation of the universe that resulted from the warrior god's victory:

> You crushed Rahab like a carcass . . .
> The heavens are yours, the earth also is yours,
> the world and all that is in it—you have founded them.
> (Ps. 89:10–11)

---

11. One of the terms used in Bible for the watery chaos preceding creation is *tōhû wābōhû*, depicted in Gen. 1:2 as the state of things before God's creative act and in Jer. 4:28 as the chaos to which the created order could revert as the result of divine judgment in response to human sin.

Rahab is one of several names for the deity who in the primordial battle sought to destroy harmony in the assembly of the gods and was challenged to mortal duel by a young member of that assembly. In the Babylonian myth the antagonist was named Tiamat (etymologically related to the word *tehom* in Gen. 1:2), and the warrior chosen to defend the divine assembly was Marduk, patron deity of the Babylonian city-state. Another name for personified chaos is Leviathan, described in Isaiah 27:1 as "the twisting serpent, . . . the dragon that is in the sea." Though variously named, the frightening reality is the same, namely, the primordial threat to the viability of all life, divine and human alike, symbolized by the salt water of the sea (i.e., the fluid that in contrast to the fructifying waters of the winter storm destroyed rather than sustained life). The stability of a universe perched precariously between life and death could be secured only by the heroism of a deity so fiercely dedicated to the maintenance of an ordered universe as to risk all in deadly combat: "You rule the raging of the sea; when its waves rise, you still them" (Ps. 89:9).

The roots of this motif in the mythology of the conflict myth are thus unmistakable. Marduk, in the fifth tablet of the *Enuma Elish*, slew Tiamat, and then with her carcass fashioned the universe. After YHWH crushed Rahab in Psalm 89, he was celebrated as founder of the universe (v. 10).

The Divine Warrior's achievement of securing cosmic order provided the metaphysical basis for the earthly monarchy responsible for establishing and maintaining order on earth. Humans, no less than the beings that inhabited heaven, lived under the constant threat of chaos in the form of famine, disease, and enemy invasion.[12] They too longed for a defending champion, a hero capable of defeating invading enemies and assuring agricultural abundance and commercial prosperity. Given the gravity of threats to human existence, the only dependable governance, according to royal ideology, was governance established in heaven and administered on earth by one designated by the king of heaven. Only through the eternally secured dynasty of such a superhuman, one elevated above the unpredictability of human contingencies, could humans hope to preserve their nation; this was the rationale of the royal paradigm. Accordingly, the royal psalms directed Israel's attention to the intimate bond between divine king and his earthly counterpart: "my hand shall always remain with him; my arm also shall strengthen him. . . . I will establish his line forever, and his throne as long as the heavens endure" (Ps. 89:21, 29).

While noting the contrast between the points of view of the narrative account of the rise of monarchy in 1 Samuel and the mythic etiology found in the royal psalms, we should not miss the echo of royal ideology in the benefits of kingship expressed by the delegation coming to the old judge Samuel: "we are determined to have a king over us, so that we also may be like other nations, and that our king may govern us and go out before us and fight our

---

12. Jon D. Levenson, *Creation and the Persistence of Evil: The Jewish Drama of Divine Omnipotence* (San Francisco: Harper & Row, 1988).

battles" (1 Sam. 8:19–20). According to the mythopoeic view that underlay ancient Near Eastern royal ideology, enemy threats, like all other threats to life, reflected unruly chaotic forces that could be effectively broken only by the agency of a Divine Warrior, who, having defeated chaos on a universal scale, proceeded to empower an earthly deputy to safeguard humans from the scourges of war, disease, famine, and every other manifestation of the pernicious persistence of chaos. The elders who came to Samuel were insisting on such a divinely empowered champion.

In returning to hymnody, we find a dramatic celebration of Israel's God-given defender against her blustering enemies in Psalm 2:6–7:

> "I have set my king on Zion, my holy hill. . . .
> You are my son;
>   today I have begotten you.
> Ask of me, and I will make the nations your heritage."

To this formulation we can compare the promise made in Psalm 89:20–23:

> "I have found my servant David;
>   with my holy oil I have anointed him;
> my hand shall always remain with him;
>   my arm also shall strengthen him.
> The enemy shall not outwit him,
>   the wicked shall not humble him.
> I will crush his foes before him
>   and strike down those who hate him."

As indicated above in the brief description of ancient Near Eastern royal ideology, kingship was inseparably linked to temple, in heaven as on earth. In the heavenly drama of myth, combat was followed by the building of a house (i.e., temple) for the victorious god. This provided the setting for the banqueting of the gods in celebration of their champion's victory and the resulting restoration of peace and prosperity. For that happy state of contentment and security to continue, however, the divine king was obliged to prove his indispensability in providing in perpetuity the food offerings required by the gods. Since it was beneath the dignity of the gods to produce their own provisions, the divine king created the human race to labor on behalf of the gods. But that innovation in turn required administration.

The answer was a structure on earth paralleling heavenly realities. A human king was appointed to organize the human economy in a manner that would provide offerings for the gods. Central to that endeavor was the temple, to which those offerings would be brought for storage and offering. In the typical ancient Near Eastern kingdom, all political, economic, and social structures radiated out from the central institution of the temple, for it was the *omphalos mundi* that secured the vital connection between human civilization and the divine realm upon which the former was dependent.

This gave awesome power to those officiating over the temple, primary among whom was the one designated by the patron deity to oversee his terrestrial affairs, the king. The gravity of refutations of the king's power and authority will be appreciated when it is remembered that in the world of royal mythology they represented a threat not only to the economic prosperity and national security of the nation, but also to the viability of the entire universe, for without the regular offerings of the temple, the gods could no longer discharge their various cosmic responsibilities. Needless to say, insurrections were crushed with incisive, brutal force. The king's authority had to be preserved from every form of human rebuke or interference, for he represented and embodied divine authority and was expected to enforce proper order with unrestrained might. Such was the nature of mediation between heaven and earth inherent in a mythopoeic construal of reality. How did that construal fit into the world of Israelite religion and politics?

While recognizing in the hymns cited above the influence of ancient Near Eastern royal ideology on Israel's concepts of kingship and temple, it is important to be equally attentive to modifications imposed by Israel's indigenous beliefs. Of preeminent significance was the growth within Yahwism of the confession that, amid sundry divine beings in the heavenly assembly, one being alone enjoyed ultimate sovereignty and authority, all others assuming subservient roles such as prosecutors (e.g., the *satan* of 1 Kgs. 22 and Job 1) and messengers (i.e., angels). Surviving the modifications, however, were traces of the functional parallelism between divine and earthly king and divine and earthly temple. Upon that link rested the exalted authority of the Davidic king and the importance of the central temple in Jerusalem. Given the degree of authoritativeness required to maintain the highly centralized hierarchy of monarchy, it is not surprising that Israel's kings were often drawn to the practical benefits of absolute monarchy.

On the most basic level, the exalted status of a king like Solomon, standing as it does in such stark contrast to the modest powers of the judges of Israel's confederacy, traces back to the notion at home in royal ideology that a special bond, shared by no one other human, existed between king and deity. According to Psalm 89:3–4, that bond is solemnized in the form of an oath pronounced by the divine King:

> "I have made a covenant with my chosen one,
>   I have sworn to my servant David:
> 'I will establish your descendants forever,
>   and build your throne for all generations.'"

One human was thus exalted over all others to represent the nation's divine patron and to secure the safety and prosperity of its inhabitants. Accomplishment of these tasks required uncommon power, indeed, divine power. Hence the correspondence between God's ruling "the raging of the sea," crushing

"Rahab like a carcass," scattering his enemies with his "mighty arm" (Ps. 89:9, 10) and God's promise to his king to "crush his foes before him" and to "set his hand on the sea and his right hand on the rivers" (89:23, 25). The Davidic king's rule was thus understood to be infused with divine power. This comes to expression in the similitude linking his reign and the perdurance of the heavenly bodies established by God's victory over chaos:

> His line shall continue forever,
>   and his throne endure before me like the sun.
> It shall be established forever like the moon,
>   an enduring witness in the skies.
>   (Ps. 89:36–37)

The king was to be considered no less a part of the eternal divine order than the sun and moon! Granted, one must recognize the element of hyperbole that was intrinsic to the hymnic-epic style of the royal psalms. This can be illustrated by reference to another royal psalm, the wedding hymn in Psalm 45, where in verse 6 the king is addressed as "God." While it would be rash to extrapolate from this that the writer actually viewed the king as a divinity, it seems clear that divine-like attributes were being ascribed to the king, a mortal exalted above fellow mortals by the God who "anointed you with the oil of gladness beyond your companions" (Ps. 45:7 [Heb. v. 8]).

That the authority of the king extended to his role in the temple cult is indicated by a divine oath in Psalm 110:4: "The LORD has sworn and will not change his mind, 'You are a priest forever according to the order of Melchizedek.'" The same psalm hints at the king's unique genesis: "From the womb of the morning, like dew, your youth will come to you" (Ps. 110:3).

Clearly, from the point of view of political ideologies, Psalms 45, 89, and 110 stem from a world far removed from that of the early Yahwistic clans or even from the simple courts of Saul and David.

We noted earlier how the limited kingship that evolved out of Israel's tribal structures was accounted for in 1 Samuel by a historical narrative. The political process was carried out by human actors responding to divine prompting within the contingencies of mundane experience. The mythic grounding given to kingship by the royal psalms, in contrast, was exempt from ordinary worldly contingencies. Kingship was established eternally as an aspect of cosmic order, for even as the Divine Warrior, in defeating chaos, secured the orderliness of the heavenly bodies and the seasons they regulated, so too he established order on earth by appointment of his deputy, the king. Like the sun and moon, the reign of the Davidic dynasty was to endure forever, a claim that could not be made for any *ordinary human* institution.

This exemption of kingship from the contingencies affecting all other human institutions, however, did not go unchallenged in Israel. We shall describe in the next chapter how the office of prophecy developed precisely out of a blunt refutation of the notion of the divine right of kings. Even in the circles most actively supportive of royal ideology, the influence of earlier Yahwistic traditions could not be quashed entirely. For the theocratic notion that there could be no king but YHWH served to restrain the claims to special status and privilege that were intrinsic parts of the royal paradigm. The sole sovereign in heaven was one who, long before the appearance of Israel's first king, had issued laws that were binding on every Israelite as the obligatory response to the sovereign's antecedent beneficence. These laws, when translated into guidelines for the mediation of divine rule within human institutions, categorically excluded the ascription of exceptional status and rights to the king or any other official. We turn to a vivid example of the continued vitality of the early Yahwistic tradition.

With verses 30–32, Psalm 89's lofty claims made on behalf of the king are interrupted by a theme reflecting the restraining counterweight of the Epic tradition. While anointed and exalted and promised a dynasty that would "continue forever," the king's descendants were not exempt from the stipulations of the divine king's Torah, but would be subject to punishment for transgression. The "but" that introduces the asseveration in verses 33–37 strains under a tremendous logical contradiction. The promise of God's eternal commitment to the Davidic line was reaffirmed, but the specter of descendants of David who "forsake my law" casts a dark shadow on the preceding divine drama that established the exceptional eternal status of the institution of monarchy. The same God who so wondrously established the Davidic kingship and promised to protect it from all foes suddenly is described as "full of wrath against your anointed" (89:38). The same heavenly king who had sworn to uphold the Davidic house forever in a shocking reversal now has "renounced the covenant with your servant" (89:39).

Embedded in the structure of Psalm 89 is thus a glaring contradiction that creates tremendous difficulty if one confines oneself to a synchronic reading. How can a hymn that had so exuberantly celebrated God's securing for David an eternal dynasty conclude with God's renunciation of that same covenant, a description of how David's kingdom had fallen to its enemies, and an imploring lament for the taunted and humiliated king (89:49–51)?

It is likely that verses 38–51 reflect the Babylonian destruction of Jerusalem in 586 BCE. The good fortunes of the Davidic monarchy had turned to calamity. Verses were accordingly added to the psalm to acknowledge the contradiction without attempting to explain it. But what can be said of the final canonical message of Psalm 89 in the form in which it was transmitted to subsequent generations?

In its canonical form, Psalm 89 places in sharp focus the problematics of monarchy. For certain "progressive" circles, the rustic form of early kingship, with constitutional limits restricting the powers of the throne and with considerable voice vouchsafed for the clans, seemed archaic. Accordingly, the case was made for a more assertive form of monarchy. But by appealing to royal ideology for enhanced political muscle and to the mythic notion of an eternal bond between divine and human kings, an institution emerged that was vulnerable to the contradictory evidence of history.

What happened in 586 BCE, from the mythic perspective of ancient Near Eastern royal ideology, was possible only as a consequence of the defeat of the patron god within the assembly of the gods, an interpretation highly problematic within the monotheistic setting of sixth-century Israelite religion. Though the trauma inflicted on the Jewish community by the Babylonian destruction of their temple and city differed in detail from that experienced nearly a millennium and a half earlier by the inhabitants of Ur,[13] the intensity was comparable. The consequence was that the more mythological versions of royal ideology that had developed within the Jerusalem court succumbed to the harsh judgment of history.

That faith in YHWH was not dealt an irreparable blow by the destruction of the central icon of the royal cult can be credited in no small part to those circles in Israel that had resisted the mythologized version of kingship, in defense of the more modest concept of a limited, constitutionally based monarchy that had accommodated itself to the theocratic principle ensconced in the Mosaic covenant and the Torah. Among the most active participants in those circles were the prophets of the divine sovereign YHWH.

ASSESSMENT OF THE KINGS OF JUDAH AND ISRAEL

Since we shall describe the position taken in relation to the monarchy by the prophets in the next chapter, we shall devote the remainder of this chapter to an assessment of how the kings of Judah and Israel positioned themselves within the tension between a constitutional form of limited monarchy compliant with the conditions of the law of the king in Deuteronomy 17 and the ancient Near Eastern ideology of the god-king. Two cautionary notes introduce our examination: (1) a critical reading of the texts will reveal no individual king to fit the mold of either unalloyed tyrant or pure saint; (2) where a text presents a king as a paragon of pure good or unmitigated evil, the modern reader must be alert to editorial bias, from which neither the Deuteronomistic Historians nor the Chroniclers were immune.

In the biblical narrative, Samuel is described as the wise arbiter of a compromise between ancient Near Eastern royal ideology and the covenantal ideal that had taken root in Yahwistic thought during the preceding two centuries of clan-based charismatic rule. That compromise, formulated in narrative form in 1 Samuel 12 and in law in Deuteronomy 17, aimed to ameliorate the conflict arising from the archaic confession that there could be no king but YHWH and the de facto adoption of monarchy. It was a middle way, based on the distinction

---

13. Cf. "The Lament of Ur," in *Ancient Near Eastern Texts Relating to the Old Testament*, ed. James B Pritchard, 3rd ed. (Princeton, NJ: Princeton University Press, 1969), 455–63.

between two levels of rule: the one authoritative, absolute, and ultimate; the other mediated, derivative, and penultimate. While ultimate sovereignty was reserved for Israel's divine king, her human kings were empowered with jurisdiction over the economic and military matters of state, but even that limited authority was contingent on their conforming their rule to the divine rule codified in the Torah. Preeminent among the restraints placed upon kings by that condition related to their treatment of subjects: not their personal goals and strategies, but God's rule as revealed in the Torah was to guide their conduct.

Introduced by the Samuel compromise was the principle that over the course of subsequent history would become foundational for any political theology claiming a biblical basis, what we have called the theocratic principle. In effect, that principle is the First Commandment, formulated in political terms: there is solely one ultimate sovereign, known through his beneficent acts in human history, whose rule on earth is mediated though the agency of human leaders. Strict conditions apply to human mediation that distinguish between the distortion of human agency in the forms of abuse of power (i.e., tyranny) and status (i.e., idolatry) and legitimate governance, which is rule that conforms to divine purpose and will. Since no human government is capable of regulating itself solely on the basis of intrinsic warrants, the right of protest and critique of any citizen must be guaranteed as an inference from the egalitarian view that knowledge of divine purpose is not the exclusive domain of any privileged class.[14]

The theological rationale for the categorical relativization of everything human was the claim that every form of government is the product of fallible, sinful human beings. Thus an unbroken line of continuity exists from Samuel to the early Christian martyrs and on down to Dietrich Bonhoeffer and Reinhold Niebuhr. This tradition declares that nationalistic idolatry can be avoided only where human authorities are exposed to the uncensored scrutiny of critics who, by reserving ultimate loyalty for an authority that transcends every historical institution and national boundary, maintain a stance independent of and uncoopted by any political regime.

In the epilogue, a monkey wrench in what may give the illusion of a smoothly running system of critique will have to be explored: the very agents entrusted with moral scrutiny, namely, individuals and communities formed around ethical values, are themselves human and vulnerable to self-deception. Indictments claiming basis in divine authority can be—and as our survey in part 1 amply illustrated, often have been—merely the expression of partisan interests and sectarian prejudices. In the Hebrew Bible this problem took the form of the struggle between false and true prophecy.[15] In the New Testament the apostle

---

14. The cultural ramifications of this "democratization" of religious practice are far-reaching and include the development of a simplified system of transmitting sacred texts (that, unlike hieroglyphs or cuneiform, is easily learned by normal citizens) and the development of the individual's sense of moral agency and responsibility.

15. Deut. 18:22; 1 Kgs. 22:28; Jer. 5:30–31; 14:14; 23:21.

Paul wrestled with the issue of discernment of spirits.[16] For the moment, it must be sufficient to issue a *caveat lector*, deferring until later a more thorough exploration of this vexed problem: criticism must be as rigorously directed at one's self and one's own party as at the other person or party. In God's *imperium*, there are no favorites, no custodians of infallible truth, only fellow sinners called together in a search of the common good and a commitment to the well-being of all.

In biblical studies it is important to move beyond theoretical discussion to specific examples. This is especially true in the case of the disputatious topic of monarchy. Kingship was a controversial and complicated phenomenon from its inception in Israel, as indicated by the conflicting biblical accounts of the life of the first king, Saul (1 Sam. 8–12). In later writings, the king could be held up as the paragon of virtue (Ps. 72), be addressed as "God" (Ps. 45:6 [Heb. v. 7]), and even shape the nation's yearning for a Messiah (Zech. 9:9–10). Or he could be denounced as the cause of the downfall of God's people (Amos 7:16–17; Jer. 22).

A monolithic understanding of kingship did not exist in Israel precisely because it was an institution stripped of its divinity, and thus exposed to moral scrutiny like any other human institution. For this reason it could be argued that Yahwistic religion exercised a secularizing effect on the notions of kingship that prevailed in the world of early Israel. That would be accurate only partially, however, for there is another half of the picture. By bringing divine presence down from heaven to earth, biblical religion opened the mundane realm to the search for evidence of God's mediated presence.

The historical fact that kingship succeeded theocracy behooved Israel's savants to clarify how divine purpose could be served by this institution. They did so, as exemplified by the transitional role played by Samuel, by proposing a form of kingship infused with and shaped by the essential beliefs and values of early Yahwism. More specifically, they did so by describing kingship in terms of covenant, that is, the contractual arrangement God made between God and humans. In the early Mosaic phase of Israelite religion, covenant was conceived of in conditional terms. To grant kings exceptions from those terms flew in the face of deep-seated Yahwistic confessions and convictions.

God in all periods of biblical history draws humans into covenant through election, reflecting the fact that the divine/human relation depends on divine initiative. Election is amenable, however, to divergent construals. On the one hand, emphasis can be placed on the *privileges* that accompany election: through election, the king is exalted above all other humans, enjoys special divine blessings, and shares in the hymns of praise raised by humans to the deity. Or emphasis can be placed on the religious and moral *responsibility* of the elected one: the king is clothed by God with the qualities of evenhanded justice and compassionate care for the weak and the poor that derive from God's own nature. New Testament writers, drawing on Isaiah 53, even discerned the definitive paragon of royalty in the willingness of Jesus to die for his people, a paradox that challenged

---

16. 1 Cor. 12:10; 14:29–33; cf. 1 John 4:1–6.

theological savants through the centuries, none of whom were able to match the eloquence of the apostle Paul in the second chapter of Philippians.[17]

While the kings of Judah and Israel who patterned their rule after ancient Near Eastern imperial models emphasized the special privileges imparted by divine appointment, those who sought to adhere to a "constitutional" understanding of limited monarchy provided tangible proof of the abiding influence of the Mosaic covenant. Within the framework of that covenant, they recognized reciprocal commitments: YHWH committed himself to support, defend, and give wisdom to those he anointed, while they in turn devoted themselves to faithfulness in worship and obedience to God's commandments. This reciprocal structure reflects the premonarchical origins of the Yahwistic communal identity discussed in the previous chapter. In effect, it flows naturally out of the nested nature of leadership characteristic of the league, whereby the paterfamilias and the clan members pledged to each other adherence to specific commitments.

In the case of kings who sought to abide by the terms of constitutional monarchy, the older Mosaic covenant and the new royal covenant were not set in conflict, with the former being construed as conditional and the latter as absolute. Instead, kingship was reshaped so as to preserve the values intrinsic to faith in YHWH. Even as the God of Israel, under the Mosaic covenant, was committed to the well-being and protection of the people, so the king as God's agent pledged himself to upholding the inalienable rights of individuals, preserving their family inheritances, extending to vulnerable classes such as widows and orphans the safeguards necessary to protect their dignity and well-being, as well as to provide efficient administration, an open and transparent judicial system, adequate military defense, and a robust economy. The people in turn promised to be loyal to their king, compliant in paying the taxes requisite for public order and dutiful when called to military service.

Our attention thus far has been focused on the viability of a reconciliation between the Mosaic and royal covenants, a comity that would draw on the strengths of both the charismatic and monarchical models of governance. At the heart of that ideal lies a dynamic that enables the twin covenants to meld and to flourish. It is the dynamic of a concept of loyalty that is propelled by the dialectical relation between ultimate and penultimate loyalties. The people on the level of day-to-day political matters commit themselves to be loyal to their king. If this were the end of the matter, to be sure, the result could be a form of tyrannical kingship with godlike reverence being paid to the human ruler. But as in the case of the graduating levels of heads of households during the league period, so too in the case of kings: while enjoying the loyalty of his subjects, the king himself was subject to the highest King, and in relation to the sovereign of the heavens and the earth he joined his people in worship and a life of humble piety and obedience as an expression of *the ultimate loyalty* that in a theocratic understanding of government was reserved for God alone.

17. Cf. Matt. 8:16–17; Luke 22:28; 1 Cor. 1:22.

In the historical examples to which we now turn, we shall examine how individual rulers related to the conditions imposed by a form of monarchy that complied with the traditional values of Yahwistic faith. Did a king respect the limits imposed on him by the model of the righteous leader cultivated by his progenitors? Did he honor commitments made to subjects as well as to God? We shall look for more than acts of piety such as prayer and sacrifice. We shall also scrutinize the lives of kings in relation to something that has tested leaders of all ages, namely, the exercise of power: Is there evidence of power sharing and respect for the division of power as a safeguard against its abuse? Is there evidence of openness to criticism, even contriteness, in the case of legitimate censure? Does a king's ruling style leave room for consultation with other than handpicked advisors and court-paid prophets?

EXAMPLES OF "LIMITED" MONARCHY
IN THE NARRATIVE LITERATURE

In the narrative structure of the Deuteronomistic History, Samuel's warning to the people in 1 Samuel 8, in response to their determination to have a king, serves as the backdrop for the long chronicle of the kings of Judah and Israel. The bitter struggle between Samuel and Saul over sacrifice and military operations adds further detail to the stage setting. The reign of David is covered extensively, due in large part to the availability to the ancient historians of two long narratives, each covering an important part of David's life. The depiction of David earns for him the distinction of being the first—and in certain ways the paradigmatic—example of a king who was respectful of the limits imposed on monarchy by Israel's indigenous religious beliefs and values. This may be attributable in part to the fact that his reign came at a time in the history of the nation antecedent to the development of the structures of full-blown monarchy. But the narrative also invites one to examine the character of David, a man who combined cunning and ambition with more laudable qualities manifested in his loyalty toward Saul, steadfastness in his friendship with Jonathan, and hospitality to the outcasts who looked to him for leadership (1 Sam. 22:2; 2 Sam. 15:18–23).

Several episodes illustrate David's openness to the counsel of the prophets serving as guardians of the core values of early Yahwism. In 2 Samuel 7, David expresses his intent to build a temple, the significance of which within ancient Near Eastern royal ideology we have already detailed. But Nathan the prophet delivers to David a word of YHWH explaining that God's manner of being present with his people was not the conventional one of dwelling in a temple, but of "moving about in a tent," that is, of a lifestyle at home with seminomads and loosely confederated clans rather than with urban cultures. David defers. But matters do not then simply revert to the hallowed customs of the past. While God's reaffirmation of the promise of a homeland underlines continuity with the past, something new is added. To the old covenant with the entire nation a new personalized covenant is added: "the LORD declares to you that the LORD will make you a house. When your days are fulfilled and you lie down with your ancestors, I will raise up your offspring after you, . . . and I will establish his kingdom" (2 Sam. 7:11–12).

The moral obligations of the king find expression in the stipulation that if an individual Davidic king disobeyed the Mosaic law, he would be punished (7:14). But the foundation of monarchy is secured with an attendant promise (one with which prophets like Amos and Jeremiah would take issue): "Your house and your kingdom shall be made sure forever" (7:16). The effort to strike a balance between the values of the league and the innovations of kingship is patently evident in the tension running through this narrative, as indeed we found to be the case in Psalm 89.

Ironically, one of David's most despicable acts illustrates with greatest clarity his openness to the terms of the Mosaic covenant. In an act befitting an absolute monarch, he gets a wife by arranging for the death of her husband (2 Sam. 11). The prophet Nathan encounters him with the indictment and sentence of the higher court that the prophet serves, that of the divine sovereign. David acknowledges the higher authority of that court through deep remorse, repentance, and fasting. From it he emerges chastened and burdened with the prophet's warning that "the sword shall never depart from your house" (2 Sam. 12:10).

Earlier we noted the sharp difference that existed in the sources available to the Deuteronomistic Historians in their dealing with the reigns of David and Solomon. Since the narrative covering Solomon's reign compensates for the lack of older historiographic sources with an account couched in legend, we may be receiving more the portrait of how later tradents pictured the ideal of kingship than an accurate depiction of Solomon's reign. But that tendentious portrait is important in its own right for one studying the politics of the Bible, for those who painted it were participants in the construction of biblical political theory.

Though the scholarly literature contains a wide range of opinions regarding the nature of Solomon's reign, our reading of the biblical and archaeological evidence suggests that Solomon did move kingship in the direction of administrative and architectural sophistication patterned after the capitals of neighboring empires. His accomplishments are ascribed by the ancient historians to Solomon's deep devotion to YHWH. The fact that the long prayer of Solomon that opens the section treating his reign resembles speeches and prayers coming at critical junctures throughout the Deuteronomistic History led Martin Noth to the plausible observation that they represent the theological interpretation of the Deuteronomists.[18] But as observed earlier, the aura in which Solomon's

---

18. Martin Noth, *Überlieferungsgeschichtliche Studien: Die sammelnden und bearbeitenden Geschichtswerke im Alten Testament* (Tübingen: M. Niemeyer, 1957).

reign was couched, while veiling biographical details, may reflect the model of monarchy that he sought, and in part was able, to institute.

Solomon's prayer in 1 Kings 8:22–53 manifests the spirituality and humility that, according to the concept of constitutional monarchy, are essential to the security and prosperity of the nation. Solomon opens the prayer by addressing the incomparable God of Israel, a God "keeping covenant and steadfast love for your servants who walk before you with all their heart, the covenant that you kept for your servant my father David" (8:23–24). Carefully held in balance are God's steadfast commitment and the king's wholehearted obedience.

The prayer gives eloquent expression to the temple theology that is one feature of the Deuteronomistic interpretation of limited monarchy. As God has committed himself to a particular dynasty, so too is God committed to a particular earthly location as the place where he makes the divine presence accessible to the people. On the face of it, this seems similar to the place of the temple in mythopoeic conceptions of absolute monarchy, in connection with which we have observed the parallelism between the heavenly house of the patron deity and the temple built and maintained by the king to serve the needs of the gods.

However, in the Deuteronomistic version of monarchy, the temple's role in relation to the deity is carefully defined so as to exclude the possibility of viewing the earthly temple as the house in which YHWH actually dwells. The archaic aniconic tradition of early Israel, that is, the prohibition against the manufacture of any image of the deity, itself safeguards against such confusion. But added to it in Deuteronomistic thought is what scholars have called "name theology." God authorizes the construction of the temple as a place where his name (*šēm*) will dwell (1 Kgs. 8:29), while God's *actual* dwelling remains in heaven (8:30). These two points are seen clearly in the prayer by comparing verse 29 with verse 30 and viewing both against the background of verse 27: "But will God indeed dwell on the earth? Even heaven and the highest heaven cannot contain you, much less this house that I have built!"

God cannot be manipulated by humans, not even empowered humans like priests and kings. Nevertheless, out of respect for the twin covenants with the people and the king, God promises to be accessible in the temple. Even then, however, God's sovereignty is safeguarded, for the prayer makes clear through numerous examples that God will hear the pleas of humans when they arise from repentant, God-fearing hearts. The twin covenants again betray roots reaching back to a common theological tradition. The king who sins will be punished, the people that sins will be punished; but God will have mercy on king and people when they repent and pray for mercy. Whether the plight should involve crop failure, disease, war, or even captivity and exile, God will hear the prayers of the repentant that are directed toward the city and house that Solomon built for God's *name*.

Further on in their history, the Deuteronomists were able to describe several other kings of the Davidic house who sought to uphold the terms of the Mosaic covenant. Of Asa they reported that he "did what was right in the sight of the

LORD," and that "his heart was true to the LORD all his days" (1 Kgs. 15:11, 14). Of Jehoshaphat they wrote, "He walked in all the way of his father Asa; he did not turn aside from it, doing what was right in the sight of the LORD" (1 Kgs. 22:43).

A later historiographic work referred to as the Chronicler (consisting of 1 and 2 Chronicles, Ezra, and Nehemiah) limits its scope to the southern kingdom of Judah. Though its chief source is the Deuteronomistic History, it seems that its authors had access to sources providing data for a more detailed account of Jehoshophat's reign (2 Chr. 17–20). This more elaborate picture comports with the brief glimpse given of Jehoshaphat in 1 Kings 22, where, in contrast to the evil King Ahab, he is portrayed as one eager to be counseled by prophets true to YHWH. According to the Chronicler, he is faithful in worship, dedicated to upholding the traditional law through judicial reform, and steadfast in trusting God during times of international crisis. His faithfulness is seen as key to the prosperity enjoyed by the nation during his reign.

Turning back to the Deuteronomistic History, we find that Hezekiah was the next to win praise, "He trusted in the LORD the God of Israel. . . . For he held fast to the LORD; he did not depart from following him but kept the commandments that the LORD commanded Moses" (2 Kgs. 18:5, 6).

In many ways, the Hezekiah we meet in 2 Kings exemplifies the Israelite model of constitutional monarchy. He is described as a leader who placed prayer and worship at the center of his decision making. Moreover, the purge of Canaanite religious relics and practices for which he is credited underscores his commitment to the central tenet of Mosaic covenant. There is no indication that he used the special entitlements associated with his office for personal gain. In instances of both diplomatic crisis and serious personal illness, his point of orientation in seeking direction was true to the law of the king in Deuteronomy 17. Moreover, he respected the assets available within the framework of checks and balances inherent in Israel's concept of limited monarchy.

When the army of the Assyrian king Sennacherib, which had already devastated all of the other fortified cities of Judah, was at the walls of Jerusalem, Hezekiah sought the counsel not only of his royal advisors, but also of the senior priests and the prophet Isaiah. As a result, religious faith, the pragmatics of international diplomacy, and domestic priorities were mutually enriched by an approach to politics that enlisted all of the available resources of the nation. The result was not a confusing mix of incommensurate ingredients, but the implementation of effective statecraft. No small part of the credit goes to the prophet Isaiah, whose moral compass was calibrated in accord with a powerful, integrative vision of God's sovereignty. On that basis Isaiah was able to extend to his king hope for a final salutary outcome of events, a hope to be sure chastened by a deep distrust of human power, especially power twisted into arrogant self-confidence by pride. To Isaiah we shall return in chapter 15.

The Deuteronomists, the Chronicler, and the prophet Jeremiah concur in ascribing to our next exemplar, King Josiah, a deep commitment to the faith and moral values of Yahwism. Particularly noteworthy is the connection made by both of the ancient histories between his "discovery of the book of the law in the temple" in 622 and the thoroughgoing reform of the cult that he carried out. Given the plausibility of the scholarly view that the "book of the law" being referred to was the Torah constituting the heart of the book of Deuteronomy, it appears that the zeal for the Lord, awakened in his heart and validated by the prophet Huldah, was rooted in the covenant formulary that shaped a limited form of monarchy consistent with the ancestral Yahwistic faith (2 Kgs. 22:11–20). It is one of the deep ironies of the history of monarchy in Israel that Josiah's covenantal fidelity did not survive his tragic death at the sword of the Egyptian pharaoh Neco, for the despotic manner of rule of his offspring led not to commendation but rather to prominence in the gallery of Israel's most blameworthy kings (Jer. 22:11–19).

From the period of the divided monarchy, Asa, Jehoshaphat, Hezekiah, and Josiah were the only kings earning positive evaluations by the Deuteronomists and the Chronicler. The northern kings fared even worse, being condemned en bloc by the older historians and ignored by the Chronicler. To be sure, a distinct historiography slants the interpretation of both of these southern-based works in favor of their half of the divided Jewish nation. Indeed, the twin themes of Deuteronomistic History are God's election of Jerusalem ("his habitation to put his name there," Deut. 12:5) and God's election of the Davidide ("your throne shall be established forever," 2 Sam. 7:16). In the case of Chronicles, a leading historiographic theme was the reunification of the divided kingdom under the Davidic house, from which follows the refusal even to acknowledge a separate rival kingdom in the north.

Shortly we shall return to the narrative sources for illustrations of kings who were influenced by the tenets of absolute monarchy. First, we turn to the traces found in the Psalter of the form of monarchy that conformed to the central theocratic principle of the ancestral Yahwistic religion, "no king but YHWH."

EXPRESSIONS OF LIMITED MONARCHY
IN HYMNIC LITERATURE

When dealing with the theme of monarchy, it is especially important to be sensitive to the functional difference between hymnic/poetic compositions and narrative/historiographic literature. While the latter seeks to give an orderly account of the history of kingship in Israel, the former in verse celebrate the glorious triumphs of kings enjoying divine favor and lament the trials and defeats they suffer in less propitious times. As we observed in the case of Psalm 89, hymns project vivid images, many of them derived from the mythopoeic celebration of kings whose stature and accomplishments loom larger than life. While any analysis of history narratives must reckon with the issue of interpretive tendencies impelled by authorial presuppositions, the hyperbolic and symbolic characteristics of hymnic literature create even greater challenges. Nevertheless, the two psalms to which we now turn enrich our understanding of important aspects of Israel's concept of limited monarchy.

Psalm 132 revolves around the twin elections that provide the etiological warrants for Israelite kingship:

> The LORD swore to David a sure oath
>   from which he will not turn back:
> "One of the sons of your body
>   I will set on your throne."
>
>   (v. 11)

> For the LORD has chosen Zion;
>   he has desired it for his habitation:
> "This is my resting place forever;
>   here I will reside, for I have desired it."
>
>   (v. 13)

The background that the psalm gives for God's choosing a royal house and a temple city recalls the narrative history, for the setting is not the heavenly drama of myth, but the historical episodes of a human life. David, out of his zeal for the Lord, endured great hardships and showed remarkable tenacity in his effort to find "a dwelling place" for the Lord, which, as verse 8 indicates, means a sanctuary for the ark that represented the invisible presence of God with the people.[19] The first point clarified by this psalm is therefore the fact that kingship in Israel was a chapter in the ongoing Epic of God's dealings with the Jewish community.

The second point provides the key to Israel's concept of limited monarchy:

> "If your sons keep my covenant and my decrees that I shall teach them,
>   their sons also, forevermore, shall sit on your throne."
>
>   (v. 12)

The rule of Israel's kings benefits from divine support, but that support is contingent on the terms of the theocratic principle that ultimately only one rule is authoritative, that of the divine king. To that heavenly king every human king must submit. The condition of obedience creates an important line of continuity with Israel's Epic tradition. It cautions against reading lofty formulations of God's covenant with the Davidic house, like Psalm 89:36–37, in terms of a divine guarantee exempt from the critique raised by other biblical texts. Monarchy in Israel will prosper and bring prosperity to its subjects, not on the basis of a mythic event antecedent to history, nor on the basis of eternal orders of creation akin to those regulating the heavenly bodies, but rather on the basis of an earlier covenant that God established with Israel long before the advent of kingship.

---

19. The so-called ark narrative in 1 Sam. 4–7 has been examined in detail by Miller and Roberts, *Ark*; see note 1 of this chapter.

Though kingship would introduce new institutions and ordinances, the laws and statutes of the Mosaic covenant could not be annulled, but remained binding on king and subjects alike, for all humans ultimately stood under the sovereign will of the only absolute king. Affirmed by Psalm 132 is thus the reciprocal relationship of divine grace and human response in grateful obedience that had been a hallmark of Israelite community from its early formative years. The historical ontology that had taken root during the league period could not be eradicated by the innovations of kings. At its core Israel was to remain a theocracy under YHWH, regardless of its mundane structures of governance at any given time. Ancestral beliefs and values thus provided the framework within which kingship, as one historical episode among many in the ongoing history of God's dealing with Israel, would have to find its place. The theo-political lesson taught by Psalm 132 is clear: when it comes to monarchy, honest interpretation must take into account the tensions in the biblical texts themselves.

Psalm 72 in turn presents the king in terms that reflect the compromise that was reached in the development of a limited, constitutional form of monarchy between the religious beliefs and moral values of early Yahwism and the innovations introduced by monarchy. The covenant that creates a special bond between God and king is described with images and similes that fashion a nimbus of glory around the king. Prayers were made that his reign might endure as long as the sun and moon and that he might be like "showers that water the earth" (72:5–6). Like the great emperors of Mesopotamia he is to have "dominion from sea to sea," to him all of the kings of the earth are to render homage, and like Abraham of old, nations are to be blessed in him (cf. Gen. 12:3).

Interspersed with prayers for his exaltation above every other power on earth, however, are equally exuberant descriptions of the king as a righteous judge and a defender of the poor and needy against their oppressors. While such rhetoric is also at home in the ideology of ancient Near Eastern kingship, the connections are unmistakable between the portrait of the king in Psalm 72 and the description in the early Yahwistic Epic of the God who heard the cries of the oppressed Hebrew slaves in Egypt and mercifully delivered them and guided them to their new homeland:

> For he delivers the needy when they call,
>   the poor and those who have no helper.
> He has pity on the weak and the needy,
>   and saves the lives of the needy.
> From oppression and violence he redeems their life;
>   and precious is their blood in his sight.
>   (Ps. 72:12–14)

What is most striking in Psalm 72 is the inseparable connection between the king's dedication to merciful justice and the prosperity and security of the land.

Verses 2 and 3 make this connection by placing the two themes side by side in syntactic parallelism:

> May he judge your people with righteousness,
>   and your poor with justice.
> May the mountains yield prosperity for the people,
>   and the hills, in righteousness.

Also striking is the linking of the description of the king's dominion over the kings of the earth (72:8–11) with his merciful treatment of the weak and the poor (72:12–14). The moral dimension of the psalmist's concept of monarchy could not be stated more clearly.

The final point to be made is that in the climactic conclusion of the psalm, praise of the king is subsumed under the ultimate praise that is raised to "the LORD, the God of Israel, who alone does wondrous things" (72:18). Not only does this create an emphatic reminder of the king's subordination to the one absolute king; it also points to the source of the qualities of just compassion that the king is to embody.

Psalm 82 amplifies the theme of God's universal justice: The God whom Israel worships presides in judgment even over the gods of the other nations and sentences them to revocation of their divinity because they have failed to "give justice to the weak" or to "rescue the weak and the needy," but instead have judged unjustly and shown "partiality to the wicked" (Ps. 82:2–4). The power with which God rules the universe is the power of compassionate justice. When divine moral law is violated by those in power, "all the foundations of the earth are shaken" (82:5). The connection between prosperity and justice therefore is based in ancient Israel on an elemental theocratic principle, a principle to which monarchy had to conform if it were to remain within the framework of Yahwistic belief. In an ultimate sense, even in the new era there remained but one king in Israel, a king who was the merciful champion of the weak and the just defender of the oppressed.

We conclude this section with reference to Psalm 22, a hymn best known as the source of Jesus' lament on the cross, "My God, my God, why have you forsaken me?" (v. 1). In it we hear of the suffering and humiliation suffered by one (identified in the title of the psalm as King David) who pleads for God, upon whom he is utterly dependent, to deliver him as he once had saved his ancestors (vv. 4–5). Even in his adversity, however, his trust in God is reaffirmed (vv. 25–26). More astonishing still is his affirmation of God's *universal* dominion in words that represent one of the most concise formulations of the theocratic principle in the entire Bible (vv. 27–28):

> All the ends of the earth shall remember
>   and turn to the LORD;
> and all the families of the nations
>   shall worship before him.

For dominion belongs to the LORD,
    and he rules over the nations.

THE LURE OF POWER: SIGNS OF THE INFLUENCE
OF THE IDEOLOGY OF ABSOLUTE KINGSHIP

In this section, we engage in oversimplification. Though the Deuteronomistic History provides a precedent by dividing the kings of Judah into the categories of good and bad, modern historians refrain from categorizing them neatly, as either those respecting the theocratic restraints on monarchy mandated by the Mosaic covenant, or those succumbing to the blandishments of ancient Near Eastern kingship ideals. After all, on which side of the ledger would be the witness to David's heinous violation of the dignity of Uriah and Bathsheba? Despite that caveat, we shall describe several kings whom the ancient historians of Israel judged to be untrue to Yahwistic beliefs and values. If unreliable as a source of knowledge of the actual figures involved, the narratives do point out traits the biblical tradents deemed to fail the moral test of the ancestral faith of their ancestors.

The Deuteronomistic account of Ahab begins with reference to the marriage alliance his father Omri had arranged between his son and Jezebel, a Phoenician princess. The tone thus set is ominous, since Ethbaal, king of Tyre, presided over a monarchy styled after the "eternal" rule of the Egyptian pharaohs. As indicated by his name, his patron god was Baal.

Ahab wasted no time in building a temple for his wife's deity in his capital city of Samaria. Conflict was soon to follow, initially between the zealous supporters of the Canaanite god Baal, namely, Ahab and Jezebel on one side, and the prophet of YHWH named Obadiah and his disciples on the other. Soon, another defender of the ancestral faith joined the fray: Elijah, named "troubler of Israel" by the king.

Ahab's political ideal is portrayed bluntly in the narrative: among the prerogatives of a king is the right to establish and support the religious institutions and practices of his state. Elijah refutes the king's version of monarchy with appeal to the only king with a legitimate claim on the devotion of the people: "I have not troubled Israel; but you have, and your father's house, because you have forsaken the commandments of the LORD and followed the Baals" (1 Kgs. 18:18).

The legend cycle that grew up around the figure of Elijah is characterized by high drama, with Elijah staging a contest between YHWH and Baal, Jezebel hotly pursuing her nemesis, and Ahab yielding to the harsh tactics of his tyrant wife by eliminating the rightful owner of an ancestral vineyard he desires for his own deployment. Though the king takes possession of the vineyard, the prophet saves the last word for God: "Because you have sold yourself to do what is evil in the sight of the LORD, I will bring disaster on you" (1 Kgs. 21:20–21). And concerning the queen: "The dogs shall eat Jezebel" (1 Kgs. 21:23).

Upon the next "bad" king, Manasseh, are heaped myriad acts that violate Mosaic Torah and repudiate YHWH's claim to sole worship (2 Kgs. 21:1–9). One particular ritual action strikes the reader as particularly heinous, the sacrifice of his own son through immolation (v. 6).[20]

Though the Chronicler added a sequel to the Manasseh account describing the chastened king repenting and being forgiven by YHWH during his incarceration in Babylon (2 Chr. 33:12–13), the Deuteronomists stick to the script of a king so out of alignment with the Yahwistic idea of limited, God-centered kingship as to bring upon Judah the devastating fate that previously had fallen upon the northern kingdom (2 Kgs. 21:10–15).

If the scales of divine justice required the wickedness of yet another king to seal the fate of a rebellious people, Jehoiakim filled the bill with an irony that echoed the righteous father/faithless son pattern of Hezekiah and Manasseh. Jeremiah drew the contrast between Josiah and Jehoiakim with these stinging words (Jer. 22:15–17):

> Did not your father eat and drink
>   and do justice and righteousness? . . .
> He judged the cause of the poor and needy. . . .
> But your eyes and heart
>   are only on your dishonest gain,
> for shedding innocent blood,
>   and for practicing oppression and violence.

Regarding the legacy of the kings deemed wicked by ancient historians and prophets alike, the sentence was clear: not monarchy per se, but those who had been anointed to lead the nation, but who refused to live within the limits of a form of monarchy that was respectful of the central tenets of the ancestral Yahwistic faith, had bought ruin upon the land.

We shall conclude this chapter with a comment regarding the ambiguous nature of Israel's second form of government.

THE DANGERS INHERENT IN MONARCHY

A strong case in defense of Israel's second form of government can be made. To begin with, the invasion of the Philistines threatened the loosely confederated tribes with annihilation and called for a centralized polity capable of organizing material and human resources into a military force capable of defending the nation. Under the leadership of Samuel a limited concept of monarchy developed that both satisfied the needs presented by the changed international situation and respected the essential beliefs and values of the religious tradition that

---

20. In 2 Kgs. 16:3 King Ahaz is also accused of human sacrifice (cf. Jer. 7:31–32; 19:5–6; 32:35).

had become established in the previous two centuries. On what basis then could one raise objections to monarchy?

On one level, the problems, no different than in the case of any other form of government, have to do with competence. If one chooses one's examples carefully, one can make either a strong case for the fittingness of monarchy for Israel's situation in the Iron Age or an emphatically negative one. Jeremiah demonstrates both options in his condemnation of Jehoiakim and valorization of his father Josiah (Jer. 22:13–17).

But is there a more comprehensive measure against which individual kings can be evaluated? There is likely to be no objection for the use of competence as a standard for assessing a public official in any setting or time period. David was competent. There is no evidence that Zimri was. More controversial is the role integrity should play in an evaluative criteriology. So long as the duties of office are fulfilled competently, what bearing do traits of character have on political performance?

The distinction between professional competence and personal character is anachronistic when applied to Israelite thought, which did not question what moderns may consider an ad hominem position, namely, that personal morality is integral to political effectiveness. At least in the mind of the prophets, the king was to serve as a model of honesty, compassion, and religious piety for the rest of the nation. This perhaps had less to do with what might be associated with pietism in modern parlance than with Israel's rigorously consistent moral view of reality. Competence in office was inseparably tied to purity of heart. A wayward heart, whether distracted by lust, greed, or self-aggrandizement, was a major obstacle in the way of performance of duty. It is for that reason that the prophets, the primary watchdogs of Israelite moral values, did not hesitate to scrutinize the personal lives of kings, priests, and nobles. There was no strict line of separation between personal behavior and public performance when it came to upholding the terms of the covenant, regardless of one's position in Israelite society.[21]

This linkage becomes particularly clear when one views the manner in which Israel's kings dealt with power. Familiar is the adage "Power corrupts, and absolute power corrupts absolutely." The centralization of power that occurred institutionally under Israel's kings for very understandable historical reasons was accompanied by the standard temptations beckoning those upon whom exceptional powers are conferred, temptations to exploit those powers for entitlements and rights that were denied their subjects. In the case of a fledgling monarchy surrounded by mighty empires, a metaphysical dimension compounded the historical/political problem. As noted earlier, to the kings of Egypt and Mesopotamia were attributed divine qualities.

---

21. In modern times, the manner in which different standards of personal morality were applied to Presidents Kennedy and Nixon is noteworthy.

The kings of Israel were not immune to the temptation to see themselves as enjoying a higher status than their subjects on the scale from human to divine. What happens to the self-image of one who receives a divine oracle announcing, "You are my son; today I have begotten you" (Ps. 2:7)? Royal and sacerdotal powers are both attributed to the king in Psalm 110, and his origins are described in mysteriously mythological terms (110:3b). When the king is addressed as "God" in Psalm 45:6, one detects the hyperbole of court style, but when this hymnic celebration of royal marriage goes on to describe the special privileges that accrue to this one exalted among mortals, this "most handsome of men" (45:2) who is distinguished from his companions by the superior quality of his cosmetics, who is showered with the gifts of the wealthy, who is pampered by a princess decked in her chamber with gold-embroidered robes and followed by her attending virgins, one is prompted to ask what effect this has on his ability to rule with wisdom, humility, justice, and a dedication to the equality of all mortals under God's reign.

Psalm 45 thus gives the reader a glimpse of a social world that stands in stark contrast to the world that produced Israel's village culture and its austere customs and mores. In the new social world of the royal court lurked the temptation for its chief resident to view himself as categorically higher in status than his fellow citizens, perhaps even as being endowed with divine attributes. With this inflated self-image came a sense of entitlement to comforts and luxury not within the reach of the average citizen. Almost certain to follow in the wake of such exceptionalism was neglect of the poor, exploitation of the weak, decay of high standards of evenhanded justice, and tolerance of cronyism and marketplace dishonesty. To be sure, not everyone in the kingdom shared the skepticism of the prophets toward the pretensions of the crown. An elite minority living close to the king as courtiers and advisors enjoyed the benefits of court life and were eager to contribute to the continued magnification of the royal office. And as the plight of Jeremiah and his ilk demonstrate, the position of whistleblower was no less hazardous then than now.

A second danger accompanied kingship. We have noted that a key element in the concept of limited monarchy was a system of checks and balances built into the governance of the nation that acted as a restraint on both personal and institutional abuses. That ordinary Israelite citizens were participants in the sharing of power is manifested in their participation in the acclamation and coronation of their kings.[22] Prophets served as counselors and critics in bringing the values of early Yahwism to bear on public policy making. Priests exercised a high degree of autonomy in administering the religious rituals and cultivating knowledge and reverence for the Torah.

The move away from limited monarchy toward a less restrained form of rule thwarted the functioning of the checks and balances that the interplay of these diverse offices provided. A bulging bureaucracy shielded the king from contact

22. 1 Sam. 11:15; 2 Sam. 2:4; 5:3; cf. Judg. 8:23–33.

with subjects. The religious cult was brought under the direct control of the crown. Prophets were silenced, often through persecution and the threat of death. Public policies were determined by a king exalted above his subjects, with the aid of counselors who were handpicked and prophets and priests living on the payroll of the royal court.

Hebrew Scripture as it was compiled and handed down to posterity was rigorously persistent in preserving, on the one hand, evidence for the historical necessity and even potential benefits of monarchy and, on the other hand, the threats it presented to the fledgling Yahwistic political ideals of compassionate justice and equality for all, ideals attainable only under the reign of a Creator transcending every form of special privilege and committed to the well-being of every one of his beloved children. In their nuanced treatment of monarchy, the historians, psalmists, and sages of Israel demonstrated the deftness with which they combined the lofty idealism of their ancestral faith and a healthy dose of pragmatism: They were insistent that ultimately Israel was to acknowledge only one king, but at the same time they were willing to forge a limited version of monarchy that would enable the nation to cope with new historical challenges while preserving robust safeguards against kingship's becoming an instrument of idolatry and abuse.

On its most basic level, the controversy over monarchy in the centuries in which kings reigned in Israel involved a spiritual struggle for the heart of the nation. At the eye of the storm in that struggle were the Hebrew prophets. To them we now turn.

Chapter 12

Prophetic Politics

THE PLACE OF THE PROPHETS WITHIN THE POLITICAL STRUCTURES OF ANCIENT ISRAEL

In three essential respects *prophetic politics* in ancient Israel preserved and adapted to new situations the theo-political legacy of early Yahwistic religion: (1) there is but one universal sovereign who rules over all nations and all creation (the theocratic principle); (2) the one true God is accessible to ordinary persons, who, irrespective of social class or lineage, can be visited by the divine Spirit and enlisted as witnesses to and agents of divine purpose; (3) the God encountered in such existential moments of calling is not a generic *mysterium* or an abstract principle, but the personal God YHWH, who had accompanied Israel from its infancy as a nation and promised to remain true to the terms of the solemn covenant through which he became their God and they his people.

This historical understanding of divine governance in human affairs stood in conflict with the fundamental claim of monarchy as it was generally construed in the ancient Near East, according to which the deity had chosen a special agent to incarnate, represent, and manage earthly affairs as a vassal manages his master's plantation. According to that ideology, prophecy, like all other human

216

activities, was obliged to conform to the policies of the royal bureaucracy and to adapt its pronouncements to the interests of the crown. The prophetic functionaries whose activities are described in texts surviving from ancient Egypt and Mesopotamia fit this type.[1] While the Israelite prophets whose writings were preserved in Hebrew Scripture were not categorically opposed to the institution of monarchy (note especially the active role of Isaiah vis-à-vis the Judean kings), the theocratic principle that they held to be inviolable precluded the possibility of accepting an earthly king as the final authority in matters of governance. In this way they manifested a line of continuity with the ancestral Yahwistic confession, "There is no king but YHWH."

The distinction between the prevailing ancient Near Eastern ideal of kingship and the Yahwistic concept of limited monarchy is illustrated vividly by comparing the figures deemed by biblical tradition to be true prophets with those who were denounced as false, for the latter closely resemble the prophetic figures found in the cultures neighboring ancient Israel.[2] The contempt for the four hundred prophets of Ahab in 1 Kings 22:6 offers a glimpse into the attitude of the prophets of YHWH toward court-appointed functionaries. The latter earned their stipend by proclaiming as divine oracles the words their king desired to hear, thereby conforming to the picture painted by the Deuteronomists of King Ahab as a king who had betrayed the religious traditions of his people and imposed on the land the alien customs and beliefs of absolute monarchy native to the culture of his Phoenician wife, Jezebel. King Jehoshaphat, on the other hand, true to what one would expect of a king portrayed by the ancient historians as a godly leader, asked King Ahab, "Is there no other prophet of the LORD here of whom we may inquire?" To which Ahab replied, "There is still one other by whom we may inquire of the LORD, Micaiah son of Imlah; but I hate him, for he never prophesies anything favorable about me, but only disaster" (1 Kgs. 22:7–8). The distinction could not be drawn more clearly.

True prophets of YHWH, unlike court prophets, were unable to manipulate their oracles to make them acceptable to kings, for the source of their moral authority transcended themselves. They were answerable to the only leader to whom they could commit their ultimate loyalty, the king of all nations, and hence they were bound to the orders of no human authority.

In Amos 3:3–8, the eighth-century prophet described the sovereign nature of his source of prophecy, concluding: "The lion has roared; who will not fear? The Lord GOD has spoken; who can but prophesy?" The same prophet stressed to the priest of the royal sanctuary in Bethel that he had proclaimed words of

---

1. See Martti Nissinen, *Prophets and Prophecy in the Ancient Near East* (Atlanta: Society of Biblical Literature, 2003).

2. In this chapter our use of the historiographic writings of the Bible will require the same effort to distinguish between information useful for historical reconstruction and the interpretations of the ancient authors that are of value primarily for the light they shed on the theo-political views of tradents like the Deuteronomistic Historians. When we proceed to the prophetic books themselves, we shall strive to secure a reliable historical footing for our reconstruction and political analysis.

judgment against King Jeroboam, not on the basis of professional credentials, but simply because "the LORD took me from following the flock, and the LORD said to me, 'Go, prophesy to my people Israel'" (Amos 7:15). The prophet Jeremiah described the inner divine imperative with a powerful metaphor: "If I say, 'I will not mention him, or speak any more in his name,' then within me there is something like a burning fire shut up in my bones; I am weary with holding it in, and I cannot" (Jer. 20:9).

Various attempts have been made to explain the phenomenon of the Hebrew prophets, sometimes with appeal to comparative data from other cultures, sometimes with reference to psychopathology, sometimes in terms of psychology. After all such attempts have been exhausted and biblical prophecy seems as elusive as ever, what remains is a description based primarily on the biblical sources themselves. This actually seems to be the most reasonable approach for two reasons. First, after comparisons with similar phenomena from other cultures, both ancient and modern, are made, biblical prophecy essentially remains sui generis. Second, in a study that is interested in the *political* function of prophecy, comparitivist and psychological explanations, while shedding light on certain formal aspects of biblical prophecy, such as the use of messenger formulae and the genre of judicial trial, cannot explain the inner dynamics of the relation between prophets and their fellow citizens. Our primary attention, therefore, must be directed to the theo-political role of the prophets within the concreteness of their native settings.

Prophecy preserved the classic theocratic principle, not only in terms of its function as messenger of the heavenly king, but also in terms of its bearing on political matters. Prophecy was coterminous with kingship in Israel, and it is safe to say that it arose and functioned in response to kingship. In relation to the innovations introduced by Israel's kings, many of them contradicting values reaching back to Israel's clan origins, prophets fought courageously on behalf of the traditional beliefs and values of the community, rooted in adherence to the fundamental theocratic principle of one sovereign.

The inability of even the most powerful and aggressive of Israel's kings to supplant the inferences drawn from that principle, like individual civil rights and inalienable land tenure, proves how deeply rooted in the Israelite consciousness its early Epic and the customs and norms inferred from it had become. Though kingship effected enormous political, cultural, and economic change and lifted Israel for a time from obscurity to regional recognition, on a deep level religious Jews remained true to their unique historical ontology as a people tracing origins solely to divine grace and living under the beneficent rule of the one true king of compassionate justice. This tenacity can be credited in no small measure to the effort of the prophets to preserve the values that their ancestors living in the age of charismatic rulers had struggled so courageously to establish.

That the contents of the prophetic message were not autogamous but betrayed roots in tradition has important bearing on the nature of prophetic politics. Prophets, ancient and modern, are often depicted as ecstatics drawing from their subjective consciousness diatribes against existing realities. They are viewed as operating as individualists rather than as members of a community, as promoting personal viewpoints rather than defending traditional values. In an earlier generation of biblical scholarship, the regnant opinion was that the prophets were the inventors of ethical monotheism. From them, according to this hypothesis, developed the *torah* tradition that became the foundation of Jewish religion. This view, most closely associated with the scholarship of Julius Wellhausen, is no longer convincing.

The prophets, while betraying a high degree of creativity in applying older norms to new situations, were not inventors, but staunch defenders of a tradition of law and an Epic-based understanding of Israelite values that had established itself as the foundation of their community long before the institution of monarchy. They felt the divine call to speak out whenever they observed that their sacred laws and identity-defining values were being threatened by alien notions.

While the social stratification, economic inequality, and elitist view of leadership that accompanied the drift toward the ideology of absolute kingship abetted the moral decline denounced by the prophets, the prophets were not so simplistic as to single out the monarchy as the sole source of corruption and depravity. They were indefatigable in condemning the sins that plague every nation, whatever its system of government, and this they were able to do thanks to the stark anthropological realism to which they subscribed, expressed most succinctly by Jeremiah: "The heart is devious above all else; it is perverse—who can understand it?" True to the classical orientation of Israel's prophets, Jeremiah in the following verse identified the only source available as a remedy to the fatal trap in which humanity was caught, the Lord who can "test the mind and search the heart" (17:10).

In terms of the metaphor introduced earlier, the prophets were guardians of a communal story, specifically, the Epic rooted in the hallowed theocratic principle of YHWH's sole sovereignty. From it they derived a moral vision that not only embraced all aspects of reality but was remarkably consistent in substance. They applied it to their different situations with a courage and freshness that was possible only for those who pictured themselves as agents of a transcendent regime that was the only utterly dependable moral force in the universe. Their understanding of that regime (often referred to in biblical tradition as the reign or kingdom of God) was as grounded in Israel's Epic, as was the communal identity of their ancestors who drew from the exodus pageant the laws and institutions that structured life in the earliest phase of Israelite history.

While deeply grounded in the religious beliefs and ethical values of an ancestral legacy, however, the prophets were not mindless traditionalists imposing ancient norms on new circumstances without thought to source and purpose. Because their beliefs and ethics were rooted in the Epic recounting the involvement of YHWH in the life of Israel, they spoke and acted with the conviction that that same God was still present in the events of *their* time.

Their application of the laws of the past thus was not mechanical or legalistic, but dynamic. Even as kindness to the alien was the only fitting behavior for early Israel, as it drew upon its memory of being aliens who were the beneficiaries of YHWH's mercy, so too during the time of Amos and Isaiah, such kindness remained the consistent way to be a people who continued to depend upon divine mercy.

The prophets accordingly reminded their listeners of the importance of maintaining the vital connection between values and their roots in the ongoing story of God's providential care. Mindfulness of their place in that story would safeguard the social justice and equality upon which political harmony depended. Conversely, forgetting, as denial of Israel's essential nature, was tantamount to national death. Hosea, in chapter 13, laments how both in its earliest history and in his own time, Israel courted calamity by betraying its true sovereign. In verses 4–7 he goes on to give a lesson in memory and forgetfulness:

> Yet I have been the LORD your God
>   ever since the land of Egypt;
> you know no God but me,
>   and besides me there is no savior.
> It was I who fed you in the wilderness,
>   in the land of drought.
> When I fed them, they were satisfied;
>   they were satisfied, and their heart was proud;
>   therefore they forgot me.
> So I will become like a lion to them,
>   like a leopard I will lurk beside the way.

Memory was thus the key to balancing a sense of indebtedness to tradition with charismatic empowerment to speak out to the present generation courageously and in a contemporary idiom. By remembering their origins in divine grace and succor, the people would find their way in a precarious world. Forgetting their past would lead to loss of identity. For once they had lost sight of the source of their moral standards in the example of divine compassion and justice, they would fall prey to the blandishments of deceptive leaders appealing to the deviousness that the prophets believed lurked in every human heart.

The prophets further believed that since the sovereign of the nations refused to allow the universe to lapse into the chaos of amorality, he would send judgments to remove evil and to lead the people back through repentance to healing. In pondering why the holy sovereign would not simply remove the stain on creation by destroying unfaithful Israel outright, the prophets were led to conclude that God too was influenced by memory:

> How can I give you up, Ephraim?
>   How can I hand you over, O Israel? . . .
> My heart recoils within me;
>   my compassion grows warm and tender.

> I will not execute my fierce anger;
>> I will not again destroy Ephraim;
> for I am God and no mortal,
>> the Holy One in your midst,
>> and I will not come in wrath.
>>> (Hos. 11:8–9)

Thus far we have stressed the similarity in form and content between prophetic politics and the politics that had emerged during the earlier period of charismatic rulers. Now we move to a distinguishing difference. Unlike the judge, who derived from the charismatic experience of call a divine mandate to shape the politics of his nation, the prophet was the recipient of a vision of a *divine* government that became the standard for evaluating and judging *this* world's governments and their leaders. Stated differently: the prophets acknowledged the place of human government in the larger scheme of universal divine rule, and whether they then placed their support behind a particular regime, or subjected it to negative criticism, or even conspired for its overthrow by designation of more suitable political leadership, depended strictly on the degree of conformity they perceived between the current government and their vision of the divine imperium.[3] The evaluative criteriology that arose out of the theo-politics of the prophets revolved around two questions: Was God's sole sovereignty acknowledged by the nation's leaders? Was that sovereignty being mediated and implemented in the structures of government in a manner capable of guarding against distortion, idolatry, and abuse?

In the following diagram we contrast the unitary structure of governance that characterized the charismatic rule of the league period with the division of power that the prophets sought to maintain during the monarchy:

Unitary rule under: šôpēṭ (judge)
                          /   \
Division of rule under: melek (king) and nābî' (prophet)

In the upper line we represent the charismatic judge (šôpēṭ) as a ruler combining civil and spiritual leadership. The lower line requires more detailed commentary.

According to the concept of kingship regnant in the ancient Near East, king and priest theoretically respected a division of responsibility in which the former exercised civil and military authority while the latter presided over the temple cult. We attach the qualification *theoretically* in recognition of the perennial struggle in which kings sought to regulate the cult and priests maneuvered to control the crown. Balance of power was not an intrinsic principle. With the

---

3. Since the objective in this general description of prophecy is to describe the relation taken to politics by those figures that tradition judged to be "true prophets," we shall not in the present context discuss the problem raised by "false prophecy," except to note that prophets from Micaiah ben Imlah to Jeremiah had to contend with rivals who gave their uncritical support to the kings from whose patronage they benefited.

introduction of kingship in Israel, the monopoly of authority soon reemerged with the king seeking to consolidate his base of power by asserting control over the cult. Solomon reached that goal with the banishment of the uncooperative priest Abiathar and installment as head of his temple cult the compliant cleric Zadok, who had lent support to his bloody campaign for succession.

So strong were the antiroyal and antiurban tendencies in Israel—or to rephrase from a theological perspective, so strong were the commitments to the religious confessions and moral ideals of early Yahwism—that the Israelite community midwifed the birth of a new office as a counterbalance to the self-aggrandizing proclivities of kingship. Whereas kingship came to be accepted as the de facto form of government—of political necessity and in order to avoid national extinction at the hands of the Philistines—the office of prophet arose as a safeguard against tyrannical forms of mediation and implementation that violated the terms of God's transcendent sovereignty, forms such as the crown's translating hymnic expressions of YHWH's reign into laws and institutions asserting the privileged status of the king over his subjects.

The fact that prophecy arose in Israel right at the time of the introduction of kingship is a bold declaration of ancestral Yahwism: while the government of the people could be institutionalized under the centralized leadership of a king, the value system of this people could not be transmuted into an ideology of special royal status and privilege by zealous monarchists. Accordingly prophecy can be credited with defense of the fundamental theocratic principle that ulti-mately Israel could have but one sovereign. Drawn from that principle was the accompanying inference that the spiritual and moral guidance and protection originating with God would remain accessible to every citizen.

Since designation of the prophet depended on neither family, class, nor pro-fession, but on manifestation of the divine spirit, in principle any member of the community could be called to prophesy, with the corollary result that the prophet represented the broad populace rather than any special interest group. Kingship thus was placed, no less than any other institution, under the watchful eye of the prophets. The mythopoetically grounded warrant for the exemption of kings from the legal restraints imposed on ordinary citizens was normal in other lands; this was not purged altogether from Israel, but was fiercely opposed by the prophets. The startled reaction of King Ahab, in encountering the prophet Elijah implanted on the property that the wicked king had seized by executing its vintner-owner, thus became emblematic: "Have you found me, O my enemy?" (1 Kgs. 21:20).

The prophetic position over against the monarchy was predicated on a con-tingency clause that applied to all human institutions, including the temple cult, the judiciary, the military, and commerce. To the extent that kings implemented the values and laws that defined God's universal rule, they would enjoy the sup-port of YHWH's spokespersons, the prophets. However, when contradictory norms were embraced, whether in the form of idolatry, tyranny, assertion of exceptional privilege, or contrived circumventions of common law, the prophets were quick to respond.

Light can be shed on prophetic politics by considering its relation to the biblical concept of covenant. In chapter 10 we described the Mosaic covenant that structured the relationship between the people and YHWH in the league period. God, having initiated that relationship through beneficent acts, established as the condition for continued blessing the obedience of humans to laws patterned after God's compassionate justice. We observed in chapter 11 that the introduction of monarchy was accompanied by appeal to another covenant with God legitimating the exceptional authority of kings. As a result, a special bond binding God and king was added to the one already binding God and the people. These two covenants ran into conflict when kings viewed the private covenant relationship that they enjoyed with YHWH as conferring upon them a privileged status elevating them above their subjects. The prophets, realistic enough to know that kingship had been introduced for complicated reasons beyond their control, ingeniously sought to resolve the problem by insisting on the integration of the two covenants, in a manner that we here depict graphically:

Mosaic Covenant (League):   YHWH >>> People

Royal Covenant (Monarchy):   YHWH >>> King >>> People

                                         > King

Twin Covenants (Prophecy)   YHWH →

                                         > People

The prophets thus relativized kingship by taking it out of the mythic realm of eternal (divine) structures and placing it on the plane of finite (human) institutions. Under such an arrangement, the king's role of ordering the political life of the nation was not disputed, but it was placed within constitutionally defined limits, limits rigorously monitored by the prophets on the basis of checks and balances safeguarded by the dialectic of twin covenants. Rather than being exempt from the laws binding common citizens, the king in Israel was to define himself as a king by being obedient in an exemplary fashion to the Torah of Moses. Jeremiah states this succinctly by contrasting King Jehoiakim, who used his office to enrich himself at the expense of the working-class members of his nation, with his godly father Josiah: "Are you a king because you compete in cedar? Did not your father eat and drink and do justice and righteousness? Then it was well with him. He judged the cause of the poor and needy; then it was well. Is not this to know me? says the LORD" (Jer. 22:15–16; cf. 2 Kgs. 23:35–37).

Relativization of the authoritative dimensions of governance, however, must not be confused with secularization, a modern concept alien to ancient Hebrew thought. As indicated by the fact that the terms of constitutional monarchy were presented as a part of Mosaic law (Deut. 17:14–20), kingship was viewed as a divinely legitimated institution. But as a historical rather than a primordial structure, it could be replaced by another model of governance, and Israel would still be Israel. We can thus picture Hosea or Jeremiah refuting the psalmist's comparing the Davidic dynasty with the eternal order of the heavenly bodies (Ps. 89:29, 36–37), for they located kinship squarely on the human side of an overarching edifice over which only one sovereign reigned.

The consistency that characterized the fundamental moral vision of the prophets makes possible the sort of general description of prophetic politics that we have formulated in the above paragraphs. But there is another characteristic of prophecy that defies generalization. It stems from the fact that the prophets were at home in Israel's Epic-grounded historical understanding of divine presence and activity. The situations in which the prophets were commissioned to discern the presence of YHWH were concrete and particular to their times. The words with which they felt compelled by God to address these situations were thus crafted to fit the specifics of the given case. While the foundational principles of prophetic politics thus can be stated in general terms, the *practice* of prophetic politics must be described by way of examples from the lives of individual prophets, who, not incidentally, also differed from one another in temperament, social class, vocation, and geographical location. The vocabulary of Amos, the southern farmer who crossed the border to address Jeroboam, the arrogant king of the northern kingdom, was perforce different from that of aristocratic Isaiah when he addressed the pious and God-fearing Hezekiah. What is more, Isaiah's earlier message to Ahaz was distinctly different from what he later communicated to Hezekiah. Continuity in fundamental vision combined with specificity in application is fully in keeping with Israel's Epic/historicist understanding of the God who, while steadfast in purpose, is encountered in the concreteness of changing human experience.

PROPHETIC POLITICS DURING THE UNITED MONARCHY

During the united monarchy, which spanned the reigns of Saul, David, and Solomon, the prophets were actively engaged in the struggle to preserve the values of early Yahwism within the context of an emerging monarchy. According to the narrative in 2 Samuel 11–12, Nathan was the first prophet on the scene, decrying the violation of the civil rights of Uriah, a Hittite foot soldier who was killed by arrangement of King David to enable him to claim for his own pleasure the hapless soldier's wife. Though David's act was by common standards an unconscionable and cowardly breach of personal moral conduct, it would have been viewed as more than a private crime by the prophets or anyone else committed to a Yahwistic notion of human dignity.

While in an absolute monarchy a foreign soldier might be viewed as property of the crown, according to the laws of early Israel he was to enjoy the same protection as a full citizen. David had committed an act of flagrant abuse of power, and with rhetorical force characteristic of the prophets, Nathan drove home to the king the repugnance of the act by telling a story about a shepherd and his pet lamb (2 Sam. 12:1–6). Already in this narrative one sees implied a principle that runs throughout biblical prophecy: humans live in a moral universe in which consequences follow actions. Yes, David is repentant. Nevertheless, his heinous act had set in motion a chain of violence that would never leave the fabled house of David, and the entire remaining story of David's reign reads like a Shakespearean tragedy.

Other reports of prophetic intervention in the affairs of the kings of the united monarchy add substance to the interrelated themes of limiting royal power and safeguarding the religious and ethical principles of early Yahwism. According to 2 Samuel 7, Nathan delivered to King David a divine message that vetoed his desire to build a temple. In the preceding chapter we gave sufficient explanation of the vital connection between monarchy and a central temple to indicate the significance of the divine demurral contained in Nathan's oracle. The final chapter of 2 Samuel describes an episode in which Gad the prophet announces divine judgment in relation to a census ordered by David. Commentators see in David's census the attempt of the central administration to fit the territorially rooted tribes into the tax districts of the new monarchy.

The remainder of the narrative dealing with the united monarchy makes scant contribution to the question of prophetic politics. In the episodes leading to Solomon's securing the throne, Nathan is pictured as a faithful supporter of the Solomonic faction. Once Solomon has expunged all opponents, built the temple, and introduced the other institutions of centralized monarchy, no further mention is made of prophetic activity—an ominous silence that sheds important light on the way the Deuteronomistic Historians and their prophetic sources viewed the issue of limited versus tyrannical rule during the Solomonic period.

The first ten chapters of 1 Kings provide a rich stage setting for the appearance of the next prophet. The reader is introduced to a royal court administering a sizable empire on the basis of structures copied from the absolute monarchies of Phoenicia and Egypt. While the modern critic will discern the hyperbole characterizing the narrative style of the author, the depiction of the general *pattern of interaction* between prophet and king likely is based on reliable tradition. The prelude to the drama that unfolds in these chapters had already been given in Samuel's warning in 1 Samuel 8. The freedom-loving clans of Israel had been forced by their king to submit to high taxation, conscription, and forced labor, measures dedicated to strengthening the royal power base.

Since forced labor was perhaps the single most egregious affront to the values of the common Israelite ("and you shall be his slaves" [1 Sam. 8:17]), it is noteworthy that the prophet Ahijah sought out the very one Solomon had appointed over forced labor, Jeroboam ben-Nebat, as the latter was fleeing for his life from the king against whom he in protest recently had rebelled. The scene depicts prophetic politics in its most activist mode. The prophet delivered the word that God had designated Jeroboam to be king over a breakaway kingdom consisting of ten of the twelve tribes. The underlying reason was divine judgment against

Solomon for apostasy and failure to uphold the Torah. To the newly designated king the prophet extended the promises and conditions of limited monarchy:[4] "If you will listen to all that I command you, walk in my ways, and do what is right in my sight by keeping my statutes and my commandments, as David my servant did, I will be with you" (1 Kgs. 11:38). Recollection of the events of David's life may lead to a sense of dismay that the adulterer king had become an example of obedience. Clearly, in contrast to unrepentant, high-living Solomon and his capricious son Rehoboam, repentant David stood tall as a paragon of godliness!

How are we to interpret the political intervention of Ahijah? Most plausibly we should view it within the framework of early Israel's concept of limited monarchy, a concept embraced by the Deuteronomists and central to the prophetic traditions upon which they drew. According to those traditions, kings ruled under conditions set by divine covenant. Their authority to rule was conditional upon their faithfulness to the higher imperium of divine government. Solomon had broken the conditions of the covenant in both of its aspects: exclusive worship of YHWH and obedience to Torah. As had been the case in David's reign, consequences were inevitable. But the divine commitment to the agreement was more tenacious than the human. The covenant with the house of David would be honored, albeit on the basis of a reduced mandate. The northern half of the kingdom would have a second chance on the basis of a parallel covenant arrangement proffered to Jeroboam.

PROPHETIC POLITICS DURING THE DIVIDED MONARCHY

A new political era began with the presence of two Israels. As late as the time of Ezekiel, right at the end of the epoch of monarchy, the political cleavage of the nation was regarded in itself as evidence of divine disfavor. How could it be deemed otherwise, when Judah and Israel were locked in frequent, deadly conflict? The prophetic vision of future healing was therefore a vision of reunion (Ezek. 37:15–23) under the covenant formulary "you shall be my people and I shall be your God" (v. 23). But reality was stubbornly resistant to the vision. This was the situation that the prophets had to face. Their commission arose within the tension between this political reality and the clear conviction, lying at the heart of their sense of national and spiritual identity, that it was God's intention that the nation live in unity as one people faithful in worship, obedient to God's will codified in the Torah, and thereby present as a blessing to other peoples. Prophetic politics thus combined visionary and pragmatic elements.[5] The

---

4. Cf. above page 223 regarding the prophetic integration of Mosaic and royal covenants.
5. See Paul D. Hanson, *The Diversity of Scripture: A Theological Interpretation* (Philadelphia: Fortress Press, 1982).

prophets were dedicated to translating the vision of divinely sponsored domestic and international harmony into the social and political realities of their times.

Evidence for the activity of the prophets during the divided monarchy comes under two categories. For the period reaching from the division in 922 BCE down to the middle of the eighth century, references to the prophets appear in the body of the historical narratives of the Deuteronomistic History and the Chronicler. From the reigns of Uzziah of Judah and Jeroboam II of Israel on down to the early Second Temple period, there are, in addition to such narrative references, separate books consisting of words attributed to the prophets after whom those books were named. Some of the prophetic books also contain scattered biographical notations. Due to the considerable scope of this material, our examples will be limited to ones that shed additional light on prophetic politics.

PROPHETIC ACTIVITY RECORDED IN THE HISTORICAL WRITINGS

Though Jeroboam is presented as a populist leader who rose to the throne of the rival breakaway nation as a defender of early Yahwistic values, the report of his reign beginning in 1 Kings 12 gets off to an ominous start. Jeroboam, we read, established shrines in Dan and Bethel and installed a calf image in each, acts for which a prophetic figure called "a man of God" roundly condemns him. With that a major historiographic theme in the Deuteronomistic History has been announced: all of its defects notwithstanding, it is the southern kingdom of Judah that is the standard-bearer of divine promise, and this because of God's initial covenant with David. The same Ahijah who earlier designated Jeroboam as the first king of the north reappears in the narrative to seal the doom of that kingdom, which can be understood historiographically as the countertheme to the theme of the Davidic promise upholding the kingdom of Judah.

Recognition of the Deuteronomistic History's political ideology does not a priori discredit its merit as a source for the political activity of the prophets it treats. Rather, each episode must be dealt with individually, using appropriate critical methods. We shall do so with the awareness that, as is the case of history writing in any period, the biblical authors and editors personally engaged in political process through their acts of interpretation and elaboration.

The most impressive and well-rounded prophetic figure to arise out of the narrative material in the Bible is Elijah (1 Kgs. 17–2 Kgs. 2). There is no good reason to doubt that two basic themes in the Elijah narrative have roots in history: (1) Ahab, a ninth-century king of Israel, promoted an ideology of kingship that was deeply influenced by the absolute kingship ideals of Phoenicia (which in turn had deep roots in Egypt of the pharaohs) and a religious syncretism that promoted the Canaanite cult of Baal alongside YHWH worship; (2) protest came from Elijah, a Gileadite from Tishbe, who sought to defend both the religious beliefs and the moral values of early Yahwism, and who did so, in a manner anticipating the career of Jeremiah, at the cost of persecution instigated by the royal house.

Over the course of the formation of the Hebrew canon, the figure of Elijah was fashioned into a defining example of the prophetic office. Regarding degrees of authority, the fact that the prophet represented the divine imperium empowered him to announce the rise and fall of the kings of the earth, contradictory appearances from the human vantage point notwithstanding (1 Kgs. 19:15–18). But the tension between the eternal and ephemeral perspectives often weighed heavily on the prophets, exemplified by the picture of Elijah receiving God's awesome command to anoint new kings over Aram and Israel and yet cowering in a cave and wishing to die. This paradox of strength in weakness is a common motif in the biblical picture of God's suffering servants. Intrinsic to this motif is an underlying assurance. Though tested to the point of bitter complaint and despair, Elijah and the chain of prophets following him ultimately stood firm in their defense of the twin Yahwistic principles that were at the heart of the Israelite concept of constitutional monarchy: exclusive worship of YHWH and obedience to divine law. At the center of Elijah's obedience was defense of the equality of every human before God. No biblical story illustrates this quality more clearly than the story of Naboth's vineyard (1 Kgs. 21). All of the earthly might and cunning that king and queen together could muster could not extinguish the prophet's godly passion for justice.

Though Elijah no doubt had every reason to feel isolated as he denounced the king in defense of a humble vintner, the story in 1 Kings 22 of the prophet Micaiah ben Imlah, a man inspired to contradict Ahab's four hundred court prophets in the name of YHWH, indicates that he was not the only one daring to speak out against abuses stemming from a non-Yahwistic political ideology. An interesting element in the Micaiah story is the approach it takes to the perennial problem of contradictory prophetic pronouncements. The sole authentication of the veracity of the prophet's message resides in heaven. This does not resolve the problem of false prophecy, but it draws attention to the profound complexity involved in the question of prophetic discernment. To this we shall return in discussing Jeremiah in chapter 16.

The stories about Elisha, Elijah's successor, display Hebrew legend making at its best. Besides providing a source of exquisite humor (what subcategory of bald-headed gentlemen other than Spirit-filled prophets can deal with disrespectful, jeering kids by enlisting the help of hungry she-bears?), the Elisha stories exude the sense of numinous mystery that enshrouded the prophets of Israel. Legends that grew up around the figures of Isaiah, Jeremiah, and Ezekiel add to the impression that the prophets of YHWH, while not infrequently deviating from conventional norms of social decorum, were nevertheless formidable figures in the public affairs of their day.

Elisha's activities went beyond the bizarre acts of an eccentric. He seemed to have earned the distinction of being the inheritor of Elijah's mantle by advising kings in matters of state (2 Kgs. 3). Finally, though, the role he plays in the chain of prophets remains minor, for the real political action quickly passes over his life to a prophetically inspired bloody revolution against the Omride dynasty, remembered for its betrayal of YHWH in favor of Baal. The prophetic choice for king is Jehu, who with fanatic zeal and remorseless cynicism pursues a bloody holy war to which fall victim not only the priests of Baal and their northern palace sponsors, but also the hapless members of royal family of the south. Here we see prophetic politics twisted into a form of violent, fanatical extremism that in modern times has been replicated by certain fundamentalist parties and regimes on the basis of a degradation of the theocratic principle into a warrant for a tyrannical form of government. It should be emphasized, however, that the Jehu episode presents an exception, not a normative paradigm of biblical prophetic politics in action. This point is made within the prophetic corpus itself, for the prophet Hosea condemned the excesses of the Jehu revolt in no uncertain terms (Hos. 1:4–5).

With this brief discussion of Elisha, we conclude consideration of those prophets known only through the references found in the Deuteronomistic and Chronicler's histories and proceed to the most extensive body of material available for our inquiry into the politics of Israel's prophets, namely, the books named after and consisting of words attributed to prophetic figures.

PROPHECY AS PRESENTED BY BOOKS ASCRIBED TO INDIVIDUAL FIGURES

Worth recalling is the following fact regarding the history of prophecy in ancient Israel: its origins coincided with the rise of kingship, even as its termination followed in the wake of the demise of institutional monarchy. We miss the significance of this shared lifespan if we attempt to explain it solely on the level of institutional structure. More was at issue than alternative forms of governance. In the interaction between prophets, kings, and citizens we witness the struggle of a people to define its identity, describe its goals, and clarify its values.

Earlier Israel was not lacking leaders devoted to preserving the beliefs and values that had been drawn from experiences reaching back to slavery in Egypt and the identity-forging events that followed. But with the emergence of monarchy, a form of governance widely associated in antiquity with a construal of reality antithetical to the way Israel had come to view the world, the task of safeguarding and revitalizing the distinctive identity that had been cultivated by the Hebrew Epic became vastly more difficult. The Rechabite refusing to adapt his seminomadic lifestyle to an urban setting or the Nazirite eschewing wine and clinging to his tent dwelling were ill-equipped for the exacting task of reformulating the principles of early Yahwism in terms viable within a radically changed world. While Amos could refer to prophets and Nazirites in the same breath (Amos 2:11–12), it is clear that the carefully nuanced political thought of the prophets bore little resemblance to the rigid traditionalism of the Nazirites.

The crisis would have been serious enough to call for a new type of leadership, if limited to the internal changes that were reshaping the Jewish homeland. But tectonic shifts were shaking the political landscape of the entire eastern Mediterranean. In the century that witnessed the rise of the first four "classical" prophets—Amos, Hosea, Micah, and Isaiah—the two Jewish kingdoms came under the iron fist of the vast and daunting Assyrian Empire. Suddenly a people living a parochial life under the patronage of its divine king YHWH had to relate his suzerainty to the god Ashur, whose imperium claimed to encompass "the four corners of the earth." A people that heretofore had contended with foreign powers roughly equal in might to itself suddenly came up against a war machine that in short order swept the northern kingdom from the face of the earth and then proceeded to reduce the southern kingdom to the status of hapless vassal.

Why even bother to examine the political strategies of the prophets, given the evidence of history that they failed to save the nation from humiliating defeat? The answer given by the prophets themselves is this: defeat at the hands of foreign powers was itself an expression of the divine suzerain YHWH's rule. Whether that is construed as a convenient rationalization or the expression of a profoundly moral political judgment will depend in large part on the interpreter's perspective. It seems reasonable to assume, however, that any opinion deserving attention be formed on the basis of careful examination of the evidence. With this goal in mind, we turn in the chapters that follow to a close reading of collections of biblical prophecy.

Chapter 13

The Politics of Amos

*Idolatrous Nationalism
and the Collapse of Moral Leadership*

Amos addressed a nation that paid scant attention to the grave threats taking shape just beyond its borders. King Uzziah of Judah and King Jeroboam II of Israel presided over an era of prosperity and national security unknown since the time of David and Solomon. But it was a prosperity and security reserved for the elite, due to the steady decay of the more egalitarian economic structures that had characterized early Israel. Once an elitist ideology was established in the royal court, it tended to spread through the larger society. The king's claim to special privileges based on the presumption of exceptional divine favor spread to the nobility, the merchant class, and religious officials. In the midst of robust economic expansion, the living standards of the poor grew grim in adverse relation to the increasing comforts enjoyed by the upper class.

The dazzle of the luxury enjoyed by the privileged few in urban centers like Samaria did not impress Amos. "Cows of Bashan" he called them (Amos 4:1). His focus was on the average person, suffering impoverishment as the price for the decadent lifestyle of the wealthy, "who lie on beds of ivory," "eat lambs from the flock," "sing idle songs to the sound of the harp," "drink wine from

231

bowls," "anoint themselves with the finest oils, but are not grieved over the ruin of Joseph" (6:4–6).[1]

Amos took his message to the streets. This signaled a shift from the pattern of the earlier prophets, who addressed primarily kings and other public leaders. Amos spoke to the people as a whole. This shift is significant. The function of the earlier prophets could be described as counseling heads of state. What prompted Amos, and subsequently the other prophets of the eighth and seventh centuries, to redirect the focus of their crusade toward the general public?

The rhetoric employed by these prophets suggests that the shift was tied to another change introduced by the eighth-century prophets that we mentioned earlier, their tendency to view the destiny of their people on the encompassing horizon of world affairs. Foreign policy was no longer limited to defending the land against neighboring petty dynasts, but had escalated to contending with the daunting force of a world empire capable of annihilating Israel from the face of the earth. Faced with such a mortally threatening crisis, the prophet found little reason to trust the smug confidence of the nation's leaders. Since the time of Samuel, the prophetic tradition had generated a harsh critique of an institution that seemed inclined to place the interests of the royal court and landed nobility ahead of the civil rights of ordinary citizens and thereby to weaken the moral and material fabric of the nation's security.

In a redirection of strategy, the prophets beginning with Amos seemed to place their bets on the general public as being a more promising audience than the elite for words of admonition and warning aimed at getting the nation off of an idolatrous track leading to calamity and back on one promising security and social justice based on the theocratic pillars of ultimate allegiance to YHWH and obedience to his righteous Torah.

We shall examine the political message of Amos in the following order. First, we shall describe two fundamental errors that he saw poisoning the nation's application of religion to politics: (1) nationalistic idolatry, in which pride of state led to repudiation of the theocratic principle of YHWH's sole sovereignty; (2) the collapse of moral leadership, resulting in flagrant violation of the compassionate justice of God as formulated in the Torah. We shall conclude by citing spheres of society in which he accused the nation of specific crimes.

AMOS'S INDICTMENT OF NATIONALISTIC HUBRIS

According to the wandering preacher from Tekoa, Israel's elemental sin was confusing two domains, God's ultimate dominion and the limited authority of the state. The distinction between the ultimate and the penultimate, attributed

---

1. Reflected in Amos 6 is an ancient drinking feast with roots reaching back to Ugarit (*marzeah*) and perduring down to classical times (*symposium*). See Philip J. King and Lawrence E. Stager, *Life in Biblical Israel* (Louisville, KY: Westminster John Knox Press, 2001), 355–57.

to Samuel in 1 Samuel 12 and subsequently cultivated in the prophetic tradition, was being repudiated by religious and political leaders alike, as they *identified* God's reign with a regime of their own making.

Amos stands tall within the canon as a witness to authentic prophecy: The prophets, while deeply indebted to their religious traditions, were not blindly bound to them, but acted as both guardians and reformers as they related the beliefs and values of earlier generations to developments in the world around them. This nuanced position can be illustrated by reference to an image widely used in early Yahwism to describe Israel's sole sovereign, namely, the image of Divine Warrior. It was God the Warrior who was celebrated in the ancient poem in Exodus 15 as the one who saved helpless slaves from their bondage in Egypt. This same Warrior led them through the dangers of wilderness and enemy harassment to a new homeland. During the league and on into the early centuries of the monarchy, God the Warrior was the source of deliverance time and again when the tiny nation faced foes many times their own size, and celebration of God's victories on behalf of the tribes of Israel constituted the heart of the nation's Epic.

Now, in the mid-eighth century, Amos sees his people threatened not primarily by foreign nations, but by their own rebellion against the God who had delivered and sustained them. The traditional image of the God of incomparable splendor and majesty had become perverted into a picture of an accommodating numen who merely reflected the interests of the nation, even at a time when those interests were corrupt and unjust. For example, for those living under the aegis of a deity viewed as national benefactor, hoarding of wealth by the powerful was viewed not as greed but the enjoyment of special divine favor.

Amos addresses the perversion of true religion through nationalistic hubris by depicting the Divine Warrior entering the battlefield, not on the side of Israel, but *against* his own people. "Alas for you who desire the day of the LORD!" the prophet thunders (Amos 5:18). The "day of the LORD" is a concept at home in Divine Warrior tradition and refers to the appearance of the deity in battle. In Amos's time it had become a rallying call for national pride. As Israel's divine patron, God could be depended on to intervene whenever Israel was threatened by foreign aggressors or whenever its economy showed signs of weakness. The image of God had been made to fit the self-image of the nation, for in the mid-eighth century both kingdoms, under King Uzziah in the south and King Jeroboam in the north, were enjoying military power and material prosperity such as had not been experienced since the golden age of David and Solomon. Why desire the "day of the LORD"? To this question the smug patriot in effect replied, "Because God will soon arrive to keep the good times rolling." Amos attacks this popular religion as an idolatrous attack on God's claim to unconditional sovereignty: "Why do you want the day of the LORD? It is darkness, not light; as if someone fled from a lion, and was met by a bear" (5:18–19).

From antiquity to the present, the most common connection of deity to nation has been the one attacked by Amos: understanding the national god to be the divine protector of the particular interests of that nation, over against the claims of other nations and their gods. Throughout history civic religion has been seen as a vital aspect of pride of country and patriotism. Faith is merged into culture as a popular construal of divine providence, and destiny is ensconced as the religious core of a body politic.

As we have seen in the previous chapter, this wedding of royal crown and ecclesial miter was an intrinsic aspect of the mythological foundation of the mighty empires of the ancient Near East. The king was the patron God's earthly representative, and as such the king was not only head of state but also the one charged with maintaining the cult. This pattern is one all too common in the world in which we live. Though the explicit trappings of the royal myth have fallen into desuetude, the identification of a nation's god with the self-interests of state is as alive today as ever, whether in an Islamic theocratic state like Iran or Pakistan, or in the minds of zealous defenders of the American notion of manifest destiny.

Amos was not a traitor or a nihilist, out of blind rage singling out his government for divine condemnation. Rather, on the basis of the theocratic principle of God as sovereign of all peoples, whose rule upheld one universal standard of justice, Amos depicted a heavenly court in which all nations were weighed on the same scale, and the indictments he cited and the judgments he announced arose from a process of examining evidence that was remarkably evenhanded and impartial.

The first two chapters of Amos read like a transcript from the pages of a world court. One by one the nations bordering Israel are brought before the judge: Damascus, Gaza, Tyre, Edom, Ammon, and Moab. The indictments are familiar to every student of geopolitics: use of excessive military force, displacement of civilian populations, violation of treaty obligations, cruelty untempered by human compassion, slaughter of civilian populations, and aggressive military moves against neighboring countries. They are all found guilty as accused, and the sentences include banishment of the head of state, destruction of military installations, and general exile.

Additionally it is to be noted that the rhetoric used in the sentences is drawn from the repertory of the Divine Warrior, with fire and storm being sent by God against the offending nations. In chapter 1 and on through verse 3 of chapter 2, the drama tracks the pattern familiar from holy war, with the patron god of a nation inflicting dreadful punishment on the surrounding nations, to the territorial, material, and military benefit of the favored nation. But Amos proceeds to deconstruct the conventional application of the pattern, as he depicts the judge, the God of Israel, concluding the session of court with the lengthiest and most thoroughly prosecuted case of all, one against the homeland itself! In this case the culpability that will bring the fall of the land is located not in international relations, but in the internal life of its citizens. The standard against which Israel is judged is the Torah, which according to Israel's Epic had been given to it as a guide to its life as a people. But rather than showing respect for the dignity of all persons and mercy for the poor and personal decency and honesty, the citizens in the land have been flagrant in their cruelty, greed, and decadence.

On the basis of that grave indictment the sentence is handed down, and it seems fittingly adapted to a people that has repudiated the God of justice and mercy: Their strength as a people will be taken away, and they will be left defenseless before their enemies. A people that has been instructed by the prophets that a nation's strength depends on its faithfulness in worship of the one true God and its obedience to his righteous laws has distorted religion into self-indulgent revelry underwritten by a lenient imposter-god. Their outrageous impudence extends to their treatment of religious leaders who attempt to call them to account: they seek to drag them into their drunken decadence, and failing, they take measures to silence them (2:12).

Amos's invective against nationalistic idolatry is poignantly expressed also in chapter 9. God has just been introduced as the creator of the heavens and the earth and the sovereign of all nations; then in verse 7 the topic of Israel's place in this whole *oeconomia* is addressed. Against the nationalistic hubris that flaunted Israel's special status and claimed as proof of this status the Epic account of the exodus from Egypt, Amos presents a God challenging the concept of exceptionalism:

> Are you not like the Ethiopians to me,
>   O people of Israel? says the LORD.
> Did I not bring Israel up from the land of Egypt,
>   and the Philistines from Caphtor and the Arameans from Kir?
>   (9:7)

Amos's courageous stand against the domestication of religion became a hallmark of prophetic politics. God's transcendence, holiness, and categorical otherness from everything earthly provided the theocratic bedrock of Israel's identity. The prophets would not allow religion to become a warrant for nationalism, or for the claims of the rich and powerful that their accumulation of excess wealth and power was a sign of special divine favor and their curtailment of human rights an exemption accorded them as an attribute of their high standing.

Even after Amos's death, his courageous testimony that God could not be co-opted retained its verve, as shown by an addition to his words found in 2:4–5. This passage addresses the question arising in Judah after the sister state to the north, Israel, had been destroyed by the Assyrians: would God's special favor toward Judah and the royal house of David spare that nation from divine judgment? Without equivocation, the disciple of Amos replied with an emphatic *no*. Using Amos's forensic structure of indictment and sentence, he states God's decision:

> For three transgressions of Judah,
>   and for four, I will not revoke the punishment;

because they have rejected the law of the LORD,
> and have not kept his statutes,
but they have been led astray by the same lies
> after which their ancestors walked.

(2:4)

From this theocratic viewpoint, a seamless fabric of justice upholds the entire universe. No human agent can rupture it with impunity. God will allow no exceptions, for to do so would throw into jeopardy the moral structure of all reality.

Amos's testimony was denounced and opposed in his time and in the times of the prophets who carried forth his legacy. The most strenuous opposition came from the highest ranks of leadership in the nation. That kings would oppose a prophet who refused to respect the special entitlements believed to accompany the highest office in the land is understandable. One might expect more personal integrity and moral courage from the official *religious* leaders, however, for was it not their primary responsibility to serve as guardians over the sacred traditions of their people? As Amos had demonstrated by basing his indictment of Israel strictly on the basis of the ancient Torah, Israel's God was a judge demanding impartial justice.

THE COLLAPSE OF MORAL LEADERSHIP AND FLAGRANT VIOLATION OF THE TORAH

Facing the either/or choice of allegiance to God or king, the cult officials of Israel placed their support uncritically behind the king. Amos was thus drawn into a second assault on the soul of the nation, a religious establishment whose leaders surrendered moral conscience in deference to the authority of the state. To be sure, under monarchy religious institutions and their functionaries were vulnerable to this evisceration of their independence, since appointments and financial support came from the royal chancellery. In 7:10–17 we find a story that sheds valuable light on the political position of the prophet in a nation in which the official religious establishment had acquiesced to the will of the king. Amaziah, the priest of the cult center in Bethel, sends a report to the king that Amos is engaged in conspiratorial activities and that "the land is not able to bear all his words" (7:10). The priest demonstrates his unconditional loyalty to his monarch by issuing an order that Amos leave the land, never again to "prophesy at Bethel, for it is the king's sanctuary, and it is a temple of the kingdom" (7:13).

The political theology of the priest Amaziah is transparent. The king enjoys legal immunity, and it is the responsibility of religious leaders to protect him from criticism, for criticism directed against the king is tantamount to conspiracy in both a political and a religious sense. In other words, the identity and destiny of the nation are inseparably tied to the personage of the king. Amos offers a concise description of the patriotic function of the place of worship: It is "the king's sanctuary, and . . . a temple of the kingdom" (7:13).

Amos's response to Amaziah's banishment order reflects a very different understanding of the relation between religion and politics. To the priest's command "never again [to] prophesy at Bethel," he responds that he cannot conform to the terms of office that regulate state-sponsored functionaries, including the professional prophets serving the king. "I am no prophet, nor a prophet's son; but I am a herdsman, and a dresser of sycamore trees, and the LORD took me from following the flock, and the LORD said to me, 'Go, prophesy to my people Israel'" (7:14–15). This statement reflects Amos's understanding of the status of a nation's government within the larger framework of cosmic rule. Its authority is strictly limited by the higher authority of God's governance of the universe. Belonging to a human society, while entailing certain civic obligations, can never bind one's conscience, for within a theocratic understanding of politics, ultimate allegiance is reserved solely for the heavenly king.

It is that king who has commissioned Amos to speak out against the crimes of King Jeroboam and the land's nobility, and the actual conspiracy that is being committed is not by Amos, but by the priest who plots with the king to silence God's mouthpiece. "The lion has roared; who will not fear? The Lord GOD has spoken; who can but prophesy?" (3:8). With this vivid image the prophet reveals the basis of his understanding of the relation between religion and politics. On that basis he repudiates the twin abominations threatening the land: political idolatry and a religious institution paying unqualified homage to human rulers.

The virulence of Amos's polemic against nationalistic idolatry and the capitulation of religion to tyranny could lead one to conclude that he was a radical categorically opposed to the monarchy and unqualified in his condemnation of ritual and cult. But Amos is more subtle on both fronts. Human government is condemned when it denies the categorical distinction between divine government and human rule and exempts leaders from the norms that apply to all citizens. The religious cult is condemned when it views ritual as a substitute for justice and compassion. Clarification of these distinctions clears the way to understand the purpose of his invective within specific spheres of life.

EXAMPLES OF AMOS'S INVECTIVE WITHIN SPECIFIC REALMS OF SOCIETY

Religion can be a very potent instrument in the hands of self-serving leaders. It offers many modes of justifying immoral behavior, so Amos found it necessary to wage battle against the perversion of religion on many fronts. Observance of holy days and ritual acts of fasting and sacrifice were seen as establishing divine favor even when the celebrants conducted their lives in dishonesty and debauchery. With biting sarcasm Amos cried out to the practitioners of such a perverted cult: "Come to Bethel—and transgress; to Gilgal—and multiply transgression" (4:4).

When the Holy Warrior comes, he will destroy both the palatial residences of the rich and their places of worship. "Seek me and live, but do not seek Bethel, and do not enter into Gilgal," the Lord says in 5:4–5. Is this because the God of Israel does not welcome the worship of grateful mortals? No. It is because these particular mortals use worship to obscure the fact that in their workaday lives they "turn justice to wormwood, and bring righteousness to the ground" (5:7). In the view of the prophet, it is blasphemous to think that the holy God could accept gifts from people who use religion as a cover for cruelty and greed. "I hate, I despise your festivals. . . . Even though you offer me your burnt offerings and grain offerings, I will not accept them. . . . But let justice roll down like waters, and righteousness like an ever-flowing stream" (5:21–24). Here we see with final clarity the objective of Amos's iconoclasm. The cult-ritual practices that he seeks to remove are the ones that obstruct the quintessential human vocation: justice and righteousness.

We thus grasp the message of Amos rightly if we recognize that his invective against both political and religious leaders is dedicated to a fundamental reform effort, one aimed at reestablishing the moral health and security of the land. But his crusade comes up against formidable obstacles, with roots reaching into the basic socioeconomic structures of a nation in which older tribal and familial structures of land ownership and commerce have been supplanted by the entrepreneurial schemes of a growing wealthy class. At the heart of the downward spiral leading to "the ruin of Joseph" Amos perceives a shocking spiritual/moral crisis: a people has forsaken its God.

While Amos's rhetoric may strike the modern reader as excessively harsh, it becomes plausible when viewed in relation to fundamental conceptual confusions,

Human Ruler	confused with	Heavenly Ruler
Institutional Religion	confused with	True Worship
Nation Israel	confused with	Family of Nations
Special Privilege	confused with	Justice and Compassion

The book of Amos is not a systematic treatise, but rather notes taken from the grassroots reform activities of a street prophet. Yet the ad hoc nature of the sayings reveals to the perceptive reader a remarkable unity of perspective. The universe displayed in Amos 5:8 is governed by

> [t]he one who made the Pleiades and Orion,
>   and turns deep darkness into the morning,
>   and darkens the day into night,
> who calls for the waters of the sea,
>   and pours them out on the surface of the earth,

who moreover is a God who does not stand by indifferently as the integrity of creation and the health of the human family are jeopardized by leaders who abuse their offices and exploit their subjects for their own gain and "who turn justice to wormwood, and bring righteousness to the ground," "but are not grieved over the ruin of Joseph" (5:7; 6:6). Speaking for a God of justice, Amos announces to Israel, "[P]repare to meet your God!" (4:12), who has forced that encounter by taking from the citizenry a man of the land and saying to him in Amos 7:15, "Go, prophesy to my people Israel."

That, in sum, is the unified picture underlying Amos's understanding of the political function of prophet. The prophet has been tutored by the history of God's relationship with Israel in the contents of the message that is to be proclaimed. Here are examples of that message within specific realms of society:

> *Government:* The God of holiness and righteousness is repulsed by those who use their offices to exploit and impoverish those below them and then use the ill-gotten spoils to support a lifestyle of decadent luxury (3:15; 4:11; 6:1–7).

> *Economics:* Excessive taxation of the common citizen leading to impoverishment is an offense to God (5:11), as is the selling of citizens into slavery for trivial debts (2:8).

> *International law:* God requires conformity to the terms agreed to in international treaties and condemns acts of cruelty and wanton destruction (1:3–15).

> *Commerce:* Dishonest trade practices, including the falsification of weights and measures, is an assault on God's reign of justice (8:5–6).

> *Judiciary:* Perverting the law so as to benefit the rich and the powerful is an offense against God (2:8), as is the suppression of evidence in court (5:10).

Amos is a realist whose honest assessment of the social/political situation in his nation is saved from nihilism only because of his vision of the grandeur and mercy of the God of the universe. The prognosis is bleak. Nevertheless, hope grounded in compassion and faith impels him to persevere in his reform efforts:

> Seek good and not evil,
>   that you may live;
> and so the LORD, the God of hosts, will be with you,
>   just as you have said.
> Hate evil and love good,
>   and establish justice in the gate;
> it may be that the LORD, the God of hosts,
>   will be gracious to the remnant of Joseph.
>   (5:14–15)

Note however the qualification: "it may be . . ." For Amos is acutely aware of the persistent disjunction between God's righteousness and the treachery of the nation that ignores the scale of justice to its own peril. As a prophet receptive to visions of God's impending action, he twice sees God's mercy prevailing over the demands of justice and leading to a reprieve (7:1–6), but in the face of a nation stubbornly rejecting its God, the drama cannot escape a foreboding undertone (7:7–9) and two concluding visions announcing a decree of irrevocable destruction (8:1–3; 9:1–4). Clearly Amos found himself near the end of his career uncertain of the outcome of his struggle as God's spokesperson. However, it was not a struggle ending in futility, for his was not a solitary voice, but one witness in a chain of prophets dedicating body and soul to God's righteous rule.

Chapter 14

The Politics of Hosea
Moral Bankruptcy and Civil Chaos

Hosea was roughly contemporary with Amos, though his career seems to have continued somewhat beyond that of Amos into the tumultuous final years of his nation, the northern kingdom of Israel. That slight chronological difference left its mark on his writings. While many of Amos's declamations offer hints of situations within the political life of the nation, the words of Hosea evoke a sense of surrealism. Israel is portrayed with lurid images taken from the realms of prostitution and crude idol cults. In contrast, the past is recalled rather nostalgically as the time when Israel lived in intimate communion with its God, not without moments of unfaithfulness, to be sure, but with an openness to divine mercy contrasting with the unmitigated depravity of the present.

Though utilizing a different idiom, it is clear that like Amos, Hosea was an astute observer of the political affairs of his time. For example, he addressed a nation whose citizens "devour their rulers" (Hos. 7:7). In fact, six kings ruled in rapid succession in the last decades of the northern kingdom's existence, four of them falling victim to assassins. He also witnessed the civil conflict referred to by historians as the Syro-Ephraimite War, in which the northern kingdom (often referred to by Hosea as Ephraim) entered into league with Syria to invade and conquer Judah, its sister kingdom to the south. The objective was to remove the

Davidic king and replace him with a ruler who would join in a revolt against Assyria. Hosea 5:8–6:6 describes the agony of civil war, in which brothers turn against brothers and those who should live in a covenant of harmony turn to foreign enemies to take sides in the battles of a house divided against itself.

The anti-Assyrian strategy failed, and the Deuteronomists reported that King Menahem of Israel submitted to Pul (i.e., Tiglath-pileser, king of Assyria), paid tribute extracted from the nation's wealthiest citizens, and thereby postponed calamity (2 Kgs. 15:19–20). The prophet interpreted the chaos of his time as the "rottenness" of a nation emptied of morality and pursuing a path toward destruction (Hos. 5:12). Menahem's momentary reprieve notwithstanding, Hosea was convinced that a final judgment was on the horizon, for ultimately the foe was not an earthly potentate receptive of blandishments and bribes, but the heavenly king, who through the shock of war would continue his effort to bring a power-crazed nation to its senses, that is, "until they acknowledge their guilt and seek my face" (5:15).

The Syro-Ephraimite incident, known to historians primarily on the basis of passages in Isaiah and 2 Kings, is the only specific historical event to which Hosea confidently can be connected. In general, an inquiry into the political activity of the prophet Hosea yields sketchier results than was the case with Amos. While it is possible to glimpse the actual political, social, and economic circumstances addressed by Amos, the surrealistic tone of Hosea's message referred to above does not lend itself well to historical reconstruction. But the provocative rhetoric may in itself suggest a political tactic on the part of the prophet. Interesting to note are his observations regarding how the people perceive the prophets and the political role that he sees the prophets playing in a land that seems hell-bent on a road to destruction. "Israel cries, 'The prophet is a fool, the man of the spirit is mad!'" (9:7). Given such a hostile reception, what tactics should a prophet adopt?

> The prophet is a sentinel for my God over Ephraim,
>   yet a fowler's snare is on all his ways,
>   and hostility in the house of his God.
>
>   (9:8)

Though charged with the solemn task of being God's sentinel—we might say, the conscience of the people, reminding them of the moral foundation that alone could secure the land—the prophet was treated like an outlaw and lived in constant fear of danger. It is not surprising to find that the prophet responded by adopting a form of language that was forceful, filled with provocative metaphors, and sweeping in its condemnation. Hosea, in adopting this mode of attack, indicates that he pictures himself in the tradition of earlier messengers of God delivering hard-hitting messages of judgment and doom, for at one point he reports God's retrospect on the history of prophecy:

> Therefore I have hewn them by the prophets,
>   I have killed them by the words of my mouth,
>   and my judgment goes forth as the light.
>   (6:5)

Hosea obviously understood it as his calling to persist in the struggle of Elijah and Amos of "hewing" the people with harsh words of judgment. His favored metaphor for Israel is that of whore, a metaphor developed elaborately in the first three chapters and then echoed in subsequent chapters:

> When their drinking is ended, they indulge in sexual orgies;
> they love lewdness.
>
> (4:18)

> [Y]ou have played the whore, departing from your God.
> You have loved a prostitute's pay
> on all threshing floors.
>
> (9:1)

The bitter irony behind the metaphor is that, for all of Israel's whoring, the yield will be nil: "Even though they give birth, I will kill the cherished offspring of their womb," God announces (9:16).

How could the nation have descended to the nadir of its entire history, thereby exposing itself to annihilation by a foreign enemy? The prophet places the blame squarely on the shoulders of the nation's leaders. In a passage developing another torrid metaphor whose translation is bedeviled by the corrupt state of the transmitted text, the king and the other high officials are likened to an overheated oven, connoting both the fiery state of their inebriation and the lewdness of their sexual escapades (7:3–7). This accusation of drunken dissipation takes on an aura of verisimilitude when viewed in light of the recurrent motif of orgies, involving both gods and earthly kings and nobility, found in literature reaching from prebiblical times, on through the history of the Hasmoneans, and extending down to the Roman Empire. It certainly presents a powerful image of incompetence, abuse of power, and reckless dereliction in the discharge of official duties.

In keeping with his duty to interpret the conditions of his time in light of Israel's religious traditions, the prophet exposes the fundamental flaw in the reigning regime: it has cut itself off from the only source of authentic government and the only authority that could give it legitimacy:

> They made kings, but not through me;
> they set up princes, but without my knowledge.
> With their silver and gold they made idols
> for their own destruction.
>
> (8:4)

We saw in chapter 11 that the basis of Israel's constitutional form of monarchy was the theocratic concept of God's exclusive universal sovereignty.[1] God alone was authorized to appoint a king as his agent in ordering the affairs of the nation through structures of human government that conformed to and

---

1. See Deut. 17:14–20.

implemented God's righteous reign. When the distinction between ultimate and penultimate was lost, and the king was no longer seen as bound to God's higher rule and divine laws and ordinances that he was to obey along with every other citizen, the restraints on the abuse of power inherent in absolute kingship were removed, opening the door to despotic monarchy and political tyranny. The parallel devolution observed by the prophet in the realm of the religious establishment is noteworthy, where the people repudiate the holy God and construct gods of their own, thereby determining their own destruction.

In brief, then, Hosea describes the following political situation: a nation faces a daunting crisis without the benefit of responsible leadership. Other passages describe the frenzied foreign policy that results. Security is sought in the increase of military spending (8:14). The government, lacking long-term objectives and moral guidelines, embarks on a mission of desperate, erratic diplomacy, turning first to Egypt and then to Assyria (7:11, 16; 8:9–10; 12:1).

The prophet, noting the futility of government cut off from moral principles, recalls the origins of kingship in Israel, when the people went to Samuel requesting a king in order that Israel might become like the other nations:

> Where now is your king, that he may save you?
>   Where in all your cities are your rulers,
> of whom you said,
>   "Give me a king and rulers"?
> I gave you a king in my anger,
>   and I took him away in my wrath.
>   (13:10–11)

Having already noted the prophet's perception of the parallel between impudence in government and in religion, it remains to consider the specific nature of Hosea's accusations against his coreligionists, the priests. In 5:1 Hosea delivers a word of judgment against both priests and the house of the king for being a "snare" to the people. In 4:4–14 he singles out the priests for an indictment suggesting that they bear the brunt of the responsibility for the horrific decline of the nation:

> My people are destroyed for lack of knowledge;
>   because you have rejected knowledge,
>   I reject you from being a priest to me.
> And since you have forgotten the law of your God,
>   I also will forget your children.
>   (4:6)

An ominous assumption underlies this indictment, namely, that the foundation essential to a nation's survival is categorically moral in nature. The calamity threatening Israel is the result of the rejection of that foundation, and those who are ultimately responsible are the religious leaders charged with the cultivation of virtue among the populace by teaching them true religion. In Israel, the priests are paid for this service, but what good are they if they abuse their office by enjoying its material benefits while utterly neglecting the duties to which they are commissioned? They eat and drink wine to excess, they whore, they cavort with false gods. The negative example they give calls to mind the piercing query of the holy, poor cleric in Chaucer, "If gold ruste, what will yren [iron] do?"[2] Hosea informs them that their sacred calling will not grant them immunity from judgment; indeed, the hereditary status of their office will not even secure the succession of their children.

What is the nature of the moral tradition that the priests have failed to nurture among the people? According to Hosea, it has two dimensions. One is the retelling of the Hebrew Epic, the story of God's delivering Israel from Egypt and with loving protection making them a nation (11:1–4). As a result of this sacerdotal neglect, "she [i.e., Israel] did not know that it was I who gave her the grain, the wine, and the oil," observes a grieving God in 2:8. Israel's tragedy becomes clear: instead of expressing gratitude in worship and obedience, Israel forgot and spurned its God and pursued a path of self-destruction (6:4). The first dimension of the priests' deleteriousness, therefore, is their failure to keep alive the story from which the people of Israel derived their very identity and sense of direction in the world.

The second dimension of the tradition entrusted to the priests is the Torah itself, the protective ordering of life that God gave Israel to assure its security and prosperity. This dimension is beautifully encapsulated in three verses:

> Hear the word of the LORD, O people of Israel;
>   for the LORD has an indictment against the inhabitants of the land.
> There is no faithfulness or loyalty,
>   and no knowledge of God in the land.
> Swearing, lying, and murder,
>   and stealing and adultery break out;
>   bloodshed follows bloodshed.
> Therefore the land mourns,
>   and all who live in it languish;
> together with the wild animals
>   and the birds of the air,
>   even the fish of the sea are perishing.
>
> (4:1–3)

The moral universe of Hosea, shared by the prophets as a whole, is here sketched with remarkable brevity. It is a universe construed in terms of a covenant between God and people. Securing the center of that universe is what we have called the theocratic principle, Israel's ultimate *loyalty*, its *faithfulness* to the Creator. Loyalty to God is kept alive through the transmission of *knowledge* in the form of the story of God's merciful acts, from creation to redemption to sustaining Israel as a people. That loyalty is properly expressed in *obedience*

---

2. Chaucer, *The Canterbury Tales*, Prologue l, 500.

to the laws God has given to foster decency and integrity within the people, a precondition for the holy God's abiding with them. Israel, misled and betrayed by its priests, has repudiated the basic principles of this moral universe. It has betrayed the source of all goodness and polluted the land with all manner of violence and sordidness, and the result is cataclysmic and inevitable: the material universe that depends upon a moral foundation enabling all of its participating communities to live in harmony collapses. Israel, the people called by God to be a source of blessing as God's agents of *shalom* in the world, has become instead a lethal source of defilement.

We are introduced here to a remarkably holistic view of reality. It is as if we are viewing a cell through an electron microscope. The nucleus of the universe is a human community, upon which is conferred by divine grace a prescription for preserving the health of the entire organism. By living true to this prescription, a robust vitality is maintained at the center that radiates outward for the benefit of the whole. The converse sadly is equally true. If the nucleus is corrupted and the integrity of the cell breaks down, the damage is not confined to the nucleus, but it emanates outward until the entire organism is consumed. Creation cannot bear up under the weight of inner rot. Implosion is the result, as a whole universe collapses. In these brief words, Hosea has explained why Israel's entire world—economic, social, and international—was crashing in upon them. Disease had established itself in the soul of the nation.

Perhaps one leaves the book of Hosea desiring a more promising prognosis. One suspects that Hosea would reply that it is the solemn responsibility of a prophet to be honest to God and people. Besides, only if Israel could be shocked into recognizing the root cause of its dilemma would there be any hope of deliverance. The prophet sees little indication of openness to the truth, and hence his message is largely in the form of threats and invective. He hits at the heart of the disease, a distorted reading of reality that confuses the penultimate with the ultimate (i.e., human government with heavenly government), false worship with true (i.e., idolatry with worship of the one God), and an empty life with the authentic life (i.e., self-indulgence with obedience).

Nevertheless, even in the face of a nation's sickness unto death, the last word is neither sickness nor death. Though covered over by layers of betrayal, the source of hope burns through the gloom in the message of Hosea:

> How can I give you up, Ephraim?
>   How can I hand you over, O Israel? . . .
> My heart recoils within me;
>   my compassion grows warm and tender.
>   (11:8)

The God who delivered slaves and gave them an opportunity to live as a free people and as a source of blessing for all nations continues to appeal to Israel, much as God's servant, the prophet Hosea, at God's behest, persists in seeking to touch the heart of a fickle lover (3:1–5). The call to Israel to reclaim its source and to reestablish its national identity on the theocratic foundation of God's order of compassion and justice abides as the raison d'etre of his hard-hitting message:

> Sow for yourselves righteousness;
>> reap steadfast love;
>> break up your fallow ground;
> for it is time to seek the LORD,
>> that he may come and rain righteousness upon you.
>> (10:12)

What is required? "But as for you, return to your God, hold fast to love and justice, and wait continually for your God" (12:6).

We have summarized Hosea's message. It remains to assess the value of his contribution to his nation. The historical fact is that Israel, notwithstanding the prophet's testimony to God's unrelenting appeal to the heart of the nation, did not survive, but fell victim to the imperialism of the mighty empire of Assyria. Does this not imply that the prophet failed in his mission? One way to dodge such a conclusion is to argue that the message of the prophets was a spiritual message, and accordingly the destruction of political Israel was inconsequential to God's plan of salvation. The souls of the faithful would be snatched in splendor out of the ashes of national calamity. Such recourse is without basis in the message of Hosea or any of the other eighth-century prophets. The divine purpose that they expounded was not removed from the political history of the nation, but inextricably tied to it. The God they proclaimed struggled for a people in the midst of their physical setting. When judgment came in the form of foreign invasion, it was not greeted as a welcomed release from the bondage of the physical world. It evoked bitter lament, such as we find in the book of Lamentations or in the lament of Jesus over the impending fate of Jerusalem (Luke 13:34).

Similarly, when the prophets looked beyond judgment, they described repentance leading to restoration of the nation. This is as true of the prophets themselves (e.g., Hos. 3:4–5) as of the disciples and tradents who collected and amplified their words (e.g., the addition of "and David their king" in Hos. 3:5 and the amplifications of the prophet's message in Amos 9:11–15). Politics, accordingly, cannot be dismissed as a peripheral sphere for the prophets. Politics is at the center of the prophetic message. This is not to deny that their grasp of God's universal reign transcended human regimes. It is only to insist that their sense of God's suzerainty was unsundered, as seen for example in the fact that it was precisely their ultimate fealty to the divine king that secured their reliability in service to their earthly king and nation.

The allegation that the fall of the northern kingdom of Israel to the Assyrian armies proves that Hosea's career ended in failure cannot be dismissed blithely and requires closer scrutiny. Might one not plausibly suggest that if the people had hearkened to the prophet's call to desist in covering over lives of dishonesty and deceit with cult ritual and had wholeheartedly renewed their covenant with

YHWH in righteousness and obedience, they would have withstood the assault of the Assyrians? Such an explanation would involve an oversimplification of both prophetic politics and the historical process in general. Regarding the latter, history is not like a chess game allowing one to go back to earlier moves and calculate possible outcomes if nations had chosen different courses of action. Chess is complex enough to make such an exercise challenging. History is vastly more complex.

The more important reason to resist resorting to simplistic formulae in the analysis of prophetic politics is the complexity of that phenomenon itself. The prophets struggled within the ambiguities of history, not with clairvoyance but with a highly principled understanding of the relation between divine and human government. From the chapters of Israel's religious Epic and on the basis of the Torah tradition growing out of that Epic, the prophets inferred a set of criteria for the behavior of leaders and their subjects that they upheld by applying them to the concrete circumstances and events of their society and world. The fundamental objective of their activity was reform based on repentance, and they did not hesitate to announce that God would bless faithfulness. Since they regarded the ultimate ruler of the nations to be YHWH, it does seem accurate to claim that they believed that no foreign power could annihilate a people living in obedience to the sovereign of the universe. The consistent opposite side of their crusade for reform was the announcement of judgment that would issue from persistence in apostasy and injustice. Taken together, these two sides of the prophetic message account for the preservation of the prophetic books, even after the fall of the northern kingdom to the Assyrians and, nearly a century and a half later, the fall of the southern kingdom to the Babylonians. To future generations, their threats of judgment continued to provide the basis for political reform, even as their promises of divine blessing held out hope for the future to the community during times of exile and foreign occupation.

All in all, the book of Hosea presents, on the basis of a consistent historiography, a political theology that continues to instruct modern readers. It reveals a universe firmly upheld by a moral foundation created and sustained by God. As for the realm of human affairs, the destiny of nations is not the result of fate or whimsy, but unfolds in keeping with a divine plan incorporating the participation of humans. Consequently, human acts have consequences, and the greater an individual or nation's strength, the greater its responsibility.

Hosea's construal of that reality is most concisely captured by the word "covenant." On its most basic level, creation flourishes or declines within the context of a relationship between God and those God has created. For humans, the implication is the choice between faithfulness and perfidy, obedience and defiance. The result is a seamless moral fabric encompassing all realms—nature and history, personal and communal, domestic and international. No realm exists in independence of the others. For example, the quality of life that a given nation provides for its citizens has a profound bearing on that nation's contribution to world harmony. The integrity of individual leaders does affect their ability to provide quality leadership for those they represent.

Chapter 15

Isaiah

The Majesty of the Holy One as the Nation's Sole Foundation

Of the biblical prophets, Isaiah provides the most comprehensive example of prophetic politics in action. He draws together with impressive lucidity the cardinal themes of the earlier prophets. Though his words, like those of all the other prophets, are not presented in the form of a systematic statement of political theology, but rather arise out of concrete situations, it is not difficult to discern a unified understanding of the relation of religious faith to political realities shaping the individual utterances. The lasting legacy of his career is evidenced both by the fact that the book transmitted under his name includes amplifications that extend over several centuries and by the extensive degree to which he was quoted and alluded to by later Jewish and Christian writers.

The book of Isaiah as a literary whole, in spite of its long history of transmission, amplification, and editing, is not a haphazard compendium of sayings and compositions. Themes and motifs developed by the eighth-century prophet recur in the section arising from the exilic period (chaps. 40–55) and in the remaining eleven chapters, which reflect conditions in the Jewish community in the late sixth and fifth centuries as it adjusted to life under Persian rule. Sorting earlier material from later is not a precise science, but in utilizing materials from the book of Isaiah for the purposes of our study of prophetic politics, we shall draw upon sayings in this section that most scholars would agree stem from the eighth-century prophet, even as in subsequent sections we shall consider the light shed on later periods by materials that most likely stem from the exile and the early Persian periods.

Readers who look to the opening lines of a book for clues to its central thesis will not be disappointed in the case of the book of Isaiah. It is a tribute to the literary sensitivity of the ancient editors that the first saying of the book, in 1:2–9, is an accusation directed by Isaiah against Israel that lays bare the rudimental failure of the nation. By opening with a summons to the heavens and the earth as witnesses, it betrays its setting as the highest court, where Israel will be tried by the most exalted of all judges. The indictment is buttressed by evidence from common human experience as well as from the natural order. Children show respect to their parents, and the beast acknowledges the one who feeds it. But incredibly, "Israel does not know, my people do not understand" (1:3).

The accusation is not a reckless insult hurled out of spitefulness, but a careful summary of the prophet's assessment of Israel's core problem: The nation has adopted a manner of behavior that contradicts both the essential identity that grew out of the centuries covered by its Epic and the elemental wisdom of its seers.[1] It is because that behavior has placed the very existence of the nation at risk that the case is accepted for trial by the highest court in the universe. Called for is a careful cross-examination of the defendant, Israel, to lay bare its fundamental error, which basically involves an epistemological fallacy that distorts reality rather than shedding light on it, perverting Israel's understanding of the meaning of existence on its ultimate level. The nation is being dragged to calamity because it has cut itself from its source and violated the theocratic principle upon which its political viability is founded. It has "forsaken the LORD, . . . despised the Holy One of Israel" (1:4).

The depth and consistency of the prophet's moral insight is reflected in the fact that all of his pronouncements in the succeeding chapters emanate from this central indictment. At issue is what constitutes a healthy, viable body politic. The arguments he formulates locate questions dealing with the nature and proper function of government on the most fundamental level of scrutiny. Human government cannot be understood apart from knowledge of the cosmic government ordered by the sovereign creator of the universe. To the twenty-first-century reader, this theo-political viewpoint may seem archaic and infused with a mythopoeic mind-set incomprehensible to a rational thinker. In our epilogue we shall set forth, contrariwise, our case: the prophet's thesis not only is applicable to our time but is as critically important now as it was in the prophet's time. The more immediate task, however, is that of understanding Isaiah's political message within the context of seventh-century Israel.

Isaiah discerns at the heart of the calamity befalling his nation the hubris that regards security and prosperity as the accomplishments of clever human leaders.

---

1. See J. William Whedbee, *Isaiah and Wisdom* (Nashville: Abingdon Press, 1971).

He sees as the only alternative to such ruinous myopia a humble submission to the one reality that transcends all human agencies and institutions. His favorite term for that reality is "the Holy One of Israel." Anthropocentric government tends to foster structures that discriminate in favor of the powerful elite over ordinary citizens and exploit the underrepresented. Theocentrically chastened government, if true to its acknowledgment that all nations and every citizen within those nations belong to a universal moral order transcending every human regime, will cultivate safeguards against the temptation to utilize political and military power for self-aggrandizing purposes. Isaiah is untiring in reminding his nation that submission to God and conformity to God's justice and mercy alone provide a secure basis for national security and prosperity, because, according to Isaiah's understanding, the universal God is not a distant and passive entity, but an active and attentive reality encountered in every corner of the nation's life.

Awareness of the presence of the Holy One became a very personal matter for Isaiah, as the result of the encounter described in chapter 6. The core of that encounter was an awesome experience of the holiness of God, over against which Isaiah and the human community he represented were exposed as sinful and unclean. Only by a divine act of cleansing could the prophet become to the nation a messenger of the Holy One. The message with which he is charged is one of dreadful impending judgment (6:9–13). Though a first reading suggests preordained calamity for Israel, viewing the passage within the context of Isaiah's overall proclamation enables one to hear the outcry of one overwhelmed by a sense of the nothingness and futility of all things human before the holiness of God. Beyond this outcry, however, there lay confidence in the reality of divine mercy that can transform nothingness and futility into a new creation. This juxtaposition of human despair and divine possibility was captured exquisitely by the later Isaiah of the exile: "surely the people are grass . . . but the word of our God will stand forever" (40:7–8).

Viewing Isaiah's mission against the background of this awesome sense of the holy center of the universe offers a key to understanding his political message. Without a grounding in that transcendent reality, all human institutions are drawn into the vortex of myopic self-service that inevitably leads to conflict and widespread devastation. It is clearly the prophet's understanding that acknowledgment by the nations and their leaders of their subordinate status vis-à-vis the divine sovereign alone provides a basis for international peace. Once the divine source of societal norms and international policy is forgotten, the moral foundation that alone can safeguard the world from lawlessness and chaos is lost.

Isaiah contrasts the holiness of the sovereign of the nations that he has experienced in his call with his own condition and the state of his nation, and his immediate response is a sense of impending doom. Though he will recover equipoise and dedicate his life to seeking to shock his people into the radical revision of their understanding that alone could save them, the overarching awareness of the nothingness of humanity before the holy God infuses his every word and gives his social and political message a sense of urgency and a poignant focus.

Though the existential experience of being in the presence of the holy sovereign of the universe infused the entire career of the prophet Isaiah with a sense of submission to the only authority that legitimately could claim ultimate allegiance, it would be a mistake to understand that experience in a vague *generic* sense as a theophanous moment or a mystical illumination. The one whom Isaiah encountered was not in a *general* sense the holy one, but rather in a very specific sense the *Holy One of Israel*, who had revealed his name intimately to Moses as YHWH and who accompanied that self-introduction with just and merciful acts that were of the very essence of the divine nature and in turn were spelled out in instructions that enabled humans to live in communion with God and at peace with one another. Accordingly, when Isaiah goes forth from the presence of YHWH to proclaim God's will for the nation, he is not inventing a new religious system, but rather calling the nation back to the God of its ancestors and admonishing its citizenry to recommit their lives to the mercy and justice formulated in their Torah tradition.

While current biblical scholarship has refuted the earlier view of the prophets as the creators of ethical monotheism, in favor of understanding them as defenders of an Epic and Torah tradition with roots in earliest Yahwism, it is at the same time clear that each prophet shaped that tradition in a particular way that reflected both personal background and the particularities of his time.

In the case of Isaiah, two traditions are drawn into a creative, symbiotic relationship. The first tradition is the one already treated in chapter 11, the royal tradition that developed within the Jerusalem-based Davidic dynasty. By emphasizing the cosmic reach of God's rule rooted in creation, this tradition served well Isaiah's insistence that the Holy One of Israel was the sole authority before which all other powers were obliged to submit. The iconography of the innermost chamber of the Jerusalem temple provides the context in which Isaiah finds himself and his people drawn into the presence of the King of Kings, out of which experience he is filled with the awesome awareness of the utter dependence of all creation on this sublime and dreadful majesty.

Even the tradition of YHWH's universal rule, however, is not left in ethereal suspension, but drawn into the concreteness of political life by being linked to a particular institution, the Davidic house. God's universal reign is not exercised directly, but through the mediation of a chosen human agent, whose God-given attributes the prophet describes in Isaiah 9:2–7 and 11:1–9. The location of that mediated rule was also specific, namely, in Jerusalem, a theme that comes to beautiful expression in Isaiah 2:2–4 and its parallel in Micah 4:1–4. The specificity of person and location of the earthly kingship, however, did not negate the universality of the rule of the sovereign represented by the Davidic king, as is clearly indicated by the expansive scope of the moral universe described by Isaiah and those following in his tradition.

Universalism, however, can devolve into the moral thinness of latitudinarianism. That this did not occur in the prophecy of Isaiah is attributable to the second tradition upon which he drew and into which he integrated all else, namely,

Israel's Epic of origins and the accompanying Torah presenting the imperatives arising from the divine acts of mercy and justice depicted in that Epic. The quality of life to which the Epic/Torah tradition called the nation bore implications for every sphere of the society. Another consequence of Isaiah's conjoining royal and Epic traditions is that the common tendency of ancient Near Eastern monarchies to accord the king exceptional privileges and status was sharply qualified, as already noted in our discussion of Deuteronomy 17:14–20.[2] The king, like every other citizen, was bound by the conditions of the Torah, indeed, he was to manifest his legitimacy by setting an example of humility before God and obedience to God's commands. Finally, by placing the origins and history of kingship within a temporal as opposed to a mythic/spatial framework, Isaiah, again in keeping with the historiographic perspective inherent in the nation's Epic, upheld the qualitative distinction between God's absolute authority and the derived, penultimate authority of mortal rulers.

An important consequence of this distinction was this: while Isaiah ascribes an important role to the Davidic king as one delegated by God to lead the country in righteousness and thereby to secure it from danger, he does not follow the customary ancient Near Eastern royal pattern of tying the deity to the monarchy unconditionally. Kingship derives its legitimacy solely as the mediator of God's will within the structures of human institutions. This explains what, apart from a clear grasp of the theocratic principle, could appear to be a contradiction within the larger Isaianic tradition, namely, the prophetic voice speaking out in Isaiah 40–55 in the wake of the collapse of the monarchy, and the temple cult announcing the perdurance of the Jewish people after the demise of the Davidic monarchy and the Jerusalem sanctuary.

Isaiah, by maintaining a creative dialectical relation between the royal and Epic traditions, cultivated a message containing profound implications for the history of political thought: God, the sovereign judge of all nations, set before all peoples, regardless of rank or class, the same instruction (*torah*), according to which evenhanded justice was to guide international policy, compassion was to govern treatment of the poor and disadvantaged, and humility was to define the posture of all mortals before the Holy One. This limit, which imposed on the vigorous claims of royal tradition the egalitarian mandates of prophetic Yahwism, undergirded Israel's sense of election with a moral foundation. God could be counted on as Israel's source of protection so long as the nation honored God and obeyed God's commandments. The nation living in righteousness in turn would uphold the ancient Abrahamic promise of being a blessing to all nations, and its central sanctuary would serve as an arbitration center to which nations could bring their disputes for resolution and as an academy where all peoples could transform tactics of war to strategies for peace (Isa. 2:5).

---

2. To be sure, royal psalms like 45 and 89 indicate that the prophetic qualifications did not go unchallenged by construals of kingship that moved in more assertive directions. See above [pages 192–99].

However, abuse of the notion of divine protection, by presenting God as a patron who would protect a nation that treated with contempt his norms of justice and decency, arrogantly claimed special exemptions and privileges, and promulgated oppressive, self-serving economic and social policies was a mockery of the Holy One and a perversion of sound understanding that would incur the punishment of the heavenly judge who presided over a moral order encompassing the entire universe.

Let us summarize what we have observed of Isaiah's message to this point. Human government can be construed aright only by understanding its proper relation to divine government. Central to the latter is the holy God, before whom all other powers are nil until they derive legitimacy as agents of God's universal reign. Isaiah recognized the Davidic king as a legitimate agent of God's reign, but only with the qualification that safeguarded the theocratic principle. The king's agency was authentic only to the extent that it mediated God's reign by faithfully implementing the Torah tradition of evenhanded justice and mercy.

From this understanding of divine and human government grow twin themes that elucidate the prophet's conception of the relation of faith to politics: (1) trust in the Holy One is the only reliable basis for a government that fosters security, peace, and prosperity; (2) human pride lies at the heart of the ruinous repudiation of God's universal rule in favor of a human regime viewing itself as self-legitimizing and ultimate. We turn now to examine these two themes.

TRUST

"In quietness and in trust shall be your strength" (Isa. 30:15b). Politicians scramble to address current problems, and military personnel rush to head off military threats. Isaiah points beyond such frantic activity to a reality that, though intangible and denied by many, represents for him the only point of reference that assures the long-term security of a nation. However, Isaiah's spiritual counsel does not meet with wide acceptance, which leads to the harsh warnings that arise repeatedly in his speeches: "Because you reject this word, and put your trust in oppression and deceit . . ." (30:12).

In 3:1–11 Isaiah paints a picture of the conditions that follow a nation's rejection of God's order of justice as the foundation of its government. It is a picture of political chaos. The public offices that are essential for the ordering of civic affairs are removed: "For now the Sovereign, the LORD of hosts, is taking away from Jerusalem and from Judah support and staff" (3:1). To be taken away are "warrior and soldier, judge and prophet, diviner and elder, captain of fifty and dignitary, counselor and skillful magician and expert enchanter" (3:2–3). So desperate is the situation that the vacuum will be filled by utterly unqualified surrogates: "I will make boys their princes, and babes shall rule over them" (3:4). The result will be anomie and anarchy:

> The people will be oppressed,
>> everyone by another
>> and everyone by a neighbor;
>> the youth will be insolent to the elder,
>> and the base to the honorable.
>>
>> (3:5)

The people desperately search for someone to rule, based on the minimal qualification of possessing a cloak: "You shall be our leader, and this heap of ruins shall be under your rule" (3:6). The offer is refused: "You shall not make me leader of the people" (3:7). How could a land come to such a deplorable, destitute state? Isaiah skips over the dozens of penultimate reasons he doubtless could enumerate and focuses in on Israel's fundamental error:

> For Jerusalem has stumbled
>> and Judah has fallen,
>> because their speech and their deeds are against the LORD,
>> defying his glorious presence.
>>
>> (3:8)

Since the nation Isaiah addresses with this lament has not yet fallen, we can assume that he still intends his bleak picture to shock the nation into recognizing its utter reliance on the Holy One. But he must also avoid another trap, that of construing divine protection in magical terms. This he manages to do by tying the royal tradition's theme of God's protection of Jerusalem to the moral imperative of prophecy. Trust in the Holy One of Israel does not imply an unconditional promise of security. Trust is rather to be the inner disposition of the individual and the nation that see themselves in the first instance and on the most basic level as belonging to the universal fellowship (*oikoumenē*) of the sovereign of all nations and wholeheartedly embrace the terms of the covenant that are intrinsic to that fellowship. Trust, as an attribute arising out of the theocratic principle, thus enables the community to live in harmony with the will of the Holy One and to be guided not by the shifting stratagems of world empires but by the steady compass of the creator of the heavens and the earth.

Isaiah formulates the inner disposition that arises from trust in the Holy One in the following ways: "Take heed, be quiet, do not fear, and do not let your heart be faint" (7:4). "If you do not stand firm in faith, you shall not stand at all" (7:9). "Do not call conspiracy all that this people calls conspiracy, and do not fear what it fears, or be in dread. But the LORD of hosts, him you shall regard as holy; let him be your fear, and let him be your dread" (8:12–13; cf. 1 Sam. 12:24). "For thus said the Lord GOD, the Holy One of Israel: In returning and rest you shall be saved; in quietness and in trust shall be your strength" (30:15). Each of these formulations is pointing to one pure truth, namely, that the only trustworthy orientation within an ambiguous, threatening world is one that is located in a reality transcending the whimsy of human designs. The prophet has in mind the same truth to which he pointed when in 1:3 he accused Israel of lacking knowledge and understanding, namely, that at its core the universe is a moral order established by a divine purpose.

Individuals and nations that establish themselves on that truth will not succumb to the pressures of blustering tyrants. Rather, they will base decisions on the conviction that policy guided by adherence to the principles of universal justice and equality will keep its focus on long-term goals and comprehensive results. This is not the same as claiming that a specific policy is revealed to a nation with God as its underwriter and guarantor. While such a claim to certainty is not uncommon among policy makers claiming guidance from on high, it involves a fundamental confusion between the perspective provided by faith and trust in the living God and the human responsibility of being diligent in the pursuit of global justice and peace. While that pursuit is a vocation shared by all fair-minded humans, those adhering to Yahwistic tradition will seek to represent with self-critical truthfulness their legacy of Scripture and tradition. Within the framework of this understanding of the role of faith in political process, failed policy will challenge chastened leaders to seek all the more diligently to "get it right," free from the prideful commitment to one course of action that can lead a nation into confrontations in which matters spin out of control. "In quietness and trust" is not an easy composure to maintain in the face of crisis, but in a world fraught with tension, it offers the only dependable path to peace.

In two passages Isaiah sketches his vision of the leader who places his ultimate trust in the reality transcending every human state, who in leading his people adheres to the universal norms of justice authored by that reality, and who seeks to be an agent of righteous compassion in the world.

The backdrop of the lovely poem in 9:2–7 (Heb. vv. 1–6) is a period of darkness and gloom, a time in which the nation lives under an oppressive, militaristic regime, a nightmare never far from Isaiah's consciousness. The description of remarkable transformation takes the form of a hymn of praise to God, to whom deliverance is credited. But the paean, while bearing marks of a Divine Warrior hymn, is not purely mythological, for God's agent in securing the governance of the people on a solid moral foundation is a king of Davidic descent. The harmonious order intrinsic to the design of the creator of the universe will become a reality through the agency of a flesh-and-blood human delegated by God. In trust and faithfulness the king will establish a lasting peace, upheld by justice and righteousness. The last line of the poem underlines the central point, as if to safeguard against equating the limited, derivative authority of the earthly king with the tyranny characteristic of the kings of the world empires: "The zeal of the LORD of hosts will do this" (9:7).

The prophet's second celebration of godly leadership is found in 11:1–10. Again Isaiah reflects within the framework of the model of government regnant at his time, monarchy, specifically, the kingship of the Davidic house. His reflection, however, goes beyond specific political models to a more fundamental truth. The authenticity of the envisioned government will lie in the fact that it is not autogenous, but derived from a transcendent source. Receptivity to power beyond self of course depends on acknowledgment of and trust in that power. It is not accidental, therefore, that the description of the endowment received by the king from God concludes with the following line: "His delight shall be in the fear of the LORD" (11:3). "Fear" in the biblical sense of the word connotes honor and respect and humility before one's superior. The verb "delight" indicates that it is the wholehearted disposition of this king to submit to the authority and follow the will of God.

In this way the king, rather than exalting himself above his subjects (cf. Ps. 45:6–9), will model for those subjects the proper posture of the human before the Holy One. His example will thus stand in stark contrast to a nation that "does not know," a people that "does not understand" (Isa. 1:2–4). Isaiah's grounding in the prophetic tradition reflected in Deuteronomy 17:16–20 is clear. The king will not "acquire more horses" and "many wives . . . and silver and gold in great quantity for himself," but will "learn to fear the LORD his God, diligently observing all the words of this law and these statutes, neither exalting himself above other members of the community nor turning aside from the commandment." God will uphold his side of the covenant by conferring upon him "wisdom and understanding," "counsel and might," "knowledge and fear of the LORD" (Isa. 11:2).

Like the honorific titles ascribed to the king in 9:6, these gifts could be perverted into claims to special status, were it not for the prior premise, namely, that the king is a mortal alongside his subjects, and that his office is not one of privilege but of responsibilities delegated to a human who is a faithful civil servant because he in the first instance is a servant of God. Gifts applied for personal advantage by the king would be gifts perverted to a use not intended by the giver. The faithful king will recognize that the qualities that establish his authority and ability to rule are not his personal possessions, but derive from the spirit of the Lord. Thus the entire consciousness of the just ruler will be formed by the sense of being the representative of a higher authority.

The hymn goes on to apply this lesson. Leadership entails judgment, but 11:3b–4 clearly states that judgment will be based not on personal discernment, but on norms the king has received from the religious Epic of community:

> He shall not judge by what his eyes see,
>   or decide by what his ears hear;
> but with righteousness he shall judge the poor,
>   and decide with equity for the meek of the earth.

The irreducible prerequisite of sound government is impartial justice. Justice tainted by partisanship or personal interest dooms a land to corruption. Justice, to be founded on dependable standards, must transcend entanglements with personal interests. The king, as the highest human model of the land, must exemplify transcendent justice. But how can he judge other than by "what his eyes see . . . , by what his ears hear"? To answer this is to solve the perplexing question of the basis of impartial justice, a question in modern times that has commanded the attention of moral philosophers from Immanuel Kant to John Rawls. The biblical answer is a religious answer: God, the judge transcending all human judges, is the source of impartial justice.

The concept of a transcendent source of moral norms is not unproblematic, because it is susceptible to the perversion of individuals and nations claiming possession of special divine gifts as a means of defending purely selfish or imperialistic goals. The problem involved in distinguishing between legitimate and illegitimate appeals to religious warrants in defense of positions taken by humans on public issues will be addressed in the epilogue. For now, we can observe that for prophets like Isaiah, the concept of divine justice is safeguarded against subjectivism, personal whimsy, and passing social trends by the sanctity ascribed to tradition. According to this view, God's will had been handed down through the ages in the Torah. The king can judge by other than the limited vision of "what his eyes see," because he judges on the basis of a received body of law that has undergone the test of the ages and thus reliably defines for a community the nature of righteousness and equity.

Since that body of law belongs to the public domain, the king is not free to manipulate it in the direction of personal self-interest. The king that does is confronted by the prophet, the guardian of the nation's memory (Epic) and moral legacy (*torah*). Thus Ahab, after engineering the execution of innocent Naboth and confiscating his land, when confronted by Elijah exclaims, "Have you found me, O my enemy?" (1 Kgs. 21:20), and Ahaz, when urged by Isaiah to trust God in time of crisis, demurs and exposes himself to the prophet's rebuke, "Is it too little for you to weary mortals, that you weary my God also?" (Isa. 7:13).

As we examine evidence regarding the political role of prophets like Isaiah, would we be justified in calling them politicians, in something resembling the modern sense of the term? Not really. They address political issues, but their perspective remains sub specie aeternitatis, which is to say, they hold up to their nation standards derived from the ideal *oikoumenē,* that governed by the Holy One. In viewing the not infrequent eccentric behavior of the prophets, it becomes especially clear that they do not fit the profile of candidates for political office, or even for committees charged with writing party platforms.

Perhaps Isaiah brings us closest to a prophet bearing at least quasi-official status in government (as a counselor to Hezekiah). But in Isaiah's case as well as that of the other prophets, the ultimate commitment to God's reign stands in the way of their dedicating themselves fully to any temporal regime or party. It is this transcendent perspective that enables the prophets to carry out their chief responsibility, serving as impartial critic and guardian of the conscience of the nation and thus making a contribution to political process that is beyond the grasp of professional officeholders and party loyalists.

HUMAN PRIDE

Thus far we have described Isaiah's understanding of sound government as predicated on a relationship of trust. It is founded on a transcendent order, and its leaders acknowledge that they serve strictly on the basis of penultimate authority delegated to them by God and with responsibility to uphold God-given moral norms. We now ask, what did Isaiah regard as the greatest threat to sound government? Not surprisingly, it is the quality that is diametrically opposed to "delighting in the fear of the LORD," namely, human pride. Isaiah relentlessly scans the political landscape of his world in search of instances of the human vice that he sees as responsible more than any other for the near-fatal condition of his nation.

In Isaiah 10 we find a prophetic attack on leaders who exempt themselves from the moral imperatives binding on their citizens, who in effect confuse their stature with the Divine. They are not bound to the mercy code's command to care for the widow and the orphan, for they write the law for themselves (10:1–4). Isaiah's survey is not limited to his own land. God, as sovereign of the nations, has enlisted the king of Assyria as his instrument in judging godless peoples, but when that instrument confuses agency with sovereignty, his hubris affronts the Holy One and inevitably leads to downfall, for it is contrary to the order of the universe that "the ax vaunt itself over the one who wields it, or the saw magnify itself against the one who handles it" (10:15–16).

Pride and the self-deception that accompanies it also contaminate the religious sphere, within which Isaiah observes worshipers using religious ceremony to conceal corruption and violence dedicated to self-gain at the expense of the weak and poor. In the tradition of Amos and Micah, Isaiah presents a God who rebukes such false piety and accepts as true worship only acts of sacrifice and praise that are accompanied by and manifested in acts of justice and loving-kindness. The God who cannot endure the hymns and sacrifices of those who return from worship only to reengage in corruption and cruelty not only condemns such blatant hypocrisy, but goes on to prescribe a clear criterion for authentic worship:

> Wash yourselves; make yourselves clean;
>> remove the evil of your doings
>> from before my eyes;
> cease to do evil,
>> learn to do good,
> seek justice,
>> rescue the oppressed,
> defend the orphan,
>> plead for the widow.
>
> (1:16–17)

With pride, pretentiousness, and deception lodged in the high places of political and religious leadership, it is not surprising to find that the lesser imitators of the high and mighty enact a vanity fair of their own. Like the "cows of Bashan" ridiculed by Amos, Isaiah holds up for biting sarcasm the "daughters of Zion" who go strutting about in their jewels, exotic coiffures, and fine garments (3:16–17). The bitterness of his condemnation will seem excessive or misogynous if one fails to see how discordant human pretension and pride are with the prophet's primal understanding of God's holiness.

Given Isaiah's awareness of the evanescence of all creatures before their creator, it is understandable that he regards human pride as the manifestation of a perverted sense of reality; to use his metaphor, it is akin to the pot confusing itself with the potter (29:16). In 2:11–22, he gives colorful expression to all manner of inappropriate exaltation of created things before the creator. Prideful human behavior, whether in relation to fellow humans in the form of expressions of superiority or in relation to God in the form of a sense of special privilege, betrays a fundamental distortion of reality. The inevitable consequence of human pride will be a final encounter with its falsity on the day when universal harmony is restored through the reduction of "all that is proud and lofty" and the exaltation of the only one worthy of worship: "The haughtiness of people shall be humbled, and the pride of everyone shall be brought low; and the LORD alone will be exalted on that day" (2:17).

The reason Isaiah focuses on pride as the fateful flaw is that it expresses the fundamental human error that undercuts the foundation for the dependable ordering of life. To those filled with their own self-importance, Isaiah exclaims in exasperation, "You turn things upside down!" (29:16). Once prideful humans are deprived of the laissez-faire environment where they can pursue corrupt enterprises with impunity and are obliged to acknowledge that the world is ordered by a righteous judge, the structure of justice that characterizes God's sovereign rule and that is summarized in Israel's *torah* tradition can become the foundation of human government. Isaiah audaciously glimpses the day in which reality will be set aright, social justice will again prevail in the land, and every human will be secured from the harm of evildoers by the protecting presence of the God of justice:

> The meek shall obtain fresh joy in the LORD,
>   and the neediest people shall exult in the Holy One of Israel.
> For the tyrant shall be no more,
>   and the scoffer shall cease to be;
>   all those alert to do evil shall be cut off—
> those who cause a person to lose a lawsuit,
>   who set a trap for the arbiter in the gate,
>   and without grounds deny justice to the one in the right.
>   (29:19–21)

While Isaiah has a clear vision of the world that lives in harmony under the just rule of God and God's delegated leaders, he does not passively await a day when God will restore social justice. Isaiah treats the vision as an urgent mandate to work on behalf of that righteous order in all areas of life. A vital aspect of that mandate is taking the offensive against injustice wherever he encounters it.

Isaiah summons the best of his poetic skills in mounting his attack, as when he draws his audience into a seemingly frivolous song of unrequited love, only to entwine them with a stinging indictment (5:1–7). In other cases he forgoes all subtlety and lists one vice after the other as cancers devastating the moral tissue of the nation. Real-estate agents are attacked for buying up land and houses and creating a market in which nothing affordable remains for the average person (5:8–10). The high life of those exploiting the poor and using their ill-gotten wealth to lubricate a debaucherous lifestyle is threatened by a harsh reversal with the celebrants "dying of hunger" and "parched with thirst" (5:11–13). Delicacy is set aside as he names the Holy City of Jerusalem "a whore," a title earned by those using bribes to buy power and paying no heed to the plight of orphans and widows (1:21–23). Even the nation's judges, responsible for preserving justice and equity, have succumbed to corruption as they "acquit the guilty for a bribe, and deprive the innocent of their rights" (5:22–23). Within such an environment, what chance is there for the cause of justice? Isaiah even views as in jeopardy those of his profession who are charged with preserving the conscience of the nation, for those in power lay down their instructions: "Do not prophesy to us what is right; speak to us smooth things, prophesy illusions, leave the way, turn aside from the path, let us hear no more about the Holy One of Israel" (30:10–11; cf. 9:15).

Emphatically, Isaiah was not one of the prophets capitulating to such blandishments. But as he observes his coreligionists, both priests and prophets, succumbing to the immorality of the society as a whole and even abetting the disintegration of ethical standards, he issues a warning of dreadful impending doom for the nation that echoes the vision accompanying his inaugural call to prophecy (cf. 28:7–22 with 6:9–13). On the horizon he glimpses a time of such utter confusion that right will no longer be distinguishable from wrong. The sacred law will sound like gibberish to consciences clouded by dissipation and self-deception.

Isaiah sums up the perversity of the situation by picturing a scene in which the rulers of the land resort to black magic by ratifying a covenant with death as insurance against calamity, "for we have made lies our refuge, and in falsehood we have taken shelter" (28:15). Even this gloomy view of the land's utter depravity, however, does not shake the prophet's conviction that God's order of justice ultimately would prevail. To those remaining faithful, therefore, his advice remains consistent with his vision of God's sovereignty: "One who trusts will not panic" (28:16). On the basis of this trust alone the prophet can cling to his hope that God's reign of righteousness would finally prevail (29:22–24).

Even with the eclipse of human hope, his confidence in the theocratic foundation of world government remains standing.

Having completed our description of the central themes in Isaiah's prophetic message and observed how he applied them to the *domestic* issues facing his nation, it remains to consider two examples of his applying his faith to *international* crises.

In the decade leading to the fall of the northern kingdom to Sargon II of Assyria in 722, Isaiah found himself drawn into the very difficult task of trying to discern what guidance could be found in Yahwistic faith for a diplomatic crisis that was threatening the very existence of both Israel and Judah. King Ahaz found himself in a dilemma defying any easy solution. The most dreaded specter on the international scene was the seemingly unstoppable advance of the superpower, the Neo-Assyrian Empire. Following an ancient pattern, Shalmaneser V, having secured the eastern and northern borders of his sprawling empire, was now marching westward, his ultimate goal being Egypt. What chance did the small nations along the Mediterranean coast have to maintain their sovereignty against such a threat? Several nations, including Syria and the northern kingdom of Israel, decided that the answer resided in an anti-Assyrian military coalition. Frustrated in their effort by the refusal of King Ahaz of Judah to join their cause, they initiated an attack on Judah in 732, aimed at removing Ahaz from the throne and replacing him with a puppet king of their choosing named Tabeel.

Ahaz's options were these: (1) Submit to the pressure of Syria and Israel and become a member of the defense alliance with the inevitable consequence of incurring the wrath of Assyria. (2) Place his nation under the protective shield of the superpower Assyria by trading national autonomy for vassal status, with the accompanying consequences of annual tribute and state recognition of the Assyrian cult. (3) Prepare to defend Judah against the Syro-Ephraimite coalition while at the same time avoiding entanglements with the Assyrians.

This episode is such an interesting case study because it entailed the kind of ambiguity that is typical of international diplomacy. The prophet is not able to pull out a Torah scroll, look up the appropriate passage, and read a definitive divine solution to the king. What he can and does do is eschew all ephemeral concerns and reach back to the center of his religious tradition, to its most fundamental teaching, its understanding of God and God's relation to world governments. The result is not a facile, pragmatic political strategy, but a courageous attempt to restore king and nation to a right relationship with the ruler of the universe. The prophet thereby identifies as his most important *political* contribution the *religious* act of pointing out to the king and his counselors the penultimate significance of all worldly realities, in comparison to the only ultimate reality, which can give humans an orientation capable of safeguarding them from panic reactions and providing a basis for responsible policy decisions, an orientation predicated on trust in the Holy One.

Isaiah demonstrates his faithfulness to his prophetic calling by resolutely resisting the temptation of being lured into the myopic pragmatics of realpolitik, instead remaining focused on the unique contribution that he as a religious leader can make to his nation, namely, calling attention to the fact that security depends on a reality that transcends the parochial interests of any single nation. Loss of this transcendent perspective quickly leads to fear before worldly powers, with the ensuing danger residing not primarily in the might of foreign armies, but in the loss of trust in God and the consequent frantic grasping after security from sources that fail. "The heart of Ahaz and the heart of his people shook as the trees of the forest shake before the wind" (7:2). To base policy dealing with national crisis on fear is to run the risk of rash decisions leading to alliances that are untrustworthy and to short-term strategies that are followed by fatal long-term consequences. Isaiah was to experience this pattern of frantic crisis diplomacy more than once in his career, as his nation vacillated from neutrality to alliance with Assyria to an anti-Assyrian pact with Egypt and then back again. The same pattern was to be repeated in the last five years of the century, culminating in Sennacherib's invasion of Judah.

Isaiah does not assume the role of secretary of state; that is, he does not outline a specific foreign policy for King Ahaz. Remaining true to his vocational mandate, he commends a frame of mind capable of allowing the king and his advisors rigorously and clearheadedly to think through the alternatives facing the nation: "Take heed, be quiet, do not fear, and do not let your heart be faint because of these two smoldering stumps of firebrands" (7:4). This he backs up with a divine assurance that, if heeded, could have had the effect of removing the immediate catalyst for panic in the royal cabinet, namely, the hostile allied offensive being staged by the "stumps," Israel and Syria, for they "shall not stand" (7:7). This announcement perhaps could be construed as an instance of the prophet's crossing the line from religious counselor to military advisor, but when one recalls Isaiah's consistent message that all attempts by mortals to challenge God's sole right to sovereignty will be brought to naught, it becomes evident that the prophet is adhering to his central theme that worldly powers usurping divine prerogatives ultimately will fail.

Isaiah next moves from what God decrees to what the king must decide for himself: Will he subscribe to the realpolitik of world powers that acknowledge no authority higher than their own and who obliterate the distinction between themselves and divine rule and thus stumble on their own pride; or will he submit to the one authority upon which genuine security can be based? The prophet put the challenge to the king in these words: "If you do not stand firm in faith, you shall not stand at all" (7:9).

The king rejects the prophet's counsel. He embraces the calculus of military power and casts his lot with Assyria. Isaiah describes that fateful decision with a vivid image: "Because this people has refused the waters of Shiloah that flow gently, and melt in fear before Rezin and the son of Remaliah; therefore, the Lord is bringing up against it the mighty flood waters of the River, the king of Assyria and all his glory" (8:6–7). Two waterways are contrasted: the channel bringing fresh water into Jerusalem, capable of sustaining the people even in time of siege; and a torrential river, raging over its banks and leaving destruction and death in its wake.

Isaiah was prescient, but not in the sense of foretelling specific future events. His image draws deeply on Near Eastern mythology, in which "the mighty flood waters" represent the powers of chaos that threaten to destroy the ordered universe. His image extends his central theme: if you reject the sole reliable basis for security, namely, the Holy One, turning instead to the pragmatics of earthly power, the result is a "covenant with death" (cf. 28:15).

Did Isaiah have a clear notion of how Ahaz's rejection of YHWH's reign and his casting his lot with Assyria would work itself out in history? There is no way of answering that question with anything approaching certainty. What can be stated confidently is that he believed that king and nation were making a serious mistake that would have calamitous consequences. A nation built upon any basis other than the theocratic foundation provided by the Holy One was doomed.

From our vantage point in history, we know that as a result of Ahaz's strategic alliance with Assyria, Judah became a vassal state, part of the terms of which was the installation of images of Assyrian gods in the Jerusalem temple. Would the course of history have been otherwise if Ahaz had heeded the prophet's counsel? In relation to this question, speculation will not get us far. What will be more promising will be an analysis of Isaiah's advice that seeks to understand the *political theology* underlying his message. While we speak anachronistically in using such a modern term, we hope to point thereby to the subtlety and depth of the prophet's application of religious faith to political issues, which subtlety and depth also revolves around a seamless relationship between domestic and international issues. While we shall end our discussion of Isaiah with this very point, we first discuss one further episode in the prophet's dealing with international affairs.

By submitting to Assyria, King Ahaz avoided the full fury of the Assyrian armies that devastated both Syria and the northern kingdom of Israel. A more stealthful conquest, however, ran its course in Judah as a result of Ahaz's diplomacy of expedience, the conquest concerning which Isaiah had issued his warning with the image of the "the waters of the River," mighty and many (8:7). Judah became yoked to Assyria as a vassal obliged to render annual tribute and to pay homage to the Assyrian deities. By the time Hezekiah succeeded his father Ahaz on the throne in 715, even this swap of liberty for security had not restored domestic tranquility. The nation that refused to make trust in God a basis for careful homeland and foreign policy continued to vacillate between rash strategic alternatives. The military pressure of the Assyrians to the north was matched by aggressive diplomatic moves by the Egyptians from the south. The land was split between two diametrically opposed geopolitical strategies. An anti-Assyrian party that had gained ascendancy in the period 713–711 and had encouraged Hezekiah to enter into an alliance led by Ashdod with the support of Egypt was opposed by a vociferous anti-Egyptian party. The Ashdodian revolt that ensued turned into a fiasco for Judah and its allies when the promised Egyptian aid failed to materialize. The hand of the Assyrian overlord fell even more heavily on the weakened and discredited vassal state of Judah. Nevertheless, the utilitarian policy of basing international decisions on the calculus of balancing imperial powers continued unabated in Jerusalem.

As the tumultuous eighth century drew to a close, neither the domestic nor the international situation had stabilized, and discerning minds had reason to fear that the outcome would be calamitous. The nation continued to be torn between pro-Assyrian and pro-Egyptian factions, with each side basing its argument on an assessment of the relative strength of the two military powers contending for the Jewish nation. What prophetic word did the prophet find to address the new crisis that was building during the years 705–701?

Recalling that Isaiah in the earlier crisis had resolutely opposed Ahaz's pro-Assyrian policy, one might expect that Isaiah would take the position of staunchly supporting the foreign policy that Hezekiah had adopted, namely, that of challenging Assyrian control of the eastern Mediterranean by expanding the borders of Judah both to the southeast into Edomite territory and westward into the region traditionally held by the Philistines. The narrative material spliced into the book of Isaiah in chapters 36–39 that largely parallels 2 Kings 18–20[3] could support this conclusion, since it portrays the prophet as standing firmly on the side of the king in the face of Assyrian hostilities, a portrait that comports with the Deuteronomist's twin themes of God's special election of Davidic king and Zion.[4] Since the Deuteronomistic History and the Chronicler's History both appear to reflect something approximating a civil religion, it is reasonable to conclude that Hezekiah enjoyed broad support in influential circles.

Though it is clear that Isaiah himself belonged to the upper echelons of the Judean society, there is convincing evidence that his consistent testimony on behalf of a politics transcending all partisanship had led him to adopt a critical position similar to that represented in modern times by Dietrich Bonhoeffer, Mahatma Gandhi, and Martin Luther King Jr. Chapters 30 and 31, from the tense period of 705–700, preserve words of the prophet expressing his strenuous opposition to Hezekiah's alliance with Egypt in an anti-Assyrian coalition. While on the surface these words could be seen as evidence for the wavering of a prophet incapable of adhering to a consistent policy, a deeper look suggests another interpretation. With his focus on the fundamental principle of trust in God's governance of worldly affairs, the prophet views Judah's current vassal status under Assyria as an aspect of divine punishment for the sins he has assailed throughout his career. That status would not be changed by military and

---

3. Aside from numerous small editorial changes and a half-dozen larger ones, the most significance divergence is found in the absence in Isa. 36 of the account of Hezekiah's payment of tribute to Sennacherib found in 2 Kgs. 18:13–16 and the absence in 2 Kgs. 20 of Hezekiah's prayer found in Isa. 38:9–20.

4. Cf. Frank Moore Cross, *Canaanite Myth and Hebrew Epic: Essays in the History of the Religion of Israel* (Cambridge, MA: Harvard University Press, 1973), 278–85.

diplomatic stratagems, but solely by a fundamental reorientation of the nation from a worldly realpolitik to a theo-politics based on unwavering trust in God.

The position underlying Isaiah's words in 30:1–5 and 31:1–3 thus is consistent with his portraits of righteous government in Isaiah 2, 9, and 11: Only when the nation and its leaders denounced reliance on worldly sources of security ("who carry out a plan but not mine" [30:1]) and submitted to the divine sovereign ("look to the Holy One of Israel" [31:1]) did the possibility of dependable policy fostering genuine peace return. This, rather than some magical notion of divine engineering, is the meaning of Isaiah's confession, "The zeal of the LORD of hosts will do this" (9:7). In the meantime, the best choice of the various undesirable alternatives was submission to the yoke of God's agent of punishment until such time as the nation's repentance and submission to YHWH would open up new possibilities. That the so-called Second Isaiah is attached to the corpus of the eighth-century prophet precisely on the basis of a prophetic judgment that such national repentance has been accomplished offers one of the most persuasive pieces of evidence for the theological congruity of the larger Isaiah corpus (40:1–2).

Consistency of theological perspective combined with realism in coping with concrete situations summarizes Isaiah's approach to international policy. While consistent in holding before king and nation the sole reliable basis for national security—namely, trust in God as the framework within which specific policy decisions were to be made—Isaiah was also mindful of the political realities of the last decade of the eighth century: Whereas the anti-Assyrian policy of the northern kingdom had led to its annihilation, Ahaz's submission to Assyria, while leading to a complicated set of religious entanglements, had the pragmatic effect of allowing the kingdom of Judah, though now demoted to client-state status, to continue to exist as a nation.

Even that modest advantage, however, would be cast to the wind, in Isaiah's judgment, by a policy that looked to Egypt for deliverance. In other words, Hezekiah's stratagem of seeking to free the land from the yoke of Assyria by relying on the military might of Egypt contradicted the same principle as did Ahaz's earlier reliance on the might of Assyria to secure Judah from the assault of Damascus and Samaria. What on the surface appears to be an inconsistent foreign policy can be recognized as the political flexibility that becomes possible when the conceptual distinction between ultimate commitments and penultimate arrangements is maintained.

Isaiah failed in his effort to bring the nation to single-hearted reliance on God, and events continued to plot a tragic decline. It is interesting to note, however, that those who chronicled the events presented Hezekiah mainly in a favorable light, as one engaged in a conscientious effort to rid the land of the accoutrements of Assyrian religion and culture. That a blend of religious and nationalistic motives underlay his actions seems likely, for it was a symbiosis abetted by the close identification of king and cult in the royal theology of Jerusalem. Given their affinities with the ideals of the Davidic monarchy, it is not surprising then that the editors of both Kings and Chronicles lift Hezekiah up as one of the paragons of godly rule, a leader dedicated to reestablishing both autonomy and the reunification of the divided state of Israel. In the words of the Deuteronomists, "there was no one like him among all the kings of Judah after him, or among those who were before him" (2 Kgs. 18:3–6).

The modern historian likely will ascribe more weight to Hezekiah's political agenda than to his religious piety: As an aspect of the king's policy to challenge the yoke placed upon his nation by the mighty empire from the northeast, he ties the security of his country to a military pact with Egypt. What the modern critic perhaps does not recognize sufficiently, however, is that it was the freedom from reliance on expedient military solutions provided by his theo-political perspective that allowed the prophet Isaiah both to unmask the actual contours of the calculating global policy of the Egyptians (i.e., Israel serves as a useful front line of defense against the archrival Assyria) and to dare to censure his king: "Therefore the protection of Pharaoh shall become your shame" (30:3). As one less tied to the prevailing royal ideology and its nationalistic tendencies than the court historians, Isaiah was able to maintain a critical position resistant alike to blind patriotism and religious fanaticism.

Due to his daring to challenge the ideology of the Davidic state, Isaiah, already besmeared by an earlier accusation of treason (8:12), was placed once again in a tense situation. The king had embarked on a policy that enjoyed wide support in official circles. A chorus of prophets provided divine assurances. Isaiah's only defense was the caustic accusation that the words of assurance they offered originated not with the Holy One but arose from a self-induced drunken stupor (29:9–10)! The populace desired the wishful thinking of the nationalistic prophets, not Isaiah's hard-hitting realism (30:8–11). National leaders, their religious cheerleaders, and a "patriotic" populace thus were conforming to the common pattern of state religion, with its emphasis on the indivisibility of a nation's self-interest and the intentions of its patron deity. Isaiah's career could have been much less stressful if he simply had conformed to the popular assumption that Judah was safe from the assault of the Assyrian armies, since God would not permit harm to be done to the people he had chosen and the land in which he dwelt. Isaiah, however, repudiated the popular nationalistic religion.

With the approach of the last years of the eighth century, neither the domestic nor the international situation had stabilized. The nation continued to vacillate between the pro-Assyrian and pro-Egyptian options, with each side basing its argument on an assessment of the relative strength of the two military powers contending for the Jewish nation. What prophetic word does the prophet find to address this desperate situation?

The basic premise of Isaiah's prophetic model remained the same as the one he presented during the Syro-Ephraimite crisis two and a half decades earlier:

> In returning and rest you shall be saved;
>   in quietness and in trust shall be your strength.
>   (30:15)

Sadly, the people refused to look to the Holy One as a refuge from the militaristic frenzy by which they were engulfed and insisted on trusting in a defense weighed in terms of military materiel: "We will ride upon swift steeds" (30:16). Specifically, the nation that during Ahaz's reign had refused to base foreign policy on trust in the Holy One and instead placed its security in the hands of the Assyrians now under Hezekiah was refusing to trust God and instead was placing its defense in the hands of Egypt. Only a superficial assessment of Isaiah's position would conclude that Isaiah has switched positions. His approach to foreign policy is consistent with the theocratic principle of classic Yahwistic faith: acknowledge the Holy One as the only sovereign deserving of fear and trust, yield yourself to that sovereign in obedience and trust, and then work out foreign policy, not in fear of human armies but in fear of God. It is hard to miss the sadness in the divine word he delivers in 30:1–5, the first two verses of which read thus:

> Oh, rebellious children, says the LORD,
> who carry out a plan, but not mine;
> who make an alliance, but against my will,
>   adding sin to sin;
> who set out to go down to Egypt
>   without asking for my counsel,
> to take refuge in the protection of Pharaoh,
>   and to seek shelter in the shadow of Egypt.

Refuge and shelter are fundamental needs of humans in an often threatening and cold world, and it pierces the heart of the prophet to find his people looking for security where it cannot be found, even as they repudiate the only true source of hope.

One senses that the prophet revisits the despairing mood of his inaugural speech to his incorrigible people (6:9–13) in 31:1–3, which begins with these words:

> Alas for those who go down to Egypt for help
>   and who rely on horses,
> who trust in chariots because they are many
>   and in horsemen because they are very strong,
> but do not look to the Holy One of Israel
>   or consult the LORD!

The prophet thereby uncovers the tragedy that he sees leading to profound suffering for his people: they are looking to the wrong source. They have confused the penultimate and the ultimate. International crises will confront every nation; policies must be developed, decisions made, defenses built, armies deployed. This is the stuff of historical existence. Religious faith does not provide explicit strategies for such challenges. While its bearing is indirect, its role is crucial, for it provides a vantage point that fosters a dependable approach to potentially deadly threats. Trust in the universal sovereign does not provide a magic wall of security around a nation. Such a concept would conform to the realms of magic and mythology, realms from which the prophets emphatically distance themselves. But trust in the Holy One saves a nation from basing its policy on illusions and false securities and provides a foundation for deliberation that is both stringently moral and rigorously realistic.

For heuristic reasons, we have separated Isaiah's treatment of international politics from his dealing with domestic issues such as honesty in business and justice in courts of law. In a summarizing statement of Isaiah's application of religious faith to politics, this separation must be surmounted, for the two realms are intertwined in his thought, for reasons that point to the heart of Isaiah's message. For Isaiah there is but one ultimate ruler, who is the author of the order upon which all reality depends for viability. Intrinsic to that order are laws regulating internal relations within a given nation and mutual obligations defining proper conduct among nations.

The nation that repudiates God's laws in its domestic life through oppressive treatment of some of its citizenry and through manipulation of religion in support of corrupt policies will eviscerate the fibers holding it together and break down the moral resources that equip it to deal effectively with international crises. In hearing Isaiah's assurance in the face of enemy attack that "in returning and rest you shall be saved, in quietness and in trust shall be your strength," it must be remembered that he is describing a quality of life that permeates all aspects of a nation's existence. Isaiah's vision of national health and world peace is remarkably holistic. This is what simultaneously lends to his message both consistency in perspective and flexibility in application.

Chapter 16

Jeremiah

The Suffering Prophet

THE BOOK AS A SOURCE

Throughout Jeremiah's career, the prophet found himself personally engaged in political events in which the future of his people stood in precarious balance. The contemporary reader is drawn into an account of those events and Jeremiah's participation in them that is gripping and characterized by a high degree of verisimilitude. Indeed, the book of Jeremiah provides a fuller description of the life and times of its prophet than does any other prophetic corpus. Utilization of this rich source for the purpose of understanding Jeremiah's political strategy is complicated, however, by two characteristics of the book.

First, one must deal with its complex composition history. This is illustrated even on the level of text recensions, where one finds that the Septuagint (Greek) version of Jeremiah is one-eighth shorter than the Masoretic (Hebrew) version. Furthermore, distinctly different styles characterize different sections of the book. One finds oracles, directed both against the leaders and people of Israel and against foreign nations, that are written in verse, while long narrative sections betray rhetorical features resembling those of the book of Deuteronomy and the Deuteronomistic History (Deuteronomy through 2 Kings).

Finally, chapters 36–44 present a sustained account, also in prose, depicting the hardships endured by Jeremiah at the hands of his opponents.[1] Included in the last mentioned is an episode from the reign of King Jehoiakim (609–598) that describes the fate of a scroll upon which, at Jeremiah's dictation, the scribe Baruch had written down "all the words of the LORD that he had spoken to him" (36:4). After Baruch had read it first to the people and then to certain officials, the scroll finally was presented to King Jehoiakim, who cut it into pieces as it was read, casting each section into the flames of a brazier. Scholars have made various attempts to identify the oracles that constituted that original scroll, as well as the "many similar words" that Jeremiah added when he gave dictation to Baruch a second time (36:32).[2]

The second characteristic of the book of Jeremiah that complicates using it as a source for describing Jeremiah's political activity is this: even the passages that with a reasonable degree of confidence are attributable to Jeremiah must be read with awareness of the highly conventionalized nature of the genres and phrases the prophet uses. Both the outward struggle and the inner turmoil of Jeremiah have been described by commentators in vivid detail, often without sufficient attention to the fact that Jeremiah's complaints are patterned after the genre of the lament, a genre found with particular frequency in the book of Psalms.

The above caveats, while behooving the interpreter to proceed with caution and with awareness of the necessarily tentative nature of all conclusions, do not negate the widely held scholarly judgment that the vivid oracles and narratives of the book do afford authentic glimpses into the activities and proclamations of an individual who, amid enormous hardship and no small measure of self-doubt, claimed to disclose the purposes of God, against which he measured the political policies and social conditions of his nation.

JEREMIAH'S LOCATION WITHIN THE RELIGIOUS TRADITIONS OF ISRAEL

In moving toward consideration of the politics of Jeremiah, it is important to note that what was stated earlier in a general description of the biblical prophets pertains specifically to Jeremiah, namely, that he speaks from within and on behalf of a classical religious tradition that had developed over the course of centuries. Even a cursory reading of his message reveals a prophet steeped in the heritage of his religious community. His references to the stories of the book of

---

1. Cf. the pioneering study of Sigmund Mowinckel, *Zum Komposition des Buches Jeremia* (Kristiania: Dybwad, 1914).

2. See especially the attempt of William L. Holladay to reconstruct the first and second scrolls of Jeremiah, "The Identification of the Two Scrolls of Jeremiah," *Vetus Testamentum* 30 (1980): 452–67. That reconstruction in turn is integrated into his two-volume commentary, *Jeremiah 1: A Commentary on the Book of the Prophet Jeremiah Chapters 1–25*, Hermeneia (Philadelphia: Fortress Press, 1986) and *Jeremiah 2: A Commentary on the Book of the Prophet Jeremiah Chapters 26–52* (Minneapolis: Fortress Press, 1989).

Genesis are numerous, as are his allusions to Israel's Epic account of the birth of a nation out of slavery. It is obvious that he felt a particular affinity with Moses, and the suggestion that he may have viewed himself as the prophet like Moses mentioned in Deuteronomy 18:15 is plausible. [3]

That Jeremiah's conceptual universe was shaped by a thorough understanding of the Torah is obvious in the big picture as well as in detail. For example, major themes of his preaching, like the inevitability of divine punishment for perfidy and the inextricable connection between blessing and obedience to God's statutes, draw deeply and persistently on Deuteronomic tradition. The Mosaic covenant constitutes the heart of his message. The following will serve as examples. In the curses in 11:3–5 and their formulaic conclusion 'āmēn, we see a pattern reflecting Deuteronomy 27:15–26. In 21:8 we read: "And to this people you shall say: Thus says the LORD: See, I am setting before you the way of life and the way of death," a clear echo of the central Deuteronomic theme of divine retribution: "See, I have set before you today life and prosperity, death and adversity" (Deut. 30:15). Moreover, he can be very creative in his application of Torah, as Michael Fishbane has shown in comparing Jeremiah 3:1 with Deuteronomy 24:1–4. [4]

That Jeremiah viewed himself as standing solidly in the tradition of the prophets is equally clear. While his dependence on the words, themes, and tone of Hosea is particularly pronounced, instances of borrowing from or allusion to Amos, Isaiah, Micah, and other prophets are also numerous.

The one religious tradition that is underrepresented in the utterances of Jeremiah is that which formed around the royal theology of the Davidic house. It can hardly be regarded as accidental that the single conceivable allusion he made to an event from the lives of Israel's kings was to David's mourning over the child born of his adulterous relationship with Bathsheba (Jer. 22:10). After all, Jeremiah shares with Hosea the distinction of being the harshest critic among the prophets of the institution of monarchy and the national cult sponsored by it. Even the concerted efforts of Josiah to reform the cult and to bring the nation into conformity with the strict standards of the Torah as legislated in the Deuteronomic Law failed to elicit the unequivocal support of Jeremiah. If Jeremiah entertained the possibility of a righteous kingship and faithful priesthood, it was in the form of an eschatological hope. [5]

The observation that Jeremiah, like the other prophets of YHWH, stood firmly within his nation's religious heritage and found the source of his identity in the Mosaic covenant and Torah, must not obscure the fact that his message bears the imprint of his personal background and temporal and geographical setting. This is illustrated most vividly by contrasting his message with that of Isaiah, a prophet who faced international crises similar in gravity to those addressed by Jeremiah.

3. Holladay, *Jeremiah 1*, 38.

4. Michael A. Fishbane, "Torah and Tradition," in *Tradition and Theology in the Old Testament*, ed. Douglas A. Knight (Philadelphia: Fortress Press, 1977), 284–86.

5. Jer. 23:1–8; cf. 36:30.

While both prophets, in their acknowledgment of only one universal sovereign, adhere faithfully to what we refer to as the theocratic principle, Isaiah attributed to the Davidic house and Jerusalem temple a more positive role in implementing God's purposes within the realm of human history than did Jeremiah. Though the picture of unusual intimacy between Hezekiah and Isaiah found in Isaiah 36–39 must be interpreted with an awareness of the historiographic tendencies of its Deuteronomistic source, Isaiah 9:2–7 (Heb. 1–6) and Isaiah 11:1–5 can be understood as Isaiah's descriptions of the divinely conferred responsibilities of a king serving as representative of God's just rule on earth. Equally evident is the abiding significance—all threats and setbacks notwithstanding—of Jerusalem as Holy City in his thought, a view expressed hauntingly in the Ariel passage in Isaiah 29:1–8 (cf. Isa. 37:33–35), a prophecy that may have contributed to the popular view of the invincibility of the temple, which Jeremiah felt obliged to refute in his so-called "temple speech" (Jer. 7 and 26; cf. 21:2).

On the basis of the above contrast, one might draw the conclusion that Isaiah belongs to the category of court prophet, whereas Jeremiah fits the description of "peripheral" prophet.[6] A closer look, however, reveals a more complicated picture. In the case of Isaiah, we find a prophet whose affinity with Zion/Davidic tradition does not inhibit him from announcing an imminent destruction of the land (Isa. 6:11–13) and from hurling a scathing rebuke against King Ahaz (Isa. 7:13–17). As for Jeremiah, we find a prophet who was sought out by Zedekiah for counsel (Jer. 37:17–21), who was able to address ambassadors of foreign nations gathered in a summit meeting with the king (Jer. 27:1–11 [cf. 1:5, 10]), and who in one case described King Josiah in a very positive light (to be sure, by way of providing a foil against which to denounce his perfidious son [22:11–17]).

Given the fact that recourse to simple categorical distinctions more often obscures than enhances understanding of a complex historical figure, it is best to approach the particular form of political activity that Jeremiah engaged in and the way in which he shaped his message to kings and populace in terms of the concrete situations he addressed and the particular theological themes and traditions upon which he drew.

Particularly with regard to the position he took vis-à-vis king and temple, it is important to note his lineage. He stems from a Levitical priestly family from Anathoth, that is, the village northwest of Jerusalem to which Abiathar had been banished by Solomon. Besides bearing historical memory of the subordination to the Zadokite priesthood that his priestly lineage had suffered at the instigation of a Davidic king, he would have witnessed personally the adverse effects on the career of his father, the priest Hilkiah, of King Josiah's closure of the countryside shrines in favor of centralization of the cult in Jerusalem under Zadokite leadership.

---

6. For a description of these two categories of prophets, see Robert R. Wilson, *Prophecy and Society in Ancient Israel* (Philadelphia: Fortress Press, 1980).

Though such particularities are not to be overlooked in an examination of Jeremiah's politics, their significance comes to clarity only in relation to a deeper dimension, namely, his understanding of the basis of his authority. Significantly, on this phenomenological level Jeremiah stands in solidarity with Isaiah and all of the other canonical prophets: The message he proclaimed was a message he believed originated with God or, in the idiom of Hebrew prophecy, a message with which he was commissioned in the divine assembly. More than any other prophet, he was forced to defend his authority by refuting other prophets who invoked the name of the same God in messages that contradicted his own and enjoyed broader popular appeal than his own harsh words. Jeremiah insisted that those prophets lacked the sole credential that mattered: they did not speak truthfully on behalf of the only authority who commanded absolute allegiance, the sovereign of the universe, the Lord God (23:18, 21–22). In times of vicious assault from those "saying, 'Peace, peace,' when there is no peace" (6:14), his refuge was solely the one extended to him by God: "But you, gird up your loins; stand up and tell them everything that I command you. Do not break down before them, or I will break you before them. And I for my part have made you today a fortified city, an iron pillar, and a bronze wall, against the whole land— against the kings of Judah, its princes, its priests, and the people of the land. They will fight against you; but they shall not prevail against you, for I am with you, says the LORD, to deliver you" (1:17–19).

Though Jeremiah could complain that not having been born would have been preferable to the task placed upon him (20:14–18), his identity was shaped by a transcendent reality to which he had surrendered his own will:

> If I say, "I will not mention him,
>   or speak any more in his name,"
> then within me there is something like a burning fire
>   shut up in my bones;
> I am weary with holding it in,
>   and I cannot.
>
> (Jer. 20:9)

Of course, this is the sort of claim made by lunatics as well, which underlines the importance of seeing the prophets, not only within the context of their individual careers, but within their canonical context. Jeremiah was no maverick harboring private illusions; he understood himself to stand in the tradition of the prophets whom God had sent from the birth of the nation to the present (7:25–26), an understanding corroborated by the living religious tradition that preserved his words within its sacred writings.

THE POLITICS OF JEREMIAH

Moving specifically to the politics of Jeremiah, we shall first describe the central theological principles upon which he constructed his message. That will provide the basis for examining the manner in which he applied his theology to the political issues of his day, both domestic and international. Finally, we shall consider whether it is possible to recover from the biblical text Jeremiah's view of the future of his nation.

Constituting the heart of Jeremiah's message is Israel's covenantal theology and its central theocratic principle of God's universal sovereignty. The themes elaborating on that core attest to Jeremiah's close ties to Deuteronomic tradition: As an act of loving-kindness, God created Israel as his people by delivering them from Egypt, guiding them through the wilderness, giving them a land as a heritage and a law through obedience to which they would be secured from harm. Sole worship of God, trust in God to the exclusion of all other allegiances, and obedience to God's will out of gratitude: these are the conditions required of the nation as their side of upholding the covenant. Arising from this covenantal identity was Jeremiah's theo-politics: Israel was to constitute itself politically by faithfully implementing God's righteous rule within the historical structures of human government.

For Jeremiah, the incomprehensible tragedy was that Israel had repudiated God's gracious initiative, abdicated its theo-political mandate, and nullified its identity (i.e., pronounced its own doom [4:18]). This tragedy comes to shocking expression in 2:5–8, where a recounting of Israel's religious Epic modulates into a parody recounting the nation's senseless denial of its sacred story: "They did not say, 'Where is the LORD who brought us up from the land of Egypt?'"[7] Saving memory had been replaced by a stupor of forgetfulness. Like a raging plague, it had infected all of the leadership classes of the society:

> The priests did not say, "Where is the LORD?"
>   Those who handle the law did not know me;
> the rulers [literally, shepherds] transgressed against me;
>   the prophets prophesied by Baal,
>   and went after things that do not profit.
>
> (2:8)

When one recalls that Jeremiah's concept of political stability was predicated on his understanding of the universal order established and maintained by God, one readily grasps the calamitous consequences of the abdication by the nation's priests, scribes, rulers, and prophets of the responsibility faithfully to implement that order within human institutions. Simply put, a people was left without a moral compass: The priests, responsible for reminding the people of God's presence in their lives, no longer sought the Lord. Scribes, trained to instruct the people in God's will as delineated in the Torah, had no personal relationship with God; indeed, "the false pen of the scribes has made it into a lie" (8:8). Rulers scoffed at divine justice, and prophets denounced God in favor of Baal. No

---

7. Full appreciation of the full rhetorical force of this "inverted" recounting of Israel's national Epic can be gained by comparing 2:4–8 with the positive formulations of the ancient credo in Deut. 26:5–9 and Josh. 24:2–13. In this regard, comparison of Ps. 105 (positive) with Ps. 106 (inverted) is also enlightening.

more reliable were the teachers of wisdom, "since they have rejected the word of the LORD" (8:9).

In the style of ancient Near Eastern treaties and reminiscent of Deuteronomy 32:1, Jeremiah called upon the heavens to witness Israel's breaking of the covenant:

> Be appalled, O heavens, at this,
>> be shocked, be utterly desolate, says the LORD,
> for my people have committed two evils:
>> they have forsaken me,
> the fountain of living water,
>> and dug out cisterns for themselves,
> cracked cisterns
>> that can hold no water.
>
> (2:12–13)

For Jeremiah, the inevitable consequence of Israel's repudiation of God's covenant was social chaos, a lawlessness in which the moral undergirding of community collapsed into deceitfulness and distrust:

> They bend their tongues like bows;
>> they have grown strong in the land for falsehood, and not for truth;
> for they proceed from evil to evil,
>> and they do not know me, says the LORD. . . .
> Their tongue is a deadly arrow;
>> it speaks deceit through the mouth.
> They all speak friendly words to their neighbors,
>> but inwardly are planning to lay an ambush.
>
> (9:3, 8 [Heb. 9:2, 7])

Falling victim to civic chaos are even the values most hallowed by a kinship-based society, the safety and succor of family and clan:

> For even your kinsfolk and your own family,
>> even they have dealt treacherously with you;
>> they are in full cry after you;
> do not believe them,
>> though they speak friendly words to you.
>
> (12:6)

One sordid side of the degraded social conditions that Jeremiah observed was that the darkness of anomie provided open season for the exploitation of the poor by cold-blooded opportunists, on whose garments were found "the lifeblood of the innocent poor" (2:34).

> For scoundrels are found among my people;
>> they take over the goods of others.
> Like fowlers they set a trap;
>> they catch human beings.

Like a cage full of birds,
    their houses are full of treachery;
therefore they have become great and rich,
    they have grown fat and sleek.
They know no limits in deeds of wickedness;
    they do not judge with justice
the cause of the orphan, to make it prosper,
    and they do not defend the rights of the needy.
                                    (5:26–28)

. . . [F]rom the least to the greatest
    everyone is greedy for unjust gain;
from prophet to priest
    everyone deals falsely.
                        (8:10b)

That the calamitous situation stemmed from Israel's repudiation of the covenant Jeremiah stated with stunning poignancy by recasting the tree metaphor of the sapiential Psalm 1 along the lines of the blessing/curse formulary of Deuteronomy 27–28:

Cursed are those who trust in mere mortals
    and make mere flesh their strength,
    whose hearts turn away from the LORD.
They shall be like a shrub in the desert. . . .
Blessed are those who trust in the LORD,
    whose trust is the LORD.
They shall be like a tree planted by water,
    sending out its roots by the stream.
                            (17:5, 7–8)

Was the situation terminal in Jeremiah's mind? Was the death of the nation inevitable? Though Jeremiah's message was overwhelmingly negative, one can properly question whether he would have gone to such lengths and endured such hardship, had he not felt called to lead Israel back to its healer, even in the eleventh hour. More to the point, among the pronouncements of Jeremiah we find appeals to the nation to return to the covenant that was the sole hope for salvation:

O Jerusalem, wash your heart clean of wickedness
    so that you may be saved.
                        (4:14)

Interestingly, one of Jeremiah's appeals to return contains an introductory note that not only reflects espousal of Josiah's ideal of a reunited nation, but also intimates that there was a greater likelihood of a positive response on the part of the remnant of the northern kingdom than among the people of Judah:

Return, faithless Israel, says the LORD.
I will not look on you in anger,
    for I am merciful, says the LORD;

> I will not be angry forever.
> Only acknowledge your guilt,
>   that you have rebelled against the LORD your God. . . .
> Return, O faithless children, says the LORD,
>   for I am your master;
> I will take you, one from a city and two from a family,
>   and I will bring you to Zion.
>
> (3:12–14)

Also worth noting is the fact that, in the narrative account of the dictation of the first scroll to Baruch, Jeremiah offers the following as the motive for Baruch's reading it to the people in the temple: "It may be that their plea will come before the LORD, and that all of them will turn from their evil ways, for great is the anger and wrath that the LORD has pronounced against this people" (36:7; cf. 26:3). It seems plausible to regard this as an accurate description of the ultimate purpose underlying not only the scattered calls to repentance but also the plethora of scathing oracles threatening imminent judgment upon the land.

The author of the second account of Jeremiah's "temple sermon" in Jeremiah 26 offers the same motive for Jeremiah's impassioned appeal: "It may be that they will listen, all of them, and will turn from their evil way, that I may change my mind about the disaster that I intend to bring on them because of their evil doings" (26:3), thereby softening the apparent (perhaps more original) contradiction in Jeremiah 7 between the preacher's appeal to the people to amend their ways so that YHWH will be able to "dwell with you in this place" (7:7) and the apparent fait accompli announced in 7:14–15 of the destruction of the temple.

While Jeremiah, at least in the earlier years of his activity, may have entertained some faint hope that his words would lead to a change of heart, in the final analysis he had concluded that seeking to convert the people from their self-destructive resolve bordered on futility. Was not Jerusalem's plight ten times more desperate than had been the case with the city traditionally epitomizing degradation, Gomorrah?

> Run to and fro through the streets of Jerusalem,
>   look around and take note!
> Search its squares and see
>   if you can find one person
> who acts justly
>   and seeks truth—
> so that I may pardon Jerusalem.
> Although they say, "As the LORD lives,"
>   yet they swear falsely.
> O LORD, do your eyes not look for truth?
> You have struck them,
>   but they felt no anguish;
> you have consumed them,
>   but they refused to take correction.
>
> (5:1–3)

In one instance, Jeremiah extrapolated from his experiences with his people a general observation of the human condition that ranks among the darkest in the entire Bible: "The heart is devious above all else, it is perverse—who can understand it?" (17:9; see also 13:23). The answer that came to him was a divine word summarizing a central Deuteronomic theme:

> I the LORD test the mind
> and search the heart,
> to give to all according to their ways,
> according to the fruit of their doings.
> (17:10)

In the final analysis, Jeremiah was convinced that God's testing and searching had proven that the efforts of the prophet to persuade Israel to return to covenant were hopeless. The trial of the people had run its course, and the sentence had been pronounced. In the language of covenant, "because of the curse the land mourns" (23:10), that is to say, the social order had collapsed under the weight of wickedness. This would best explain the deep pessimism underlying a theme that seems to have characterized Jeremiah's final years, namely, that he was forbidden by God to intercede on behalf of the people (7:16–20; 11:14–17; 14:11–12; 15:1–2). All that remained for the prophet to do in anticipation of the impending calamity was to state clearly the cause . . .

> Have you not brought this upon yourself,
> by forsaking the LORD your God,
> while he led you in the way?
> (2:17)

. . . and the effect. The rupture in world order resulting from Israel's perfidy was not confined to the political realm, but would engulf all of creation:

> I looked on the earth, and lo, it was waste and void;
> and to the heavens, and they had no light.
> I looked on the mountains, and lo, they were quaking,
> and all the hills moved to and fro.
> I looked, and lo, there was no one at all,
> all the birds of the air had fled.
> I looked, and lo, the fruitful land was a desert,
> and all its cities were laid in ruins,
> before the LORD, before his fierce anger.
> (4:23–26)

How can one fit such pessimism into the covenantal view that Jeremiah held of the world as a moral universe, overseen by a just and merciful God who had called Israel out of slavery to be his holy people (2:1–2)? The answer lies in a tragic sense of solidarity that Jeremiah felt with the most innocent victims of the impending disaster: the poor, those betrayed by their leaders, the powerless who were vulnerable to the exploitation and abuse of their shepherds. Out of this sense of solidarity arose a fierce moral indignation against those bringing on the calamity that came to expression in stinging oracles of judgment. Though psychologizing on the basis of highly stylized compositions is a risky endeavor, the following passage breaks with the conventional language found in many of Jeremiah's complaints and seems to reveal the prophet's deepest feelings:

> My joy is gone, grief is upon me,
>   my heart is sick.
> Hark, the cry of my poor people
>   from far and wide in the land:
> "Is the LORD not in Zion?
>   Is her King not in her?"
>   (8:18–19)

Jeremiah must have felt compelled to respond to this agonizing sense of God's abandonment felt by the poor. The rage that he felt on their behalf doubtlessly was intensified by the contrast between their misery and the prosperity flaunted by their oppressors, rage expressing itself in questions akin to Job's, which reveal Jeremiah's personal struggle with the perennial question of divine justice: "Why does the way of the guilty prosper? Why do all who are treacherous thrive?" (12:1).

One cannot deny the stark truth that Jeremiah leaves his readers with open questions. What point is there to keep appealing to those hopelessly addicted to evil, not only enjoying the spoils of their robbing the poor, but responding to the prophet's accusations with protestations, "I am innocent; . . . I have not sinned" (2:35), and deluding themselves with the notion that the covenant was intact by addressing God as "my Father, . . . the friend of my youth" (3:4)? In spite of his faithful testimony and patience in suffering, "No one repents of wickedness, saying, 'What have I done!'" (8:6).

Let us summarize Jeremiah's central theo-political message before moving on to describe the specific instances in which he applied it to the issues of his day. Jeremiah shared with his fellow prophets a covenantal theology upholding a consistently moral view of reality grounded in the sole sovereignty of YHWH. The creator and lord of all creation did not leave its inhabitants without guidance regarding what fosters life and what leads to death. Among the families of the nations, God had revealed to Israel in its Epic and its Torah a clear description of the manner of life that led to *shalom* and the theocratic basis for sound government that would foster justice at home and peace among nations:

> If you return, O Israel, says the LORD,
>   if you return to me,
> if you remove your abominations from my presence,
>   and do not waver,
> and if you swear, "As the LORD lives!"
>   in truth, in justice, and in uprightness,
> then nations shall be blessed by him,
>   and by him they shall boast.
>   (4:1–2)

JEREMIAH'S POLITICAL MESSAGE: SOCIAL INJUSTICE
AND THE THREAT OF PUNISHMENT

In the initial years of his career, Jeremiah proclaimed that God was engaging in a final struggle to bring a nation on the brink of disaster, due to its forgetting its origins in God's grace and placing its trust in human stratagems (17:5–6), back to its senses through repentance, that is, a change of direction away from self-determination to submission to God's order of justice.[8] Corrupt leaders were abusing their political offices for self-gain. Smooth-talking prophets were garnering popular support by invoking God's name to give assurances that everything would be all right and that no enemy would be able to defeat Israel. In the face of such failure to heed the eleventh-hour call, what was God's word to the nation? Jeremiah's chastened political message grows out of that question. To that message we now turn.

Perhaps due to his somber assessment of the moral depravity of his society, the number of oracles dealing with social justice issues is not large. Moreover, most of those utterances are couched in conventional terminology, making the specific nature of abuses under attack hard to identify. Like Hosea, he describes Israel's wickedness with the use of sexual metaphors (3:1–2) that today have a misogynist ring (2:23–25; 4:30–31; 5:8). Another group of sayings revolves around the theme of idolatry. He reserves particular vitriol for his attacks on the prophets of both the north and the south, the former for leading the people away from YHWH to Baal, the latter for adultery, lies, abetting the designs of evildoers, and spreading wickedness and ungodliness (23:13–15).

The picture one gets is that of a breakdown of all of the virtues constituting civil decency: "Everyone is greedy for unjust gain; from prophet to priest everyone deals falsely" (8:10–12). What Jeremiah describes is a society crippled by a corrupted leadership class, economically ravaged by the exploitation of the working class, and cast into the chaos of everyone looking after one's own gain, a situation that deteriorated precipitously as the vise of enemy armies tightened on the land.

From Jeremiah's theocratic perspective of God's universal sovereignty, the social disintegration that he witnessed around him had to be interpreted within the wider context of the cataclysmic international changes enveloping his world: "This is the city that must be punished; there is nothing but oppression within her" (6:6b). Decay at the heart inevitably led to a collapse of the whole, spurring the prophet to query the bearing of the struggles between the Babylonians, Egyptians, and Assyrians on his bankrupt nation. According to the narrative of Jeremiah's call to the prophetic office, he early on believed that the agent of God's judgment was an enemy from the north (1:13, 14–15; cf. 4:6; 5:15–17; 6:1, 22–26). While different conjectures have been advanced for the identity of the foe he had in mind at an early stage of his career (e.g., the Scythians), it

---

8. The concept "turning/repentance [*šûb*]" is of central importance to Jeremiah (see William L. Holladay, *The Root Šubh in the Old Testament, With Particular Reference to Its Usages in Covenantal Contexts* (Leiden: Brill, 1958).

is apparent that as Judah devolved into political turmoil under the vacillating leadership of Josiah's sons, he came to believe that God's chosen instrument of punishment was Babylon (20:4–6; 21:8–10; 27:12–15).

Since the consequences of breaking the covenant affected all dimensions of reality, Jeremiah's identification of Babylon as the specific historical agent of God's punishment did not exclude his identifying other instruments of divine judgment, such as drought (14:1–10), the sword and famine (14:18), and bereavement (15:5–9). He was simply drawing from the standard ancient Near Eastern repertory of covenant curses to emphasize that for those who repudiate God's rule, there was no escape (cf. Deut. 28). That repertory in turn reflects the ancient recognition that those various scourges did not afflict their victims singly, but in ghastly unison:

> And when they say to you, "Where shall we go?" you shall say to them: Thus says the LORD:
>
> Those destined for pestilence, to pestilence,
>   and those destined for the sword, to the sword;
> those destined for famine, to famine,
>   and those destined for captivity, to captivity.
>   (15:2)

JEREMIAH'S POLITICAL MESSAGE: INTERNATIONAL POLICY

It is not possible to draw a sharp distinction between Jeremiah's domestic and international politics, due to his theocratic view of Israel as a part of God's universal sovereignty. His position on the foreign-policy alternatives available to Judah accordingly was tied to his diagnosis of Israel's spiritual and moral condition. Since the norms against which he measured the latter were determined by the covenant binding God and people in a relationship of mutual commitments, it was not a static position. We have noted that his initial threats were accompanied, and apparently motivated, by an appeal to the nation to repent of its wickedness and return to trust in God and obedience to the Torah. As for clues to the concrete setting of that appeal, it is interesting to note that Norbert Lohfink finds evidence in Jeremiah 30 and 31 that the young Jeremiah lent his support to Josiah's efforts to reunify the north and south, a program that likely blended the king's zeal for religious reform with his geopolitical ambitions, awakened by a perceived weakening of Babylonian hegemony in the area.[9] When one adds

---

9. Norbert Lohfink, "Der junge Jeremia als Propagandist und Poet," in P.-M. Bogaert, *Le Livre de Jeremie* (Leiden: Brill, 1981), 351–68. The passages Lohfink cites are 30:5–7, 12–15, 18–21; 31:2–6, 15–22, to which William L. Holladay, in accepting Lohfink's argument, makes the modest additions 31:1aαb and 9b (Holladay, *Jeremiah 2*, 27).

to this evidence the positive picture Jeremiah presented of Josiah in 22:15–16, it seems reasonable to conclude that, until 609, he believed that repentance was still possible. On the basis of 3:11–14, one might even assume that he felt that Israel's return would set an example for the more recalcitrant Judah.

The bitter experiences of subsequent years conspired to harden his position. The death of Josiah and the political ineptness and ethical weakness of his sons, the utter failure of Jeremiah's efforts to reverse the moral decline of his society, the personal abuse he suffered at the hands of the land's religious and political leaders, and the Babylonian army's reassertion of its unrivaled power in the defeat of the Egyptians at Carchemish in 605 congealed into a somber conclusion: Judah had been tried in the heavenly court that determines the destiny of all nations and been found guilty. The sentence was military defeat and deportation to Babylon. Jeremiah's political views over the course of the calamitous years from the exile of the nation's top leaders in 598 to the final destruction of Jerusalem in 587 can be understood as inferences drawn consistently from that verdict and sentence.

Jeremiah did not stand alone in viewing the events of his nation and world within the framework of God's universal rule. Isaiah's seemingly enigmatic words delivered in YHWH's name to Israel come to mind: "Keep listening, but do not comprehend; keep looking, but do not understand" (Isa. 6:9).

In witnessing a massive accumulation of evidence of the people's incorrigibility, Jeremiah and Isaiah both seem to have come to the dread conclusion that the point had been reached where the nation's allegiance to a policy of self-indulgence and self-determination was so definitive as to exclude categorically any possibility of submission to the transcendent reality who was the sole reliable basis for domestic order and international peace. Expressed within the conceptuality of ancient Israel, the evidence had been weighed in the divine court, the accused had been found guilty, and the sentence had been rendered. Something like that understanding best explains the words of Isaiah 6:10:

> Make the mind of this people dull,
>   and stop their ears,
>   and shut their eyes,
> so that they may not look with their eyes,
>   and listen with their ears,
> and comprehend with their minds,
>   and turn and be healed.

It would be a mistake to construe this divine command as the application of a static metaethical principle. Rather, it arises out of a struggle between God and people occurring within a covenantal framework. Similarly, in the case of Jeremiah, one can best understand the shift from pleading for a return to God to conceding the futility of intercession as based on a sober assessment of the concrete situation faced by the prophet. Here too, one is not dealing with the prophet's application of a timeless mandate. If in the last hour, the people would repent, God's mercy would readily be extended. Jeremiah 5:1 goes so far as to extend Abraham's argument to its outer limit: It would be sufficient to elicit God's pardon to discover "one person who acts justly and seeks truth"! But all Jeremiah witnesses around him is a populace stubbornly resolved to live in defiance of God's commands.

To continue the former strategy of pleading for return would amount to futile pandering. Honesty in the face of imminent catastrophe demanded a new, candid response: Pleas for divine mercy, fasting to elicit God's pardon, intercession by the prophets, sacrifices by the priests, diplomacy, and any other human efforts had run up against the harshest of moral conclusions: a point is reached in the life of individual or nation when human efforts are rendered useless over against a conclusive divine judgment, a judgment sealed by the proven incorrigibility of the people.

It is erroneous, therefore, to view Jeremiah's "new" position as a fundamental change in his thinking. It is rather consistent with his foundational belief in God's universal sovereignty. As far as international relations are concerned, this means that Egypt or Assyria or Babylon can rightfully figure into Judahite international policy only if they are commissioned by God to play a role in divine purpose. In a word coming from an early stage in Jeremiah's career, he already cautioned against a realpolitik that was based on human calculus:

> What then do you gain by going to Egypt,
>   to drink the waters of the Nile?
> Or what do you gain by going to Assyria,
>   to drink the waters of the Euphrates?
> Your wickedness will punish you,
>   and your apostasies will convict you.
> Know and see that it is evil and bitter
>   for you to forsake the LORD your God;
>   the fear of me is not in you, says the Lord GOD of hosts.
>   (2:18–19)

With these words Jeremiah appeals to the theocratic principle of Yahwistic faith: the sole sovereignty of God. All other powers are penultimate; that is to say, their force is strictly derivative. Where they derive their assignment from God, they are to be reckoned with; where their authority is self-generated, they are ephemeral and not to be feared (see Isa. 7:3–9). On this basic point, Jeremiah stands firmly within the classic faith of both early Israelite religion and prophetic Yahwism. He reaffirms the conviction of Samuel in 1 Samuel 12:24: "Only fear the LORD," and of Isaiah in Isaiah 30:15: "In returning and rest you shall be saved; in quietness and in trust shall be your strength." In harmony with his own understanding of God's stature he delivers this divine message to the kings of the world: "It is I who by my great power and my outstretched arm have made the earth, with the people and animals that are on the earth, and I give it to whomever I please" (Jer. 27:5).

Surely recourse to words of impending calamity was not a turn made blithely by Jeremiah. With deep anguish he witnessed that Israel had chosen to "trust in mere mortals" and cast its destiny with "mere flesh." Rather than enjoying the blessings of those "whose trust is the LORD," it would experience the curses of a mortal enemy, Babylon (17:5–8). Since that enemy was not only exercising its own power, but ultimately was being used as an agent of the ruler of all nations, the only course of action available to Israel was submission to the Babylonians. Moreover, the sentence was not short-term, as claimed by Jeremiah's rival, Hananiah, but of such duration as to necessitate settling down as a captive people and engaging in normal personal and economic activities that contributed to the stability of the Babylonian state (Jer. 28–29).

The vitriolic response of Jeremiah's opponents was immediate. Was his not an egregious act of treason? Was he not calling into question the central tenets of the ancestral faith, God's election of David (and his descendants) as king, and Jerusalem as his sanctuary? Was Jeremiah not simply an agent of the Babylonians, abetting their military objective of destroying Judah?

There is no reason to doubt that the persistent theme running through the narrative of Jeremiah's "passion," that is, of his being treated as a dangerous enemy of state, accurately reflects reality, as does the leitmotif of his Houdini-like escapes, thanks to the support of the influential Shaphan family (26:24). The following verse gives classic expression to the political ploy used by leaders of all ages to repress dissent: "Then the officials said to the king, 'This man ought to be put to death, because he is discouraging the soldiers who are left in this city, and all the people, by speaking such words to them. For this man is not seeking the welfare [šālôm] of this people, but their harm'" (38:4).

Dissent, according to their reasoning, especially in times of crisis, is nothing less than treason! The tense confrontation calls to mind an accusation Jeremiah had directed against his adversaries, the corrupt priests and prophets: "They have treated the wound of my people carelessly, saying, 'Peace, peace [šālôm šālôm],' when there is no peace [šālôm]" (6:14). Jeremiah's position is clear: The condition of the nation is so grave that it is not his indictment, but rather the comforting words of his rivals that constitute treason. The refusal of the political leadership to acknowledge the accuracy of Jeremiah's description of the nation's state of health simply confirmed the terminal state of their spiritual sickness. Their position recalls what Isaiah had called a "covenant with death" (Isa. 28:15).

The rot has extended right to the head of the body politic, a point made bluntly in the continuation of the above narrative, where King Zedekiah testifies to his own pathetic weakness with these words to his officials: "Here he is; he is in your hands; for the king is powerless against you" (38:5). What the narrative makes clear is that Zedekiah, trapped in the decline of the Davidic house, is powerless to divert the destruction of his kingdom or even to save himself from the fate Jeremiah earlier had proclaimed against Jehoiakim: "He shall have no one to sit upon the throne of David, and his dead body shall be cast out to the heat by day and the frost by night" (36:30).

A CLOSER LOOK AT JEREMIAH'S CRITIQUE OF KING AND TEMPLE

Jeremiah's scathing attack on Jehoiakim and his announcement of the impending destruction of the temple attest to the rhetorical power of this prophet. As was noted in our discussion of psalms originating in the official royal cult, the notion of a uniquely lofty status bestowed by God upon the Davidic king and the closely related concept of God's special tie to the temple in Jerusalem not only were fostered within the royal court but also became part of the Torah tradition in the book of Deuteronomy, from which source they were enlisted as the twin historiographic themes by the Deuteronomistic Historians. We also have observed that David and Zion occupy an important place in the prophetic thought of Isaiah. Especially at the point of the most serious threat ever to the existence of the Davidic kingdom, many in Judah looked to the divine promises inherent in this two-point theologoumenon as a source of desperately needed hope. Was it not reckless of Jeremiah to single out these cherished intertwined institutions as objects of harsh critique? An answer to this question is best pursued by examining several relevant texts.

In 21:12 Jeremiah summarizes the solemn responsibility of the king in terms as familiar to ancient Mesopotamian inscriptions as to Deuteronomic Law (17:14–20) and Isaiah's inaugural poem (9:2–6 [Heb. 1–5]):

> Execute justice in the morning,
>   and deliver from the hand of the oppressor
>   anyone who has been robbed. . . .

Because the king possessed power vastly superior to anyone else in the land, his responsibility to uphold justice was commensurately weighty. Justice was most poignantly executed on behalf of those most vulnerable to exploitation, the poor. Where proper exercise of power in defense of the oppressed was discarded in favor of leveraging royal stature for personal gain, an atrocity unfolded that evoked divine wrath. With a keen eye on his target, Jeremiah affixes to his formulation of royal responsibility the following threat:

> . . . or else my wrath will go forth like fire,
>   and burn, with no one to quench it,
>   because of your evil doings.

Jeremiah's indictment and sentence of Jehoiakim were expressed in graphic detail in the woe oracle in 22:13–19. The fact that the political scruples of this descendant of Levitical priests from Anathoth were untethered by deference to a high royal theology may contribute to the vitriolic tone in his pronouncements against Jehoiakim. However, the substance of his critique cannot be dismissed as a simple product of blind antiroyal ideology. On the deepest level it was Jeremiah's clear grasp of the central theocratic principle of Yahwistic faith that induced his conviction that the king's legitimacy was contingent strictly on his faithful implementation of the divine justice and compassion expressed in the Torah, whereby he would serve as an example for the entire nation. It is note-worthy that Jeremiah does not portray the king as a fearsome tyrant, but as a pathetically inept weakling who cowers before Jeremiah's honest assessment of the situation, while creating an illusory sense of security by using resources badly needed for social reform and national defense to build a gaudy palace. To add to this travesty of integrity, he presses his subjects into service and then reneges on paying their wages (22:13–14).

Out of his moral indignation arose words that are among the most trenchant in the Jeremiah corpus:

> Are you a king
>   because you compete in cedar?
> Did not your father eat and drink
>   and do justice and righteousness?
>   Then it was well with him.
> He judged the cause of the poor and needy;
>   then it was well.
> Is not this to know me?
>   says the LORD.
> But your eyes and heart
>   are only on your dishonest gain,
> for shedding innocent blood,
>   and for practicing oppression and violence.
>   (22:15–17)

The ignominy of the king is so extreme as to assure that his donkey death will not even elicit lamentation (22:18–19).

Regarding the question of whether Jeremiah was being reckless in attacking the twin pillars upon which the Jerusalem populace desperately placed their hope for deliverance, we are guided by his lament over the plight of the victims of the king's dereliction: "Hark, the cry of my poor people, from far and wide in the land: 'Is the LORD not in Zion? Is her King not in her?'" (8:19). For Jeremiah the fun-damental truth underlying his judgment on Jehoiakim was this: This earthly king had betrayed the heavenly king, thereby annulling his title and legitimacy to rule. Sadly, due to the Davidic king's abdication of his divinely commissioned respon-sibility, the poor people of the land would experience the absence of the Lord, and their suffering would be of the horrendous nature described in the book of Lamentations, a corpus fittingly attributed by tradition to Jeremiah.

Of course, the answer thus given, namely, that Jeremiah's pronouncement of judgment on Jehoiakim was justified by the magnitude of the suffering his dereliction had brought upon the people, is reasonable only on the political level, where it is undeniable that the innocent members of a nation suffer along with the guilty. The deeper question of theodicy, however, remains unresolved by Jeremiah. Rather, he reiterates it: "Why does the way of the guilty prosper? Why do all who are treacherous thrive?" (12:1). While the fact that many of the rich and powerful did not escape the wrath of the Babylonians may have offered some scant palliation to the aging Jeremiah, it is likely that to his dying day in Egypt, he continued to be haunted by "the cry of my poor people."

The cry of the poor provides the backdrop also for the second text calling for our closer attention, where the untiring foe of special entitlements for the ruling class intones an iconoclastic attack on the magical notion of religious shrines, notwithstanding the fact that the particular shrine in question was the second pillar upon which the threatened populace sought to prop up its hope. While scholarly debate will continue over which version of Jeremiah's "temple sermon" should be accorded priority and over the extent of Deuteronomistic editorializing in Jeremiah 7, only excessive cynicism will lead to attribution of the account's provenance to pure fancy, rather than to memory of a stunning episode in the prophet's life.

We think it likely that at some point in the final decade of the seventh century, Jeremiah appeared in the gate of the Jerusalem temple and issued a harsh warning in a desperate attempt to shock his people back to their senses, that is, to a penitent return to the historic beliefs and values that constituted their national identity. Evidence of ongoing revision of that momentous speech and its narrative framework only testifies to the central importance it retained for the self-understanding of those who sought to live as faithful heirs to the prophetic tradition.[10]

On the basis of Jeremiah 7:1–15 it is understandable how this prophet contributed to our vocabulary the term "jeremiad," for it ranks among the most powerful sermons ever preached. With surgical incisiveness, the prophet lays bare the spiritual condition of his "patient," contrasting true worship with worship that is nothing more than a reckless attempt to hide gross immorality. Taking the positive point first, we find Jeremiah articulating an understanding of authentic existence that does not belittle the role of worship, but clothes it in moral integrity, by tying it inseparably to trust and obedience: "For if you truly amend your ways and your doings . . . , then I will dwell with you in this place, in the land that I gave of old to your ancestors forever and ever" (7:5a, 7).

Here we find what amounts to a hendiadys that secures *shalom* for the land and its inhabitants: a people living in faithfulness to the covenant creates a hospitable setting for God's presence, from which presence alone issues forth

---

10. I completely agree with Jack Lundbom's assessment of the relation between the ipsissima verba of Jeremiah and later additions: "The book also contains reflections by others who look at Jeremiah's life and preaching from a distance, and these form a second theological component no less important than the component of theology that derives from the prophet" (Jack R. Lundbom, *Jeremiah 1–20*, Anchor Bible [New York: Doubleday, 1999], 571).

security and well-being. The concrete contents that the prophet places within that hendiadys are a summary of the moral life epitomized in the Ten Commandments: "act justly one with another, . . . do not oppress the alien, the orphan, and the widow, or shed innocent blood in this place, . . . do not go after other gods" (7:5–6).

In contrast to this eloquent picture of life in harmony with God is placed a description of the chaotic conduct of the people: "you steal, murder, commit adultery, swear falsely, make offerings to Baal, and go after other gods" (7:9). Stridently they have twisted the Torah into a mocking antithesis amounting to an assault on the heart of the nation's very identity. Even that does not exhaust their disgrace. Reciting what amounts to a magical incantation, "This the temple of the LORD, the temple of the LORD, the temple of the LORD," they continue their twisted procession by entering into the presence of God and confidently announcing, "'We are safe!'—only to go on doing all these abominations" (7:4, 10).

God will not be mocked or deceived. "I too am watching," God declares. As proof that God will not tolerate this perversion of the house called by his name into a den of robbers, a historical precedence is elicited, "Shiloh, where I made my name dwell at first" (7:12). Like Shiloh, the temple in Jerusalem would be destroyed! Magical manipulation of God can have no place in Israel, a nation with a religious heritage based on the inseparability of worship and the ethical life.

JEREMIAH'S POLITICAL MESSAGE IN THE WAKE OF THE BABYLONIAN CAMPAIGNS OF 597–587

Jeremiah had adapted his message in the last years of the seventh century to his conviction that the nation had crossed a line that made calamity inevitable. So too, in response to the unfolding of that calamity, Jeremiah turned to address a new, complicated set of circumstances: a nation stripped of self-rule; a population split, some remaining in Judah and some living as exiles in Babylon; and a community puzzling over the future of promises that had been central to its religious heritage and sense of national identity, namely, a homeland, a sanctuary, God's presence and blessing.

The source material treating this period belongs preponderantly to portions of the book that betray editorializing in a Deuteronomistic style. Yet the major themes are presented with such consistency as to suggest that Jeremiah's message is preserved in its essentials. Here we proceed to examine two poignant sample texts.

Chapter 24 describes a vision the prophet received shortly after the deportation of Jehoiachin (sometimes called Jeconiah [24:1]) in 597. Jeremiah sees two baskets of figs, one good and one spoiled, in front of the temple. The former symbolizes the exiles in Babylon, the latter those who remained in Judah after the king and the upper echelons of the Jewish community had been taken away. In effect, the curses of the covenant are placed upon the latter (24:9–10), whereas the exiles are described as recipients of God's blessing in the form of protection and eventual return and lasting establishment in the land, where the gift of a new heart will reestablish the covenant between God and people (24:6–7).

If this vision is basically reflective of the political position Jeremiah took after 597, as seems likely, it is evident that Jeremiah subscribed to a partisan ideology simplistic in form and unsympathetic to the plight and rights of those remaining in Judah. That this reductionary, dualistic picture subsequently evolved into a canonical paradigm is understandable, given the key role that the Babylonian *gola* came to play in the development of Second Temple Judaism. As for Jeremiah, his bias in favor of the exiles can be best understood as an extension of his understanding that the destruction of Judah and submission to the Babylonian conquerors were a divine sentence of guilt and punishment. The rigidity with which he adhered to this view allowed no room for a parallel carrier of future blessing, namely, the people, mainly of the laboring class, who remained in Judah after the waves of deportation had been completed.

Chapter 42 describes another group that fell into the category of those falling outside of Jeremiah's notion of election and future promise. Its background is the aftermath of the culminating assault of the Babylonian armies that had reduced city and temple to ashes. Zedekiah, who ruled under the authority of the Babylonians in the period between the deportations, had been blinded and taken into exile, while Gedaliah, whom Nebuchadnezzar had appointed governor of the subjugated state, had fallen victim to assassins. An anxious group, fearing the reprisal of the Babylonians and contemplating flight to Egypt, appealed to Jeremiah to consult the Lord on their behalf. However, once Jeremiah had returned to them with a word obviously contrary to their intent, namely, that they were to remain in the land, they defiantly proclaim that they will go to Egypt, the express purpose being to escape further war and deprivation.

Against their stratagem, Jeremiah announces God's will: they are to remain in the land of Judah. If in obedience they remain in the land, they will be recipients of promises resembling those given earlier to the "good figs," that is, to the *gola*! In the case of their defying this divine mandate and fleeing to Egypt, the curses of the covenant would descend on them; that is, they would become recipients of the curses earlier pronounced upon the "bad figs," those remaining in the land! Does not comparison of chapters 24 and 42 reveal a blatant contradiction?

Answering this question would be simplified if one of the accounts could be traced to Jeremiah and the other attributed to the hand of a later tradent. The problem is that the accounts are stylistically so similar as to suggest a common literary history. A more complicated solution therefore is preferable: with a high degree of verisimilitude, the narratives in question picture a prophet striving to discern God's will in a hastily changing, chaotic situation. The constant is this: the calamity that had happened was decreed by God as just punishment on the people. What was now required on the part of the people was abandoning all pretenses of self-determination and accepting the punishment. For the exiles addressed in chapter 24, this meant accepting the exile as the avenue God had chosen for punishment that would lead ultimately to restoration of the nation; in contrast, those left in Judah after the first deportation continued to live under the curse that would visit the land calamitously ten years later.

In the case of chapter 42, the prophet, under the conviction that the sifting of the population that had occurred in 587 once again was according to divine will, warns the people left in Judah not to imagine that they could deflect divine punishment by, in effect, contriving an alternative exile by fleeing to Egypt, but to accept life in Babylonian-occupied Judah as their destiny. The major theme in 42:1–43:7 of the rejection of the prophet's advice, followed by flight into Egypt, prepared for the story in chapter 44 of the apostasy of the Egyptian refugees, which in tradition eventually modulated into an etiology of the heretical status of the Jewish enclaves in Egypt.

In spite of obvious editorial reshaping in both chapters, there is no reason to doubt the veracity of the basic picture of Jeremiah continuing his role of offering political counsel on the basis of his discernment of divine intent. It is noteworthy that later editors preserved both accounts, in spite of the obvious lack of consistency between them. Had both narratives been purely the product of Deuteronomistic authors, it is unlikely that such tensions would have been built into the text. As for the significance of ambiguity for the larger question of the application of core beliefs to political realities, it will be a topic to which we shall have occasion to return.

Thus far we have traced Jeremiah's politics through three phases. Consistent throughout are his core beliefs: YHWH alone is the sovereign ruler of all nations, and any nation that repudiates that transcendent regime is doomed. From among the nations, YHWH has entered into a covenant with Israel. If Israel is obedient to the terms of that covenant, blessings will come to Israel, and through Israel to the nations. Disobedience will lead to curses, culminating in destruction of the nation. When applied to changing conditions, these core beliefs lead to different strategies: first, appeals to a disobedient people to repent and return to God; then, announcements of judgment combined with refusal to intercede, reflecting a sense of finality in God's decision to execute the sentence of punishment; finally, advice to accept Babylonian rule as an expression of divine will.

Already in the third phase, in words directed to the Babylonian exiles (24:6–7), Jeremiah pointed to a fourth period lying beyond judgment, in which a chastised and repentant people would return to YHWH and live in obedience to their God in a world delivered from the Babylonian oppressor. Jeremiah understood that restoration of the covenant bond between God and people was the abiding purpose of God's actions, even during times of darkest doom. This is evident in occasional words from Jeremiah's early ministry. Jeremiah 6:9 draws on the metaphor of gleaning grapes to point to hope beyond judgment on the basis of "the remnant of Israel." Now, after the calamity inflicted by Babylon on the nation, Jeremiah could address that remnant with a word of hope.

The movement from the theme of punishment to restoration is similar to that found when one moves from Isaiah 1–39 to Isaiah 40–55, the difference being that in the case of the book of Isaiah the announcement of penalty paid and the arrival of God's salvation is made by a "disciple" of Isaiah, not the prophet himself, whereas in Jeremiah, the same individual spans the whole development of divine address, from punishment to restoration. The obvious reason is that Jeremiah lived on both sides of the Babylonian conquest.

As in the case of the narratives recounting the last years of Jeremiah's life, so too, in the passages describing the restoration to come, it is difficult—probably impossible—to separate Jeremiah's pronouncements from the elaborations of that theme coming from the tradents who preserved and further shaped the words of and stories about the prophet. Especially in the case of the so-called book of consolation (chaps. 30–32), efforts at sorting out words of Jeremiah from later elaborations are not as productive as observing that in this section one finds an eloquent expression of hope rooted in Jeremiah's conviction that God's plan ultimately would prevail. Envisioned is a future in which the tragedy of a people, chosen by God for peace and blessing, for both themselves and the nations of the world, but negating that great promise through apostasy and disobedience, finally would be transformed, by divine grace, into a drama of healing and *shalom*.

The transformation would not be the result of a change in God's universal rule, according to which peace and justice flourished wherever communities acknowledged God's sovereignty in worship and obedience and human regimes conformed to the standards of justice and mercy defined by the Torah. No, it would be the result of a new initiative consistent with that sovereignty and expressing its unique quality of loving-kindness: God would attend to the source of human behavior, effecting an inner transformation of the heart in which deviousness and perversity (Jer. 17:9) would be replaced by a loving embrace of God's will. After tracing Jeremiah's ministry through torturous twists and turns and reading words predominantly addressing a people broken by its rejection of God's way, we come to a final testimony to God's faithfulness that takes the form of a vision of a future in which God's initiating grace is answered by the trust and obedience of the covenant community.

Jeremiah's message of restoration beyond judgment is the same in essentials as that proclaimed by Ezekiel and the herald of Isaiah 40–55: the scattered of both the northern and southern kingdoms would be returned, would live in freedom and safety in the land of Israel, and would be guided by leaders embodying in their lives and implementing in their structures of government God's righteous rule. At the same time, the particular religious and political historical sensitivities of each prophet influences the specific themes he develops or omits. For example, Ezekiel envisions a restoration in which the temple and the Zadokite priesthood are central, Second Isaiah mentions the temple in only one passage, while Jeremiah completely omits temple and Zadokite priesthood from his vision of the future.

Infinitely greater than thematic differences among the canonical prophets is the distance that Jeremiah sets between himself and the prophets he declares to be imposters. Perhaps the most profound difference revolves around the nature of the vision of restoration. Whereas the false prophets made light of the weight of sin that doomed the nation and "treated the wound of [God's] people carelessly, saying, 'Peace, peace,' when there is no peace" (Jer. 6:14), Jeremiah, as background to his words of comfort and hope, insisted on the gravity of the situation, using the terminology of medical science: "Your hurt is incurable, your wound grievous. There is . . . no medicine for your wound, no healing for you" (30:12–13). Jeremiah took with utter seriousness Israel's experience of God's wrath, in keeping with his understanding of the moral structure of the universe, where wickedness cannot be ignored: "I will by no means leave you unpunished" (30:11). In contrast to the facile promises of Hananiah of an immediate return to the good times of the past, Jeremiah described the past as an unbroken chain of heedless repudiations of God's Torah, that is, a history of damnation. Blithe promises of a prophet could not break that chain. Only one physician was equal to the task, and it was upon the word of that healer that Jeremiah based his vision of the future: "For I will restore health to you, and your wounds I will heal, says the LORD" (30:17a).

It would be tantamount to repeating the misperception of the false prophets to treat Jeremiah's vision of restoration dismissively. The themes constituting that vision address in breadth and depth the mysteries of human political existence in antiquity as much as in the contemporary world.

Restoration to political health (and there can be no denial that Jeremiah had in mind the reconstitution of a concrete state consisting of northern and southern kingdoms and organized under duly appointed leadership) would not be possible if the citizens deluded themselves into thinking that they could persist in repudiating God's claim on their lives, continue living the "good life" blending self-indulgence with scornful defiance of the Torah, and expect to enjoy security and prosperity. Jeremiah describes graphically the about-face that alone could prepare Israel for restoration to statehood:

> Indeed I heard Ephraim pleading:
> "You disciplined me, and I took the discipline;
>   I was like a calf untrained.
> Bring me back, let me come back,
>   for you are the LORD my God."
>   (31:18)

Repentance alone prepared the human for God's transforming power of the inner being that would renew the covenant on a new basis: "This is the covenant that I will make with the house of Israel after those days, says the LORD: I will put my law within them, and I will write it on their hearts; and I will be their God, and they shall be my people" (31:33).

This reaching for a deeper grounding for religious fidelity and moral integrity reflects the seriousness with which Jeremiah reckoned with his nation's bleak past. As he looks to the future, the doomsayer who concluded that national catastrophe was inevitable and traced its source to the human heart, devious and perverse, saw no alternative future short of a thoroughgoing spiritual transformation, one that only God could effect: "I will give them one heart and one way, that they may fear me for all time, for their own good and the good of their children after them. . . . I will put the fear of me in their hearts, so that they may not turn from me" (32:39–40).

Health within the inner self of all its citizens did not exclude, but provided the basis for, the other dimension of a sound society and nation, namely, viable and trustworthy religious and political institutions and honest and competent leaders. Jeremiah reached back to his heritage and announced that God would provide, from the house of David, "a righteous Branch . . . and he shall execute justice and righteousness in the land. . . . And this is the name by which it will be called: 'The LORD is our righteousness'" (33:15–16). But even after political stability returned and integrity took up residence in the highest office in the land, Israel was not to forget that good governance was founded upon something vastly more enduring than well-intentioned human leaders. Therefore it remained the prophet's responsibility to point to the only source of lasting justice and well-being: "Then I myself will gather the remnant of my flock out of all the lands where I have driven them, and I will bring them back to their fold, and they shall be fruitful and multiply. I will raise up shepherds over them who will shepherd them, and they shall not fear any longer, or be dismayed, nor shall any be missing, says the LORD" (23:3–4).

Amid the flux and turmoil of human affairs, Jeremiah adhered steadfastly to the theocratic core of his political thought: There existed only one source for the transformation prerequisite to a future of *shalom* among the peoples of the earth and for the structures of governance capable of fostering justice and equality for all citizens, that source being the sovereign God upon whose universal reign the viability of every human institution depended. And as important as the infinite power of the sovereign one was the compassionate nature of his rule, for it provided the model that was to be implemented by the provisional governments of the world:

> I have loved you with an everlasting love;
>> therefore I have continued my faithfulness to you.
>>>> (31:3)

It may seem odd to conclude our discussion of one of God's most hard-hitting spokespersons with the theme of love. But one of the most striking features of the politics of Jeremiah is the tenacity with which he traced divine love and faithfulness through times others used as evidence of God's either having abandoned Israel or having conceded victory to the purportedly more powerful gods of the victorious enemy. The divine love he described, to be sure, was not a pampering love, but a tough love, one that remains salient for anyone seeking to gain an adequate perspective for understanding the complex relationship between religion and politics.

Chapter 17

Ezekiel

Calamity, Ritual Cleansing,
and Restoration

THE BOOK AS A SOURCE

Moving from the thought world of Jeremiah to that of Ezekiel gives one the sense of traveling to a vastly different land. Though our discussion of Jeremiah 7 indicated that Jeremiah's thinking was influenced by the ritual traditions of his community, he was inclined to view the political happenings of his time through the lens of a covenant theology and in terms of historical categories. The lens that Ezekiel used was more thoroughly shaped by the world of ritual, and both his critique of his nation and his construal of a future that would redress the fatal mistakes of the past are imbued with the language of the Priestly Writing and, more specifically, the Holiness Code.

As a historical source, however, Ezekiel poses for the modern critic challenges similar to those encountered in the book of Jeremiah. The book played a vital role within circles involved in the rebuilding of Judea after the return of exiles in the last third of the sixth century, and they did not hesitate to make additions that applied the prophecy of Ezekiel to the specific challenges of their time, such as the rivalry between priestly groups (44:6–16; 40:46b; 43:19; 45:4–5;

46:19–21, 24; 48:11).[1] Later still, the apocalyptic ruminations of a visionary seeking to bridge the considerable gap between the divine promise of "my sanctuary is among them forevermore" in 37:28 and the actual implementation of Ezekiel's restoration program in chapters 40–48 gave rise to chapters 38 and 39 and the grotesque figure of Gog of Magog. Separating out other more subtle additions, especially in chapters 34–37, is more difficult, and scholarly opinion varies widely, but in these cases what one is dealing with is less a departure from Ezekiel's message than embellishments in the spirit of the prophet.

While it is clear that later tradents played an important part in shaping the book of Ezekiel, the extreme position of C. C. Torrey that the book is a pseudepigraphical work from the third century BCE has been rejected by the scholarly world in favor of the view that the larger part of Ezekiel derives either from the sixth-century prophet himself or from disciples elaborating on his message in response to changing conditions.[2] We can thus proceed to describe the politics of Ezekiel with reasonable assurance that they are within the ken of rigorous scrutiny.

EZEKIEL'S LOCATION WITHIN THE RELIGIOUS TRADITIONS OF ISRAEL

Ezekiel's familiarity with the major religious traditions of his people is evident throughout the book, though as we shall see in our examination of the theology underlying his political position, he commonly gives those traditions a creative twist to serve a point. Like Hosea and Jeremiah, he draws on the exodus and the Sinai traditions. YHWH's election of David receives his attention, as does the deity's chosen dwelling place, though his avoidance of the specific name Zion suggests a certain distancing in relation to connotations current in his time. His mention of Noah, Daniel, and Job gives an indication of his detailed knowledge of his people's stories, though he is silent in relation to the patriarchal legends. The myth of Eden plays an important part in his vision of the future, while Canaanite notions of the netherworld influence his picture of the fate of the world's rulers. Pride of place, however, is enjoyed by priestly traditions: first, in the broad sense of his developing common sacerdotal tropes like defilement and cleansing; secondly, in his specific citing of laws drawn from the Holiness Code and other halakic sources.[3]

---

1. See Antonius H. J. Gunneweg, *Leviten und Priester*, FRLANT 89 (Göttingen: Vandenhoeck & Ruprecht, 1965).

2. E.g., Walter Zimmerli, *Ezekiel 1*, trans. Ronald E. Clements (Philadelphia: Fortress Press, 1979), 68–74; Joseph Blenkinsopp, *A History of Prophecy in Israel* (Philadelphia: Westminster Press, 1983), 166–68.

3. Note especially how the laws of Lev. 19 echo through Ezek. 22:7–8 and the prominence given to the Sabbath law in Ezek. 20:12, 20; 22:8. See also Ezek. 22:29; 45:10–12; and 47:22–23.

Of particular theological significance is the manner in which he depicts both Israel's depraved historical past and the vision of future redemption with the language of ritual (cf. Lev. 16). Also unmistakable are the affinities of his restoration plan with the sacred precincts of Israel's wilderness encampment described in the Priestly Writing. All of these priestly accents make more noticeable the scant reference to the covenant theology of the Deuteronomic tradition that was central to the thought of Jeremiah, thereby providing literary evidence for the divergent backgrounds of the prophet from Anathoth and Jerusalemite priest-prophet.

The nearly irresistible desire to move from literary deposits to biographical details is riddled with hazards, well illustrated by portraits in the scholarly and quasi-scholarly literature of Ezekiel as schizophrenic, epileptic, or catatonic. True, the biblical narrative describes actions that could suggest mental pathology, but, as in the case of the often bizarre activity of Isaiah, one must keep in mind that the prophets enacted what they felt divinely commanded to do; those who transcribed the stories of the prophets treated them not as normal individuals but as holy figures possessed of a higher spirit. Even after placing proper restraints on our imagination, however, it seems hard to deny the general veracity of the book's consistent description of Ezekiel as an eccentric character who, more in the style of the ecstatic prophets of the early monarchy than their successors, was drawn up almost to the point of identification into the message he felt called by God to proclaim. How else is one to understand his being designated by God as "a sign for the house of Israel" (12:6, 11; 24:24, 27)? Or his witnessing the "likeness of the glory of the Lord" borne by a vastly enhanced version of Elijah's fiery chariot? Or his being transported back and forth between Jerusalem and Babylon by God's spirit, and eating and discovering "as sweet as honey" the heavenly words that he was to speak to the house of Israel?

By his own contemporaries in exile, Ezekiel, his unusual traits notwithstanding, was esteemed as a spiritual leader, as indicated by the fourfold reference to his being consulted by elders of the community.[4] Not only the elaborate plan for recovery contained in the book, but also his ruminations on the solemn demands placed on the true prophet give ample evidence that Ezekiel was indeed a highly educated and creative counselor who provided a sense of cohesion and direction to a people at a critical junction in their history.

THEOLOGICAL PRINCIPLES
INFORMING EZEKIEL'S POLITICS

Central to Ezekiel's understanding of reality was the kebôd yhwh (glory of God), that is, the presence of God in the midst of the people, upon whom their well-being was entirely dependent. The concept was not new to Ezekiel. According to the priestly tradition upon which he freely drew, the history of the presence

---

4. Ezek. 8:1; 14:1; 20:1; 33:31.

of God's *kebôd* began with Israel's infancy in the wilderness (Exod. 16:7) and continued in the community's worship, first in the portable sanctuary and then in the Jerusalem temple, where, for example, Isaiah experienced the awesome encounter that shaped his entire career. It is on the basis of his understanding of the mysterious, yet palpable nature of the *kābôd* that Ezekiel interpreted and responded to the unprecedented events that unfolded before him.

Without the presence of God's glory in the temple, Jerusalem's viability was nil. The urgent tone of Ezekiel's prophecy—and in this point it is in agreement with Jeremiah's message—stems from a central tenet of Yahwism, namely, that no earthly image or structure could *guarantee* God's presence.[5] The events leading up to and culminating in the destruction of Jerusalem by the Babylonians in 586 therefore pressed upon the prophet Ezekiel questions combining theological, moral, and liturgical facets: Under what conditions can the *kebôd yhwh* dwell amidst the people? When is the point reached where it is forced to withdraw?

Once the calamity had occurred, moreover, the question did not disappear, but was transformed into a new form while yet preserving the underlying theologoumenon: What was required to restore conditions hospitable to the return of God's *kebôd*? Those questions gave both substance and structure to Ezekiel's political ruminations. Moreover, they were accompanied by a leitmotif that, though formulaic in nature, adds depth to Ezekiel's interpretation of the central significance of God's presence. Repeatedly divine pronouncements are punctuated with the recognition formula, "and you/they shall know that I am God," which also can appear in variant forms, for example, "and they shall know that I, the LORD, have spoken in my jealousy" (5:13).[6] All human sentimentality is stripped before the daunting image of a God who does everything ultimately for one reason, that proper glory may be ascribed to his holy name. If viewed anthropocentrically, the concept suggests an inordinate conceit. In Ezekiel's thought, however, it drives the notion of the limits of human language when speaking of God.

Moreover, another theological concept places beyond doubt that Ezekiel's understanding of divine knowledge and God's glory implies neither vanity nor caprice. That is the theme of God's pledge. God speaks of his initiating activity toward Jerusalem in terms of courtship, "I pledged myself to you and entered

---

5. A story from an earlier calamitous period no doubt contributed to the rich connotations attached to Ezekiel's use of the concept "glory of God." In that story the armies of Israel have suffered a disastrous defeat at the hands of the Philistines, and a messenger brings the aged priest Eli the tidings: "Your two sons also, Hophni and Phinehas, are dead, and the ark of God has been captured." Eli falls over backward, breaks his neck, and dies, but the grim reaper's work does not stop. Phinehas's pregnant wife hears, goes into labor, gives birth, and then dies, but not before naming the child Ichabod (meaning, "alas, the glory!") and explaining, "The glory has departed from Israel, for the ark of God has been captured" (1 Sam. 4:12–22).

6. The most complete study of this formula (*Erweiswort*, or "proof-saying") was written by Walter Zimmerli in German in 1953 and has appeared in translation in *I Am Yahweh*, trans. D. W. Stott (Atlanta: John Knox Press, 1982), 1–28. See also Walter Zimmerli, *The Fiery Throne*, ed. K. C. Hanson (Minneapolis: Fortress Press, 2003), 87–89.

into a covenant with you" (16:8). Even after the relationship had been ravaged by Jerusalem's habitual infidelity, and dreadful consequences were on the horizon, God reinvokes the theme of covenant, which in turn becomes the basis for hope for a salvific future (16:59–63). Similarly, the history of Israel's perpetual rebelliousness in chapter 20 both begins with the divine oath (20:5–6) and is moved through subsequent stages (v. 15) to its culmination under the direction of God's binding himself to his word (v. 33).

Clearly, a lofty transcendent orientation characterizes Ezekiel's theology. He views all of reality in relation to a deity who is enveloped in radiant splendor, yet presents himself to the faithful community in the form of the dazzling effulgence Ezekiel names with the priestly technical term, *kebôd yhwh*. This deity directs the history of Israel and the nations in such a way that they may come to know that he is God. But the course of history is not accordingly capricious, for God has bound himself by oath to a covenant relationship with Israel that ultimately will be fulfilled. It is through the lens of this theology that Ezekiel addressed the difficult political issues of his day.

EZEKIEL'S POLITICAL MESSAGE: DOMESTIC POLICY

Making sense out of Ezekiel's political pronouncements is no easy task. Jeremiah's deep pessimism regarding human nature at times makes it difficult to fathom how any room was left for the prophet's reform efforts. However, certain of his pronouncements invoke the traditional covenant concept of God's extending to the nation the options of obedience leading to life and rebellion leading to death, thereby safeguarding his theology against collapsing into determinism.

But comparison with Hosea and Jeremiah reveals a profound ambiguity in Ezekiel's understanding of God's relation to Israel's past. While both of these earlier prophets accused Israel of heinous forgetfulness and ingratitude toward YHWH, they could nevertheless point to the time of the wilderness sojourn as one in which Israel was faithful to the covenant, thereby identifying a historical precedent for the possibility of repentance and return. In contrast, Ezekiel rewrites the traditional Epic so as to eliminate any reference to a time of obedience. Already at the beginning in Egypt, and on through the wilderness, conquest, and subsequent history under judges and kings, the history is one of unmitigated sin (chaps. 16, 20, and 23). Throughout that history, God's intent to destroy the people outright was prevented by one consideration alone, "for the sake of my name, that it should not be profaned in the sight of the nations" (20:9).

Making the picture even more puzzling is Ezekiel's account of laws and statutes God gave to the people while they were in the wilderness. Naturally, the giving of the law on the wilderness mountain of Sinai comes to mind. This story, though itself sullied by Israel's rebelliousness, clearly portrays the statutes and ordinances given by God as reflective of God's own righteousness and provided for Israel's benefit. Unprecedented in biblical or postbiblical literature is the divine word relayed to Ezekiel in 20:25: "Moreover I gave them statutes that were not good and ordinances by which they could not live." What motive could possibly lie behind this seemingly deceptive act on God's part? Ezekiel's favorite leitmotif supplies the answer: "that they might know that I am the LORD" (20:26).

In recalling Ezekiel's lofty vision of the glory of God directing events in accord with the divine name, can one escape the picture of a deity determining the course of history and Israel being swept along by the consequent world happenings? When one adds to this picture Ezekiel's emphasis on God's originating oath and covenant with Israel, and notes that they provide the basis for the remarkable turnaround Ezekiel foretells, in which the pattern of rebellion that was present throughout Israel's history would be supplanted by the glorious restoration of a people living in fidelity to the covenant *forever* (16:60–63; 20:40–44), it is hard to escape the conclusion that Ezekiel's historiography assumes a drama scripted from heaven. Humans enter that glorious new era, not through the act of repentance in response to prophetic appeal, but as a result of divine surgery, through which a heart of stone is replaced with a heart of flesh (11:19; 36:24), and divine intervention, through which ravenous shepherds are forced to yield to a faithful servant, David (34:1–24).

In this scenario, has human agency been entirely removed? Is human politics even a relevant category in studying Ezekiel, or is it entirely supplanted by divine government? Another way of formulating this question is this: Has the historiography underlying Ezekiel's treatment of Israel's past and future carried him beyond the perspective of prophetic eschatology, into the thought world of apocalyptic determinism?

Before settling on the conclusion that Ezekiel has trumped human freedom with divine determinism, another theme found among his utterances needs to be considered: describing moral consequences in terms of individual responsibility, a theme buttressed by admonitions detailing the duties incumbent upon the prophet as sentinel. Ezekiel rightfully has been credited with challenging the traditional notion that posterity is punished for the sins of its forebears. Ezekiel 18:2 recites the proverb, "the parents have eaten sour grapes, and the children's teeth are set on edge," only to hear God repudiate it in the powerful language of oath (v. 3) and replace the traditional notion with a new ethical principle: "it is only the person who sins that shall die" (vv. 4, 20). As if to make sure that no misunderstanding could arise, the prophet goes on to enumerate every conceivable variation on the theme (18:5–29; cf. 33:10–20). Fitting into this structure of just punishment is also the role of the sentinel to proclaim God's words of warning, for here too dereliction of duty would lead to punishment of the offending party (3:17, 21; 33:1–9).

Stress on the moral responsibility of the individual seems to run counter to the notion of history being a drama determined from beginning to end by divine fiat. Can one deduce from Ezekiel's stress on individual responsibility a conscientious effort on his part to call the people to account? If so, his task must have seemed daunting, given God's inaugural characterization of Israel as "rebels . . . impudent and stubborn" and the elaboration of that grim character profile in the prophet's lurid historical epitomes. Yet, unless for the sake of saving Ezekiel from inconsistency one engages in the arbitrary exercise of deleting all words of admonition, it must be concluded that Ezekiel followed the practice of his predecessors in urging repentance. The following passage is representative of his appeal: "Repent and turn from all your transgressions; otherwise iniquity will be your ruin. Cast away from you all the transgressions that you have committed against me, and get yourselves a new heart and a new spirit! Why will you die, O house of Israel? For I have no pleasure in the death of anyone, says the Lord GOD. Turn, then, and live" (18:30b–32).

If the above admonition captures an authentic aspect of Ezekiel's message, it would seem to follow that the dire threats of judgment in chapters 5, 6, and 7 were not perfunctory announcements of divinely preordained events, but rather part of a prophet's effort to awaken the moral conscience of his compatriots. Similarly, genuine righteous indignation can be recognized underlying the particularly scathing words he reserved for the prophet, priest, elder, king, and prince, leaders whose dereliction of duty was hastening calamity (7:25–27). Perhaps the words concluding God's ominous command to the prophet to mime the fugitive going into exile by toting baggage through the streets of Jerusalem accurately express the precarious balance in the prophet's mind between hope and futility: "Perhaps they will understand, though they are a rebellious house" (12:3; cf. 14:1–5).

How then is one to interpret the obvious tension in Ezekiel's thought between ascription to divine determination of all that had happened and would happen in history, in seeming obliteration of human freedom, and appeal to the people to exercise their responsibility as moral agents? One option is simply to say that Ezekiel contradicted himself. The other is to inquire further to see whether in the tension there resides a nuanced understanding of Israel's existential dilemma.

A starting point would be the laws that Ezekiel holds up as the standards against which Israel was to be measured. The fact that the Sabbath law takes pride of place (20:12, 20; 22:8) points in the direction of a worldview that is shaped by a ritualized understanding of reality. Also worth considering is the fact that, in drawing on other laws, he seems to rely heavily on the formulations found in the Holiness Code. For example, in addition to Sabbath observance, prohibition of idol worship, honor of parents, protection of aliens, and just weights and measures are all found in Ezekiel *and* in Leviticus 19.[7] In seeking to uncover the significance of this connection, it is well to remember the theme underlying the Holiness Code's formulation of law, pointing as it does to the goal of obedience, a theme formulated in phrases such as, "You shall be holy, for

---

7. Ezek. 20:12, 20, 24; 22:3, 7–8, 29; 47:22–23; 45:10–12; Lev. 19:3–4, 33–36.

I the LORD your God am holy" (Lev. 19:2), "for I am the LORD; I sanctify them/
you" (Lev. 22:16, 32).

For Ezekiel, as for the Holiness Code, true Israel is a holy people in whose
midst dwells the holy God. The cardinal threat to its existence is not moral turpitude, but defilement. Violation of ethical precepts can be redressed by repentance and return (Ezek. 18:27). Defilement of the land through the sacrilege of
idolatry, profanation of Sabbath, and degradation of the body through lewdness
pollute the land and repudiate the sacral order that is God's construal of the
universe, thereby forcing the withdrawal of the glory of God with the inevitable
consequence of the collapse of the nation.

One of Ezekiel's political positions, his partisan support of the exilic community, in opposition to those who remained in the land of Judah, while seeming highly arbitrary from a modern point of view, is consistent with his ritual
understanding of politics. Israel exists where God is present; so it is entirely fitting that Ezekiel's pronouncement regarding land claims was placed, in the final
redaction of the book, within the context of the description of the withdrawal of
the *kebôd yhwh* to Babylon. Ezekiel's reasoning has the precision of a syllogism.
Those remaining in Jerusalem make their case against the exiles: "They have
gone far from the LORD; to us this land is given for a possession" (Ezek. 11:15).
Ezekiel's oracle responds: "Though I removed them far away among the nations,
and though I scattered them among the countries, yet I have been a sanctuary
to them for a little while in the countries where they have gone" (11:16). The
reasoning is clear: because the land has become defiled, God's presence departs
and takes up residence elsewhere, there becoming a sanctuary for the exiles.
The political implications of this judgment are enormous; the future of Israel,
assured by God's oath, lies with the exiles, not with those left in Judah.

In 24:1–13 Ezekiel uses the symbol of a rusted cooking pot to depict the
terminal condition of Jerusalem on the eve of the final Babylonian assault. What
is interesting is that his description breaks out of the semantic field of culinary
arts into another realm that betrays his most fundamental viewpoint, the realm
of ritual defilement. Jerusalem as chef bears the epithet "the bloody city," well
earned by the crassness of its treatment of blood:[8]

> For the blood she shed is inside it;
>   she placed it on a bare rock;
> she did not pour it out on the ground,
>   to cover it with earth.
>
>   (24:7)

More serious than the alluded-to violence leading to bloodshed is the sacrilege incurred in disposing of the blood so as to defile the earth, a heinous act
that cannot go unpunished; but even as the pot is so decayed as to defy efforts to
restore it, so too divine efforts to cleanse the bloody city are to no avail:

---

8. Cf. Lev. 17:13.

Yet, when I cleansed you in your filthy lewdness,
   you did not become clean from your filth;
you shall not again be cleansed
   until I have satisfied my fury upon you
                                          (24:13)

Ezekiel's worldview, consisting of sacral order as the context for the life of obedience to the commandments, is visible also in chapter 22, where the introduction Ezekiel provides for his elaborate indictment emphasizes blood-guilt, defilement, and idolatry (22:1–4). It also explains the peculiar inclusion—among ethical laws prescribing behavior toward parents, the alien, and the poor—of accusations pertaining to uncovering a father's nakedness and to violation of women during menses (22:10; cf. 18:6). Found in no other prophetic list of indictments, their inclusion by Ezekiel points graphically to pollution and defilement as that which stains and consumes the heart of the nation.

At base, destruction of sacral order results from the obliteration of the distinctions that safeguard the sacred from the profane. Of all leadership classes in a society, the priesthood bears the primary responsibility for upholding these distinctions. It is therefore no accident that as the second bookend to the long indictment in chapter 22, Ezekiel turns to Israel's leadership, with the lengthiest accusation reserved for the priests: "Its priests have done violence to my teaching and have profaned my holy things; they have made no distinction between the holy and the common, neither have they taught the difference between the unclean and the clean, and they have disregarded my sabbaths, so that I am profaned among them" (22:26).

While princes, officials, prophets, and the people of the land have also committed heinous acts (vv. 25, 27, 28, 29), only the priests, in "making no distinction between the holy and the common, the unclean and the clean," have entered the *Walpurgisnacht* where their behavior has assaulted the very being of YHWH, "so that I am profaned among them."

Of paramount importance in analyzing Ezekiel's approach to politics are chapters 8–11, for there the indictment of those who *profane* YHWH, stated in one single verse in chapter 22, receives elaborate treatment that spans four chapters and culminates in a description of the consequence of YHWH's being profaned *among them*: namely, God's glory departs from their midst and migrates to join the exiles in Babylon. Language is pushed to its limit in a description of the most horrendous abominations imaginable that have become the surrogate rituals of the temple! In the sanctuary that God had chosen as his dwelling place, mock worship is being performed to idols deriving from Canaanite, Egyptian, and Mesopotamian religion, with the officiants taking comfort in the assurance that "[t]he LORD does not see us, the LORD has forsaken the land" (8:12). The bitter irony of course is that they are as wrong on the former point as they are right on the latter. While YHWH in fact sees sharply and in lurid detail what is going on, he states tersely the effect of their blasphemies, "to drive me far from my sanctuary" (8:6).

The shocking drama presented in Ezekiel 8–11 provides a framework for the previously raised question: Does the tension between Ezekiel's appeal to the people to repent and his announcement of a judgment that gives the appearance of an inevitable result of divine determination constitute a blatant contradiction? The fact that Ezekiel's position vis-à-vis repentance resembles more that of Jonah than Isaiah or Amos could lead one to such a conclusion. However, once Ezekiel's ritual construal of reality is factored in, an alternative answer suggests itself. While he dutifully discharges his obligations as sentinel by attacking the iniquity of the people, it would seem that on a deeper level he is conscious of a perduring defilement that contradicts the sacral order constituting the sine qua non of the nation's existence. The remedy for such defilement exists within the ritual structure of the temple, where God has installed priests responsible for sacrifice and atonement. What happens when the temple and the priesthood themselves become defiled? God, who cannot dwell amid defilement, is forced to leave, with the collapse of the nation following as an inevitable consequence!

What of the oath by which God had committed himself to the covenant binding Israel and God? Since the covenant is of divine origin, like God's holiness it cannot be annulled. But given the nation's obduracy, there is only one available recourse, namely, God's directly assuming administration of the purifying rituals that are capable of ridding the people of the curse of defilement, rituals entailing both the refining fires of military conquest and the cleansing ablutions of sacred water.

While on first appearance, therefore, it may seem that Ezekiel's worldview is deterministic, leaving no room for politics in which humans play a role, deeper scrutiny reveals that Ezekiel's entire strategy involves politics. To be sure, on a socioeconomic level, Ezekiel's involvement seems anemic compared to that of Isaiah and Jeremiah. But if one evaluates Ezekiel against another standard, that of ritual politics, a richly detailed plan comes into view. It divides into two parts, a description of the past and a program for the future. The present, sandwiched in between, is dominated by the rapidly unfolding calamity, bringing to a climax the wages of a past of unmitigated iniquity and defilement. As such, it leaves little opportunity for social reform, in the classical prophetic sense. This explains Ezekiel's concentration on past and future, a point corroborated by the sudden, unmediated shift in his historical reviews from shocking descriptions of Israel's depraved past to glorious pictures of the impending reign of peace.

Noteworthy in the contrast between past and future is Ezekiel's ascription of agency. In his historical résumés, the people of Israel are the actors, often under the guise of a lewd maiden. In the visionary descriptions of the future age, God is the actor. In the former case, the result of human action is unmitigated disaster; in the latter, divine action produces an eternal paradise.

Multiple are the traditions and themes gathered by Ezekiel into his picture of the future. Principal among them are King David, the Jerusalem priesthood, Sinai, Eden, and Day of Atonement.

Ezekiel's portrait of the future consists of two phases.[9] In the first, described in portions of chapters 34 and 36 and in the powerful dry-bones image of the revivification of the people Israel in chapter 37, God takes several actions to remedy a situation that from a human vantage point is hopeless. First, God rids the people of the shepherds (i.e., leaders) who have exploited and scattered the sheep, and God personally becomes their shepherd, mercifully attentive to their wounds and needs. Structurally, the picture is one of direct, unmediated theocracy. Without apparent concern with consistency, YHWH announces, "I will set up over them one shepherd, my servant David. . . . And I, the LORD, will be their God, and my servant David shall be prince among them" (34:23–24).

Next, God addresses the proven depravity and inability for self-correction of the people, a condition described in chapter 20 as calling for obliteration in the manner of the generation of the flood, were it not for God's concern for the divine name. Since Ezekiel described the corruption of the people primarily in the ritual language of defilement, it comes as no surprise that in chapter 36 YHWH's intervention is depicted in terms of the ritual ministrations assigned in Leviticus 16 to the high priest on the Day of Atonement: "I will sprinkle clean water upon you, and you shall be clean from all your uncleannesses, and from all your idols I will cleanse you" (36:25).

What assurance is there that though cleansed, the oft-repeated reversion to defilement and deprivation would not recur? In a novel move, YHWH introduces a radical solution: "A new heart I will give you, and a new spirit I will put within you; and I will remove from your body the heart of stone and give you a heart of flesh. I will put my spirit within you, and make you follow my statutes and be careful to observe my ordinances. Then you shall live in the land that I gave to your ancestors; and you shall be my people, and I will be your God" (36:26–29).

In this manner, the cardinal divine attributes Ezekiel ascribed to God are reconciled with the prophet's deeply pessimistic portrait of human nature. God upholds the covenant with Israel to which he has bound himself by oath. God satisfies the conditions prerequisite to his actions: "It is not for your sake that I will act" (v. 32). The lofty divine epistemology expressed repeatedly in the book is preserved: "Then the nations that are left all around you shall know" (v. 36).

---

9. The appearance of two phases, the first described in chapters 34–37 and the second in chapters 40–48, may stem in part from the final editorial shaping of the book. It seems probable that the basic vision in chapters 34 and 36—of future restoration under a Davidic prince ruling on God's behalf over a divinely cleansed and obedient people—stems from Ezekiel, like the basic program in chapters 40–48 of a restored temple community made possible by the return of the glory of God to Jerusalem. If this is the case, one is on solid textual ground in describing Ezekiel's vision of the future as consisting of God's ritual cleansing of Israel, followed by his presentation of the plans for the restored community. In political terms, this would constitute a blending of direct and mediated theocracy, construed along sacerdotal lines.

At the same time, the problem of human incorrigibility will be solved: "I will make you follow my statutes." Out of all this emerges a new human, immunized from relapse by the implantation of a new heart and secured in obedience to God's will through the gift of a new spirit, the latter attribute vividly illustrated in the vision that immediately follows, the vision of the God breathing his spirit into the dry bones.

The theological and anthropological prerequisites are thereby in place for the concrete implementation of the restoration. With the curse annulled, the fruitfulness of the land will be restored like Eden and the devastated cities rebuilt (36:29–36). Northern and southern kingdoms will be reunited under David (37:15–26). Finally, the crowning jewel is set in place: "I will make a covenant of peace with them; it shall be an everlasting covenant with them; and I will bless them and multiply them, and will set my sanctuary among them forevermore" (37:26).

From the rigorous ritual perspective of Ezekiel, the conditions have been met for the one remaining move necessary for the restoration of Jerusalem, the return of the glory of God. As Ezekiel had witnessed the departure of the *kebôd yhwh* in 11:22–23, so too he witnesses its return in 43:1–5: "and the glory of the LORD filled the temple." In contrast to certain other visions of the restoration of Jerusalem that remain suspended on an ethereal level,[10] Ezekiel's vision includes a blueprint complete in every detail, one, moreover, that is to be made public and acted upon (40:4). But Ezekiel's blending of themes drawn from the wilderness and Sinai traditions with the lavish imagery of the Eden myth (chap. 47) assures that the resulting picture depicts no mere earthly habitation, but one worthy of the Holy One who is creator and sovereign of all that exists and suitable for the people that he gathers from the nations.

The ritual/mythic aspects of the program of restoration presented in Ezekiel 40–48 must not obscure the specific political measures it seeks to implement, which enables us to trace a move in his vision of the future from a political model of direct theocracy to mediated theocracy. For Ezekiel, while audaciously describing a brilliant new era of peace and prosperity for Israel, does not neglect depicting the institutions and political arrangements that will implement God's universal rule within the mundane structures of human rule. Since he names David as the shepherd chosen by God to represent his just rule, it is obvious that Ezekiel does not jettison the Davidic tradition. However, he does stipulate provisions to guard against the illegitimate forms of mediation that led to the downfall of Judea's kings and the ruin of the nation, including idolatry, apostasy, and self-indulgence at the cost of their subjects.

The first provision surfaces in the key verse, 34:24: "And I, the LORD, will be their God, and my servant David shall be prince [*nāśî'*] among them." Ezekiel's suppression of the term *melek* (king)—which as was pointed out in chapter 11 resonates both etymologically and thematically with the ideology of absolute

10. Isa. 60:17–22; Rev. 21:1–4.

monarchy—in favor of *nāśī'* (prince) clearly is a conscious move to return the political office of "chief of state" to its traditional, limited Yahwistic origins.

Ezekiel's picture of political structures in force during Israel's infancy not surprisingly derives from the Priestly Writing, which hallows his program with the powerful warrant of Mosaic authorship. In Numbers 1 and 2, Moses follows YHWH's instructions for organizing the tribes, each under its designated *nāśī'*. As Jon Levenson has correctly observed, in designating his head of state as *nāśī'*, "Ezekiel sought to bring the institution of monarchy under the governance of the Sinaitic covenant."[11] Though the specific form of the restraints Ezekiel imposed on the Davidic office differed from the formulation in Deuteronomy 17:14–20,[12] the underlying intention is similar. In relation to the Torah, Israelite rulers do not hold an exceptional position, but are subject to the commandments like any other citizen (43:7; 45:8–9).

The particular ritual concerns of Ezekiel come to expression in the second major provision he stipulates against the abuse of royal authority. Banished will be the Solomonic architectural linking of the holy (i.e., the sanctuary) and the profane (i.e., the royal courts) and the accompanying practice of burying kings at the threshold of the temple (43:6–9).[13] That Ezekiel was particularly concerned to end the de facto control by the kings of Judah over the temple cult is also evident in one detail he adds to his plan for allotment of the land. Whereas in all other respects it is modeled after his favored Priestly Writing archetype, he creates a buffer between Judah (the royal tribe) and Aaron (the holy priesthood) by inserting between them the Levites (minor priests) (48:9–14). No other detail could indicate more clearly the overweening liturgical importance for Ezekiel of maintaining adequate separation between the sacred and the profane. One readily recalls Ezekiel's rebuke in chapter 22 of the Jerusalem priests who "made no distinction between the holy and the common, . . . the unclean and the clean" (22:26).

EZEKIEL'S POLITICAL MESSAGE: FOREIGN POLICY

Ezekiel's position regarding foreign policy arose from the same core of ritual-theological principles that informed his domestic policy. Prosperity and security depended on a corporate life of sanctity providing the setting for God's dwelling in the midst of the people. Since Israel had hardened itself into a position of repudiating the Torah, and its priestly leadership had degraded the ritual center responsible for atonement into an idolatrous mockery of God, the destruction of the land was inevitable. It was clear to Ezekiel, as it was to Jeremiah, that the divinely designated instrument of judgment was Babylon.

11. Jon D. Levenson, *Theology of the Program of Restoration of Ezekiel 40–48*, Harvard Semitic Monograph Series 10 (Missoula, MT: Scholars Press, 1976), 69.
12. See chap. 12 above.
13. See Zimmerli, *Ezekiel 1*, 59, and Zimmerli, *Fiery Throne*, 55.

From this core Ezekiel consistently extrapolated his foreign policy. The first point was that any effort to resist the Babylonian armies was futile, since they ultimately were under the command not of a human leader but the divine sovereign of all nations. The second point, congruous with the positions of Isaiah during the earlier Syro-Ephraimite and Assyrian crises and of Ezekiel's contemporary Jeremiah, was that strategies involving defense alliances with other nations were doomed to failure, again because they pitted human force against divine decree.

Ezekiel 17 contains the prophet's classic pronouncement against the decision made in 592 by Israel's leadership, to appeal to Egypt for aid as a part of an anti-Babylonian alliance (see Jer. 27). Ezekiel is instructed by the Lord to "propound a riddle, and speak an allegory to the house of Israel" (Ezek. 17:2), and the ensuing utterance is about a vine and two eagles. The first eagle breaks off the top of a cedar and carries it off to "a land of trade, . . . a city of merchants" (v. 4). After this figurative account of Nebuchadnezzar's deposing Jehoiachin to Babylon, the poem describes the eagle taking a seed from the land and planting it, where it becomes a low vine, referring to the Babylonian king's setting up Zedekiah as vassal. Then enters the second eagle, who transplanted that vine "to good soil by abundant waters," but the poem ends with foreboding questions about its destiny, questions that convey Ezekiel's dire warning against Zedekiah's basing the nation's defense against Babylon on an alliance with Psammetichus II of Egypt.

The alliance came to naught, as Nebuchadnezzar ruthlessly reimposed control over the region. But Zedekiah's heedlessness to both prophetic warnings and the harsh lessons of history was remarkable. His military dalliance with Egypt was resumed several years later, and indeed, as reported in Jeremiah 37, Psammetichus's successor Hophra in 588 led his army against the Babylonian forces besieging Jerusalem, only to retreat back to the homeland, thereby leaving Jerusalem at the mercy of the superior power of Nebuchadnezzar. The warning to King Zedekiah issued by both Jeremiah and Ezekiel was thus fulfilled: "Pharaoh's army, which set out to help you, is going to return to its own land, to Egypt" (Jer. 37:7b).

Jeremiah's further commentary also coincides with Ezekiel's position, as is seen in a comparison of Ezekiel 30:20–26 with the following passage: "Do not deceive yourselves, saying, 'The Chaldeans will surely go away from us,' for they will not go away. Even if you defeated the whole army of Chaldeans who are fighting against you, and there remained of them only wounded men in their tents, they would rise up and burn this city with fire" (Jer. 37:9–10). The situation is the same as that faced by Gideon, but in reverse! Numbers and military might are meaningless against those drawn to battle at God's command, whether the combatants belong to the tribes of Israel or to a foreign army.

The section of the book of Ezekiel that deals most extensively with foreign affairs is chapters 25–32. Here condemnation of Egypt is developed extensively and unsparingly (chaps. 29–32), reflecting a bitterness no doubt crystallized by

the retreat in 587 of Pharaoh's army, which left Jerusalem isolated in its exposure to the assault of Nebuchadnezzar's ruthless forces:

> . . . [Y]ou were a staff of reed
>   to the house of Israel;
> when they grasped you with the hand, you broke,
>   and tore all their shoulders.
>   (Ezek. 29:6b–7a)

Though it is difficult to sort out Ezekiel's words from those of later contributors, consistently through the oracles against Egypt the once-powerful
nation on the Nile is condemned in strongest terms for the hubris by which it
claimed divine status in a manner reminiscent of the king of Babylon in Isaiah
14:12–20.

We have noted earlier that a sharp turn in Ezekiel's message coincides with
the fall of the nation in 587. God's judgment was not a negation of the covenant
with Israel, but the means by which the obstacles to that covenant, constructed
by Israel's obduracy, were removed. We have also seen how God took personal
charge of transforming depraved Israel into an obedient people. It remains to be
seen what effects this turn had on the position taken by Ezekiel and subsequent
redactors toward neighboring nations besides Egypt.

Most notable about the collection of oracles against foreign nations is the
absence of Babylon. In contrast to Jeremiah (and those who supplemented his
words in Jer. 50–51), Ezekiel does not look beyond the role Babylon played in
God's plan as the instrument of divine punishment. After 587, to be sure, Ezekiel turned to a description of the future, but as we have seen, it is an idealized
future, in which restored Israel is described in terms blending imagery from the
Priestly Writing's picture of the tribes in the wilderness with motifs drawn from
mythical Eden. This disinterest in the details of post-587 history is also to be
seen in his failure to mention Nebuchadnezzar's installation of Gedaliah as governor, the latter's being murdered by Ishmael son of Nethaniah, and subsequent
events in the land of Judea.[14] The promise of restoration resides in the exiles,
and from that perspective the future is depicted categorically along two lines: the
glorious reestablishment of the sacral community in its land, and the elimination of the threat posed by other nations.

Accordingly, the foreign policy that comes to expression in the oracles against
the nations is driven by an idealism that is the opposite, dark side of the brilliant promise of restoration found in Ezekiel 40–48. Second in coverage to
Egypt is Tyre (chaps. 26–28), first depicted as exulting over the fall of Jerusalem
(26:2), but then condemned, like Egypt, for its cruelty to other nations (26:17)
and its hubris (28:2). In 28:12–19, Tyre's previous dwelling in Eden is lavishly described, but whereas Ezekiel in chapter 37 describes in Edenic terms the

---

14. The fact that the book of Jeremiah (chaps. 40–41) describes the events of this period in detail
is readily explained by that prophet's personal involvement.

restored land that Israel will occupy, it is Tyre's expulsion from Eden that is the theme of the oracle in Ezekiel 28.

Later tradents filled out the number of foreign nations condemned to seven by adding oracles against Ammon, Moab, Edom, and the Philistines in chapter 25 and Sidon in 28:21–23. The former four are attacked for their gleeful, exploitative response to Israel's fall. The thematic kernel of this group lies in the accusation leveled against Edom, who "acted revengefully against the house of Judah," which reflects its combining cowardice and treachery in despoiling a land left defenseless by the Babylonian devastation, an act that earned for Edom the distinction of being depicted as archenemy of God's people in numerous Second Temple period writings. The Sidon oracle amounts to a "rider" attached to Tyre to fill out a traditional poetic parallel.

Running as a leitmotif throughout the oracles against the nations is the proof-saying "then you/they shall know that I am the LORD," which integrates all of the pronouncements dealing with foreign matters into the same theologoumenon that governed Ezekiel's treatment of domestic affairs: one principle alone determines the course of history, the principle of God's self-glorification, which is Ezekiel's unique rendition of the classic theocratic principle of ancient Israel's theo-politics.

SUMMARY OBSERVATIONS

Ezekiel's central political message came to expression in *theological* terms: without a sound spiritual core, the nation was doomed. The specific shape of his theo-political message was determined by his distinct, priestly worldview; that is, it was construed in terms of ritual defilement and purity.

Significant in Ezekiel's message is the tension between one explanation of the destiny of Israel strictly in terms of unilateral divine activity and another that factors in the importance of human attitudes, decisions, and actions, that is, the tension between direct and mediated theocracy. This tension can be depicted most succinctly by contrasting two quotations: "Repent and turn from all your transgressions. . . . [G]et yourselves a new heart and a new spirit!" (18:30–31). "A new heart I will give you, and a new spirit I will put within you . . . and make you follow my statutes" (36:26–27).

The apparent conflict between these two statements must be analyzed against the background of Ezekiel's emphasis on God's glory and the divine name as the basis of all events, an emphasis buttressed by the centrality in his thought of "knowledge of God." Ezekiel does not eliminate the importance of human agency, which, after all, is an essential component of the mutuality of divine and human relations in covenant tradition upon which Ezekiel repeatedly draws.[15]

---

15. The term "covenant" occurs frequently: 16:8, 59, 60, 61, 62; 17:13, 14, 15, 16, 18, 19; 34:25; 37:26; 44:7. The covenant formulary appears in: 11:20; 14:11; 36:28; 37:23, 27.

The issue with which Ezekiel struggles is Israel's historically proven inability to obey, an issue that leads to the incisive intervention of God in providing a new heart and a new spirit. But if God in turn will "make you follow my statutes," is not human freedom annulled by divine determination? Ezekiel's message avoids falling entirely into such predestination by a subtle move. Immediately on the heels of the description of God's replacing a heart of stone (i.e., forgetfulness and hence disobedience) with a heart of flesh, appears this sentence: "Then you shall remember your evil ways, and your dealings that were not good; and you shall loathe yourselves for your iniquities and your abominable deeds" (36:31).

God's initiative has not destroyed the human agent, but restored it to wholeness by reviving memory of sinful deeds leading to a feeling of shame.[16] Incorrigible Israel was characterized by denial of all wrong. Obedient Israel has been given the capacity to repent and claim its new heart and spirit by the restoration of knowledge, knowledge of who God is ("that you may know . . .") and knowledge of who Israel is ("you shall be my people, and I will be your God"). In light of that restored knowledge comes awareness of both its lostness and the path to redemption: "I will sprinkle clean water upon you, and you shall be clean from all your uncleannesses" (36:25).

While Ezekiel's penetrating analysis of the ambiguities of human moral agency pushes biblical thought in important new directions, his exposition of foreign policy remains traditional. One aspect of that exposition, which continues the line of thought of his contemporary Jeremiah, while on the surface perhaps suggesting fatalism and isolationism, is much deeper. His message that resistance to the Babylonian attack was futile (since Babylon was acting as an agent of divine judgment) was based on an assessment of Israel's moral condition as being beyond correction, short of the shock of lost nationhood and subjection to a foreign power.

Of course, whether one regards his position as treason or an act of profound moral courage and even patriotism depends on how one evaluates his assessment of the moral and spiritual state of his nation. One's evaluation of his stand against any anti-Babylonian alliance would be similarly determined. While the issues raised here require further reflection in light of the hermeneutical guidelines outlined in the epilogue of this book, it should be noted here that Ezekiel's position is not that of a maverick, but of one standing solidly in the tradition of the prophets, which has elicited theological thought through the ages.[17]

The final facet of Ezekiel's foreign policy that requires comment comes to light in the so-called "oracles against the nations" (chaps. 25–32). The case of Egypt is unique, since through the analysis of Ezekiel 17:1–10 we have seen that his negative attitude toward the "aid" offered by Egypt was shaped by actual

16. For an insightful treatment of moral identity in Ezekiel, see Jacqueline E. Lapsley, *Can These Bones Live? The Problem of the Moral Self in the Book of Ezekiel* (Berlin/New York: Walter de Gruyter, 2000).

17. One can call to mind, for example, Luther's category of "the left hand of God" and Bonhoeffer's raising the question after the Nazi occupation of Paris of the possible providential role of Hitler.

historical events. To a different category, it seems, belongs the condemnation of Tyre, Ammon, Moab, Edom, and the Philistines. Again, though, Edom is to some degree a special case, due to its role in the sacking of Jerusalem after its fall. Here it seems that the most one can do is to seek to understand these utterances, in which later voices are added to those of Ezekiel, in light of the profound hurt to national pride suffered in the calamity of 587. In effect, the serious question of the threat to both national and religious identity posed by foreign nations is answered by a categorical divine judgment upon all of them, which amounts to the kind of dualistic construal of the world that characterizes later apocalyptic and Manichean thought. To go beyond such empathy by seeking to find any kind of theological guideline to the treatment of foreign nations that can be of use to later generations seems unpromising.

Chapter 18

Isaiah 40–55

Exile and the Renewal of Hope

Restoration

As can be seen clearly in the message of the prophet Ezekiel, the impact of the Babylonian conquest of Judah on the political and religious institutions of Israel was enormous. In this chapter, we shall move beyond the magisterial vision of restored Israel found in the book of Ezekiel to several other projections of the future recorded in writings from the exilic and early postexilic periods.

Within the beautiful poetic message contained in Isaiah 40–55 from the anonymous writer of the Babylonian exilic community commonly called Second Isaiah are found a number of divine pronouncements that, while not constituting anything as complete as the program found in Ezekiel 40–48, nevertheless present an audacious sketch of political organization that the author envisions as arising out of Israel's punishing experience of military defeat and captivity in a foreign land.[1] Second Isaiah interprets the tragedy of the past as God's judgment on a people who stubbornly refused to abide by the Torah given to them by God (42:23–25). In light of that bleak history, this prophet describes a reconstitution

---

1. The position initially presented by C. C. Torrey in 1930 and subsequently reformulated by James D. Smart (*History and Theology in Second Isaiah: A Commentary on Isaiah 35, 40–66* [London: Epworth Press, 1967])—namely, that Isaiah 40–55 stems not from a leader of the exilic community in Babylon but was written in Judah—remains unconvincing to most biblical historians.

of Israel under forms of leadership designed to safeguard against the failed ways of the past and to build a community on the foundation of divine justice and compassion under the terms of a renewed covenant.

One group of pronouncements confronts head-on the most stinging proof of the political failure of the Judean monarchy, the fact that the nation, deprived of its homeland and its religious center, now lived as a captive community in Babylon. If the kings of the Davidic house had proven themselves to be helpless before the military might of the Babylonians, what possible source of deliverance could be discerned on the geopolitical horizon?

In a move that is truly astonishing, when viewed against the popular legends celebrating the martial prowess of the founder of the Davidic house (2 Sam. 5–23) and the strict injunction in the Torah not to "put a foreigner over you" (Deut. 17:15), Second Isaiah describes as the agent anointed by God to deliver Israel from its captors not a native ruler but the ascendant Persian monarch Cyrus, who in Isaiah 45:1 is designated by YHWH in terms traditionally reserved for Israel's native leaders, *měšîḥî* (my messiah).[2] That Second Isaiah could identify the military objectives of a foreign ruler with the purposes of YHWH is noteworthy in two respects. It indicates that the prophet is an astute observer of international events. It also represents a dynamic theology of history in its placing the traditional Israelite notion of God's involvement in the affairs of this world within an international framework that stretches older categories in new directions.

Recent studies have pointed to numerous examples within the Hebrew Bible of the reinterpretation of earlier laws so as to make them relevant to new situations.[3] At times, the new application preserves in substance the meaning of the earlier law; at other times, it radically changes or even reverses the sense of the older formulation.[4] Michael Fishbane, whose scholarship has played a pioneering role in stimulating such studies, captures the dynamic of inner-biblical exegesis in the following concise formulation, in which *traditum* refers to "the content of tradition" and *traditio* to "the process of transmission": "while the *traditio* culturally revitalizes the *traditum*, and gives new strength to the original revelation, it also potentially undermines it."[5]

2. Following the Septuagint (LXX).

3. A particularly convincing example of this approach is Bernard M. Levenson, *Deuteronomy and the Hermeneutics of Legal Innovation* (New York and Oxford: Oxford University Press, 1997).

4. This phenomenon is demonstrated by Joachim Schaper in reference to the reinterpretation of Deut. 23:2–9 by Ezek. 44:6–9 on the one hand and by Isa. 56:1–8 on the other ("Rereading the Law: Inner-Biblical Exegesis of Divine Oracles in Ezekiel 44 and Isaiah 56," in *Recht und Ethik im Alten Testament*, ed. Bernard M. Levinson, Eckart Otto, and Walter Dietrich [Münster: LIT, 2004], 125–44). The starting point for Schaper's study is a question raised by Michael Fishbane: "Could it be that Ezek 44:6–9 is an application of this pentateuchal passage [Deut 23:2–4] to exclude such types [i.e. "foreigners and uncircumcised males"] . . . and that Isa 56:7, which announces that YHWH will bring (*hăbîʾôtîm*) the foreigners and the uncircumcised to perform holocaust and meat sacrifices (cf. Ezek 44:11!), is a rebuttal of these exclusionist claims *on the basis of the same text?*" Michael Fishbane, *Biblical Interpretation in Ancient Israel* (Oxford: Clarendon, 1985), 142n98.

5. Fishbane, *Interpretation*, 15.

It is not only the laws of the past that were the object of reinterpretation, but also the central topoi of Israel's Epic. In Isaiah 43, YHWH reveals that the deliverance to come derives from divine initiative, which is illuminated by describing it in terms of the earlier exodus from Egypt (Isa. 43:15–17). Then, as if to release the imagination from bondage to older forms of thought and to free it to imagine daring new initiatives, YHWH announces:

> Do not remember the former things,
>   or consider the things of old.
> I am about to do a new thing;
>   now it springs forth, do you not perceive it?
> I will make a way in the wilderness
>   and rivers in the desert.
>
> (43:18–19)

Taken together, verses 15–17 and 18–19 provide a classic example of the inner-biblical dialectic of simultaneously *revitalizing* and *undermining*. The same God who according to the Epic delivered Israel's ancestors from slavery in Egypt is about to act again on behalf of the Babylonian exiles, but in a dramatically new way: not through the agency of a native-born equivalent of Moses but through a Persian warrior named Cyrus, designated by YHWH as his *messiah*! The revitalization of the exodus motif simultaneously serves to undermine another tradition, the theologoumenon developed within the royal court and the Jerusalem temple of God's unique bond with the Davidic king (e.g., Pss. 2 and 89), according to which the king was the recipient of God's eternal covenant and of special divine blessings. For, as indicated by Isaiah 55:3, that covenant and those special blessings are now extended to the *entire* community:

> Incline your ear, and come to me;
>   listen, so that you may live.
> I will make with you an everlasting covenant,
>   my steadfast, sure love for David.

On the basis of the texts we have thus far considered, is there any indication that Second Isaiah addressed the kinds of concrete institutional structures that are prerequisites for rebuilding a political body? Though Ezekiel's reversion back to the figure of the *nāśîʾ* ("prince") from the Priestly Writing's version of the Epic implied a sharp curtailment of the prerogatives of the Judahite kings, it at least drew upon a political model of Israel's past, namely, charismatic rule. But what model is suggested by the declaration that, in place of the Davidic king, *all* who harkened to the prophetic call would become recipients of the eternal covenant and its blessings, a declaration elaborated on in Isaiah 61:5, where the priestly office is similarly democratized and in Isaiah 56:1–7, where Deuteronomic law is reversed to admit foreigners and eunuchs into the temple?

While it is undeniable that the message of Second Isaiah projects a highly idealistic vision of the nation's future, it seems unwarranted to exclude it from the body of texts promising to illuminate the range of political reflections that arose in the aftermath of the Babylonian destruction. Indeed, the verses that may go the furthest in shedding light on the question of the political model guiding Second Isaiah's thought are the most idealistic and mysterious of all, the so-called "Servant of YHWH" passages in 42:1–7; 49:1–6; 50:4–9; 52:13–53:12.

In the first seven verses of Isaiah 42, one hears echoes of traditional descriptions of the ideal Davidic king (e.g., Isa. 11:1–5): YHWH's anointed one is endowed with the spirit of YHWH and will serve faithfully as an agent of God's justice. But a notable difference is this: the king in Isaiah 11 is imbued with might and approaches his judiciary duties in the incisive manner characteristic of royalty:

> [H]e shall strike the earth with the rod of his mouth,
>   and with the breath of his lips he shall kill the wicked.
> (11:4b)

The administrative style of YHWH's servant, according to Isaiah 42:2–3, breaks with the model of royal might and splendor:

> He will not cry or lift up his voice,
>   or make it heard in the street;
> a bruised reed he will not break,
>   and a dimly burning wick he will not quench.

The astute reader may retort that in the second Servant Song the Servant is given a "mouth like a sharp sword," and is described as "a polished arrow" (49:2). That the rhetorical force of these terms differs from the thrust of Isaiah 11, however, is indicated emphatically by the complaint of failure uttered by the Servant in 49:4. The resulting paradox of divine commissioning and human powerlessness is pushed further in verse 6: The scope of the Servant's charge is extended beyond Israel to the nations, indeed, "to the end of the earth." Finally, the tension approaches the breaking point in verse 7, where the Servant is portrayed as "one deeply despised, abhorred by the nations, the slave of rulers," before whom, nevertheless, "kings shall see and stand up, princes, and they shall prostrate themselves," not, to be sure, because of any intrinsic attribute of the Servant, but "because of the LORD, who is faithful, the Holy One of Israel, who has chosen you."

The language of chosenness and of agency in the execution of divine justice in 49:1–7, as well as in 42:1, suggests that the commission of the Servant, while clearly not in the customary mode of kingship, nevertheless addresses the same areas of human governance covered in an earlier period by the Davidic kings. The final two Servant passages press even further the emphatically counterregal qualities of this chosen one. According to 50:6, he submits to the physical abuse and insults of adversaries and, more remarkably still, according to the last of the four Servant passages, he gives up his life as a sin offering for the healing of what is described metaphorically as a straying flock of sheep (53:4–12).

In the interpretation of any body of literature, it is important to strive to understand the issues being addressed and the mode of discourse being applied to the task by the author. In asking of Isaiah 40–55 what it contributes to our knowledge of politics in the Bible, this much seems clear: (1) The Servant Songs seek to address perceived failures of earlier structures of governance with statements, authoritatively presented as divine pronouncements, that propound a radically new vision of governance. (2) Since this new vision is presented in terms whose idealism transcends even the mytho-theocratic construal of the future proposed by Ezekiel 40–48, great care must be taken in extrapolating from it data deemed relevant to the description of biblical politics as a whole or, even more emphatically, insights bearing on the relevance of biblical politics to contemporary political theology. We shall return to the question of abiding relevance in the epilogue.

As for the question of the place occupied by Second Isaiah's vision within the larger picture of biblical politics, we find that it leads directly to the next topic, namely, the political program of restoration sponsored by the prophets Haggai and Zechariah.

Chapter 19

Haggai and Zechariah
A Temple-Centered Vision of Restoration

LOCATION WITHIN PROPHETIC TRADITION

Often emphasis in biblical scholarship on the points of difference existing between different biblical writers and traditions obscures the common ground that they share. Before considering the next political stage of development emerging out of the Babylonian conquest and the exile, it is important to recognize that in the case of Jeremiah, Ezekiel, Second Isaiah, and the prophets Zechariah and Haggai, a common grounding in the national Epic, the Torah, and prophetic tradition is clearly evident. Consider these words from the passage introducing the book of Zechariah:

> Do not be like your ancestors, to whom the former prophets proclaimed, "Thus says the LORD of hosts, Return from your evil ways and from your evil deeds." But they did not hear or heed me, says the LORD. Your ancestors, where are they? And the prophets, do they live forever? But my words and my statutes, which I commanded my servants the prophets, did they not overtake your ancestors? So they repented and said, "The LORD of hosts has dealt with us according to our ways and deeds, just as he planned to do." (Zech. 1:4–6)

In addressing his audience in the year 520, Zechariah made it clear that his message stood in continuity with "the former prophets" and that he, like them, stood in the service of the "words and statutes" of the Lord of hosts. Historical events were not the result of blind chance, but were influenced by the conduct of a nation in response to divine law. In the final two chapters of his collection of prophecy, Zechariah repeats his sense of standing in a particular tradition by again making reference to "the former prophets" (7:7) and restating God's words and statutes (7:8–14 and 8:14–17). In this way he created a framework for his visions and accompanying oracles that depicted the universe in which Israel lived as a moral universe. The horrific calamity that resulted in loss of nationhood stemmed from the noncompliance of earlier generations to God's word delivered by the prophets. Based on this harsh lesson from the past, Zechariah fashioned his message as a call to repentance, a summons for the people to return to a life of obedience. The same is true of Haggai, as indicated by his extended indictment and call to action in 1:3–11. To a large extent, both of these reformers were firmly rooted in the tradition of the prophets who preceded them.

While it would be remiss to overlook the affinities between Zechariah and Haggai and their predecessors, it also would be misleading to overlook hints in their proclamations of a transformation in political policy that was to characterize the century following the exile, a transformation in no small part due to international political developments resulting from the rapid ascendancy of the Persian Empire and ensuing repercussions within the Jewish community. In the verses from the first chapter of Zechariah cited above, the distinction between former prophets and prophets of the present points not only to continuity but to change as well, as highlighted by the description of God's "words and statutes" as capable of "overtaking" the sinner, a notion echoed by the retributive activity ascribed to the huge flying scroll in Zechariah 5:1–4.

In complementary manner, the role of prophet was diminishing at the same time that the stature of the Torah as a distinct entity functioning to define and maintain community order was being enhanced, a process leading up to the situation in the time of Ezra, when the Torah of Moses had come to enjoy the status of the legal charter of the Jewish community. This new status, in turn, was in step with the official policy of the Persians requiring subject provinces and subprovinces to produce an official code of law defining a standard of conduct capable of providing the stability and reliability required of a vassal state in a vast and often restive empire.

The process of consolidating the legal norms of Jewish religion went hand in hand with changes in leadership roles in the decades following the return of exiles to Judah. Whereas during the period of monarchy Israel's prophets played a central role in alerting the nation to the social and political implications of divine will, on the basis of appeal to existing codes like the Book of the Covenant and Deuteronomy as well as through the pronouncement of fresh oracles, in the period during which the Torah was being codified as the community's definitive norm the role of prophet was eclipsed by that of savants trained to interpret the law and apply it to new situations.

Though neither biblical nor extrabiblical sources provide sufficient evidence to enable us to reconstruct a clear succession, these savants over the course of the following centuries from the Persian to the Hellenistic and Roman periods would be designated variously as priests, Levites, scribes, seers, and finally rabbis. Later we shall return to the topic of the enhanced status of Torah and the pivotal importance that this ascribed to those trained in its interpretation. But first, more must be said about the fluidity and change that characterized the last third of the sixth century.

HISTORICAL CONTEXT

The reshaping of Judah into a commonwealth subject to a foreign power did not occur without intracommunity strains, since accompanying the authority to interpret and apply the law to new situations came enhanced influence and prestige. Nor did tradition provide an unequivocal answer to the question of who was the legitimate interpreter of divine law, as can be seen in the stories in the Pentateuch of conflict between different leadership groups, as well as in the conflicting versions of priestly genealogies in the Pentateuch, 1 Chronicles, Ezra, and Nehemiah. In fact, the past could be drawn upon to support the claims of different groups. (1) Had not God clearly declared that the sons of David were his chosen representatives and guardians of his house of worship?[1] (2) Had not God spoken to his people in the past through his servants the prophets, from Moses down to Jeremiah and Ezekiel?[2] (3) Who was it that stood before God at the altar and administered atonement for the sins of the people? Was it not the priests of the family of Zadok?[3] (4) Finally not to be forgotten were the Levites, who faithfully taught God's law to the people and who unequivocally pointed out to them the alternatives between which they were obliged to choose, obedience and life or disobedience and death.[4]

When one combines the rich diversity present in Israel's religious traditions with the sea change thrust upon the Jewish community by the new reality of Persian hegemony—that is, a foreign power that simultaneously encouraged the development of local religious customs and laws and imposed an absolute oath of loyalty and a heavy levy of tax and tribute on its vassal states—it is not hard to understand why the period from Zechariah and Haggai to Nehemiah and Ezra was a time of flux. From this time came a reordering of institutional and leadership structures that not only assured the survival of the Jewish community through the Persian period, but sketched the contours of a polity that would

1. 2 Sam. 7:8–17; Ps. 110.
2. Deut. 18:15–22; Hos. 6:5.
3. Ezek. 40:46; 43:18–21.
4. Deut. 33:8–11.

remain essentially intact within the centuries of development of rabbinical Judaism, beginning with the Pharisees.

In a process of developing institutional structures and orders of leadership that would meet the new challenges presented by the Persian hegemony, different groups drew upon the precedents of the past that they believed held most promise, both for their personal interests and for the viability of the community at large. Though the literary deposit of the period contains evidence of contention between different groups extending all the way down to the time of the completion of the Chronicler's History (ca. 350 BCE), any effort to reconstruct the history from 538 to 400 confronts the fact that the final form of the biblical texts treating this period reflects primarily the viewpoint of the ascendant priestly party, the Zadokites. If, however, we seek to glimpse the transformative political developments of that period—which glimpse is essential for assessing the magnitude of the achievement represented by the reconciliation of conflicting groups evidenced by the final edition of the books of Chronicles, Ezra, and Nehemiah—we must strive to understand even the most enigmatic of the texts arising from the early Persian period.

Of great significance for the future of the Jewish community was the rebuilding of the Jerusalem temple. In the planning for an expeditious rebuilding of the temple, the interests of the Persians and the leaders of the returning exiles converged, as can be seen by comparing the Edict of Cyrus preserved in Ezra 6:3–5 with Haggai 1–2 and Zechariah 1–8. Understandably, circles that identified Israel's past glory and future promise with the Davidic dynasty and the Jerusalem temple, with which it was closely associated, believed that the key to prosperity and security was to be found in restoring the institution that was not only the center of worship but also the equivalent of a modern center of banking, commerce, and international relations.[5]

The temple with its multiple functions was of keen interest not only to those laboring to restore the viability of their native Jewish community. The Persians also had a deep vested interest in a strong temple institution. The economic costs of administrating and policing its vast territory were enormous. Without the reconstitution of the temple treasury with a well-trained staff, the collection of taxes and the regular payment of tribute could not be conducted with the efficiency and regularity mandated by a huge bureaucratic regime.

The construction challenges were formidable, involving first the removal of the debris of the old temple left by the Babylonians, next leveling the temple precincts to provide a platform for the new structure, then laying foundation stones, and finally erecting the edifice itself. A reflection of the difficulties and setbacks experienced is reflected in the narrative in the book of Ezra. Though containing contradictions and inconsistencies due to editorial activity spanning many decades, it is likely accurate in citing an unsuccessful attempt by

---

5. See Gary A. Anderson, *Sacrifices and Offerings in Ancient Israel: Studies in Their Social and Political Importance* (Atlanta: Scholars Press, 1987).

Sheshbazzar to commence construction soon after the arrival of exiles in 538, followed by a similarly aborted initiative by Zerubbabel shortly thereafter, with completion coming only with the prophetically inspired building campaign in the years 520–516/5.

The ideological and administrative considerations relating to the phenomenon of temple rebuilding in postexilic Judah were no doubt similar to those arising in any ancient Near Eastern society. Key to temple building and dedication rituals in antiquity was the role played by the king. According to the mythology of kingship in eastern Mediterranean empires, the prosperity of a state was dependent on the beneficence of the patron deity. The earthly representative of the patron god was the king. It was his responsibility to build the earthly habitation of the chief deity, which also served as the storehouse for the gifts offered to the resident god and his retinue. From this follows the function of the temple as central treasury of the state.

In the Jerusalem temple of the Davidic kings, despite certain changes in the mythic trappings due to Israel's focus on one deity, the central role of the king and the economic importance of the temple remained intact. This fact is seen clearly in the biblical account of Solomon's temple building and dedication, as well as in the involvement of subsequent kings, like Josiah, in temple renewal. Throughout the period of monarchy in Israel, therefore, the essential lineaments of the familiar ancient Near Eastern pattern were preserved: it was the king who presided over the building and rededication of a state's central sanctuary; all other officials, including priests, derived their appointments and functions from his command.

This leads to the puzzling questions of the role played by members of the royal house of David in the temple rebuilding activities of the years immediately following the return of the Babylonian exiles and their disappearance after the temple had been dedicated. In the narrative chronology provided by the biblical sources, we have already noted that the first scion of the house of David mentioned is Sheshbazzar (Ezra 1:8–11; 5:14–16).[6] The information provided is very sketchy; he is described as the leader ("the prince" [*hannāśîʾ*] in Ezra 1:8 and "governor" [*peḥāh*] in the Aramaic report in 5:14) who led the first wave of exiles back to Judah, bearing the gold and silver vessels of the earlier temple and then attempting to set in place a foundation. While there is no reason to doubt the veracity of the former accomplishment, serious questions linger regarding his involvement in actual temple construction, since Zerubbabel is also credited with laying the foundation. Suffice it to say that Sheshbazzar was authorized by the Persians to lead those who wished to return to Judah, perhaps on the basis

---

6. The fact that he among the leaders referred to in Ezra and Nehemiah is not given a patronym plausibly has been explained by Sara Japhet as due to an editorial *Tendenz* (Sara Japhet, "Sheshbazzar and Zerubbabel—Against the Background of the Historical and Religious Tendencies of Ezra–Nehemiah," *Zeitschrift für die alttestamentliche Wissenschaft* 94 [1982]: 94–96). His Davidic ancestry is generally accepted in the scholarly literature (most recently, see James C. VanderKam, *From Joshua to Caiaphas: High Priests after the Exile* [Minneapolis: Fortress Press, 2004], 8–10).

of their assumption that his family legacy would enhance his chances of consolidating a community struggling to reconstitute its public offices and institutions,
not to mention to refurbish its tarnished national identity and social solidarity,
both essential facets of the Persian imperial design.

One can only speculate why, after an apparent faltering attempt to get temple
construction underway, Sheshbazzar fades from the scene, to be replaced by
the second governor, a direct descendant (grandson) of King Jehoiachin named
Zerubbabel. The contrast between the faint mention of the first governor and
the enthusiastic celebration of the second could not be greater, thanks to the
spirited campaign of two prophetic contemporaries of Zerubbabel, Haggai and
Zechariah. Before analyzing the vigorous rebuilding activity that their words set
in motion, it is important to locate their perspective in relation to the alternative
visions of restoration and the role of the Davidide that had arisen during the
period of deep searching in the aftermath of 587.

It was during the exile that the monumental historical work known to scholars as the Deuteronomistic History, spanning Deuteronomy to 2 Kings (minus
Ruth), took its final shape. It is noteworthy that it ends with a report that the
Babylonian King Evil-merodach released King Jehoiachin from prison and
extended to him dining privileges in the king's presence.[7] In this way, a national
history that had ended with the darkest of tragedies, complete devastation of
homeland and destruction of its central shrine, offered the reader a departing
glimmer of hope. The deposed king, though held captive under the custody
of the conquerors, had at least been allowed to shed his prison garments and
become the recipient of a royal stipend. The pious Judean reader was likely to
have asked, could this be evidence of a providentially directed first step toward
the restoration of the former glory of the Davidic house?

In contrast, the book of Jeremiah contains an oracle of the Lord definitively
announcing the demise of the Davidic house (Jer. 22:24–30):

> Thus says the LORD:
> Record this man as childless,
>   a man who shall not succeed in his days;
> for none of his offspring shall succeed
>   in sitting on the throne of David,
>   and ruling again in Judah.
>   (Jer. 22:30)

Less vitriolic, but equally pessimistic regarding the future prospects of the
Judahite dynasty was Second Isaiah, who announced God's plan to transfer the
covenant and its attendant blessings from the Davidic house to the populace in
general (Isa. 55:3).

As for Ezekiel, while the thematic links between him and Haggai and Zechariah are significant enough to lead some scholars to conclude that the latter

---

7. 2 Kgs. 25:27–29.

were drawing on the plan set forth in Ezekiel 40–48,[8] a deeper scrutiny reveals a complex portrait of the relation of past to the envisioned future. Against the background of a scathing criticism both of the Judean monarchy and of the temple priesthood, Ezekiel describes a future in which the role of the king would be simplified to resemble the "prince" of Israel's tribal past, whereas the Zadokite priesthood would be elevated to preeminence as God's representatives in a temple-based theocracy.

It is clear that Haggai and Zechariah, from among the alternative restoration strategies available, placed the prophetic office enthusiastically in support of a maximalist program of reestablishing the structures that existed before the devastation wreaked by the Babylonians. While it would have been possible for these prophets to appeal to oracles of both their predecessors and contemporaries (e.g., in the book of Jeremiah, Isa. 40–55, and Isa. 56–66) to present the devastation of 587 as proof of God's annulment of the covenant with the Davidic house, it is not difficult to recognize the popular appeal of a campaign that heralded a descendant of David in the company of a Zadokite high priest as called and empowered by God to return the torn and humiliated nation to its former royal splendor.

Much of the rhetorical force of their messages derives from their application of an ancient ritual pattern to the situation of Judah in the last decades of the sixth century, the ritual of the refounding of the state temple by a triumphant king. That ritual looks back upon a period of decline into chaos in which enemy forces disrupted the prosperity of the land and in which the specter of anarchy was visible in all areas of society. All this was about to change as the result of the advent of the savior king as temple builder. The day of the laying of the foundation stone was one of great excitement and rejoicing ("consider from this day on," Hag. 2:18), for it represented a new creation, in which the nation's patron deity, through the mediation of his human deputy the king, restored order and thus recreated peace and prosperity.[9]

The emotional pitch of the language was further amplified in Judah's case by combining the ancient ritual pattern with the emergent messianism that increasingly was to infuse Jewish and then Christian eschatology. Against this conceptual background is to be understood the theme of reversal that permeates Haggai's proclamation in the year 520 and that reaches its climax in a royal oracle in which YHWH describes Zerubbabel's role in terms of a cosmic assize resulting in the reordering of the geopolitics of the entire earth:

> Speak to Zerubbabel, governor of Judah, saying, I am about to shake the
> heavens and the earth, and to overthrow the throne of kingdoms; I am

8. E.g., Joachim Jeremias, "Hezekieltempel und Serubbabeltempel," *Zeitschrift für die alttestamentliche Wissenschaft* 52 (1934): 109–12.

9. See A. Petitjean, "La Mission de Zorobabel et la Reconstruction du Temple. Zach. III,8–10," *Ephemerides Theologicae Lovaniensis* 54 (1966): 54ff., for a detailed description of the parallels between Zech. 3:8–10 and Mesopotamian cornerstone ceremonies, including the cornerstone inscription, rites of purification, and the promise of blessing.

> about to destroy the strength of the kingdoms of the nations, and over-
> throw the chariots and their riders; and the horses and their riders shall fall,
> every one by the sword of a comrade. On that day, says the LORD of hosts,
> I will take you, O Zerubbabel my servant, son of Shealtiel, says the LORD,
> and make you like a signet ring; for I have chosen you, says the LORD of
> hosts. (Hag. 2:21–23)

This oracle is unique in the Hebrew Bible in its identification of messianic deliverer with a historical Jewish figure, Zerubbabel, a contemporary leader situated at the center of the political activity of the nation and eligible as an heir to the Davidic throne! Needless to say, the lofty rhetoric of the oracle raises the question of its bearing on the Persian policy of zero tolerance for seditious moves on the part of a vassal state or any hint of encroachment on another vassal. In this case, the issue goes far beyond the suggestion of an impending border violation to the announcement of an earth-scorching campaign by the local deity of the vassal state of Judah that would result in the reordering of the power structures of the world and the universal triumph of YHWH and his earthly representative, Zerubbabel.

The blatancy of this challenge to imperial policy is striking. In the Persian scheme of things ultimate authority resided exclusively in the imperial cult, and while gods of the vassal states were to be tolerated, their subservience to the Persian imperium was unconditionally mandated, as reflected in the prayers and sacrifices that subject peoples were expected to offer up in their local sanctuaries on behalf of the Persian monarch.[10] Haggai, however, announced that YHWH was about to intervene with such defiant force that "the throne" and "the strength" of "the kingdoms of the nations" would be overthrown. Moreover, he promised to take Zerubbabel as his "servant" (a familiar royal title) and make him "like a signet ring" (connoting divine authority; cf. Jer. 22:24!), all of this on the basis of divine election ("for I have chosen you").

In the lofty language of royal ideology (see Ps. 89), Haggai's oracle announces an abrupt break with the treaty stipulations by which the Persians bound Judah to the terms of a compliant vassal. The argument that Haggai 2:20–23 and the other visions and oracles of Haggai and Zechariah 1–8 would have been viewed by the Persians as unthreatening eschatological speculation is unconvincing,[11] as we shall later demonstrate on the basis of evidence from the books of Zechariah, Ezra, and the Chronicler. Though it is possible that the Persians were not informed immediately of the speeches of Haggai and Zechariah, it is hard to imagine that much time would have elapsed before their notorious spy system took under surveillance the claims being staked out for the Davidic prince Zerubbabel.

---

10. Ezra 6:8–12: ". . . so that they may offer pleasing sacrifices to the God of heaven, and pray for the life of the king and his children" (v. 10; cf. also 9:9).

11. Carol L. Meyers and Eric M. Meyers, *Haggai, Zechariah 1–8: A New Translation with Introduction and Commentary* (Garden City, NY: Doubleday, 1987).

In older biblical scholarship, it was common to laud the tolerance of the Persians toward their subject states, or to stress the "enlightened policy" of Cyrus and Darius I in contrast to the earlier harshness of the Assyrians and Babylonians. Recent studies have corrected this misleading view, pointing out that while stable provincial economies and well-administered local temples were a required part of the empire's financial and military policy, the slightest hint of nationalistic self-assertion would not have been tolerated. On the other hand, to assume categorically that a prophet like Haggai would not have participated in actions that could have been interpreted as insubordination is to ignore the ubiquity of rebellions against mighty overlords throughout ancient Near Eastern history. Sara Japhet captures the atmosphere in Judah during the active years of Haggai and Zechariah succinctly: "It was an era of ferment, and from the little we know it seems to have been marked by messianic stirrings and expressions of hope for liberation, independence and redemption. These hopes were linked to the figure of Zerubbabel son of Shealtiel, the living scion of the House of David."[12]

To understand Haggai and Zechariah and their audience, one must be able to imagine their sense of nostalgia for both the beauty of the temple and the splendor of the royal court, a beauty and splendor that would have grown rather than diminished in the years of exile in a foreign land (see Pss. 122, 126, 137). Hardly to be overestimated is the power inherent in the picture of Zerubbabel as David redivivus coming to the temple site with construction tools and foundation stone in hand, to the accompaniment of a divine oracle teeming with the lofty language of the ancient Near Eastern temple refounding ritual. Here the yearning listener meets the long-awaited temple-founding king, a dazzling figure, in every way worthy of his descent from the house of David and Solomon:

> "This is the word of the LORD to Zerubbabel: Not by might, nor by power, but by my spirit, says the LORD of hosts. What are you, O great mountain? Before Zerubbabel you shall become a plain; and he shall bring out the top stone amid shouts of 'Grace, grace to it!'"
>
> Moreover the word of the LORD came to me, saying, "The hands of Zerubbabel have laid the foundation of this house; his hands shall also complete it. Then you will know that the LORD of hosts has sent me to you. For whoever has despised the day of small things shall rejoice, and shall see the plummet in the hand of Zerubbabel." (Zech. 4:6b–10a)

When one scrutinizes certain other formulations in the visions and oracles of Zechariah, a picture takes shape that, while resembling in essential features the one found in Haggai, also betrays shades of difference. For one thing, the oracle in 4:6b–10a is the only instance where Zechariah names his Davidic hero. Other references are more veiled and may reflect awareness of the danger of transgressing the border set by the Persians between cultivation of robust domestic

---

12. Japhet, "Sheshbazzar," 79.

cultural and religious structures, on the one hand, and initiatives that could be interpreted as in any way seditious, on the other. This may be the reason Zerubbabel is referred to in the oracle in 3:6–10 indirectly as "my servant the Branch" ('abdî ṣemaḥ). "Branch" is the designation used also in 6:12.

Nuanced differences aside, it is significant that both Zechariah and Haggai depart in an important respect from the normal pattern of the ancient Near Eastern temple-founding ritual that had remained essentially intact in preexilic Judah. Rather than Zerubbabel officiating as primate, with priests serving as his assistants, here we find a relationship of *parity* between the royal figure and the high priest. As a political model, the diarchy Haggai and Zechariah describe is unique, a fact underscored by the emphasis on equality found in the heavenly discourse in the central vision in Zechariah ("these are the two anointed ones who stand by the Lord of the whole earth" [Zech. 4:14]), as well as in the oracle in chapter 6 ("There shall be a priest by his throne, with peaceful understanding between the two of them" [Zech. 6:13b]). The most likely cause underlying this modification of the ancient Near Eastern pattern is Judah's vassal status under the Persians. Except at the risk of incurring reprisals for treaty violation, the leaders of Judah cannot showcase the full-blown royal apparatus of an autonomous state.

Taken as a whole, therefore, we see in the oracles and visions of Haggai and Zechariah tension between two poles: outright rebellion against the Persian overlord, and compliance with imperial policy.[13] As the position taken was mixed, so too would be the final results. Before describing the political structures that would emerge, however, we need to describe the polity that was emerging within the Persian Empire during the time of Haggai and Zechariah's activity.

PERSIAN IMPERIAL POLICY

In a concerted effort to consolidate what under Cyrus and Cambyses had remained a sprawling and rather disorganized empire, Darius I (522–486) instituted a centralized form of rule with twenty satrapies, whose satraps in turn were responsible for the strict oversight of the governors of the provinces under their jurisdiction. It is significant that Zerubbabel bears the title "governor of Judah" (paḥat yĕhûdā) in the opening verse of Haggai. Though in earlier scholarship skepticism was expressed as to whether the application of the title to Zerubbabel in this verse was anachronistic rather than historically accurate,[14] it now seems

13. Japhet has formulated the complexity of Zechariah's message thus: "The attempt to view Zechariah's stand as a consistent whole usually takes into account only one side of his sayings, and sees him either as a preacher of revolt, a 'conspirator', or as someone who puts an absolute division between Israel's future salvation and political reality of today" (Japhet, "Sheshbazzar," 79).

14. Albrecht Alt argued that Judah was not accorded the status of province by the Persians until the time of Nehemiah, a position adopted by numerous subsequent scholars (Alt, "Die Rolle Samarias bei der Entstehung des Judentums," *Kleine Schriften zur Geschichte des Volkes Israels II* [Munich: C. H. Beck, 1953], 333ff.).

clear that as far back as the time of Cyrus II's 538 edict, Judah, like Samaria, was integrated into the Persian system as a province and that, during the time of the rebuilding of the Jerusalem temple, Zerubbabel was indeed the duly appointed governor.[15]

His responsibilities, accordingly, would have included maintaining order in his vassal state, demonstrating fealty to the Persian crown through timely delivery of tribute, and avoiding appearances of any design to establish autonomy or expand jurisdiction beyond the borders of Judea itself. Against this background, it becomes clear why the political leader of the newly reorganized Jewish state, though of direct Davidic descent, bears the title of governor rather than king. Though Haggai and Zechariah draw upon the model of the preexilic monarchy, they are obliged to adjust native tradition to the conditions set by Persian imperial policy.

Within the Persian system, the importance of the chief administrator of the temple was equally well defined. While the office of high priest in the strict sense is not attested in the preexilic period, references to equivalent functionaries are found.[16] What is even clearer is that, within the Persian system, an authoritative supervisor over the temple hierarchy was a prerequisite both for the collection of the temple tax upon which local administrative authorities depended and for the ingathering of the tribute owed by the province of Judah to the Persian crown.

Supporting the diarchy of governor and high priest would have been a rather elaborate bureaucracy, hints of which are found in the biblical sources. Acting in an advisory capacity to the governor would have been a council of elders, representing the most influential families and their commercial interests. Under the high priest would have been a college of priests, an entity that will concern us further, due to the tensions inherent in it because of the competing interests of rival priesthoods. While deferring to the next chapter a description of several other politically active groups and quasi-parties, we conclude our general description of Persian administrative organization with reference to the broadest stratum of civic involvement, the assembly of citizens, a loosely organized entity that assembled in times of crisis to express its concerns to the authorities.

While a surface reading of the received texts might suggest that in Judah traditional structures of leadership could have been adapted quite easily to fit the formal requirements of imperial rule, a more rigorous scrutiny reveals that under the influence of historical roots, communal identity, and future hope, tensions between Persian policy and native tradition were sure to arise, especially within an environment charged with the messianic hope that out of the ashes of humiliating defeat God was committed to restoring the former glory of the nation. Against the background of such nationalistic yearning, it is understandable that prophets seeking to revive the spirits of a foundering nation would draw on the one tradition that more than any other celebrated the glory of Israel:

---

15. Japhet, "Sheshbazzar," 80.
16. E.g., Exod. 28:1–5.

the tradition of God's election of Jerusalem and David, that is to say, the royal tradition.

THE POLITICAL POLICY OF HAGGAI AND ZECHARIAH

Without careful attention to the concrete situation that Haggai and Zechariah faced, including the complex interplay between native tradition and Persian policy, the political significance of their messages is missed. Specifically in the case of Zechariah, continuity with the classic prophetic theme of Israel's history of rebellion against God's Torah and the urgent need for repentance is clear. Equally clear is the specific choice he makes from among the competing visions of restoration, which choice is already evident Zechariah 1:14, where, in answer to the question "How long will you withhold mercy from Jerusalem and the cities of Judah?" the Lord answered, "I am very jealous for Jerusalem and for Zion." Zechariah understands God's presence in the affairs of state in terms of the familiar royal theologoumenon combining the designation of Jerusalem/Zion as God's earthly dwelling place with the election of David as anointed ruler.

Zechariah thus joined ranks with Haggai in a courageous effort to place the prophetic office in the service of a restoration program emphasizing continuity with Judah's preexilic past. They announced that the restoration of stability and prosperity was tied to the reinstitution of the monarchy, in the qualified form mandated by Judah's vassal status, and the rebuilding of the temple cult, understood now as a part of the much larger Persian fiscal administration. That they, in spite of the new reality of Persian hegemony, construed their program as the revival of the institutions and offices that existed before the Babylonian destruction is indicated by the two figures they named as incumbents of the royal and sacerdotal offices: Zerubbabel, a prince of the house of David, and Joshua, son of Jehozadak ben Seraiah, and thus a direct descendant of the last Zadokite chief priest of the first temple.

Given the complexity of the situation they addressed, both from a domestic and an international point of view, it is not surprising that the spirited effort of the prophets Haggai and Zechariah to restore the political structures of the preexilic era was only partially successful. That it was successful in the most important respect, assuring the survival of the Jewish community, speaks volumes for the flexibility, durability, and resourcefulness of the Jewish political legacy they inherited and adapted to their new situation. A key to that success was their ability to galvanize broad-based support behind the rebuilding of the temple and infuse that huge undertaking with the material and financial resources that the Persians had made available and without which it is inconceivable that the central cultural and religious symbol of Judah could have been finished.

Regardless of how splendid the edifice was, however, it would not have provided the economic and spiritual vitality required by a viable state if it were not for their also managing to cultivate the requisite civil and religious leadership.

In the first instance, this was accomplished by their consolidating the sacerdotal authority of the community for the next two and a half centuries firmly in the hands of the Zadokite priesthood. This was a victory that did not come without struggle. In writings from the preexilic, exilic, and early postexilic periods, writings including narratives, legal texts, and prophetic sayings, one finds traces of flux, competition, and at times hostility among priestly groups.

The priestly genealogies preserved in the Hebrew Bible also reflect a high degree of creativity on the part of different priestly families seeking to establish their authority, especially by tracing ancestry back to Aaron or Moses, that is to say, to the most authoritative figures of Israel's past, hallowed by their intimate association with God's disclosure of the Torah on Mount Sinai. The importance of the prophetic oracle in establishing the legitimacy of the Zadokites and specifically of the Zadokite high priesthood is obvious. The very presence of the books of Haggai and Zechariah in the Bible attests to the authority ascribed to these two figures.

Zechariah 3 demonstrates with utmost clarity the contribution of Zechariah to establishment of the high priesthood under the leadership of the Zadokites. Depicted is a scene out of the divine assembly in which the Zadokite high priest Joshua stands before the Lord with "the Prosecutor" (*haśśāṭān*) situated alongside of him to accuse him. The Lord, in defense of Joshua, rebukes the Prosecutor, describing the priest as "a brand plucked from the fire." A ritual proceeding follows, in which Joshua's "filthy clothes" are removed, in place of which he is attired in a clean turban and apparel, in symbolical enactment of the removal of his guilt. This proceeding becomes the basis, finally, of Joshua's installation as head of the temple, which is accompanied with the assurance of his continued access to the members of the divine assembly.

Besides providing the testimony of the divine assembly that Joshua is henceforth the legitimate head of the rebuilt temple, the text raises the question of why he first had to be cleansed of filthy attire and the guilt it symbolized. While his years spent in a foreign land may provide a partial explanation, it seems likely that the description of a heavenly prosecutor accusing him and of God's personal intervention on his behalf addressed charges raised by parties contesting Joshua's credentials. In other words, the text may reflect ongoing rivalry among priestly families and disputes over sacerdotal rank, an interpretation whose plausibility is enhanced by the presence of other biblical texts reporting priestly conflicts.[17] At any rate, what more powerful proof could supporters of Joshua provide than a description of a heavenly court and its presiding judge YHWH handing down its decision on the matter!

A clue to the source of the challenge to the primacy of the Zadokite high priest Joshua is found in the book of Ezekiel. In the stratum of the book that can be attributed to the prophet himself, a distinction is made between the priests who officiate at the altar and those who serve as assistants, a distinction similar to that

17. E.g., Num. 12 and 16.

found in the priestly stratum of the Pentateuch between Levitical priests (i.e., Aaronides) and Levites. While the Levites in this view are not vested with the full sacrificial rights of the priests, their status certainly is one commanding respect.

Shocking, therefore, is a passage, clearly secondarily added to Ezekiel's own words, in 44:6–16, in which the Levites are listed alongside "foreigners, uncircumcised in heart and flesh," who are denied access to the temple. Even more shocking, and found nowhere else in the Bible, is the reason given for their exclusion: "But the Levites who went far from me, going astray from me after their idols when Israel went astray, shall bear their punishment" (Ezek. 44:10). Clearly, in a period after Ezekiel's career, a bitter dispute erupted between the Levites and the Levitical priests, "the descendants of Zadok, who kept the charge of my sanctuary when the people of Israel went astray from me" (44:15). While the interpolated passage in Ezekiel 44:6–16 creates an aetiology for the suppression of the Levites, and Zechariah 3 defends the Zadokite high priest against his accusers (most plausibly understood as "the Levites"), we shall later comment on other biblical passages in Isaiah 56–66 and Malachi that reflect the opposite point of view.

The candidate that Haggai and Zechariah supported for high priest became well established as leader of the Jewish community and was able to bequeath his office to later generations in a succession reaching all the way down to the second century BCE. However, the Davidide they championed as incumbent for the other half of the diarchy did not enjoy the same success and permanency in office, in spite of the fact that Haggai and Zechariah presented the two of them as inseparably connected in their program of restoring the institutions of the preexilic monarchy. In the references to Zerubbabel and Joshua in Haggai (Hag. 1:12, 14; 2:2, 4), the picture is one of inseparable cooperation. Zechariah uses language suggesting that they are the designated agents of God in bringing about eschatological promises (Zech. 3:8–10; 4:12–14). The passage in 6:9–14 develops this language further, echoing Zechariah 3:8 in referring to Zerubbabel as "Branch" and then describing the relationship between the Branch and the high priest: "Here is a man whose name is Branch: for he shall branch out in his place, and he shall build the temple of the LORD. It is he that shall build the temple of the LORD; he shall bear royal honor, and shall sit and rule on his throne. There shall be a priest by his throne, with peaceful understanding between the two of them" (Zech. 6:12–13).

The central drama of the enigmatic passage Zechariah 6:9–14 revolves around the collection of silver and gold and the fashioning of "crowns" ('ăṭārôt). Since 'ăṭārā (sing.) / 'ăṭārôt (pl.) is a word used for the crown of kings rather than priests, the usage here reflects the innovative leveling of the dignity and authority of the two members of the diarchy, as described earlier. The continuation of the narrative, however, is hardly what the reader expects: "Take the silver and gold and make *crowns*, and set [it] on the head of the high priest Joshua son of Jehozadak" (Zech. 6:11), where one would have expected "and set them on the heads of Joshua son of Jehozadak and Zerubbabel son of Shealtiel."

There follows an oracle that, much in the spirit of 4:6b–10a, announces the temple building of "the Branch" and describes the harmony of relationship between the royal and sacerdotal members of the diarchy. The passage ends with one further instruction: "And the [other] crown[18] shall be in the care of Helem, Tobijah, Jedaiah, and Hen son of Zehaniah, as a memorial in the temple of the LORD" (6:14).

While the Masoretic Text and the versions bear the marks of scribal interventions, any effort to reconstruct the circumstances that led to the apparent change from a double crowning to the crowning of the high priest and the deposit of the crown intended for the royal figure in the temple as a memorial to his role in its construction unavoidably involves speculation. In 1938 Julius Morgenstern suggested that the text reflects the intervention of the Persians in response to what they perceived as activities revolving around the Davidide Zerubbabel that broke the terms of the vassal treaty by which Judah was bound, a hypothesis that, in light of the messianic rhetoric found in passages like Haggai 2:20–23 and Zechariah 4:6b–10, is plausible but impossible to prove.

What can be concluded is what is of most significance for understanding the political structures that were to emerge in the years after the completion of the temple. The history of the text of Zechariah 6:9–14 reflects an adjustment made by the Jewish community from a polity modeled on preexilic structures of a diarchy of Davidic king and Zadokite priest—and no doubt infused with hopes for a return to the legendary glory of the golden age of David and Solomon—to the more modest yet durable polity that would serve the community throughout the remaining two centuries of Persian rule. This policy consisted of an unbroken succession of Zadokite high priests, responsible for the conduct of the temple cult and for the collection of taxes designated for local administration as well as the tribute exacted by the occupying power, and *non-Davidic* governors, answerable to the satrap of Abar-nahara for the preservation of civic order in the land.

Emphasis needs to be placed on the fact that, regardless of what fate befell Zerubbabel, he was the last Judahite governor belonging to the house of David. It is also significant that the change was not due to the lack of eligible offspring, since Zerubbabel had two sons, Meshullam and Hananiah (1 Chr. 3:19), one of whom under normal circumstances should have succeeded him. A policy change on the part of the Persians clearly had taken place, and with the cessation of the Davidic governorship a concomitant enhancement of the authority and prestige of the Zadokite high priest no doubt followed.

A complete picture of the political structure of Judah beginning in the last years of the sixth century requires attention to the emergence of a third office, one occupied by individuals commonly referred to as scribes, who were trained

---

18. In contrast to "crowns" in v. 11, in this verse (14) the spelling is defective (i.e., lacking the *waw* of the plural), which, since the following verb is in the singular, should either be read as the alternative singular form *hāʿăṭeret* or understood as a harmonizing emendation.

in the interpretation of the Torah, the body of Mosaic law that as we noted earlier was emerging as the "charter" of the Jewish community. While having roots in priestly praxis,[19] the "office" of interpreter would develop in directions not confined to priestly prerogatives, as we shall see when we turn to the time of Nehemiah and Ezra and describe the activities of Ezra, a priest tracing his ancestry to Aaron and designated as "a scribe skilled in the law of Moses" (Ezra 7:6).

THE POLITICAL LEGACY OF THE RESTORATION PERIOD

The latter half of the sixth century BCE was a period of political ferment. Building upon Jeremiah's and Ezekiel's visions of renewal of the Jewish people following the ruinous results of the Babylonian conquest, Second Isaiah audaciously announced YHWH's choice of the Persian king, Cyrus, as his instrument for delivering captive Israel and providing them with the opportunity to rebuild the nation. For Second Isaiah, the renewal of God's covenant with his people, prepared for by judgment and repentance, enlarged the previous focus of the mediation of God's earthly rule on the house of David to an embrace of the whole community.

Spiritual leadership, on the other hand, was invested in the enigmatic figure of the Servant of YHWH. While Second's Isaiah's identification of Cyrus as God's "anointed one" contributed to the Jewish community's political accommodation to foreign rule, the portrait of the Servant of YHWH assumed an important place in the repertory of themes utilized by later visionaries.

The books of Haggai and Zechariah, together with a critical reading of Ezra 1–8, provide a rich source for describing theo-political developments in the last two decades of the sixth century BCE. That period began with a prophetically inspired movement to reestablish the royal/sacerdotal regime of the royal house of David and the Zadokite priesthood. The terms used to describe Zerubbabel's divine mandate reflect a kingship model that virtually fuses the dominion of the Davidic ruler with the universal dominion of the divine sovereign YHWH. In jeopardy were both the strict restraints placed by the classical Yahwistic theocratic principle on all forms of mediation of divine rule and the prospect of accommodating the religious tenets of Jewish faith with the new political reality of Persian rule.

The mysterious disappearance of the royal member of the diarchy prepared the way for an epoch-making development in biblical political history. Earlier prophets, by identifying various foreign rulers as mediating agents of YHWH's earthly dominion, had prepared the way for a major switch in political thinking. Israel could preserve its identity as God's people under a form of government in which the Persians provided oversight over political institutions, while the

19. Cf. Hag. 2:10–13. Another stream that can be seen feeding into the new office of Torah interpreter is that of the Levitical teaching activity that reaches back to preexilic times.

religious life of the Jewish community was regulated by native leaders expertly trained in the ancestral laws and customs. Since Israel's God remained sovereign over all nations, the theocratic principle that constituted the heart of Yahwistic political thought was preserved at this critical point in history, with God's rule being mediated by a new form of diarchy, a Persian/Jewish partnership.

Chapter 20

The Jewish Commonwealth and a Politics of Accommodation

Judah during the time of Zerubbabel and Joshua was characterized by changes that bridged the gap from the political structures of the Davidic monarchy and the Jerusalem temple to the institutions of a vassal state living under Persian rule. Though some of the oracles of Haggai and Zechariah suggest that for a short time hopes for restoration of the religious and civil edifice of earlier times were rekindled, textual clues embedded in the final form of Zechariah 1–8 indicate that nationalistic aspirations were forced to yield to compromises driven by the realities of foreign occupation. The incomplete nature of that evidence would have left conclusions regarding those adaptations in the realm of speculation, were it not for the picture of the Judean commonwealth that is provided in the literary corpus to which we now turn, namely, the books of Ezra, Nehemiah, and Chronicles.

Genealogical lists may seem like a strange place to begin discussion of the politics of Judea during the restoration period and the Jewish commonwealth that followed (ca. 520–330 BCE), especially in light of the fact that contradictions exist between genealogies purporting to cover the same groups and that scholars have produced divergent reconstructions, based on the assumption that the lists have suffered from scribal errors such as haplography. As unpropitious a starting point as they may seem, however, we are able to draw two conclusions. Firstly, the lists of priests in Nehemiah 12:10–11 and 22, though themselves harboring a major contradiction, nevertheless establish beyond reasonable doubt that the high priesthood was filled throughout the Persian period by an unbroken succession by Zadokites who were direct descendants of Joshua, the first high priest of the Second Temple. Secondly, where the evidence must be gleaned from even more tenuous material, namely, a combination of biblical references, supplemented by seals and jar impressions discovered through archaeological excavations, plus inscriptional evidence coming from Elephantine (a Persian-period Jewish military colony in Egypt), this conclusion can be drawn: after the first two governors of postexilic Judah, who as we have seen were Davidic descendants, came a succession of provincial Judean governors, ruling under the authority of the satrap of Abar-nahara, who were of *non-Davidic* descent.

What this reveals is that the careful balancing of power between the two most influential dynasties of preexilic Judah, the royal house of David and the sacerdotal family of Zadok, had ceased, with the disappearance of the former and the survival of the latter. This change would inevitably carry with it implications for the distribution of power and authority among the religious and civil offices. In the present chapter, we shall witness a transformation of political structures that would produce the basic lineaments of Jewish community for centuries to come.

As sources for inquiry into the politics of Judea in the fifth and fourth centuries BCE, the books of Ezra, Nehemiah, and Chronicles present notorious difficulties. Even the question of whether Ezra preceded Nehemiah or vice versa is mired in endless debate. The objectives of the present study would be lost if we allowed ourselves to be drawn into the myriad unresolved literary and historical questions that continue to exercise scholars.

On the other hand, simply to ignore the fact that our source materials have reached their present form through a complicated process of composition and redaction would lead to a grossly inaccurate reconstruction. The procedure we have chosen is this: first, we shall ferret out of Ezra 7–10 and Nehemiah 1–13 details regarding the political structures that seemed to have been in force during the period in which these two leaders were active (the latter half of the fifth century BCE). Since a large portion of the material incorporated into these writings (aside from the many lists and documents imbedded in the narrative) is accepted by most scholars as stemming from the memoirs of Ezra or Nehemiah, it provides, when read critically and in the light of all available extrabiblical evidence, a fairly reliable basis for reconstructing the politics of the period.

There is undeniable truth in the claim that aretalogical writings often preserve, alongside legendary embellishments, authentic historical reminiscences. However, care must be taken in dealing with the multilayered texts of Ezra and Nehemiah, lest political views reflecting the times of later writers and editors go undetected, and lead us to anachronistic interpretations. Such care is especially important in the case of Ezra 1–6. While it contains an account of the period from Cyrus's edict of 538 down to the dedication of the temple in 515, its political point of view reflects a later period, perhaps the early fourth century BCE.[1] Therefore we shall bring the first six chapters of Ezra into the discussion after we have examined the earlier strata of the books of Ezra and Nehemiah.

Finally, our attention will turn to the Chronicler's History, a work that, while drawing on diverse sources and bearing the marks of two or three editorial recensions, probably reached its present form at some point between 400 and 300 BCE.

POLITICAL STRUCTURES IN JUDEA DURING THE CAREERS OF EZRA AND NEHEMIAH

The most reliable sources of information for the activities of Ezra and Nehemiah and the political situation in Jerusalem at that time are what scholars loosely refer to as their memoirs.[2] In the case of Ezra, this encompasses mainly Ezra 7–9 and Nehemiah 8:1–9:5. In the case of Nehemiah, the memoir consists of Nehemiah 1–7; 11:1–2; 12:31–43; and 13:4–31 (minus various later additions).

Though some scholars have drawn attention to textual and historical ambiguities to argue for a reversal of the order of Ezra preceding Nehemiah, recent scholarship has largely rejected that revision and upheld the traditional chronology, according to which Ezra arrived in Judea in 458 BCE (the seventh regnal year of Artaxerxes I), and Nehemiah's first visit commenced in 445 (the twentieth regnal year of Artaxerxes I). Actually, for our objective of depicting the political situation in the latter half of the fifth century, the chronological question is of little consequence, for both of these leaders appear to have worked within a religious and civil order that by their time had become fairly well established, an order that they in turn helped to refine and stabilize.

Before turning specifically to the question of Ezra's "office," it is necessary to describe the international situation within which the Jewish community found itself in the mid-fifth century BCE. The political framework providing the parameters to which it was obliged to conform was laid out in the policy for vassal states that Darius I, building upon the previous efforts of Cyrus and Cambyses, had established in the course of his organizing the sprawling empire into twenty satrapies. Judea (*Yehud* in the documents of the time) was a district within the province of Abar-nahara. Administrative responsibility pertaining to civil matters and matters of compliance belonged to the local governor of Judea (e.g., Nehemiah), who reported to the governor of Abar-nahara, in this case Tattenai,[3] who in turn, in the highly structured bureaucracy of the Persian

---

1. Note the anachronistic references to Ahasuerus (=Xerxes) (486–65) and to Artaxerxes (465–24) in Ezra 4:6–23.

2. The qualifier "loosely" is necessary in light of evidence of considerable editorial revision, including the rearranging of material, the change from first to third person, and the insertion of extensive material, including rescripts and genealogical and demographical lists.

3. See Ezra 5:3 and 6:6–13.

Empire, reported to the Ushtani, satrap of Babilii-Ebirnari, that is, the entire territory reaching from Babylon to the eastern Mediterranean coast.[4] Matters of cult and local custom, on the other hand, were under the charge of the community's religious leadership. In the case of Judah, this entailed the temple hierarchy, namely, the Zadokite high priest, assisted by the priestly orders consisting of priests and Levites.[5]

Below the overarching canopy upheld by the governor and high priest were organizational structures that the Persians allowed to grow out of local customs and historical precedents in the individual provinces. In the case of Judea, it is clear that clan identity continued to play an important role in community organization, thus preserving a phenomenon that persisted throughout the monarchy of the preexilic period, according to which the royal bureaucracy imposed a centralized system of conscription and taxation on the land but never succeeded in obliterating the sense of clan allegiance on the local level. It seems likely that the tenacity of clan identity was one of the factors enabling the Jewish community to emerge from the trauma of national calamity and a succession of foreign overlords as a viable political and religious entity.

Evidence for the perdurance of traditional social structures is found in the role played by the "heads of the ancestral houses." These heads, as noted in the previous chapter, were also designated with the traditional title of "elders" (zĕqēnîm). They formed an advisory council to the governor that played an important role in times of community crisis and decision making.

Israel's monarchy also left its legacy in the continued role played by "nobles" (ḥōrîm) in the affairs of state. Not surprisingly, they are pictured as defending special privileges over against the common citizen, which position led to a confrontation with the reform-minded governor Nehemiah. Joseph Blenkinsopp has convincingly argued that the term yĕhûdîm, while of course used in some cases to refer to members of the Judean community in general, in other cases refers to the upper class constituted by those who had returned from exile, in contrast to commoners consisting of members of the laboring class ("the poor of the land" [dallat hāʾareṣ]), whom the Babylonians had allowed to remain in their homeland.[6]

Two other groups involved in the political affairs of the Ezra and Nehemiah period are district administrators (śarîm, [in Neh. 2:9 the term refers to Persian military officers]) and "officials" (sĕgānîm, apparently petty government officers). They too seemed to line up with those opposed to Nehemiah's reforms.

---

4. During the reign of Artaxerxes II, that huge satrapy would be divided into its two constituent parts.

5. Anachronistically, 2 Chronicles, in the course of its description of Jehoshaphat's judicial reform, projects back the division of authority that became standard during the Persian period: "See, Amariah the chief priest is over you in all matters of the LORD; and Zebadiah son of Ishmael, the governor of the house of Judah, in all the king's matters" (2 Chr. 19:11).

6. Joseph Blenkinsopp, *Ezra–Nehemiah: A Commentary*, Old Testament Library (Philadelphia: Westminster Press, 1988), 68.

Rounding off the roster of political players is a group differing from all of the above in two respects. They are not native to Judea, and, from a Persian viewpoint, they are of equal or superior status to Ezra and Nehemiah. The individuals in question are Sanballat of Samaria, Tobiah the Ammonite, and Geshem of Kedar ("the Arab"), in relation to whom mention is also made to "the Ashdodites." Sanballat ("the Horonite") is known from the Bible, as well as the Elephantine letters and the historian Josephus, as governor of Samaria and a member of the family that for generations had held the gubernatorial office under the Persians. It seems likely that in the other three instances we are dealing with local leaders appointed by the Persians as governors in their respective provinces. The role that they play is consistent throughout the narrative, that of interfering in the efforts of the leaders and inhabitants of Jerusalem and Judea to rebuild their nation.

The style of opposition that they practice is all too familiar to modern readers from the practices of the warlords in contemporary Somalia, Afghanistan, and Iraq, involving deception, intrigue, shifting alliances, and resort to assassination and armed conflict when persuasion and cunning alone fail to achieve the desired goals. A further dimension of difficulty is added by the fact that in the case of Sanballat and Tobiah, agitators have made inroads into the upper echelons of Jerusalem society, Sanballat through the marriage of his daughter into the high priest's family,[7] Tobiah through his close relationship with the priest Eliashib.[8] The history of the Tobiad family's meddling in the affairs of the Jerusalem temple community extends all the way down to the Hasmonean period,[9] and their survival technique in a very dangerous world is illustrated by an episode included in Nehemiah's memoir, namely, a plot against Nehemiah's life attempted by Tobiah's henchmen, who are called "his lords of the oath (ba'ălê šebû'â),"[10] that is to say, members of a brotherhood sworn to secrecy, loyalty unto death, and ruthlessness. Clearly, Nehemiah was not manifesting paranoia in surveying the fortifications of Jerusalem on the day of his arrival in the cloak of night and in keeping his workers at combat-ready status!

Beyond the different offices and groups just described, one further element of the organizational structure of Judea needs to be mentioned, namely, "the assembly [qahal]," which was the meeting of the citizenry for purposes such as resolving the crisis revolving around mixed marriages (Ezra 10:7–14), the public reading of the Torah (Neh. 8), disputation over the charge of injustices perpetrated by the wealthy against the poor (Neh. 5:1–13), and religious celebrations such as dedication of the rebuilt city wall (Neh. 12:27–43). The influence of this broadest of all bodies derived not from an officially invested mandate, but rather

---

7. Neh. 13:28.
8. Neh. 13:4–5.
9. This stage of the Tobiad family history is well documented in the Zenon papyri. See C. C. Edgar, *Zenon Papyri in the University of Michigan Collection* (Ann Arbor: University of Michigan Press, 1931).
10. Neh. 6:18.

from the sympathy and support both of the traditional leadership groups (such as the elders and heads of families) and of the royal appointees such as Ezra and Nehemiah. The flexibility of this arrangement is illustrated by the proceeding described in Ezra 10, where the enormity of the task of addressing every instance of mixed marriage, compounded by inclement weather, was resolved by setting up a commission, consisting of family heads, with judiciary powers to render decisions and determine punishments (Ezra 10:14–17).

The above offers about as complete a picture of the political organization of Judea in the mid-fifth century as the evidence permits. While it offers necessary background for an understanding of the "offices" of Ezra and Nehemiah, one further note is called for. While this picture conforms to the general pattern of orders of governance in the vassal provinces of the Persian Empire, it is clear that political expediency necessitated deviations from the norm, including the ad hoc commissioning of special envoys in response to specific concerns arising within the royal court assembled in Persepolis or in the summer residence in Ecbatana. Especially in the case of Ezra, recognition of this category of ad hoc appointments is essential.

The most valuable single source for depicting Ezra's "office" is Ezra 7:1–26, a third-person narrative describing his commission from the Persian king to travel to Jerusalem. Especially valuable information is found in the imperial edict in Aramaic in 7:12–26, an archival document bearing distinct marks of authenticity.

Ezra 7:1–10 first sets the stage by placing Ezra's official visit to Judea in the seventh year of Artaxerxes, which, since Artaxerxes I is likely the referent, means 458 BCE.[11] The text then goes on to provide an intriguing double title for Ezra. First, his priestly pedigree is elaborately detailed. His lineage traces back to Zadok and ultimately to Aaron (vv. 1–5), which is to say that this expert in the Torah of Moses can trace his roots to the priest who was present at Sinai when that law was first revealed, a claim that could not be rivaled! Alongside being a priest of the purest pedigree, he is also described as "a scribe skilled in the law of Moses that the LORD the God of Israel had given" (v. 6). This office he held, moreover, not merely as a formal profession, but as a passion rooted in his innermost being, "for Ezra had set his heart to study the law of the LORD, and to do it, and to teach the statutes and ordinances" (v. 10). He is both a model of the Israelite obedient to the law and a teacher intent on promulgating the sacred tradition.

As if Ezra's qualifications for being an interpreter of the Torah were not already well established, his dual title is presented once more in the introduction to the text of Artaxerxes's commissioning rescript: "the priest Ezra, the scribe, a scholar of the text of the commandments of the LORD and his statutes

---

11. An alternative would be to identify the Persian emperor in question with Artexerxes II, which would place Ezra's arrival in the year 397 BCE, an interpretation that creates more problems than it solves.

for Israel" (v. 11). Not only did Ezra carry a dual title, priest and scribe; he also enjoyed dual sponsorship, of both a heavenly and an earthly king, as described by the following envelope construction (aba): He was entrusted with "the law of Moses that the LORD the God of Israel had given; and the king granted him all that he asked, for the hand of the LORD his God was upon him" (v. 6). Ezra is accordingly a mediator serving both a divine suzerain and a human suzerain, the former native to his own culture, the latter foreign.

After this elaborate introduction to the emperor's *envoy extraordinary* in 7:1–11, the decree authorizing his mission appears in verses 12–26. First, "Artaxerxes, king of kings," greets "the priest Ezra, the scribe of the law [*dātā*] of the God of heaven." Then the following instructions are given: (1) The emperor decrees that any of the people of Israel, whether priests or laity, who wish to go to Jerusalem may do so. Doubtlessly motivating Artaxerxes's action is his resolve to continue the policy initiated by Cyrus and Cambyses of providing the wherewithal necessary to maintain Judea as a stable and reliable buffer state, situated strategically in relation to both Egypt and Greece. The decree then turns to the specific responsibilities of the envoy. (2) Ezra is "to make inquiries about Judah and Jerusalem according to the law of your God, which is in your hand." The activity of "making inquiry" about a specific contemporary situation in light of the Torah is the quintessential act of a "scribe skilled in the law of Moses," whether in the time of Ezra, in the era of the sages known to Sirach, or, for that matter, in the generations of the rabbis leading to the Mishnah and Talmud and beyond. Ezra thus arises from the specific circumstances of his time as the harbinger of an office that would become the most important one in the community that was both rooted in ancient Israel and adapting itself to live in an ever-changing world.

In this manner, we can make sense of Ezra's office, specifically within the context of Jewish history. But how does his role of making inquiry about Judah and Jerusalem according to the law of his God fit into the purposes of those who actually issued the commission, namely, the Persian emperor Artaxerxes or, as Ezra 7:14 more broadly specifies, "the king and his seven counselors"?

Important light on this question is shed by a directive issued at an earlier date by the predecessor of Artaxerxes I, Darius I (520–486). It pertained to the codification of Egyptian law in that southern satrapy. In two respects Darius's order offers a close parallel to the assignment given to Ezra in Judea: First, Darius's action was taken shortly after he had crushed the revolt of Aryandes, satrap of Egypt, in 518, and can be seen as part of an effort to strengthen militarily strategic frontiers of a sprawling empire that presented obvious difficulties for the distant royal capital to administer. Second, the Persian emperor, in a manner analogous to the later appointment of Ezra, commissioned a native Egyptian scribe named Udjahorresnet to travel to his homeland to reorganize the "houses of life," that is, the scribal schools. Though the project was overseen by the new satrap, Pharnadates, it is clear that Darius kept himself informed regarding the sensitivities of the local population and wanted the local law code, recorded in both imperial Aramaic and the local demotic Egyptian, to be accurate and definitive.[12] In both cases the intent was to strengthen the stability of provinces within the Persian Empire, perhaps with special attention to regions like Egypt and Judea that were situated in militarily strategic locations.

From the Persian point of view, Ezra was dispatched to evaluate the internal viability of Judea on the basis of its traditional system of law and, where necessary, to deal with cases of nonconformity. Again, the geopolitical aspect of his assignment was important, inasmuch as Judea occupied territory that was of critical importance for the defense of the Persians, with direct exposure to Egypt and straddling routes that would be utilized by Greeks making a beachhead at any one of the ports between Ashkelon and Dor. More specifically, the timing of Ezra's commission coincided with an event posing a major threat to Persian control of the eastern Mediterranean. In 460 BCE the Attic-Delic League, led by Athens, initiated a major naval assault against Persia and Egypt, resulting in the defeat of the Persian army, the death of the satrap Achaemenes, and the transfer of control of the Palestinian and Phoenician coastland from the Persians to the Delian League. It would be straining credulity to regard the fall of Memphis to the Greeks in 459 and the dispatch of Ezra by the Persian royal court in 458 as a mere coincidence. The Greek menace was at the threshold of the Persian Empire, and Judea straddled that threshold![13]

Third, Ezra brings with him resources of silver and gold, contributed by the emperor and members of the Jewish exilic community, together with sacred vessels belonging to the Jerusalem sanctuary. All of this comports with the central importance ascribed by the Persians to provincial temples, due to their function as the treasuries into which taxes were gathered both for use in underwriting the costs of the local religious and civil institutions and for assuring timely delivery of the tribute levied by the imperial administration. Of course, the role of the temple as the heart of the religious vitality of the Jewish community would have made this aspect of the mission especially sacred for the devout scribe Ezra.

Fourth, exemption from taxation is decreed for all temple personnel, presumably out of recognition of their crucial role in the operation and enforcement of the temple-based internal revenue system. Since the vastly expanded temple staff may have represented as much as 10 percent of the total population, this provision exacerbated the tax burden of the common citizens.

Fifth, the next assignment in the edict is especially noteworthy: "and you, Ezra, according to the God-given wisdom you possess, appoint magistrates and judges who may judge all the people in the province Beyond the River who know the laws of your God" (v. 25). Responsibility for appointment of magistrates and judges normally would be invested in the provincial governor, thus raising the question of the extent of the authority that the crown had invested in Ezra.

12. J. Blenkinsopp, "The Mission of Udjahorresnet and Those of Ezra and Nehemiah," *Journal of Biblical Literature* 106 (1987): 409–21.
13. See Othniel Margalith, "The Political Role of Ezra as Persian Governor," *Zeitschrift für die alttestamentliche Wissenschaft* 98 (1986): 110–12.

Also out of the ordinary is the extension of his jurisdiction to Jews throughout the province of Abar-nahara. Such details corroborate our suggestion that the office to which the Persians appointed Ezra was that of *envoy extraordinary*. It is interesting to note that, in addition to his skill in the scribal profession, he is endowed with "God-given wisdom." That wisdom was a mark of the most highly esteemed members of the scribal guild is suggested by the description of Ahiqar, a counselor in the royal court of Esarhaddon, as "a wise and ready scribe."[14] The central importance of wisdom in the scribal circles is also seen clearly in the corpus preserving some of the most eloquent examples of the sapiential tradition, The Wisdom of Jesus Son of Sirach.[15]

Significant for the subsequent development of the scribal office is the combining of administrative responsibilities, such as the appointment of judges and magistrates, with the teaching of Torah: "and you shall teach those who do not know them [i.e., the laws of your God]." The elevation of the scribal office at the expense of other offices is also evident when one recalls that matters pertaining to the law were traditionally under the aegis of the priesthood (Deut. 17:18; 31:9–13, 24–26; Jer. 2:8a; 18:18). In other words, the mandate Ezra receives from the Achaemenid king combines elements variously associated with civil ruler, priest, and scribe, a phenomenon introducing a new challenge into Israel's struggle to preserve the theocratic principle of God's sole sovereignty and the accompanying requirement of legitimate mediation and implementation.[16]

The unusually high level of authority conferred upon Ezra comes into view in relation to the punishments designated by the decree for those found guilty, namely, death, banishment, confiscation of property, and imprisonment. The legal basis upon which Ezra and his magistrates and judges are to base their sentences is twofold, "the law [*dātā*] of your God and the law [*dātā*] of the king." Does this imply the identification of Mosaic and Persian law, or their compatibility? It seems most likely that the latter is intended, since the two laws would pertain to different spheres.[17] For example, an official refusing to release

14. A. Cowley, "The Words of Ahikar," in *Aramaic Papyri of the Fifth Century B.C.* (Oxford: Clarendon Press, 1923), col. 1, line 1, 212 (trans. on p. 220). For a description of the international scope of the scribal profession, see Jonathan Z. Smith, "Wisdom and Apocalyptic," in *Visionaries and their Apocalypses*, ed. Paul D. Hanson (Philadelphia: Fortress Press, 1983), 101–20.

15. It is questionable whether his priestly status (which, in light of questions raised by the dubious genealogy attributed to him in 7:1–5, may not be legitimate) carried any weight in the Persian mind.

16. Whether it is appropriate to designate the polity of the Jewish commonwealth during the Persian period "theocratic" (or alternatively "hierocratic") depends on definitions. Some scholars argue that since political decisions within Judah were normally made by the governor, with priests and elders contributing mainly as advisors, the term "theocratic" is inaccurate (e.g., Joachim Schaper, *Priester und Leviten in der achaemenidischen Zeit* [Tübingen: Mohr Siebeck, 2000]). However, since the Torah of Moses was recognized as the authoritative basis of community order, and in light of the increasingly important role that scribes played in deciding matters of community rule, it seems that "theocratic," if understood in a broad sense, does capture a central feature of the Jewish commonwealth of the Persian period.

17. Perhaps the relation between the two laws is analogous to the relation between the Torah of Moses and the law of the king (*mišpaṭ hammelek*) in 1 Sam. 8:9–19 (cf. Deut. 17:18–20).

funds for payment of the imperial tax would fall under Persian law, as would an officer accused of plotting revolt. On the other hand, domestic issues such as the abuse of lending laws and marital conflicts would be tried under Jewish law. As for punishments, they more readily fit Persian criminal law than the stipulations of Jewish *torah*. Perhaps it was in determining the relation of the two judicial systems that "the God-given wisdom" that Ezra possessed came into play!

Narrative sections of the book of Ezra fill out the skeletal description of Ezra's duties in Artaxerxes's decree. While the Persians were primarily concerned with stability and the uninterrupted flow of tax revenue, it seems clear that Ezra's priority was the restoration of holiness in a community that through assimilation was in jeopardy of losing its unique identity as God's people. Ezra's attention turned first to the phenomenon of mixed marriages, in vogue not only among the laity but among the priests and Levites as well. Since there is no explicit proscription of exogamous marriages in the Torah, Ezra is engaging in a manner of halakic interpretation—that is to say, an interpretation that sharpens or extends the applicability of a law beyond its original intent—that later became common practice in strict sectarian groups like the Qumran community.

In such cases, it is important to identify the underlying principle that is guiding the interpretation. The fundamental issue as Ezra perceived it is revealed by the juxtaposition of the two verbs that structure the narrative in Ezra 9–10: "mixed itself" (*hit'ārebû*) and "separate yourselves" (*nibdelû*). While satisfying the interests of the Persians by addressing an issue threatening the stability of the community, Ezra's zealous attack on mixed marriages reveals the deeper religious purpose of calling the Jewish community back to the purity that was a prerequisite for God's dwelling in their midst. The latter function, to be sure, reflects the priestly status claimed for Ezra in Ezra 7:1–5, since preserving the holiness that alone maintains the unique identity of Israel as God's people lies at the heart of sacerdotal vocation.

The picture of the priest-scribe Ezra proceeding with focus and incisiveness on behalf of restoring holiness in the land reflects the specific legal tradition to which he adheres, namely, the one codified in the Priestly Writing, where separation (*bdl*) of defilement from holiness occupies center stage as the only way of preserving the identity and, indeed, the very existence of Israel as God's chosen people.[18] This central theme underlying Ezra's action lends plausibility to the suggestion that the "law of Moses" that Ezra brought back from Babylon was a version of the Priestly Writing, possibly even the completed five books of Moses, or Pentateuch, a hypothesis that cannot be proven but is very plausible. At the very least, it is clear that Ezra based his reform work on the tradition underlying the Priestly Writing, which, as we have seen, was the same tradition framing the conceptual world of the earlier Zadokite priest, Ezekiel.[19]

18. *bdl*: Ezra 8:24, 28; 9:1f.; 10:8–11, 16. Cf. Lev. 10:10; 11:45–47; 20:24–26. It is the care for holiness that is the duty of Aaron according to P (e.g., Exod. 28:36ff.); cf. Klaus Koch, "Ezra and the Origins of Judaism," *Journal of Jewish Studies* 19 (1974): 180.

19. Ezek. 22:26; 44:23.

In spite of the impossibility of describing the precise relationship between the component strata of Pentateuchal law (the Priestly Writing [P] and the Holiness Code [H]) and the books of Ezekiel, Ezra, and Nehemiah, it is clear that the same threat to the existence of Israel as God's people serves as the backdrop, namely, the threat of blending into its pagan environment, resulting in the defilement[20] of holiness and the consequential destruction of the essential quality enabling God to dwell in the midst of God's people.

P and H, whose narratives situate them in the preconquest wilderness period, present difficulties for one seeking to identify the specific sociopolitical situation they are addressing. In this respect, the book of Ezekiel is of more help as background to understanding Ezra's mission, since passages like Ezekiel 8–11 give graphic portrayal of the alleged defilement within the community, which according to the priest-prophet reached all the way to the temple personnel and resulted in the departure from the land of the glory of the Lord (*kebôd yhwh*) and the consequent destruction of the Jerusalem temple. Confronted with a situation in which, through marrying foreigners, "the holy seed has mixed itself with the peoples of the lands, and in this faithlessness the officials and leaders have led the way" (Ezra 9:2), Ezra clearly found himself contending with a life-and-death struggle for the preservation of Israel that ranked in lethal potentiality with the one with which Ezekiel had struggled.

Numerous other details in Ezra's memoirs and the third-person reports of his activities similarly reflect his affinities with H and P and their sacerdotal concerns, including his attention to the proper conveyance of the temple vessels, ample subsidization for sacrificial offerings and for the salaries of the temple functionaries, and the proper celebration of the Feast of Tabernacles. However, in one final activity of Ezra that we shall describe, his *scribal* persona again comes to the forefront. This activity is described in Nehemiah 8, a chapter that scholars agree originally belonged to the Ezra memoir. If its original position was after Ezra 9–10, the recommitment of the people of Israel to covenantal holiness, through repentance and separation from the defilement incurred through intercourse with the peoples of the lands, prepares the way for celebration of the new year and the reading of the Torah.

Nothing could depict more clearly the exalted status that was ascribed to the Torah in the time of Ezra than this festive event. The people request Ezra to bring the Torah of Moses that he has conveyed from Babylon. Standing above them on a platform, flanked by priests, and amid solemn celebration, he reads, day on end, the contents of the Torah, which the Levites interpret for the people. It is not difficult to recognize this event as an etiological moment foreshadowing a community constituted by the reading and interpretation of Torah and producing Targumim (interpretive translations from Hebrew into Aramaic [the common language of the people in the Second Temple period]) and halakic

---

20. Ezra 9:11 enumerates the dangers of being contaminated by mixing with the "peoples of the lands": "unclean land," "pollutions," "abominations," "uncleanness."

interpretations that would grow in number until finally being collated in the Mishnah.

The momentousness of the occasion is expressed in the final verses of the account, in which we sense a nostalgic return to Israel's tribal origins as "the heads of ancestral houses, . . . with the priests and the Levites," gather with Ezra to study the Torah and then hearken to its words by building booths and reenacting that ancient festival as it had not been done since "the days of Jeshua son of Nun" (Neh. 8:13–18).

The fact that Ezra's own mission to Judea was followed in a short time by the arrival of Nehemiah raises questions about the extent of Ezra's success, especially in light of the fact that Nehemiah describes measures he took in response to many of the same problems to which Ezra had attended. It is impossible to avoid the basic historiographic issue of the relation of the Ezra of history to the Ezra of legend. In the final biblical version of the Ezra story, he emerges as both a second Moses[21] and a forerunner of the scribe, that is, the wise interpreter of Torah who would serve within Judaism during the following several centuries as the community leader par excellence, with a practical significance outstripping that of both priest and governor.

While the richness of the interpretive strands enfolding Ezra removes the historical figure several stages from the critic's view, it seems hard to explain the verisimilitude of the Ezra memoirs, replete with archival materials and historical details, without postulating the career of a remarkable leader, who, while not enjoying unqualified success, nevertheless set Judaism on a path that would prove reliable for centuries to come, even to the present time. That his life story was embellished with details deriving from the practices of the wise scribes who inherited the profession he largely inaugurated only adds to the luster of the one who in the eyes of the Persian emperor possessed sufficient skill and wisdom to be commissioned as *envoy extraordinary* and who in the eyes of the rabbis of the Tannaitic era would have been worthy of receiving the Torah from God on Sinai, had Moses not already done so.

We turn now to Nehemiah, who, after serving in the presence of the emperor as a personal attendant, with his overlord's pledge of support was dispatched to Judea in the year 445 BCE, a mission necessitated according to the opening words of the book of Nehemiah by a disaster that left Jerusalem unfortified. Once again, we see convergence of Jewish and Persian concerns, with Nehemiah distressed over the degraded state of community life in the homeland and with the Persians facing another military crisis in the region, this time involving a revolt by Megabyzus, satrap of Abar-nahara.

Like Sheshbazzar, Zerubbabel, and Ezra before him, Nehemiah led a group of returning exiles, though unlike Ezra, who insisted on relying solely on divine

---

21. Cf. Koch, "Ezra," 73–97, who presses the parallelism between Ezra and Moses to the limit, though the fact that the typology he develops has deep roots in the rabbinical writings is readily apparent.

protection, Nehemiah willingly accepted the escort services of the imperial army and cavalry. This detail already points to a difference in approach between the *priest-scribe* Ezra and the *governor* Nehemiah (5:14), a difference underscored by the contrast between Ezra's utter reliance on divine mercy manifested in the benefactions of the Persian king and Nehemiah's more pragmatic linking of divine blessing with his own human action: "The God of heaven is the one who will give us success, and we his servants are going to start building" (Neh. 2:20).[22] While Nehemiah credits God as the ultimate source of protection and success, throughout his memoir, one sees a courageous leader, endowed with engineering, military, and administrative skills, marshaling the meager material and human resources available to him to rebuild the wall, correct abusive lending practices, and provide defense against enemy intruders. One response to his followers' expression of dread before the threats of their enemies is typical: "Do not be afraid of them. Remember the LORD, who is great and awesome, and fight for your kin, your sons, your daughters, your wives, and your homes" (Neh. 4:14).

In the case of Nehemiah, no less than Ezra, the question of the nature of his "office" is an interesting one. In large part, his activities fit what can be defined as the responsibilities of a governor within the Persian system. Thus he addressed the question of the security of Jerusalem by restoring fortifications that had been destroyed by an undocumented calamity, and when a neighboring governor and his allies encroached upon his territory and plotted against his life, he dispatched himself with the cleverness and courage required of a clan leader within an intrigue-filled political environment.[23] Also belonging quite naturally to the domain of provincial governor were his systematic transfer of rural families to the underpopulated city of Jerusalem and his sweeping economic reforms.

Against the background of our discussion of the vital role local temples played in the Persian bureaucracy,[24] it is very understandable that Nehemiah would have placed the prestige of his office behind purging the temple of inappropriate elements and reorganizing its personnel.[25] Not only did he evict the well-connected Ammonite Tobiah from a chamber in the temple provided for him by a priest named Eliashib (13:4–9) and drive away one of the sons of the high priest Jehoiada, who had married a daughter of Nehemiah's old enemy Sanballat. He also reinstated proper payments to the Levites and other temple personnel and appointed a priest, a scribe, and a Levite as treasurers over the temple storehouses.

---

22. This contrast is made by Sara Japhet, "Sheshbazzar and Zerubbabel—Against the Background of the Historical and Religious Tendencies of Ezra–Nehemiah," *Zeitschrift für die alttestamentliche Wissenschaft* 94 (1982): 74–75.

23. Nehemiah likely would have been better prepared to deal with the rival warlords of Somalia, Afghanistan, and Iraq than have most Westerners!

24. Darius II in 419 personally issued an order to the Jewish colony at Elephantine in Egypt to observe the Festival of Unleavened Bread (perhaps Passover was also included in the order, but the text is only partially preserved). See Cowley, *Aramaic Papyri*, No. 21, 60–65, in B. Porten and A. Yardeni, *Textbook of Aramaic Documents from Ancient Egypt*, vol. 1, *Letters* (Winona Lake, IN: Eisenbrauns, 1986), col. I, line 1, 212 (trans. on p. 220).

25. Cf. Ezra 2:62–63.

While most of the activities described in Nehemiah's memoir thus fit the profile of a provincial governor, there are a few episodes in which Nehemiah renders halakic interpretations that resemble functions one might sooner associate with the scribal office. In Nehemiah 5:1–13 he responds to "a great outcry of the people and of their wives against their Jewish kin." They complain of lending practices that are bringing them to economic ruin. Their plight was one endemic to traditional agrarian societies, where tenant farmers are legally required to surrender a large percentage of the crop to wealthy landowners. Even in normal times, the economic situation was precarious, since in addition to payment of rent-in-kind they had to produce sufficient surplus to pay for sizable temple and imperial taxes. In the case of crop failure, the delicate balance between solvency and bankruptcy collapsed, since seed for the next planting had to be borrowed and property provided as collateral to secure the loan. With interest rates as high as 60 percent per annum,[26] the results dreaded by the people seemed inevitable, namely, loss of fields and sale of children to slavery.

Nehemiah's response gives a portrait of a very unusual governor, as he takes incisive action based on an innovative interpretation of Torah. In effect, he took the commandments in Exodus 22:25–27 (Heb. vv. 24–26) and Deuteronomy 24:10–13 and combined them with the laws of release in Leviticus 25. Not only are the wealthy lenders required to return the interest payments they have collected; they are to restore everything that has been seized through foreclosure on unpaid loans. The slate, in other words, was to be wiped clean, as in a jubilee year!

In other instances as well, Nehemiah describes activities in which the governor engages in halakic interpretations and applications that adumbrate the techniques of the later scribes. In Nehemiah 13:10–14, he takes action against an abuse denounced in Malachi 3:8–10, the withholding of the Levitical tithe, that is, the provisions that enabled temple servants to perform their duties undistracted by the need to produce their staples. In Nehemiah 13:23–27, he draws upon the Torah (Deut. 23:4–9) and combines it with a moral extrapolated from the Solomon narrative in 1 Kings 11, as he renews the campaign against mixed marriages begun by Ezra.

Nehemiah's attack on those defying Sabbath law by engaging in all sorts of commerce reveals a particularly innovative halakic maneuver, for Nehemiah 13:15–22 is based on the interpretation of Deuteronomy 15:12–14 found in Jeremiah 17:21–22, the latter being "a remarkable instance of inner-biblical legal exegesis,"[27] in that it adds to the Pentateuchal law the command "to carry in no burden through the gates of Jerusalem on the Sabbath day" and includes it as part of what God had commanded at Sinai.

---

26. Cowley, *Aramaic Papyri*, No. 10, pp. 29–32.

27. Michael Fishbane, *Biblical Interpretation in Ancient Israel* (Oxford: Clarendon, 1985), 132. Relevant here is Fishbane's entire discussion of the relation between Deut. 5:12–14; Jer. 17:21–22; and Neh. 13:15–21 on pp. 129–34.

A POLITICS OF ACCOMMODATION IN RESPONSE
TO PERSIAN HEGEMONY

The vitality of the Jewish community and the richness of the traditional sources that sustained it could not be illustrated more vividly than they were in the mid-fifth century. As if the trauma of defeat and destruction of native institutions in the Babylonian period had not dealt a sufficiently devastating blow, the failure in the waning years of the sixth century to restore the Davidic monarchy added to the demoralization of the struggling community. The book of Malachi testifies to the fact that the spiritual and material impoverishment of the community that Haggai had sought to reverse through his promotion of the temple rebuilding program under the Davidide Zerubbabel and the Zadokite priest Joshua continued to plague Judea a half century later. That was the situation that Ezra and Nehemiah were deployed by the Persian court to redress.

Adaptation, in the sense of a dynamic strategy combining continuity and change, describes the response chosen by the leaders of the Jewish community in the mid-fifth century. Indeed, the fact that Ezra and Nehemiah applied their talents in accommodating cherished traditions to the new situation, rather than repeating Haggai and Zechariah's program of seeking to replicate the political and religious institutions of the preexilic period, goes far in explaining their success. A clear testimony to that success was the emergence of new forms of leadership and a political strategy of accommodation that proved effective on into the Hellenist and Roman periods and beyond. So it was that, due in large part to the courageous and wise initiatives of Ezra and Nehemiah and the cooperative hand of several Persian leaders, the political model of accommodation joined the repertory of political strategies suitable under particular circumstances for upholding the theocratic principle of Yahwistic faith.

As in the case of the models of charismatic rule and monarchy, however, political and spiritual viability did not spontaneously arise out of accommodating policies; it was contingent on unswerving allegiance to God's sole sovereignty and diligence in implementing the qualities of divine governance in human institutions. While each model was vulnerable to the perennial temptations of abuse of power and nationalistic idolatry, the model of accommodation presented a new challenge, mediating YHWH's rule within a regime that did not acknowledge the ultimate universal authority of Israel's heavenly sovereign. Given the fact that in the centuries ahead the Jewish people would live under a sequence of foreign powers—Persian, Greek, Roman—it seems inevitable, though no less tragic, that we shall enter a stage of our study characterized by enormous struggle and frequent persecution. The fact that the end result was not the death of an ancient culture, but its further political and religious growth, accounts for an enrichment of human history that transcends simple quantification.

Above we noted the importance of the dynamic of continuity and change in the resilience of the Jewish community in the Persian period. An important instance of continuity with the past and adaptation to the present was the preservation of traditional checks and balances within the new structures of leadership—a notable achievement when one considers how thoroughly the actual offices had changed. Accordingly, many of the responsibilities that had belonged to the king in the earlier era were assumed by the governor, especially responsibilities pertaining to the maintenance of civil order and to the collection of tax revenue, but including as well attention to certain aspects of the cult.

To be sure, the governor was no longer patron of the temple in the manner of the Davidic kings. The appointment of priests was not his prerogative, and temple funding flowed not from his personal coffers but from an economic partnership consisting of the Persian crown and the Jewish community as a whole. Nevertheless, given the role of the temple as the state treasury within the Achaemenid administrative structure, the governor also had a stake in its orderly functioning (Neh. 13:13).[28] Moreover, while Nehemiah's innovativeness in extending the bearing of the law to the specific problems of his time resembled characteristics sooner associated with scribe than governor, even in the domain of religious reform he stood in the tradition of the righteous king, as expressed in narratives about Solomon, Jehoshaphat, Hezekiah, and Josiah and in prophetic oracles like Isaiah 9:2–7 (Heb. vv. 1–6) and 11:1–5.[29]

Adaptation, in the sense of a strategy blending continuity and change, also describes the career of Ezra. While his priestly background accounts for his deep concern with the restoration of purity in the Jewish community, the highly original way in which he remolded the scribal office can be regarded as his most significant achievement. When Artaxerxes I appointed him as a scribe,[30] he was dealing with an office with deep roots in the ancient cultures that the Persian Empire had absorbed through conquest. The office of scribe also had a long history in Israel, reaching back at least to the early monarchy. In most cases, the

---

28. This responsibility is vividly illustrated in the generation after Nehemiah by a letter sent by Yedoniah (apparently the high priest) of the Jewish colony Yeb on the Nile to the then-governor of Judea, Bigvai (Bagoas), in which he petitions the governor for a subvention for the rebuilding of their destroyed temple. Several details make this example of the relation of governor to temple unusual: Josephus reports that Bigvai, unlike Nehemiah, is Persian, not Jewish (Josephus, *Ant.* 11.7.1); the petitioners are seeking support for a temple that is not even in the province over which Bigvai has jurisdiction; and they report that they have also made their appeal to Delaiah and Shelemiah, the sons of Sanballat, governor of Samaria. These oddities place in bold relief the categorical nature of the governor's obligations vis-à-vis the temple of his subjects. Moreover, the letter, in a sentence recalling Ezra 6:10, makes explicit the way in which this local temple fits into the larger pattern of the imperial cult: "and they shall offer the meal-offering and incense and sacrifice on the altar of the God Ya'u on your behalf, and we will pray for you at all times, we, our wives, our children, and the Jews" (Cowley, *Papyri*, No. 30, ll. 25b–26).

29. Michael Fishbane points to the "historical analogy between the actions of Mesopotamian kings and Nehemiah" in his discussion of Nehemiah 10 (Fishbane, *Interpretation*, 30–31). That Nehemiah's *'ămānā* ("covenant") in Neh. 9:38 (Heb. 10:1) resembles in certain ways the *mišarum* of Mesopotamian kings, whereby they sought to restore to health the socioeconomic structures of their domain, is an example of continuity covering a time span even exceeding that of the history of ancient Israel.

30. Akkadian: *šapiru,* Aramaic: *sapra'*.

scribes in the Bible are mentioned as part of the royal bureaucracy.[31] In certain narrative contexts where a fuller description is given of their activities, however, they serve as envoys on behalf of the king, thus foreshadowing Ezra's role in the service of Artaxerxes.[32] Baruch, Jeremiah's amanuensis, may also be seen as part of the background to Ezra's function as a reader of God's word (Jer. 36:4–10).

More important in understanding the significance of Ezra's reading of the Torah to the assembled community is his priestly identity, for according to the book of Deuteronomy the public reading of the Torah every seventh year during Sukkot was the duty of the Levitical priests (Deut. 31:9–13, 24–26; see also 17:18). Continuity stands creatively in tension with change in this case too, for according to Nehemiah 8–10, Ezra not only read the Torah, but engaged in its teaching and halakic interpretation extending its meaning to new situations.

THE POLITICAL STRUCTURE OF JUDEA IN THE MID-FIFTH CENTURY

Beyond the above description of the offices of Ezra and Nehemiah, what can we say in general regarding the political organization of Judea in the mid-fifth century? The pattern of governance that becomes visible in the memoirs fits what is known about the conditions placed on vassal states within the Persian Empire. Responsibility for social law and order, fiscal stability, and peaceful relations with other vassal states fell under the aegis of the governor. Nehemiah's attention to the adherence of the populace to their native system of law, the proper organization of the temple, and repair of damage to public buildings and fortifications comports with these responsibilities. But none of the fusing of the office of governor with symbols drawn from the royal ideology of the Davidic house that occurred in the time of Zerubbabel is to be found in association with Nehemiah. Indeed, in one case Nehemiah reports that he took incisive action to repudiate the charge that his building activities were motivated by royal aspirations: Sanballat, citing the supporting testimony of Geshem, hurls at Nehemiah the accusation, "[Y]ou and the Jews intend to rebel; that is why you are building the wall; and according to this report you wish to become their king. You have also set up prophets to proclaim in Jerusalem concerning you, 'There is a king in Judah!'" (Neh. 6:6b–7a). The accusation, echoing the prophets Haggai and Zechariah's heralding the building activities of Zerubbabel with the invocation of royal symbolism, is emphatically repudiated by Nehemiah: "No such things as you say have been done; you are inventing them out of your own mind" (Neh. 6:8).

31. 2 Sam. 8:17; 20:25; 1 Kgs. 4:3; 2 Kgs. 12:10 (Heb. v. 11); 18:18, 37; 19:2; 22:3–12; Jer. 36:10.
32. 2 Kgs. 18:18–27; 19:2–7; 22:14–20.

Turning next to the institution that played a central role in the polity of the Persians, while at the same time symbolizing for the Jews God's abiding presence, the following characteristics of the temple emerge from the sources: leadership is in the hands of the Zadokite high priest Eliashib, while the priesthood is divided into the priests who officiate at the altar and the Levites, who, while subordinate, are treated with honor and respect (Neh. 13:30–31). Moreover, in step with the growing status of the written Torah, the Levites win new importance as translators and teachers and interpreters of the law, as is vividly described in Nehemiah 8:7–9.

The bipartite sacerdotal structure found in Ezra and Nehemiah reflects the pattern set forth by the Priestly Writing. Other temple precinct functionaries like singers and gatekeepers are mentioned (Ezra 7:7), though they are not integrated into the elaborate Levitical genealogical structure found in the final edition of Chronicles.[33] In general, however, the temple organization, like the governorship, comports with the general polity of the Achaemenids.

More difficult to fit into this picture of Persian provincial polity is the role of Ezra. He is a priest (but not the high priest) engaged not only in activities normally associated with the sacerdotal office, such as attending to the proper functioning of the temple cult, but in areas one might associate sooner with gubernatorial duties, such as appointing members of the judiciary and enforcing punishment on lawbreakers. Then again, he takes upon himself the priestly duty of the "sons of Levi" in the public reading of the Torah, followed by halakic interpretation, anticipating the function of the later scribes.

The most plausible way to understand the place of Ezra in structures of governance in the Persian period is that the assignment given to him by the Persian emperor was broader than can be fit into the confines of a single office within the provincial bureaucracy. He was an *envoy extraordinary*; that is, his assignment was to investigate conditions in the province of Judea that had raised concerns within the Persian central administration, with authorization to take whatever measures he deemed necessary to restore stability in the region (Ezra 7:14). In executing the mandate he had received, Ezra engaged in activities that do not fall neatly into the categories of priest and scribe. Rather, we find a blending of functions enriched by "God-given wisdom" (Ezra 7:25) that can be seen as making a significant contribution to an office that in subsequent periods would be called scribe, sage, and rabbi.

The office of scribe rose to prominence within the Jewish community of the Second Temple period due to its ability to adapt to the changing conditions that are inevitably a normal part of the life of a people living as subjects of a foreign power. That the office of scribe flourished beyond the Persian to the Hellenistic and Roman periods, and with the exception of the century of indigenous Hasmonean rule, on through subsequent centuries, is testimony to the resilience of a

---

33. All of this adds plausibility to viewing the composition of the memoirs of Ezra and Nehemiah as occurring between the creation of P and the completion of Chronicles.

covenantal polity based on an authorized charter (Torah) that under the care of wise interpreters was applied anew to each generation of the faithful, regardless of where they found themselves in the world.

EZRA 1–6

Earlier we noted that the first six chapters of Ezra, though containing an account of events in the late sixth century, actually were composed at the final stage of the growth of Ezra and Nehemiah. They reflect a world in which the restructured offices we have just described performed the dual roles of maintaining the stability expected by the Persians and the purity required by the Torah. Gone, at least for a time, were the days begetting messianic dreams of a restored Davidic kingdom dwelling securely and enriched by the offerings of the nations.

In place of eschatological hopes of an ideal kingdom, one finds accommodation to a far from perfect world, one in which national autonomy has yielded to foreign rule and in which the community lives under the recurrent threat of hostile neighbors. This scaled-down level of expectation has firm roots in the careers of Ezra and Nehemiah, who in a sense can be seen as the pioneers who blazed the trail into an era marked by a pragmatic modus vivendi. Ezra is portrayed as harbinger of that era in a long prayer of repentance and supplication, in which he offers thanks for circumstances that, while far from ideal, appear in a relatively favorable light against the background of bleaker times past:

> But now for a brief moment favor has been shown by the LORD our God, who has left us a remnant, and given us a stake in his holy place, in order that our God may brighten our eyes and grant us a little sustenance in our slavery. For we are slaves; yet our God has not forsaken us in our slavery, but has extended to us his steadfast love before the kings of Persia, to give us new life to set up the house of our God, to repair its ruins, and to give us a wall in Judea and Jerusalem. (Ezra 9:8–9)

An even more realistic picture of life as an occupied people is given further on in Ezra's prayer: "Here we are, slaves to this day—slaves in the land that you gave to our ancestors to enjoy its fruit and its good gifts. Its rich yield goes to the kings whom you have set over us because of our sins; they have power also over our bodies and over our livestock at their pleasure, and we are in great distress" (Neh. 9:36–37).

The edict of Artaxerxes itself states succinctly one of the principles of the mode of accommodation that would govern the new era. Henceforth the Jews would live not exclusively under the law of their God, nor even under the law of their God complemented by the ordinances of a native king (1 Sam. 8:9), but would be bound to "the law of your God and the law of the king," the king in this case being the *Persian* emperor (Ezra 7:26). What is revealing in this verse is reference to a political model balancing two orders, religious and civil, which as we have seen arose in Israel in the place of the more monolithic charismatic structure of the tribal confederacy. With the further change coming in the Persian period, the replacement of the royal authority of the native Davidic dynasty with the royal authority of a foreign power, a new balance of powers was called for, resulting in the policy of accommodation that we have traced to the initiatives of Ezra and Nehemiah.

The classic expression of this policy comes in Ezra 6:8–12, where by royal decree provision is made for the building of the temple in Jerusalem and for underwriting the costs for sacrifices. However, unlike the case of the first temple, when Israel's own king, Solomon, was issuing the orders and paying for the expenses, under the conditions of the new era it is the foreign king, Darius I, who is directing and financing the project. The interests of the new patron could not be expressed more clearly than in Ezra 6:10: "so that they may offer pleasing sacrifices to the God of heaven, and pray for the life of the king and his children." The same parallelism between Israel's God and the Persian crown is expressed in Ezra 6:14b: "They finished their building by command of the God of Israel and by decree of Cyrus, Darius, and King Artaxerxes of Persia."

I believe Sara Japhet is correct in interpreting another detail in Ezra 1–6 as reflecting the degree of caution exercised by its editor(s) to remove all suggestion of Davidic nationalistic aspirations: The Davidic origins of Sheshbazzar and Zerubbabel are nowhere mentioned in those chapters![34] The only royal presence presiding over the affairs of the Jewish nation is that of the king of Persia, a situation adumbrated by the Cyrus oracle of Second Isaiah (Isa. 44:24–45:7).

In considering the generally peaceful conditions between the Jews and their foreign overlords that prevailed during the Persian period, one is led to inquire into the underlying causes. Because the party wielding the greatest influence inevitably is the occupying party, it is common to tout the purported "enlightened" nature of Persian foreign policy. When one contrasts the treatment of conquered peoples by the Assyrians and the Babylonians with that of Cyrus and Darius, it seems evident that this theory is not without merit. But two considerations commend a more complex interpretation: (1) The Persians were able to maintain control over their vast empire for two centuries, on the basis of a foreign policy dedicated not to promoting the well-being of vassal states, but to maintaining them as reliable allies and buffers against their major rivals, first the Egyptians and then the Greeks. (2) From the Jewish side, the first iteration of the policy of accommodation did not arise during Cyrus's reign, but a generation earlier, while the Babylonians held sway over their Jewish captives.

Already at that time, we read that Jeremiah, after having interpreted the fall of Jerusalem in terms of divine judgment on an unfaithful people, advised the exiles to settle down for several generations in Babylon, to engage in their agrarian activities, to marry and produce offspring, and to "seek the welfare of the city where I have sent you into exile, and pray to the LORD on its behalf, for in its

34. Japhet, *Sheshbazzar*, 72–73.

welfare you will find your welfare" (Jer. 29:5–7). In this poignant formulation of the policy of accommodation, we find clear evidence of its roots in the classical prophetic tradition. It is a policy, to be more precise, that could arise after the nation fell to foreign conquest, thanks to the prophetic and, before that, early Yahwistic theocratic principle of one sovereign God, the ruler of all nations. Israel's monarchy and nationhood in general stood in relation to that principle only as provisional, contingent categories. Loss of its native dynasty, even loss of its national autonomy, did not jeopardize the sole rulership of Israel's true sovereign, YHWH. Nor did it mark the end of God's promise for the final restoration of God's people. But that would have to await God's own time, be it Jeremiah's seventy years, or Daniel's revision to seventy times seven years!

CHRONICLES

The historical work comprising 1 and 2 Chronicles serves as a fitting source with which to conclude this chapter, since it can be seen as the culmination of a trajectory beginning with Haggai and Zechariah, continuing through Ezra and Nehemiah, and concluding with the final edition of Chronicles.

There is a wide diversity of scholarly opinion on the history of composition of Chronicles, as well as on the relation of 1 and 2 Chronicles to Ezra and Nehemiah. The long-held view that the latter are compositionally part of the Chronicler's History has been challenged, in my mind persuasively, by scholars like Sara Japhet, Hugh Williamson, and Ralph Klein, who, especially by pointing to thematic differences, argue that Ezra/Nehemiah should be viewed as a separate work.[35] The similarities, both linguistic and thematic, that are used as evidence by those who still argue for the longer Chronicler's History, are best understood as evidence of adherence to a common tradition rather than common authorship.

Without getting into the complicated problem of the composition history of Chronicles (and there is evidence that it went through two or three editorial stages), it seems clear that the final edition was completed at a date somewhat later than the completion of Ezra/Nehemiah. Chronicles thus serves as a witness to certain aspects of organization within the Jewish community during the period 400–350 BCE.

The policy of accommodation to the Persian rule that we witnessed in Ezra and Nehemiah and the basic harmony that resulted from Judah's leaders' implementing the policy of indigenous control over religious and social life, while honoring Persian hegemony in all international and military matters, continue to be reflected in Chronicles. The tension over the question of the role of the

---

35. Sara Japhet, "The Supposed Common Authorship of Chronicles and Nehemiah Investigated Anew," *Vetus Testamentum* 18:330–71; Ralph W. Klein, "Book of 1–2 Chronicles," in *The Anchor Bible Dictionary,* 1:992–1002, a position Klein retains in his Hermeneia commentaries (*I Chronicles* [Minneapolis: Fortress Press, 2006] and *II Chronicles* [Minneapolis: Fortress Press, 2012]).

Davidic house in affairs of state, which was evident in Haggai and Zechariah and can be detected as an abiding concern in Ezra 1–6, has disappeared. No aura of messianic hope hovers over the figures of David and Solomon, who are viewed as esteemed leaders of Israel's past whose abiding significance for political institutions was etiological rather than eschatological. David and Solomon are portrayed, indeed celebrated, as the founders of the temple, its rituals, and its elaborate sacerdotal structure. They thereby serve as historical warrants for the legitimacy, indeed central importance, of the Second Temple and its personnel.

H. G. M. Williamson has studied in detail one of the most interesting features of Chronicles, namely, the complex organizational structure of the temple personnel attributed to David.[36] The primacy of the Zadokite priests as those with exclusive rights to altar sacrifice, traceable to the Priestly Writing and emerging intact out of the flux of the early years of the Second Temple, remains unchallenged in Chronicles.[37] The spotlight, nevertheless, rests on the Levites, whose ranks are increased by the addition, alongside the traditional Levitical assistants to the priests, of three formerly nonpriestly classes: officers and judges, gatekeepers, and singers.

While the resulting numerical increase likely had the effect of magnifying the relative prestige of the priests over the Levites, it also built a legacy that would shape the organizational structure of the temple for centuries to come, a structure that would lend permanency to the different classes of minor temple personnel. In this way Chronicles carries a step further the rehabilitation of the Levites to which Ezra and Nehemiah had already contributed. That this objective was intentional on the part of the Chronicler is indicated by the depth of the genealogies provided for each of the families of Levites.[38] We can assume something like this reasoning: should history repeat itself, and the legitimacy of particular temple singers or gatekeepers be questioned (and there is no reason to doubt that such challenges were recurrent), the outcome could be more promising than the one recorded in Ezra 2:62, where certain priests returning from exile and lacking proper genealogical documentation "were excluded from the priesthood as unclean."

Another theme in Chronicles that reflects a distinct political viewpoint has to do with the historical division of Israel. In the books of Ezra and Nehemiah the territory that prior to the Assyrian conquest of 722 had belonged to the northern kingdom of Israel was portrayed as a threat to the stability of Judea, due to the intrusion of Samaria's governor, Sanballat, into local Judean affairs and the

---

36. H. G. M. Williamson, "The Origins of the Twenty-Four Priestly Courses. A Study of 1 Chronicles xxiii–xxvii," in *Studies in the Historical Books of the Old Testament*, VTSup 30 (Leiden: Brill, 1977), 251–68.

37. Williamson ("Origins") identifies a secondary stratum in 1 Chr. 23–27 and elsewhere in which the superiority of the priests over the Levites is given added emphasis.

38. The Chronicler's utilization of genealogy to establish the legitimacy of the different Levitical groups is paralleled by the provision of an honorable genealogy for Zadok (1 Chr. 6:3–8, 50–53 [Heb. 5:29–34; 6:35–38]) as a correction of unclarities (especially Zadok's descent from Eli, whose priestly line he was to supersede!) created by other priestly genealogies.

mixed ancestry of its inhabitants. An earlier generation of scholars viewed the tension between Judea and Samaria that is depicted in Ezra and Nehemiah as evidence of the "Samaritan schism." Since it now seems clear that the definitive break between Judea and the Samaritans did not occur until the time of John Hyrcanus, the altercations occurring in the fifth century appear to have involved specific conflicts between Jerusalemite and Samarian leaders, rather than a permanent division between two religious communities.

The position set forth by Chronicles assumes not only that the break between north and south is not permanent, but that it stands in opposition to divine intent. Though the prominent role played by David and Solomon in the Chronicler's account of Israel's history could have provided the background for depicting the reunification of the kingdoms by a messianic Davidic deliverer who would revive the glory of Israel's golden age, a more restrained approach is taken. The age of David and Solomon is presented as the prototype of the Jerusalem community of the present, centered around its holy temple and opening its gates to the inhabitants of all of the ancient tribal allotments. While not imbued with the messianic enthusiasm of Haggai 2:20–23, and indeed reconciled, it would seem, with the modus vivendi of accommodation to Persian rule, nevertheless the geopolitical position taken vis-à-vis the north is an audacious one: since Israelites from all of Israel, from the north as well as the south, are legitimate heirs to the temple community founded by David, the current cleavage is an unnatural one.[39]

In Chronicles, the theme of reunification is developed by highlighting aspects of Israel's history in a manner that goes beyond the Deuteronomistic *Vorlage*. For example, Hezekiah is presented as zealous for the temple in a way reminiscent of Solomon, as he issues a call to both Judah and Israel, "from Beer-sheba to Dan," to join together in joyous celebration of the Passover, the likes of which had not been witnessed "since the time of Solomon son of King David of Israel" (2 Chr. 30:1–9). At other points in the narrative, Chronicles gives expression to the possibility of repentance and the return of Israel to the sacral community gathered around the temple (2 Chr. 11:13–17; 13:4–12; 15:9–15).

THE POLITICS OF JUDEA CIRCA 400 BCE

An account of the political situation in Judea circa 400 must include four spheres of power: (1) the Persian central administration, (2) the local provincial governor, (3) the high priest and the Jerusalem temple, (4) the scribes of the Torah.

---

39. This theme is not new, having come to expression in Ezekiel in the image of the joining of two sticks into one (Ezek. 37:15–23) and in Zechariah, where that image is inverted, producing an announcement of impending judgment (Zech. 11:7–14).

blueprint for
Rome?:

The Persian Central Administration

The Achaemenid Empire maintained control of its twenty satrapies through a combination of military might and administrative efficiency, with the enormous operational costs being covered in large part by tax assessments levied against all of the vassal states. It entertained zero tolerance of insubordination, and its notorious spy network was ever watchful to report signs of insurrection, so as to crush the offenders before the affected region could be destabilized.

Although threats to Persian sovereignty within satrapies as widespread as Egypt, Syria, and Babylonia were successfully repulsed, the external threat posed by the Greeks was relentless and increased as the decades passed. It was this latter threat that made the internal stability and fealty of the vassal states strategically a matter of highest priority.

The Local Provincial Governor

In the year 408, Bagoas was the governor of Judea. His appointment by the Persians represented a significant evolution of that office. As already noted, after the tenure of Sheshbazzar and Zerubbabel, individuals of Davidic descent no longer filled the office of governor. Nehemiah, appointed in 445 BCE as governor of Judea by the Persians, though not a descendant of David, was a devout Jew, deeply committed to the religious integrity and purity of his people. Bagoas, however, who was probably Nehemiah's successor, not only was appointed by the Persians but was himself Persian, which indicates a sharpening of the division between the cultural-religious sphere, which remained under Jewish leadership in the form of the high priesthood, and the sphere of civic affairs, now under the aegis of a non-Jew.

While matters of internal stability and peaceable relations with neighboring provinces attended to by Nehemiah would continue to be a part of the governor's responsibility, the Torah-based religious reforms to which Nehemiah committed the resources and prestige of his office would pass to the incumbents of other offices. The result was, in terms of inner-communal politics, the enhancement of the third and fourth spheres of power, to which we next turn.

The High Priest and the Jerusalem Temple

Letter 30 of the Elephantine Papyri verifies not only that Bagoas was governor of Judea in the year 408, but that Johanan was the high priest.[40] This Johanan is listed in the genealogical list in Nehemiah 12:22 as the (son and) successor of Joiada.[41] With regard to offices and political spheres in this period, what Letter 30 reveals is that the governor of Judea was regarded as one whom Jedaniah, the high priest of the Yeb temple (Elephantine), could implore for help, even

---

40. "We sent to Johanan the high priest and his colleagues the priests who are in Jerusalem" (Cowley, *Aramaic Papyri*, l.18).

41. The parallel list in Neh. 12:10 names Joiada's son Jonathan, which is clearly a mistake. Both lists are obviously secondary additions (or were updated after Nehemiah's time).

though an earlier appeal to the Jerusalem high priest had failed to bring results. What is reflected is the continuation of Persian policy, according to which provincial temples, due to their administrative and economic importance, were to enjoy imperial support. It is also noteworthy that Jedaniah acknowledges that he has also "sent a letter in our name to Delaiah and Shelemiah," sons of Sanballat the governor of Samaria, who were by 408 likely functioning as the successors of their aged (or deceased) father. What is indicated is that from the perspective of the syncretistic leadership of the Jewish colony in Yeb, it was good politics to curry the favor of the Samarian leadership for their cause, especially under circumstances where the Jerusalem high priest had failed to respond.

Letters 33 and 34 add one final detail, namely, that the offerings envisioned for the rebuilt temple in Yeb, while including meal offerings and incense, were to exclude animal sacrifices. An instruction to this effect came, according to Letter 32, from Bagoas and Delaiah, and in Letter 33 it is acknowledged by Jedaniah. It would thus seem that while the temple at Yeb was not regarded to be as blatantly schismatic as the Leontopoline temple, it was not equal in status to the Jerusalem temple. From the perspective of Jews in the Diaspora, the ancient Holy City was still regarded as their spiritual center.

Unfortunately, the desire for information about the functioning of the Jerusalem temple itself at the end of the fifth century is answered mainly by silence. What we have already extrapolated from the Chronicler basically exhausts the extent of our knowledge. The high priesthood was a hereditary position reserved for the Zadokites. A *clerus major*, that is, a priest authorized to serve at the altar, was a fellow Zadokite, who traced his ancestry all the way back to Aaron. Assistants to the altar priests, as well as singers, doorkeepers, and various other temple functionaries greatly expanded the ranks of the Levites.

Beyond such matters of rank and organization of personnel, however, is the much more important question of religious significance of the temple for the Jewish commonwealth. As celebrated in the Psalms, the performance of which the Levitical musicians were responsible for, the temple was the divinely chosen place where the faithful came into the presence of their Lord. It was there that the daily and special offerings were presented to God as gestures of gratitude and for the forgiveness of sins. It was there as well that their representative before God, the high priest, performed the yearly ritual of Yom Kippur for purifying the sacred precincts and banishing the accumulated sins of the people. All in all, the temple retained the primordial quality of *omphalos mundi*, defining the geographical, indeed the cosmic, center of the life of the Jewish community and symbolizing the eternal covenant that was the basis of their peoplehood.

The Scribes of the Torah

The most significant change emerging in the Jewish community during the Persian period revolved around the Torah, including its codification, its rise to iconographic status, and its becoming the object of a dynamic process of interpretation within the emerging guild of professionals called scribes. The Persian

Empire in less than a century would succumb to Alexander, and the Hellenistic regimes would in turn fall to the native rule of the Hasmoneans, who themselves would be supplanted by the occupational forces of Rome. Unsuccessful attempts at regaining Jewish independence finally would culminate in the destruction of the Jerusalem temple itself. That Judaism continued to flourish and develop through calamity and tumultuous regime change is in no small measure due to the inner transformation it underwent during the Persian period.

An adroit refashioning of the way in which the theocratic principle was applied enabled YHWH's status as Israel's sole sovereign to be preserved, in spite of the nation's loss of political autonomy. This possibility was inherent in Israel's theo-political thought from earliest times, due to its break with the mythopoeic worldview of the major cultural centers of the Near East. According to the perspective of the Hebrew Epic, the source of human government was not a timeless and immutable heavenly prototype, but rather a covenant relationship initiated by God and carried out within the context of human history. Deity was not tied to a specific sacred place and one imperial regime, the rise and fall of which evidenced the fate of the divine patron. The source of political understanding extended to Israel consisted of the stories of God's presence in the life of the nation, involving promises, commandments, blessings, punishments, from which Israel derived an understanding of the attributes of the one God that were to be implemented in its political institutions and social structures.

As we have observed repeatedly, the path leading from divine example through legitimate mediation to faithful implementation in human government of the justice and mercy constitutive of YHWH's universal rule was one beset with temptations, including abuse of delegated authority, nationalistic idolatry, and diplomatic entanglements. Especially important in summoning the nation back to covenant fidelity was the consistent witness of the prophets to evidence of God's universal sovereignty in all the events of history. When traditions developed that equated monarchy and temple with divine rule, prophetic critique arose that insisted that the existence of nations and their dynasties and temples was contingent on the quality of their relation to the divine suzerain. Should they deny their provisional status, feign autonomy or unconditional surety of divine favor, or actively oppose divine ordinances of justice and compassion, they would fall victim to their hubris. While historical traumas like the destruction of holy temple and city in 587 BCE and again in 70 CE shook the community to its roots,[42] they resulted ultimately in underscoring the one reality that was dependable and capable of overcoming every historical adversity. Thus the words of a prophet who earlier had witnessed the destruction of temple and Jewish nationhood became inscribed on the heart of the Jewish people:

42. Compare the book of Lamentations with Mark 13.

> The grass withers, the flower fades,
>> when the breath of the LORD blows upon it;
>> surely the people are grass.
> The grass withers, the flower fades;
>> but the word of our God will stand forever.
>>   (Isa. 40:7–8)

With the loss of independence and the temple, Torah, both as representation of the Lord's presence and as expression of divine will, came to be embraced as the covenantal charter of the Jewish people. The same dynamic process of critique, interpretation, amplification, and adaptation that characterized the growth of the Epic and Torah traditions from the beginning of Jewish history continued through the growth of the oral Torah alongside the written Torah. Appropriately, it has been averred that the fifth century BCE witnessed the birth of Judaism. From a political point of view, the parallel statement can be made that out of the Persian period came the political theology that equipped the Jewish community to live through historical moments both bright and bleak with a constancy that defies rational explanations.

Chapter 21

Isaiah 24–27, 56–66;
Ezekiel 38–39;
Zechariah 9–14; Malachi

*Dissent and the Dawning
of Apocalyptic Politics*

EARLY APOCALYPTIC ADDITIONS

In the last chapter we traced the development of a political theology that enabled the Jewish community not only to survive the vicissitudes of historical change, but to nurture a dynamic covenantal concept of peoplehood that laid a sturdy foundation for centuries to come. We suggested that a key to this development was the way in which continuity and change were maintained in a vibrant tension. While the ravages of war and the vicissitudes of exile had destroyed much, a sense of identity was preserved on the basis of the ancestral Epic and the Torah of Moses, in which the devout recognized the path and the guidelines that God had laid out for them, which, if followed, promised to lead to the covenantal blessings of health, peace, and prosperity. That the community did not become locked into structures that would be ill suited for survival in a rapidly changing world was due to the fact that the Torah and its narrative context, while deemed dependable and trustworthy, were found amenable to adaptation and amplification through the skillful exposition of scribes. The political payoff was significant; the leaders of the Jewish commonwealth were able to develop a politics of accommodation that acknowledged the political hegemony of the Persians while preserving the core beliefs and values of the ancestral Jewish tradition.

The dialectical process of preservation and adaptation, however, was not always a smooth one. Controversies often flared up over divergent interpretations of the ancestral tradition. As is often the case in human history, the destabilizing effects of partisan conflict were answered through the consolidation of leadership, with the consequent marginalization of minority groups and suppression of their cherished beliefs and dreams of the future.

As a consequence, the decades following the completion of the Second Temple in 515 BCE were marked by the consolidation of power and the gradual emergence of an authoritative body of teachings. While it would be a long path before canonical standards would be established, the reform activities of Ezra and Nehemiah can be seen as early stages in the long process of distinguishing between teachings that faithfully interpret Torah and sectarian misapplications. A window on that process is opened by Ezra 2:62, which reports that among the priests returning to Judea with Ezra, some lacked documentary proof of their credentials, "and so they were excluded from the priesthood as unclean."[1] When Ezra and Nehemiah applied their rigorous interpretation of Torah to the issue of mixed marriages, a definition of Jewish identity was implemented that excluded rival understandings. These two examples draw attention to the fact that perennially in the realm of politics there are both winners and losers. Having focused in our chapter on the Jewish commonwealth on the winners, we now turn to the losers. But as we do so, we need to qualify that distinction in light of the fact that some of the writings of the latter were included in the final canonical form of the Bible, indicating that in the minds of the sages divergent viewpoints and interpretations were deemed worthy of preservation and ongoing study.

With this reminder of the relative tractability of scribal tradition, we turn to texts that give expression to early stages of a political model we designate as apocalyptic politics, which in the sixth through fifth centuries BCE functioned as a politics of dissent. At issue was a political strategy promulgated by certain minority groups steadfastly upholding a viewpoint opposed to the ascendant accommodationist policies of the leaders studied in the previous chapter.[2] Not only do these texts furnish evidence of the liveliness of discourse that occurred

---

1. For a discussion of other excluded priestly groups, see Joachim Schaper, *Priester und Leviten in der achaemenidischen Zeit* (Tübingen: Mohr Siebeck, 2000), 186–88.

2. The dynamism and adaptability of the scribal Torah tradition can be traced to a mode of perception cultivated in early Israel and never abandoned, namely, a historical perspective opposed to the mythopoeic worldview that prevailed in the ancient Levant. That perspective, conducive to the lively reinterpretation of received tradition described in the previous chapter, went a step beyond reinterpretation to preserving enigmatic writings often incongruent with the mainstream views emerging among the governing elite, a phenomenon that cannot be explained apart from a deeply rooted Hebrew historicist perspective according to which the often messy arena of human affairs was regarded as the location of divine encounter. Rather than leading to the absolutist posture characteristic of mythopoeic cultures, Jewish prophetic and scribal tradition developed an interpretive praxis within which rival interpretations were often tolerated. In the course of the shaping of the biblical corpus, such rival interpretations came to be treated as complementary rather than

within the Jewish community during the Second Temple period. They also document the early stages of a tenacious alternative to the pragmatic policies of the elite circle of Jewish leaders acknowledged as the legitimate representatives of the Jewish community by the Persians. This alternative, after coming to early expression in additions to the books of Isaiah, Ezekiel, and Zechariah and an anonymous writing that came to be known as Malachi (which we shall examine in this chapter), resurfaced robustly in the political struggles of the second century BCE. It left as a textual legacy chapters 7–12 of the book of Daniel, as well as 1 and 2 Maccabees and the sectarian writings of the Dead Sea community of Qumran (which will be our focus in later chapters).

The writings to which we now turn cannot be contextualized in isolation from other texts, for they contain scant indication of historical or political setting. The only hope for reconstructing their provenance lies in relating them to the historical events and religiosocial developments that are documented elsewhere, especially in the books of Haggai, Zechariah, Ezra, and Nehemiah. The resulting reconstruction will remain tentative, given the fragmentary and often enigmatic nature of the writings themselves. It also should be kept in mind that the texts to be discussed do not flow smoothly in a chronological progression out of the historiographic writings dealt with in chapter 20. Our procedure will involve more "backing and filling" than constructing an orderly historical account.

In the interest of providing a sense of direction in the murky waters we now enter, we recall the key historical development of the early restoration period. Chastened by the harsh consequences of a prophetically inspired but failed wedding of a program for rebuilding temple and civic structures to a messianic vision of a restored Davidic monarchy, the Zadokite priests and allied leadership groups adapted prophetic and royal traditions in such a way as to mute eschatological themes in deference to Persian imperial policy. In a dissenting response to that realpolitik, anonymous visionaries gave shape to an alternative future hope by drawing from earlier prophecies vivid descriptions of imminent divine intervention, defeat of the nations, and the establishment of Jerusalem as the city of God, to which the peoples of the earth would bring their offerings. We now turn to an examination of the expressions of dissent and the apocalyptic perspective that took shape in the writings attributable to those visionaries.

ISAIAH 56–66 (THIRD ISAIAH)

Embedded in royal psalms as well as in several of the prophetic books is the motif of the gathering of the nations to Jerusalem. Its origins can be traced to ancient Near Eastern imperial ideology, according to which the reigning king

---

as mutually exclusive. See Paul D. Hanson, *The Diversity of Scripture: A Theological Interpretation* (Philadelphia: Fortress Press, 1982).

was the earthly representative of the patron deity. A successful king exercised his power by extending his dominion over the four corners of the earth, even as he demonstrated his piety by gathering the wealth of the nations into the central sanctuary of the empire. It is a motif that not only reflected the geopolitical pretensions of pharaohs and kings, but also enjoyed substantiation in the tributes and tariffs they were able to extract from vassal states through conquest and occupation.

As we observed earlier in the chapter on ancient Israel's monarchy, this motif came to expression in both historiographic and hymnic works stemming from the period of the Davidic monarchy and even enjoyed partial fulfillment through the successful conquests of David, Solomon, and Jeroboam II. It subsequently was reapplied as an eschatological topos in postexilic prophetic oracles envisioning, after divine judgment and national repentance, an incisive new action taken by God the Divine Warrior to reestablish Israel as a sovereign state and as recipient of the wealth of the nations.[3] After that it became part of the standard repertory of eschatological motifs used by apocalyptic visionaries, including those representing the dissident groups we shall now discuss.

Chapters 56–66 of Isaiah consist of hymns, laments, and oracles that often take up themes from Isaiah 40–55, reapplying them to the circumstances of the early years of the restoration. They can be situated as roughly contemporary with Haggai 1–2 and Zechariah 1–8.[4] Our initial question is this: how does the message found in Isaiah 56–66 (Third Isaiah in the parlance of critical scholarship) relate to the prophetic pronouncements of Haggai and Zechariah, pronouncements functioning to lend oracular support to the temple rebuilding program of Zerubbabel and Joshua?

It is first important to note the similarities: both announce the reversal of the adversity of the past and the divinely initiated inauguration of a new era of peace, security, and prosperity. Moreover, in both cases, the center of the redemptive divine act is Jerusalem, and more specifically, its sanctuary. In other words, the authors of Third Isaiah share with Haggai and Zechariah the vision of God's restoring the scattered people of Judah to their homeland, a vision entailing the defeat of Israel's enemies by its God and the subsequent service rendered to Israel by the nations.

The earliest sections of Third Isaiah are 57:14–21 and 60:1–62:12. The former applies the images of Second Isaiah's inaugural vision (Isa. 40:1–11) to a new situation, that of the first waves of exiles—shortly after they have returned to the land of Israel—facing the daunting task of rebuilding their devastated homeland. An assuring word of "the high and lofty one who inhabits eternity, whose name is Holy," and who dwells "in the high and holy place," is imparted to "those who are contrite and humble in spirit" (57:15). Expressed vividly is the complete reliance of the returning displaced persons on their Savior God.

---

3. Isa. 45:14–17; 51:4–8, 9–11; 52:7–10; 54:1–3, 11–17.
4. Some parts of Isa. 56–66 may stem from later than 515, e.g., 56:1–8; 60:19–22; and 66:17–24.

The idealism and optimism continuing in Isaiah 60–62 suggest that this unit also stems from the period shortly after Cyrus's edict of 538 and the return of the first exiles to Judah. An image drawn from the eighth-century prophet Isaiah (Isa. 9:2 [Heb. 9:1]), namely, the bursting forth of light into the thick darkness that has covered the earth, introduces the motif of the ingathering of scattered Israel and the pilgrimage of the nations to Zion (Isa. 60:4–22; 62:5–11). Caravans of camels will stream to Jerusalem led by kings and bringing abundant resources for the refortification of Jerusalem and the rebuilding of the central sanctuary. This will inaugurate an era of peace, righteousness, and prosperity. In Isaiah 62:1–4 the voice of one epitomizing the profile of the Servant commissioned by the Lord in Isaiah 42:1–4 joyously announces the arrival of the jubilee year.

While the vision of the ingathering of the scattered sons and daughters of Israel and the influx of the wealth of the nations is also found in Haggai and Zechariah, a closer scrutiny reveals a striking difference: Haggai and Zechariah, while embellishing their oracles with mythic motifs, promote a detailed program for rebuilding a working government, one led by individuals they name and structurally patterned after the Davidic monarchy and the preexilic temple priesthood. In contrast, Third Isaiah, rather than announcing the appointment of known figures to specific offices, depicts a utopian realm in which YHWH's sovereignty is celebrated and the nations of the earth supply the wherewithal for restoring temple and land to unprecedented splendor. Envisioned is an Edenic habitation in which *all* citizens are righteous and sanctified as priests of the Lord and ministers of God. In a city whose walls are named Salvation and gates Praise, a redeemed people glorifies God amid prosperity and lasting peace.

It is not difficult to understand why later editors attached this highly visionary depiction of Israel's future to Isaiah 40–55 (Second Isaiah), for the latter had announced God's appointment of a foreign king who would release the captives of Israel and then rebuild Jerusalem and its temple (Isa. 44:24–45:7), leading to a joyous eschatological banquet celebrating the extension of God's covenant with David to the entire community (Isa. 55:1–5). Notwithstanding the obvious thread of continuity from Isaiah 40–55 to Isaiah 60–62, however, a significant shift in perspective is apparent. Manifested in Isaiah 40–55 is a historical grounding more akin to Haggai and Zechariah than to Isaiah 60–62. The most vivid exemplification of Second Isaiah's historical realism is his naming the historical agent God had picked to deliver captive Israel: God had anointed Cyrus, the Persian warrior-king whose defeat of Babylon and sweeping conquests along the eastern Mediterranean had reshaped the geopolitical map of that part of the world.

A careful balance between vision and realism is thus maintained by Second Isaiah. To be sure, the message of hope he extends to captive Israel is enriched with poetic images of a miraculous transformation of wastelands into fertile gardens and the glorification of a restored nation. Other elements of his message, such as the temporal dualism implicit in the distinction between a past that is to be forgotten and the new thing that God is about to create, and his reference to the dragon of ancient mythology as the archenemy of God's people, foreshadow later apocalyptic writings (Isa. 43:18–19; 51:9). However, his relating YHWH's deliverance to the historical events unfolding in his world establishes a secure connection of his message to the stage of human history. In the period of transition from prophetic to apocalyptic eschatology, it is that tie that places Second Isaiah's message theo-politically closer to Haggai and Zechariah than to the visionary author of Isaiah 60–62, who includes no reference to a divinely appointed Persian messiah.

From the vantage point of our present study, the degree to which an individual or a group relates its vision of the future to the actual circumstances of its time is of great importance. For a person of faith concerned about global peace and the quality of life of all humans, events as they unfold in the world of human affairs are not matters of indifference. Contradictions between what a community hopes for and what it experiences cannot be brushed aside. Erroneous prophetic announcements cannot be corrected blithely with clever recalculations or pious excuses. There is no denying that relating one's prophetic vision to historical happenings involves greater risk than safeguarding one's message under the protection of the immutability of mythical imagery.

Second Isaiah, like the Hebrew prophets before him, followed the risky course of keeping his prophetic message connected to the real world in which he and his people found themselves. At the same time, he refused to reduce the future of his people to the pragmatics and constraints of worldly power. Ultimately he believed human agents served divine purpose. God's purpose for Israel did not end with the Babylonian conquest of Jerusalem. Nor was it completed with the restoration of structures of governance in Judea in the late sixth century BCE.

Though hopes ran high with completion of the temple in 515 BCE, we have seen that a period of crisis followed. Unlike Second Isaiah's announcement of Cyrus's release of the exiled Jewish community, Haggai's and Zechariah's promise of a new golden age under the Davidic prince Zerubbabel and the Zadokite high priest Joshua failed to dawn. Survival of the nation necessitated retreat into a pragmatic compromise, leading to what we have called a politics of accommodation. Rather than Jewish sovereignty under the "two sons of oil," submission to the authority of this world's new imperial power imposed radical concessions. The concept of Davidic rule had to be jettisoned, while the Zadokite high priest was obliged to place the temple at the service not only of the God of Israel, but also of Darius I, king of Persia. The political entity that emerged was not the unalloyed embodiment of their eschatological vision, but at least it was a *Jewish* commonwealth, granted certain prerogatives for ordering its *internal* affairs, of which the most important pertained to Torah and temple ritual.

However, not all followers of YHWH were convinced that Darius was an agent of divine purpose. Within the context of a community whose official leaders were struggling to establish institutions suitable for life under foreign rule, a rival plan was emerging. Its roots can be traced to the bold vision of restoration already depicted in Isaiah 60–62. Since it did not specify organizational details for the resettled Jewish nation, it was less vulnerable to the contradictions of history than the "blueprint" of the politically ascendant party. The reorganizing of community structure would be accomplished not by Jewish leaders in partnership with a foreign power, but by God alone. Those remaining faithful even unto death would know that the time of vindication had arrived when all their (and God's) enemies had been eliminated, enemies within their nation, like the Zadokite priestly elite, and enemies without, like the Persian overlords. It was only after God's victory that they would be reinstated in their sacred offices as God's servants.

The visionary absolutism that was being cultivated by dissenting enclaves forms the backbone of apocalyptic politics. It is a political position that manifests no inclination to adjust vision (or ideology) to reality or to work out compromises with rival parties or foreign authorities. Instead it behooves adherents either to withdraw from situations they cannot change and await the day of final reckoning, when God would destroy all opposition, or hurl themselves into suicidal participation with the angels in the end-time battle.

We turn now to passages from Isaiah 56–66 that appear to come from a period of increasing tension between leaders and dissidents over strategies for restoring the people Israel in their homeland. In them we can trace the unfolding of the trajectory of absolute trust in the ultimate victory of Israel's God over all rivals, accompanied by an indifference to translating that victory into the nuts and bolts of political and ecclesial structure. The passages we shall discuss fit two categories, those that condemn all who oppress the chosen remnant and those that renew the promise of everlasting blessing for God's suffering servants.

In the lament in 63:7–64:11 several features of the emerging apocalyptic perspective come into view. Israel's early history is recounted as an ideal era in which YHWH acted personally to redeem his people: "It was no messenger or angel but his presence that saved them" (63:9 *ketib*). But in the present time, the lament continues, God is absent, the remnant of the faithful is not even acknowledged by those in authority ("Abraham/Israel," 63:16), and the sanctuary has been snatched away by adversaries (63:19). Out of their anguish they plea to YHWH to act as in the days of old, that is, by destroying his enemies and striking the nations with terror. The perspective is visionary in the sense that obstacles, stemming both from inner-community conflict and foreign hostilities, must be eradicated directly by YHWH. Attention to human agency and the pragmatics of political implementation is absent.

In Isaiah 58–59 egregious abuses are condemned. The people fast, but in their fasting display callous disregard for the poor and the homeless. Rather than honoring the Sabbath, they pursue their business dealings. They make a travesty of the court system by turning it into an instrument of injustice and oppression serving the rich and the powerful against the impoverished. In this entire diatribe the author stands within the tradition of Amos, Hosea, Isaiah, and Jeremiah, and indeed, he denounces many of the abuses against which his contemporaries Haggai and Zechariah contended and with which Nehemiah in his generation struggled. The hallmark of these two chapters, however, is the resolution announced. It does not involve a priestly ruling such as reported by Haggai and Zechariah (Hag. 2:10–14; Zech. 7:1–14) or the imposition of authority of office combined with righteous indignity that lent clout to Nehemiah's reforms (Neh. 5:1–13; 13:4–31). Rather, the denouement that comes in Isaiah 59:15b–20 is a depiction of YHWH's direct, unmediated intervention ("there was no one to intervene," 59:16) and a dazzling display of the Divine Warrior's fury: "wrath to his adversaries, requital to his enemies; to the coastlands he will render requital" (59:18).

In Isaiah 63:1–6 YHWH acts again, this time against foreign enemies.[5] In a scene reminiscent of Anat's rampage against her foes in Ugaritic mythology, Israel's God is depicted trampling enemies as one treads the winepress. Once again, he acts alone:

> I looked, but there was no helper;
>   I stared, but there was no one to sustain me;
> so my own arm brought me victory,
>   and my wrath sustained me.
> I trampled down peoples in my anger,
>   I crushed them in my wrath,
>   and I poured out their lifeblood on the earth.
>   (Isa. 63:5–6)

The reader may ask, when and where was this dramatic battle to take place? It is a mark of the oracles in Isaiah 56–66 that neither historical dates nor human agents seem to be of concern. In contrast to this suspension of time and place, we have observed that in Haggai and Zechariah, the human agents of change were named, even as their oracles were precisely dated, and although those dates may reflect the chronological interests of the final editor (likely the author of 1 and 2 Chronicles), they comport with the political realism of the two prophets themselves. Characteristic of the material in Isaiah 56–66, by contrast, is the absence of historical indicators, whether in the form of allusions or dates. That absence is in keeping with the ethereal orientation of the visionary author(s). When dealing with divine drama, human agents and the particularity of concrete historical settings are not important.

It would be wrong, however, to infer that the oracles and hymns of Third Isaiah originated in a vacuum. Though the recourse taken is to a transcendent realm and a divine actor, it is recourse in response to a lived situation, one difficult to reconstruct but leaving traces that can be teased out of the texts. Broadly speaking, we can detect signs of inner-community conflict. For example, in Isaiah 65, after an announcement of God's wrath against the pagan abominations

---

5. As elsewhere in postexilic writings, Edom is cited in this passage as Israel's archenemy, reflecting an animosity born of the treachery displayed by the Edomites when they pillaged Judah, after it had been rendered defenseless by the Babylonian army.

of a group brazenly laying claim to a superior holiness that separates them from ordinary people,[6] a striking divine word is pronounced:

> As the wine is found in the cluster,
>   and they say, "Do not destroy it,
>   for there is a blessing in it,"
> so I will do for my servants' sake,
>   and not destroy them all.
>   (Isa. 65:8)

This metaphor is followed by a series of blessings and curses, the blessings to "my servants," the curses against those "who forsake the LORD." The contrast depicts a sharply divided community. But who are the rival parties?

A clue is found in the final nine verses of Isaiah 65 and the first five verses of the next chapter. This passage is introduced by words that echo and then enlarge upon the divine promise recorded by Second Isaiah in 43:18–21:

> For I am about to create new heavens
>   and a new earth;
> the former things shall not be remembered
>   or come to mind.
>   (Isa. 65:17)

Here YHWH promises a new creation featuring a quality of life not known since before the banishment of Adam and Eve from Eden. No attention is given to human agency, human institutions, human politics. Attention to such matters is called for no more than it was in the first creation.

Isaiah 66 begins with a heaven/earth parallelism that continues the transcendent perspective of the preceding passage: "Heaven is my throne and the earth is my footstool." But the idyllic rhapsody ends abruptly, interrupted by a sharp divine interrogation of those who would build a house (i.e., temple) for YHWH: "What is the house that you would build for me?"

Viewed in isolation, this interrogation eludes explanation. Is it a hymnic celebration of YHWH's transcendence, unattached to a specific setting?[7] Is it a direct criticism of the particular temple building program promoted by Haggai and Zechariah?[8] The enigma is not removed entirely by the following verse (66:3), though it becomes clear that what is denounced is the conduct

---

6. Cf. Isa. 65:5 with Ezek. 44:19.

7. Jon D. Levenson, "The Temple and the World," *Journal of Religion* 64 (1984): 275–98. Cf. Valeri Stein, *Anti-Cultic Theology in Christian Biblical Interpretation: A Study of Isaiah 66:1–4 and Its Reception* (New York: Peter Lang, 2007).

8. Cf. Isa. 66:1 ("What is the house [*bāyit*] that you would build for me?") with Hag. 1:8 ("build the house [*bāyit*], so that I may take pleasure in it and be honored." Another possible translation of the Isaiah verse is: "Where could you build a house for Me?" (TANAKH, Jewish Publication Society, 1999). In either case, YHWH is stating a truth that lies at the heart of biblical faith: there is no need for which the Creator of the heavens and the earth is dependent upon humans. See Paul D. Hanson, *The Dawn of Apocalyptic* (Philadelphia: Fortress Press, 1975), 161–208.

of sacrificial rites in the temple, either because they are pagan in substance or equivalent to pagan abominations, because those offering them are unfit, due to defilement.

Light is shed on the setting and message of Isaiah 66:1–3 by the two verses that follow. Those being indicted are the same ones who came under divine judgment in Isaiah 65, that is, those who forsake YHWH by turning a deaf ear[9] and yet flaunt a self-proclaimed exceptional holiness.[10] They are blind, clueless, cowardly community leaders who are responsible for the undoing of the righteous and the devout (cf. 56:9–57:2). They are the Israel that does not acknowledge the oppressed remnant appealing to YHWH (63:16). In the final accounting, they will be put to shame while God's servants will rejoice (65:11–15). Until the final judgment, they continue to mock the visionary faith of those "who tremble at [YHWH's] word" (Isa. 66:2b and 66:5a) and to apply their earthly power to banish the faithful from the temple community (66:5).[11]

The response adopted by the excluded group is the one that often is the only one deemed available by politically disenfranchised parties: they await YHWH's unmediated intervention on their behalf, which, ironically, will originate in the contested temple (66:6). The present time is a time of trial, but as in the case of the pain of labor preceding human birth, final vindication is assured by God, as well as wealth and security, which, true to the topos of the final ingathering to Jerusalem, will be supplied by the nations (66:7–14). In the last verses of the visionary group's collection of oracles,[12] the tragic division rending the Jewish community reaches a shuddering climax:

> [A]nd it shall be known that the hand of the LORD is with his servants,
>   and his indignation is against his enemies.
> For the LORD will come in fire,
>   and his chariots like the whirlwind,
> to pay back his anger in fury,
>   and his rebuke in flames of fire.
> For by fire will the LORD execute judgment,
>   and by his sword, on all flesh;
>   and those slain by the LORD will be many.
>
>   (66:14b–16)

9. Cf. Isa. 65:1–2 and 12 with Isa. 66:4.

10. The rhetoric here is bitterly hostile against individuals claiming priestly sanctity, but whose incense and burnt offerings are not sweet smelling to YHWH, but "a smoke in my nostrils, a fire that burns all day long" (Isa. 65:5).

11. The verb *nadah*, translated "reject" in the NRSV, "in later Talmudic usage acquired the technical meaning of 'excommunicate' in reference to expulsion from the synagogue" (James Muilenburg, *Isaiah*, in *Interpreter's Bible* (New York: Abingdon Press, 1956), 5:764.

12. Isa. 66:17–24 consists of later additions.

ZECHARIAH 9–11 (SECOND ZECHARIAH)
AND ZECHARIAH 12–14 (THIRD ZECHARIAH)

The compositional and editorial process that led through various stages of growth culminating in the canonical shape of the biblical books did not occur in a vacuum. We have seen how Isaiah 56–66 both built upon and departed from various aspects of the message of Isaiah 40–55. We now turn to see how three short appendices at the conclusion of the Minor Prophets similarly betray interpretive responses to Haggai 1–2 and Zechariah 1–8.

Earlier we observed that Haggai and the first eight chapters of Zechariah provide the Bible's most direct witnesses to the foundation laying and rebuilding of the Second Temple. We were able to detect in Zechariah 6:9–14 early signs of a strategy of accommodation that would mute eschatological themes handed down by earlier prophets, in favor of a political model of partnership with the Persian occupation. This strategy comes to full expression in the later recounting of the period of return from exile, temple construction, and community building found in Ezra 1–6. But not all expository responses to Haggai and Zechariah in the Bible share the policy of downplaying an eschatological vision of the future and reconciling divine purpose with Persian dominion over Israel.

Zechariah 9–11 (Second Zechariah), Zechariah 12–14 (Third Zechariah), and Malachi each bear the title *maśśāʾ děbar yhwh* ("An Oracle, the Word of the Lord"), indicating that they were anonymous collections until becoming editorially attached to the Minor Prophets, the first two as additions to the book of Zechariah, the third as a separate booklet that propitiously rounded off the Minor Prophets scroll to twelve books.[13]

The function of these three appendices can be compared to the instances of halakic midrash (i.e., reinterpretations of specific Torah ordinances) contained in the memoirs of Ezra and Nehemiah. Using the term loosely, they might be designated as prophetic midrashim, implying that they provide reinterpretations of the messages found in Haggai and Zechariah 1–8, aimed at making sense of the received tradition in relation to the changed situation facing the protagonist group or groups.

Recalling Michael Fishbane's identification of two modes of intertextualism, *revitalization* and *undermining*,[14] and extending the concept of midrash to the prophetic material at hand, we can recognize a clear instance of reinterpretation in its *undermining* mode. Rather than being muted in these appendices, the eschatological dimension of the received texts is amplified; rather than being accommodated, the purported dominion of any suzerain besides God is subjected to an announcement of impending annihilation. What we encounter, therefore, are oracles shaped by undermining midrashic reinterpretations

---

13. What was originally a *nomen agentis,* "my messenger" (*malʾākî* [3:1]), came to be clothed with a new meaning as a proper name, the prophet Malachi!

14. Michael Fishbane, *Biblical Interpretation in Ancient Israel* (Oxford: Clarendon, 1985), 15.

reacting to the pro-Persian policy being pursued by the Zadokite temple leadership and governors of Judea.

Turning first to Zechariah 9–10, we find a scenario seriously undermining the foreign policy that had become official in Judea, namely, the policy of the Jewish community living in conformity with the terms set by the foreign occupation and the Zadokite-led temple staff dutifully collecting taxes for the Achaemenids and offering up prayers for the Persian emperor and his family. In chapter 9 YHWH as Divine Warrior is depicted conducting a campaign to conquer the vast territory reaching across the Persian province of Abar-nahara and then returning in triumph to Jerusalem to take up watch, intended to protect the temple from ever again falling into foreign hands. In the entry hymn in Zechariah 9:9–17, the eschatological theme of universal conquest celebrated in Haggai 2:20–23 is not muted, as had become the strategy within official Zadokite circles, but elaborated. While echoing the martial imagery of Haggai's oracle, it heightens the transcendent dimension: This time YHWH does not deputize a Davidic prince as his servant, but takes personal, unmediated command. Even the mysterious reference to daughter Zion's king (Zech. 9:9) is not explained by identifying him with a historical figure like Zerubbabel (cf. Hag. 2:23). The hymn, in other words, bears the marks of an apocalyptic vision.

Zechariah 10 continues the description of YHWH's conquest and repatriation of his people. Why he is obliged to take personal command of the military campaign and the ingathering of the scattered nation is answered in Zechariah 10:3:

> My anger is hot against the shepherds,
>   and I will punish the leaders,
> for the LORD of hosts cares for his flock, the house of Judah.

The theme of unfaithful shepherds (i.e., community leaders), taken from Ezekiel 34 and developed further in Zechariah 11:4–17, is a suitable vehicle for an apocalyptic politics of dissent. The direction of borrowing is from Ezekiel 34 to Second Zechariah, and a date in the late sixth or early fifth century is likely. The "undermining" mode of reinterpretation serves the dissidents' purposes well by replacing the official program of restoration with a vastly different vision of YHWH's plan.

The starting point for the shepherd passages in Ezekiel and Zechariah is the same: the shepherds (i.e., leaders of the people) are condemned for exploiting and abusing their sheep, rather than caring for them. There the similarity abruptly ends. Ezekiel goes on to describe God's promise that he would rescue the sheep from the hands of the wicked shepherds by becoming their *personal* shepherd to return them to their land and heal them and feed them and then set over them his servant David. In contrast, in the Zechariah passage YHWH raises up over the already battered flock a shepherd who outstrips the earlier shepherds in brutality: "For I am now raising up in the land a shepherd who does not care for the perishing, or seek the wandering, or heal the maimed, or nourish the healthy, but devours the flesh of the fat ones, tearing off even their hoofs" (Zech. 11:16). What is the source and intent of this unspeakably grim message?

Light is shed on this question by the undermining reinterpretation in Second Zechariah of another symbolical text from Ezekiel, namely, 37:15–27. In that passage Ezekiel is commanded to take two sticks, representing the kingdoms of Judah and Israel, and to fuse them into one, thereby performing a virtual enactment of the reunification of the Jewish people into one nation. The Chronicler's History, with its clear prounification policy, indicates that in the period from which Second Zechariah stems, the issue of drawing the north back into the union was very much alive. Against this background Zechariah 11:4–17 would appear to be a repudiation of reunification, at least under the existing Zadokite-led, pro-Persian Jewish commonwealth.

Due to the depravity of the incumbent leadership, YHWH is portrayed as a proponent not of greater unity but of deeper division. Accordingly, "the shepherd of the flock doomed to slaughter" reports, "I took my staff Favor and broke it, annulling the covenant that I had made with all the peoples" (11:7, 10), and "then I broke my second staff Unity, annulling the family ties between Judah and Israel" (11:14). That we are dealing with a politics of dissent is obvious, but the question persists: why this blunt repudiation of the *Pax Persica*, which constituted the backbone of the official Jewish leadership's foreign policy, and rejection of the ideal of reunification of north and south, sought already by Josiah and enjoying the support of the authoritative compilers of 1 and 2 Chronicles?

The most plausible explanation would seem to be that the harsh repudiation originates in a group rejecting the claim of the Persian-backed Jewish authorities that the Jewish commonwealth as presently constituted is in accord with divine purpose. But what is their alternate vision of God's plan for his people?

The graphic depiction in Zechariah 9 and 10 of YHWH reclaiming a territory surpassing that of Solomon's kingdom and resettling on it a people gathered from the nations suggests that theirs is a vision of a Jewish nation liberated from all foreign powers, living in holiness, and bending the knee to no authority save YHWH. Though the ideal of a people living in the purity safeguarded by the Lord's house in their midst and upheld by obedience to the Torah was one shared by dissidents and Judean officialdom alike, the point of dispute was Israel's relation to the dominions of this world and the agency deemed capable of restoring the living covenant between God and people. The vision displayed in Second Zechariah denounces a pragmatic politics of accommodation in favor of belief in YHWH as the sole agent capable of reconstituting a unified people. From this can be inferred a more comprehensive understanding of the conflict: the Judean leadership, in settling for the terms of the *Pax Persica*, has betrayed the terms of God's covenant with Israel by placing alongside of YHWH a rival authority, thereby setting the stage for further conflict, both within the community and among the nations.

Third Zechariah (Zechariah 12–14), the second pamphlet appended to the Minor Prophets, extends the trajectory of dissident visions. First, we shall describe the apocalyptic drama of chapters 12–13. It opens with a siege, directed by YHWH, against Jerusalem, in which "all the nations of the earth" participate. Suddenly, through a ruse, YHWH turns Jerusalem and Judah into instruments of judgment to which the nations fall victim. This elimination of the nations prepares the way for further divine initiatives, one leading to a solemn ritual of mourning involving the upper echelons of Jerusalem, another providing water "to cleanse them from sin and impurity."

The cleansing process is carried a step further with the removal from the land of "the names of the idols" and "the prophets and the unclean spirit" (13:2), that is, obstacles standing in the way of the fulfillment of YHWH's purposes. Finally, YHWH orders the sword to strike his shepherd (apparently in continuation with the enigmatic report in 11:13–17). This act of divine judgment results in a scattering of the sheep, destruction of two-thirds of them, with the remnant subjected to refining and testing, culminating with a purified and faithful community and renewal of the covenant:

> They will call on my name,
>   and I will answer them.
> I will say, "They are my people,"
>   and they will say, "The LORD is our God."
>   (Zech. 13:9)

While many details in this account remain puzzling, the central plotline is clear: A vision of the future begins with an international conflict leading to a destruction of the nations, and ends with a purging of Israel through which the covenant people is reunited with their Lord. In this vision, the restraints of historical process and limits of human capacity are of no concern, since YHWH alone initiates and directs the action. Rival powers are summarily eliminated, as God alone gathers to himself his undefiled, faithful community.

Zechariah 14 introduces a new unit with the announcement that "a day is coming for the LORD." The end-time scenario that follows gives yet another account of how YHWH will transform a present world of chaos into the purity and perfection of God's reign. The action will be initiated by YHWH's gathering "all the nations against Jerusalem to battle" (14:2). In what gives the appearance of a magnified replay of the sixth-century BCE Babylonian debacle, the Holy City will fall, followed by looting, rape, and the exile of half of the population. At that point YHWH, accompanied by his heavenly legions, will intervene with a might that alters the very topography of Jerusalem, creating out of the Mount of Olives a processional way for the victorious Divine Warrior. Further transformations follow in rapid succession: a change in the seasons, the irrigation of the land with living waters that flow forth from Jerusalem,[15] and

---

15. The temple as the source of life-giving waters is a topos tracing all the way to the reign of Shulgi (ca. 2094–2047 BCE) of the Third Dynasty of Ur.

further rearrangement of the topography of the land, which will be leveled into a plain, with Jerusalem alone rising in eternal splendor, befitting the city of God's own choosing.

With this total transformation of the land, preparation has been completed for the coronation festival: "And the LORD will become king over all the earth" (14:9a). In this proclamation resides the core hope of the visionary group. There is but one dependable basis for enduring *shalom*. Every human effort to bring peace, to unite the scattered, and to secure the land has had only the opposite effects of increased conflict and further fragmentation, for unity cannot be built upon the divisions that inevitably arise within human institutions. "On that day the LORD will be one and his name one" (14:9) is the only dependable formula for the healing of broken Jerusalem, "and it shall be inhabited, for never again shall it be doomed to destruction; Jerusalem shall abide in security" (14:11).

Jerusalem's security, however, is not an end in itself, for Jerusalem is not merely a human habitation, but the earthly dwelling place of the Holy One. Defended by a divine plague from every potential enemy and enriched by the gifts of the nations, Jerusalem will be the pilgrimage site, not only for the faithful remnant of Judea; "all who survive of the nations" will gather to celebrate the Feast of Booths (14:16). Transformed Jerusalem will be well prepared for the influx of pilgrims, the entire city having become a sacred precinct. Nor will it be thwarted for lack of sacrificial vessels, for "every cooking pot in Jerusalem and Judah shall be sacred to the LORD of hosts, so that all who sacrifice may come and use them to boil the flesh of the sacrifice" (14:21a). Furthermore, the pilgrims will be saved from the distraction of traders using the temple to display their wares, for all traders will be expelled as the din of commerce surrenders to the intonations of worship (14:21b).

Comparison of the vision in Zechariah 14 with the message of the prophet Zechariah (chaps. 1–8) indicates that the final canonical shaping of the book of Zechariah was not an arbitrary one. At the heart of Zechariah's mission was the restoration of Jerusalem and its temple as the dwelling place of God's glory and a home for God's people, where they would be secure from the harm of hostile nations.[16] Zechariah 14 envisions events that would create such a Jerusalem. However, when we subject to the scrutiny of intertextual interpretation the relation of Zechariah 1–8 to the booklets in chapters 9–11 and 12–14, an important dimension of reinterpretation becomes visible, even to the point of undermining earlier connotations.

Specifically, undermining can be detected in a reformulation of Israel's divinely appointed future that implies a sharp critique and correction of the policy of the official Judean leadership. YHWH's purpose with his people would come to fulfillment not through collaboration with this world's powers and accommodation to their imperial designs, but solely through YHWH's defeat of those world powers and his establishment of his unrivaled and uncompromised

16. See Zech. 1:12–17 and 2:1–5 (Heb. 2:5–9).

universal sovereignty. On the long trajectory from prophetic to apocalyptic eschatology, Second and Third Zechariah mark a point well advanced toward the latter. The same will be true of the third booklet attached to the Minor Prophets, the book of Malachi.

THE BOOK OF MALACHI

We have already noted that anonymous material such as that preserved in Zechariah 9–14 is notoriously difficult to contextualize, due to a lack of clear historical references. A more indirect approach, however, can lead at least to tentative conclusions, an approach that seeks to utilize perceptible connections to thematically related texts.

The final editor(s) of Zechariah 9–14 and Malachi saw sufficient affinities between the three booklets comprising these chapters to introduce them with parallel titles (Zech. 9:1; 12:1; Mal. 1:1). Latter-day historians are well advised to see what evidence of connections they in turn may find, and in the course of our examining Malachi, we shall take that advice. Sufficient points of contact are found between Malachi's oracles and the memoirs of Ezra and Nehemiah to commend interpreting the former in light of the latter and proposing a Judean setting in the first half of the fifth century BCE.

The central invective in Malachi is directed against the altar priests of the Jerusalem temple, the Zadokites, suggesting that ethical standards regulating the institution that, in the eyes of both the people of Judea and the Persians, served as the nerve center of Jewish society had declined precipitously since the ebullient days of Joshua and Zerubbabel. Most shocking is the accusation that the very ones responsible for ritual purity and compliance with the Torah are the chief offenders.

The depths of the depravity of the Zadokite temple priests is captured by Malachi in the exasperation ascribed to YHWH: "Oh, that someone among you would shut the temple doors, so that you would not kindle fire on my altar in vain" (Mal. 1:10a). This sharp repudiation of the ministrations of the altar priests calls to mind the vitriolic sarcasm hurled at the self-proclaimed holy ones in Isaiah 65:5, who warn, "Keep to yourself, do not come near me, for I am too holy for you"; in the case of those priests, God's disdain is the same: "These are a smoke in my nostrils, a fire that burns all day long."

Specifically at issue in Malachi is utter disregard for the quality of the animals being offered, which amounts to an egregious affront to God, from whom the priests are withholding the respect that one takes for granted even in the presence of a human governor (Mal. 1:8). The punishment threatened by God fits the crime: God will spread the excrement of their blemished offerings on the faces of the priests (2:3)!

The moral depravity of the priests also engulfs their parallel responsibility as teachers of the Torah. Informing the prophetic invective in this case is Moses' final words commending Levi and his offspring, who alongside faithfulness in altar service demonstrated their covenant fidelity in teaching Israel the Torah:

> For they observed your word,
>   and kept your covenant.
> They teach Jacob your ordinances,
>   and Israel your law.
>   (Deut. 33:9b–10a)

The contrast between faithful Levi and the corrupt priests could not have been drawn more sharply than in Malachi: Levi "revered me and stood in awe of my name" (Mal. 2:5), the priests "despise my name" (1:6). "True Torah [NRSV "instruction"] was in his mouth, . . . and he turned many from iniquity" (2:6); they "have caused many to stumble by [their] Torah [NRSV "instruction"]" (2:8). Levi walked with the Lord "in integrity and uprightness" (2:6); they "corrupted the covenant of Levi" and "have not kept [YHWH's] ways but have shown partiality in [their] Torah [NRSV "instruction"]" (2:8–9). The two indictments against the priests are conclusive: desecration of the altar and false teaching of the Torah.

The book of Malachi paints a vivid picture of the crisis that Ezra and Nehemiah were sent by the Persians to rectify. The points of contact are many. Among those indicted in the mixed marriages that Nehemiah and Ezra sought to dissolve were priests (Ezra 9:1; 10:5, 18–24; Neh. 13:28), an issue addressed as well in Malachi (Mal. 2:11–16). In Malachi 3:8–12 another egregious neglect of duty on the part of the priests is condemned, namely, their failure to "bring the full tithe into the storehouse, so that there may be food in my house" (Mal. 3:10).

Recall that Nehemiah had "appointed as treasurers over the storehouses the priest Shelemiah, the scribe Zadok, and Pedaiah of the Levites" (Neh. 13:13), who contended with the priest Eliashib's emptying out a storeroom designated for "the tithes of grain, wine, and oil, which were given by commandment to the Levites, singers, and gatekeepers, and the contributions for the priests" (Neh. 13:5), so as to provide accommodations for his relative Tobiah; that he had dealt at length with the solemn obligation of the people to be faithful to the laws regulating tithes (Neh. 10:35–39); and finally, that he had to take incisive action against the officials failing in their duty to gather the tithe from which the Levites derived their provisions. Then one gains a more concrete picture of the gravity and complexity of the offenses triggering the divine curse in Malachi 3:8–12 against those who rob God of his due.

One final point of contact between Malachi and Nehemiah becomes visible through comparison of Nehemiah's reform efforts on behalf of the poor who were being exploited by their wealthy neighbors (Neh. 5:1–13) with YHWH's threat of judgment against those who oppress the vulnerable in Malachi 3:5. The source of injustice and cruelty traces up the chain of command to the highest ranks, as reflected in Malachi's indictment of priests who "have not kept my ways but have shown partiality in [their] Torah [NRSV "instruction"]" (Mal.

2:9b). The response to this distortion by both the anonymous prophet and Nehemiah the governor was outrage, for to them Torah was not an abstract ideal, but a path guiding the feet of the righteous in their everyday affairs and calling for most incisive action when it intersected with the path trodden by the poor, the vulnerable, and the exploited.

It is thus apparent that the author of Malachi holds much in common with Ezra and Nehemiah in the areas of cultic and social reform. On another level, comparison reveals a divergence of perspectives. This is the level addressing the removal of obstacles to the just society and the fulfillment of the covenantal blessings of shared prosperity and universal *shalom*, a level on which we find Ezra and Nehemiah staunchly advocating a realpolitik of accommodation with the Persians, and Malachi subscribing to the more visionary denouement of incisive divine intervention. In looking to the future, Malachi, like Third Isaiah, Second Zechariah, and Third Zechariah, gives voice to his contempt for the regnant Zadokite hierocracy and its alliance with the Persians. This places him in the company of a dissident faction and an eschatological perspective unfolding in the direction of an apocalyptic politics. This world's institutions and their caretakers have become agents of evil. Hope for redemption lies solely in God's intervention. God's faithful servants can endure the present fallen order by focusing on the glorious age to come.

In distinguishing between diverging trajectories, there is a danger of slipping into oversimplifications. As a cautionary measure, it is necessary to emphasize the significant overlap between the official party and the dissidents in the period of the restoration and commonwealth. Though some scholars have construed the difference between the mainstream and the apocalyptic minority in terms of the centrality of law in the former and an emphasis on (intervening) divine grace in the other, this polarity is supported by no textual evidence.

Shared by both is the conviction that strict adherence to Torah is the foundation of Jewish society. Both acknowledge the importance of the temple cult as the place where the glory of Israel's God was celebrated through hymns and sacrifices and where the rites essential for maintaining the purity of the nation were performed. Equally clear is that Ezra, Nehemiah, and Malachi share the conviction that disobedience to the Torah and neglect of laws and ordinances regulating purity and defilement were placing in jeopardy the health and vitality of the nation. The Persians, for reasons of their own military and economic needs, placed their support behind the stability of the temple and local cultic apparatus, support that was embraced by one side and not the other.

Ezra and Nehemiah exercised their political skill by committing the nation to a strategy of collaboration with the Persians, a pragmatic tactic in which the nation traded political autonomy for the social and political stability that enabled a religious community to live in conformity with its traditional statutes and the cultic rites that maintained the purity of the land. In the implementation of this modus operandi, Ezra and Nehemiah were actively engaged, serving simultaneously as agents of their God and obedient appointees of the Persian state. Their activities were wide ranging, from repairing fortifications to enforcing ethical standards in the marketplace to assuring proper provisions for temple personnel.

It is on the level of strategy and agency that Malachi manifests his adherence to a different trajectory. The current leaders had failed in their administration of temple ritual and Torah instruction. Stepping into the calamitous breach was God himself, and the only delegation of responsibility God makes is appointment of a heavenly herald to prepare for his arrival: "See, I am sending my messenger [malʾākî] to prepare the way before me, and the Lord whom you seek will suddenly come to his temple" (Mal. 3:1). "The day of his coming" mentioned in verse 2 echoes the ancient tradition of the Holy Warrior. Since defilement is a central problem in Malachi, the similes "like a refiner's fire and like fullers' soap" (3:2) are poignant. The result of this direct divine intervention will be eradication of the altar desecration spelled out in lurid detail earlier in Malachi and restoration of purity in the temple precincts. In clear demonstration of the inseparability of cultic practice and ethics, YHWH's initiative moves from temple reform to the restoration of social justice in the land. Malachi thus adds his testimony to Micah's divine question par excellence: "What does the LORD require of you?" Religion is hollow that does not attend to the rights of the oppressed worker, the widow and orphan, the alien (3:5).

We are reminded once more of the transcendent dimension of apocalyptic politics by the denouement in the final ten verses of the book of Malachi: those humans who will be spared in the final judgment, namely, those whose names are written in "a book of remembrance," "who revered the Lord" (yirʾê yhwh), and are a "special possession"[17] of the Lord, will be enlisted into the ranks of the Divine Warrior on the *dies irae* to "tread down the wicked" (4:3 [Heb. 3:21]). Thus entering the stage of end-time drama is the divine-human partnership that will become a hallmark of latter apocalyptic writings. It is a partnership differing from the pragmatic agency carried out by Ezra and Nehemiah within the day-to-day issues of their community. It is agency on a cosmic scale that awaits its full expression in Daniel, *1 Enoch*, *4 Ezra*, and, most elaborately of all, in the Dead Sea community tractate, *The War between the Sons of Light and the Sons of Darkness*.[18]

EZEKIEL 38–39

In the book of Ezekiel, after a messenger had come to the prophet with the announcement that Jerusalem had fallen to the Babylonian invaders (Ezek. 33:21), a series of oracles in chapters 34–37 turns the narrative from the theme of judgment to promises of a brighter future. Corrupt leaders would be replaced by the

---

17. The Hebrew word here for "special possession" is the same one used in Exod. 19:5, where it stands in parallel to "a priestly kingdom and a holy nation."

18. See chap. 23.

just rule of YHWH and his servant David; Israel would live in obedience to the Torah and be at peace with the nations and with the realm of nature; and its cities would be rebuilt for a growing population. These chapters end with a fitting summary, namely, God's promise to make with Israel an everlasting covenant of peace and to place his dwelling place in its midst, all according to the ultimate purpose that runs as a leitmotif through the book, that "the nations shall know that I the LORD sanctify Israel, when my sanctuary is among them forevermore" (37:26–28).

Thematically, chapters 40–48 follow directly upon the promise in the last verse of chapter 37, for in those nine chapters Ezekiel receives in a vision a detailed plan for the rebuilding of the land of Israel, featuring at its center the temple, from which issues copious water for the transformation of wastelands into a paradise.

How are we to explain the rude intrusion of chapters 38–39 into the organic narrative development from chapter 37 to chapter 40? The reader has been prepared to receive an elaboration of the joyous news of rebirth of the nation, but these two chapters plunge into the depths of a calamity categorically more horrific than the devastation wreaked by the Babylonians. We have been led to believe that God's judgment on Israel had accomplished its intended result in repentance leading to the blessings of the covenant; instead, curse fills the air in the form of miscreants from the pits of hell. How are we to explain the apocalyptic drama of Ezekiel 38–39?

The highly enigmatic myth-charged drama of these two chapters is best explained as a codicil editorially inserted at a relatively advanced stage of the growth of the Ezekiel tradition to update the prophet's message, in light of what its author(s) regard(s) to be an alarming turn of events. A clue to the nature of the reversal is found in the description of the land against which God directs the international coalition led by Gog, "a land restored from war, a land where people were gathered from many nations" (38:8). The scorching new attack, so fierce and so final as to invoke horrendous mythic imagery, would strike out against the community that had reestablished itself in the homeland after returning from exile. Why was this new attack on "the mountains of Israel" necessary? Has YHWH resorted to sadistic whimsy? Had not the nation already been sufficiently punished (according to one prophet, even punished in double measure, Isa. 40:2)? Was not the time of return from exile a time for rebuilding foundations that would secure lasting shalom, much in the spirit of Haggai's and Zechariah's messages?

Ezekiel 39:7 may offer a key to understanding the undermining intent of these two chapters: "My holy name I will make known among my people Israel; and I will not let my holy name be profaned any more, and the nations shall know that I am the LORD, the Holy One in Israel." The purpose underlying God's directing the new assault on Israel, followed by a scorching offensive marshaling all the forces of heaven and earth against the invading nations themselves, is consistent with the central theme of the prophet Ezekiel himself, namely, the summation of all meaning in one purpose, the universal manifestation of the knowledge of God, first in Israel and then throughout the entire world. The first goal was accomplished in the Babylonian destruction: "Then they shall know that I am the LORD, when I have made the land a desolation and a waste because of all their abominations that they have committed," Ezekiel quoted YHWH as saying. Absent evidence that Israel had taken that harsh lesson to heart, the latter-day Ezekiel updates and expands on the lesson, "that the nations shall know."

The savant who took it upon himself to update Ezekiel's vision of Israel's post-587 recovery seems to have shared the eschatological perspective of Malachi, who portrayed YHWH's view of the horizon thus: "From the rising of the sun to its setting my name is great among the nations, and in every place incense is offered to my name, and a pure offering, for my name is great among the nations, says the LORD of hosts. But you profane it when you say that the Lord's table is polluted, and the food for it may be despised" (Mal. 1:11–12).

Malachi was addressing a nation, and in particular its religious leadership, that, by defiling itself with ritual and ethical wrongdoing, was creating a situation equal in gravity to the one that had led to the destruction of the first temple. Malachi envisioned the denouement in the form of a final, incisive act of judgment and cleansing by YHWH on the fearsome "day of his coming" (3:1–2), for only through that refining fire could the insidious pattern of defilement be broken and the creation of a holy nation be accomplished: "Then the offering of Judah and Jerusalem will be pleasing to the LORD as in the days of old and as in former years" (3:4).

The perspective from which the author of Ezekiel records his vision is closely akin to Malachi's. He witnesses a community struggling to reestablish itself after national calamity, only to be caught in a downward spiral of defiance vis-à-vis the Torah and defilement of the altar, leading toward an even more frightening abyss. While consistent with Ezekiel's theology of communal sanctity in honor of God's holiness, the crisis witnessed by the latter-day Ezekiel elicits an urgent redux. As a condition for the fulfillment of God's covenant of everlasting righteousness and peace, a final divine act of cleansing must occur, a cleansing so thorough as to lead God to summon as his agent of judgment the mythic figure Gog, whose hosts will wantonly destroy until preparation is completed for a sacrificial banquet on such a gigantic scale as to accommodate "the birds of every kind and all the wild animals" (Ezek. 39:17).

Only with the completion of that dread divine act could a sanctified Israel be restored and God's name be known, at home and among the nations. The finality of that apocalypse is underscored with a closing divine promise that recalls God's promise to Noah's generation: "and I will never again hide my face from them, when I pour out my spirit upon the house of Israel, says the Lord GOD" (Ezek. 39:29).

ISAIAH 24–27

The so-called Isaiah Apocalypse shares honors with Ezekiel 38–39 for the difficulties it presents for anyone seeking to situate it historically or politically. Yet no case can be made for excluding it from a discussion of a visionary trajectory within the literature of the Second Temple period, since its centrality in discussions regarding the biblical roots of Jewish apocalypticism is beyond dispute.

A sinister announcement marks the beginning of this unit of tradition:

> Now YHWH is about to lay waste the earth and make it desolate,
> and he will twist its surface and scatter its inhabitants.
>
> (24:1)

What justification is given for this dreadful divine initiative? The answer arises out of the inner sanctum of Second Temple theology. The earth has been *defiled,* and as we have observed in the proclamations of Ezekiel, Malachi, and the author of Ezekiel 38–39, a defiled land is one from which the glory of God is forced to withdraw, which seals its fate for calamity.

A theologoumenon that is explicit in the Hebrew text can nevertheless be obscured in translation, and this is the case with the rendering of Isaiah 24:5 in the NRSV: "The earth lies polluted under its inhabitants." The resulting lection is one lending itself in a liberal Protestant pulpit to a sermon on the modern ecological crisis, but the original intent addresses another realm, though one no less comprehensive in scope. In the Torah ordinance in Numbers 35 dealing with the heinous assault on the universal moral order represented by homicide, the Hebrew verb translated above as "polluted" (*ḥānēp*) is in synonymous parallelism with the verb *ṭāmēʾ*, that is, "defiled." No objection need be made to the translation "polluted," so long as the connection of that verb to the intricate edifice of priestly Torah is not lost.

To paraphrase: the inhabitants of the land have engaged in activities producing a defilement so severe as to drive God's saving presence from their midst.[19] The remaining half of verse 5 completes the indictment: "for they have transgressed the laws, violated the statutes, broken the everlasting covenant." The ergo that follows in verse 6 arises inevitably from the theological principle that would have been held by every adherent of the Jewish faith in the Second Temple period:

> Therefore a curse devours the earth,
>   and its inhabitants suffer for their guilt;
> therefore the inhabitants of the earth dwindled,
>   and few people are left.
>
> (24:6)

The covenant theology that informs this judgment derives from the heart of the Mosaic Torah tradition. The book of Deuteronomy presents that theology eloquently and elaborately. God graciously has given Israel a choice, to follow the path of obedience to Torah that leads to blessing, or to take the path of disobedience that leads to curse. Curse envelops both the natural and

---

19. The complete script of that drama of divine expulsion is preserved in Ezek. 8–11.

the political realms. Accordingly, in Isaiah 24 not only is the devastation of the natural environment described (Isa. 24:1), but also the overturning of the social order (24:2). But the curse in its penetration into the corrupt social fabric of the nation is not an end in itself, for even as in the case of the implosion of the natural realm, divine purpose is ineluctably guiding the process.

The point at which the Isaiah Apocalypse intersects with the other texts we have discussed under the rubric of "the visionary trajectory" is precisely the point midway between the description of the fallen state of human and natural realms and the divine response. In chapters 59 and 63 of Isaiah, the key phrase was *ʾên ʾîš*, that is, there was *no one* to intervene—no one, that is, except YHWH. The same end of human possibilities is encountered in Isaiah 24, where, after a turbulence in nature that is a ubiquitous motif in theophanic texts,[20] the Divine Warrior enters the fray, personally engaging "the host of heaven in heaven, and on earth the kings of the earth." The offenders are punished, the heavenly bodies shudder in shame, and the king of the universe rises up to reign, manifesting his glory before his elders (24:21–23).

Viewed as a whole, Isaiah 24 describes the basic pattern of conflict and victory that we have encountered in the other texts discussed in this chapter. The following three chapters fill out that pattern at various points.[21] For example, 25:6–10 describes the banquet for all people, which is held in celebration of YHWH's final victory, reminiscent of the Feast of Booths in Zechariah 14:16–21 and the banquet of birds and beasts in Ezekiel 38–39. Isaiah 25:10b–12 introduces Moab as the prototype of the hostile nations cast down by the Divine Warrior. Chapter 26 invites the reader to witness the hymn of praise sung by the redeemed nation. And finally, the mythic dimensions of that Warrior's battle are fleshed out in 27:1, where he slays Leviathan, the monster of the primordial sea. Together these motifs and images constitute a thesaurus that both draws on earlier mythic traditions and will become the source drawn upon by subsequent generations of visionaries.

Finally, what can we suggest regarding the setting and message of Isaiah 24–27? Like Ezekiel 38–39 it addresses a community threatened by the curse of defilement (cf. Ezek. 39:24), that is, a dire crisis in which the very institution provided by God to preserve the purity of the land has been perverted by those entrusted with its sanctity, and in which the upper echelons of the society are accomplices in the defilement of the land. It is not accidental that after the leveling of status between priest and laity in Isaiah 24:2, all of the other polarities that are dissolved revolve around economic structures: slave/master, maid/mistress, buyer/seller, lender/borrower, creditor/debtor. Reflected schematically is the fallen social and economic order with which Nehemiah contended and whose offenders Malachi excoriated.

---

20. Isa. 24:17–20; cf. Deut. 33:2; Judg. 5:4–5.
21. See William Millar, *Isaiah 24–27 and the Origin of Apocalyptic* (Missoula, MT: Scholars Press, 1976).

Thus revisited is a theme rooted in Torah and reapplied by Jewish prophets and seers of all ages. The laws and statutes of the covenant so blatantly violated according to Isaiah 24:5 are not sentimental relics or abstract formulations, but living guidelines for a healthy community, which, if repudiated, will lead to the ravages of the curse on the land and its inhabitants. Hosea's lesson had not been forgotten (Hos. 4:1–3).

We can summarize the lessons taught by the texts produced from within a growing trajectory of dissent with two points: (1) First a cautionary note: the proponents of the early stage of apocalyptic politics are not distinguished from their opponents by a negative view of strict Torah observance or temple ritual, though their dissatisfaction with their specific rivals in sacerdotal and gubernatorial offices is clear. (2) The chief wedge that is setting the divergent trajectory of the dissidents revolves around perception of the agency that will serve to bring to fulfillment the blessings of the covenant. For the visionary authors of the texts we examined in this chapter, the answer will not be found in the hands or resourcefulness of heroes like Nehemiah, but solely in divine intervention into a humanly hopeless situation. Only after YHWH, the commander of the heavenly hosts, defeats all enemies and takes up his reign in Jerusalem, will the legitimate leaders of the state be able to reassemble and recapture their sense of direction by bowing before the glory of the Holy One.

Chapter 22

Sapiential Politics in Proverbs, Sirach, Job, and Ecclesiastes

THE ELUSIVE NATURE OF THE SAPIENTIAL WRITINGS

The entity we shall describe in this chapter is elusive. To ignore it would be to commit a serious omission. To deal with it in connection with other biblical books, while an option, would fail to draw sufficient attention to the distinctive features that belong to the pattern of thought we call sapiential politics.

The elusiveness of the biblical and apocryphal writings referred to variously by the noun "wisdom" or the adjective "sapiential" resides in the nature of the entity itself. Wisdom defies borders, whether temporal or spatial. She (and we use the female pronoun because of the common personification of wisdom as female) is described as present with God as an assistant in the creation of the world. She also is present throughout the world and reveals herself to sages in nations far beyond Israel.

Small wonder then that traces of wisdom are found in the historiographic writings of the Bible, as well as in the Psalms and the prophetic books. In terms of structuring the present study, it would have been possible to place the material of this chapter alongside our discussion of the Chronicler, for the latter's accommodationist and universalist tendencies comport with central themes in the sapiential writings. While recognizing the fluidity of the borders demarcating the writings categorized as wisdom, there nevertheless remains something sufficiently distinctive about its political position to justify treatment in this separate chapter.

THE ROOTS OF WISDOM

Given the elusive nature of wisdom, it should come as no surprise that scholars have been unable to come to an agreement on how to account for its origins. One argument traces the roots of biblical wisdom to the clans of Israel in the premonarchy period, within which setting fathers purportedly instructed children in the commonsense rules that increased the likelihood of success in life and built up a defense against habits and activities that increased the chances of failure.[1] Referring to the ubiquity of collections of advice and rules of protocol designed for future rulers and administrators in ancient Egypt and Mesopotamia and the clear evidence of borrowing from such foreign sources on the part of biblical sages,[2] many scholars point to the royal court in Jerusalem as the setting of wisdom, a position corroborated by the considerable attention paid to kings and those who serve them in the biblical wisdom material.[3] Since with the demise of the monarchy in 587 the temple in Jerusalem inherited many of the functions formerly conducted in the royal court, it seems probable that the cultivation of wisdom traditions continued within the courts and chambers of the temple in the Persian and Hellenistic periods.

There is no reason why the above theories need to be treated as exclusive of one another. Propounding wisdom sayings and discourses need not be viewed as the prerogative of any single group within a society.[4] Indeed, the argument for a diversity of sources is corroborated by the variety of materials, from the straightforward advice offered by parents to children to highly philosophical and theological reflections on creation, good and evil, and the motivations underlying different kinds of human action.

In turning to the designations used for purveyors of wisdom in the biblical historiographic writings of the monarchy period, the range again is broad. Not only is uniformity in the terminology lacking, but the *nomen agentis* most commonly associated with wisdom in later tradition, "sage" (*hākām*), is absent from the narratives containing the most frequent references to those offering advice within royal circles, namely, the narratives about David and Solomon in

1. Erhard Gerstenberger, *Wesen und Herkunft des apodiktischen Rechts* (Neukirchen-Vluyn: Neukirchener Verlag, 1965).
2. Cf. Prov. 22:17–24:22 with the Egyptian text, "Instructions of Amenemope," in *Ancient Near Eastern Texts Relating to the Old Testament*, ed. James B Pritchard, 3rd ed. (Princeton, NJ: Princeton University Press, 1969), 421–24.
3. R. N. Whybray, "The Sage in the Israelite Court," in *The Sage in Israel and the Ancient Near East*, ed. John G. Gammie and Leo G. Perdue (Winona Lake, IN: Eisenbrauns, 1990), 133–39.
4. James L. Crenshaw, "The Sage in Proverbs," in Gammie and Perdue, *Sage*, 205.

the books of Samuel and Kings. Instead, the following designations are found: "advisor" (*yôʿēṣ*), "friend" or "friend of the king" (*reʿa* or *rēʿĕh hammelek*), and "scribe" (*soper*). In addition, generals,[5] priests, and prophets[6] are also found offering their counsel.

What is being reflected is likely several layers of advisors to the king, beginning with an inner circle ("cabinet") consisting of "the scribe" (*hassōpēr*), who perhaps served as the secretary of state, "the friend of the king" (*rēʿĕh hammelek*), perhaps equivalent to the chief of staff, the military commander, and finally the chief priest, who as an appointee of the king enjoyed the rank of a high officer. Supporting this inner circle were likely many other advisors, perhaps with specialties in different areas of statecraft, and scribes, many of them responsible for keeping administrative and economic records. Specific crises no doubt called for special assignments, as illustrated by the account in 2 Kings 18 of the "Rabshakeh" and two other emissaries sent by Sennacherib demanding Hezekiah's surrender to the Assyrian army. There we read, "When they called for the king, there came out to them Eliakim son of Hilkiah, who was in charge of the palace, and Shebnah the secretary [*hassōpēr*], and Joah son of Asaph, the recorder [*hammazkîr*]" (2 Kgs. 18:18//Isa. 36:3). What we see in action here is the king's negotiating team, consisting of the chief palace administrator, the secretary of state, and the head scribe, charged with recording the transactions. The narrative also draws attention to another of their skills, namely, acting as translators, obviously an important role in negotiating foreign affairs.

Though the connection between the structure and functions of the Jerusalem royal court and the full-blown wisdom collections found in Proverbs, Job, Ecclesiastes, and even Sirach and the Wisdom of Solomon is not explicit, it can be inferred from various pieces of evidence.

First, there is recurrence in the wisdom writings of the theme of rulers and those who serve them. We will also find in Sirach reference to the extensive travels of that particular scribe. Then of course there is the association of Solomon with wisdom in 1 Kings 10, in superscriptions appearing in the book of Proverbs, in the tradition identifying Koheleth (Ecclesiastes) with Solomon, and in the apocryphal Wisdom of Solomon. Moreover, in Proverbs 25:1, King Hezekiah is credited with copying some of the proverbs of Solomon.

Another chain leading from preexilic traditions to the period of the most intense activity involving the collecting and writing of sapiential works pertains specifically to the title of *sōpēr* or "scribe." Most famous among the scribes of preexilic Jerusalem was Baruch, Jeremiah's amanuensis who read his master's scroll of prophecies to the people gathered in the temple.[7] Also of note is the specific chamber within which the reading took place, namely, "the chamber of Gemariah son of Shaphan the *sōpēr*." The Shaphan referred

---

5. E.g., Joab's advice to David in 2 Sam. 19:5–7.
6. E.g., Isaiah in relation to Ahaz in Isa. 7:18 and to Hezekiah in 2 Kgs. 19:5–7 (// Isa. 37:5–7).
7. Jer. 36.

to is the patriarch of an influential scribal family who served as King Josiah's most trusted advisor.[8] His family displayed remarkable courage in offering its support to Jeremiah at a time when the royal court of Jehoiakim plotted to silence him with death.[9]

The family of Shaphan was not the only scribal group mentioned in the book of Jeremiah, however; for the prophet is also recorded as attacking scribes, who through their interpretation of the Torah allegedly twist it into a lie.[10] Clearly scribal circles were not always of a common mind, a characteristic manifested, for example, by their conflicting attitudes toward foreign nations.[11]

The most important link in the chain connecting preexilic scribalism to the scribes of the Second Temple period is one particular figure, namely, Ezra, "the scribe of the Torah of Moses," who—in contrast to those boasting in Jeremiah's time, "we are wise, and the Torah [NRSV "law"] of YHWH is with us" (Jer. 8:8), only to apply their "false pen" to pervert its meaning—is remembered as the paragon of the faithful scribe. The link joining the generations of scribes that Ezra represents could not have been expressed more clearly than in *Sifre Deuteronomy* §48, 12: "Had it not been for those who arose and preserved Torah in Israel, would not the Torah have been forgotten? Had it not been for Shaphan in his time, Ezra in his time, and R. Akiba in his time, would not the Torah have been forgotten in Israel?"

The central topic of this passage, Torah, indicates that the scribal link in the chain connecting preexilic Jerusalem with developments in the Persian period involved far more than continuity of nomenclature within a professional guild. In chapter 20 we described the sea change that had occurred during the careers of Ezra and Nehemiah, when the earlier emblem of nationhood, the Davidic monarchy, was supplanted by Torah, the covenant charter of God's people. It was also a time in which the fluidity of prophecy as the primary mode of divine revelation was being superseded by a new mode of discerning God's will and purpose, namely, interpretation of the Torah of Moses, canonized in writing and providing a durable foundation for the community's identity as God's people. This change was the catalyst for a tremendous surge in the importance and prestige of the expert interpreters of Torah, the scribes.[12]

From the time of Ezra on, any group seeking to be recognized as speaking authoritatively on behalf of Jewish tradition could do so only by demonstrating

---

8. Cf. 2 Kgs. 22:9–20.

9. Jer. 26:24; 36:11–19.

10. Jer. 8:8–12. Cf. Isa. 29:14b.

11. Cf. Sir. 39:4 with Sir. 36:1–22.

12. It is significant that the *terminus technicus* for an oracular consultation with a prophet (lidrōt) in 1 Kings 22:8 is used to describe Ezra's dedication to study of the Torah in Ezra 7:10. See Michael Fishbane, "From Scribalism to Rabbinism: Perspectives on the Emergence of Clasical Judaism," in Gammie and Perdue, *Sage,* 441–42. Fishbane also points to the expression "the hand of YHWH," applied to Ezra in Ezra 7:6 and 9, as another point of connection with the phenomenon of revelation through the prophets (e.g., Ezek. 1:3) (Michael Fishbane, *Biblical Interpretation in Ancient Israel* [Oxford: Clarendon, 1985], 441).

thorough knowledge of and unswerving reverence for the Torah. This was true of a historian like the Chronicler, of the visionaries who added their revisionary interpretations to earlier prophetic writings, and finally, of those who contributed to the growth of the wisdom writings during the Persian and Hellenistic periods. As we now turn to describe the distinctive political ideas found in the sapiential works, we shall be reminded also of continuities running from the royal court of Davidic Jerusalem to the wise scribes of subsequent centuries, even as we shall recognize numerous connections between the books of Ezra, Nehemiah, and Chronicles and the wisdom writings.

If one were to seek a concept to serve as a bridge from the Ezra tradition, especially as it came to its mature expression in Ezra 1–6, and the sapiential writings, "accommodation" would be a viable candidate. For those belonging to the generation of Ezra and Nehemiah, as well as for many who succeeded them as civil and religious leaders of the community in the first century and a half of Hellenistic rule, there was a robust degree of realpolitik in their strategy of cooperation with foreign sovereigns. After all, only those cultivating apocalyptic visions of a divine intervention that would destroy all foreign rivals and establish universal rule emanating out of Jerusalem were willing to challenge the existing world empires, given the devastating consequences that were sure to follow in the event that the Deity failed to act!

In the sapiential writings, one finds the explicit development of what remained inchoate in Ezra and Chronicles, namely, the extension of the notion of accommodation to world powers to envisioning God as the architect of an all-inclusive cosmic order. As God ruled the universe on the basis of principles of order and harmony, so too God authorized the rule of mortal kings, whose responsibility it was to uphold those same universal principles on earth. What we witness in this development is an audacious adaptation of the theocratic principle to a world in which Jewish life could no longer be sheltered from the influence of world-crusading cultures, beginning with the Persians and followed by Hellenism. The all-encompassing *oikonomia* that suffuses the sapiential writings thus depicts an order extending from the customs and norms regulating personal and family life to the laws governing international relations. We shall now describe the layered structure of that divinely authored universal order, considering first God's sovereign rule over the cosmos, then the mediation of that rule through God's appointment of earthly magistrates, and finally, the implementation of divine order to all aspects of state, society, family, and individual.

DIVINE RULE OVER THE COSMOS

The starting point for political reflection in Proverbs and Sirach is divine politics, that is, God's creation of a cosmos that is ordered in all of its aspects on the basis of laws embodying divine wisdom and understanding:

YHWH by wisdom founded the earth;
   by understanding he established the heavens;
by his knowledge the deeps broke open,
   and the clouds drop down the dew.
                        (Prov. 3:19–20)

Sirach 16:26–17:24 draws upon themes from the Torah (Genesis–Deuteronomy) to describe how every creature has its place in this eternal order, how humans enjoy a special endowment of knowledge of good and evil and the capacity to fear God and offer God praise. While God "appointed a ruler for every nation," Israel enjoys a special relationship with God and an added moral responsibility.

Sirach 39:16–35 directs the reader's attention to the providential ordering of both time and space:

"All the works of the Lord are very good,
   and whatever he commands will be done at the appointed time. . . .
No one can say, 'What is this?' or 'Why is that?'—
   for everything has been created for its own purpose."
                        (Sir. 39:16, 21)

The following lines from Sirach 42 reveal the refined sense of philosophical reasoning that characterizes this particular sage:

He has set in order the splendors of his wisdom. . . .
Nothing can be added or taken away. . . .
   [E]ach creature is preserved to meet a particular need.
All things come in pairs, one opposite the other,
   and he has made nothing incomplete.
                   (Sir. 42:21, 23b, 24)

In a similar vein, chapter 43, in a survey of the cosmos that reminds one of the wise scribe's heavenly journey in *1 Enoch*, celebrates the creator who has ordered the heavens and all of the wonders of nature in one sublime orchestral display.

THE MEDIATION OF DIVINE SOVEREIGNTY
THROUGH HUMAN RULERS

The unrivaled authority of God's universal sovereignty sets the parameters for legitimate human rule. According to the sages, such rule is characterized on one side by strict divinely ordained limitations on the authority of human rulers, on the other by the lofty empowerment of the king by his heavenly patron. As we turn to this seemingly paradoxical juxtaposition, we first consider the limits built into the sapiential notion of divinely appointed kings.

The starting point for understanding sapiential politics is the categorical distinction between the eternal reign of God and the evanescence of kings and their empires, which rise and fall at the behest of the divine sovereign:

> Sovereignty passes from nation to nation
>   on account of injustice and insolence and wealth.
> How can dust and ashes be proud?
>   Even in life the body decays.
> A long illness baffles the physician;
>   the king of today will die tomorrow. . . .
> The beginning of human pride is to forsake the Lord;
>   the heart has withdrawn from its Maker. . . .
> The Lord overthrows the thrones of rulers,
>   and enthrones the lowly in their place.
> The Lord plucks up the roots of the nations,
>   and plants the humble in their place.
>   (Sir. 10:8–10, 12, 14–15)

The categorical distinction between the ultimate and the penultimate that lies at the heart of the sage's political perspective could not be formulated more poignantly. The nature of the link that connects them is not abstract, but existential, revolving around "injustice and insolence and wealth." Moreover, the quality of heart that this distinction requires of the king is clear, namely, fear of God and humility before the Maker; for the opposite quality of human pride manifests ignorance of the cardinal principle of political authority, and its deadly consequence is inevitable, as Isaiah of Jerusalem had insisted[13] and another sage confirmed,

> Pride goes before destruction,
>   and a haughty spirit before a fall.
>   (Prov. 16:18)

This lesson is applied by adding to a normal royal court procedure a chastening qualification. In Proverbs 20:18 we find the *conventional* protocol:

> Plans are established by taking advice;
>   wage war by following wise guidance.

But the theocentric orientation of Jewish wisdom adds to court protocol this stark *qualification*:

> No wisdom, no understanding, no counsel,
>   can avail against the LORD.
> The horse is made ready for the day of battle,
>   but the victory belongs to the LORD.
>   (Prov. 21:30–31)

13. See esp. Isa. 14:12–21.

In other words, man proposes, God disposes, or more eloquently,

> The human mind plans the way,
>   but the LORD directs the steps.
>   (Prov. 16:9)

One hears an echo of the warning in Jeremiah 9:23, beginning with "Do not let the wise boast in their wisdom," when one reads,

> Do you see persons wise in their own eyes?
>   There is more hope for fools than for them.
>   (Prov. 26:12)

The only safeguard against the abuse of authority by human rulers is thus acknowledgment of the time-honored theocratic principle that stipulates the antecedent ultimate authority of God. Hence the emphasis on "fear of God" as the beginning of wisdom (Prov. 1:7; 9:10), to which Proverbs 15:33 adds the complementary quality of humility:

> The fear of YHWH is instruction in wisdom,
>   and humility goes before honor.

From this truth Sirach draws important epistemological implications that every leader and advisor does well to heed:

> Reflect upon what you have been commanded,
>   for what is hidden is not your concern.
> Do not meddle in matters that are beyond you,
>   for more than you can understand has been shown you.
> For their conceit has led many astray,
>   and wrong opinion has impaired their judgment.
>   (Sir. 3:22–24)

Such a cautionary note is particularly noteworthy within the context of wisdom writings, characterized as they are by a high level of intellectual curiosity and an audacity to investigate all things, from the heavens above to Sheol below. It is a sign of the rigorous, theologically driven critical perspective of biblical wisdom that the limits of human understanding are acknowledged. In the place of conceitedness, stubbornness, self-assertiveness, and a proud spirit, Sirach 3:29 commends a more prudent alternative: "an attentive ear is the desire of the wise."

We turn next to the other side of divine appointment, namely, the empowerment of human rulers. Against the background of the "infinite qualitative distinction" upheld by Israel's sages between divine and human government, the degree of authority they ascribe to kings and the corresponding subservience required of subjects may seem incongruent. On what basis could a political model that is structurally hierarchical and socially conservative also include provisions for defending the principles of justice and evenhanded treatment of citizens of all classes? The only source capable of generating a defense against the common tendency of autocratic regimes to devolve into despotism was rooted deeply in the ancestral faith of Israel, namely, the tradition of the strict subordination of human kingship under the cosmic rule of the divine sovereign. The key question that guides our inquiry into sapiential politics thus arises from the theocratic principle that we found to be of central importance during the earlier periods of charismatic rulers, kings, and prophets: Are the policies the sages outline for mediating and implementing God's sole sovereignty adequate for safeguarding God's authoritative rule, or are they vulnerable to the abuses traditionally plaguing highly centralized forms of mediated rule such as monarchy, hierocracy, and aristocracy?

The following passages state clearly that the rule of the king is an extension of God's universal dominion to the realm of humans. As such, human government is to embody the qualities that characterize God's eternal order.[14] For the king serves as a mediator, a conduit of divine purpose, whose example in turn defines the conduct of his subordinates:

> The king's heart is a stream of water in the hand of YHWH;
>   he turns it wherever he will.
>   (Prov. 21:1)

> By me [i.e., God's hypostasis Wisdom] kings reign,
>   and rulers decree what is just;
> by me rulers rule,
>   and nobles, all who govern rightly.
>   (Prov. 8:15–16)

> The government of the earth is in the hand of the Lord,
>   and over it he will raise up the right leader for the time.
>   (Sir. 10:4)

A powerful consequence follows from this intimate tie between divine and human rule: once the king is regarded as God's deputy on earth, disobedience to the king's commands takes on an awesome theological dimension. To disobey the king is to disobey God, and indeed to incur the wrath of God. The king thus becomes the agent of divine wrath:

> A wise king winnows the wicked,
>   and drives the wheel over them.
>   (Prov. 20:26)

That the resulting definition of appropriate civil conduct is conservative in nature is an understatement. A policy of unquestioning allegiance that categorically denounces the right of citizens to challenge their monarch follows:

14. Cf. Ps. 89.

My child, fear the LORD and the king,
　　and do not become involved with those who seek change;[15]
for disaster comes from them suddenly,
　　and who knows the ruin that both can bring?
　　　　　　　　　　　　　　　　　　　(Prov. 24:21–22)

Two aspects of the above passages, the parallelism between God and king and the insistence on the citizen's absolute loyalty to the king, remind one of the ancient Near Eastern ideology of absolute kingship that, as we noted in chapter 11, infused the hymnody of the Davidic court (e.g., Pss. 45 and 89). While the mythological trappings of that ideology are virtually absent from Proverbs[16] and Sirach, traces of the ambience of a lofty view of kingship are present. Of the three things described as "stately in their stride," the climactic example is "a king striding before his people" (Prov. 30:29–31; cf. Prov. 19:12). Strict deference of courtiers before the king is stressed (Prov. 25:6–7; cf. Prov. 23:1–3; Sir. 7:4–7). In the case of the book of Proverbs, it is evident that the model of good government is a high form of monarchy, in which the king's word is absolute and supported by a plethora of court advisors:

Where there is no guidance, a nation falls,
　　but in an abundance of counselors there is safety.
　　　　　　　　　　　　(Prov. 11:14; cf. Prov. 15:22)

THE WELL-ORDERED SOCIETY

In moving from divine dominion over the cosmos and correspondingly the earthly king's rule over a nation to the attributes of a well-ordered civil society, we are not surprised to find an ideal of stability secured by law and order and requiring a compliant citizenry:

Free citizens will serve a wise servant,
　　and an intelligent person will not complain.
　　　　　　　　　　　　　　　　(Sir. 10:25)

The laws and customs of a well-ordered society derive from the Creator and are thus part of the eternal structure of the universe. The different economic classes and the professions into which they are divided are not the results of chance or of human organization, but, rather,

In the fullness of his knowledge the Lord distinguished them
　　and appointed their different ways. . . .

15. Following the translation of Robert Gordis, who describes it as "the most conservative passage in the Bible" (Robert Gordis, "The Social Background of Wisdom Literature," *Hebrew Union College Annual* 18 [1943]: 117).

16. See, however, Prov. 16:15.

Like clay in the hand of the potter,
   to be molded as he pleases,
so all are in the hand of their Maker,
   to be given whatever he decides.

(Sir. 33:11, 13)

Rights are defined according to what is fitting for a given social class. To take slaves as an example,

Fodder and a stick and burdens for a donkey;
   bread and discipline and work for a slave.
Set your slave to work, and you will find rest;
   leave his hands idle, and he will seek liberty.
Yoke and thong will bow the neck,
   and for a wicked slave there are racks and tortures.
Put him to work, in order that he may not be idle,
   for idleness teaches much evil.
Set him to work, as is fitting for him,
   and if he does not obey, make his fetters heavy.

(Sir. 33:25–30)

In like manner, the categories of riches and poverty, male and female, holy and profane are fixed parts of a society determined by laws originating with the Creator (Prov. 10:15; Sir. 42:14; Sir. 33:12).[17] In the case of Sirach, we are able to locate this class structure in an actual social setting, for in his account of the trades in 38:24–39:11, he accentuates the importance of the privileges of the elite for the cultivation of the finest aspects of culture. Of course, at the top of the pyramid of the professions is his own, that of the scribe (Sir. 39:1–11)!

The social ideal that comes to light in the passages from Proverbs and Sirach that we have cited is unabashedly conservative. Given its twin premises of divinely conferred central authority and a class structure based on divinely authored natural law, one might expect that further scrutiny would fill out the picture of a society tyrannical and oppressive in nature. That this is not the case stems from two further dimensions of political reflection in these writings: (1) a distinction between ideal ruler and actual historical incumbents, and (2) a counterpoint to the theme of regal authority, expressed in verses dedicated to the theme of social justice.

First, we take note of the distinction between ideal and actual rulers. The assumption underlying this contrast is important to recognize. It is the king's sacred responsibility to embody in his rule God's laws as they are revealed in the Torah. As we shall see in the next subsection, both Proverbs and Sirach draw consistently on the Torah of Moses in their specification of the norms that are to regulate the good society. But what is to be done by the pious believer in a

17. Perhaps the most egregious proverb in the whole of Wisdom literature is Sir. 42:14:

Better is the wickedness of a man than a woman who does good;
   it is woman who brings shame and disgrace.

land governed by a ruler who repudiates God's law and, rather than fearing and glorifying God, devotes his energies to personal gain at the cost of the impoverishment of his subjects and denial of their judicial rights and human dignity? That Sirach saw this as a problem, in spite of his lofty view of divinely instituted kingship, is apparent from this teaching in 10:1–3:

> A wise magistrate educates his people,
>> and the rule of an intelligent person is well ordered.
> As the people's judge is, so are his officials;
>> as the ruler of the city is, so are all its inhabitants.
> An undisciplined king ruins his people,
>> but a city becomes fit to live in through the understanding of its rulers.

Sirach is not the first to struggle with the contradiction between the concept of the ideal ruler and the behavior of actual incumbents. One can compare, for example, the description of the *ideal* Davidide in Isaiah 9:2–7 (Heb. vv. 1–6) and 11:1–5 with the prophet's account of his tense confrontation with the *actual* Davidic King Ahaz in Isaiah 7. The resulting paradox comes to clear expression in Proverbs 16:10–11:

> Inspired decisions are on the lips of a king;
>> his mouth does not sin in judgment.
> Honest balances and scales are YHWH's;
>> all the weights in the bag are his work.
> It is an abomination to kings to do evil,
>> for the throne is established by righteousness.

Secondly, we turn our attention to a counterpoint that qualifies the autocratic, hierarchical notion of governance coming to expression in many sayings in Proverbs and Sirach. This counterpoint develops around the themes of charity toward the poor, restorative justice in the courts, honesty in commerce, and personal integrity. We have suggested that the metaphysically grounded notion of governance found in these writings bears the traces of a wider ancient Near Eastern political ideal. But what is the source of the reformist themes that glisten like quartz dikes running through a Precambrian geological formation?

In a fascinating venture into the history of religion, Sirach in chapter 24 charted the long journey of Wisdom, from her primordial home in the divine assembly, to travels through the heavens and the depths of the abyss, then over the sea and the land where she exercised her influence over all the nations, until finally she found her resting place on Zion amid the people of Israel, there to identify herself with "the book of the covenant of the Most High God, the law that Moses commanded us" (Sir. 24:23).

The significance of this identification of Wisdom (*hokma*) with the Law (*torah*) has long been recognized. It points to the hermeneutical program to which Philo of Alexandria and other Jewish intellectuals of the Hellenistic period were devoted, namely, the presentation to the citizens of Athens and

Alexandria of Judaism as the most advanced of all cultures. As the fierce conflict within Judaism to which we shall turn in the next chapter indicates, this apologetic program was filled with hazards. Would the soul of the religion of Moses simply be overwhelmed by the wisdom of the Muses?

The border-crossing ecumenism of the wisdom tradition provided the foundation upon which Jewish apologetics developed. Yet, despite the clear traces of Hellenistic influence in his reflections, even Sirach viewed himself not as an assimilationist, but as a faithful devotee of the Torah of Moses. In the texts to which we now turn, light is shed on our earlier question regarding the reconcilability of subjugation under royal authority and protection of the rights of normal citizens. What becomes apparent is that the themes of impartial justice in the courts, mercy on behalf of the poor, and fairness in commerce derive from the abiding authority of the ancestral values embedded in the Torah and defended by the prophets. The point/counterpoint tension can thus be traced to the intellectual exchange resulting from the confluence of beliefs and values of Israelite religion with rules and customs that were cultivated by sages of all nations under the broad umbrella of Hellenism.[18]

In a world of enormous religious and political diversity, Jewish sages like Sirach were keenly aware of the need for strong governing authorities. But they insisted that kings and magistrates, together with those they governed, could maintain civil order only if they built upon a solid moral foundation, the building blocks of which they located in their ancestral faith:

> By the blessing of the upright a city is exalted,
>   but it is overthrown by the mouth of the wicked.
>   (Prov. 11:11)

Once stability is traced to the moral qualities that characterize the upright, emphasis shifts from the metaphysical warrants and despotic powers claimed by tyrant kings to the attributes that mediate God's universal rule of justice and mercy to the realm of human government.

In the sayings of Proverbs and Sirach one discovers a rich description of the qualities belonging to persons of integrity, such as honesty, faithfulness in personal and family relations, discipline, and industry. As the above proverb observes, from citizens possessing these virtues arise the viability and strength of a civil society, even as the vices of the wicked lead to its undoing.

The social dimensions of the city of the upright are brought to light in sayings describing the concrete acts through which individuals of all classes are knit together in harmony. In contrast to the dispassionate description in Proverbs 10:15 of the poor person's condition as a given, we find in Proverbs 31:8–9 an impassioned appeal for advocacy:

---

18. Cf. Jonathan Z. Smith, "Wisdom and Apocalyptic," in *Visionaries and Their Apocalypses*, ed. Paul D. Hanson (Philadelphia: Fortress Press, 1983), 101–20.

Speak out for those who cannot speak,
    for the rights of all the destitute.
Speak out, judge righteously,
    defend the rights of the poor and needy.

What is more, defense of the rights of the poor is more than a pious act. In dealing with those discarded by society, one is dealing directly with the Creator:

Those who oppress the poor insult their Maker,
    but those who are kind to the needy honor him.
                  (Prov. 14:31)

It is impossible to imagine a more profound grounding for social policy than this, and it is not surprising to find the same thought, again with the negative/positive parallelism, on the lips of the Son of Man in the Gospel of Matthew: "Truly I tell you, just as you did/did not do it to one of the least of these who are members of my family, you did/did not do it to me" (Matt. 25:40, 45).

In Sirach, the plea for advocacy again rings out, reaching a climax with an echo from the story of slaves who cried to God and were delivered (Exod. 3:7–8; 6:5), an echo that in the Torah served as a motive clause capable of piercing through human apathy (e.g., Exod. 22:21–27 [Heb. vv. 20–26]):

My child, do not cheat the poor of their living,
    and do not keep needy eyes waiting.
Do not grieve the hungry,
    or anger one in need.
Do not add to the troubles of the desperate,
    or delay giving to the needy.
Do not reject a suppliant in distress,
    or turn your face away from the poor.
Do not avert your eye from the needy,
    and give no one reason to curse you;
for if in bitterness of soul some should curse you,
    their Creator will hear their prayer.
                  (Sir. 4:1–6)[19]

Similarly in the realm of commerce, God is introduced as a partner with full, active interest:

Honest balances and scales are the LORD's;
    all the weights in the bag are his work.
        (Prov. 16:11; cf. Prov. 11:1)

In the realm of jurisprudence, the central theme of Torah and prophetic commentary of impartiality is reaffirmed (Prov. 18:5; 24:23–25). Another

---

19. Cf. Prov. 11:17, 25; 22:9, and cf. Exod. 3:7 and 6:5.

forensic theme at the heart of Torah and the prophets comes to expression in Proverbs 22:22–23:

> Do not rob the poor because they are poor,
> or crush the afflicted at the gate;
> for YHWH pleads their cause
> and despoils of life those who despoil them.

At times, specific details of Torah legislation are revisited, no doubt because of the devastating effects their violation had on the poor, for example, the prohibition of moving landmarks (Prov. 22:28; 23:10; cf. Deut. 19:14; 27:17; Hos. 5:10).

With the catena of Torah and prophetic themes that we have traced in the wisdom writings fresh in mind, a final prophetic motif sounds entirely congruous:

> To do righteousness and justice
> is more acceptable to the LORD than sacrifice.
> (Prov. 21:3)[20]

This particular theme, distinctly more at home in the prophetic critique of all institutions than in the sapiential realm of divinely ordained harmony between all divisions and levels of governance, underscores the main question arising from the point/counterpoint tension that we have observed. Is it the result of incompatible worldviews simply being placed alongside of each other?

That would be an overly simple answer, for what we encounter is a profound synthesis. The basic sapiential theme that the Creator is the source of the laws governing not only the cosmos but all nations is not contradicted by the affirmation of teachings derived from Moses and the prophets. What this affirmation reflects is the abiding influence that ancient Israel's particular understanding of God's mediated presence in human affairs had on the thought world of sages and scribes engaging in lively discourse with their counterparts in other centers of learning like Athens and Alexandria.

Though, until one gets to the mid-first century BCE, the exodus tradition does not gain a prominent place in the sapiential writings, it is clear that from the earliest discernible stages of development, wisdom in Israel was shaped by beliefs and values that were distinctly Jewish. The result is not the folding of wisdom into Torah, the prophets, or the historiographic writings, but rather the deepening of its reach into the perennial questions of the sages, questions regarding the order of the cosmos, the political policies of a secure nation, the moral dimensions of a healthy society, and the ethical qualities of a person of integrity.

---

20. Cf. Isa. 1:10–17; Amos 5:21–25; Mic. 6:6–8.

WISDOM IN CRISIS: JOB AND ECCLESIASTES

The tensions between traditional beliefs and new insights that we have witnessed within Proverbs and Sirach are minimal compared to the fundamental challenges raised by two other books, Job and Ecclesiastes. With them the pursuit of wisdom by the sages of Israel entered a period of crisis. Yet both of these books enrich our study of biblical politics through their application of the tools par excellence of the sages in all cultures: careful observation of all facets of human experience and application of rigorous rational inquiry to the resulting compendium of knowledge.

The crisis addressed by Job arises on the level that we identified as the starting point of the sapiential inquiry into politics, namely, God's governance of the cosmos. It was on the basis of the evidence they found in nature and in the behavior of humans that the sages drew the inference that divine rule was characterized by order and dependability. From that metaprinciple mortals in turn were able to extrapolate a corresponding order and dependability that provided the basis for a secure nation, stable society, and prosperous citizens.

Job's life experiences, however, led him to doubt the justice and trustworthiness of God's governance. The rules that any reasonable observer could expect of a well-ordered regime, namely, congruous rewards and punishments, were blatantly violated by the deity Job encountered amid unmitigated personal tragedy (Job 21). Job is depicted as a man morally upright and religiously pious who is forced to endure horrendous suffering and loss and the bafflement of witnessing the wicked prospering. His defiant approach to God seems entirely reasonable and fair:

> Oh, that I knew where I might find him,
>   that I might come even to his dwelling! . . .
> There an upright person could reason with him,
>   and I should be acquitted forever by my judge.
>   (Job 23:2, 7)

Rather than providing a forum for such reasonable discussion, however, God presents an elaborate display of his overwhelming power through the agency of primordial beasts at home in ancient Near Eastern mythology, accompanied by a tirade of questions that leaves Job humbled and speechless (Job 38–41).[21] The modern reader may well share Job's sense of bafflement! What possible light can such a tour de force of divine might cast on metaethical questions of divine justice and inferences to be drawn from divine dominion for human government? One could exclude the book of Job as irrelevant to an inquiry into biblical politics, by insisting that it deals with relationship between God and the individual; but Job's challenge is too broad to be narrowed down to the personal level. Job

---

21. A particularly insightful contemporary interpretation of the book of Job is found in the Interpretation Series: J. Gerald Janzen, *Job* (Atlanta: John Knox Press, 1985).

challenges the entire moral order upon which all nations and all of nature are founded. If the accusations he hurls at God have any validity, human civilization is thrown into crisis!

Yet sensitive commentators have discovered that it is precisely in its unflinching struggle with theological paradox and ethical bafflement that the book of Job makes its unique contribution. Nested in a Bible that through the ages has been hijacked by the comforting theologoumenon that God is bound to the retributive principle of rewarding the righteous behavior of individuals and nations and punishing wickedness,[22] the book of Job sets forth the life of a singularly upright man whose inexplicable suffering and loss call into question every tidy, predictable formula for understanding the laws that govern divine rule and its manifestation in human affairs. The book's radical critique of popular belief clears the way for a stunning reaffirmation of the Bible's most trenchant lesson about politics, namely, that for the person of faith, the alpha and omega point of obedience is acknowledgment of the sole sovereignty of God, even when conventional human notions about "just deserts" are contradicted by "bad things happening to good people." In Hebrew Scripture, no mortal displays that cardinal theocratic principle (and its idolatrous distortion in mortal claims to divine certainty) more authentically than the irascible Job, who holds tight to the infuriating Holy One, even as he dares to refute the justice and fairness of his elusive divine judge.

Job's refusing to let go is not in vain; the end point of his relentless, passionate search is not the dark hole of the nihilist, but the peaceful repose of the faithful God-fearer, whose harsh existential lessons have enabled him to shed the peripheral and absorb into the very fabric of his being the single most important truth, the only proper posture of the mortal before the Almighty:

> I had heard of you by the hearing of the ear,
>   but now my eye sees you;
> therefore I despise myself,
>   and repent in dust and ashes.
> (Job 42:5–6)

Turning to the second outlier among the sapiental writings of the Bible, we observe that the book of Ecclesiastes resembles in theme and tone the ponderings

---

22. A mechanical notion of divine retribution underlies the lesson in divine moral order that Job's friends, Eliphaz, Bildad, and Zophar, relentlessly and mercilessly preach to him. The concept of divine rewards and punishment is one of the most difficult theological problems. Its roots in biblical tradition are deep. Indeed, retribution is woven inextricably into the Deuteronomic understanding of covenant. Any moral philosophy that is built upon belief in God's righteous, universal rule cannot avoid dealing with the question of the manifestation of that rule in human experience. Where belief in divine providence devolves into idolatry, however, is at the point where human theories encroach upon God's sole sovereignty. An example is provided by Job's friends, who can present the connection between upright behavior and prosperity and its corollary evil/punishment as a universal law to which God is bound and God's (self-appointed) human agents can explain to the less enlightened.

of the Greek Cynics. Though participating in the empirical/inductive approach of the sages that we have already essayed, the Preacher's conclusions did not lead to a portrait of a reasonable and fair universe: "I said in my heart with regard to human beings that God is testing them to show that they are but animals. For the fate of humans and the fate of animals is the same; as one dies, so dies the other. They all have the same breath, and humans have no advantage over the animals; for all is vanity" (Eccl. 3:18–19).

As distinctions between orders of creation dissolve, so too do the just deserts accruing to the righteous and the wicked, which leads the Preacher to a morally capitulating conclusion: "In my vain life I have seen everything; there are righteous people who perish in their righteousness, and there are wicked people who prolong their life in their evildoing. Do not be too righteous, and do not act too wise" (Eccl. 7:15–16).

Following from this conclusion is his well-known recommendation, carpe diem: "Go, eat your bread with enjoyment, and drink your wine with a merry heart" (Eccl. 9:7a).

Though the book of Ecclesiastes does not provide much reflection on politics, what few words it offers are decidedly on the side of the status quo: "Keep the king's command because of your sacred oath. Do not be terrified; go from his presence, do not delay when the matter is unpleasant, for he does whatever he pleases. For the word of the king is powerful, and who can say to him, 'What are you doing?'" (Eccl. 8:2–4).

One also finds scattered references to a social class structure that is not to be questioned:

> Do not curse the king, even in your thoughts,
>   or curse the rich, even in your bedroom;
> for a bird of the air may carry your voice,
>   or some winged creature tell the matter.
>   (Eccl. 10:20)

Correspondingly, the inversion of proper status is a sign of evil:

> I have seen slaves on horseback,
>   and princes walking on foot like slaves.
>   (Eccl. 10:7)

It has been argued that the book of Ecclesiastes marks the "shipwreck" of the wisdom tradition.[23] It seems more accurate to recognize in its message a poignant challenge to that tradition, one, moreover, that seems to be consistent with the searching, inquiring empirical approach that was intrinsic to the intellectual adventures of scribes over the course of several millennia and across the ancient world. It should be added, however, that especially in the case of Sirach

---

23. Walther Zimmerli, *Die Weisheit des Predigers Solomo* (Berlin: Alfred Topelmann, 1936).

and Ecclesiastes, one witnesses the encounter with the powerful philosophical movements of the Hellenistic world.[24] It was that encounter that would lead to the flash point that inaugurated a crisis of the magnitude of the Babylonian siege of Jerusalem four centuries later.

THE THEO-POLITICAL LEGACY
OF THE SAPIENTIAL WRITINGS

The contribution made by Wisdom to politics does not come to us as a blueprint, but as a portrait of an open-ended process of political discernment. To this one may object, Are not the books of Proverbs and Sirach filled with rules for good government? Yes, but those rules are assembled in a manner exposing inner tensions and even contradictions that oblige the reader to ask questions such as, How does a powerful ruler maintain order in an unorderly world without repressing the rights of ordinary people? How do justice and mercy blend in a good society? Furthermore, it is inconceivable that the ancient tradents who shaped the biblical canon were not conscious of the huge qualifications Job and Ecclesiastes raised for anyone, ruler or citizen, who searched the Wisdom writings for policies that were both faithful to the central tenets of Jewish religion and viable in a world of constant change.

We have noted many examples of faithfulness to central tenets, e.g., injunctions to show mercy to the destitute, to practice honesty in commerce, and to protect the rights of all classes of people. Foundational to all such ethical injunctions was unwavering adherence to the theocratic principle of God's sole authority, even in instances where human experiences contradicted facile understandings of that principle. Having located the sapiential writings securely within the religion of Abraham and Moses, is there anything that we can identify as Wisdom's unique contribution?

One could point to evidence of accommodation to the expanding cultural and philosophical world into which the Jews were cast, first by Babylonian conquest, followed by Persian colonization, and culminating in the more subtle, lasting cultural hegemony of Hellenism. In chapter 20 we already have credited Ezra with the highly effective adaptation to a world without Jewish national autonomy we designated as "the political model of accommodation." While it would be possible to explain Wisdom's role in terms of an elaboration on Ezra's model, an important point would be lost. The *unique* contribution of Wisdom was this: alongside other paths to knowledge of God, such as historical events, dreams, and oracles, God has endowed humans with reason, through the proper exercise of which God's sons and daughters can discover important

---

24. In the case of Job, antecedents are to be found in the ancient cultures of Mesopotamia and Egypt. See Leo G. Perdue, *Wisdom Literature: A Theological History* (Louisville, KY: Westminster John Knox Press, 2007), chaps. 4, 6, and 7.

truths about virtues and vices, integrity and deceit, life-sustaining government and life-destroying tyranny.

Wisdom doesn't simply throw reason "into the ring" as a sixth political option. It has been appropriated in this way by rationalist political scientists ancient, medieval, and modern. The biblical sages integrate Wisdom's pathway into the service of the God who has accompanied Israel from Egyptian slavery to the present. To this long relationship she offers her gift, safeguarded from epistemological distortion and idolatrous abuse by the only attribute befitting any being—as human as Job or as heavenly as Sophia—before their Maker, namely, humility.

Chapter 23

The Apocalyptic Politics of the Book of Daniel and the Dead Sea Scrolls

THE COMPOSITE NATURE OF THE BOOK OF DANIEL

The figure of Daniel, as it takes shape over the course of the book's twelve chapters, provides an ideal segue to the next phase of politics in ancient Israel. In the first six chapters, Daniel is portrayed as a God-fearing sage in a foreign court. Though his people live under the changing policies of pagan rulers, they enjoy the protection of the only true ruler of the universe, before whom even the earth's mightiest kings are brought to tremble (Dan. 6:25–27). Reflected is the situation of the Jewish community during the period of Ptolemaic rule over Judea in the third century BCE, a situation not dissimilar to the Persian period, with the Jews living under a rather benign foreign hegemony on the basis of the political model of accommodation promoted by Ezra and Nehemiah.[1]

Skillfully, an editorial link is created between Daniel 1–6 and 7–12 by reapplication of the historiographic pattern of four world empires (representing the total compass of human civilization) found in chapter 2 to the début of the four

---

1. The fictive setting of the tales in Daniel 1–6 is the Neo-Babylonian Empire, but the distance of the author from the Babylonian period is betrayed by the mistakes found in the chronology of the Babylonian kings in these six chapters.

chaos monsters in chapter 7 that inaugurates the climactic conflict unfolding at the threshold between this world and the world to come.

While the first six chapters of Daniel include the portrait of foreign rulers who through the miraculous protection of God over his people can be brought to acknowledge "the God of Shadrach, Meshach, and Abednego," in Daniel 7–12 not a glimmer of hope remains for peaceful coexistence with the kings of the earth. However, a transcendent hope lies beyond the monstrous potentates of this world. To the seer are revealed events transpiring in heaven that will culminate in the destruction of all opponents of God, the conferral of universal reign to the Son of Man and his holy ones, the awakening of the righteous to eternal life, and the elevation of the wise, righteous teachers (*maśkîlîm*) of God's people to celestial glory.

Viewed historically, the book of Daniel follows the pattern of midrashic reinterpretation that we have already observed in additions to the books of Isaiah, Ezekiel, and Zechariah. Daniel 1–6 reflects the conditions of the *Pax Persica* (538–332) and the *Pax Hellenica* (332–190), a long period of relative peace in which the foreign occupiers generally upheld a policy of toleration of Jewish religion and culture. Daniel 7–12, in contrast, can be dated to the reign of Antiochus IV Epiphanes (175–164), a reign interpreted from the viewpoint of the pious author as the final assault of evil on the holy ones of the Most High, to be followed by God's intervention and conferral of kingship to his chosen Son of Man and the vindication of God's faithful people.

While the retention of the name Daniel for the recipient of the end-time visions affirms that a single divine purpose spans the entire history of Israel, the shift from relatively peaceful relations between occupier and occupied in the first six chapters of Daniel to a situation of persecution and martyrdom in the last six is marked by the shift from the genre of wisdom tales describing the life of Daniel and his companions in the foreign court to apocalyptic visions depicting the foreign rulers as agents of primordial chaos, who after their final season of wanton cruelty were destined to be annihilated. As pronounced as was the change in the situation of the Jews, however, from the perspective of heaven to which Daniel was privy, all remained consistent with the divine plan disclosed long before to the prophet Jeremiah (Jer. 25:11; 29:10), inasmuch as the seventy-year captivity that he had predicted now was understood by the seer to signify seventy weeks of years (Dan. 9:24–27).

THE UNRAVELING OF THE MODEL OF ACCOMMODATION

As observed in chapter 20, the Jews for three centuries had lived in relative peace according to the terms of the *lex judaica,* which on the Jewish community's side of the agreement entailed a policy of accommodation. While final authority in all matters pertaining to taxation, international relations, and the military security of the empire was vested in the foreign ruler and his advisors, domestic affairs such as religious beliefs and rituals, as well as the laws regulating interpersonal and community relations, were conducted on the basis of Jewish law and custom. Not surprisingly, that modus vivendi easily broke down in times of conflict, a phenomenon reflected in the earliest strata of *1 Enoch*.[2]

At this juncture it may be helpful to recall the organization of Judea's political and religious institutions during the Persian and early Hellenistic periods. Serving as a link between the imperial court and the local population was the provincial governor, who at times was Jewish and in other instances foreign. Institutional continuity was in large part assured by the office of high priest, whose Zadokite incumbents were selected on the traditional hereditary principle of the eldest son succeeding the father.[3] As noted in the previous chapter, the relatively new office of scribe, while lacking the historical depth and ritual splendor of high priest, was of great practical significance for the daily life of the Jewish community, providing as it did an unbroken chain of interpretation and reapplication of Torah to ever-changing historical situations.

The vital role played by scribes as community leaders facilitating the adjustments and adaptations required of a people living under foreign domination can be glimpsed by comparing two figures separated by over two centuries, Ezra and Sirach, the former being in effect the founding father of the scribal tradition, the latter being the sage who fostered the modus vivendi that helped many progressive Jews to reconcile the ancestral faith to the learned schools of Greek philosophy. For both of these figures, accommodation was the key to political viability of an ethnic religious minority. Even as Ezra laid the foundation that made it possible for the Jewish commonwealth to live as a subject people under the Persians and yet maintain its traditional beliefs and customs, Sirach provided a model for Jewish survival within the cosmopolitan environment of a headstrong pan-Hellenism that sought to dissolve all ethnic and religious boundaries.

While Ezra's legacy served the Jewish community well for several centuries, however, Sirach's contribution was to prove more problematic, due not to any fatal flaw in the theo-political model that he had inherited from Ezra, but due instead to a sharp deterioration in political conditions in the eastern Mediterranean during his time. On a magnitude equal to the challenge of secular modernity to orthodox Judaism and Christianity in the seventeenth and eighteenth centuries of our era, nascent Judaism in the second century BCE encountered a daunting threat to its very identity in the face of the strident world movement of Hellenism.

Although the primary sources for Jewish history in the second century BCE, Daniel and 1 and 2 Maccabees, tend to oversimplify a complex cultural conflict

2. George Nickelsburg, *1 Enoch 1: A Commentary on the Book of 1 Enoch, Chapters 1–36; 81–108*, Hermeneia (Minneapolis: Fortress Press, 1980), 62–65, 165–73.

3. The irregular succession that ensued upon the death of Simon I in the third century BCE likely was due to the fact that the legitimate successor to the high priesthood, his son Onias II, was still a minor, a situation entirely different than the chaos that broke out in the ruthless sacerdotal infighting of the second century BCE.

by depicting two basic parties, one plotting to supplant Torah faith with Greek religion, the other willing to die in defense of the ancestral traditions,[4] a critical reading of all of the relevant ancient witnesses, such as that provided by Viktor Tcherikover, Martin Hengel, and Klaus Bringmann,[5] reveals a wide range of tactics adopted by groups that expressed their openness or opposition to the new wave of Hellenistic thought and practice.[6]

The signs of ecumenical openness are manifest. For example, the translation of the Hebrew Scripture into Greek (the Septuagint) no doubt reflects the desire of many Diaspora Jews for rapprochement with their intellectual environment. Another sign of openness is the identification of *torah* with *sophia* (universal wisdom) in Sirach 24. Finally, it was within this Jewish intellectual current that Philo of Alexandria, and later the pro-Roman Jewish historian Josephus, flourished.

While it would be inaccurate to regard the translators of the Septuagint, the author of Sirach, or Philo as traitors to their ancestral religious traditions, certain other prominent Jews sought to push the adoption of the Hellenistic way to a point that understandably elicited condemnation by more conservative circles. The high priesthood itself fell victim to such collaborators, as the tragic history of the last loyal Zadokite high priest, Onias III, indicates. Remembered by tradition as a staunch defender of the temple and its treasury against pillaging and defilement, Onias opposed the efforts of the conniving Simon of the priestly tribe of Bilga to open the gates of the temple to Seleucus IV's general, Heliodorus.

The faithful priest was able to forestall calamity for only a short time. With Antiochus IV's accession to the throne in 175, Onias suffered the humiliation of witnessing his brother Jason's purchase of the high priesthood for a huge payment of silver. From his new position, Jason aggressively contributed to the transformation of Jerusalem into a Greek city, though a mere three years later he in turn lost his office to a higher bidder, Menelaus, the brother of the ever-conniving Simon of Bilga. To add insult to injury, Menelaus was not a Zadokite, and thus officially he was unqualified for the office. Thus it was that affairs located at the heart of Jewish faith reached their nadir point as the supreme head of the temple, in a bitterly ironic turn, became the catalyst for "the abomination that makes desolate."

Antiochus used the fierce rivalry between Jason and Menelaus as pretense for his invasion of the Holy City and the temple, while the high priest Menelaus in turn robbed the temple treasury in the desperate attempt to pay off his debt to

---

4. This position remained basically intact in Elias J. Bickerman's classic study, *From Ezra to the Last of the Maccabees: Foundations of Post-Biblical Judaism* (New York: Schocken Books, 1962).

5. Viktor Tcherikover, *Hellenistic Civilization and the Jews* (New York: Atheneum, 1970); Martin Hengel, *Jews, Greeks, and Barbarians: Aspects of the Hellenization of Judiasm in the Pre-Christian Period*, trans. J. Bowden (Philadelphia: Fortress Press, 1980); Klaus Bringmann, *Hellenistische Reform und Religionsverfolgung in Judäa* (Göttingen: Vandenhoeck & Ruprecht, 1983).

6. In the Greek ideal, the rigorous physical activities of the *gymnasium* were inextricably tied to the study of science and philosophy.

the Seleucid overlord. As seems inevitable, the tragic life of Onias ended amid all this turmoil, for while he was on a peacekeeping mission to the imperial center of Antioch, he fell victim to an assassination plot of the infamous high priest Menelaus and his unscrupulous brother Simon, two individuals who were key players in setting the stage for the Maccabean War.

Before turning to that conflict, we can mention briefly, as an example of hellenizing Jews whose interests seemed primarily economic in nature, the house of Tobiah, a commercial family whose meddling in temple affairs reached all the way back to the time of Nehemiah, and whose political tenacity was due in part to the dexterity with which through successive generations they were able to intervene in Jerusalem affairs and then retreat to their hinterland redoubt to regroup and plot anew.

With this brief historical account, we have entered the world of the primary groups from which the actors of the Maccabean/Hasmonean period would be drawn. They include the deposed high priestly family of the Zadokites, the devout Torah-true laity that came to be called Hasidim, prominent and well-educated families who to various degrees were open to Hellenism as a source of enriching their Jewish religion and culture, members of commercial families seeking to strengthen their economic ties, and cabals of conniving opportunists willing to strike deals with anyone promising riches, whether temple officials, Seleucid rulers, or representatives of Rome. Among those genuinely motivated by religious commitments, perspectives varied from the sober realism of the wisdom tradition to the visionary worldview of apocalypticism. How such a divided community would deal with the new degraded form of Hellenism represented by Antiochus IV Epiphanes is the question to which we now turn.

THE IMPOSITION OF PAN-HELLENISM

For the citizens of Judea, the second century BCE was ushered in with an anomaly. The transfer of power from the Ptolemies of Egypt to the Seleucids of Syria, which resulted from the victory of Antiochus III ("the Great") over Ptolemy V in the battle at Panion in the year 200, was greeted with enthusiasm and high hopes for enhanced freedoms and improved economic conditions. The Seleucids were well versed in the tactics of imperial propaganda. Antiochus III had garnered popular support through tax concessions and promises of new levels of Jewish self-determination. Even the most progressive among the Jerusalem elite were ill prepared for the radical shift in policy introduced by Antiochus IV Epiphanes upon his assuming the throne in 175.

At the heart of the politics of accommodation framing the relation of Jews to their Persian and Ptolemaic overlords in the fifth, fourth, and third centuries was a twin concession made by the overlords in return for fealty on the part of the vassals, namely, tolerance of Jewish law and a favored tax status. This mutually beneficial arrangement was about to change. Aggressive opportunism on the part of certain members of the Jerusalem elite conspired with Seleucid imperialistic designs to nullify the long-standing *lex judaica*. It would be oversimplifying matters to construe the resulting bloody conflict strictly as a religious war or even as a clash of civilizations, the religion of Moses versus the philosophy of Hellas.

Opposing religious values and ideologies played a part, but basic human vices also fanned the flames of conflict; for example, unfettered political ambition allied to rampant economic greed created bedfellows who were less interested in preserving religious tradition or promoting a universal political philosophy than in gaining personal wealth and power. If one adds to the latter carousing and debauchery, one defines the ethos that created a hotbed wide enough to accommodate Jewish high priests, Seleucid kings, Tobiad robber barons, and finally officials representing the Roman government.

There is no reason to doubt that Antiochus IV Epiphanes (sarcastically named Epimanes ["mad man"] by Polybius) was a major instigator of the debacle described symbolically by Daniel and historiographically by 1 and 2 Maccabees. The missionary zeal of spreading the "superior" culture of Hellenism at least provided a front for his despotism, but the tolerance of native cults that characterized earlier Hellenistic kings was suspended. This was due no doubt in part to his desperate need to seize from occupied countries the gold and silver required to pay the huge punitive tribute he had incurred from the Romans in the wake of two failed military campaigns against Egypt. Since temple treasuries contained the greatest concentration of wealth in ancient capitals, it was most convenient for Antiochus that in Menelaus he had access to a high priest with keys in hand to serve as his personal guide into the vaults of the central holy place of the Jews.

Under Menelaus the conversion of Jerusalem into a Greek *polis* proceeded rapidly. It featured both an acra (a citadel for the Greek soldiers) and a gymnasium. Male participants in the new Greek lifestyle underwent surgery to remove their mark of Jewish identity, circumcision, and many Jews submitted to laws aimed at eradicating traditional practices deemed contradictory to the universalism of Hellenism, such as study of the Torah, observance of Sabbath, the daily temple sacrifice, and the annual Jewish festivals. The darkest atrocity occurred in 167 BCE with the desecration of the temple through the sacrifice of a pig upon the altar and installation of the symbol of Zeus Olympus in the Holy of Holies.

With lightning speed, the policy of accommodation that had served the Jewish community well for three centuries had abruptly collapsed. From the time of Ezra to Sirach, the terms dictated by the foreign ruler included the abdication of national sovereignty, but in the realm of religious belief and practice and ethnic customs, the Jews through most of that period enjoyed the freedom to order their own affairs. Judaism accordingly emerged as a vital entity that could grow and thrive, even as a community politically subject to a foreign regime, since its identity derived from those aspects of life that the Persians and the Ptolemies safeguarded from outside interference.

Antiochus IV, however, imposed on the Jews a radically different polity, by abandoning the policy of tolerating local beliefs and customs generally practiced by Alexander and the generals who succeeded him, and implementing in its place an aggressive program of hellenization, in the course of which his mercurial nature expressed itself in ruthless suppression of those who sought to preserve their ancestral ways.

Among the upper echelons of Jewish society in Egypt, Judea, and the Transjordan, however, there were individuals and families that seemed to sense little conflict between their interests and the Hellenistic ideals that followed in the wake of Antiochus's occupation of their homeland; at least they found that the advantages of collaboration outweighed the liabilities. Though it is impossible to be certain what ideological considerations might have been melded into their embrace of Antiochus, it seems that the Tobiads, some of the Oniads, and members of the priestly tribe of Bilga were able to rationalize that the developments of their time served as an example of Sirach's identification of Torah with universal wisdom (Sir. 24). As for Antiochus, to the extent that the Hellenic ideal of Alexander the Great was still alive in his thought, he may have regarded the transformation of Jerusalem from the center of an ancient and not terribly enlightened regional cult to a beachhead of Hellenism on the eastern Mediterranean as a giant step out of a dark age into the brilliance of a new era.

Though many different attitudes toward Greek culture existed among the Jews in Judea, as well as in Egypt and other parts of the Diaspora, the Maccabean picture of two sides, the faithful and the apostate, did in a general sense describe the crisis that came to a climax with the profanation of the temple in 167 BCE. While "progressives" initially may have welcomed as beneficial the opening of the gymnasium in Jerusalem and a curriculum that included the Greek philosophers, it is less likely that any but the most opportunistic and unscrupulous would have greeted with enthusiasm the emblem of a foreign god in their temple or the proscription of study of Torah. At any rate, the summons to resistance that was issued by Mattathias and his sons in the year 167 BCE galvanized a broad coalition and isolated collaborators like Menelaus as hellenizing apostates.

Daniel 7–12 translates that division into the cosmic symbolism of the forces of chaos and God's holy ones, locked in the climactic, end-time battle. Whereas 1 and 2 Maccabees describe a course of action in which the faithful are drawn into actual historical combat to defeat the Seleucids and their Jewish allies, the book of Daniel dismisses such tactics as but "a little help" and takes the apocalyptic posture of patiently accepting persecution and martyrdom while awaiting God's incisive intervention.

THIS WORLD AND THE WORLD TO COME
IN THE VISIONS OF DANIEL

Chapters 7–12 of the book of Daniel present in highly dramatic form an interpretation of events that fits the pattern of what we have called apocalyptic politics. In supplementary sections to the books of Isaiah, Zechariah, and Ezekiel, we saw examples of a political viewpoint that was moving in the direction of apocalyptic under the pressure of inner-community struggles. In Daniel 7–12, the apocalyptic reading of history is driven by world forces pressing upon the Jewish community from the outside, namely, the forces of hellenization and the aggressive imperial policies of Antiochus IV. Unmistakable references in chapters 7, 8, and 11 to the extreme actions taken by that Seleucid king against the religion of the Jews confirm as the date of composition of these six chapters the year 167 BCE.

The bleak dualistic assessment of reality that is the hallmark of apocalyptic politics comes to expression in chapter 7 in a description of this world's kingdoms as embodiments of mythic chaos monsters arising out of the sea. Drawing on the ancient historiographic pattern of four world kingdoms, what later in the book are unmasked as the kingdoms of Babylon, Media, Persia, and Greece (i.e., Alexander and the separate Hellenistic kingdoms that succeeded him) are represented by mythological beasts reminiscent of those the creator god of primordial times fought and slayed in the course of creating the world.[7]

This traditional pattern was given the pithy designation *Endzeit wird Urzeit* by the German scholar Hermann Gunkel in a groundbreaking study published in 1895,[8] thereby calling attention to the cyclic worldview of myth that increasingly influenced the apocalyptic seers, a view according to which the events marking the end time recapitulate the events that produced the world in its infancy. History has been brought to this final assize by the blasphemy and wanton hubris of a ruler who exalts himself above the one true God.[9] Though those faithful to God must endure terrible suffering in evil's final orgy of violence, their deliverance is imminent; however, it will not occur within the context of this world, but will be a part of God's establishing an eternal kingdom in heaven.

What is the intended political meaning of this apocalyptic interpretation of the debacle catalyzed by Antiochus IV? Taken literally, it seems to break sharply from the politics of Israel's prophets, who, while issuing urgent threats of impending doom interpreted as God's judgment on Israel's sin, looked beyond judgment to a restoration of historical Israel in its homeland.

The relation between the apocalyptic writings in Daniel and prophetic books like Isaiah involves both continuity and change. In subsequent visions in the book of Daniel, we shall find additional descriptions of salvation in otherworldly terms, in connection with which we shall elaborate on the *change* side of the

---

7. The best-known version of the ancient Near Eastern creation myth is the *Enuma Elish* (*Ancient Near Eastern Texts Relating to the Old Testament*, ed. James B Pritchard, 3rd ed. [Princeton, NJ: Princeton University Press, 1969]), 60–72. A discussion of reflexes of this myth both within the Bible and in nonbiblical texts can be found in Paul D. Hanson, *The Dawn of Apocalyptic* (Philadelphia: Fortress Press, 1975), 299–316.

8. Hermann Gunkel, *Schöpfung und Chaos in Urzeit und Endzeit: Eine Religionsgeschichtliche Untersuchung über Gen. 1 und Ap. Joh. 12* (Göttingen: Vandenhoeck & Ruprecht, 1895).

9. The motif of imperial hubris, best known from its classical expression in ancient Greek and Latin texts, was already developed in Israel's prophetic period. A vivid example is found in Isa. 14:12–21.

relationship. First, it is important to direct our attention to a basic theological tenet in Daniel 7 and 8 that stands in *continuity* with classical prophecy, namely, the theocratic principle that constitutes the heart of Yahwistic political thought through its long history of adaptive iterations.

Central to ancient Israel's Torah tradition and the prophetic politics that derived from it is the affirmation that there is only one ultimate ruling authority in the universe, namely, the Holy One of Israel. A corollary of this cardinal commandment is that any ruler who fails to acknowledge that authority and abdicates his responsibility as a mediator to implement the qualities of God's universal rule in appropriate structures of governance is placing himself under the curses of an eternal covenant. The description of the heavenly courtroom in Daniel 7:9–18, in which judgment is pronounced upon the kingdoms of this world that violated that theocratic principle, is thus on a fundamental level in harmony with prophetic politics and the covenantal tradition upon which the prophets drew.

Daniel 9 is developed around another theologoumenon that stems from the heart of Israel's religious heritage. The chapter consists of the prayer of supplication that Daniel lifts up to God. It gives expression to the covenant theology of Israel as formulated with particular clarity in the book of Deuteronomy. It acknowledges God's upholding his side of the covenant in steadfast love, but goes on to confess Israel's sin and rebellion in refusing to obey the Torah and turning a deaf ear to God's messengers, the prophets. The calamity that the nation faced thus was not the creation of a human ruler. It was God's judgment, the unfolding of the curses of the covenant under which Israel had fallen already in the early stages of its life as nation.[10]

Following the classic structure of the genre, Daniel moves from confession to supplication by imploring God's mercy not "on the ground of our righteousness, but on the ground of your great mercies" (9:18). God responds with a promise of deliverance, but in keeping with the gravity of the offense, it is not to be instantaneous: "Seventy weeks [i.e., seventy years multiplied by seven] are decreed for your people and your holy city: to finish the transgression, to put an end to sin, and to atone for iniquity, to bring in everlasting righteousness, to seal both vision and prophet, and to anoint a most holy place [or "thing" or "one"]" (9:24).

Even this part of Daniel's prayer conforms to the classic prophetic model, as found, for example, in the original formulation in Jeremiah 25, of a period of seventy years (versus Hananiah's promise of immediate restoration) as the required period of punishment, or in the assurance given through God's messenger to Jerusalem that she had "served her term," "her penalty is paid," "she has received from the LORD's hand double for all her sins" (Isa. 40:2).

---

10. The classic formulation of the blessings and curses of the covenant is Deut. 27–28. See Klaus Baltzer, *The Covenant Formulary* (Phildadelphia: Fortress Press, 1971), 86–87.

Given these continuities with classical themes, what are the innovations found in Daniel that lead us to invoke the category of apocalyptic politics? We have already seen the mythic dimension and the dualistic construal of reality in chapters 7 and 8. Now we shall describe two other features favored by apocalyptic seers, the *vaticanum ex eventu* account of history and the transcendental denouement, which are found in chapters 10–12.

Daniel, after three weeks of preparatory fasting, is visited by an angelic messenger[11] who makes reference to the struggle transpiring in heaven between Michael and himself on one side and the prince of Persia (to be followed by the prince of Greece) on the other (chap. 10). Events in heaven are thus revealed as the source of the stages of history the messenger proceeds to describe in chapter 11. Human history is thus subsumed under a more significant sphere, since earthly struggles are a mere reflection of goings-on in heaven. Two dimensions of the worldview of apocalyptic are thus evident: the sharp division between fallen past and brilliant future, and an equally significant division between epiphenomenal terrestrial happenings and archetypal celestial events.

The history of the Persian and Greek wars and their impact on the Jewish community is sketched without ascription of names to the dramatis personae, but with sufficient detail to enable identification.[12] The violence of these wars reaches a climax in the career of Antiochus IV, who directs his assault against the "the holy covenant" and the temple and its rituals (Dan. 11:30–31). In Daniel 11:32–35 Antiochus's alliance with hellenizing Jews and the revolt fomented by the Maccabees are alluded to:

> He shall seduce with intrigue those who violate the covenant; but the people who are loyal to their God shall stand firm and take action. The wise among the people [*maśkîlê'ām*] shall give understanding to many; for some days, however, they shall fall by sword and flame, and suffer captivity and plunder. When they fall victim, they shall receive a little help, and many shall join them insincerely. Some of the wise shall fall, so that they may be refined, purified, and cleansed, until the time of the end, for there is still an interval until the time appointed.

Here perhaps more clearly than in any other passage in Daniel, the apocalyptic politics of the seer comes to expression. The broad-based revolt of the Maccabees against Antiochus is acknowledged, but its significance is judged minimally ("a little help"). The reason seems clear: from the apocalyptic perspective of the writer, hope for the vindication of the righteous lies not in human efforts to regain Jewish independence, but in induction into an everlasting kingdom transcending human history. The function of the present battles against Antiochus is construed martyrologically: "Some of the wise shall fall, that they may be

---

11. The context suggests that this angel is Gabriel (cf. Dan. 8:16; 9:21).

12. *The New Oxford Annotated Bible,* or any of the other critical annotated editions of the Bible, can be consulted for the identification of the animal actors of Dan. 11 and the historical figures they represent.

refined, purified, and cleansed, until the time of the end" (11:35). Chapter 12 fills out the picture of salvation as the transcendence of death:[13] After "a time of anguish, such as has never occurred since the nations first came into existence, . . . everyone who is found written in the book" shall be delivered (12:1), and many of the dead shall awake, either to "everlasting life" or "everlasting contempt" (12:2), with a special place of honor being reserved for the aforementioned martyred *maśkîlîm*, who will shine in the sky like stars. Finally to be noted is a striking contrast: unlike the messages relayed to Israel's prophets, which were to be proclaimed publicly,[14] obviously with the intent of leading the people to repentance and their nation to security within the framework of the covenant, Daniel is instructed to "keep the words secret and the book sealed until the time of the end" (12:4).

THIS WORLD AND THE HASMONEAN MONARCHY

There is no way to determine how many Jews shared the apocalyptic viewpoint of Daniel 7–12. It is reasonable to assume that adherents were more likely to live in Jerusalem and its environs than in the Diaspora, where the influence of Hellenism was pervasive. We can surmise further that there were more adherents of the otherworldly apocalyptic orientation during the most intense period of Antiochus's assault on the religious traditions of the Jews than in years prior or subsequent. Indeed, it has been noted often that one of the primary functions of apocalyptic writings is to provide a bulwark for faith during times of persecution. We shall return to the question of apocalyptic politics later, when we look beyond the canonical writings to the sectarian writings of the Dead Sea community of Qumran. Our next task, however, is to examine the politics of a movement that was to succeed in restoring the independence of the Jewish nation under the political structure of monarchy. Like Israel's first monarchy, it embodied a theo-political model designed to secure the autonomy of the Jewish state and to safeguard ancestral beliefs, values, and customs from outside contamination. Its commitment to national independence set it apart from the policies vis-à-vis foreign rule of both apocalyptic politics (patient suffering under an evil foreign power in anticipation of God's end-time intervention) and the politics of accommodation (finding a mutually agreeable manner of coexistence with the occupying power).

Accompanying our examination of Israel's second monarchy will be the same questions we raised in relation to the earlier Davidic monarchy: How did the Hasmonean dynasty measure up to the theocratic mandate of mediating the qualities of divine rule through the structures of governance they developed?

---

13. Cf. John J. Collins, "Apocalyptic Eschatology as the Transcendence of Death," *Catholic Biblical Quarterly* 36 (1974): 21–43.

14. E.g., Amos 3:8; Isa. 6:9; Jer. 7:1–5.

Did their rule reflect the righteous standards of God's universal reign, or did they abuse their power in ways that made a mockery of justice and fostered idolatry rather than exclusive worship of the one God?

Initially, the revolt initiated by Mattathias Maccabeus and his sons seems to have held true to the beliefs and values of the ancestral faith. Not surprisingly, their initiatives enjoyed broad support from the populace. The rallying point was the Torah and the ancient customs and rites that were indivisibly associated with Jewish identity, for they had become the target of Antiochus's campaign to transform Jerusalem into a Hellenistic city-state. Already under the leadership of Judas, the religious and political aims of the insurrection became clear, namely, the restoration of temple sacrifice and the establishment of the political independence of the Jewish nation. The former was accomplished before Judas's death in 161 BCE, the latter only two decades later, after recurrent conflict and even times when the Maccabean effort seemed destined to fail.

The richest sources for the history of the Hasmoneans are the books of 1 and 2 Maccabees. First Maccabees is an interpretation of events with the clear intention of valorizing the Maccabees and justifying the Hasmonean claim to rule, against critics pointing to their lack of either Davidic or Zadokite pedigree. Second Maccabees preserves an epitome of a history written by Jason of Cyrene focusing on the temple and its personnel.[15]

The propagandistic agenda of 1 Maccabees is not hard to understand against the background of the growing inner-community tensions that followed in the wake of the popular uprising led by Judas. The anti-Seleucid alliance began to erode as various pious groups did not see the wholehearted return of the nation to obedience to the Torah for which they had fought. Many began to suspect that the political ambitions of Judas and especially his brothers Jonathan and Simon had overtaken their religious zeal as the primary motivation for their ongoing military campaigns. Traditionalists already may have viewed Judas's diplomatic initiatives with Rome as a new opening to the contamination of their ancestral beliefs by pagan influences that they had fought to eliminate. Though passages like 1 Maccabees 3:19–22 may have been intended to place Judas in the tradition of the judges (šōpĕṭîm) of Israel's early history, another likeness, that of the Greek hero, would have reinforced the fear that the Hasmonean rapprochement with Greece and Rome would actually abet rather than impede the spread Hellenism.

When Jonathan succeeded Judas he raised the level of alarm among the pious, not only by continuing the strategy of realpolitik in strengthening ties with

15. A major historiographic problem (not atypical of histories of that age) vexes attempts to reconstruct and evaluate the restoration undertaken by the Maccabees: 1 Maccabees is zealously pro-Hasmonean; 2 Maccabees has a distinct pro-temple bias; and as we have seen, Daniel is couched in the cryptic idiom of apocalyptic. As for the sectarian writings of Qumran, the fierce anti-Jerusalem-leadership bias is blatant. See the fine discussion of historiography and historical reconstruction in Daniel J. Harrington, SJ, *The Maccabean Revolt: Anatomy of a Biblical Revolution* (Wilmington, DE: Michael Glazier, 1988), 9–16.

Rome and Sparta, but also by solidifying his personal authority in laying claim to the office of high priest. No doubt, many Jews accepted his incumbency as preferable to that of Menelaus. Others were perhaps relieved to have the uncertainty caused by the vacancy in the office of high priest that existed 159–152 BCE ended by Alexander Balas's appointment of a man with the proven military and diplomatic skills of Jonathan.[16]

But an ongoing source of bitter opposition was the priestly family of the Oniads, now living as fugitives in Egypt and having the painful memory of the assassination of Onias III and the usurpation of the highest sacerdotal office reinforced by the waxing power of an illegitimate priestly dynasty, a dynasty, moreover, that in their judgment had reversed the policy of fighting in defense of the ancestral faith against Hellenism to the expedient politics of alliances with the Seleucids and the Romans. It has even been suggested that the leader of the schismatic Essene community of Qumran, referred to in the Dead Sea Scrolls as "The Teacher of Righteousness," may have been "the son or brother of Onias III."[17] At any rate, there is abundant evidence that "the Teacher" was a Zadokite, and in his teaching he combined vitriol against the Hasmonean leadership of Jerusalem with the creation of a strict Torah community in the wilderness, which prepared for the day in which its members would join the heavenly host in winning back control of the temple. We shall discuss in more detail below the animosity toward the Hasmoneans that developed at Qumran.

Simon, in succeeding Jonathan in 142 BCE, took the final step toward absolute rule, by consolidating in his person the historically separated high offices of the nation, civil and sacral: "So Simon accepted and agreed to be high priest, to be commander and ethnarch of the Jews and priests, and to be protector of them all" (1 Macc. 14:47). This he was able to do by building on the military victories of Jonathan and exploiting a bitter conflict between the rival claimants to the Seleucid throne, Trypho and Demetrius II, which in 142 BCE led to Jewish political independence and freedom from tribute and taxation. Continuing the precarious game of balance of power, he solidified his international standing through a renewal of treaty relations with Antioch, Rome, and Sparta. With great fanfare the assembly of the people issued a proclamation that was engraved on bronze tablets and exhibited prominently on Mount Zion:

> The Jews and their priests have resolved that Simon should be their leader and high priest forever, until a trustworthy prophet should arise, and that he should be governor over them and that he should take charge of the sanctuary and appoint officials over its tasks and over the country and the weapons and the strongholds, and that he should take charge of the sanctuary, and they he should be obeyed by all, and that all contracts in the

16. One of the historiographic techniques utilized by the author of 1 Maccabees is drawing parallels between the heroes of the past commemorated in the Deuteronomistic History and the sons of Mattathias. Jonathan, for example, is presented in language recalling both the earlier judges of the tribal confederacy and King David (1 Macc. 9:30, 73).

17. Harrington, *Revolt*, 120.

country should be written in his name, and that he should be clothed in purple and wear gold. (1 Macc. 14:41–43)

With this proclamation the Hasmoneans completed their clean sweep of the highest offices of the land. Simon, a man with a claim to neither Zadokite nor Davidic pedigree, now possessed administrative authority even outstripping in compass that of David and Solomon. The checks and balances that had been maintained by the separation of the offices of king, chief priest, and prophet were thereby dissolved, "until a trustworthy prophet should arise," whenever that might be![18] Though presented by 1 Maccabees in a manner intended to reflect the earlier monarchy of David and Solomon, the foreign influence deriving from the Greco-Macedonian sphere abetted the formation of what went far beyond the limited monarchy of the Davidic house.

Indeed, it would be accurate to classify it as a *despotic tyranny,* in which the flaunting of luxury and rampant debauchery, characteristic of courts of the tyrant kings of neighboring kingdoms, became a way of life. Even the pro-Hasmonean book of 1 Maccabees concludes with the report of the violent death of Simon and his sons as they caroused in the banquet hall of Ptolemy son of Abubus, governor of Jericho.[19] As for those devout souls adhering to the theocratic principle of God's ultimate authority and the responsibility of earthly rulers to mediate the qualities of divine governance in their style of rule, the signs of impending national calamity must have been overwhelming.

In keeping with the intrigue endemic to the despotic court, one son, John Hyrcanus (clearly the most clever and thus within the pagan world of tyrant rulers the best suited for kingship), managed to escape the massacre that had claimed the lives of his father and brothers and to seize the throne. Perpetuating the dual office of priest-king, he ruled in grand style, securing with the benefit of Roman support the broad reaches of his realm militarily, minting his own coins, and through his long thirty-one-year reign placing on a firm footing the dynastic claims of his descendants.

It is not solely the historiography of the court scribes that portrays Hyrcanus as a David or Solomon redivivus, for it is clear that his conquests were motivated in no small measure by the strategy of regaining control of the lucrative trade routes running from Egypt to Damascus and from the Mediterranean through the region of the Nabateans to the spice markets lying to the southeast. But he too failed to win the support of all of his subjects, for not only did the Essenes in their wilderness refuge continue to cultivate "perfect hatred" for their enemies in Jerusalem, but the increasingly powerful party of the Pharisees, with whom he originally enjoyed cordial relations, withdrew its support in protest against his resolute retention of the office of high priest. Predictably, the Pharisees were punished harshly by Hyrcanus for their disloyalty.

---

18. Josephus (*Ant.* 13.300) explicitly states that God had endowed Hyrcanus with civil, high priestly, *and* prophetic authority.
19. 1 Macc. 16:11–17.

After the one-year reign of Aristobulus, Alexander Jannaeus cultivated further the luxurious court style of Hellenistic despots, with revenue for support of regal extravagance derived from further conquest, in the course of which captives were subjected to ruthless cruelty. In response to widespread protests against his debaucherous lifestyle, he slew his own subjects by the thousands, according to Josephus in *Antiquities,* book 13.

After something of a respite from internal strife and a healing of wounds between the Hasmoneans and the Pharisees during the nine-year reign of Jannaeus's widow, Alexandra, the political situation deteriorated drastically in the following decade, a dark period marked by civil war between the contending heirs to the throne, Aristobulus II and Hyrcanus II. For the Romans, who since Judas's day had remained staunch supporters of the Hasmoneans against the Syrians and assorted other enemies, matters in Judea had become so chaotic as to threaten their own imperial interests in the eastern Mediterranean. With Pompey's triumphal entry into Jerusalem in 63 BCE, the independent reign of the Hasmoneans came to an end.

Needless to say, when measured against the criteria of the Yahwistic theocratic principle, its shortcomings were colossal: abuse of power for self-gain, violation of the rights of its citizens, debaucherous living, cruelty to any dissenting parties that dared to question their policies and style of rule, and an idolatrous refutation of the ultimate authority of the sole sovereign. Only as a distant memory could pious God-fearers recall the theocratic ideal of the king who read Torah daily and dedicated his reign to the righteous rule of the only universal sovereign.

THE DEAD SEA SCROLLS:
AN APOCALYPTIC COMMUNITY ORGANIZED
AS AN ARMY OF GOD AWAITING THE FINAL BATTLE

Josephus, in a frequently cited passage, identifies three distinct philosophies within the Jewish community of his time, Sadducees, Pharisees, and Essenes.[20] Recognizing that his choice of the term "philosophies" stems from his desire to be intelligible within the cultural milieu of his Roman patrons, scholars feel comfortable substituting the term "parties" as a more suitable designation for the leading groups that emerged in the last two centuries BCE. This tripartite division also has proven useful as a means of distinguishing between the major theo-political movements active in the Hasmonean period and beyond. For our purposes, it allows us to present in comprehensible fashion the cultural/religious demography of Hasmonean and Roman Judea at the time of the birth of the Essene community at Qumran.

---

20. Josephus, *War* 2.119.

We begin with the Sadducees, whose name etymologically derives from the Zadokite priestly party. Though descendants of the family from whom arose the long succession of Jerusalem high priests, the loss of that office and the rapidly changing circumstances of the Hasmonean and Roman periods led to the emergence of a distinct profile that is reflected, with certain minor differences, in all of the known sources covering that era. According to both the New Testament and the rabbinical writings, the Sadducees were theologically conservative (e.g., in denying the resurrection of the dead and limiting the scope of their Scripture to the Torah) and politically and economically pragmatic, a posture serving well the wealthy and internationally fluent families that constituted their ranks. Though in the New Testament they are frequently mentioned with the Pharisees as opponents of Jesus, the rabbinical writings give what is clearly a more accurate portrait of the Sadducees as opponents of the Pharisees.

No doubt in part due to their combining a progressive approach to interpretation of Torah with the preservation of a clear sense of identity within their table fellowships (ḥābērōt), the branch of the Pharisees following the teachings of Hillel emerged by the year 200 BCE as the normative Judaism of the rabbis and the fountainhead of the Mishnah and Talmud that define Jewish faith down to the present. The Sadducees, on the other hand, failed to adapt to changing times and disappeared as a force within Judaism.

Though the historical sources are not of the nature that give historians of religion a basis for a clear account of the origins of the Pharisees and the Essenes, the most plausible theory is that originally they shared a common provenance in the widespread movement of the Torah faithful (hasidim) that gave its active support to the revolt of the Maccabees against the Seleucids and their Jewish collaborators. The circumstances that led to their separation into two distinct parties are to be found in the decades following the rededication of the temple in 163 BCE.

We already have observed how, in the crisis that broke out in 167 BCE, those zealous for the Torah accepted Judas's leadership as the deliverer sent by God to save the nation from a powerful pagan enemy, a view bolstered by a typological connection drawn between his campaign and that of the early judges like Gideon. The unprecedented assault on the heart of Jewish faith made by Antiochus reinstituted the traditional institution of holy war, according to which Sabbath law temporarily could be suspended, for when humans fight in the service of God, they are engaged in a ritual akin to worship.

We have also noted that the broad coalition began to unravel amid prolonged warfare in the following two decades. The goal of reclaiming the temple had been accomplished, and the extended Maccabean conquests began to blur the distinction between religious goals and political/economic objectives. Jonathan and Simon increasingly came to resemble the professional warriors of their opponents. Reliance on God's spirit yielded to a greater and greater reliance on alliances, which included treaties with the kings who succeeded Antiochus IV to the Seleucid throne and the precarious game of playing one of the Seleucids off against the other during the times of contested succession. Though the distinction between Essenes and Pharisees was never clear-cut, due to the considerable overlap in the tenets of their faith, the sectarian writings of Qumran indicate that a structural break did come, and it was largely of a theo-political nature. This requires further explanation regarding the background of these two groups.

In sharp contrast to the Sadducees, the Pharisees and the Essenes both believed that the structures of this world would be altered dramatically at the time when God's messiah came to inaugurate a reign of eternal righteousness and peace. But differences between the two parties arose over the questions of the relation of that reign to the historical institutions of temple and monarchy and to the role that humans would play in its inauguration. Disputes also arose within Pharisaism. For example, Rabbi Akiba's support of Bar Kokhba's revolt against Rome in 130 CE (at least in the portrayal of his position in Talmudic tradition) resembles in some respects the eschatology of the Dead Sea Scrolls; but in the mid-second century BCE the Pharisees generally displayed a willingness to work with the Hasmoneans as well as the Romans in a way that was inconceivable for the Essenes. However, the Pharisees' insistence that the Hasmonean rulers and the temple priests remain true to the high moral standards of the Torah not infrequently led to the wrath of noncompliant kings and priests. Such was the case during the brief tenure of the high priest Alchimus, when the Pharisees' protest to his blatant degradation of the sacerdotal office led to severe reprisals.

Though the blending of religion and politics during the tenure of Jonathan and then Simon doubtlessly gave occasion for concern, the Pharisees, from their pragmatic perspective, would have taken into account that the emerging Hasmonean dynasty had the benefits of reestablishing Jewish control over the temple and promised to bring a higher degree of stability to the land than had characterized the previous two decades. Further, Simon's capture of the Jerusalem citadel (acra) in 141 BCE must have carried significant symbolic meaning; the enclave of the pagan conquerors that also served as the den of their apostate Jewish supporters was finally removed from its location in the heart of the Holy City.

In terms of political strategy, it thus seems justifiable to identify as a characteristic of the Pharisees during the Hasmonean period a pragmatic approach to the governing authorities. They were willing to tolerate much, so long as this world's rulers, both native and foreign, maintained conditions that enabled the faithful to remain true to their religious traditions and practices. As a consequence, their relationship with the Hasmonean kings ran the gamut from conditional support to active opposition, and the treatment they got in return ranged accordingly from respect to persecution. In terms of our typology of political models, moreover, we can recognize a close similarity between the theo-politics of the Pharisees of this period and Ezra's earlier policy of accommodation.

Extending our vision even further, we can recognize in the strategies that originated with Ezra and were developed further by the Pharisees the roots of a theo-political policy that would provide the foundation for Diaspora Judaism for centuries to come. In that policy we can recognize the adaptation of the classic theocratic principle to the political situation that was to be experienced by the scattered Jewish communities for centuries to come, namely, life under a foreign regime. In that adaptation, non-Jewish rulers—unconsciously to be sure, as was earlier the case with Cyrus—were regarded as divinely appointed authorities with the twin mandate of ruling justly as mediators of God's universal sovereignty and of safeguarding the rights of their Jewish subjects to follow their ancestral beliefs, customs, and practices. This was the theo-political policy adopted as well by the apostle Paul and many other early Christian leaders.

The Essenes, the third party described by Josephus, differed from the Pharisees less in matters of doctrine than in the theo-political position they espoused. Like the Pharisees, they staunchly defended the central tenets of the Jewish faith, such as Sabbath observance, circumcision, and in general strict adherence to the Torah. In contrast to the Sadducees and again like the Pharisees, they did not limit Scripture to the five books of Moses but included the Prophets and the hagiographa, and they believed in angels and the resurrection. The points at which they differed with the Pharisees, points that led to their splitting off from those whose early history they shared, had to do in large measure with their assessment of the relation of the realities of this world to the promise of the world to come. In a word, it was their judgment that this world, including the Jerusalem leadership and the foreign powers with whom those leaders interacted, stood under the curse of divine judgment and was soon to be destroyed in a final assize.

With the exception of Josephus's brief description of the Essenes and a small number of other scattered references, knowledge of their origins, beliefs, and practices derives from the scrolls discovered in the middle of the last century at Qumran. Though the scrolls themselves include no direct identification of the Qumran community with the Essenes, most scholars feel confident on the basis of the nature of the community organization and teachings described in their sectarian writings—such as the *Community Rule* and *The War of the Sons of Light against the Sons of Darkness*—that its members were in fact Essenes.

In order to grasp a historical understanding of the nature of their beliefs, in particular the apocalyptic orientation of their politics, it is necessary to consider the few hints available regarding their origins. One source is found among the writings that they copied and interpreted, for alongside the biblical manuscripts of Qumran are found the fragmentary remains of books not found in the Hebrew Bible. Of particular interest are *1 Enoch* and *Jubilees.*[21]

21. This distinction between the biblical books and apocryphal and pseudepigraphic writings is anachronistic when applied to the various Jewish groups of the Hellenistic and early Roman periods, for there is no proof in their own writings that *1 Enoch* and *Jubilees*, for example, were not regarded as authoritative in a manner equal, say, to prophetic books or even the Psalms. It should be noted, however, that the Torah enjoyed a position of preeminence in all of the emerging Jewish parties.

The simple fact that the scribes of Qumran painstakingly reproduced copies of such extrabiblical writings indicates that they ascribed to them a degree of authority akin to the prophetic and hymnic books that they also copied and interpreted. What are the hints that these books contain relative to the origins of the Essenes? For one thing, they assume a solar calendar that was also regarded as normative at Qumran, but was at odds with the lunar-solar calendar upon which the Jerusalem priesthood based its ritual. This may appear to modern eyes as a trivial matter, but the sharp indictment contained in *1 Enoch* 2–5 against the sinners who were violating the cosmic order obeyed even by the heavenly bodies indicates the degree of seriousness with which the calendrical dispute was waged.

It does not require a lot of imagination to picture the monks of Qumran witnessing the growing discrepancy between the seasons and their "divinely given" calendar and accusing the Jerusalem leadership of throwing the entire cosmos into disarray, when the problem actually stemmed from a defect in their solar calendar, namely, its lacking the intercalations required to synchronize the seasons with the cycles of the moon and the sun! In a bizarre way not uncommon among modern apocalyptic movements, religiously based "science" was producing the very signs that corroborated the sect's belief that the world was spiraling toward its final descent into chaos.

The apocalyptic timetable that led the Qumran community to expect the imminent end of this world comes to vivid expression in two accounts of world history in *1 Enoch*. Following the historiographic pattern of *vaticanum ex eventu* that also lies behind Daniel 10–12, the author of the apocalypse of weeks in *1 Enoch* 93:1–10; 91:12–19 and the animal apocalypse in *1 Enoch* 85–90 attributes to the antediluvian hero Enoch an overview of history reaching from *Urzeit* to *Endzeit*. After all, who could have been in a better position to possess such extraordinary prescience than that ancient hero of whom it was reported, "Enoch walked with God; then he was no more, because God took him"?[22]

Particularly noteworthy with regard to the sectarian roots of the covenanters of Qumran is the description in the animal apocalypse of the temple rebuilt by Zerubbabel and dedicated by the Zadokite high priest Joshua,[23] the very temple that served as the home of the alleged apostate priests who were the archenemies of the banished Essenes. On account of the unclean offerings presented by the officiating priests upon the altar, that temple was deemed by God as polluted from its very inception (*1 Enoch* 88:113–14)!

Since the animal apocalypse belongs to one of the oldest strata of *1 Enoch*, it is possible to trace the anti-Jerusalem-temple tradition to which the Essenes of Qumran subscribed back to the third century BCE. Are the roots of that tradition even older? Though one enters the realm of speculation in making the following suggestion, it is the most plausible explanation of an otherwise puzzling

---

22. Gen. 5:24.

23. The figures in Israel's past are presented as various kinds of animals, but their referents are transparent to the reader who is familiar with the details of ancient Israelite history.

piece of evidence. The book of Malachi gives expression to a stinging critique of the presiding temple priesthood, that is, the Zadokite high priestly family. At the heart of that critique is precisely what the author of the animal apocalypse identified as the basis for divine condemnation of the institution of the Second Temple: "O priests, who despise my name. You say, 'How have we despised your name?' By offering polluted food on my altar" (Mal. 1:6b–7a).

The textual evidence cited above suggests that, though it deviated from the tradition that emerged as normative during the Hasmonean and Roman periods[24] and was used by the Jerusalem hierocracy to defend their legitimacy, another tradition persisted that disputed the claims of the officiating priests of the Jerusalem temple. Whether actual historical continuity between the proponents of that minority tradition and the author of the animal apocalypse and finally the members of the Qumran community can be established is less important than the realization that the tradition of polemic against the temple priests that surfaced in Malachi and the animal apocalypse suited well the polemics of the Essenes of Qumran, even though the temple leadership they were attacking was no longer Zadokite, but Hasmonean.

So they copied and studied the writings ascribed to Enoch as a source shedding light on their own place in history and describing the events soon to occur, namely, the destruction of the Jerusalem temple and its apostate leadership and God's reviving his true priesthood to reclaim Jerusalem, to construct a new, undefiled temple, and to inaugurate the blessed kingdom.[25]

The next question is, who provided the initiative to reach back to this dissident religious tradition as an aid to gaining self-understanding, as a warrant for defying the authority of the nation's central leadership, and as an authoritative basis for establishing an alternative Israel as a sanctified priestly community in the Judean wilderness? This question brings us to two further hints regarding Qumran origins, the enigmatic teacher of righteousness and his nemesis, the wicked priest.

That the Essenes of Qumran took the position of categorical denunciation of the Hasmonean claims to miter and throne, rather than the more accommodating position of the Pharisees, is bound up with the personal history of their founder and religious leader, the teacher of righteousness. That he was himself of Zadokite lineage is clear; that he as eldest son of the deposed and martyred Onias III was the legitimate heir to the Zadokite priesthood is possible.[26] At any rate, the vitriol vis-à-vis the Jerusalem hierarchy that imbues the biblical commentaries ascribed to him speaks for itself. The *pesher* on Habakkuk 2:12 in the *Habakkuk Commentary* serves as an example: "the interpretation of this [passage] relates to the False Oracle who caused the assembly to go

---

24. As reflected by 1 and 2 Maccabees and Wisdom of Solomon.
25. Only one section of *1 Enoch* has not been found at Qumran, the so-called parables or similitudes in chapters 37–71, chapters that represent the latest addition to the Enochian Pentateuch.
26. Harrington, *Revolt*, 120.

astray in building a city of vanity in blood and establishing a congregation in falsehood."[27]

While the view of the future held by the Pharisees contained elements that were distinctly eschatological in nature (such as belief in the resurrection of the dead and anticipation of the eternal kingdom that God would inaugurate through his anointed one [*messiah*]), the Essenes embraced a worldview going beyond prophetic eschatology to what we can confidently call apocalyptic. Humanity, they believed, was divided between the righteous, that is, the members of the Qumran community, and the condemned, that is, apostate Jews and all foreigners. For the moment, the world had been conquered by God's enemies in a vile intermingling of the Jerusalem elite with foreign potentates. Foremost among the apostate Jews was the enigmatic figure called the wicked priest. The Dead Sea document *Psalms of Joshua* in commenting on Joshua 6:26 announces: "and behold an accursed man, a son of Belial has come to power to be a trapper's snare to his people and ruin to all his neighbors."[28]

It is not surprising that the identity of the wicked priest (aka "son of Belial") has piqued the interest of scholars, bearing as it does on matters of dating the scrolls, as well as contextualizing the message contained in them within the history of the Hellenistic and Roman periods. The two most viable candidates for the historical figure behind this scurrilous epithet are the younger brothers of Judas Maccabeus, Jonathan and Simon.[29] The Qumran commentator depicts the wicked priest as voraciously greedy for personal power and wealth and willing to violate the very ordinances and statutes that he was charged to uphold, by exploiting the people and singling out the teacher of righteousness and his followers for harassment and persecution.

Viewed through the apocalyptic lens of the sectarians of Qumran, either Jonathan or Simon could fit the description of such an agent of Satan, for both of them were instrumental in seizing priesthood and kingship from their legitimate heirs and leading the nation further and further away from its holy covenant. Restated in theo-political terms, the dissidents in the Judean wilderness viewed the Hasmonean takeover of the nation as a violation of the theocratic principle, a blasphemous stratagem in which God's sovereignty was repudiated through rejection of the mediating structures God had instituted to implement his rule over his people, namely, the twin offices of Davidic prince and Zadokite priest.

Against this background, the raison d'etre of the Qumran community becomes clear. They felt called to be the true Israel in exile in the present "age of wickedness." In their wilderness refuge, they were to preserve the covenant through obedience to the Torah in every detail and in all spheres of life.

---

27. Translation of Frank Moore Cross, *The Ancient Library of Qumran* (New York: Doubleday, 1961), 116.

28. Ibid., 114.

29. A small number of scholars point out similarities between the description of the wicked priest in the scrolls and the high priest Alcimus, who was appointed by Antiochus V and held office in the years 161–159 BCE.

Through detailed interpretation (*pešer*) of Torah, the Psalms, and the Prophets, they sought to uncover how the events of the end time unfolding around them were foreshadowed in the words of Scripture. For such esoteric understanding they looked to the one they reverently called the teacher of righteousness.

In anticipation of God's glorious intervention, they conducted their lives according to a sacramental pattern adumbrating the coming heavenly kingdom and a strict daily regimen safeguarding the holiness that was a prerequisite for their participation in the final battle, in which they, alongside God's heavenly hosts, would destroy the wicked leaders of Jerusalem, their followers, and their foreign allies.

Though they left the final obliteration of the evildoers in the hands of God, they took it upon themselves to outline in minutest detail the strategy and weapons with which they would engage when God summoned them to fight the final battle in the company of angels against the agents of evil.[30] The institutional structures that regulated their life together were both backward-looking, in that they emulated the Israelite encampments during the period of wilderness wandering, and anticipatory, in that they adumbrated the final heavenly banquet. Though such melding of tenses may seem confusing, it is perfectly at home in a worldview lavishly infused with the otherworldly perspective of myth.

In the shadow of contemporary apocalyptic figures like Jim Jones, David Koresh, and the 9/11 hijackers, it is easy to denounce the absolutism and self-righteousness of the covenanters of Qumran as a political posture that, while predicated on a death wish for all the rest of humanity, had the effect of sealing their own fiery ending. Through the inspired teaching and biblical interpretation of their teacher, they believed they had come into possession of divine truth regarding the imminent end of this world, the destruction of all apostates, Jewish and Gentile, and their own eternal destiny as God's chosen people. Compared with the accommodationist politics that guided the mainstream Jewish community from Ezra to Sirach to the Pharisees, the apocalyptic politics of Qumran represents a stark and politically sinister alternative.

We have little room in our modern sense of tolerance and ambivalence regarding truth for their cultivation of "perfect hate" toward all others. But like all writings from antiquity, the Dead Sea Scrolls should be understood within their historical context, with attention being given especially to the strategic shift made by the Hasmoneans from the accommodationist policy of Ezra and his scribal descendants to a much more aggrandizing position. What impelled that shift?

Due to the tolerant imperial policy of the Persians, Ezra and his ilk, while submitting to the political authority of a foreign regime, nevertheless were able to preserve the core religious and ethical values that defined the ancestral Jewish faith. In other words, they preserved the theocratic principle by attributing the

---

30. The title of the writing describing preparation for the impending battle points to the dualistic worldview of the Qumran community: *The War of the Sons of Darkness against the Sons of Light.*

rule of the Persians to divine appointment and limiting its authority to political matters such as security, commerce, and civil order. Within that pragmatic/provisional framework, they were able to continue their exclusive worship of the one true sovereign and obedience to his commandments.

Under the Hasmoneans, however, the politics of accommodation that incorporated a viable strategy to preserve the ancestral faith spiraled downward into a capitulation of that faith to policies that made a mockery of the Mosaic law, practices that constituted an idolatrous repudiation of the Holy One of Israel, and a court style that flaunted wanton luxury, lewdness, and debauchery. Beginning already with Simon and reaching a tragic climax during the reigns Alexander Jannaeus, Aristobulus II, and Hyrcanus II, one finds a ruthless realpolitik that contradicted the hallowed theocratic principle of God's sole authority and blatantly broke the terms of the covenant that defined the identity of Israel as God's people.

The consequence of Hasmonean apostasy parallels the tragic end of the Davidic dynasty, though its descent into the calamity of foreign invasion was much more rapid, and its final chapters lack anyone resembling the pious, tragic figure Josiah or the sliver of hope for the future of the Davidic house offered by the Deuteronomistic History's concluding report of Jehoiachin's release from his Babylonian prison cell (2 Kgs. 25:27–30).

This is not to deny that the early battles of Judas Maccabeus could be portrayed by the author of 1 Maccabees as a virtual reenactment of Joshua's conquest of Canaan. And the expansion and consolidation of Judea under his brothers Jonathan and Simon and his nephew John Hyrcanus could be framed to resemble the geopolitical successes of David and Solomon. In less than a half century, a province of the Seleucid Empire, subject to the changing attitudes of Hellenistic kings toward their ancestral religion and customs, had gained independence and a certain degree of national security through treaties with Rome and Sparta. At that point the similarities end.

Unlike the previous monarchy, in which a division of religious and civil authority was acknowledged—albeit often begrudgingly—by Davidic king and Zadokite high priest, in the new monarchy royal and sacerdotal prerogatives were combined. While consolidation of power may eliminate the inevitable tensions built into the old arrangement, what emerged was an autocratic presumptuousness destroying the checks and balances that created space for prophets to struggle in defense of the ethical and religious values of the ancestral traditions. While the book of 1 Maccabees paints a picture of widespread popular support of the Hasmonean regime, its double claim to priesthood and kingship lacked credence to many, given the fact that it legitimately could claim neither Zadokite nor Davidic descent. Moreover, the faint praise given by the Hasidean author of Daniel 7–12 to the revolutionaries ("a little help") indicates that support from the strictest adherents to Torah tradition was qualified from the beginning, eventually leading to two sources of opposition, the community of exiles at Qumran, whose weapons were mainly confined to the arsenal of the Divine

Warrior, and the increasingly powerful party of the Pharisees, whose politics of accommodation in the manner of Ezra would outlive the Hasmoneans and preserve for future generations a tradition of ardent commitment to the Torah of Moses and a lively tradition of interpretation and application to new settings and situations.

Having sought to shed light on the perils that led the Essenes to their apocalyptic politics and drawn attention to the accommodationist policy of the Pharisees, it is only fair to ask what contributions were made by the Hasmoneans to the realm of biblical politics. First, it was no mean achievement to stop the aggressive assault of the proponents of pan-Hellenism, to restore the temple to its ancestral functions and purpose, and to create circumstances under which Jews could remain true to the Torah without fear of persecution by foreign intruders. Secondly, the demonstration of the ability of insurgents to defeat and overthrow the professional armies of one of the world's greatest powers contributed enormously to the identity and pride of the Jewish people, as is still evident today in the annual celebration of Hanukkah. The breakdown in the legacy of the Hasmoneans, however, came not from international policies, but matters closer to home.

In terms of political models, the monarchy as it took shape under the Hasmoneans embodied the systemic weaknesses of the Davidic monarchy, including openness to the despotic tendencies of neighboring states and diplomatic entanglements arising from international treaties (in this case, with Rome and Sparta, in an attempt to neutralize the influence of eastern powers like Syria). What is more, through the repression of opposition and critique, the Hasmonean priest-kings assumed the license to break the restraints of limited monarchy, such as that legislated in Deuteronomy 17, and to utilize their newly consolidated central power for self-service and aggrandizement. This can be illustrated by way of a few examples.

The lure of power that lurks in the shadow of monarchy can be detected already in Jonathan's political exploitation of the dispute between the Seleucid rulers Demetrius and Alexander Balas, culminating in his emergence as high priest and commander of a large army in 152 BCE. The next step was taken by Simon, who to much fanfare, according to the emphatically pro-Hasmonean 1 Maccabees, "accepted and agreed to be high priest, to be commander and ethnarch of the Jews and priests, and to be protector of them all" (1 Macc. 14:47).

In spite of the lavish praise heaped upon him by 1 Maccabees, the underreported part of the story is hinted at ominously by the nature of his death in 134 BCE, as described in 1 Maccabees 16. Indulging in lusty Roman banquet style to the state of inebriation, he falls victim to the sword of his son-in-law, would-be usurper of the throne Ptolemy son of Abubus. His son John Hyrcanus, however, manages to thwart the budding coup, exterminate his rivals, and secure the throne. The new king thus assumes rule under inauspicious circumstances, recalling the chaotic succession history of the northern Israelite kings Elah and Zimri in the ninth century BCE.

To understand the apocalyptic politics of the Qumran covenanters against the background of the last decades of Hasmonean rule that we detailed does not lead to an uncritical affirmation of their political strategy. It does point, however, to a tragic and recurrent phenomenon in human history. Abuse of power, sharp polarization, uncompromising religious or ideological disputes, withdrawal of dissenters from involvement in affairs of cult and state exploited as an opportunity for further despotic imposition of authority by those in power: such is the pattern that can eviscerate the moral armament of a people and break down its defenses against foreign conquest. It remains for us to describe the culmination of that tragic process in the further unfolding of Jewish history in the Roman period.

THE END OF THE HASMONEAN MONARCHY AND THE BEGINNING OF ROMAN OCCUPATION

One of the favorite historiographic techniques employed by the author of 1 Maccabees was typology, by means of which he could point out how the heroes of the Hasmonean family recapitulated the actions of Israel's ancient judges and kings. History itself seemed to have lent its hand to that technique once again in 63 BCE, when Pompey invaded Jerusalem and permitted his troops to enter and thus desecrate the temple, for he thus took his place alongside of Nebuchadnezzar and Antiochus IV in the chain of foreign invaders who violated the sanctity of the Holy City and its central sanctuary. Although more than a century would pass before the temple was actually destroyed by the Romans, the occupation of Jerusalem by Pompey in 63 BCE became a tragic landmark in the long, complicated history of relationships between the Jews and their Gentile neighbors.

As we have already noted, the Hasmoneans over their century of reign had created many enemies among pious Jews. Their usurpation of the prerogatives of Davidic king and Zadokite high priest, their prioritizing power and wealth over maintenance of ritual sanctity and Torah observance, their entanglements with foreign powers, and finally, the outright decadence of their court style made it inevitable that those groups of dissidents struggling to fend off the corrosive effect of foreign influence and to restore sanctity in the land would draw upon a traditional theologoumenon as the key to understanding Pompey's conquest: Pompey was the instrument God had chosen to punish Israel for its repudiation of God's sole sovereignty.[31]

It is fortunate that there has survived from the period immediately after Pompey's conquest a composition that provides a theological interpretation of that event equivalent to the interpretation of Antiochus IV's occupation of Jerusalem found in Daniel 7–12. Though employing a literary genre different from

---

31. This theologoumenon found its classic formulation in the book of Deuteronomy. In 2 Kings it was applied specifically to the fall of Samaria in 722 and the destruction of Jerusalem in 587, and in Daniel 9 to Antiochus IV's desecration of the temple.

Daniel, the *Psalms of Solomon* (*Pss. Sol.*) concurs with Daniel in acknowledging that the awesome assault of a foreign world power cannot be repulsed by human might alone and that those suffering for their faith must trust in God to send his chosen deliverer. God's deliverer, according to this pseudepigraph, will stand in sharpest contrast to the unfaithful (Hasmonean) kings who recently had brought upon Jerusalem the humiliation of foreign occupation. He will be a descendant of the house of David, anointed by God to free Israel from the contamination of sinners and apostates, as well as from its Gentile adversaries, and to resanctify the temple and draw the people back into their covenant relationship with God. The result will be the era of justice, peace, and prosperity long awaited by God's people.

Though a mid-first-century-BCE date and a Jerusalem provenance can be regarded as secure, the identity of the group whose views are expressed in the *Psalms of Solomon* continues to be debated by the scholars, with the two most likely candidates being the Pharisees and the Essenes. The close thematic affinities between the *Psalms of Solomon* and Daniel 7–12, however, may suggest a manner of understanding the community behind *Psalms* that is preferable to trying to establish either Pharisee or Essene authorship.[32] As noted above, the visions of Daniel can be attributed to the *hasidim*, a broad movement of pious, observant Jews that only later began to develop distinct traits that could be identified as Essene or Pharisee. There may well have continued on into the first century BCE a broad coalition of the pious who believed that the Hasmoneans had betrayed their divine mandate and who waited for God's anointed king to liberate the nation, restore theocratic rule, and renew the covenant on the basis of obedience and true worship. This more flexible view would also be compatible with the expression of hatred for the enemy and longing for the day of revenge in which the Messiah would lead them alongside the heavenly hosts into a climactic battle that is found in both the *Psalms of Solomon* and the sectarian writings of Qumran.

Though the specific identity of the group from which the *Psalms of Solomon* arose remains uncertain, what is of signal importance for our study is the clear portrait they give of one of the theo-political views that existed in the period leading up to the life of Jesus, the birth of Christianity, and the development of rabbinical Judaism. While this view has roots in earlier biblical political models, it betrays traits that combine tradition with innovations in a way that contributed to the perspective from which many heirs of the biblical tradition would view the tumultuous events of the first and second centuries CE.

---

32. One should keep in mind that the party divisions described by Josephus involve a retrojection of a later construct to the first century BCE and the imposition of distinctions on a sociopolitical situation that would have been characterized by considerable fluidity between groups and in which perhaps the majority of the Jewish population would not have been conscious of diverging theological and philosophical tenets. This latter point would pertain especially to the distinction between Essenes and Pharisees, whose beliefs were in most ways very similar and whose major identifying characteristic was common opposition to the Sadducees.

With regard to political models, the *Psalms of Solomon* combines charismatic, monarchic, and apocalyptic elements. The dominant theological framework within which the reflection of the book develops is Deuteronomistic; that is, the underlying assumption is that those who are obedient to the Torah and faithful to the ordinances of the covenant will be blessed, whereas sinners and apostates, along with their Gentile allies, will suffer punishment and exclusion from the prosperity enjoyed by God's chosen people (*Pss. Sol.* 14:1–5; 15:4–9). But into this traditional retributive theology the course of recent history had thrown a rude contradiction: The pagan warrior Pompey had entered Jerusalem, broken down the defenses protecting the temple, and profaned the holy sanctuary (*Ps. Sol.* 2:1–2). Where was the divine protector?

Unlike the persistent questioning of divine justice that lies at the heart of the book of Job, these psalms, rather bluntly and without the philosophical sophistication of Job, draw on the traditional theologoumenon mentioned above to resolve—or perhaps more accurately, to gloss over—the intractability of the paradox: The people of Israel, and especially the members of the Hasmonean royal house, have sinned so egregiously[33] that God has sent Pompey to punish them.[34] This punishment, moreover (and here a theme present in sapiential tradition also comes to expression), is God's disciplinary act intended to drive the people to repentance and return them to their God (*Ps. Sol.* 13:9–10). But once the pagan instrument of God's judgment has completed his assignment, he will grow arrogant in mockery of God's sole majesty and will come to a horrific end (*Ps. Sol.* 2:26–29).[35]

The juxtaposition of Deuteronomistic retributive theology and description of the conquest of Jerusalem by the Romans creates such a sharp contradiction that some have suggested that the *Psalms* alluding to the degeneracy of the Hasmoneans and Pompey's conquest, namely *Psalms of Solomons* 1, 2, 8, and 17, were added to a collection of earlier psalms that adhere more closely to a more traditional Deuteronomistic notion of divine retribution. For even the reference to that conquest as divine discipline seems forced in relation to a verse such as *Psalm of Solomon* 7:3: "Discipline us as you wish, but do not turn (us) over to the gentiles."

Whether one explains the thematic inconcinnities and theological contradictions of this writing by postulating the growth of these psalms over time or by assuming a lack of integrative skill on the part of the author, the writing as we have received it bears painful testimony to the recurrence of the spiritual trauma that had been experienced at another momentous point in Israel's history, namely, the occasion of Josiah's death in 609 BCE on the field of battle against

---

33. "They exalted themselves to the stars [cf. Isa. 14:13]. . . . they were arrogant in their possessions, and they did not acknowledge (God). . . . their lawless actions surpassed the gentiles before them; they completely profaned the sanctuary of the Lord" (*Ps. Sol.* 1:5–8).

34. *Ps. Sol.* 2:7.

35. "pierced on the mountains of Egypt" alludes to Pompey's death in Egypt in 48 BCE, the victim of the Caesar's assassins.

Pharaoh Neco II as reported in the Deuteronomistic History (2 Kgs. 23:29–30). With that similarity the comparison ends, for while the Deuteronomist offers only the slightest hint of a future for the house of David (2 Kgs. 25:27–30), the *Psalms of Solomon*, due to the apocalyptic orientation of its author(s), develops a glowing promise unrestrained by the ordinary limits of history and human politics.

This promise is made all the more spectacular by being projected against the background of a kingdom described in terms of utter wickedness and depravity, thereby conforming to the pattern of temporal dualism found in most apocalyptic writings: a past age of unmitigated evil soon to be supplanted by a glorious new age through the intervention of God. Given this pattern, however, it is natural to ask, to what extent is the degeneracy of the Hasmoneans exaggerated by dint of this apocalyptic worldview? Obviously, one must reckon with a historiographic *Tendenz* in the *Psalms of Solomon,* one that is diametrically opposed to the favorable bias toward the Hasmonean dynasty found in 1 Maccabees.

In the eyes of the first-century-BCE pious community, the Hasmonean kings were usurpers of the offices rightfully belonging to the house of David and the descendants of Zadok.[36] Moreover, their indulgent lifestyle and tyrannical manner of rule were so depraved as to scorn God's exclusive sovereignty and the theocratic principle that constituted the foundation for Israel's understanding of legitimate government. While the vitriol of political polemic and the dark hues of apocalyptic no doubt influence the lurid images of the *Psalms of Solomon*, there is no good reason to doubt that the overall picture they present of the Hasmoneans is basically accurate. To conclude contrariwise would be to overlook the foreshadowing of decline found in 1 Maccabees and to reject the picture painted by Josephus of the rampant abuses, degeneracy, and cruelty that had become a regular part of the life of the last generations of the Hasmoneans.[37] It would also fail to shed light on the most likely motive for Pompey's invasion and occupation of Judea, namely, the need to quell the civil war between the rival claimants to the Judean throne, Hyrcanus II and Aristobulus II, a war that was exacerbating tensions in a part of the world that already was causing the Romans much grief. That the political failures of the Hasmoneans were being abetted by rampant decadence, unrestrained greed, and lust for power seems undeniable.

The picture given by the *Psalms of Solomon* of the religious and moral malfeasance of the Hasmoneans thus must be accepted as more than the propaganda of one party against its rivals. The final generations of the Hasmoneans had assimilated the excesses of the pagan imperial courts. The author could not have missed the irony. The fateful effect that foreign influence had had on Solomon was being magnified before their very eyes to an extreme unprecedented in Jewish history: "There was no sin they left undone in which they did not surpass the

36. *Ps. Sol.* 17:6.
37. 1 Macc. 16:11–17 and Josephus, *Wars* 13.1. Adding to the credibility of both of these sources is that the author of 1 Maccabees writes his history from a pro-Hasmonean perspective and the historian Josephus claimed Hasmonean ancestry!

gentiles" (*Ps. Sol.* 1:8). Solomon had lost part of his kingdom on account of his sin. The Hasmoneans went the remaining distance and lost the entire kingdom. Rather than setting an example of godliness for their subjects, they lived lives of utter depravity:

> In secret places underground was their lawbreaking, provoking (him),
>   son involved with mother and father with daughter;
> Everyone committed adultery with his neighbor's wife.
>   (*Ps. Sol.* 8:9–10a)

They outdid even the offenses of the priests repudiated in an earlier age by the prophet Malachi:[38]

> They stole from the sanctuary of God as if there were no redeeming heir.
> They walked on the place of sacrifice of the Lord,
>   (coming) from all kinds of uncleanness;
> and (coming) with menstrual blood (on them),
>   they defiled the sacrifices as if they were common meat.
>   (*Ps. Sol.* 7:11–12)

When the pious protested, or called attention to the commandments of the Torah or the statutes regulating temple sacrifice, their priest-kings did not hesitate to hang them from crosses on the outskirts of Jerusalem as an example to others who might be tempted to join the pious protests. Like Jeremiah, they were experiencing persecution and were led to ask what possible response was humanly available in the face of such flagrant disregard for the justice and mercy of the Torah. Like Jeremiah, they concluded that the time for calls to repentance and reform was past. The heavenly judge's sentence had been handed down. God had appointed a pagan conqueror to be the agent of his judgment. As Nebuchadnezzar earlier had acted as the rod of God's anger, Pompey invaded Jerusalem and established the Roman occupation that would end Jewish national autonomy. "God exposed their sins in the full light of day" (*Ps. Sol.* 8:8a). "[F]or there rose up against them a man alien to our race" (*Ps. Sol.* 17:7b).

Of course, that agent was not the promised deliverer, but rather the one sketching into the end-time scenario the final act of part one, the *dies irae*. *Psalm of Solomon* 17 moves the reader from that act describing the final judgment to part two, which announces the arrival of the deliverer who is anointed by God to inaugurate the eternal blessed kingdom.

The promise of one sent by God to save his people from their enemies is not an innovation, but rather constitutes a renewal of the ancient divine promise to David:[39]

---

38. Mal. 1:6–14; 2:1–16.
39. 2 Sam. 7:8–17.

Lord, you chose David to be king over Israel,
and swore to him about his descendants forever,
that his kingdom should not fail before you.
(*Ps. Sol.* 17:4)

Though the eternal promise cannot be nullified, it has been interrupted, for the monarchy was seized by an illegitimate dynasty, displacing for a time the house of David:

Those to whom you did not (make the) promise,
they took away (from us) by force;
and they did not glorify your honorable name.
With pomp they set up a monarchy because of their arrogance;
They despoiled the throne of David with arrogant shouting.
(*Ps. Sol.* 17:5b–6)

For the purpose of removing the illegitimate monarchy (i.e., the Hasmoneans), God enlists "a man alien to our race" (*Ps. Sol.* 17:7), Pompey. But far from being a benign deliverer, he too degrades Jerusalem with pagan practices, which the apostates among the people readily embrace. Verse 20 of *Psalm of Solomon* 17 serves as the turning point, with this summary of the dire situation in the land:

From their leader to the commonest of the people,
(they were) in every kind of sin:
the king was a criminal
and the judge disobedient;
(and) the people sinners.

Driven from their Holy City, living as "refugees in the wilderness" (*Ps. Sol.* 17:17), the devout cry for help to God:

See, Lord, and raise up for them their king,
the son of David, to rule over your servant Israel.
(*Ps. Sol.* 17:21)

Like the holy Warrior of Israel's infancy as a people, the anointed deliverer will first purge the land of both the violence of the Gentiles and the apostasy of their Jewish collaborators.[40] Then he will reconstitute the people by distributing "them upon the land according to their tribes" and replace the wicked rulers of the earth: "He will judge peoples and nations in the wisdom of his righteousness" (*Ps. Sol.* 17:28–29).

---

40. In keeping with the imagery of holy war, the divine judge does not rely on the force of human warriors, such as "horse and rider and bow" (*Ps. Sol.* 17:33), but utilizes a far more effective weapon, "the word of his mouth" (*Ps. Sol.* 17:24).

The prophetic vision of the messianic age, especially as it is depicted in the book of Isaiah, is about to dawn. Jerusalem will be restored to holiness, the nations will return the scattered children of Israel as gifts to their homeland. The vision of Isaiah 60–62 will be established:

> There will be no unrighteousness among them in his days,
>   for all shall be holy,
>   and their king shall be the Lord Messiah.
>
> (*Ps. Sol.* 17:32)

"Lord Messiah" is of course a remarkable title,[41] a title, moreover, that is imbued with the most complete description of "the messiah" in all of early Jewish literature. He incorporates all of the characteristics attributed to the ideal king by the prophets Isaiah, Jeremiah, and Ezekiel, characteristics of wisdom, mercy, righteousness, power, and understanding (*Ps. Sol.* 17:34–43).[42] The day promised in chapter 34 of Ezekiel will dawn, when the kings who devoured their sheep through their own greed and violence will be replaced by God's chosen servant, David, who will bind up their wounds and feed them and protect them from all harm.

Since the *Psalms of Solomon* provides us with a unique glimpse into the manner in which one group of pious Jews viewed their uncertain future at a crucial point in the history of both Judaism and Christianity, it is important to ask, what manner of theo-political vision do we have in these *Psalms?*

In truth, it is a vision that combines elements of several of the political models found in the Hebrew Bible. Certainly, the manner of the Divine Warrior's conquest, the distribution of the land according to tribal allotments, and the description of his rule in terms of judging peoples echo the charismatic policies and practices of the tribal period. Though his manner of rule is described in lofty terms, he faithfully serves as the servant of the "king over the heavens" (*Ps. Sol.* 2:30a), again in keeping with the hallowed theocratic principle of early Yahwism. That is to say, he does not rule on his own authority, but rather as the agent through whom God mediates his universal rule over his human subjects.

But those charismatic elements freely intermingle with the decidedly monarchical descriptions of the son of David's reign. The promise that God gave to David and his son Solomon of an eternal kingdom is about to be fulfilled on the day when "their king shall be the Lord Messiah."

But this reign will not be a continuation of the history of the Davidic dynasty chronicled by the Deuteronomistic History and Chronicles. Unlike David and Solomon, whose sins are conspicuously reported (especially in the former opus), "he himself (will be) free from sin" (*Ps. Sol.* 17:36). Of course, one must not overlook the transcendent connotations that are developing during the late

---

41. "Lord" was at home in the imperial cult of Rome, and "Messiah the Lord" finds an echo in the New Testament, e.g., Luke 2:11.

42. E.g., Isa. 9:1–6 (Eng. 9:2–7).

Second Temple period around the titles found in the *Psalms*, like "messiah," "lord," and "son of David." As for the people, we are informed that "all shall be holy." And the land will be secure from all enemies and blessed with abundance (*Ps. Sol.* 17:29–32, 44).

The restraints imposed on earthly rulers, even Davidic kings, do not apply in this vision, nor do the international threats and domestic wrongs that are an inevitable part of every nation's history. Have we then entered the realm of apocalyptic? We have already noted that the temporal pattern of evil age/blessed age reflects the dualism of an apocalyptic worldview, as does the mythic depiction of a Divine Warrior who intervenes to destroy all that is wicked on the earth and to establish an eternal reign of *shalom*.

Here too, however, it is important to note that key themes found in most full-blown apocalyptic writings are absent. Though "transcendence of death" is identified as the essential mark of apocalyptic by an authority on the subject,[43] resurrection does not figure into the future promise in *Psalms*. Nor does the spatial dualism that places the paradisiacal realm in a heavenly realm transcending the mundane. Though cleansed of all imperfection, the Davidic monarchy to come is situated in Jerusalem and in the land of Israel, thereby reconstituting the kingdom of David and Solomon.[44]

Essentially what we find in the *Psalms of Solomon* is an eloquent description of the future hope that was being cultivated within a broad stream of the Jewish community in the half century before the Common Era, a concept of a messianic reign that transcended the limits of Israel's previous monarchies, but nonetheless remained recognizably anchored in this world.

---

43. John J. Collins, "Apocalyptic Eschatology as the Transcendence of Death," *Catholic Biblical Quarterly* 36 (1974).

44. This terrestrial localization of the messianic kingdom represents the most common view within rabbinical tradition.

Chapter 24

Roman Occupation
and Jewish Political Responses

The period of the Roman occupation of the Jewish homeland that commenced with Pompey's conquest in 63 BCE was characterized by enormous political instability. Just one century earlier, the seemingly miraculous twin events of the defeat of the foreign tyrant Antiochus IV and the establishment of Judea as an independent kingdom had awakened expectations of a return to the splendor and national pride of the era of David and Solomon. The pious warriors who rallied behind Judas Maccabeus and lived to sing praises to their national and spiritual liberator could not have anticipated the reconquest of their land by an even mightier empire a century later. Sadly, many of them *did* witness a development that threatened to nullify the political and religious triumph of their generation, the descent of the Judean monarchy into a degenerate state that made it virtually indistinguishable from the neighboring pagan empires and vulnerable to enemy conquest.

Within the turmoil and uncertainty of the mid-first century BCE, the Jewish community split into factions marked by sharp disagreement over the strategy best suited for regaining national autonomy and rebuilding a stable government. We shall describe the major alternatives that arose amid that struggle, noting how each revived features from the political models of earlier Israelite history and how one of them finally emerged from the chaos of oppression, rebellion, and crushing defeat with a time-tested credibility that commended itself to the leaders of the Jewish community for centuries to come.

We begin our discussion where we ended the previous chapter, namely, with *Psalms of Solomon (Pss. Sol.)*. Its response to Pompey's conquest of Judea in 63 BCE is so vivid as to suggest that its author(s) wrote from firsthand experience. The vision for the future that it sets forth was sufficiently opaque to be amenable to interpretations yielding widely divergent political strategies, two of which proved to be of particular significance in determining the course of Jewish history in the Roman period and beyond: one urging revolt and leading to national calamity, the other cultivating a policy of coexistence that secured for Judaism a future amid the rise and fall of world empires.

Of particular interest for our purposes is *Psalm of Solomon* 17, a psalm interlaced with references to Hebrew Scripture. Especially prominent are the two monumental covenant traditions associated with the figures of Moses and David.

First, the doctrine of retribution central to the Mosaic covenant is enlisted to explain the tragic loss of national autonomy to the Romans. The pious community out of which the *Psalms of Solomon* arose was well acquainted with the suffering and persecution suffered at the hands of the Hasmonean kings by those insisting on strict adherence to the Torah. Drawing on a trope incorporated into Hebrew prophecy by Isaiah, Jeremiah, and Ezekiel, *Psalm of Solomon* 17 describes "a man alien to our race" as the agent chosen by God to punish an apostate monarchy and a sinful populace. That man was the celebrated Roman general Pompey.[1]

Equally rooted in antecedent tradition is the second motif, namely, God's faithfulness to his covenant with David (see 2 Sam. 7, Ps. 89). From the house of David, God, in God's own time, would anoint as "Lord Messiah" a deliverer who would cleanse the land of corrupt royal and religious leadership, thrust out the foreign legions, and reestablish the glory of Israel and its ascendancy over the nations. God's chosen king would be faithful to the Torah as formulated in Deuteronomy 17:14–20, for he would eschew excess wealth and military might and place his trust solely in the true king of the universe ("the Lord himself is his king," 17:34). He would be endowed with God's spirit of wisdom and

1. Josephus portrays Pompey in a favorable light as a religious and virtuous liberator, respectful of the temple and its sacred accoutrements, who, in breaking through the defenses of Jerusalem, refrained from plundering it in the manner of Antiochus IV, but rather set out to restore proper order to the central cult of the Jewish community. It seems likely that Josephus had in mind Cyrus the Mede as he was described by Second Isaiah (Isa. 44:23–45:7), a parallel that extends further inasmuch as Josephus, like Second Isaiah (Isa. 42:23–25), identifies his own people (specifically the rival contestants for the throne, Aristobulus and Hyrcanus) as the cause of the national calamity (*Ant.* 14.4). Opposition to native kings arising from the Jewish populace did not end in 63 BCE. Both Herod the Great and the succeeding members of his dynasty were plagued with opposition, often spearheaded by the Pharisees, who enjoyed broad support among the common citizens. The lingering aspirations of the Hasmonean house also led to tensions during the Herodian period, as exemplified by the revolt of Judas, son of Hezekiah, in Sepphoris in 4 BCE.

understanding (cf. Isa. 11:2–5), thereby fulfilling the promise in Ezekiel 34:12–14 that God would set over his people a true shepherd from the house of David.

Psalm of Solomon 17 represents an important stage in the development of the political model of kingship. Though the classical theocratic principle that ultimate kingship belongs to God alone is upheld, we do not find a categorical rejection of monarchy. In fact, the history of God's relation to the house of David gives testimony to a deep covenantal commitment of deity to the anointed human ruler. But commitment is clearly distinguished from indulgence, for God's favor is inextricably tied to the obedience of the king to God's will as expressed in the Torah, a principle that was ensconced in the law of the king in Deuteronomy 17. As God's chosen servant, the Davidic king was to mediate the justice and compassion that lay at the heart of the universal divine imperium. Within the context of Jewish faith, monarchy could be defended as a legitimate form of rule only if the behavior of king and court manifested unconditional submission to the king of the universe. This theocratic principle alone explains the recurrent coexistence in Israelite history of rigorous critique of kingship and deep longing for the return of God's anointed ruler (i.e., messiah).

Events that followed in the wake of Pompey's conquest illustrate the opaqueness of the divine promises in *Psalm of Solomon* 17, for they set, for many generations to come, a pattern of contradictory messianic understandings extrapolated by different groups from the same eschatological traditions. To those following in the tradition of Daniel and *4 Maccabees,* emphasis was placed on the fact that deliverance would come solely through divine initiative, thereby behooving the pious to prepare patiently through prayer, merciful acts, and, when necessary, suffering and death. To more zealous types drawing inspiration from the heroic acts of the five sons of Mattathias, the psalm's prophecy of holy war against the Gentile rulers who had violated the sanctity of Jerusalem was taken as an invitation to identify (or appoint!) the promised messianic leader and to muster all who were willing to join in revolt against the foreign adversary.

For a century and a half, these two strategies, often drawing on the same scriptural warrants, struggled against each other for the allegiance of the Judean and Galilean populace. During the same time, a third position developed the opportunistic stratagems of the Herodians, often in consort with the aristocratic temple leadership, namely, a policy of collaboration with the Romans. Since the aristocratic temple leadership consisted primarily of Sadducees, it is a major challenge to locate this rather amorphous group in the political landscape of the late Second Temple period, a challenge to which we shall return.

Whether in regard to the Sadducees or to any other Jewish party or movement, it is tempting to rely simply on the authority of Josephus, who neatly parsed the political landscape of his native land into four "philosophies." The question must be raised, however, whether his categories are reliable and, if they are, how they can be correlated with the three strategies we have described above.

At first glance, one might be inclined to identify the tactic of nonviolent messianic eschatology with the Pharisees, the more aggressive insurrectionism with "the Fourth Philosophy" (which most likely is to be identified with the group Josephus and other writers of his time call Zealots), and the strategy of collaboration with the Sadducees. Since Josephus's writings contain the most complete description of the diverse Jewish groups active during the Roman period, any effort to understand the political landscape of Judea and Galilee of that time must attend to his references, but this must be done with caution and a careful weighing of other sources, given the fact that a high degree of fluidity characterizes the political strategies of the various Jewish groups, as they are forced to adjust to major changes in the structure of Roman government and the shifting foreign policies that came as a consequence. Caution behooves us therefore to focus on specific events and figures mentioned in the sources as a basis for extrapolating a general picture of the religious and political situation in Judea and Galilee in the period leading to the Jewish revolts of 66–73 and 132–135 CE.

Before proceeding to an analysis of the strategies adopted by the various Jewish groups in their dealing with the Roman occupation, two cautionary notes are called for. (1) In spite of the fluidity and diversity that characterized Jewish religion and politics before the Tannaitic period, Second Temple Judaism in large part was characterized by a shared nucleus of beliefs and practices drawn inferentially from what we have called the theocratic principle, chief among them being exclusive worship of the one God of Abraham and Moses, obedience to the Torah as the unique expression of God's will, and devotion to the temple as God's chosen dwelling place amid his chosen people.[2] These core beliefs and practices were preserved and transmitted in the forms of commandments, hymns, prophecies, laments, and biblical narratives retelling the story of God's election and guidance of the children of Israel over the course of their history. (2) Only a minority of the Jewish population of Judea and Galilee actually identified with one of the religious "parties." The vast majority, consisting mainly of small landowners, tenant farmers, and day laborers, shared the core beliefs of their more educated compatriots and observed the stipulations of the Torah to the extent that the exigencies of life permitted.

Given the historical and geographical particularity of the story-embodied, identity-giving religious heritage shared by rich and poor alike, it was inevitable that Roman occupation of the land treasured as God's gift to the sons of Abraham, Isaac, and Jacob would be viewed widely as an offense against God and as an indication that the fulfillment of God's promises to his people remained a future hope. It is precisely in relation to that hope, however, that we find widely divergent views regarding the political response to the Romans that their religion called for.

With the exception of the local clients of the Romans, namely, the Herodians and their devotees within the temple leadership, whose status and wealth derived from their foreign patrons, the Jewish populace shared a deep discomfort with

---

2. See Seth Schwartz, *Imperialism and Jewish Society, 200 B.C.E. to 600 C.E.* (Princeton, NJ: Princeton University Press, 2001), 49–66.

foreign rule. But that discomfort did not lead to a unified strategic plan, in part because the nation's story, or Epic, contained political models ranging from the policy of accommodation to the foreign overlord, promoted by Ezra, to denunciation of all compromise and a call to revolt, the hallmark of the Maccabees. That diversity of response was not the product solely of diversity within the received tradition, but also was influenced by changes that occurred in Roman policy, ranging from tolerance for the beliefs and practices of the Jews in certain periods to the imposition of emperor worship in others.

The year 6 CE illustrates the complexity of the political situation in Judea and Galilee. Herod Archelaus, the son of Herod the Great who had ruled as ethnarch over Judea since his father's death in 4 BCE, proved incapable of dealing with the growing unrest among a Judean populace stirred up by a series of religiously inspired revolts. With chaos gripping the land, Jews and Samaritans joined in a rare alliance by appealing to the Romans to intervene. Taking swift action, the Romans responded by deposing Archelaus and appointing a prefect reporting directly to Rome, thereby making Judea a province of the Roman Empire. Galilee, on the other hand, remained under the rule of another of Herod's sons, the Herod (Antipas) of New Testament infamy. Since that dual arrangement remained in force until the year 36 CE, it constitutes the political background of the New Testament narrative describing the short public career of Jesus of Nazareth centered in Galilee and the tragic events that transpired after his pilgrimage to Jerusalem in 30 CE, matters to which we shall turn in the next two chapters.

Because of the religious importance of Judea and the symbolic significance of the Jerusalem temple in Jewish eschatology, it is understandable that unrest and instances of revolt against the Romans occurred primarily in that part of the Jewish homeland. In contrast, relations between the Romans and their subjects in Galilee were relatively stable. The fact that Antipas was allowed to retain his jurisdiction over Galilee and Perea for thirty years after his brother Archelaus was deposed bespeaks his success in maintaining order within his jurisdiction. That accomplishment cannot be attributed solely to his political and diplomatic prowess, however. It stems in part from the disposition of a Galilean populace apparently less inclined to the assertion of self-rule than their coreligionists in the south.[3]

Specifically with regard to the political situation at this time in the southern heartland of the Jewish faith, it is possible to recognize a general similarity to conditions prevailing at the beginning of Seleucid rule over Judea two centuries earlier: In both cases, the population was sharply divided by opposing attitudes toward the presence in the land of an alien regime. In the period with which we are now concerned, we find that certain circles welcomed the arrival of the new foreign authority as promising improvement over the oppressive rule of

3. The exceptions to this general contrast between Judea and Galilee center on hellenized urban centers such as Sepphoris, Tiberias, and Gischala. For a thorough study of Galilee during this period, see Sean Freyne, *Galilee from Alexander the Great to Hadrian 323 BCE to 135 CE* (Wilmington, DE: Michael Glazier, 1980).

Archelaus, who like his ruthless father did not hesitate to slaughter those who posed a threat to his authority. Other groups saw in the onerous tribute levied by the Romans a repudiation of God-given religious liberty and hence a mandate for violent resistance. Still others resigned themselves to the shift from one bad situation to another, out of the belief that only in a time of God's choosing would redemption finally come to Israel.

Unfortunately, efforts to add clarity to the political landscape of Judea and Galilee in the first decades of the Common Era are confounded by disagreements among modern scholars on a crucial point. The dilemma is inevitable and involves the double challenge lodged at the heart of every historical reconstruction: the accounts of events given by ancient historians, such as Josephus, are influenced by their political allegiances and ideologies, even as modern scholars in turn are influenced by theirs.[4] In relation to Josephus's report of the events occurring in the decade following King Herod's death,[5] for example, Richard Horsley argues that the insurrections led by Judas of Gamala and Zadok the Pharisee were fueled by the robust support of the peasantry.[6] Other scholars, appealing to sociological studies of insurrection movements in general, suggest that to call the uprisings of this era peasant revolutions is to overlook the fact that resistance to foreign occupation generally comes from the upper echelons of society, with the working poor preoccupied with the daily pursuit of life's necessities and more interested in maintaining conditions conducive to physical survival than in ideologically or religiously motivated regime change.[7] Sean Freyne has provided detailed historical/textual evidence that supports the more theoretical models provided by social scientists.[8]

Though questions regarding the political situation in Judea and Galilee in the first century of the Common Era remain, it seems that the pieces of evidence provided by Philo, Josephus, the New Testament, and several Roman historians fall short of supporting the theory of a widespread peasant revolution. When, as in the case of Josephus's chronicles, references are made to particular insurgents, the profile fits educated, economically viable community leaders, rather than subsistence peasants and day laborers. Accordingly, a more nuanced understanding of Jewish responses to Roman occupation must be developed than is provided by the general category of peasant revolt.

---

4. The hermeneutical and historiographic principles that shaped Josephus's interpretation of Jewish history are complex. He himself claims to be a Pharisee. But he expresses deep respect for the priestly leadership of a nation that he believes should model itself after a theocracy, that is, a people ruled by God through God's designated priests. In addition, of course, he seeks to present himself as loyal to his patron, the Roman emperor.

5. *Ant.* 18.4–23 and *War* 2.118.

6. Richard A. Horsley, *Jesus and Empire: The Kingdom of God and the New World Disorder* (Minneapolis: Fortress Press, 2003), 53–54.

7. For references, see Christopher Bryan, *Render to Caesar: Jesus, the Early Church, and the Roman Superpower* (Oxford and New York: Oxford University Press, 2005).

8. Freyne, *Galilee.*

As noted earlier, for all those who based their identity on the core beliefs and values of the ancestral Jewish faith, the Roman occupation categorically was in violation of God's will. But their history did not testify univocally to the response such a crisis called for. It told, on the one hand, of leaders like Ezra and Nehemiah who accommodated the ancestral faith to foreign imperial administration and indicated that prayers were to be offered in the temple for the emperor and his family, on the basis of the quid pro quo that their submission to foreign rule would be matched by freedom to worship their God, follow the Torah of Moses, and maintain the sacred rites of the temple in Jerusalem. On the other hand, that same history contained stories of divinely inspired insurrection, as when the sons of Mattathias revolted against Antiochus IV Epiphanes, a foreign king who callously violated all of their core beliefs. Stories both of cooperation and revolt, mediated by later enigmatic prophecies, such as those found in *The Psalms of Solomon*, were thus available as warrants for those devising strategies for dealing with the foreign occupation, making discord virtually inevitable. In addition, the nature of the specific actions taken at different times was influenced both by individuals and groups within the Jewish community and by policy makers in Rome and their Palestinian-based prefects and generals.

Since another paradigm found in Jewish Scripture featured prophets who did not hesitate to pronounce judgment on rulers both native and foreign,[9] it is not surprising that figures like Judas of Gamala, Zadok the Pharisee, and Athronges of Judea rose to prominence by announcing in the name of the God of Israel the imminent destruction of the Romans. They issued a call to revolt patterned after the holy wars of old, thereby raising messianic hopes in the hearts of the many pious Jews who responded to their provocative proclamations.

The violent stratagem of such zealots and insurrectionists was strengthened enormously when the Roman emperor transgressed the most central and solemn of all Jewish confessions, that there is one God alone worthy of worship (i.e., the theocratic principle). Accordingly, the most egregious theo-political development in the period of Rome's control of Judea and Galilee was Augustus Caesar's laying claim to the divine titles *Lord* and *Savior* and describing the *Pax Romana* as a universal order of peace secured for the world by its new divine benefactor, the *divi filius,* the son of the recently divinized Julius Caesar.[10] In due course we shall witness how that frontal assault on the sole lordship of the God of Israel provides the focal point around which the political debates arising within the movement initiated by Jesus of Nazareth revolved. Before turning our attention to the politics of the New Testament, we will complete our general description of the Jewish community's varied responses to the political crises of the first two centuries of the Common Era, especially in light of the claim to divinity by Augustus Caesar.

---

9. The figures of Elijah, Isaiah, Jeremiah, and Ezekiel all contributed to the paradigm of the prophet as king-maker/breaker.

10. See Helmut Koester, *From Jesus to the Gospels* (Minneapolis: Fortress Press, 2007), 206–7.

Our synthesis of Josephus's testimony with the other available sources allows us to categorize the political strategies developed within the Jewish community living under Roman occupation under three general policies, each with roots in the nation's political history: collaboration, accommodation, and resistance. Obviously, a wide range of variation existed within each of these categories. *Collaboration*, whether exercised by the Herodians or by temple officials, could be tempered by sensitivity to local customs and beliefs, or it could translate loyalty to the Roman overlord as warranting the suspension of the rights of the governed. *Accommodation* ran the gamut from cooperation with the foreign authorities to a prima facie civility that actually served as a cover for more subversive goals. *Resistance* could fall at any point along the continuum from passive to nonviolent to overtly hostile opposition.

We begin with the option of collaboration as practiced in the first instance by the members of the dynasty of the son of the Idumean king Antipater, Herod the Great. The Herodians, ever aware of their half-breed status and the tenuousness of their claim to kingship in the eyes of most Jews, viewed collaboration with the Romans as best serving their political ambitions of holding on to their rule over the Jewish nation and maintaining sufficient Roman military subvention to suppress politically motivated challenges to their royal claims. There were challenges from descendants of the Hasmonean royal family, as well as religiously motivated challenges arising from groups upholding the sanctity of temple, land, and Torah, for example, the Pharisees, the Essenes, the Zealots, and what Hillel Newman has designated "halakhic Sadducees."[11] As for the Jerusalem Sadducees, whose livelihood and social status were intertwined with the Jerusalem temple bureaucracy, the practice of parlaying an alliance with the Romans into the enhancement of their personal standing was not uncommon. This practice was abetted by the meddling of Herod and his sons in the process of sacerdotal appointments.

Likely outnumbering such co-opted Sadducees were those—primarily though not exclusively living beyond the confines of the capital city—who remained steadfast in their understanding of the ancestral faith. Unfortunately, efforts to understand the political position of the Sadducees in the Roman period are hampered by a lack of source material. As the historical losers in the competition with the Pharisees for leadership of the Jewish community, they did not leave behind a chain of tradition equivalent to the rabbinical writings, from which, with caution, information can be extrapolated for use in historical reconstruction. When in Talmudic literature Sadducean rulings are described and contrasted with those of the rabbis, it is only to be expected that the debate will be biased in favor of the latter. A further regrettable fact is that archaeologists and historians have yet to discover a library of Sadducean writings equivalent to the

11. Hillel Newman, *Proximity to Power and Jewish Sectarian Groups of the Ancient Period: A Review of Lifestyle, Values, and Halakhah in the Pharisees, Sadducees, Essenes, and Qumran*, Brill Reference Library of Judaism 25 (Leiden: Brill, 2006), 38–39.

Dead Sea Scrolls or the Cairo Geniza.[12] As for the ancient historians, Josephus is the best source, but his description is sketchy, and though he claims a priestly family background, his contrasts between Pharisees and Sadducees by and large reflect a pro-Pharisee bias.

Though the situation facing modern scholars is far from ideal, the following description of the (halakic) Sadducees can be given with a reasonable degree of confidence. Socioeconomically, they enjoyed a loftier status than the Pharisees, which on the one hand gave them political leverage in dealing with the governing authorities and in voicing their opinions in the Sanhedrin, but on the other hand alienated them from common citizens who favored the greater openness of the Pharisees to their needs and concerns. Buttressing their sense of superiority was their historical claim to sacerdotal preeminence within the Jewish community, which revolved especially around the office of high priest, a claim to which even the Herodians paid heed. At any rate, it was a prerogative to which they held fast right down to the destruction of the Jerusalem temple.

Though credible challenges have been raised to the traditional view that the Sadducees held to a rigid adherence to the written Torah that disparaged halakic study, the basic distinction between a conservative interpretive tendency among the Sadducees and the more progressive halakic approach of the Pharisees and their descendants, the Tannaitic and Amoraic rabbis, retains its validity. Hillel Newman offers a poignant example of this contrast. At issue was the question of whether the name of the ruling (non-Jewish) regime could be affixed to a divorce certificate. The affirmative rabbinic response was based on the pragmatic principle of keeping peace with the governing authorities. The Sadducees took the opposite stand: to encroach on the authority of the law in this manner "offended the honor of Moses and Israel, which they considered as 'permanent' compared with the honor of the rulers."[13] This specific case exemplifies the hermeneutical progressivism that led the Pharisees and their rabbinical descendants to accept the authority of an oral Torah, whereas the Sadducees were guided by a literalism that more tightly limited authority to the five written books of Moses (the Torah in the strict sense). The same scriptural conservatism explains their rejection of the position of the Pharisees and later the rabbis that scriptural status could be attributed to two additional sections of the Tanakh (Hebrew Bible), the Nebi'im (prophets) and the Ketubim (writings), though the preeminent status of the Torah was never in question.

From these differences in halakic practice and determination of the compass of the canonical writings there follow certain differences in ritual and doctrine. For the Sadducees, adherence to a belief in the eternal validity of the temple-based sacrificial laws in the Torah thwarted any program of reapplying those laws to life outside of the temple. Belief in the resurrection and an eschatological

---

12. Though the teacher of righteousness was likely a Zadokite priest, the view that the sectarian writings of Qumran can be understood as representative of a Sadducean position remains unconvincing.

13. Newman, *Proximity*, 220.

hope centering on the messiah of the house of David, being based not on the Torah but on the Prophets and Writings (especially the Psalms), were embraced by the Pharisees and rejected by the Sadducees. When we come to discuss the Pharisees, we shall note how these differences placed the Sadducees at a distinct disadvantage to the Pharisees in meeting the challenge of interpreting ancestral traditions in light of subjugation to Rome and the destruction of the temple.

We turn now from the collaboration of the Herodians and their sacerdotal adherents and the conservativism of the halakic Sadducees to groups that took more critical positions vis-à-vis ruling authorities, positions that covered a wide range from nonviolence to aggressive terrorist action.

Two of those groups, the Essenes and the Pharisees, shared a common ancestry among the pious believers (Hasidim) of the Maccabean period. At the heart of their Torah-centered piety was the belief that ultimate devotion was to be reserved exclusively for the God of Israel, a belief shared as well by the more revolutionary groups. The strategy of collaboration, because it invited compromise with competing loyalties, was categorically rejected. But whether exclusive devotion was translated into accommodation or resistance depended on differing modalities of belief and the interpretive methods applied by specific groups to determine the meaning of Scripture for new historical periods and circumstances unanticipated by the ancestral traditions.

In proceeding to circles resorting to resistance, we encounter problems, chief among which is the attempt to understand the relationship between the various groups and individuals mentioned by Philo, Josephus, the New Testament writers, and the rabbis. The principal groups are the Sicarii, the Zealots, the Essenes, and Josephus's Fourth Philosophy.[14] Some of the individuals in question are Judas the Galilean, Zadok the Pharisee, and Athronges the Judean.

Judas, Zadok, and Athronges belong to a broad category of insurrectionists characterized by resistance to the occupying power for a mixture of nationalistic, religious, and personal reasons. Though conforming to the "Maoist (or Mosaic!) stratagem" by originating in a social stratum exempt from the groveling subsistence economy of the exploited victims of society, their success depended on the degree to which they were able to exploit the grievances of the broader populace. In 6 CE, Judas and Zadok were able to interpret the imposition of direct Roman rule over Judea and the accompanying increase in the burden of taxation placed upon an already impoverished peasantry in religious terms, as an attack on the God-given liberty of the Jews and on the sanctity of their land. Their absolutist mentality, stoked by messianic illusions, excluded all possibility of compromise, thereby exacerbating divisions within the Jewish population and exposing the land to inevitable Roman reprisals. Though their message and

---

14. Two possible candidates for Josephus's Fourth Philosophy are the Sicarii and the group he and other writers of antiquity refer to as the Zealots. Another group mentioned by Josephus is the *Therapeutai*, consisting of conventicles of desert monks scattered over Egypt, whose beliefs and lifestyle resembled in some respects the Essenes of Qumran. In relation to the theo-political trajectory we are following in this chapter, the *Therapeutai* have scant bearing.

strategies resemble in some ways the groups to which we next turn, there is no evidence that they belonged to a movement or sect surviving beyond their own time and place in history.

The Sicarii, on the other hand, do betray characteristics of a movement. Active in the 40s and 50s of the Common Era, they can be designated as terrorists on the basis of their strategy of mingling among the population and stabbing (hence their name, derived etymologically from "dagger") those they viewed as collaborators with the Roman enemy, that is, members of the aristocracy as well as the wealthy mercantile class. During the chaotic years of the First Jewish Revolt, they were so prominent in exacerbating the infighting among the rival groups within the local resistance that more moderate Jews, such as the Pharisees, drove them out of Jerusalem, whence they fled to Masada and their final suicidal death as they faced the assault of the Romans in 63 CE.

The Zealots are even more clearly recognizable as a movement. It is perhaps even legitimate to apply to them the designation of *sect,* understood in the sense of a group that gains its identity by asserting the sole legitimacy of its understanding of ancestral traditions against the leading authorities of their religious community. Their formation as an anti-Roman movement in Jerusalem in the years 67–70 CE may have followed their flight from Galilee as the Romans advanced southward toward the capital city. Once they had regrouped in Jerusalem, they cast themselves into the cauldron of Jewish infighting, lashing out against the high priest, the aristocracy, other insurrectionist groups, and with any remaining strength, the foreign foe, the Romans.

Next we turn to the Essenes, whose origins trace back to the beginning of the Hasmonean period and whose historical kinship with the Pharisees we noted in the preceding chapter. We consider the Essenes before the Pharisees, due to the fact that they belong to the category of groups adhering to the political option of resistance.

Our most valuable source for the identity of the Essenes is the library discovered by a Bedouin goatherd searching for a lost member of his flock on the shores of the Dead Sea in 1946–47. The focus of our present study would become blurred if we were to engage in a reevaluation of the extremely complex set of issues that divide scholars over the question of the identity of the copyists and authors of the Dead Sea Scrolls, namely, the inhabitants of the community that occupied for a period just short of two centuries the site of Khirbet Qumran on the northwestern bank of the Dead Sea. For me, the preponderance of evidence still weighs in favor of the view held by a majority of scholars, that the Qumran community consisted of Essenes who had fled from Jerusalem under the leadership of a deposed Zadokite priest, to whom they ascribed the title "teacher of righteousness."[15]

---

15. See James C. VanderKam, *The Dead Sea Scrolls and the Bible* (Grand Rapids: Eerdmans, 2012). An alternative, and in my judgment less convincing, identification tying the Qumran community to the halakic Sadducees has been argued by Newman, *Proximity.*

Leaving open for the moment the question of whether their apocalyptic vision of violent destruction of their enemies places their politics in the category of passive or active resistance, it is clear that they were dissidents, who, having broken with the Hasmonean leadership of the Jerusalem temple community around the middle of the second century BCE, fled to their wilderness enclave to await God's new initiative. In their view, the Jerusalem from which they had fled was defiled, corrupt, illegitimate, and under the judgment of God. Their withdrawal from the daily politics of the Hasmonean regime and the ritual life of the Jerusalem temple was in their view the only way to protect themselves from the defilement that had engulfed Jerusalem. The monastic community that they established would keep alive God's eternal covenant with his people Israel, for in the wilderness they were to be God's temple, undefiled, obedient, and awaiting God's return in judgment and mercy.

According to their apocalyptic vision, the world's final assize was approaching. The world was divided between the sons of light and the sons of darkness. Their current isolation from politics was not categorical but strategic. God was about to inaugurate a holy war against all that opposed his rule, and that included both Jews and Gentiles, for example, the Hasmonean priest-kings, their compromising temple collaborators, the Romans (*kittim*), and the fallen angels. The strict ritual purity that they maintained prepared them for the holy war in which they would fight in the company of the angelic hosts against the sons of darkness, to cleanse the land and to prepare for the final reign of peace under the chosen messiahs of Levi (Aaron) and Judah.

The Essene community of Qumran thus provides a vivid example of the model of apocalyptic politics. Inherent in that model was the tension between the alternatives of escape into a vision of celestial glory and religiously inspired revolt, aimed at hastening divine intervention in the realm of a fallen humanity. Since in the apocalyptic community's worldview the signal for switching from passivism to military action depended on a message from heaven, the role of the inspired teacher or prophet in unlocking the secrets of Scripture was essential to the community's process of decision making. Regrettably, little is known about how, if at all, the fundamentally important office initially filled by the teacher of righteousness was handed down to later generations. As the Roman threat loomed larger and larger on the western horizon, was the community left without the instructions of an inspired interpreter? Several related questions remain unanswered. What was the relation of the Essenes to the other groups that eschewed the options of collaboration and accommodation? Is the resistance of the Qumran community to be classified as active, violent, passive? Did it vary over time?

With regard to the important question of the Qumran community's understanding of its religious heritage and the means to be used for determining the meaning contained in Scripture for its own time, we have the benefit of commentaries produced at Qumran on biblical books such as Nahum and Habakkuk. The *pesher* method developed in these commentaries purportedly unlocked the secrets that these writings had long revealed regarding the end-time events Qumran covenanters were now witnessing. The outcome of the present crisis as thereby disclosed to them constituted their secret knowledge and was known to no one else. Their vindication was at hand; their place of honor as true Israel and as God's chosen priesthood was soon to be fulfilled. Or so they believed.

While the basic facts of Qumran origins are known (persecution suffered under the Hasmoneans Jonathan and Simon, leading to flight from Jerusalem by a group of strictly observant Jews, led by a Zadokite priest ["the teacher of righteousness"]), little is known about its ending, thus bedeviling attempts to answer many of our questions. This much regarding the final days of the Qumran community, however, can be extrapolated from the larger historical panorama of the Roman period. In facing a Roman command that tolerated no dissent, regardless of whether or not they entered the fray militarily in application of the bombastic rhetoric of their document *The War of the Sons of Light against the Sons of Darkness,* the members of the Qumran community experienced the brutal fact that whatever may be the validity of their vision of celestial victories, on earth the armies of the Romans determined the fate of the peoples they conquered. As was the case with all groups that defied the might of Rome, the covenanters of Qumran experienced in their final earthly battle crushing defeat and the death of their community. But more was at stake. Among the political options tested by different groups during the Second Temple period, the option of ideological absolutism suffered a stinging defeat when the Qumran apocalypse collapsed under the daunting power of imperial Roman army.

We return to the question of how to designate the political strategy of the Qumran group. A comparison of Daniel 7–12 with Qumran writings suggests that for most of their history they followed a path of nonviolent resistance in relation to both native and foreign authorities and powers. Whether in their last dark hours they resorted to arms may never be known, though it should be noted that no weapons were found among the ruins at Khirbet Qumran, thus lending credence to the suspicion that the grand schemes of war spelled out in their writings were primarily the products of apocalyptic imagination.

In light of this picture, it seems unwarranted to place the Essenes in the same political category as the Zealots. On the basis of evidence from Josephus and the New Testament, the Zealots can be understood as the authentic advocates of the option of sectarian resistance, calling for violent opposition to the enemies of Israel. While the possibility remains that some of the Essenes cast themselves into the fray in a final suicidal attack on the Romans in 63 CE, the political strategy that they had cultivated over the life of their community has closer affinities with that propounded by Daniel 7–12, one of patiently awaiting the initiative of God to defeat the enemy and to reward the faithful with eternal peace. Of the imminence of a final battle in which apostate Jews and pagans alike would be destroyed and the remnant of the undefiled would be vindicated, they entertained no doubt; however, the consummation of that denouement rested not in human hands but in the hands of God. As modern historians, our evidence is limited to the sphere of human events.

To this point, affinities between the Essenes and the Pharisees are apparent. But more needs to be said of their understanding of the bearing of ancestral tradition on their response to the events of the world around them.

At this point we encounter a categorical difference between the Essenes (at least as we know them though the Dead Sea Scrolls) and the Pharisees (at least as we know them through Josephus, the New Testament, and rabbinical sources). In contrast to the dialectical approach that guided the interpretation of Scripture among the Pharisees and their rabbinic descendants, the Essenes of Qumran (and likely also the Sicarii and Zealots) approached interpretation, not through the lens of a hermeneutic holding in tension interpretation of Scripture and reflection on the complexities of contemporary events, but through application of a key unlocking absolute truth that negated the beliefs and practices of all rivals. In applying the *pesher* method of interpretation, the teacher of righteousness of Qumran claimed to discover the secrets of heaven and thereby to present to his followers what God was about to do in the world.

Such epistemological absolutism, predicated on exegetical certainty, left no room for discussion with coreligionists representing different perspectives or with emissaries presenting the policies of governing imperial powers.[16] God's remnant in the wilderness, chosen to preserve true Israel, alone held the key unlocking the meaning of Scripture, enabling it to foretell the future. But when historical events conspired to contradict its "certain" predictions, its own destiny succumbed to that of the group from which it had split (the Pharisees) and their more subtle epistemology and hermeneutics that aspired to preserve the ancient Mosaic tradition within the context of an interpretive discourse that did not trump the dynamics of historical change with absolutist claims but acknowledged the limitations of human understanding and the inevitability of misjudgments in the face of ambiguity.[17] Thus it was that sectarian withdrawal combined with ostracism within the broader Jewish community resulted in the peripheralizing and rendering obsolete of the Essene movement.

If any members of the Essene community were present in Jerusalem in the chaotic years of 67–70, the best they could have done to contribute to their community's future would have been either to join cause with the Pharisees or to follow in the path of one of their coreligionists, John the Baptist, who saw fit to bequeath his movement to one of his disciples, Jesus of Nazareth. To summarize, the future of the political legacy of the Bible rested not in the hands of

16. There is good reason to believe that the Zealots held to an epistemological absolutism, though regrettably the rich source material provided by the Dead Sea Scrolls for the Essenes is not matched by a similar discovery pertaining to the Zealots.

17. We make this historical observation in full awareness of the agility of absolutists, ancient and modern, to keep revising their purportedly biblically warranted prophecies of the final assize in the face of the contradictory testimony of history (à la Herb Armstrong and Hal Lindsey).

Sadducees or Essenes, but in the ranks of the Pharisees and their cousins, the followers of the son of Joseph.

A final comparative word should be added regarding the political positions of the Essenes and another party in the fray, the Zealots. While the Zealots held in common with the Qumran covenanters an animosity toward both the Jerusalem leadership and the Roman occupation, they differed in the political strategy they drew from their dualistic worldview. Eschewing the eschatological equivocation of the sectarian writings of Qumran, the Zealots translated into the call to armed revolt their certainty that both the Jewish leadership and the Roman armies were enemies of God. Holy war was not a category to be decorated by florid descriptions of inscribed weaponry or limited to celestial strategies, but was to be put into practice by slaying all of the enemies of God, Jewish apostate and Roman idolater alike.

A full description of how the strategy of violent resistance fared in the history of the Roman period would fill a book. For our purposes, it is enough to point out that, like the model of collaboration, it held no future. Beginning with Herod's death in 4 BCE, continuing though the implementation of direct rule by the Romans in 6 CE, and on to the Jewish revolt of 66 CE that ended in the Roman destruction of the temple in 70 and finally the suicidal departure from this world by the Zealots on Masada in 73, the Zealots' employment of armed resistance contributed a tragic paragraph to the chronicle of failed extremist political strategies.[18] Far from achieving its goals of liberating Israel, it sacrificed its adherents to its foes and led to the tightening of the Roman fetters on the surviving Jewish population. Consequently, among the Jews the model of violent resistance increasingly came to be regarded as self-discrediting and thus to be avoided.

But violent resistance as a political strategy could never be banished entirely. For, in spite of its contributing role to some of the darkest moments of Jewish history, it was a model that resurfaced as a source of hope at times when foreign rulers threatened the cherished values and practices of the Jewish community. Indeed, in little over a half century after the First Jewish Revolt against the Romans, it provided the paradigm for yet another futile attempt to overthrow the Romans by force, and, astonishingly, the leading proponents of violent resistance in that case were members of the party generally characterized by a balance between the courage to express dissent and political savvy in negotiating differences vis-à-vis coreligionists and foreign authorities alike, namely, the Pharisees. It is to the party of the Pharisees that we now turn, since they are the chief representatives of the third political option found within Judaism of the Roman period, namely, accommodation.

---

18. Though the revolt centering in Alexandria in 115–117 CE also documents the futility of the strategy of violent resistance in the history of Jewish relations to foreign regimes, it opens up the vast topic of the politics of the Jewish Diaspora, and thus lies beyond the scope of the present study.

Any attempt to describe the Pharisees from their origins among the pious (Hasidim) during the conflicts of the Maccabean period through the Hasmonean and Roman periods and finally to the period after the Second Jewish Revolt, when their legacy passed on to the traditions of rabbinical Judaism, must be prepared to deal with complicated and often conflicting pieces of evidence. In comparison, the task of describing the politics of the Essenes or the Zealots was relatively simple, the reason having much to do with differing theo-political modalities. Whereas the latter groups were characterized by an absolutist attitude toward the authority of Scripture and its meaning in relation to current events, the Pharisees held in balance an acceptance of the normative nature of Scripture and a willingness to adapt Torah statutes and ordinances to changing conditions. The balance, to be sure, was commensurate with the political posture of the Pharisees, a posture of involvement that included willingness to utilize the levers of politics to advance their own notions of state and religion.[19]

This dialectical approach in relation to religion and politics was visible from the beginning of the history of the Pharisees, when a split between Essenes and Pharisees occurred over the choice of separation from the taint of politics or engagement with political processes aimed at reform. For the Essenes, the aggrandizing politics of the Hasmoneans, which was visible already during the lifetime of Jonathan and Simon, led to withdrawal into the wilderness in the effort to preserve their purity from the defilement of the masses. The Pharisees, contrariwise, sought to work for reform within the order of regnant authorities, both native and foreign.

In the early years of the conflict with the Seleucids, the Pharisees supported the military initiatives taken by the sons of Mattathias against Antiochus IV that resulted in the liberation of Jerusalem and the rededication of the temple. Though the political aggrandizement of Jonathan and Simon no doubt strained the alliance, their support continued on into the reign of John Hyrcanus. Hyrcanus's resort to an increasingly opulent and secular court style, however, evoked the harsh criticism of leading Pharisees. The king responded by switching his allegiance to the Sadducees, an alliance that continued through the short reign of Aristobulus I and the much longer reign of Alexander Jannaeus (103–76). For a brief time the Pharisees again took advantage of the favor of Queen Salome Alexandra (76–66) to avenge themselves of grievances against

19. See Newman, *Proximity*. Though limiting his analysis to the Hasmonean period on the grounds that occupation by a foreign entity adds a variable that obscures the definitions he seeks to clarify, Newman's distinction between "regime-powered dissenting groups" and "independent-powered seceding groups" sheds light on the position taken by the Pharisees during the Roman period, since it derives from the theo-political strategy developed by the Pharisees in the century preceding Pompey's invasion. According to Newman, the Pharisees, as the primary representatives of the "regime-powered dissenting groups," while maintaining a critical stance vis-à-vis ruling authorities, nevertheless remained engaged in politics, with the intention of exerting influence from within existing structures and steering public affairs and societal norms in directions advantageous to them, rather than seceding on the basis of an ideological/theological vision claiming divine authorization for radical change, in the manner of the Essenes and the Qumran group.

their opponents, but their period of political influence abruptly ended during the civil war fought between the two claimants to the Hasmonean throne, Hyrcanus II and Aristobulus II. It seems likely that the Pharisees were among the people that appealed to the Romans to end the chaos being wreaked by their native kings and to assume direct control of their nation. We have already commented on the likelihood that *Psalm of Solomon* 17 reflects the anti-Hasmonean position of the Pharisees at the time of Pompey's invasion in 63 BCE.

The political clout of the Pharisees remained weak during the reign of Herod the Great, for whom maintenance of a firm hold on a populace that took umbrage at his half-Jewish pedigree entailed appointing priests (normally from the Diaspora) who swore allegiance to him and withholding his wrath only from religious groups that refrained from criticizing his cruelty, immorality, and cynicism. The grievances of the Pharisees found expression in the delegation that traveled to Rome after the death of Herod in 4 BCE to request the replacement of native kingship with reorganization of Judea as a Roman province.

The political fortunes of the Pharisees did not improve in 4 BCE, or in 6 CE, the year in which Herod's son Archelaus was removed as ethnarch of Judea and a Roman prefect was installed as ruling authority over that province. For the maintenance of civil order and for the gathering of the taxes payable to Rome, the new regime followed the pattern similar to that of the Persians during the time of Ezra and Nehemiah, that is, utilizing the services of the native official best situated to act as buffer between rulers and subjects, namely, the high priest. Due to the historical ties of that office to the Sadducees and the aristocratic bond that unified the interests of temple personnel and wealthy Jerusalem Sadducees, the Pharisees during the period 6–66 CE were relegated to the political periphery.

Though eclipsed politically by their religious rivals, the Pharisees' influence over the general Jewish populace actually grew during the Roman period.[20] Since most Jews detested the Roman occupiers and distrusted the collaborating Jewish temple leaders, the party that remained outside of and even in opposition to the political and religious leadership came to be regarded as their advocates. This strengthening of their base of popular support played a major role in the emergence of the Pharisees over all rivals as the authentic representatives of Judaism after the two Jewish revolts. The consequence of most significance was that it was their halakic tradition that lived on among the rabbis of Yavneh and the later academies of Torah study.

But before that period of ascendancy was to dawn on the Pharisees, the most difficult period of their entire history was to intervene, a period consisting of two crises that would test both their political judgment and their religious wisdom to the breaking point.

The first crisis revolved around the turmoil of the First Jewish Revolt (66–73 CE), in which rival Jewish groups fought to promote their own agendas with

---

20. Cf. Josephus, *Ant.* 13.15.5 and 18.1.3.

more energy and passion than they collectively mustered against the Romans. It was a time when the navel of the universe, to which Isaiah and Ezekiel looked for the establishment of universal peace, seemed ravaged by the catastrophic assault on Zion prophesied in Jeremiah 1, Ezekiel 38–39, and Zechariah 12. Adding to the calamity was the fact that the ranks of the archetypal foe from the north consisted not only of Romans, but also Jewish Zealots, pursued by the Syrian division of the Roman army under the command of legate Lucius Vitellius and fleeing desperately over the border into Judea. Desperately, leading Pharisees sought to form a centrist movement to negotiate a plan for preventing the destruction of temple and Holy City. But when in 66 CE it became clear that war was inevitable, they joined forces with those willing to put aside differences to banish from Jerusalem terrorists who were wantonly killing Romans and fellow Jews alike and to prepare for the Roman offensive.

As part of the Jewish defense initiative, the Jerusalem council appointed Josephus to serve as governor of Galilee. Under difficult circumstances exacerbated by disunity among the populace and lack of materiel, he prepared for Vespasian's attack. The following year, he was captured, but in a remarkable display of political savvy he announced that Vespasian would become the next Roman emperor. This demonstration of newly affirmed loyalty was not forgotten by the rising star of Rome; when Vespasian in fact did assume the throne, he rewarded Josephus with a pension that enabled him to devote his life to writing the two histories of the Jewish people that remain our most important extrabiblical sources for the events of the period.

Though Josephus's acceptance of Roman patronage could be viewed as an act of treason, several considerations paint a more complex picture. Josephus's disdain for fanatical insurrectionists and self-appointed messiah-saviors is well documented.[21] Though his claim to membership in the party of the Pharisees is open to question, his theo-politics in certain respects reflects that of the Pharisees: He preferred accommodation to the foreign regime, over assertions of independence that risked bloodshed. His priestly way of thinking likely leaned toward preference for a theocracy led by priests over other political models. But political pragmatism perhaps can be identified as his overweening predisposition, and under the circumstances of his time, including the chaos of disunity among the contending Jewish parties and movements and the social and economic fractures that the failed revolt had produced, it is not hard to understand how an intellectual as complex as Josephus came to embrace civility within the Roman imperium as the best option available, not only to him personally but to the Jewish people as a whole.

---

21. Josephus is emphatic in his condemnation of the ill-fated revolutionary movements of insurrectionists like Simon and Zadok. Indeed, he blamed such revolutionary stratagems for the calamitous defeat suffered by the Jews in the revolt of 66 CE. His rebuke of the firebrands whose messianic claims threatened to destroy the very nation they set out to liberate went so far as his identifying Vespasian as God's anointed deliverer of the Jewish people (*War* 6.312–13).

Beyond political pragmatism, was Josephus also motivated by religious considerations? Did the tradition of YHWH choosing the Persian emperor Cyrus as his messiah-deliverer, who would release and restore captive Israel, play a role in the understanding of one as well versed in Hebrew Scripture as Josephus?

Bearing indirectly on such questions, and of importance in itself in regard to the theo-politics of the Pharisees, is the legend handed down in rabbinical literature about Yohanan ben Zakkai. According to the legend, ben Zakkai, having fled from besieged Jerusalem, won the support of the Roman emperor Vespasian through a remarkable piece of political exegesis. According to his interpretation of the words of Isaiah 10:34, "And the Lebanon shall fall by a majestic one," "Lebanon" referred to the temple constructed by Solomon with cedars provided by Hiram from Lebanon, and "a majestic one" referred to Vespasian. The legend goes on to describe how the Roman general (who was soon to become emperor) was so pleased that he granted Yohanan ben Zakkai's request for the restoration of the rabbinic academy at Yavneh.[22]

Clearly, one must take into account the legendary nature of the story of Yohanan ben Zakkai. But as has long been recognized, legends frequently develop on the basis of a historical memory and even in their embellishments can capture something of the deeper significance of the originating episode. In support of this view in relation to the rabbinical tale of ben Zakkai is the known fact that the academy at Yavneh, to which he had gathered from Jerusalem surviving Jewish leaders (with Pharisees prominent among them), enjoyed the support of the Romans. It was within that academy of Torah study that an intellectual conduit was established through which the central teachings of the Pharisees continued to develop, thereby setting the trajectory that would produce the Mishnah (ca. 200 CE) and finally the Babylonian Talmud (ca. 400 CE).

It thus seems reasonable to conclude that this legend captured the essence of ben Zakkai's religious wisdom and political savvy: At a critical turning point in Jewish history, he was able to practice the politics of accommodation in such a careful balancing act as to keep peace with the pagan overlord and at the same time remain faithful to Mosaic religion and cultivate community structures that enabled the continued growth and flourishing of Judaism during the imperial Roman period.

We should be reminded that in striking this balance, ben Zakkai was not engaged in pure innovation, but was drawing on a policy that had taken deep root within the politics of the Pharisees long before the First Jewish Revolt. According to the corroborative testimony of Philo[23] and Josephus,[24] the legitimacy of the Roman imperium was acknowledged by the Jews in the form of daily temple sacrifices offered on behalf of the emperor. Significantly, there is no indication in the historical records that the Pharisees, who on numerous prior

---

22. Jacob Neusner, *Development of a Legend: Studies on the Traditions concerning Yohanan Ben Zakkai* (Leiden: Brill, 1970).

23. Philo, *Leg.* 157, 232, 317.

24. Josephus, *War* 2.19, 409.

occasions had demonstrated their willingness to die rather than compromise their loyalty to the one God, remonstrated with the temple leadership over the daily offering of a bull and two lambs. If, as seems likely, they found no contradiction between this ritualization of the penultimate authority of the Roman emperor and their ultimate loyalty to God, they were following the precedent set by the archetypical scribe of the Torah of Moses, Ezra, who in the fifth century BCE had chosen the path of accommodation to the Persian emperor under circumstances similar to those experienced anew by the Jews under the Romans.[25] Yohanan ben Zakkai cautiously trod the same path in his own time.

As in the individual cases of Josephus and ben Zakkai, so too in the case of the Pharisees as a group, one could attribute the policy of accommodation to an unbridled realpolitik or cynical opportunism leading them to embrace any strategy capable of enhancing their influence at the expense of rival groups like the Sadducean priestly family of Boethus or Hasmonean aspirants like Hezekiah. But this would not account for the numerous instances of Pharisees' paying for their opposition to the ruling authorities with their blood, during both Hasmonean and Herodian times. It also offers inadequate explanation of their practice of restraint on occasions when one might have expected them to join the ranks of more radical groups, occasions like the death of Herod in 4 BCE. In explaining the acts of the revolutionaries who did take up arms on such occasions, Josephus offered this description of the Fourth Philosophy: "they have an inviolable attachment to liberty; and they say that God is to be their only Ruler and Lord."[26] But was this not the theocratic position of the Pharisees as well? If they were led by political motives alone, might they not have allied with the insurrectionists to execute vengeance on their old enemies once and for all? These are questions that will be revisited, for they will prompt us to describe the subtleties inherent in the theo-politics of the Pharisees that set them apart from both the Sadducees and the Zealots.

First, however, a final traumatic episode in the life of the Pharisees remains to be addressed, one that on the surface may seem to undermine the case we have been building for the Pharisees being practitioners of the via media, one that may seem even to place them within the political option of violent resistance practiced by adherents of Josephus's Fourth Philosophy. That episode was the Second Jewish Revolt against Rome in 132–35 CE, a tragic event in which the contribution of leading Pharisees—in contrast to the situation in 66 CE—was not to restraint and the exhausting of all alternatives to war before joining in the last-ditch attempt to defend the land against the devastating wrath of the Romans, but to taking the initiative in providing a decisive divinely sanctioned catalyst for revolt.

There is no reason to question the testimony of Josephus that a major impetus for revolt against the Romans beginning in 132 CE came from the Pharisees.

25. Ezra 6:9–10.
26. *Ant.* 18.1.6.

Before attributing this change in policy to a radical shift in political philosophy, however, it is important to recognize a fundamental difference in the gauntlet thrown down by Emperor Hadrian compared to the actions of the Roman leadership in the earlier war. We shall argue that the aggressive initiative taken by Hadrian represented such a direct assault on the center of Jewish belief that accommodation, though the traditional policy of the Pharisees, was rendered untenable if obedience to the First Commandment and the theocratic principle was to be upheld. The situation was not unlike the crisis thrust upon an earlier generation of the Jewish nation by Antiochus IV Epiphanes in 167 BCE. In the face of an imperial command to worship an idol, exclusive allegiance to the God of Israel mandated the radical response of holy war!

The crisis unfolded as follows: In 131 CE Hadrian visited Jerusalem and announced plans for an ambitious building project that would replace the rubble of Jerusalem with a new city, Aelia Capitolina. The jewel in the crown of this sparkling city was to be a temple dedicated to Jupiter Capitolinus, erected on the site of the ruins of the Jewish temple. The "abomination of desolation" that Antiochus had visited upon the Holy City roughly three centuries earlier was about to be reenacted!

What followed fit a pattern well attested in biblical tradition. A prophetlike figure appeared on the scene and spoke on the authority of the God of Israel. In this case the divine spokesperson was a Pharisee with impeccable credentials, Rabbi Akiba. Drawing upon Numbers 24:17, a verse already imbued by Jewish sages with messianic connotations, Akiba announced in 132 CE that Simon ben Kosba was Bar Kokhba, the deliverer chosen by God to muster the faithful to liberate Israel from the Romans and their blasphemous plan to establish pagan worship on Zion.

For a brief time prophecy seemed to reach for fulfillment. The Romans retreated, Jerusalem was liberated, and ben Kosba ruled over the new state for three years with the historically significant title of Nasi. We can only imagine the excitement that swept over the Jewish homeland: On the threshold of the propitious seventieth year after the destruction of the temple by the Romans, God had intervened in human history and through Bar Kokhba's successful campaign was preparing for the rebuilding of the temple and the restoration of Israel under a king of the house of David. The ancient promises of Jeremiah and Ezekiel and the restatement of those promises in the collection of writings that we earlier suggested expressed the eschatological yearnings of the Pharisees, *The Psalms of Solomon,* were being fulfilled before their very eyes!

The messianic fervor was imprinted on the coins minted by the new liberation regime, on which the date was recorded as "the first/the second year of the redemption of Israel." The period of messianic exaltation, however, was short-lived. Though the Romans had suffered an embarrassing military defeat, it is not surprising that they soon regrouped with sufficient strength to settle accounts. No less than twelve legions were committed to the campaign, and the resulting devastation marked a nadir point in Jewish history.

The magnitude of the challenge thrust upon the Pharisees, and upon the Jewish religious community in general, was tantamount to the one occasioned in the late sixth century BCE by the Babylonian destruction of Jerusalem. The replay of that tragedy was made more bitter by comparison with another calamity, namely, Antiochus's defilement of the temple in 167 BCE. In that case, there was a far different outcome, celebrated to this day during Hanukkah: the crushing defeat of the foreign enemy and the reconsecration of the temple through the heroic military efforts of the sons of Maccabee.

The theological dilemma raised for the Pharisees by this calamity was one lodged at the heart of their biblical heritage. Their God, unlike the gods of the pagan pantheons whose internal battles accounted for the rise and fall of cities and nations, was proclaimed to be the sole God of the universe. All that transpired in human history was according to this God's purpose. But what purpose could be found to explain an event in which the dwelling place of Israel's God was razed to make room for the temple of Jupiter?

Closer scrutiny of this tragic point in Jewish history, however, reveals an irony imbued with theological significance. In contrast to the victory of the Maccabees, which led to an increasingly secular form of national independence and ended in calamity and subjugation to an empire mightier than the one from which it had been liberated, the defeat of 132 CE, like the defeat of 587 BCE before it, set in motion a period of profound theological and political reflection and discovery. As if purified by fire, the Pharisees reached back to their traditional political policy of accommodation, and upon it they constructed a model of community that would enable Judaism not only to survive horrendous new calamities in the centuries to come, but to continue to develop religious and ethical norms and practices that would contribute not only to its own flourishing but to the enrichment of human civilization in general.

It is by no means certain that a nonpartisan observer of the first century CE would have picked the Pharisees, from the various parties and movements active in the Jewish community at that time, as the group destined to shape normative Judaism. After all, the practitioners of the politics of collaboration, the Sadducees, benefiting from their wealth, international commercial ties, priestly pedigree, and temple-based connections with the Roman regime, appeared to control the levers of influence that matter in the realm of politics. As for the hearts and passions of the general populace, did not the messianically charged message of the patriotic resistance, the Sicarii, the Zealots, and the Fourth Philosophy, carry the talisman of Jewish pride that preserved the memory of Joshua, David, Judas, and the sons of Maccabee?

An interesting question emerges: what was it in the position of the Pharisees, as both political underdogs and ideological moderates, that situated them favorably in relation to the inexorable march of history toward the philosophical and scientific revolutions that, after gestation in the fertile thought world of the high Middle Ages, would give birth to modernity? Was it not their expanding the circles of those included in intellectual inquiry from the aristocratic elite to educated representatives of an emerging middle class? In connection with this democratizing tendency, is there not to be detected a movement toward a dialectical form of reasoning that placed tradition in a lively conversation with unfolding historical and cultural developments? Perhaps it is accurate to see in the Pharisees and their heirs in the rabbinical tradition the intellectual precursors of such architects of Western civilization as Averroës, Maimonides, Erasmus, Luther, Calvin, and Spinoza.

More than anything else, the Pharisees were interpreters of their religious tradition. This in itself, of course, does not account for their unique contribution to Western religion and philosophy, for the Essenes and the halakic Sadducees also attributed central importance to the sacred writings. The difference arises in the way in which received traditions were related to an ever-changing world.

In contrast to the Sadducees, the Pharisees did not limit sacred Scripture to the five books of Moses. They viewed their own biblical interpretation as continuing the long tradition of ongoing revelation that had added the prophetic, hymnic, and sapiential writings to their canonical corpus. Nor did they limit God's presence and God's revelation to the temple and its (primarily Sadducean) priesthood. As Jacob Neusner has pointed out, they drew from Exodus 19:3–6 the important lesson that all the children of Israel were called to study the Torah and to apply it, in all its aspects, to their daily lives.[27] The progressive position of the Pharisees proved to be in tune with the views and convictions of most Jews. Their progressive view of scriptural authority and revelation enabled them to apply ancient traditions to situations not addressed or anticipated in the written Torah.

The destruction of the temple in 63 CE proved to be a crucial test for all religious parties. The tactics of the insurrectionists had ended in calamity, and Josephus undoubtedly speaks for many of his countrymen when he places blame squarely on those seeking to regain national freedom through the force of arms. The Zealots and the Essenes, with their absolutist hermeneutic, disappeared from the stage of history. A temple lying in ruins presented a different kind of challenge to the Sadducees, for their conservative hermeneutics tied the applicability of much of the Torah to the ritual functions of that central symbol of traditional Jewish religion. For them, the relevance of the elaborate sacrificial laws had become perplexingly problematic, a dilemma exacerbated by the fact that the vocations of the Sadducean temple priests suddenly had been abolished.

Unlike the Sadducees, for whom the Jerusalem temple represented the irreplaceable center of Jewish faith, the Pharisees had discovered that the central meaning of Judaism continued to be found in the Torah even after the temple's destruction. This discovery inspired their audacious reinterpretation of ancient laws to reveal fresh meaning for an age vastly different from that of Moses and

---

27. Jacob Neusner, *Invitation to the Talmud: A Teaching Book* (New York: Harper & Row, 1988), 40.

the prophets.[28] Even the laws specifically regulating the temple tithes and sacrifices were reapplied to life without the temple and—for the increasing number of Jews living in the Diaspora—to life outside of the Holy Land of Israel. Nothing less than a liberating experience of the first order was the discovery that the spirit behind the command to tithe was fulfilled in the giving of alms to the poor, and the equivalent of temple sacrifices in a templeless world was an act of loving-kindness.[29]

The righteous and compassionate nature of God, which was the source of all of the statutes and ordinances of the Torah, was no less active in the world after the destruction of the temple than it was before. The openness of the Pharisees to the new thing that God was doing created an open door for Judaism to enter a changing world with renewed vitality and direction. It is thus understandable that in the era after the two Jewish revolts, the disappearance of the Essenes and the declining influence of the aristocratic Jerusalem Sadducees were accompanied by the increasing favor with which the Pharisees were regarded as inspired teachers divinely chosen to lead the nation through the present crises to the future promised by God, both in this world and in the world to come.[30]

Depending on one's perspective, one could regard the Pharisees as religious radicals or as religious reformers. The former view would place emphasis on the way they reinterpreted laws regarding temple ritual so as to make them applicable to life in a templeless world. The latter view is the one we prefer, and for reasons that reach back further in the history and religion of Israel.

Over the course of the long history of politics in the biblical and postbiblical period, amid many different tactics and even distinct different political models, one *principle* perdured as guardian of the sine qua non of biblical political theology: the theocratic principle that the only government that commands the unqualified, ultimate allegiance of the faithful is the rule of God. Accordingly, obedience for the religious Jew living within any political setting—be it

---

28. Shaye J. D. Cohen explains the reason for the relative ease with which the rabbis (in the first century CE, more properly to be designated Pharisees) were able to adjust to the post-70 world: "Apparently because the piety of second temple Judaism had prepared the rabbis for a temple-less world. . . . The Regimen of daily prayer, Torah study, participation in synagogue services, and observance of the commandments sanctified life outside the temple and, in effect, competed with the temple cult, just as the new lay scholar class, the scribes and others, in effect competed with the priests. After the destruction of the temple, which must have been felt keenly in all reaches of the population, what could have been more natural than to take the extra-temple piety that had developed in the preceding centuries and view it as the equivalent or replacement for the temple cult?" (Shaye J. D. Cohen, *From the Maccabees to the Mishnah* [Philadelphia: Westminster Press, 1987], 218).

29. No single text captures the dialectical position of the Pharisees and the rabbis after the destruction of the Jerusalem temple in 70 CE more poignantly than the oft-quoted midrash in *Avot D'Rabbi Nathan,* which reads in part: "The Temple is destroyed. We never witnessed its glory. But Rabbi Joshua did. And when he looked at the Temple ruins one day, he burst into tears. 'Alas for us! The place which atoned for the sins of all the people Israel lies in ruins!' Then Rabbi Yohanan ben Zakkai spoke to him these words of comfort: 'Be not grieved, my son. There is another way of gaining ritual atonement, even though the Temple is destroyed. We must now gain ritual atonement through deeds of loving-kindness'" (*Avot D'Rabbi Nathan,* 94:5).

30. See Josephus, *Ant.* 13.15.5 and 18.1.3–4.

a confederation of tribes, a monarchy, or a commonwealth ruled by a foreign power—was defined as single-minded submission to God's reign.

From this major premise of the First Commandment the Pharisees, like the prophets before them, inferred their political strategies. The categorical distinction between God's eternal, universal rule and the changing, ephemeral rule of this world's masters required flexibility, for compromise in relation to this central commandment, which constituted idolatry, took different forms, depending on the specific historical context. Even as there was no biblical warrant for claiming that charismatic rule, or monarchy, or any other political model provided an immutable blueprint for an independent nation of Israel, so too there was no scriptural basis for arguing that any particular strategy, such as accommodation or resistance, was mandated for every situation in which the Jewish community fell under foreign rule. Political models and strategies could be evaluated against one standard alone: the supernal imperative of God's universal reign. Accordingly—and here we take examples from the Roman period—collaboration with the Romans that interfered with obedience to the Torah was unacceptable, as was, most emphatically, any fealty to the emperor that infringed on God's sole claim to worship. On the other hand, calls for suicidal strategies dedicated to establishing a native government—be it in the form of a revival of monarchy under the Hasmoneans or a theocracy under a self-acclaimed national savior—were predicated on a fundamental confusion between the heavenly realm (the ultimate) and the mundane (the penultimate), and thus involved another kind of idolatry, also calling for denunciation. The categorical distinction between God's ultimate reign and all human governments, and the practical inference that the latter derived their legitimacy solely by conforming to the norms of God's reign, left open another, often startling possibility, namely, that God can choose foreign leaders and nations to fulfill his purposes for Israel and the world. Thus God's agent in punishing Samaria was the Assyrian Tiglath-pileser, even as God chose Nebuchadnezzar as his agent of judgment on Judah. Cyrus was named by God as his "messiah" appointed to restore the exiled Jews to their homeland. Though no Jew could accept Caesar Augustus's claim to divinity or the identification of his reign with the long-awaited peaceable kingdom, recognizing certain of his actions as in harmony with God's will was a possibility at home within the prophetic worldview inherited and cultivated by the Pharisees.

Underlying the complexity of the politics of the Pharisees is the fact that their theo-political philosophy did not benefit from the immunity enjoyed by utopian schemes constructed upon the vision of eternal structures free of earthly contact, and thus unaffected by the contradictory evidence of human history. Their future hope rather was dedicated to the restoration of a *historical* entity with distinct lines of continuity with the kingdom of David and Solomon. This historical orientation necessitated making judgments on the ruling principles and policies of current governments, both native and foreign. It required contrasting the nature of existing regimes with the qualities that would characterize the rule of God's anointed leader, qualities derived from their understanding of God's universal rule. It implied finally the most hazardous dimension of their political position, namely, recognizing and adding their support to that anointed one when he entered the stage of history.

Exercising their theo-political responsibilities over against foreign or native regimes that manifestly did not conform to the ultimate norms of God's rule proved to be far simpler then declaring a particular individual to be God's new David. The reason is clear. Relating to current native or foreign regimes that were not claimed to be messianic was carried out within the framework of what in Augustinian and Lutheran tradition eventually would be formulated as a two-kingdom theory: while no earthly kingdom could be identified with God's kingdom, every earthly kingdom stood under the judgment of God's kingdom.

But what happens when a biblically rooted religious movement identifies a particular historical regime with the reign of God, as both the disciples of Jesus and the Pharisees did in the first two centuries of the Common Era? We have indicated that in the case of the Pharisees, the identification of Kosiba's government with the messianic kingdom was withdrawn after it crumbled before the reassertion of Roman imperial power. Along with that recantation was drawn a lesson in restraint in the realm of messiah naming. The result was that the eschatological kingdom and the messiah who would deliver and restore Israel were bracketed from normal political process and assigned to a rather nebulous future age.

This observation must not obscure the contribution that belief in the final coming of the messiah-deliverer would continue to make within Judaism. Indeed, the notion of the universal peace, justice, and prosperity that God intends for all creation remains at the heart of Jewish political theory and action. That notion is conveyed by a Hebrew word that has entered everyday vocabulary: šālôm, the restoration of all realities and relations to the wholeness that comes only in communion with God. Less well known is the term tiqqûn ʿôlām, the repair or restoration of the universe which for many Jews gives expression to the vision inspiring their efforts to alleviate hunger, sickness, and world conflict. In the chapters to follow, we shall delve into the questions of how the Jesus movement and the early church dealt with its identification of Jesus as the messiah and what inferences were drawn into Christian political thought from the multivalent image of the kingdom of God.

Before entering into a discussion of politics in the New Testament, and in anticipation of our reflection in the epilogue on the bearing of biblical tradition on contemporary issues of religion and politics, we shall comment on the assertion that allowing biblical "certainty" to be undermined by acknowledgment of ambiguity within the text inevitably results in moral relativism. Were the Pharisees and the rabbis that followed in their tradition of creatively reinterpreting Scripture in light of changing realities relativists?

A distinction, albeit anachronizing, should be made: the secular relativism that is in vogue in the postmodern world is a metaphysical relativism, that is, a belief that there are no universal truths. A more nuanced—and in my mind convincing—relativism is often overlooked: though the viability of the intricate cosmic order assumes certain abiding regularities, the limitations that are intrinsic to the human condition deny any individual or group access to absolute certainty regarding those verities. The nub of the problem becomes epistemological. Within the context of this distinction, we can understand the position of the Pharisees over against their rivals, the Sadducees and the Essenes (as well as the Zealots and adherents to Josephus's Fourth Philosophy) by referring to the dialectic cultivated by the Pharisees and rooted in the Bible itself. The Pharisees held to a worldview that distinguished between the one universal order, which was ultimate in duration and purity, and all remaining realms, which were penultimate and transient and, in relation to "the Good," imperfect at best and diabolical at worst.[31]

The considerable flexibility that the Pharisees were able to exercise in dealing with foreign and domestic powers alike was predicated on the subordination of all earthly powers under God's ultimate authority. Whether Hasmonean, Zadokite, or Roman, all potentates, sacerdotal as well as political, were utterly subordinate to God. Accordingly, political action taken in relation to any regime, whether native or foreign, had to be weighed against the claims of the heavenly king. So long as the earthly ruler did not inhibit the duty of the Jews to worship God exclusively and to follow God's commandments unstintingly, a great deal of room for accommodation to his authority was available, and Yohanan ben Zakkai and his colleagues demonstrated just this fact. But when Hadrian constructed on the site of the Jerusalem temple the temple of Jupiter, the categorical threshold of *status confessionis* had been crossed.

Once the modern mind is able to enter into the thought world of those who believed that human affairs ultimately were subject to divine providence, and further, can appreciate the firm belief of the Jews that God would honor his promise to restore their land to liberty and eternal peace under his anointed ruler, the conclusion drawn by Akiba, that the time of Israel's redemption had come, can be understood as fitting within the framework of the dialectical philosophy of the Pharisees.

It was within the framework of that same philosophy that the disastrous outcome of the revolt had to be interpreted as well. The result was that a very high threshold was set for attributing validity to any specific messianic claim, whether it was made by Christians or arose from within the Jewish community. In general, the role that apocalyptic speculation would play in rabbinical thought was curtailed. When themes originating in the apocalyptic writings of the Second Temple period did resurface in medieval times, they were applied not to political speculation, but rather to mystical exercises through which the pious individual

31. Both the dangers and benefits of introducing modern concepts into an analysis of ancient phenomena should be recognized. In the case of the dialectical relation of the ultimate to the penultimate, the danger is that of imposing modern categories on earlier cultures for whom the underlying philosophical considerations were not operative, whereas much insight can be gained through attention to commonalities that transcend the limits of time and specific worldviews.

sought to experience the splendor of the divine realm. An example of such exercises is found in the *hekhalah* texts inspired by the visions of the seven heavens such as one finds in *1 Enoch* 14. Similarly, in *merkabah* mysticism tracing back to the book of Ezekiel, contemplation focused on the chariot throne of the deity served as a pathway toward the individual's entry into a transcendental experience. Movements inspired by messianic/apocalyptic themes did arise, such as the bizarre episode connected with Nathan the prophet and Shabbatai Tzwi in 1666. Such phenomena remained on the fringe of the Jewish community and were met with not even the modicum of tolerance with which various forms of mystical contemplation were treated by the rabbis.

That political extremism directed against non-Jewish rulers did not reappear within the Jewish communities scattered throughout the Diaspora may seem surprising, given the fact that, unlike the Christian church in the medieval period, Judaism developed neither a political entity equivalent to the Holy Roman Empire nor a normative central administrative structure like the papacy. This contrast, as is oft observed, explains in part why Judaism did not develop a tradition of creedal orthodoxy. Identity was defined regionally rather than universally, and in local communities what defined the Jew over against others was a life orchestrated by festivals, rituals, and obedience to the commandments of Torah as they were interpreted by their rabbis. Also contributing to the political moderation of the Jews over their long history of living in the Diaspora was a feature closely related to the restraints it placed on apocalyptic speculation, namely, the view that it lived in an era in which God no longer revealed his will directly through prophets, a postprophetic period in which God's commandments were written down, to be studied and applied by learned teachers whose interpretations were collected in the Mishnah, Talmud, Tosefta, and commentaries.

Once the contrast is drawn between Judaism and Christianity, however, it would be wrong to conclude that Judaism perdured without the benefit of administrative structures. Rather to be noted is that such structures did not simply copy foreign models, however much specific legal details and technical terms can be traced to Roman and Christian sources. The growth was from within and drew upon indigenous roots tracing all the way back to Roman times.

As pointed out earlier, the year 70 CE marked a turning point in the destiny of the various Jewish parties and movements. Also to be noted is the effect that that cataclysmic event had on the offices and institutions of the Jewish community. The ruling court (Sanhedrin) that previously was led by the high priest and consisted of a mixture of priests and laity, Pharisees and Sadducees, whom the high priest deemed suitable for trials involving accusations of religious violations, underwent a major transformation. With the destruction of the temple came the loss of the high priests' seat of power. The gap was filled by the growing influence, both in Palestine and the Diaspora, of the rabbis, a development related directly to the waxing importance of the Torah as the source of Jewish identity, in place of the Jerusalem temple.[32] The head of the newly constituted ruling body was named *nāśî*, that is, patriarch. The fact that the Romans, beginning in the interbellum period and continuing after 130, recognized the patriarch as the official spokesperson for the Jewish community both enhanced his prestige and hastened the expansion of his authority beyond strictly religious matters, to matters of internal and international policy. What remained essentially unchanged through this period of the evolving role of the patriarch and eventually the rise of separate regional patriarchates was the political philosophy originating with the Pharisees, which enabled Jewish communities to live at peace as subjects of non-Jewish rulers on the basis of the quid pro quo of civil obedience in return for religious freedom. That this political model was violated repeatedly over the centuries by hostile regimes constitutes a tragic history that only underscores the tenacity with which the Jewish community sought to live at peace with their political overlords.

The bedrock upon which were constructed the dialectical political philosophy and dynamic hermeneutic during the Second Temple period and beyond was none other than the First Commandment and its inherent theocratic principle. From the central confession that Israel is to acknowledge no God besides YHWH, the tradents of the Bible and the chain of rabbis that followed deduced the distinction between ultimate and penultimate authority.

Before concluding our discussion of Jewish political thought and action in the Roman period, we must make brief mention of the birth and development of what philosophically was the most extreme of the strategies for coping with the physical world, namely, Gnosticism.[33] Simon Magnus, described in the eighth chapter of the biblical Acts of the Apostles as a magician, developed by the time of Justin Martyr (100–165 CE) into the eponymous head of a gnostic movement. In the polemical writings of the church fathers, various other gnostic sects are described, with the one following the teachings of the second-century Alexandrian Basilides being the most influential and widespread. Though differing among themselves in the complicated systems of thought characteristic of such sects, they held in common the denunciation of the physical world as the product of a recusant demiurge and disseminated among their followers the secret knowledge (*gnosis*) whereby their true essence or soul could be released from the prison of the flesh.

Though reflecting influences as wide-ranging as Jewish apocalyptic speculation and Neoplatonism, the specifically Christian forms of Gnosticism ascribed to Jesus a key role as the Savior sent by the unknown God to release the faithful from the prison of the material world created by the demiurge, who in Christian Gnosticism is identified with the god of the Old Testament. Given their

32. Cf. Cohen, *Maccabees*, 107–8.
33. For an excellent study of the major Gnostic writings, see Elaine H. Pagels, *The Gnostic Gospels* (New York: Vintage Books, 1989).

denunciation of the material world and the corporeal self, it is not surprising that the gnostic groups were detached from the political activities of their various societies. Indeed, their lifestyle of choice was ascetic, and as is seen in the extensive library of gnostic writings discovered in 1945 in the Upper Nile site of Nag Hammadi, they built their communities—not unlike the apocalyptic community of Qumran—in the isolation of the hinterland.

Chapter 25

The Politics
of the New Testament

PROBLEMS RAISED BY THE COMPOSITION HISTORY
OF THE BOOKS OF THE NEW TESTAMENT

A prima facie reading of the New Testament by one unacquainted with critical biblical scholarship likely would give the impression that its twenty-seven books contain in a straightforward manner all the information needed to write a detailed description of the politics of Jesus and the early church. Not only do the Gospels provide a narrative beginning with Jesus' birth and ending with his resurrection, but the book of Acts continues the narrative on through the life of the early church and the journeys of the first missionaries, into which the teachings and narratives of Paul's letters and the other epistles can be fit. In addition, the book of Revelation describes the way the church under persecution by the Romans understood the coming glorious victory of those who remained faithful unto death.

That same reader, upon a second reading, may begin to detect a more complex relationship between the text and history. The chronology of events differs among the Gospels; tensions are detected in policy toward the Romans as depicted by different writers; and even the apostle Paul's political views vary as one reads the corpus of letters attributed to him and compares them with the accounts in Acts describing his relations with Roman authorities.

It is always possible to harmonize conflicting materials, both by explaining differences as evidence of development in the minds of individuals and groups and by suggesting that different situations called for different policies. Neither of these considerations can be dismissed out of hand, and indeed some seeming discrepancies can be illuminated in that manner. It is another matter entirely, however, to predicate in principle the inerrancy of the New Testament writings. This is the step taken by some scholars, particularly among those adhering to the principles of fundamentalism.

In defense of their position such scholars draw attention to the lack of consensus among those applying higher-critical methods in relation to matters such as the chronology of the events in the lives of Jesus and his disciples, the words that can be attributed to Jesus, and the number of Pauline letters that are attributable to the apostle Paul himself.

Given the wide disparity of conclusions drawn by critical scholars regarding the texts providing the basis for studying the politics of the New Testament, it is not surprising to witness confusion among lay readers. Consequently, some turn their backs on scholarly literature entirely and accept the inerrancy of the biblical writings as a matter of faith. Others come to the conclusion that the Gospels and Epistles not only are unreliable historically, but in substance offer nothing relevant to contemporary political and social issues. These currents issue forth in two diametrically opposed attitudes toward Scripture, the one providing biblically based personal comfort for those willing to defer to authoritarian leaders in matters pertaining to the public realm, the other fostering a secularist viewpoint that categorically excludes all religious considerations from the public forum.[1]

We witness the consequence of this split in what has been described by a number of vivid metaphors and contrasts: the battle for the Bible, culture wars, blue states/red states, liberal democracy/republican ideals. Pollsters, the media, and political advisors have treated this bifurcation as a phenomenon akin to the race for a World Series championship. Political outcomes in elections have become vulnerable to the marketing of political extremes that stifle the cultivation of policies worthy of bipartisan support. Even in the primaries leading up to national elections we are made privy to graphs revealing who is leading in filling coffers with unregulated campaign contributions as candidates prepare for the final battle.

Seldom has attention been drawn to the fact that such dumbing down of political strategy is directly related to the dumbing down of civil discourse and the public understanding of the role moral values and religious beliefs should play in determining domestic and international policies. Lazy citizens incapable of, or at least resistant to, coping with complex issues demand and then are intellectually hobbled by unambiguous polarities: the evil guys/the good guys, greedy capitalists/compassionate liberals, patriots/world citizens, advocates of economic growth/guardians of our fragile planet, world trade/buy local.

---

1. For an insightful critique of the inadequacy of the approach taken to the Bible by many contemporary readers, see Harvey Cox, *How to Read the Bible* (New York: HarperCollins Publishers, 2015).

The resulting dualistic construal of the world is implicitly alluring, for it banishes ambiguity and the resulting need for intellectual struggle, the airing of differences, and the careful weighing of complex data, in favor of absolute truths and falsehoods that require partisan loyalty and a hostile division between *us* and *them*. It should come as no surprise that this neo-Manichean *political* mentality is aided and abetted by absolutist *religious* attitudes resulting in a clash of civilizations between feuding ideologies placing their adherents in a mental lockdown so confining as to extinguish the ability to relate to other perspectives.

It is our argument that the cultivation of willingness and skill to deal openmindedly with complicated political issues correlates positively with patience and tenacity in studying the richness and complexity of Scripture. The converse correlation is equally true: The one whose mind is ideologically predisposed to uphold one political position regardless of changing circumstances or new evidence likely is one who holds firmly to an absolutist religious understanding. Caveat lector: The religious right or the so-called neocons do not hold a monopoly on absolutism! Many liberals, while open to arguments of fellow party members, are viscerally opposed to the issues raised by conservatives, Evangelicals, or, God forbid!, fundamentalists!

The above paragraph is a not so subtle argument against the simple Manichean universe of absolute truths, in favor of the more perplexing universe, in which no human possesses an infallible key to unlocking (whether in a scriptural tradition or in a political philosophy) the one truth that trumps all alternatives. But this argument in turn must be safeguarded against a false inference that it implies a moral relativism in which any truth claim is as worthy of adoption as any other truth claim, a position that leads to moral chaos.

We therefore call attention to the importance of what in earlier chapters emerged as the foundation of political reflection at all stages of biblical history, the theocratic principle predicating the existence of two realms: the realm of divine governance, which alone claims the ultimate allegiance of its citizens, and the realm of human governance, whose governing authorities have legitimate claim to no more than the penultimate allegiance of its citizens, and that allegiance only to the extent that its institutions and policies mediate and implement the qualities inherent in the ultimate rule of God.

This distinction between two realms reflects a clear philosophical premise lying at the heart of biblical ontology: While dynamic and ever unfolding in new dimensions and directions, the world is not mired in perpetual confusion and eternal flux. Reality is robustly constructed, governed by laws that maintain cosmic order, and directed by an underlying purposefulness that includes both a beginning (creation) and an ultimate goal (universal *shalom*). That orderliness and purposefulness is not arbitrary but has a source, namely, God's universal sovereignty. God's realm transcends the realm that is inhabited by humans and is marked by limit and imperfection. But within the covenantal relationship God established with creation, God has revealed the divine nature to the faithful and has enabled those who mold their lives after that nature to recognize that life in the human realm can reflect the order and purposefulness of the peaceable kingdom. Indeed, they are called to live in wholehearted dedication to the triumph of peace and justice over conflict and inequality. Political engagement is one of the modes through which they fulfill that calling.

The narratives and laws and prophecies of the Bible thus provide the foundational truth upon which believers build their faith communities and cultivate the perspective by which they are guided in their engagement with political issues. Tested over a long span of history, the Bible has proven to be a trustworthy and in many respects a unique resource. However, only by distorting its intrinsic historical-covenantal character can one take the further step of the inerrantist in ascribing to the Bible timeless infallibility in answering every question raised by today's world.[2] To make the claim to absolute, exclusive, perfect truth erases the distinction between what can be known by God alone and what is within the grasp of humans. Stated philosophically, it entails a fundamental epistemological error; stated theologically, it abets idolatry by confusing divine attributes with qualities within the reach of mortals.

Moving from this philosophical-theological reflection back to the question of methods of interpretation, we formulate the issue at stake as follows: To claim that humans can possess absolute truth on the basis of a Bible that is inerrant in all matters is to engage in a serious categorical confusion, the mind of the creator with the mind of the creature. To move from this confusion to constructing a political theology advanced as God's politics is to confuse two realms whose identities should be kept distinct on the basis of an "infinite qualitative distinction"[3] between God's rule commanding ultimate allegiance and the realm of all human governments, imperfect by nature, and entitled to no more than penultimate allegiance, and that only to the extent that they conform to the justice and mercy constituting God's reign.

The basic point can be related to politics thus: since the categorical distinction between the mind of God and the mind of humans implies that full and perfect incorporation of God's justice and mercy will be accomplished by no human regime, public discourse must avoid absolute truth claims, thereby opening up the public forum to the legitimacy and importance of differing points of view. These remarks anticipate themes that will be treated systematically in our epilogue, but at this point they serve the function of enabling us to proceed to a description of the approach we shall take to the writings of the New Testament.

While reaffirming with earlier generations of the faith community that the authors of the New Testament writings, both in their oral and literary stages,

---

2. Martin Luther and John Calvin used vivid metaphors to stress the genuine human dimension of the Bible, Luther calling the Bible "a worm of a book" compared to the Greek and Latin classics, Calvin referring to Scripture as God's stuttering as evidence of the extent of his reaching down to humans.

3. Here we are extending Kierkegaard's oft-quoted theological formulation to the realm of political theology, in Søren Kierkegaard, *Purity of Heart Is to Will One Thing*, trans. Douglas V. Steere (New York: Harper & Bros., 1938).

were interpreting and adding to an inherited scriptural tradition that bore testimony to God's will and purpose, we at the same time recognize that we have at our disposal linguistic and historical methods that reveal a greater complexity in the composition history of the New Testament than was recognized by premodern readers. This observation does not imply for us a superior perspective for grasping the will and purpose of God found in the Bible.[4] What it does suggest is this: For modern interpreters of the Bible to reject the tools and methods that their scholarly contemporaries utilize as a matter of course in studying other bodies of literature and in reconstructing the history of other ancient cultures would be to contribute to a methodological weakness that would not only discredit their studies in the minds of learned colleagues but also foster a schizoid worldview among those who read their biblical-theological writings in search of religious and political insight.

The application of philological and historical methods to the New Testament will entail both similarities and differences in comparison to the Hebrew Bible. Some of the similarities are these: testimony to God's nature, to God's purpose and will, and to the inferences to be drawn from both for the governance of human communities and nations will be found in writings of human beings, who formulate the truths revealed to them within the concreteness and limitations of their own languages and worldviews. This requires attention to the genres they employ and the nature of the message thereby conveyed. Myths must be distinguished from legends, which in turn must be distinguished from hymns and historiographic works. Appreciation of all such marks of the genuine humanity and historicity of the authors in no way should diminish the wonder with which the person of faith witnesses the purpose and will of a God who has chosen to be known to humans without obliterating the nature of what it means to be human.

Differences in comparison to the Hebrew Bible also are to be recognized. Though Moses and Jesus can be seen to resemble each other in the role they play as founders of Judaism and Christianity, the words purporting to come from these two figures raise different sets of questions. To begin with, whereas the historicity of Moses for centuries has been questioned by some scholars and cannot be proven due to the lack of extrabiblical attestation,[5] the historicity of Jesus is corroborated by extrabiblical sources—most important of which are the works of the Jewish historian Josephus—and is doubted by no serious scholar.

---

4. In the preface to his commentary to Paul's Letter to the Romans, Karl Barth defines his understanding of the relation between the historical confessions of the Christian faith and modern scholarly method with his usual candor: If forced to choose between the two, he would side with the confessions, but he hastens to add that he can draw upon both by placing the best that modern critical method offers in the service of the historical faith (Karl Barth, *The Epistle to the Romans*, trans. E. C. Hoskyns [London: Oxford University Press, 1933], 1–2).

5. The general picture given by biblical tradition of a leader and lawgiver who played an indispensable role in the formation of the Jewish people is historically plausible, though it has been embellished over the centuries with legendary elements. See Paul D. Hanson, *The People Called: The Growth of Community in the Bible* (1986; repr., Louisville, KY: Westminster John Knox Press, 2002), 17–24.

Similarly, the enormous effort that has been expended in seeking to reconstruct the life of Jesus and to sort out the *ipsissima verba* of Jesus from words attributed to him by later tradition has no parallel in scholarship dealing with the five books of Moses. These differences are only to be expected of scholarship focusing on two figures vastly separated from each other in time. Though we could continue in describing other similarities and differences, the above examples suffice and allow us to move on with an approach applying the historical tools used earlier in our study of the Hebrew Bible, adapting them to be sure to the unique properties of the New Testament writings.

The methodological challenges are not ended once one chooses to employ the tools of historical-critical research for reconstructing the politics of Jesus and the early leaders of the Christian movement. For more controversy rages *among* those applying historical-critical methods than between critical scholars and literalists. The situation is analogous to that noted by Eugene Borowitz, in which closer affinities typically exist between liberal Christians and reformed Jews than between reformed and orthodox Jews or between liberal and fundamentalist Christians.[6] In the field of biblical studies, much has been gained through the mollification of traditional divisions. One of the chief gains is the enrichment of scholarship that comes from discourse benefiting from divergent perspectives.

ORGANIZATION OF OUR STUDY OF THE POLITICS OF THE NEW TESTAMENT

Having situated our approach within the field of New Testament studies, we now need to specify more precisely how we intend to organize our study. Preliminarily, we need to acknowledge the implications of our view that the Gospel narratives are not literal records of Jesus' life and sayings, but are interpretative accounts that, while drawing on earlier sources, including collections of authentic Jesus sayings, nonetheless bear the imprint of four distinct theological perspectives. While in fundamental agreement regarding the major events of Jesus' life, the message he proclaimed, and the manner in which he related to the ruling religious and political authorities of his time, their distinct perspectives both complicate and enrich our analysis.

Next, we must factor into our approach the distinction now established among critical scholars between the letters of Paul and the writings penned by disciples in his name. Whereas traditional scholarship treated the entire Pauline corpus as the oeuvre of a single writer, the more recent effort to distinguish between Pauline and post-Pauline letters has made it possible to trace developments in political policy as the church grew from first generation to second and third. The situation is similar in dealing with the enigmatic contribution of the book of Revelation to the political thought of the New Testament. While an

6. Eugene B. Borowitz, *The Masks Jews Wear* (New York: Simon & Schuster, 1973).

earlier generation generally accepted the traditional identification of John of Patmos with the writer of the Gospel of John, we now can discern the way in which scattered, persecuted fledgling churches defended the ancient theocratic principle with a magnificent proclamation of the ultimate triumph of God's sovereignty over every idolatrous imposter.

Having set the coordinates for our study, we can now describe the steps we shall follow in investigating the politics of the New Testament. Already at this point, though, we encounter another scholarly conundrum. While seeking to avoid the excesses that accompany an overly confident reliance on historical-critical methodology, especially when it is combined with blatant cynicism regarding the motives guiding the apostle Paul and the tradents who shaped the four Gospels, we shall continue the approach used in previous chapters by delineating the stages through which the New Testament writings passed before they reached their canonical form.

Critical assessment of the New Testament writings with an eye to questions of sources, editorial shaping, and layers of theological interpretation will be a necessary part of this approach. It will result in the following steps of investigation: (1) Through a careful reading of the Gospels, we shall first delineate what we believe can be identified as the words and acts of the historical Jesus pertaining to the realm of politics, and on that basis seek to describe the strategies he employed in dealing with the religious and political authorities of his time, such as the temple hierarchy, the Pharisees, and the provincial officers of Rome. (2) Then we shall discuss the theo-political principles and policies of Paul as they can be extrapolated from letters attributable to the apostle himself. (3) Finally, we shall follow the theo-political strategies that unfold in the post-Pauline writings, including Hebrews and the book of Revelation, and in the final canonical version of the four Gospels.

Though these three steps do not differ radically from the ones followed by premodern scholars, one significant difference stands out. In our approach, description of the politics of Jesus entails the difficult task of distinguishing between the words and acts of the historical Jesus (chap. 26) and the interpretations of the followers of Jesus who shaped what they received—in light of their Easter and post-Easter experiences—into confessional narratives of the life of the one whom they believed to be the Messiah Deliverer, not only of Israel but of all peoples of the world.[7]

The endeavor to recover what can be known of the Jesus of history is a difficult one, having in the last two centuries produced widely divergent results and no small degree of contention. The reasons why scholarly consensus has eluded and no doubt will continue to elude those engaged in the search are clear. On the one hand, as is the case in dealing with any figure of antiquity, the sources are fragmentary and shaped by the interpretative interventions of

---

7. In the case of Matthew and Luke, the narrative of Jesus' life extends from his nativity through his passion and death and on to his resurrection on the third day. In the case of Mark, it begins with his baptism by John the Baptist and ends with his death and resurrection.

tradents who write from their particular theological, ideological, and political viewpoints. On the other, modern interpreters are equally influenced by agendas of their own, born of what in German hermeneutical scholarship is designated as *Vorverständnis,* prior understanding or perspective. These two obstacles have led some scholars, both in the more distant and recent past, to dismiss the search for the Jesus of history as an endeavor destined to discover less of the historical Jesus than the profile of the modern historian.[8]

Given the vast array of methods and results associated with the search for the historical Jesus, it is necessary to situate our own approach against the background of a brief retrospective.

THE HISTORY OF HISTORICAL JESUS RESEARCH

Throughout the centuries spanning late antiquity, the medieval period, and the Reformation, the narrative of the New Testament Gospels in their received form was deemed a reliable source for the details of the life of Jesus. This sense of confidence in the accuracy of the Gospels was called into question as the result of the rise of the historical-critical method in the eighteenth century.[9] The historical-critical method rests on the assumption growing out of the Enlightenment that the provenance and meaning of documents of the past were to be recovered through the application of tools fashioned by human reason in its search for truth. The writings of the Bible were not exempt from critical scrutiny, inasmuch as the category of supernatural revelation was rejected by an approach insisting that all literature be understood as the creation of human beings within the conditions of human existence and the limits of human understanding.[10]

Not surprisingly, the Jesus that survived the rational scrutiny of the critical historians of the eighteenth and nineteenth centuries was one stripped of

8. The classic formulation of this criticism was aimed at Adolf von Harnack by the controversial Roman Catholic Fr. George Tyrrell: "The Christ that Harnack sees, looking back through nineteen centuries of 'Catholic darkness,' is only the reflection of a Liberal Protestant face, seen at the bottom of a deep well" (*Hard Sayings: A Selection of Sayings and Meditations* [London: Longmans, Green & Co., 1898]).

9. For a more detailed account of the history of the search for the historical Jesus, see Paul D. Hanson, "We Once Knew Him from a Human Point of View," in *Who Is Jesus Christ for Us Today: Pathways to Contemporary Christology,* Michael Welker Festschrift, ed. Andreas Schuele and Günter Thomas (Louisville, KY: Westminster John Knox Press, 2009), 203–18.

10. Exerting considerable influence on the study of the New Testament writings was Troeltsch's insistence that Christianity, like any other religious phenomenon, had to be subjected to scientific historical analysis if it was to be taken seriously by modern thinkers. Excluded from investigation into the historical Jesus were references to transcendence or appeals to categories such as revelation or the doctrinal authority of the church. See Ernst Troeltsch, Der Historismus und seine Probleme (Tübingen: J. C. B. Mohr, 1922). The most emphatic rejection of this notion of "scientific" historiography came from Karl Barth: "We must open our eyes and see this quite particular history: God becomes man, the Word was made flesh, it lived in the midst of men. . . . One must clearly either accept this 'myth' as history itself, and call all the other histories myth, or otherwise refuse the Christian 'myth' and remain with the human notion of history" (Barth, The Faith of the Church [New York: Meridian Books, 1958], 98).

supernatural characteristics, for example, notions of divinity and acts falling under the category of the miraculous. From the pioneering work of Hermann Samuel Reimarus (1694–1768) to David Friedrich Strauss's *Leben Jesu* (1835–36), the portrait of a teacher of lofty ethical values emerged, values resembling the finest of moral reasoning of that time. Most importantly, this was a Jesus who could be esteemed by the modern thinker without sacrifice of the intellect and without embarrassment within university circles. Far from conceiving of their role as that of destroying the essence of Christianity, these German scholars, like their Deist counterparts in Britain, deemed their endeavor essential to preserving the legacy Christianity had to offer to an emerging modern world.

Like so many other parts of the liberal intellectual edifice bequeathed by the Enlightenment, the original quest's detailed construction of the Jesus of history rapidly unraveled within the intellectual ruptures of the fin de siècle. Specifically, in 1909 Albert Schweitzer's study *The Quest of the Historical Jesus*[11] proved to be the coup de grace, by offering a scathing critique of an approach that utterly failed to attend to the historical principle of interpreting a historical figure within his or her original setting, rather than simply dressing that figure in the clothes of the modern interpreter. Far from being the genteel teacher fitting right in with the participants in the seminars and salons of Berlin and Paris, Schweitzer's teacher was a fiery Jewish prophet announcing the imminent end of the world. Rather than going on to integrate the eschatology of Jesus into an interpretation that bore relevance for the modern world, however, Schweitzer dismissed such teaching as irrelevant and proceeded to a tour de force of his own by boiling down the lasting legacy of Jesus to the concept that became the basis of his lifelong dedication to serving humanity, namely, "the fatherhood of God and the brotherhood of Man."

The most influential theological development to grow out of Schweitzer's demolition of the first quest came in the decades between the world wars, from the New Testament scholar Rudolf Bultmann. Though firmly established as a leading authority on the growth of the New Testament traditions, his assessment of the value of seeking to recover the historical Jesus was resoundingly negative. His primary reason was not the difficulty encumbering the quest for the historical Jesus, but rather resided in a theological principle that he believed derived from the heart of the gospel: the eternal meaning of Jesus Christ was grasped solely by faith in the *kerygma* (i.e., the post-Easter church's proclamation of the risen Christ), and any attempt to secure faith on the shaky speculations of historical reconstructions was theologically misguided. Exquisite is the irony that the New Testament scholar most frequently vilified as heretical in conservative evangelical circles shared their attitude toward historical-critical reconstructions as detrimental to faith!

To be sure, the similarity ends there, for in contrast to the evangelical's reliance on a literal reading of the Gospel narratives, Bultmann developed an

---

11. *Von Reimarus zu Wrede: Eine Geschichte der Leben-Jesu-Forschung* (Tübingen: J. C. B. Mohr [Paul Siebeck, 1906]).

existentialist interpretation dependent on the philosopher Martin Heidegger, in summing up the Gospel as the urgent call to humans to decide for or against the authentic life of love and service offered by God in Christ.

Neither the tombstones marking Schweitzer's historiographic onslaught nor Bultmann's theologically based dismissal could repress for long the quest for the historical Jesus. From my term of study in Heidelberg, Germany, in the early 1960s, I still remember vividly the excitement with which students were reading Günther Bornkamm's *Jesus of Nazareth,* the first fully developed contribution to a stage of historical Jesus studies that has been called "the second quest," written, ironically, by one of Bultmann's star students![12] Bornkamm's study incorporated the methodological approach to the writings of the New Testament that had been developed by his teacher, resulting in a reconstruction of Jesus' life that was less ideologically driven and more textually based than its predecessors. Moreover, the growth of tradition from early sources to the final shape of the Gospel narratives was seen more in terms of crystallization of sayings and episodes tracing back to Jesus and continuity of theological interpretation from the eschatological teaching of Jesus himself to the resurrection faith of the post-Easter church than of distortion by disciples of their master's earlier simple ethical message. Continuity is also stressed by another of Bultmann's star students, Helmut Koester, who finds in "Jesus' celebration of common meals in anticipation of the 'messianic banquet' and the story of his suffering and death" the roots of the early church's eschatology.[13]

The impetus for the most recent chapter in the history of Jesus research, the "third quest," derives from the Jesus Seminar, organized in 1985 by the New Testament scholars Robert Funk and John Dominic Crossan. The Jesus Seminar has sought, through the application of historical methods, to identify the authentic sayings of and stories about Jesus both in the canonical Gospels and in noncanonical writings like the *Gospel of Thomas.* Its operating premise is essentially the same as that of the original quest that grew out of the rationalism of the Enlightenment; all supernatural elements, such as miracles and attributions of divinity to Jesus, a priori must be attributed to later tradition. What emerges as the corpus of authentic Jesus sayings are ethical teachings (the similarity to Reimarus and Strauss is striking), to which some of the leading protagonists of the third quest add a degree of specificity from the realm of comparative religion: Jesus is a teacher in the style of the Cynic philosophers.

It would be misleading to imply, however, that unanimity has emerged from the research of the third quest. No doubt, Albert Schweitzer's penetrating eye would once again detect a striking resemblance between the individual quester's

---

12. Credit for setting "the second quest" in motion is generally attributed to Ernst Käsemann, who in a 1953 address to a gathering of Bultmann former students set forth the challenge to reexamine the issue of the historical Jesus in light of recent studies on the growth of New Testament tradition and on the basis of a specific authentication criteriology.

13. Helmut Koester, "The Memory of Jesus' Death and the Worship of the Risen Lord," *Harvard Theological Review* 91, no. 4 (1998): 335–50.

Jesus and his or her own worldview and social agenda. Peasant itinerant, Cynic teacher, folk revolutionary are all possible products of the inventive mind beginning with a catalogue of disconnected sayings, lacking historical setting and narrative context, and thereby requiring an outside interpretive model to bring them into a comprehensible pattern of meaning.

For the student of the New Testament who finds the above method to recover the authentic words of Jesus arbitrary and the a priori exclusion of an eschatological dimension to Jesus' teaching reductionary and theologically impoverished, two alternative approaches are available: (1) whether in accord with the literalist position of conservative evangelicals and fundamentalists or the existentialist position of Bultmann, the entire search for the historical Jesus can be dismissed as misdirected, or (2) one can describe and then pursue what is believed to be a more promising avenue for learning what can be known about the historical figure, Jesus of Nazareth. The latter option is our choice for the following reasons: (a) Differing from those who dismiss the legitimacy of the search for what can be known about the historical Jesus, we believe—without naively claiming that certainty is within reach—that a plausible picture of the historical Jesus can be drawn on the basis of a historically valid methodology. (b) Given the objective of our study, namely, to describe the political models and strategies found in the Bible at all stages, it is indefensible to ignore the fact that Jesus was a historical figure who lived in a specific time and political setting, and rather mandatory to seek to learn what the available sources can contribute to our understanding of his politics. (c) Given our understanding of the theology of the Bible in terms of the dynamic growth of understanding occurring within the concreteness and thickness of history, it is of key importance to inquire into the stage in that dynamic process that represents the foundation of the Christian understanding of the world and specifically of the relation of faith to the political, economic, and social realities of human civilization. That stage is recovered by rigorous research into the life of Jesus of Nazareth.

THE METHODOLOGY USED IN THIS STUDY FOR UNDERSTANDING THE POLITICS OF THE HISTORICAL JESUS

The approach we take to the historical Jesus is indebted to the studies of Albert Schweitzer, Günter Bornkamm, Norman Perrin, Helmut Koester, and John Meier. It is in fundamental disagreement with the rationalist reductionism of the first quest represented by Reimarus and Strauss and with the methods of the heirs to that legacy constituting the leadership of the Jesus Seminar.

The parameters within which we shall conduct our investigation in chapters 26–30 are these: (1) We begin with the assumption that by application of a set of criteria developed by Bornkamm, Perrin, and Meier it is possible to distinguish, with a reasonable degree of confidence, between the sayings and acts of the historical Jesus and the interpretive additions of Jesus' followers in the post-Easter period.[14] (2) Eschatological themes revolving around God's promises to restore Israel and, through the agency of his anointed one (Messiah), to restore the long-awaited peace, justice, and mercy of God's universal reign are essential parts of the teachings and practices of Jesus and can be torn from the repository of authentic Jesus traditions only through the imposition of models or criteria alien both to the ancient Jewish/Roman world in which he lived and to a theological understanding that is sensitive to the biblical texts themselves. (3) A line of continuity can be followed from the teachings and acts of the historical Jesus to the letters of Paul, the post-Pauline writings, and the theological interpretations that came to expression in the narratives of each of the Gospel writers. Continuity, to be sure, is to be distinguished from stenographic transmission, for the distinctive contributions of successive generations involved more than editorial rearranging or even redactional reshaping of received material.[15] When, for example, one contrasts the theme in Mark's Gospel of Jesus' admonishing the disciples to keep to themselves the messianic significance of his actions with Jesus' command to the Gerasene in Luke, "Return to your home, and declare how much God has done for you" (Luke 8:39), it is not difficult to recognize the distinct theological perspectives that are shaping the narratives of those two Gospel writers. This having been said, it is even more important to be aware of the fundamental difference between recognizing a growth of tradition from Jesus' acts and teachings to the letters and Gospel narratives shaped by the early apostles and attributing, in the manner of scholars like Funk and Crossan, later layers of tradition to leaders of the early church who twisted the purportedly simple ethical teachings of the peasant teacher Jesus into a drama of supernatural intervention by a divine savior that served the aim of establishing authority over an institution aspiring to universal influence and power. Luke Timothy Johnson is correct in rejecting such cynical interpretations as warranted neither by the biblical texts themselves nor by the specific environment out of which they arose.[16]

We shall turn to the biblical texts in due course. But first it will be helpful to point out how the reduction of the historical Jesus to a teacher in the style of wandering Cynic philosophers grows out of a failure to understand the specific environment within which he lived and carried out his ministry.

In turning to the Greco-Roman world for the ideal type with which to describe Jesus, critics have diverted attention away from the primary religiocultural environment of which he was a part. Not only was Jesus born of Jewish parents, but his education was in the Jewish tradition. In his teachings he drew

---

14. Ben F. Meyer prefers to speak of indices rather than criteria in *The Aims of Jesus* (Eugene, OR: Wipf & Stock, 2002), 86–87.

15. See Helmut Koester, *Paul and His World* (Minneapolis: Fortress Press, 2007), 105–17, and Norman Perrin, *Jesus and the Language of the Kingdom: Symbol and Metaphor in New Testament Interpretation* (Philadelphia: Fortress Press, 1976), passim.

16. Luke Timothy Johnson, *The Real Jesus: The Misguided Quest for the Historical Jesus and the Truth of the Traditional Gospels* (San Francisco: Harper Collins, 1996).

on the law and the prophets and the hymns of ancient Israel, not on the philosophical dialogues and dramas of the ancient Greeks.

For this reason, the path leading to a proper understanding of Jesus' politics is the long path that we have taken in part 2, chapters 9–24. There we came to recognize political models (charismatic rule, monarchy, prophecy, religious commonwealth, wisdom, apocalypticism) with which he was acquainted and ideal types (expounder of Mosaic law, king, prophet, seer) against the background of which he could understand his own calling. In Jewish Scripture he encountered both the will of his heavenly Father, to which he submitted in obedience, and a universal divine purpose, which alone provided the overarching framework within which he could grasp the significance of the events of his own life and world around him.

Recognizing the native environment within which Jesus was raised and in which he labored does not exclude the importance of taking notice of influences from the wider world we designate with the terms "Greco-Roman" and "Hellenistic." Indeed, as we have seen in previous chapters, the religion of Israel from the very earliest period was enriched through contact with neighboring cultures, leading, for example, in the Second Temple period to writings like Ecclesiastes, Esther, Judith, and 2 Maccabees. But to assume that the essential nature of the culture that formed the thought world of Jesus was Greco-Roman is to overlook the central stream of belief and values that formed the heart of the Jewish faith at the fin de siècle and that clearly distinguished it from pagan religions and practices.

An equally indispensable segment of the path one must tread to grasp the environment of which the historical Jesus was a part is the one we followed in the previous chapter. Jesus was a citizen of a Jewish nation that was occupied by a foreign world power and administered by religious and political figures who were either indigenous and owing their careers to the Romans or Roman officers sent to the eastern provinces to maintain order over restive populations. Whether Jesus ever encountered a wandering Cynic philosopher remains in the realm of speculation (a vacuous realm rife with interpretive possibilities!). That Jesus encountered members of parties and movements representing the political alternatives available to his compatriots in dealing with the occupying force is undeniable (a fact placing strict limits on interpretive possibilities!).

In describing the environment of the Jewish people in the period between Pompey's conquest in 63 BCE and the two major Jewish revolts, we established the essential cultural-political framework within which to situate our study of the Jesus traditions of the New Testament.[17] Of necessity, we will have to ask how Jesus related to groups exercising the diverse strategies of collaboration, accommodation, and resistance.

---

17. Ben Meyer offers a one-sentence indictment of previous scholars for their neglect of Jesus' historical and cultural background: "They accordingly tended to overlook the larger history which Jesus himself inherited and in which he lived and moved, each presenting only so much 'background' as was necessary to make his idea of Jesus intelligible" (Meyer, *Aims,* 19).

Chapter 26

The Politics of Jesus

IN SEARCH OF THE HISTORICAL JESUS AND HIS POLITICS

We believe that the approach holding the greatest promise of recovering what can be known about the Jesus of history and his politics involves three dimensions, *background, context,* and *text,* which is to say: (1) a clear understanding of the religious/cultural tradition within which he was raised, (2) an awareness of the historical/political/religious context within which he lived, (3) a method of studying the narratives about Jesus and the words ascribed to him capable of revealing the central themes of his proclamation and the political significance of his actions.

Each of these dimensions of inquiry requires reconstruction from less than complete or unambiguous evidence. The resulting picture of Jesus and his politics must be judged on the basis of its plausibility over against other reconstructions.

In the previous chapter we laid the foundation for the task we now undertake, namely, to ascertain all that we can about the politics of the historical figure Jesus of Nazareth. Our questions will be sharply focused: Is the primary *background* against which to understand the acts and words of Jesus the Hellenistic world or the world of ancient Israel? To what extent is knowledge of the historical/political *context* of the Jewish homeland under the Romans, in which one finds competing political strategies regarding the appropriate response to the foreign occupation, necessary for understanding the life of Jesus? Finally, as we turn to detailed scrutiny of the New Testament *texts* themselves, can we recover a cogent portrait of the message and activity of Jesus and a satisfactory understanding of the relation between the words and acts attributable to him and the reshaping of those words and acts by his disciples that culminated in the four Gospels? To these three questions we now turn.

BACKGROUND

In beginning with the religiocultural tradition that constitutes the background for our inquiry into the life of Jesus, it will be helpful to compare the nature of the sources available for the study of the life of Jesus with those constituting the corpus probed by Pauline scholars. In the case of Paul, scholars have the benefit of at least six New Testament epistles written by the apostle himself, plus letters written in his name that apply Pauline themes to new settings, and finally narratives in the book of Acts that interlard historical details with themes characteristic of aretalogies. Specifically with regard to the religious tradition within which Paul was educated, Acts 22:3 contributes the valuable detail that Gamaliel, the highly regarded Pharisee and grandson of the venerable Hillel the Elder, was his teacher, a pedigree of which the apostle was justifiably proud.

In contrast, the instruction Jesus received in the religious traditions of his ancestors is illuminated only indirectly, on the one hand by legendary narratives (Luke 2:41–52; Mark 1:21–22; Matt. 7:28) and on the other by inferences drawn from the fact that the words attributable to him in the Gospels are saturated with allusions to and quotations from Hebrew Scripture. Additionally, many of the speech forms, narrative themes, and methods of scriptural interpretation that give shape to the teachings of Jesus in the Gospels are also familiar to us from rabbinical tradition. The significance of these affinities will not be lost when, in the next section, which focuses on the *context* of Jesus' life and mission, we draw inferences regarding his relation to the Jewish parties of his time. While the above mentioned sources are rich and often alluring (as the broad array of Jesus portraits in both scholarly and popular literature attests), our reconstruction of the message and activity of the Jesus of history necessarily will involve extrapolation from softer evidence than is available for Paul of Tarsus.

Two options present themselves to the one who would choose to move beyond the fragments of evidence provided by the sources to a reasonably intelligible picture of Jesus' religious and cultural background. One either moves outside of Jewish culture to find an *ideal type* on the basis of which to fit the disconnected pieces into a comprehensible pattern (such as *peripatetic teacher* or *itinerant miracle worker*), or one identifies within Judaism a *prototype* whose characteristics accord with what critical study of the relevant texts discloses about the historical Jesus. We follow the latter strategy, for not only does it seem inherently sensible to privilege Jesus' native heritage in that search; it is of even greater significance that the search for the historical Jesus reaches a significantly higher level of credibility through the discovery that a specific prototype indigenous to biblical tradition provides an exceptional match with what can be recovered from the sources about Jesus of Nazareth, namely, the prophetic figure of the *Servant of God*. While it is significant that the leaders of the post-Easter church found in the figure of the Servant a key to understanding the relation of Jesus to God the Father, our detailed examination of texts in the following section of this chapter will present evidence that Jesus himself recognized in prophets like Elijah, Jeremiah, and the Servant of Isaiah 40–55 a pattern and design that illuminated the events of his own life.

As in the lives of those biblical figures, his faithfulness to God and compassion for others evoked scorn and abuse, rather than understanding and acclaim, from many of his contemporaries. Yet even in the face of dreadful suffering, he held steadfast to his conviction that in the events of his life God was at work for the redemption of Israel.[1]

Not only can we best understand Jesus' vocation in light of the biblical figure of the Servant; it is also in relation to that figure that we open a window on the meaning of metaphors, topoi, and themes found in the Gospels that are rooted in his ancestral faith. The metaphor that most poignantly captures his understanding of that faith is the kingdom of God. Stemming from Hebrew Scripture and elaborated on in Jewish apocalyptic writings and in the preaching of John the Baptist, it rose to preeminence in Jesus' proclamation. The story of Jesus' life in all four Gospels manifests a central aim, an aim that confidently can be attributed to Jesus himself, namely, restoration of the universal harmony intended by God from the beginning, involving both a renewal of creation and the redemption of sinful humanity.[2]

Central to Jesus' understanding of the kingdom of God and underlying everything he said and did was belief that in its totality the world was the creation of his heavenly Father. Yet his vision of the present age was a tragic vision. Intended to be a world that embodied God's justice and mercy, in which all its living beings dwelt in harmony, the present world was scarred by cruelty, sickness, and inequality, for creatures had turned against their creator. Because the rupture was relational rather than metaphysical, the only avenue that could lead to healing was repentance, for repentance opened the door to reconciliation of

---

1. See Helmut Koester, *Paul and His World* (Minneapolis: Fortress Press, 2007), 93–117, for a detailed analysis of the crucial importance of the biblical image of the Suffering Servant in the early church's efforts to understand the life of their Lord. While Koester is very cautious in seeking to peer behind the applications of the Servant to Jesus in the various layers of the Gospels, he avers that the description of the Servant in Isaiah 52:13–53:12 played an important role in Jesus' understanding of his own life and mission (oral communication).

2. The indivisibility of creation and redemption in Hebrew Scripture has been described poignantly and in detail by Terence E. Fretheim, *God and World in the Old Testament: A Relational Theology of Creation* (Nashville: Abingdon Press, 2005).

estranged children with a forgiving Father. Central to Jesus' teaching was thus a robust reaffirmation of the classic theocratic principle of Hebrew Scripture: turn back to God, submit to God's sovereignty, become a covenant partner in the redemptive process, beginning with the individual and radiating outward until Israel and all nations are united as members of God's kingdom.[3]

The kingdom theme is announced in the first recorded public words of Jesus: "The time is fulfilled, and the kingdom of God has come near; repent, and believe in the good news" (Mark 1:15). In response to John the Baptist's inquiry from prison as to whether he was "the one to come," Jesus replied, "Go and tell John what you hear and see: the blind receive their sight, the lame walk, the lepers are cleansed, the deaf hear, the dead are raised, and the poor have good news brought to them. And blessed is anyone who takes no offense at me" (Matt. 11:4–6).

The significance of such deeds goes beyond indication that a skilled physician had appeared in Galilee. In a world in which both physical impairments and poverty were regarded as tangible evidence of bondage to powers beyond normal human control, Jesus' healing acts were interpreted as signs of the dawning of a new liberating order, and his followers were beginning to identify him with "the one to come," that is, the long-awaited redeemer of Israel. What Jesus and those in his circle of disciples were experiencing was accordingly something other than the noteworthy accomplishments of a solitary magician or miracle worker (types familiar to the Galilean countryside); they were witnessing in the lives of ordinary people signs that the centuries-long promise preserved by Israel's prophets was being fulfilled. The world was being healed, one cripple, one indigent, one prisoner at a time (Isa. 2:2–4; 42:1–9; 61:1–4; Jer. 33:14–16; Ezek. 34:11–24). But even amid such hopeful signs, Jesus' tragic vision persisted: "Blessed is anyone who takes no offense at me"—words anticipating the bitter resistance that the agents of God's healing order would encounter. The same sense of sober realism comes to expression in enigmatic words immediately following Jesus' answer to John the Baptist's emissaries, "From the days of John the Baptist until now the kingdom of heaven has suffered violence, and the violent take it by force" (Matt. 11:12).

In spite of Jesus' clear-headed realization that God's reign would be resisted and his own service would entail suffering, his ultimate trust in the triumph of righteousness burst forth in an exuberant moment of rejoicing upon the return of his disciples, with their report that the healing effects of God's kingdom were reaching out to villages throughout Galilee. "I watched Satan fall from heaven like a flash of lightning," Jesus exclaimed (Luke 10:18).

When we turn to examine texts that we regard to be reliable sources for the teachings and acts of Jesus, we shall fill in the picture of the obedient Servant

---

3. While it is clear that in the first instance Jesus viewed his calling in relation to the children of Israel, the eschatological framework that he shared with the Hebrew prophets envisioned as the final goal of God's purpose the inclusion of all nations in the reign of justice, peace, and shared prosperity.

from Nazareth whose aims and yearnings were directed by a sense of the world-transforming power that was reshaping the lives of those around him. Here we simply add one further observation. Our identification of the prototype of the Servant found in Hebrew prophecy as most suitable for illuminating the life of Jesus and our specification of the metaphor of the kingdom as best capturing the heart of his message and mission actually converge in producing a unified picture. For it was in the figure of the faithful and often suffering Servant of the Lord, cultivated and embodied by the prophets, that the central hope of the restoration of Israel within God's reign of justice and mercy came to fullest expression.[4]

Viewing Jesus against the background of the biblical figure of Servant and the tradition of the kingdom of God brings into sharp focus an important biblical topos, for Jesus understood that he had been sent to restore the *covenant* into which God had called the children of Abraham. The ancient church custom of naming the two parts of the Bible the Old and New Testaments (i.e., "covenants"), while laboring under the weight of an implied supersession of the former by the latter, does point to the source of the unity of Christian Scripture in covenant.[5] Though the concept of covenant cannot encompass all of the themes and traditions found in the Bible, it does draw attention to the fact that the drama unfolding over the course of biblical history is a drama occurring within the context of the covenantal relationship between God and the community responding to God's call. That drama began with God's creation of a *good* world and God's response to the threat to that creation posed by human wickedness by calling forth a people to provide testimony to divine righteousness and compassion as the sole source of human hope.

What defines the drama as tragedy is the stark fact that the very people commissioned to be an example and a source of blessing to all nations joined in the rebellion against its Maker. God did not abandon the world, but continued the struggle for the hearts of that rebellious people and for the redemption of the world by designating faithful servants who accepted suffering and death as the cost of discipleship. We believe that Jesus understood his life as one growing out of and continuing the vocation of those called to suffer in the service of the God who would not abandon his creation to chaos, but in the proper time would accomplish what was intended from the beginning, a creation healed of all brokenness and unified in universal justice and loving-kindness within the safety of a restored covenant.

---

4. Cf. Luke 11:49–51. For an excellent study of the tradition of the suffering prophet, see Odil Hannes Steck, *Israel und das gewaltsame Geschick der Propheten: Untersuchungen zur Überlieferung des deuteronomistischen Geschichtsbildes im Alten Testament, Spätjudentum und Urchristentum*, WMANT 23 (Neukirchen-Vluyn: Neukirchener Verlag, 1987).

5. Preferable are the designations "First Testament" and "Second Testament." Many biblical scholars have adopted the term "Hebrew Scripture" for the former, in which case the latter is designated "Christian Scripture" and is seen to encompass both sections of the Bible in the versions canonized within different parts the church.

In proposing that a prototype, a central metaphor, and an ancient topos, all deriving from Hebrew Scripture, can help us recover a cogent picture of the historical Jesus, we are clearly reaching beyond the canons of historical positivism, especially regarding the positivist's insistence on an *objective, scientific criteriology* purporting to draw a clear line between the *authentic* and the *spurious*. For we believe that in ancient scriptural traditions the line between origins and the history of the interpretation of origins is porous, marked more often by continuity than by ruptures. Fortunately we are in good company in rejecting the minimalism of positivism, for historians ever since the classical studies of R. G. Collingwood in the middle of the last century have cultivated methodologies that recognize the unique blend of art and science that is essential to meaningful historical reconstruction.[6]

In more recent years the decline of positivism, abetted by its hardening into an imperious form of historical-critical method in biblical studies, has led to a pendulum swing among some scholars in the opposite direction. Under labels such as "new literary criticism," "reader-response criticism," and "postmodernism," the argument is made that historical questions are irrelevant to the study of biblical texts and that such texts should be approached strictly as literature. While such an approach is perfectly suitable for scholars choosing to limit the study of the Bible to its literary and aesthetic qualities, for those seeking to understand the politics, religion, and theology of the Bible, the exclusion of the historical dimension is ill fated.[7] Fortunately, a more promising path is available, one that involves a search for the historical setting and original meaning of the biblical texts, chastened by sober recognition that those texts offer the historian incomplete evidence, evidence that has been refracted through the interpretative lens of its witnesses and thus must be interpreted with caution.

Having described the first dimension of our approach to the study of the politics of Jesus, namely, an adequate understanding of his religious and cultural background, we move to the second dimension, the historical/political/religious context of his life work.

CONTEXT: GALILEE AND JUDEA UNDER THE ROMANS

In chapter 24 we described in broad terms the difficult circumstances in which the Jews living within their ancestral homeland found themselves during the Roman period, a period beginning with Pompey's invasion in 63 BCE. For their first six decades the Romans authorized limited native rule under the dynasty of the loyal vassal Herod. The last vestige of Judean political autonomy was lost in 6 CE, when Herod Archelaus, son of Herod the Great, was removed

6. R. G. Collingwood, *The Idea of History* (Oxford: Clarendon Press, 1946).
7. In German scholarship the dynamic of a history of interpretation that lives from and amplifies the originating experience is called *Wirkungsgeschichte,* and the consciousness of the interpreter is called w*irkungsgeschichtliches Bewusstsein.*

from power due to his incompetence in enforcing order upon a restive Jewish population. Judea was placed under the direct rule of the Romans. Galilee, on the other hand, which was the setting for most of Jesus' public career, remained under Herodian rule for another three decades, with another of Herod's sons, Antipas, managing to maintain a delicate and often precarious balance between demonstrating his political loyalty to the Romans and his religious piety to his Jewish subjects.[8]

As we turn to a more specific focus on the situation within the Jewish homeland during the time of Jesus' short public career—which lasted approximately two years and ended with his death circa 30 CE—it is important to recognize the contrast between political conditions in Galilee and those in Judea, for only then can we explain the sharp difference between the relative tranquility that seems to have characterized his Galilean ministry and the religious and political conflicts with political and religious authorities in Jerusalem that marked the tumultuous days culminating in his execution.

The Gospel narratives suggest that the Galilean countryside was populated largely by a peasant class consisting of small landowners and tenant farmers, as well as marginalized classes such as day laborers and vagrants. The parables told by Jesus reflect a similar demography. The overweening challenge faced by a population living on the edge of destitution was that of providing sufficient daily sustenance for themselves and their dependents so as to avert the ever-present threat of debt slavery.[9] Politically what this economics of subsistence produced was a largely compliant population, due not to an ideologically based policy of cooperation with the Romans, but to the all-consuming burdens of daily life.

It is therefore no accident that when insurrections occurred in the north, they were confined to cities like Sepphoris, Tiberias, and Gischala, where Hellenistic and Roman influences and international mercantile connections had resulted in an affluent, educated class capable of plotting and occasionally engaging in religiously and ideologically motivated resistance.[10] The Gospel narratives and the sayings of Jesus that they preserve reflect in the first instance relationships between Jesus and the lower ranks of the society. Though the Gospel narratives mention a few propertied benefactors like Mary and Martha who provided Jesus'

8. The relative tranquility that Antipas was able to preserve as tetrarch of Galilee and Perea over his long term of office (4 BCE–39 CE) bespeaks considerable talent as a ruler. The major conditions placed on local dynasts by the Romans were maintenance of peace in their domain and a steady flow of revenue in the form of taxes and annual tribute. These conditions he obviously met. Additionally, however, any indication of insubordination was swiftly punished, which Antipas learned to his regret when his request for promotion to kingship from Emperor Caligula led to banishment in 39 CE. The other side of maintaining peace of course concerned the local population, in relation to which he seemed to enjoy more respect than had his brother Archelaus in Judea, by safeguarding the freedom of worship and displaying his own Jewish piety through pilgrimages to Jerusalem for major festivals. In this way he managed to confine dissent to the more extreme fringes of the Galilean population.

9. "Give us *today* our daily bread" was not a perfunctory request!

10. Seth Schwartz, *Imperialism and Jewish Society, 200 B.C.E to 600 C.E.* (Princeton, NJ: Princeton University Press, 2001), 129–61.

itinerant ministry with occasional support, the vast majority of those drawn to Jesus were from the lower ranks of society, ranging from commoners managing to live just above the poverty level to those resorting to begging or pilfering as a means of procuring daily bread. The precarious line between those two groups was drawn by taxation and the arbitrary forces of nature that could bankrupt a peasant farmer in a single season. It is not surprising that the needs such common folk brought to Jesus often involved mental and physical ailments that are the by-products of their poverty and deep yearnings for the simple necessities of life, like food for their languishing bodies and shelter for their struggling families. Strategizing for the overthrow of the Roman occupation found scant room in lives revolving around the daily ordeal of making it through to tomorrow.[11]

Such was life in Galilee during Jesus' days of traveling from village to village, preaching to the crowds that gathered around him, and feeding and healing those whose hands reached out to him for help in the midst of misery from which they saw no escape apart from a radical reordering of political and economic structures.

Jesus gained a wide following among the poor, due to his message that the God who intended no individual to live in poverty and brokenness of body or soul had delegated him to proclaim and initiate the alternative order for which they yearned. At the top of his guest list were those who sought what Jesus came to deliver, bread for the hungry, release to those in bondage, and comfort for those living in sorrow. The bonding experienced between Jesus, his plainspoken disciples, and the tenacious crowds that followed him defined in an earthy way the characteristics of the kingdom of God. Sadly, though, not all accepted the invitation, including those whose earthly possessions benumbed awareness that the pearl of great price was not of this world of material pleasure and false security, but was the gift of God to the merciful and the pure of heart.

When we turn to the second region serving as the context for part of Jesus' life, namely, Judea, we find political circumstances that were generally more volatile than those found in Galilee. We have already noted that the Romans found it necessary to establish direct rule over Judea already in 6 CE, while allowing Galilee to be ruled for several more decades by Herod Antipas. In the period 26–36 CE the Roman prefect in charge of the province of Judea was Pontius Pilate, a figure legendary for his mercurial temperament and harsh style of rule. As reflected in his choice of Caesarea Maritima as his residence and administrative center, he elected to remain aloof from the daily affairs of his Jewish subjects and showed no interest in understanding their traditions, customs, and aspirations. His trips to Jerusalem on religious holidays like Passover were not motivated by respect for the Jewish way of life, but by fear that tensions created by the arrival of huge throngs of pilgrims might break out in violence,

11. As suggested in chapter 25, hypotheses arguing for broad-based peasant uprisings by the Galileans against the Roman occupation lack the support of either contemporary historical sources or the New Testament. See Sean Freyne, *Galilee from Alexander the Great to Hadrian 323 BCE to 135 CE* (Wilmington, DE: Michael Glazier, 1980).

and that such violence, if escalating into widespread bloodshed, could taint his professional image in the eyes of the emperor.

It would be an oversimplification to ascribe the ruthlessness with which Pilate repressed anti-Roman demonstrations to his cruel mentality alone. Political unrest was endemic among the Jewish inhabitants of Judea and had plagued native and foreign leaders alike ever since the beginning of the Roman occupation in 63 BCE, a phenomenon perhaps inevitable, given the centrality of its symbols and institutions in the history of the Jewish nation. Not only did the national Epic enshrine the tradition of God's election of Israel to be a free people governed by its native leaders; its sacred traditions had transformed the nostalgia of a golden age under David and Solomon into an eschatological vision of a future messiah (anointed one) who would restore the liberty of the Jewish nation and usher in an age of unprecedented peace and prosperity. Celebrated by historians and psalmists alike were brave warriors of the distant and more recent past: Gideon, David, Hezekiah, and Judas Maccabeus. The gaps in the official history of persecution by pagan conquerors and vindication by divinely ordained deliverers were filled in with legends of women of courage like Judith and Esther who carried on the tradition of Deborah and Jael.

In chapter 24 we drew attention to *Psalm of Solomon* 17 as evidence of the fervent longing that existed, in the wake of Pompey's invasion, for a messianic deliverer of the house of David. Alongside such longing were to be found the noneschatological, shrewdly calculating positions of the Herodians and temple Sadducees. The net result was that the Romans could depend on no single party as representing the Jewish nation, but were forced to choose from the contentious rivals—all of which were looking after their self-interests—the one that best aligned with the imperial policies of Rome.

Abetting the tenuousness of Pilate's grip on the volatile Judean population was the anemic nature of his power base: The only military asset under his direct command was a modest retinue of local recruits, meaning that any major crisis requiring intervention at the level of legionary force placed Pilate at the mercy of the Syrian legate to whom he reported, Lucius Vitellius. This humiliating state of dependence pertained to matters of local administration as well, as demonstrated by the fact that the Jerusalem high priest who presided during Jesus' public ministry, Caiaphas, was an appointee not of Pilate but of the living symbol of Pilate's lack of autonomy, Vitellius!

There is always a danger in historical reconstruction of achieving clarity by oversimplifying complex situations, a tendency common among scholars who portray the Romans as the embodiment of unalloyed evil and then indiscriminately group together as revolutionaries the followers of John the Baptist, Jesus of Nazareth, and the self-appointed Jewish messiahs who from time to time trumpeted the imminence of the final battle for Jerusalem. Though recognition of the volatility of the political situation in Judea helps us understand the events leading to Jesus' execution during Passover 30 CE, it must lead neither to an overly idyllic picture of Galilee, where instances of resistance to Roman rule were not unknown, nor to an overly negative picture of the way the Romans applied their imperial power in Judea.

In dealing with the native populations of the eastern Mediterranean, the Romans viewed themselves as a civilizing agency in a barbarous world. Far from being a province governed without political and judicial institutions, Judea was administered on the basis of civil structures tracing back to the Greek city-states and refined by Roman leaders who looked upon themselves as the descendants of Aeneas. In relation to earlier periods in Jewish history, especially as regards political arrangements between the occupying power and the local officialdom, life under the Romans at its best resembled life under the Persians during the era of Ezra and Nehemiah.

While matters of international policy and taxation were controlled by the Romans, in part through the deputation of local authorities for carrying out specific tasks involving the local population (e.g., temple personnel under the oversight of the high priest were responsible for the collection of the revenue owed to Rome), matters pertaining to native religious practices and local customs were left to the Jewish leaders themselves, as were the courts of law, with the exception of cases involving crimes liable to capital punishment.[12]

The importance of maintaining an accurate picture of Roman rule will become apparent when we come to interpret specific texts, such as the classic formulation of "render unto Caesar," attributed to Jesus, and the apostle Paul's admonition for respect of the governing authorities in Romans 13. Richard Horsley—whose contributions to our understanding of the Roman background of the Gospels are formidable—at times sets up dichotomies that obscure the complexity of the political landscape of Judea during Roman times. Oversimplification is often magnified by the admiring students of influential scholars like Horsley: "Horsley urges the reader to see the analogy between the Roman Empire, against which Jesus and Paul struggled, and the American empire in which contemporary American readers of the Bible live," reports Max Myers.[13] Here an overly generalized historical analysis leads both to a blurring of the differences in strategy adopted by Jesus, his immediate disciples, and subsequent generations of the church and to an insufficiently nuanced treatment of the bearing of biblical politics on contemporary realities. The consequence can be unfortunate, namely, that the potential contribution of biblical theology to political reflection in our own time will be lost to those concluding that biblical scholars lack the historiographic rigor required of those seeking to relate ancient history to contemporary realities.

12. The involvement of the high priest Caiaphas in the trial of Jesus before Pontius Pilate, if historically accurate, would be an anomaly.

13. Max A. Myers, "Hermeneutics in the American Empire: Toward an Anti-Imperialist Theology," in *The Bible in the Public Square: Reading the Signs of the Times*, ed. Cynthia Briggs Kittredge, Ellen Bradshaw Aitken, and Jonathan A. Draper (Minneapolis: Fortress Press, 2008), 95.

CONTEXT: JESUS IN RELATION
TO THE JEWISH PARTIES OF HIS TIME

In moving beyond a general description of the context of Jesus' public career, it is important to investigate the relation between Jesus' political position and those of the main Jewish groups and parties of his time.

In terms of political influence, it is clear that the high priest and members of the Jerusalem aristocracy, including religiously lenient Sadducees, were preeminent. Their privileged positions were maintained on the basis of demonstrated loyalty to the Romans, combined with concerted efforts to maintain law and order within the indigenous population, a dual portfolio filled with internal tensions. Matters were complicated by the fact that political preeminence did not coincide with religious popularity within the Jewish population, for the party favored by the general populace was that of the Pharisees, a group comprised of lay leaders dedicated to an ancestral covenant that tolerated no rivals to the one God of Israel and that enjoined uncompromising adherence to the Torah of Moses.

Conspicuously dissimilar to the latitudinarian strategy of the Herodians and the collaborating wing of the Sadducees, the resolute position of the Pharisees repeatedly had incurred the wrath of both local leaders and occupying forces, from Hasmonean times down to the period of the Jewish revolts. Finally, stirring up the situation through unmitigated belligerence against both the Romans and their own Jewish leaders were insurgent groups whose messianic overtures awakened longing for the liberation of the Jewish homeland from the foreign occupiers.

The majority of the Jews of Judea and Galilee during the Roman period, however, were formally affiliated with none of the parties vying to represent the Jewish people. Most of those who were drawn to Jesus' teachings came from that nonpartisan majority. Nevertheless, in the course of his travels, Jesus found himself confronted with the political positions of the Herodians, the high priest and other temple personnel, the Pharisees, the Sadducees, and even individuals influenced by more revolutionary ideologies.[14] By sifting through the words and actions attributable to Jesus, we find evidence pointing to his own political attitudes and the way they related to the political strategies of other Jewish teachers and leaders. We turn now to a general description of Jesus' relations to the Jewish groups that shared with him this tragic time in history, postponing until later a more detailed examination of those relations on the basis of specific texts.

Jesus' attitude toward Herod Antipas and the *Herodians* in general is captured by the epithet that he reportedly applied to the executioner of John the

14. We do not include in our discussion another group, the Samaritans, who by the time of Jesus' ministry had become a separate religious sect whose adherents figure into the political background of Jesus' life only tangentially (e.g., the story about Jesus and the Samaritan woman at the well [John 4:4–42] and the parable of the Good Samaritan [Luke 10:29–37]). This is not to deny that the inclusion of Samaritans in traditions about Jesus functioned in an important way to highlight what was undeniably a part of Jesus' eschatology, namely, that the compass of the kingdom of which he believed he was a part extended beyond the conventional boundaries that religious leaders of his time had drawn.

Baptist, namely, "that fox" (Luke 13:32). It is an attitude that he shared with all Jews who remained faithful to their ancestral religion, for the accumulation of crimes against the devout perpetrated by the Herodians stretched across the decades, from the bloody massacres of Pharisees conducted by Herod the Great to the ruthless repression of those who placed loyalty to the God of Israel ahead of tolerating the iniquitous policies and practices of Herod's sons.

Evaluating Jesus' relation to the *Sadducees* is more complicated. In chapter 24 we credited the research of Hillel Newman with demonstrating the need to distinguish between different positions vis-à-vis Jewish tradition among the Sadducees. Especially important is his calling attention to halakic Sadducees, a group whose interpretations of Torah, he avers, betray affinities with some of those found in the commentaries of Qumran. While we can assume that Jesus would have found little common ground with the elite Sadducean families who had cast their lot with the Herodians, it is conceivable that he engaged not only Pharisees but also halakic Sadducees in disputations over Torah interpretation.

In seeking to move beyond conjecture to more specific comparisons, however, a major obstacle is encountered: since all four canonical Gospels in their present form are the products of authors writing in a period after Judaism and Christianity had divided into distinct religious communities, they do not provide historically verifiable information on the nature of the relationship between Jesus and members of the rival Jewish parties and movements. The frustrating consequence is that in the Gospels one commonly finds Pharisees and Sadducees lumped together as Jesus' interlocutors (e.g., Matt. 23), thereby obscuring differences between those two parties, as well as distinctions within the ranks of the Sadducees.

In addition to the New Testament Gospels, the sources with which one is left are the descriptions Josephus offers of four Jewish philosophies and scattered references in later rabbinical sources. Here too the question of historical reliability is raised by the facts that Josephus, writing under the influence of commitments and biases of his own, betrays a style tailored for a non-Jewish audience, while the rabbis, themselves heirs to the tradition of the Pharisees, pay scant and less than evenhanded attention to the interpretive traditions of the Sadducean rivals they have successfully supplanted.

Though less than ideal, we have no choice but to continue the line of inquiry begun in previous chapters, one combining a critical reading of extrabiblical sources—in this case Josephus and the rabbis—with an equally rigorous scrutiny of the layers of tradition in the New Testament Gospels that transmit words attributed to Jesus and narratives describing episodes in his life bearing on his relation to his coreligionists, as he seeks to negotiate the precarious path of remaining loyal to the kingdom of God while living in a world governed by the Roman imperium.[15]

---

15. As explained elsewhere, I do not find in the noncanonical gospels information regarding the historical Jesus that adds to what is known from the New Testament writings.

We begin with Josephus, his writings containing the only explicit description of the Sadducees surviving from antiquity, which description, moreover, synchronizes reasonably well with evidence gleaned from rabbinical sources and the New Testament. In contrast to Jesus and the Pharisees, the Sadducees recognized as authoritative only the books attributed to Moses, namely, the first five books of the Bible. The dynamic hermeneutic evident in the halakic application of Torah to new situations practiced by Jesus and the Pharisees stands in stark contrast to the literalism of the Sadducees. The implications of this more formalistic hermeneutic are twofold: The religious life of the Sadducees was strictly defined by Mosaic statutes and ordinances, whereas areas not covered by the Torah were dealt with on terms framed by the prevailing world order. Similarly, teachings based on parts of the Hebrew Bible that were not accorded scriptural status by the Sadducees, namely, the Prophets (Nebi'im) and the Writings (Ketubim), were excluded from their body of beliefs—for example, eschatological themes like the coming messianic/Davidic kingdom, the resurrection of the dead, and the active role in divine governance of angelic beings.

The eschatological themes rejected by the Sadducees resided genially within the teachings of the Pharisees and Jesus. The theological basis for the latter alignment is not hard to explain. Jesus shared with the Pharisees a progressive view toward Scripture and tradition, a fact manifested by his referencing not only the Torah, but also the Prophets (Nebi'im) and the book of Psalms, which belongs to the third section of the Hebrew Bible, the Writings (Ketubim). In applying interpretive techniques with affinities to those used by the Pharisees, Jesus developed an eschatology that included belief in the ongoing cosmic struggle for dominion between God's angelic hosts and the minions of Satan, confidence in the final victory of God and God's messiah in the inauguration of a universal reign of peace, and belief in the resurrection of the dead. In terms of relationships, it is thus clear that Jesus' appropriation of the Jewish heritage resembled more closely that of the Pharisees than that of the Sadducees.

Having come to recognize the considerable theological overlap between Jesus and the Pharisees, we now move to compare how he translated into political acts his faith in the ultimate victory of God's messianic reign with the political strategies of the Pharisees. The theo-political options available to Jews living under the Roman occupation were collaboration, accommodation, and various forms of resistance. In chapter 24 we described the political policies adopted by the Pharisees in the wake of the First and Second Jewish Revolts. In what ways did Jesus ally himself with the theo-political philosophy of the Pharisees? In what ways did he differ?

We begin by observing that the biblically based, yet flexibly applied hermeneutic of the Pharisees seems to accord with the strategy followed by Jesus as he wrestled with the challenge of sorting through the competing claims of Caesar and his God. We recall that the theo-politics of the Pharisees revolved around the foundational theocratic principle of subordination of every human government to the only ultimate ruling authority in the universe, that inhering in the sovereignty of God. Enjoined by this axiom was the renunciation of any earthly regime that arrogated itself to a status rivaling God's claim to the exclusive devotion of human subjects.

Unlike the Herodians and the collaborating wing of the Sadducean party, the Pharisees could not align themselves with a realpolitik based on acceptance of the Roman claim of providentially determined universal sovereignty. When imperial pretense modulated into the decree that subject peoples bow before deities other than the God of Israel, the Pharisees were obliged to move from the politics of accommodation to dissent. The particular form of dissent to be adopted could be determined only through the dialectical hermeneutical process of relating a living tradition of scriptural interpretation to the concrete realities of ever-changing historical/political situations.

This is a process that any absolutist ideology, ancient or modern, will condemn as morally relativistic and religiously compromising. But it is a process that we believe is consonant with the heart of the faith of ancient Israel, being rooted in the Torah of Moses, preserved in the hymnody of the tribes of Israel, audaciously recorded and augmented by the prophets, reapplied to a new age by the sages and their heirs the Pharisees. This process was extended to an even wider horizon by those finding in Isaiah's metaphor of a "light to the nations" and Jonah's commission to preach to the Ninevites a mandate to extend the membership of the people Israel to the furthest reaches of God's family.

Perspective can be gained on understanding the relation between the politics of Jesus and the politics of the Pharisees by augmenting our discussion to include what we know about the position of the other dissenting parties, particularly the one best known to us, the Essenes.[16]

In their understanding of the relation of this world to God's plan for history, the Essenes sided with the Pharisees and Jesus against the Sadducees by holding to the eschatological vision of the final advent of God's Anointed One to deliver the people Israel from their enemies and to inaugurate an era of eternal peace. A serious divergence arose on the level of relating that eschatological vision to politics. While both Jesus and the Pharisees responded to the Roman occupation from the perspective of prophetic eschatology, the Essenes viewed their world and the entire cosmos through the lens of a full-blown apocalyptic eschatology.[17] With that worldview came an ontological dualism that described this world as a realm ripe for destruction in a grand assize conducted by God and God's sanctified combatants, both angelic and mortal. The *pesher* method of interpretation used by the scribes of Qumran lent itself to this bleak view of the world, since it claimed to uncover the hidden meaning of Scripture for events ineluctably leading to the rapid end of this world. The dialectic relationship

16. As indicated in chapter 24, I believe that the Qumran community was Essene, and accordingly I draw upon the Dead Sea Scrolls as a reliable source of information about that Jewish "party."

17. For a detailed description of the similarities and differences that exist between prophetic and apocalyptic eschatology, see Paul D. Hanson, *The Dawn of Apocalyptic* (Philadelphia: Fortress Press, 1975), 10–12.

Sadducees

temple

Pharisees

between this world and the world to come, characteristic of the hermeneutics of
Jesus and the Pharisees, together with the elements of interpretive multivalence
and flexibility inherent therein, was absent in the absolutism of the Essenes.

Lodged in the apocalyptic worldview was a categorical dismissal of involvement in this-worldly politics. Politically speaking, the position of the Essenes
falls under the general category of dissent, specifically dissent in the form of
withdrawal. Their rejection of the Roman imperium and a temple-based priestly
bureaucracy that was in league with the Romans was categorical. Their vision
of the future depicted a heavenly battle leading to the overthrow of the Romans
(aka the *kittim*) and their Jewish supporters, and the restoration of God's universal reign, in which those who had remained obedient to the Torah would
regain their positions of priestly leadership. The point at which the Essenes differed from the Zealots and the Sicarii hinged on tactics. Rather than engaging in
violent acts aimed at exterminating the enemy, their policy involved withdrawal
from political engagement and maintenance of strict communal obedience and
purity in preparation for *God's* intervention to destroy the illegitimate rulers and
to vindicate the faithful remnant as God's chosen nation of priests.

Though their eschatology was lurid in its elaboration of end-time warfare,
there is no indication that they resorted to arms, even in the throes of the final
onslaught of the Romans. There is no archaeological evidence that they possessed
arms other than the fantasy arsenals that fill large sections of their war manual.
Without denying the importance for their spiritual identity of the descriptions
of cosmic carnage in the War Scroll, from a historical perspective it seems that
the members of the Qumran community followed the path of passive dissent
commended by Daniel 7–12. Within the context of an apocalyptic worldview,
however, passive dissent is no less total in its denunciation of strategies of political coexistence with the occupying power than is active dissent in the form of
armed resistance, as practiced by the Zealots and Sicarii. It is in this respect that
the position taken by Jesus in relation to the Romans and their Jewish collaborators aligns itself with the Pharisees rather than the Essenes.

The difference in the political implications that arise out of the two kinds of
eschatology is pronounced. The apocalyptic eschatology of the Essenes supplied
categorical distinctions and a definitive end-time scenario that left no room for
pragmatic compromises with rival parties. Its absolutism inoculated the Essenes
against the kind of historical ambiguities that prompted the Pharisees to shift
their stance vis-à-vis the Romans.[18]

"Accommodation" is the term that represents the middle ground taken
by the Pharisees between the collaboration of the political Sadducees and the
resistance—whether in withdrawal or revolt—of the Essenes and the Zealots.
Though holding in common with the Essenes an eschatological vision of God's

18. As we observed in chapter 24, the leaders of the Pharisees in the Second Jewish Revolt
resorted to the Zealot-like tactic of violent resistance that prima facie seems to contradict their earlier
eschewal of violence in favor of maintaining peaceful relations with the Romans, a policy that fits
our category of accommodation.

final defeat of their enemies and the restoration of the righteous remnant of Israel, the political inferences the Pharisees drew from that vision distinguished them from groups that shunned the porous boundaries characteristic of city life and withdrew to a monastic life in the wilderness characterized by self-regulated sanctity and utopian community structure. The Pharisees rather sought to maintain their purity within a sullied world in which secular and sacred existed side by side. While in contact with defilement in their day-to-day activities, they depended on the sanctity of their table fellowships (*ḥābûrā*) to provide space in which their faithfulness could be nurtured and sustained. Living "in the world but not of the world" of course presented a much more difficult existential challenge than living apart from a world whose validity is denied on the basis of a divine archetype. How did the Pharisees navigate within this precarious vortex of clashing worlds?

Rather than representing an internal contradiction, the pragmatic *political* policy followed by the Pharisees was a corollary of their foundational theocratic principle: the belief that ultimately there is only one legitimate government, the universal imperium of God. Since human regimes were passing and in God's time would be supplanted by the kingdom inaugurated by the divinely appointed messiah, only contingent loyalty could be paid to such regimes, a loyalty contingent, that is, upon a given regime's tolerance of the religious practices and beliefs of the Jewish people. Such penultimate loyalty, in the interim before the messiah came, left considerable room for active engagement on the level of ordinary political negotiation and policy making. This dialectical view is the political posture inherent in what in the course of our study we have associated with prophetic eschatology. Accordingly, it is perfectly reasonable to view the Pharisees as descendants of the prophets of ancient Israel. In my judgment, it is that legacy that lived on in the theo-politics of Jesus.[19]

First to be noted is that Jesus shares with the Pharisees a dialectical understanding of the relation of this world and the world to come. The roots of this understanding can be traced to the theocratic principle that God alone can claim ultimate sovereignty and to the political inference that follows, namely, the relativization of every human regime. But the belief shared by the Pharisees and

19. It is understandable how one could raise objections to this conclusion. Does the New Testament not attribute to Jesus words that seem to fit more the worldview of the Essenes than the Pharisees? Does he not announce the nearness of the kingdom of God? These legitimate questions can be addressed adequately only when we enter into a close analysis of individual words and acts attributed to Jesus. But two preliminary remarks are in order. (1) Within the thought of the Pharisees, there existed eschatological views ranging from the expectation of imminent divine intervention to more restrained messianic hopes. Within this range, Jesus would fall more in line with the former view than the latter. (2) In the wake of the destruction of the temple in 70 CE, the words of Jesus regarding God's redemptive action on behalf of his people were reshaped from an increasingly apocalyptic perspective, as can be seen in an analysis of texts like Mark 13. However, the reshaping should be understood as an amplification of Jesus' teaching about the future rather than as a substantial alteration, since Jesus' utter commitment to God's reign and his confidence in its final fulfillment in the history of his people were amenable to retranslation into the topoi of apocalyptic eschatology when abetted by crises such as the calamity of 70 CE.

Jesus that the sovereign whose ultimate authority relativizes all human institutions was also the creator of this world disallowed their denouncing all things worldly, in the categorical manner of the Essenes and the gnostics. Instead, signs of the presence of God's reign in the midst of the ephemeral structures of this world were to be heralded. An important consequence, in the case of Jesus' teaching, was a lively tension between intimations of God's kingdom experienced within the circle of the faithful and their yearning for the fullness of that kingdom. When we turn to the parables of Jesus, it will become evident that the tensive relationship between "realized" and "futuristic" eschatology offers a key to grasping their often elusive meaning.

To this must be added another perspective Jesus shared with the Pharisees, namely, a dynamic understanding of the relation between Scripture and tradition, based on a progressive hermeneutic and vivid sense of the role of divine inspiration in the interpretation of the sacred texts and their application to contemporary life. This dynamic understanding of the Scripture/tradition dialectic lay at the root of disputes between Jesus and the Pharisees. How were differences in the interpretation of Scripture, and specifically Torah, to be adjudicated? That question inevitably led to the question of authority. Only those endowed by God and properly trained were authorized to interpret Scripture.

The dispute over authority between Jesus and his Jewish compatriots comes to expression in the following passage from the Gospel of Luke: "One day, as he was teaching the people in the temple and telling them the good news, the chief priests and the scribes came with the elders and said to him, 'Tell us, by what authority are you doing these things? Who is it who gave you this authority?'" (Luke 20:1–2).[20]

The gauntlet thrown down before Jesus was serious. From the point of view of his compatriots, he was exercising an authority with which he had not been duly invested, that is, he was a false prophet. For his authority to have been legitimate, it should have originated within and been regulated by conventions designed to thwart the ever-present danger of false teaching. In reference to Paul's preconversion zealotry against followers of the Way, a story in the book of Acts attributes to Ananias of Damascus words that reflect the conventional understanding: "[Saul] has authority from the chief priests" (Acts 9:14). Contrarily, from the perspective of the Jewish leaders contending with Jesus, his authority rested on his *own* claim. Hence his interpretations of Torah, often radical in the challenges they raised for the teachings of the scribes and Pharisees, were not only false, but blasphemous. Regarding the communal and political implications of his liberal *halakoth*, the freedoms he accorded his disciples regarding Sabbath observance, ritual laws regulating diet, and contact with

20. We shall return to the issue of authority in relation to Jesus' teachings in greater detail in the next section, *Texts*. Other passages relevant to this question are Matt. 7:28–29; Luke 4:6; John 5:25–27.

disease threatened the spiritual identity and solidarity of the Jews at a time when the Romans were threatening their very existence!

The explanation of why the religious controversies between Jesus and the Pharisees hinged on the question of authority cannot be understood apart from understanding the nature of ancient Israelite religion. In previous chapters we have described the origin and development of Yahwism in terms of a historical ontology. In the religions of Israel's imperial neighbors, truth claims were predicated on the concept of a timeless myth prescribing the immutable structures of the divine realm as the template for human government. In contrast, the religion of Israel developed as a narrative account of God's engagement in the life of a people chosen as an instrument of a creative and redemptive plan. Scripture originated not as a timeless archetype, serving for all time as the pattern for human government, but as a story of the relationship initiated and maintained by God with Israel. This story was translated into the ordering of human community and its forms of government by way of inferences drawn from the nature of the initiating deity, inferences understood as conditions ensconced in the covenant between God and people and establishing the basis for harmony between God and people and among people and nations. The single most poignant designation of that twin harmony is *shalom*.

The historical ontology intrinsic to the origins of Israel's Epic guided the growth process that generated a normative body of writings (Torah + Prophets + Writings), as well as an ongoing history of interpretation of those writings. The overarching term that is descriptive of this entire process is *tradition*; tradition in turn explains the central role of authority in the disputes between parties offering conflicting interpretations of their common Scripture.

Because ancient Israelite religion, with its open-ended historical ontology, was not insulated against influence from the pervasive mythopoeic worldview of its cultural environment, Hebrew Scripture does include occasional allusions to a static view of the world that on the surface may seem to support a fundamentalist notion of inerrant divine word. For example, the plan for the tabernacle that Moses received from God in Exodus 25:9 is called a *tabnît* ("blueprint"). Of course, the text most frequently cited by defenders of an infallible Bible is 2 Timothy 3:16, "All scripture is inspired by God." But if one's method of interpreting Scripture embodies the same understanding of historical development that we have traced in the growth of the Bible itself, then proper discernment of the meaning of the biblical writings will be regarded not as application of timeless truths to contemporary situations, but as an act of discerning the meaning of biblical traditions for the new situations within which communities of faith find themselves. In the teaching of historical Christianity, such discernment is the gift of the Holy Spirit, present within the assembly of those responsive to God's will.[21]

---

21. See Paul Achtemeier, *Inspiration and Authority* (Peabody, MA: Hendrickson Publishers, 1999).

For those subscribing to this dynamic understanding of the interpretive process, the question of true and false teaching persists, much in the manner that the issue of true and false prophecy repeatedly surfaced in biblical times. This is simply to recognize that the question of authority is inherent and unavoidable in the hermeneutical exercise of extending the meaning of Scripture into new situations within religious traditions—such as rabbinical Judaism and classical Christianity—that view God as a dynamic presence encountered in a living scriptural heritage rather than as the author of a compendium of lapidary truths demanding strict enforcement.

It is precisely because both Jesus and the Pharisees engaged Scripture using a historically imbued hermeneutic that they came into conflict. Both believed that the meaning of Scripture reached beyond its original setting to new situations. Both believed that the interpretive process was guided by divine inspiration. In cases where conflicting interpretations emerged, the need to differentiate between legitimacy and error could not be avoided. Inevitably, the vexed issue of authority could not be put to rest. When we turn to specific texts, we shall consider the diverging inferences drawn by Jesus and the Pharisees regarding the conditions mandated by Scripture for membership in the people of Israel.

Conflict also flared up over the perilous question of how to relate God's rule to the claims of the Roman Empire. The Pharisees and Jesus, as well as Pharisees among themselves and followers of Jesus among themselves, while in agreement on the foundational principle underlying every iteration of a political strategy—the sole ultimate authority of the one God—came to differing strategies for relating God's sovereignty to earthly regimes. This was the inevitable consequence of the categorical distinction that we find at the heart of biblical theo-politics, namely, the distinction between God's reign and every human regime. While the central commandments of sole worship of God and renunciation of every manner of idol that safeguard the core biblical testimony to God's exclusive reign are normative, the translation of those imperatives into policies and strategies for dealing with human governments remains proximate, being conditioned by the flux of history and the limits of human wisdom. Misjudgments and errors are endemic to such an ambiguous endeavor.

In their understanding of the relation of Scripture to life in the present, both Jesus and the Pharisees recognized the function of ongoing divine inspiration that made interpretation a dynamic religious practice, rather than a mechanistic exercise. With courage and audacity, they studied Scripture with the expectation that new insights would be revealed regarding the application of received tradition to new situations unanticipated by Moses. They disputed with one another over divergent conclusions, while holding in common the core beliefs of their shared ancestral faith.

Religious controversies, though politically unremarkable in normal times, can spiral out of control in times of political instability. It is against such a tense political background that we can understand the tragic deepening of the conflict between Jesus and the Jewish authorities and its entanglement in

Pilate's desperate struggle to maintain order in a volatile situation over which he had limited control. Suddenly the divergent teachings of the itinerant Galilean prophet became a threat to the stability of a Jewish community living in a precarious relation to an oppressive foreign occupying power.

In subsequent decades, the calamitous outcome of the two Jewish revolts would demonstrate emphatically the legitimacy of the fear of dire consequences resulting from sectarian groups defying the authority of Jewish leadership. Even in the prerevolt period, however, the dangerous mixture of inner Jewish community dispute and Roman anxiety over the prospect of anarchy erupting in the eastern provinces of the empire proved lethal for the teacher from Nazareth. Whether under more tranquil political conditions the disputes between Jesus and the Pharisees on matters of Torah interpretation might have been conducted in the discursive style familiar from later rabbinical writings is intriguing to contemplate but impossible to answer.

Reference to one incident described in all four Gospels and regarded widely among critical scholars as authentic, namely, Jesus' rebuke of the merchants and moneylenders in the temple courtyard, begins our transition from generalized observations regarding the relation of Jesus' theo-political worldview to that of the other Jewish parties toward the more tangible world of disputation and conflict, a move that will continue in the next section, where we examine a larger number of relevant texts. Both the time and the location of this event are significant. Jesus has made the journey of a faithful pilgrim from Galilee to the Holy City to celebrate Passover. But instead of finding in the sacred precincts of the temple a place where he can offer his thanks and praise to God, he finds the clamor of vendors hawking their merchandise and the noise and redolence of animals being sold for sacrifice, to which he reacts by overturning tables and driving out the merchants and declaring, "It is written, 'My house shall be called a house of prayer'; but you have made it a den of robbers" (Matt. 21:13; Mark 11:17; Luke 19:46).

What light does this story shed on Jesus' politics? Mercantile activity, as such, had long been a normal part of temple life in the commercial centers of the ancient Near East, as already indicated by five-thousand-year-old business dockets from Mesopotamia that are among the first attestations of writing. Typical was the white temple of the Sumerian city-state of Uruk, a complex combining what today would be called banks, hostels, commodity exchanges, and royal treasuries, that is, all of the institutions forming the hub of a thriving economy. The money changers and vendors encountered by Jesus in Jerusalem at Passover 30 CE were professionals plying a very ancient trade, and Jesus' act of turning their tables understandably provoked ire and dismay. How can we understand its religious and political significance?

An adequate explanation must begin with reference to the central point that emerged above in our discussion of the background to Jesus' life and message: Jesus must be understood in relation to the Hebrew prophets and within the context of the Jewish community living under Roman occupation. In this episode Jesus applies a technique practiced by prophets like Isaiah, Jeremiah, and Ezekiel, namely, the enactment of a *sign act* aimed at capturing the attention of onlookers.[22] In the present case, the sign poignantly is wedded to words that underline the unbroken trajectory connecting Jesus' ministry to that of the Hebrew prophets, for his terse message weaves together verses drawn from the books of Isaiah and Jeremiah, the former from an eschatological passage envisioning the day when the true purpose of the temple would be realized ("for my house shall be called a house of prayer for all peoples" [Isa. 56:7b]), the latter from a speech Jeremiah is reported to have delivered in the precincts of the Jerusalem temple decrying the debasement of that true purpose ("Has this house, which is called by my name, become a den of robbers in your sight?" [Jer. 7:11]).

The temple-cleansing incident thus exemplifies how a clear grasp of Jesus' background in the religion of his people is essential to understanding the significance of his own political actions. Prophecy originated in ancient Israel in part as a protest movement against the reimposition of ancient Near Eastern royal ideology on the fledgling Yahwistic community, an ideology predicated on identification of the central temple of the state with the authority and political interests of the monarchy. Thus Amos condemned Jeroboam II and his compliant priest Amaziah, who insisted that the prophet had no right to speak out against the king at the central shrine Bethel, which Amaziah revealingly designated as "the king's sanctuary" and "a temple of the kingdom" (Amos 7:13).

Isaiah, though enjoying closer relations with the royal court, was equally severe in denouncing any perversion of worship by the privileged and elite of Judah (Isa. 1:10–17). Jeremiah repeatedly exposed himself to the wrath of the king and to accusations of treason by insisting that the temple could convey no solace to those who viewed it as a guarantee of national security while they flagrantly violated the commandments and treated God's sanctuary like "a den of robbers." It is very possible that Jesus also shared with the seer of Zechariah 14 a longing for the day when the temple would be restored to its true purpose: "And there shall no longer be traders in the house of the LORD of hosts on that day" (Zech. 14:21b).

As was the case in previous periods of Jewish history, so too in Jesus' time diverse functions were carried out in the Jerusalem temple complex, and different attitudes were expressed regarding those functions. In the temple incident, Jesus can be identified as an adherent of a prophetic tradition that condemned activities that obscured or obliterated the central meaning of the temple, namely, as dwelling place of the God of mercy and justice. His citation of the words from Jeremiah is thus understandable. Out of devotion to the one God, Jesus rose up against rivals, rivals that were not limited to idols, but could include any representation or activity that detracted from worship and true piety. Like the

22. Cf. Isaiah's walking naked and barefoot (Isa. 20), Jeremiah's carrying a yoke on his shoulders (Jer. 27–28), and Ezekiel's baking barley cakes over a fire fueled by human dung (Ezek. 4:9–15), all at the command of God as signs of impending judgment.

Pharisees at a later date taking their stand against Hadrian's plan to dedicate his temple to Jupiter, Jesus sought to drive out those who threatened to overwhelm God's sanctuary with activities completely at home in other temples in the Roman Empire, but which from his prophetic perspective made it indistinguishable from a den of robbers.[23]

Those singled out for judgment by his prophetic invective likely would have seen nothing objectionable in their commercial activities. As we have seen, the native Jerusalem hierarchy, led by Sadducean priests, used the temple complex as home base for its wide-ranging activities. These included gathering local tax revenue as well as the annual tribute owed to Rome, overseeing the daily rituals and annual feasts that constituted the Jewish calendar, managing the finances of a large priestly bureaucracy, and accommodating foreign dignitaries visiting Jerusalem on official business. That individual entrepreneurs would press the limits of decorum to maximize their own interests within the context of such a multifaceted institution is not surprising. Nor is it surprising that one nurtured in the prophetic tradition of the temple being the house of God would react with a stinging indictment of their commercial activities. In so doing, Jesus was living true to the tradition of Jeremiah and Amos, while the temple officials who issued the vending permits could be likened to an earlier figure remembered by tradition as one placing loyalty to an earthly master above fear of the Lord, Amaziah, priest of Bethel![24]

The temple incident also places in a clear light the distance between Jesus' eschatology and that of the Essenes: Though Jesus' emphasis on the imminence (and proleptically speaking, immanence) of the kingdom of God calls to mind many of the eschatological themes of the sectarian writings of Qumran, his choice of a prophetic jeremiad as the means of excoriating the vendors and money lenders, rather than an announcement of a divinely initiated apocalyptic assize, demonstrates his choice of political engagement rather than monastic withdrawal, and his dedication to reforming the temple rather than consigning it and all his rivals and adversaries to an end-time judgment. The dialectical tension between the kingdom as present and the kingdom yet to come thus becomes visible within the walls of the temple. What is more, his enacting a sign act rather than fomenting an armed revolt manifests the distance between his prophetic strategy and the violent apocalyptic tactics of the Zealots and the Sicarii.

The temple-cleansing story thus adds credence to the opinion that, when viewed within the context of the Jewish parties of the Roman period, Jesus' political position lies closest to that of the Pharisees. Specifically with regard to religious beliefs, it also locates Jesus solidly within the core of beliefs of the ancestral faith as they had been preserved and fostered by the leaders of the

---

23. While no direct illusion to Ezekiel 8 is made in the accounts of the temple cleansing, it is not impossible that that lurid depiction of temple profanation also informed Jesus' words and action.

24. Amos 7:10–17.

Pharisees: "sole worship of the God of Abraham and Moses, obedience to God's will as recorded in the Torah, and devotion to the temple as the place chosen by God for their worship and sacrifices."[25] In driving out those who were carrying on commerce in the temple, Jesus not only demonstrated his reverence for the edifice that for him was the house of his heavenly Father, but he gave expression to his awareness of belonging to the long succession of prophetic guardians of the sanctity of the temple as a place of undistracted worship and prayer.

Inextricably related to his devotion to the temple was his passionate commitment to the exclusive worship of the one God. What he encountered were intolerable impediments to what in his mind was the central purpose of the temple, to be a house of prayer. This core belief found poignant narrative expression in the temptation story related by Matthew and Luke and alluded to in Mark, where Jesus replies to Satan's temptation with the words of Deuteronomy 6:4: "It is written, 'Worship the Lord your God, and serve only him'" (Matt. 4:10// Luke 4:8).[26]

The Gospel tradition thus draws attention to Jesus' adherence to what we have identified as the foundational theocratic principle of Yahwistic faith, exclusive worship of the one God, even as it illustrates Jesus' obedience to the Torah as the unique expression of God's will.[27] Another episode, found with slight variations in all three Synoptic Gospels and bearing distinct marks of authenticity, emphasizes the degree to which for Jesus the oneness of God and the status of Torah as the unique expression of God's will are inseparably linked. In answer to a question put to him by a lawyer[28] regarding the ranking of the various commandments, Jesus responds by quoting the Shema Israel: "The first is, 'Hear, O Israel: the Lord our God, the Lord is one; you shall love the Lord your God with all your heart, and with all your soul, and with all your mind, and with all your strength" (Mark 12:29–30). To this quotation from Deuteronomy 6:4 he adds a second from Leviticus 19:18 expressing the inseparability of belief and morals in biblical faith: "You shall love your neighbor as yourself." In a single word event, offering the clarity of a pebble hitting the mirror surface of an alpine pond, Jesus thus communicates his understanding of the core of his ancestral faith, its uniquely authoritative source, and the inseparability of love of God and love of neighbor. As we shall elaborate later, the widely based ascription of this core of beliefs to Jesus in the Gospels provides a solid argument for historicity.[29]

25. See Schwartz, *Imperialism and Jewish Society*, 49–66; Hillel Newman, *Proximity to Power and Jewish Sectarian Groups of the Ancient Period* (Leiden: Brill, 2006), 53–73.

26. Supporting the view that Jesus' aim was reform of the temple, not its destruction, is the solid textual testimony to his practice of pilgrimage to the Jerusalem temple to worship (John P. Meier, *A Marginal Jew: Rethinking the Historical Jesus* [New York: Doubleday, 1991], 1:349.

27. See above note 25.

28. In Matt. 22:35, the lawyer is identified as a Pharisee; in Mark 12:28 he is designated as one of the scribes; in Luke 10:25 he is identified simply as a lawyer.

29. Jesus' citation of Jer. 7:11 in the temple-cleansing story also depicts another important affinity, namely, Jesus, like the Pharisees, included the Prophets in the body of writings regarded as authoritative.

Of the three above-mentioned tenets of Jewish faith, Jesus' relation to "obedience to the Torah" is the most likely to raise questions in the minds of readers and therefore calls for further comment. The Gospel of Matthew poses a conundrum in the so-called Sermon on the Mount by depicting Jesus as a second Moses who ascends a mountain and expounds the Torah:

> Do not think that I have come to abolish the law or the prophets; I have come not to abolish but to fulfill. For truly I tell you, until heaven and earth pass away, not one letter, not one stroke of a letter, will pass from the law until all is accomplished. Therefore, whoever breaks one of the least of these commandments, and teaches others to do the same, will be called least in the kingdom of heaven; but whoever does them and teaches them will be called great in the kingdom of heaven. For I tell you, unless your righteousness exceeds that of the scribes and the Pharisees, you will never enter the kingdom of heaven. (Matt. 5:17–20)

This interesting hermeneutical reflection is followed by a series of interpretations of specific laws (i.e., midrashim) following this pattern, "You have heard that it was said, '. . .' But I say to you, '. . .'" In each case the prodosis (which varies slightly from case to case) cites one of the commandments from the Torah, while the apodosis modifies the commandment, in the direction of a more stringent signification.

In these verses Matthew is shaping tradition in such a way as to provide his readers with his understanding of Jesus' relation to the Torah of Moses. It follows that one cannot simply regard Matthew's formulation as a verbatim of Jesus' thought. However, in anticipation of our examination of texts attributable to the historical Jesus, we can suggest with a reasonable degree of confidence that the understanding of the role of interpreter offered by Matthew reflects the dialectical method of interpretation practiced by Jesus, which in turn betrays deep roots in the interpretive practices of the scribes and Pharisees. The spirit of that approach is captured in a pithy saying also found in Matthew: "Therefore every scribe who has been trained for the kingdom of heaven is like the master of a household who brings out of his treasure what is new and what is old" (Matt. 13:52).[30]

If we relate the central features of the expository method of the Pharisees and their heirs the Tannaim and Amoraim to what can be gleaned from the Gospels about Jesus' treatment of Scripture, the following points emerge: (1) Disputation over the meaning and application of specific Mosaic laws was a central feature of the interpretive praxis of the Pharisees, both in relation to rulings enjoined by Sadducean scholars and variant positions taken by other Pharisees.[31] (2) The hermeneutic practiced by the Pharisees was not static and literalistic,

---

30. See Krister Stendahl, *The School of St. Matthew, and Its Use of the Old Testament* (Philadelphia: Fortress Press, 1968).

31. Particularly notable are the divergent positions taken by Hillel and Shammai in their interpretations of particular Mosaic laws.

but dynamic and open to the abiding role of inspiration, making them sensitive to the meaning a given statute or ordinance acquired when applied to a new situation. (3) Light is shed on the disputes between Jesus and the Pharisees over matters of praxis and belief by two further considerations, first, the understanding they *shared* of the dynamic relation between Scripture and the world they lived in, and second, the *conflicting* conclusions they drew due to diverging eschatological views.

The Pharisees were guided by the vision enshrined in *Psalm of Solomon* 17 of God's raising a righteous king from the house of David, while Jesus was guided by a sense of the immanence of God's restoration of both Israel and all nations, leading to an era of universal *shalom*. Both of these eschatological views have deep roots in Hebrew Scripture. The view of the Pharisees was implemented proleptically in the restoration movement of Ezra and Nehemiah following the Babylonian exile. To be sure, one major deficit remained, namely, the continued subjugation of the Jews under a foreign power. Visible in prophetic writings that also stem from the early Persian period is the alternative eschatological vision, namely, of God gathering the scattered tribes of Israel into their homeland, together with foreigners from all parts of the world who chose to worship the one God and to obey his commandments.[32] When we suggest that it is this understanding of the awaited restoration that informs Jesus' interpretation of Jewish tradition, we are not claiming that he subscribed to the apostle Paul's later notion of an explicit Gentile mission. Jesus viewed his mission within the framework of God's covenant with Israel, a mission that we can be confident he sought to pass on to his disciples: "Go nowhere among the Gentiles, and enter no town of the Samaritans, but go rather to the lost sheep of the house of Israel" (Matt. 10:5–6). At the same time, the burden he bore for the salvation of his people did not thwart his understanding of a divine mercy so inclusive as to attend to the pleas of a Canaanite woman (Matt. 15:21–28).

In generations subsequent to the lifetime of Jesus and his circle of followers, learned disputations between Jesus and the Pharisees over matters of Torah interpretation were escalated into bitter invective between what had become two separate and competing religious communities. Two examples of the effects of invective on Christian polemical writings were the hardening of the distinction between law and gospel in the writings of the apostle Paul and the blurring of distinctions between different parties within Judaism through the undifferentiated use of the term *Ioudaioi* (Jews/Judeans) in the Gospel of John.[33] This transformation of learned disputation into bitter invective and finally unspeakable violence represents one of the most horrific tragedies of human history.

---

32. See Isa. 56:1–8; 66:18–23; and 60:1–7.
33. See Daniel J. Harrington, *God's People in Christ: New Testament Perspectives on the Church and Judaism* (Philadelphia: Fortress Press, 1980).

TEXT

We move now to the third dimension in our approach to describing and understanding the politics of the historical Jesus, namely, a rigorous examination of relevant New Testament texts. It will be helpful to begin by contrasting our understanding of the suitability of biblical traditions about Jesus for historical reconstruction with the position taken by "questers" like Robert Funk and John Dominic Crossan.[34] The central issue concerns the reliability of the chain of tradition through which Jesus' words and narratives were preserved and interpreted before being written down in their present canonical form. The questers emphasize the magnitude of the gap (temporal, ideological, and political) between the historical Jesus and the Jesus Christ proclaimed by the apostle Paul and presented by those who gave shape to the Gospels. They argue that the resulting canonical portrait is a distortion of the "real" Jesus, a distortion driven by the ambitions of early church leaders who stood to benefit from the transformation of a collection of moral teachings and practical narratives into an ecclesiology and a body of doctrine that elevated Jesus to divine status and them to the position of authoritative guardians of a new imperial religion.

It is our judgment that the resulting reconstruction of the life and teachings of the "real" Jesus itself distorts a tradition in which the message and acts of the historical Jesus, including his understanding of his own role in the realization of God's reign of compassionate justice, were interpreted and applied to new situations by succeeding generations of disciples in a manner that both preserved the significance of their religious movement's founding events and related them to new situations. Rather than distortion, the process the historian can follow from the words and acts of the historical Jesus to the teachings of the apostle Paul and the accounts of the evangelists and latter New Testament authors continues the time-tested dialectic of reverence for tradition and audacious reapplication that characterizes both Hebrew Scripture and the writings of the rabbis.

Recognition of the blending of faithfulness to the past and sensitivity to the present that lies at the heart of this understanding of tradition does not impose blindness to the human aspects of tradition history. For example, the particular shaping of their source materials by the Gospel writers and Paul will be interpreted with an eye to their particular religious and political agendas within their specific historical milieus. Indeed, this recognition secures a sound basis for the application of the kind of rigorous *Ideologiekritik* that must play a part in the interpretation of all writings, both ancient and modern. In the present study, the attempt at evenhandedness will result in a much more positive view of the relation between the Jesus of history and the Jesus of the apostle Paul and the Gospels than one finds in the "distortion theory" of the most prominent questers.

---

34. See Paul D. Hanson, "We Once Knew Him from a Human Point of View," in *Who Is Jesus Christ for Us Today: Pathways to Contemporary Christology,* Michael Welker Festschrift, ed. Andreas Schuele and Günter Thomas (Louisville, KY: Westminster John Knox Press, 2009), 203–18.

It is not possible to elicit definitive proof for the rightness of our approach to the texts reporting the acts and sayings of Jesus, over against alternative readings. Such certainty lies beyond the grasp of the student of ancient history, where plausibility and the most felicitous accounting for what evidence is available set the parameters of a method necessarily blending aspects of art and science. However, it is important to keep in mind the nature of the culture with which we are dealing in interpreting the writings of the New Testament, namely, a culture in which tradition was the medium through which memory of identity-building events was kept alive in narratives that grew through adaptation to changing circumstances.[35]

Such an understanding of the way in which tradition grows is entirely at home within the Jewish milieu in which Jesus was raised.[36] Those who were dedicated to carrying on the task inaugurated by the Galilean teacher-prophet did not gather for table fellowship with the "academic" intention of recording as many Jesus sayings as they collectively could recall. Rather, they celebrated the memory of the one whose Spirit they still experienced in their midst, a memory rich in stories as well as words, a memory that provided the narrative context within which the deepest significance of the sayings and acts of Jesus could be grasped, a memory that provided the basis for their developing the strategies and structures of a community life that would be appropriate to the purpose to which they felt called.

While the neopositivist's approach winnows the received tradition until only an allegedly uncontaminated historical core remains, and then fleshes out the surviving verbal abstraction with the aid of a foreign model (e.g., Cynic philosopher), historical understanding seeks to recover the reality of the historical Jesus through a reading, at once critical and empathetic, that strives to glimpse the trajectory that extends from words and acts originating with Jesus to the reliving and retelling of those words and acts in the memory, often ritually reenacted, by succeeding generations of disciples.[37]

---

35. Ben F. Meyer, after a close analysis of 1 Cor. 11:23–24; Phil. 2:6–11; and formulas occurring in the discourses in the Acts of the Apostles, highlights the importance of memory as a link between the historical Jesus and the early church: "The overarching fact is that Palestinian Christianity was nourished on the memory of Jesus" (Meyer, *The Aims of Jesus* [Eugene, OR: Wipf & Stock, 2002], 69). Helmut Koester specifies the primary carrier of memory, namely, ritual, especially the communal celebration of the meal commemorating their Lord: "Here is what I imagine happened after the death of Jesus. . . . [T]he friends and disciples of Jesus did what they had always done in the company of Jesus: they gathered together, read the Scriptures, sang psalms, and prayed as they broke the bread and blessed the cup. When they did this, they realized that Jesus was mysteriously present among them" (Koester, *Paul and His World* [Minneapolis: Fortress Press, 2007], 100).

36. The central role played by memory in the growth of ancient Israelite tradition is described by Brevard S. Childs in *Memory and Tradition in Israel* (Naperville, IL: A. R. Allenson, 1962).

37. N. T. Wright, on page 9 of his "Introduction" to Ben Meyer's *The Aims of Jesus*, draws attention to an important aspect of the relation between a historical figure and the traditions that preserve and build upon the memory of that figure: "the deepest meanings of a historical character's intentions and achievements are found not simply in his own recorded words and actions but in the traditions they generate."

In eschewing the false certainties of neopositivist "scientific method," historical understanding seeks to regain an accurate picture of Jesus that preserves the dimension of divine wonder that inspired the first generations of his followers. Any interpretative strategy that excludes that dimension seriously abridges the sources available to the one seeking to comprehend the essential reality of the historical Jesus.

The phenomenon of memory and interpretive continuity that is central to the way we approach the biblical traditions about Jesus can be illustrated by reference to the "words of institution" found in 1 Corinthians 11:23–25, which Paul introduced with the words, "For I received from the Lord what I also handed on to you." For the reader sensitive to the ritual setting lying behind this introduction, its bearing on the question of historical understanding is substantial. What the first generation of the church realized is that in gathering together to partake of bread and wine, they were in the presence of the one who regularly had gathered his disciples for supper and most notably did so on the eve of his being delivered up to those who sought his life. Here we see an example of the concrete setting within which the memory of Jesus' life and words was preserved, interpreted, amplified, and ritually reenacted, namely, within the community gatherings of the disciples in the decades following Jesus' death, gatherings which, like the ḥăbērōt of the Pharisees, were centered around the basic life-giving elements of bread and wine enriched with the study of God's Word.

As we come to the end of our description of the method that will guide us as we seek to identify within biblical texts words and acts attributable to historical Jesus, it is important to be reminded that we are not proposing a criteriology capable of achieving a definitive separation of historical source material from the layers of interpretation that were added by later generations of believers. Our expectations must be more modest. Together with attention to the *background* of Jesus in Jewish tradition and the *context* of his life within Galilee and Judea during the era of Roman occupation, the method for textual study that we have outlined, by combining historical criticism with awareness of the lines of continuity existing between sources, memory of those sources, and theological reformulation and interpretation, provides a heuristic framework that fosters historical understanding by restraining the ever-inherent danger of construction in one's own image and safeguarding the independence and integrity of the biblical materials themselves.

NARRATIVES THAT SITUATE JESUS IN HIS JEWISH MILIEU

After stating as his objective the composition of "an orderly account" on the basis of careful examination of "events . . . handed on to us by those who from the beginning were eyewitnesses" (Luke 1:1, 2), Luke the historian includes in his narrative of Jesus' early years his circumcision (2:21), his presentation in the temple by his parents in compliance with Torah (2:22–24), and his tarrying in the temple to engage in discussion with its teachers (2:41–51). While these stories cannot be understood *sensu stricto* as historical, they nevertheless contribute to historical understanding in the sense that we have described earlier. Luke is not creating from pure fancy a setting for the chief protagonist of his story that is alien to Jesus' background, but is supplying his readers with vignettes that enable them to situate Jesus in his Jewish milieu. Luke's technique accordingly is neither documentary nor purely fictive. His objective is what contemporary literary critics call verisimilitude, that is, a depiction that vividly portrays Jesus within the cultural and religious setting in which he was born and raised and developed into adulthood. To the reader familiar with the world of Palestinian Jews during the Roman period, Luke's narrative rings true. That quality continues to resonate with the sensitive reader today.

When we affirm the verisimilitude of Luke's introductory chapters, we are not presenting a revolutionary new finding. To begin with the observation that Jesus was a Jew whose parents followed Jewish customs and taught their children the tenets of their religious tradition is to be less inventive than those who begin with the suggestion that Jesus was an itinerant Cynic teacher. Since we are embarked on the search for historical understanding, rather than novelty or attention-getting new discoveries, we are content to have our picture of Jesus' early years enriched by Luke's idyllic vignettes.

Legends, such as the one depicting the young Jesus in learned discussion with temple teachers, whatever relation they may have to actual episodes preserved in the memory of parents and friends, function as explanations of what those in the circle of Jesus' followers observed, namely, his thorough understanding of Hebrew Scripture and tradition. That understanding was manifested in the richness with which his words were imbued with biblical citations and allusions. When one recalls the religious landscape of Galilee during the years of Jesus' youth, a plausible answer can be given even to the question of the identity of his teachers. In all likelihood, they were members of the preeminent circle of lay expositors of the Torah, the Pharisees, who saw it as their mission to preserve in the memory of younger generations the precious heritage that established their identity and their place in a largely pagan world eager to vilify their covenant as a scandal and to force them to assimilate to the universal religion of the divine emperor.

The plausibility of this suggestion is strengthened by three further observations: (1) The Pharisees, alone among the religious Jewish parties of the Roman period, were enabled to reach out to commoners such as the sons of merchants and farmers, for they were restrained neither by the elitism of the Sadducees nor by the disdain cultivated by the Essenes for those choosing to live in the villages and cities dominated by a foreign power. (2) The rich grounding of Jesus' teachings in all three sections of the more inclusive Bible of the Pharisees (in contrast to the exclusive Torah Scripture of the Sadducees), the progressive interpretive methods he employed, and the genres (e.g., parables and wisdom sayings) that he utilized as vehicles of his message all reflect the influence of the Pharisee teachers who opened up for him the path from village parochialism to empire-shaking political engagement.[38] (3) Not to be forgotten is the eschatological dimension of the worldview of the Pharisees, which invited their students to envision a new creation of universal justice and shared prosperity that no world empire could accomplish, one that could be inaugurated solely by the creator of all peoples through the agency of his *messiah*.

The introduction to Luke's Gospel accords with our view that background, context, and awareness of the link with the past provided by tradition must all be taken into account in the search for a historical understanding of Jesus of Nazareth. In a vivid narrative style, Luke portrays a homey, intimate version of what in previous pages we have sought to accomplish in the idiom of modern scholarship, namely, a depiction of the setting within which Jesus' words and actions become comprehensible within a specific sociopolitical milieu. The two modes of presentation are not mutually exclusive; instead, when combined they provide a thicker sense of context, resulting in a more profound historical understanding of the specific words and life experiences of Jesus.

The net result of this synthetic approach is salutary historically as well as theologically. What we encounter in the Gospels is not a catalogue of sayings inserted into collections of disjointed narratives, but rather sayings and narratives that invite us to glimpse a teacher and healer who understands his vocation in light of a prophetic calling to be a servant of God at a moment in history in which God was acting to restore the people of Israel through repentance and recommitment to the covenant. But what is a teacher without a classroom?

By diligently sifting through the available sources, we are able to bring into focus not only the unique Jewish teacher-prophet Jesus, but also the audience gathering around him from the villages he visits, an audience drawn mainly from the poor and the ordinary who recognize in Jesus one not only manifesting solidarity with them in their suffering under Roman occupation, but also revealing to them a message that transforms darkness and gloom into light and hope. Contrary to the official propaganda being broadcast by the Roman cult of the divine emperor, the mightiest power in the universe—indeed, the Creator of the universe—is the patron not of Caesar, but of the meek, the poor, and those persecuted for their refutation of idols. In his teachings and acts, they learn another lesson: the invitation he brings is not the invitation to suicidal sacrifice but to commitment to a power not of this earth, the power of love, a power alien to the understanding of those who rule by the sword and ultimately more powerful than all of the military arsenals of the world. The Jesus we glimpse in the words and narratives of the Gospels speaks thus to those who are willing to consider the invitation to a strategy other than the doomed strategy of dominion by force of arms, an invitation that in effect reads, "Fear not, your well-being is not

---

38. I suspect that I am not alone in having been empowered—whether in a junior high school classroom, a Sabbath or Sunday school discussion, or a scout troop meeting—by a teacher who opened up a world beyond the limits of hometown or neighborhood.

controlled by the governments of this world. They rise and fall, all mysteriously in the service of the one true sovereign, whose reign is established not by force, but by meekness, willingness to look out for the neighbor, and submission to a peaceful reign that reserves no privileged positions, but is inclusive of all who accept all-embracing love as the polity of the peaceable kingdom."

The eschatological theme of the imminence of God's reign pervades all that Jesus said and did. In continuity with the prophets of ancient Israel, he announced that in spite of the ostentatious claims of worldly empires, the signs of the inbreaking of a new order of justice, peace, healing, and shared prosperity were visible to those who viewed the world from the perspective of faith in the God of Israel. The eschatological dimension of his message flowed directly from the clarity with which he articulated the foundational principle of biblical faith that served as the starting point for all of the political strategies found in the Bible: the theocratic principle affirming the sole sovereignty of God and the concomitant relativization of all earthly governments and authorities. To view the prophetic eschatology that runs throughout the New Testament as an add-on by later churchly leaders is to turn historical understanding on its head: epigones become credited with the extension of the central themes of Hebrew Scripture to a wider world, while Jesus is relegated to a caricature as an outlier propounding moral platitudes that fail to connect with the urgent concerns of a people longing for redemption and restoration.

Jesus' eschatology, by pointing to signs of God's reign in the lives of his followers, distanced itself from the gnostic view of salvation, according to which the physical world was a prison from which the spirit had to be released. The world that the heavenly Father had created, while ravaged by those who sought to establish their personal dominion through brute force, was the one for whose liberation and restoration to its God-intended wholeness Jesus believed he was called. It is also important to note, however, that the profound bearing of Jesus' eschatology on political theory can also be jeopardized by being construed in strictly this-worldly terms. As important as was the community of forgiveness and love that Jesus gathered around him and as significant as were acts of healing and feeding and consoling, they were signs of a much deeper process of transformation, one that the prophets could imagine as nothing less than the creation of a new heaven and a new earth!

An earlier generation of New Testament scholars introduced the categories of realized and futuristic eschatology, with some emphasizing one or the other as capturing the true meaning of Jesus' message, especially as it came to expression in the parables. Closer to the truth are those who insisted on seeing tension between the two, not as an unresolved contradiction in Jesus' thought, but as a dialectic functioning to preserve a profound understanding of the life of discipleship in a far from perfect world. Where God's love comes to expression in a visit to the imprisoned, a meal prepared for the one living in hunger, or care for the victim of illness or injury, God's reign of compassion and justice is entering this imperfect world, and those who witness such acts enacted in obedience to their Lord can rejoice over signs of the healing of a broken world.

At the same time, an essential aspect of a theo-political policy that is true to the biblical heritage will be the insistence that the redemption intended by God is not completed until there is not a single child going hungry to bed at night, not a single political prisoner remaining in chains, not a single peasant suffering exploitation and deprivation. In the biblical view of the world, realism *and* idealism, pragmatism *and* vision delineate the dynamic field of faithful discipleship. God's love for the world God created is fully present in the hot meal given to a homeless person on a cold winter night in a church basement's provisional shelter. At the same time it is important not to lose sight of the location of a specific *miṣwāh* within a cosmic drama that began with a purposeful act of divine creativity and that will not cease to unfold until every constellation and every galaxy and every creaturely inhabitant within them is restored to God's all-embracing *šālôm*.

THE POLITICS OF JESUS AS EXPRESSED IN HIS WORDS AND ACTS

In all four Gospels, the reader is introduced to the colorful figure of John the Baptist, who serves as a ligature securing the connection between the Hebrew prophets and Jesus of Nazareth. Reference to Isaiah 40:3 serves to place John and Jesus in an eschatological trajectory by relating them to the ancient promise of God's final restoration of true Israel (Matt. 3:1–2; Mark 1:4; Luke 3:4–5; John 1:23). This eschatological orientation is enriched by tying John to the divine promise appearing at the conclusion of the prophetic books of the Bible: John is the Elijah-like figure announced by Malachi as the one who would prepare the way for the day of the Lord's coming (Mal. 4:5–6 [Heb. 3:23–24]), a day when "once more you shall see the difference between the righteous and the wicked, between one who serves God and one who does not serve him" (Mal. 3:18). The narrative in 1 Kings had described Elijah as a prophet carrying out, amid suffering and persecution, his commission to declare the heavenly judge's indictment against the wicked. The book of Malachi, in connection with its announcement of Elijah's return to earth,[39] makes it clear that the category "the wicked" was not an empty abstraction, for it quotes the indictment of the divine judge specifying their transgressions: "against the sorcerers, against the adulterers, against those who swear falsely, against those who oppress the hired workers in their wages, the widow and the orphan, against those who thrust aside the alien, and do not fear me, says the LORD of hosts" (Mal. 3:5).

---

39. Elijah, according to 2 Kgs. 2:11, ascended to heaven in a fiery chariot, thereby being available for a reappearance at the crucial turning point of the ages.

John the Baptist, with his stern theme of repentance, proved to be a fitting link in the chain of witnesses to God's indictment against iniquitous people and God's defense of innocent victims of oppression.

Though the theological significance of John and the way in which his career modulated into that of Jesus were elucidated by the biblical tradents with the aid of a conventional method, namely, typology, the essential traits of the historical John were not lost. He belonged to the class of prophetic figures who regarded the moral depravity of his time as a sign of impending divine judgment. Intoning the central theme of his biblical predecessors, he called for repentance as the only way to escape the wrath to come. Though the brief account given of his message accentuates divine wrath, when he is viewed against the background of Hebrew prophecy, it becomes evident that he belongs to the line of witnesses who yearned for the redemption of Israel and searched for signs of the advent of the anointed one God had promised to send to restore his captive people.

In his particular portrait of John the Baptist, Luke inserts an interesting question-and-answer session between audience and prophet that highlights the theme we found in Malachi's portrayal of Elijah redivivus: the apocalyptic message of impending divine judgment is rooted firmly in the moral imperative of the Torah. Even as Malachi announced that the judgment was the consequence of egregious abuse of the dignity and rights of the most vulnerable members of the society, John is portrayed as instructing the multitudes and then specifically tax collectors and soldiers how they are to conduct their lives so as to avoid impending divine wrath: practice the central law of love for neighbor by sharing food and clothing, conduct your profession as civil servant in honesty and integrity, and do not abuse the authority and power invested in you as a soldier (Luke 3:10–14).[40]

Here, as will be the case throughout his Gospel, Luke homes in on the inseparability of God's rule and the moral mandate of the covenant to show mercy and practice justice. John the Baptist's announcement of impending divine wrath, according to Luke, is not a reckless outburst of sectarian fury, but is rather a passionate plea for a people to come to their senses through repentance and to return obediently to the Torah. Israel's present captivity had a clear cause, namely, repudiation of the life-giving covenant relationship that God had extended to his people. The message demanded by the present moment was clear, as it had been when spoken in their time by Amos, Hosea, Isaiah, Jeremiah, Ezekiel, and Malachi: Repent! Far from being an innovator, John carries on the testimony of the long line of God's servants, the prophets. Fittingly, he is associated with his typological precursor Elijah. The divine wrath invoked by Israel's disobedience was immanent and terrifying. The only option available to humans to avert impending calamity remained unchanged: "repentance for the forgiveness of sins."

40. See François Bovon, *Luke 1: A Commentary on the Gospel of Luke 1:1–9:50*, Hermeneia (Minneapolis: Fortress Press, 2002), ad loc. 3:10–14.

Where does the historical John, to the extent that the layers of tradition drawn upon and elaborated on by the writers of the Gospels and the Acts of the Apostles allow us to discern, fit into the picture we gave in chapter 24 of the Jewish parties of the time? The nature of his diet and the description of his garb comport with his harsh message of impending judgment and the urgent call to repentance to suggest that he belonged to one of the wilderness communes brought to light through discoveries in the Judean wilderness.

Though the paucity of textual evidence places severe restraints on the extent to which we can describe John's theo-politics, it would seem in general that John had little interest in or patience for debate with his audience regarding specific political strategies. The fate of the nation was seen in categorical terms, with the only hope for escape found in the invitation to join a countercommunity centering around repentance and baptism. He appears on the scene as an outsider, and his call to repentance is a summons to renounce the evil world and through the cleansing of baptism to be gathered to the remnant of the true Israel that would be spared the wrath to come. These various pieces of evidence cumulatively suggest that, within the Jewish parties of his time, John's profile most closely fits that of the Essenes. Since the Essenes relied on the conversion of new adherents to sustain their celibate communities, the description of John's attracting a circle of followers comes as no surprise, even as specification of baptism as the rite of initiation available to the repentant comports with evidence from the Dead Sea Scrolls and the architectural remains at Khirbet Qumran.

Among those who responded to John's proclamation by submitting to baptism in the Jordan was Jesus of Nazareth. As scholars have noted, there is no reason to doubt the historicity of this event, for disciples emphasizing the uniqueness of Jesus in the salvation history of Israel would not invent a story depicting their Master as the disciple of another charismatic leader.[41] The same applies to words Jesus uses to describe John found in both Matthew and Luke (<Q): "a prophet . . . and more than a prophet" (Matt. 11:9). This is high praise indeed, expressive of Jesus' esteem for the one who initiated him into his own prophetic vocation, praise extended even further with the words, "Truly I tell you, among those born of women no one has arisen greater than John the Baptist" (Matt. 11:11a). But high praise can lead to hero worship, a phenomenon comfortably at home in the Roman imperial cult, but excluded a priori in the politics of the kingdom, where all human measures of status and worth dissolve before the glory of the sole sovereign of the universe. Jesus concludes his tribute to John with a statement preserving the categorical distinction between this world and the world to come: "the least in the kingdom of heaven is greater than he" (Matt. 11:11b).

---

41. Tradition addressed the potentially compromising fact of Jesus' original discipleship under John the Baptist with the formulation found on the Baptist's lips in the Gospel of John, "He must increase, but I must decrease" (John 3:30).

John would have agreed, for the core theme of his preaching, the nearness of God's reign, envisioned an order of shared blessing, compared to which the realities of this world would be emptied of all significance. It was that theme that evoked the wrath of the minions of worldly power and sealed with his blood the end of his preaching career and his initiation into the martyr guild of Israel's suffering prophets. The cause of his death arose directly from his instance that there was only one king entitled to exercise absolute authority, a king who would tolerate no rivals. Herod Antipas, following a practice that was habitual in the history of his family and endemic to regimes claiming absolute authority over their subjects, sought to preserve his power against rivals by imprisoning the one daring to denounce his hubris. But in John's case, as in the lives of Socrates, Jesus, Blandina, Gandhi, and Martin Luther King Jr., the tyrant was blinded by his imperiousness from recognizing that in seeking to silence his most outspoken critic, he magnified that prophet's witness to the king under whose judgment all earthly tyrants fall.

Imprisonment, however, did pose an immediate problem for one called to prepare for the coming of the kingdom and that kingdom's messiah: The narrative proceeds to deal with John's pondering, who would continue the work he had begun? Stories that had begun to circulate about the extraordinary deeds of one of his followers, Jesus of Nazareth, led him to ask: "Are you he who is to come, or shall we look for another?" Jesus' reply interprets his own acts of healing and proclamation of good news to the poor on the basis of his Jewish tradition: They were to be understood as signs of the inbreaking of God's kingdom (Isa. 29:18–19; 35:5–6; 26:19; 25:8; 61:1–2). John, as he faced his executioner, was, we hope, sustained not alone by the conviction that the crusade to which he had devoted his life had not been futile, but also by confidence that God had anointed the one he had baptized to restore faithful Israel.

Although the eschatological theme of God's kingdom constituted the heart of the proclamation of both John and Jesus, closer examination indicates a difference in emphasis. Though the sources are very limited in the case of the Baptist, it seems apparent that his message stressed one aspect of the kingdom of God, namely, the divine wrath that would prepare the path to repentance. Though not neglecting the prophetic theme of judgment, Jesus' sayings and acts are infused with the other side of the kingdom theme, namely, the joy with which Jesus witnessed evidence that in his life God's redemptive work was being accomplished.

To be sure, Jesus did not gloss over the brutal force with which the powers of this world opposed God's initiative: "From the days of John the Baptist until now the kingdom of heaven has suffered violence, and the violent take it by force" (Matt. 11:12). Indeed, both in a chronological and a thematic sense, it appears that Jesus, in harmony with the pattern found in the book of Malachi, built his message of salvation upon the foundation of John's urgent call to repentance. But in his healing acts, as well as those of his followers, he found occasion for the kind of jubilation captured in the remarkable image with which he responded, according to [...] sent out before him: "I wat[...] (Luke 10:18).

Found in both Matthe[...] explicit contrast between hi[...] drinking, and they say, 'H[...] drinking, and they say, 'Lo[...] tors and sinners!'" (Matt. 11[...] with little variation in all th[...] cal explanation for the differ[...] and the Pharisees and that [...] the disciples of the Pharisees fast, but your disciples do not fast?' Jesus said to them, 'The wedding guests cannot fast while the bridegroom is with them, can they? . . . The days will come when the bridegroom is taken away from them, and then they will fast on that day'" (Mark 2:18–20 and par.).

What light do these passages shed on Jesus' relation to John the Baptist and the Pharisees? The contrast between the world-renouncing, ascetic lifestyle of John on the one hand and Jesus' intermingling with "tax collectors, publicans, and sinners" on the other reflects differences among the Jewish parties of the Roman period and corroborates a suggestion made earlier in this chapter. While John manifests the world-denial of the Essenes, Jesus' interacting with people outside of his own religious circle both resembles and amplifies the view of the Pharisees, of living in the world but not of the world. Later we will have occasion to add specificity to our description of areas where Jesus' religious practices resemble those of the Pharisees (e.g., the importance of table fellowship as a celebration of God's covenant with Israel), as well as points of dispute (e.g., the interpretation of laws regulating purity and defilement). First, we want to preview the fundamental tenets of Jesus' politics and the theological understanding that shape them.

THE KINGDOM OF GOD AS CENTER
OF JESUS' THEOLOGICAL UNDERSTANDING

John had been imprisoned and was soon to be executed. But the prophetic task to which this second Elijah had been called was far from completed.[42] At the point of the violent termination of John's ministry, Jesus experienced the summons of his heavenly Father to gather together a circle of disciples as the next step in

---

42. Given the roots of Jesus' teaching in the eschatological tradition of the Hebrew prophets, the centrality of the concept of the kingdom of God in his message comes as no surprise. The argument for this etiology rather than one appealing to ideal types at home in Hellenistic culture has been made earlier in this chapter and will not be repeated here. Corroborating our conclusion regarding Jesus' roots in the prophetic-eschatological tradition is John Meier's observation that the density of attestation of the topos kingdom of God in the Synoptic tradition contrasts "sharply with the relative dearth of the phrase in early Judaism and the rest of the New Testament" (Meier, *Marginal*, 2:239).

God's renewal of faithful Israel. His understanding of his vocation was molded by knowledge of his religious heritage. A central part of God's purpose as delineated by Hebrew Scripture was the commissioning of one nation to serve as a blessing for all nations. That nation had a checkered history, exemplifying faith and courage under leaders like Abraham, Moses, and Joshua, but stubbornness and even treachery under kings like Ahab and Jehoiakim.[43]

Evidence that God remained steadfast in his partnership with Israel was to be found in the history of prophets who defended God's sole authority and contended for the hearts of the people, often at the cost of ridicule and abuse. Ezekiel gave succinct expression to the prophetic understanding of Israel's God: "As I live, says the Lord GOD, I have no pleasure in the death of the wicked, but that the wicked turn from their ways and live; turn back, turn back from your evil ways; for why will you die, O house of Israel?" (Ezek. 33:11). In particular, the prophetic notion of divine commission as the call to vicarious suffering and death on behalf of a sinful people, found in the Servant Songs of Second Isaiah, helped shape Jesus' understanding of his own role in God's redemptive plan.[44]

We have described the period from Pompey's conquest in 63 BCE to the time of Jesus as a time blending political confusion with religious yearning for the restoration of a free, righteous Israel. On the basis of *Psalm of Solomon* 17, we drew attention to the centrality of messianic hope in the vision of pious Jews living under the Roman occupation: "and their King will be the Messiah [and] Lord. . . . The Lord will himself be his king." While Jesus' understanding of how his role related to messiahship is one of the most debated questions in the history of Jesus research, there is no credible basis for denying that central to his vision of the future was the belief that his generation was witnessing the dawn of God's kingdom and that the meaning of his life was defined by participation in the kingdom's coming.

There is no evidence, however, that he aspired to kingship over a reconstituted monarchy in the literal sense defined by *Psalm of Solomon* 17 and exploited by self-appointed messiahs like Judas son of Hezekiah and Simon son of Joseph. The kingdom that he envisioned was eschatological in nature, and the king whom he served was the heavenly king of the universe. While his allegiance to that king served as the normative basis for his social and political actions, translation of divine kingship into human politics entailed not a literal transfer of absolute canons of authority from God to human rulers, but the requirement that human regimes and their designated rulers conform to the standards implicit in the theocratic principle of God's rule over the entire creation, as they came to expression in Hebrew Scripture.

---

43. For an insightful analysis of the manner in which the Deuteronomistic tradition made theological sense out of the blatant contradictions between faithfulness and disobedience in the book of Joshua, see Rachel M. Billings, *"Israel Served the Lord": The Book of Joshua as Paradoxical Portrait of Faithful Israel* (Notre Dame, IN: University of Notre Dame Press, 2013).

44. See especially Isa. 52:13–53:12.

While this understanding left room for human government, it categorically subordinated the latter to the only government commanding unconditional allegiance. Accordingly, the legitimacy of the regimes of this world was to be derived not from claiming heavenly warrants for unlimited authority, but from concrete demonstration in the day-to-day affairs of state that human officials were serving as faithful agents of the heavenly king by implementing in their institutions the justice and compassion inherent in the reign of the sole sovereign of the universe.

Clear evidence that Jesus repudiated any notion of an identification or a one-to-one correspondence of human and divine monarchy (which is the premise of the ideology of the divine right of kings in both antiquity and medieval times) is found in the flexibility with which he draws upon first one political model and then another in this political statements. By this fluidity he is either proving himself to be muddle-headed in his political thought, or he is serving notice that his allusions to human models of government are intended as metaphors, in their concatenation shedding light on a profound understanding of political process, rather than as literal prescriptions. We believe the latter to be the case.

Quantitatively, the political model that finds the most frequent expression in the words of Jesus is that of monarchy. This is not surprising, since the tradition of David as faithful shepherd of his people occupies a central place in the political legacy of Hebrew Scripture.[45] But the prophetic indictment of many of Israel's kings for perfidy and idolatry militated against an appeal to the Bible to claim monarchy as the only divinely appointed form of human government.[46] It is noteworthy that in turning to the history of his people for a model suitable as a guide for organizing his disciples, Jesus looked to the era before the introduction of monarchy to the organization of early Israel under twelve *tribes*. That he chose *twelve* disciples is in itself rich in symbolic significance. Moreover, in a saying preserved by Matthew and Luke (<Q), Jesus specifies the office to which the disciples are appointed: "You will sit on thrones judging the twelve tribes of Israel" (Luke 22:30//Matt. 19:28).[47] The quality of rule conveyed by this allusion to premonarchical, tribal Israel is that of the intimacy and relative simplicity of village life. This usage, however, does not diminish the significance of the frequent allusions to the more centralized polity of kingship in Jesus' teachings.

What then is the significance of the juxtaposition of different topoi like kingdom, judge, and tribe in Jesus' teachings? It would seem to reflect the following view: though human structures of government are elicited throughout Scripture to clarify aspects of God's mediated rule, literal readings inevitably obscure rather than enhance understanding of something as complex and even perilous as the adaptation of divine governance to the structures of human rule. Like therapeutic lasers targeting a malignant tumor from different angles, Jesus

---

45. E.g., Ezek. 34.
46. E.g., Jer. 22 and Zech. 11.
47. This saying is carefully analyzed in Meier, *Marginal*, 2:135–39.

addresses the relation of the kingdom of heaven to the political realities of his time by drawing first on one, then on another model. For example, he expresses the unconventional demography of God's reign by reference to the patriarchs: "I tell you, many will come from east and west and will eat with Abraham and Isaac and Jacob in the kingdom of heaven, while the heirs of the kingdom will be thrown into the outer darkness" (Matt. 8:11–12; cf. Luke 13:28–29 [<Q]). The net effect of the intertwining of diverse biblical models is to connote the multifaceted splendor of a form of rule that adequately can be described by no single human political model. Taken together, they enrich the eschatological vision of Jesus and at the same time snatch it from the possession and control of any human ideology.

We now turn to texts containing sayings attributable to Jesus and narratives recounting acts of the historical Jesus that shed light on the centrality in his thinking of the kingdom of God.[48] Of preeminent significance is the prayer that he taught his disciples, for it locates with utmost clarity the heart of Jesus' faith. First, in continuity with Hebrew prophecy and in harmony with the traditional Jewish prayer, the Kaddish, he yearns for the preparation that alone can set creation on the path toward renewal, the sanctification of God's name as the *alpha* point of all reality. Only when the entire universe acknowledges its source and sustainer can it manifest *šālôm* in all its parts.

The supernal glory of God provides the theocratic foundation upon which those who love God can proceed to pray for the advent of God's kingdom. The Kaddish eloquently expresses the link: "Magnified and hallowed be his great name in the world [or age] that he has created according to his good pleasure; may he cause his kingdom to reign [i.e., may he establish his kingdom] . . . in your lives [i.e., in your lifetime] and in your days and in the lives of the whole house of Israel, very soon and in a near time [i.e., in the near future]."[49]

All of Jesus' words and all of his actions were committed to the coming of God's kingdom, that is, the reign of the one who would establish justice, equality, peace, and shared prosperity throughout creation. In this prayer for God's kingdom we find the unifying theme around which all that Jesus said and did revolves and finds its deepest meaning.

It is of utmost importance to grasp aright Jesus' understanding of the kingdom of God as it related to the events of the world around him. As reflected both in his drawing metaphors from different political models and in his disassociating himself from insurgent groups like the Zealots and the Sicarii, he did not regard the kingdom as a nationalistic movement that was to compete with, and by superior force supplant, rival earthly regimes. Nor did he concur

---

48. It has been suggested that a more appropriate translation of βασιλεία τοῦ θεοῦ would be "reign of God." Because of its preserving the connotations connected with the biblical metaphor of royal rule more accurately than alternative translations, we choose to stick with the translation "kingdom of God," while acknowledging that it is problematic if not understood within its ancient historical milieu and in its metaphorical linguistic function.

49. Meier, *Marginal*, 2:297–99.

with the Essenes' view of the coming kingdom as a mandate to withdraw from involvement in the day-to-day affairs of society. Speculation as to the time of the kingdom's debut and the signs foretelling its arrival represented for him a distraction from its true meaning.

His own disciples seemed as confused as modern interpreters often are about the relation between the immediacy of the kingdom and its future dimensions. John Meier has properly explained that to frame the question of the tense of the kingdom in exclusive terms of either present or future is to miss its rich symbolic meaning, to which a tensive quality is essential.[50] The reality of the kingdom of God was experienced in the most common daily acts, like giving a loaf of bread to one in hunger, speaking a word of comfort to the bereaved, and blessing little children. But its limitless embrace reached out spatially to encompass the most distant constellations, a wonder that has become all the more astonishing with the discoveries of modern science, including the amazing images transmitted back to earth by the Hubble space telescope, which place within our ken events approaching the moment of the big bang. Temporally as well, the kingdom burst open conventional human categories as it addressed everyday matters of food and shelter while simultaneously glimpsing the heavenly banquet.

God's kingdom was the reality that enriched Jesus' response to every person he met, every danger he encountered, and every question that was pressed upon him. It follows that our effort to understand the meaning of God's kingdom and its significance for the contemporary world must begin, not with a philosophical formulation that resolves all tensions and contradictions, but with careful study of the concrete events in which Jesus perceived the kingdom's coming and the sayings and parables in which he opened up for his followers glimpses of the reality that alone explained life in its myriad aspects.

From the first petition of the Lord's Prayer, it becomes clear that for Jesus the coming of God's kingdom was inextricably tied to obedience to God's will. Accordingly, "thy kingdom come" and "thy will be done" were not separate events for which his disciples were to pray, but one dynamic phenomenon in which the kingdom unfolded and flourished through obedience to the will of the heavenly Father. What Jesus yearned for, lived for, and died for was the reunification of all of reality through the alignment of this world with the realm of God's reign: "on earth as it is in heaven." The universe would be restored to its intended wholeness when all that exists lived in harmony with the loving nature of its Creator. This central truth that enfolds theology and ethics in inseparable union is grasped in the rabbinical teaching that on the day in which all of the children of Israel were obedient to the Torah, the messiah would come.

Among the gems that depict with especial clarity Jesus' understanding of the kingdom of God are the Beatitudes. Their dual appearance in the Sermon on the Mount in Matthew 5 and the Sermon on the Plain in Luke 6 is best accounted for by recognizing Q as the common source drawn upon by the two

50. Ibid., 10.

Gospel writers. The four blessings in Luke—pithy, unadorned, and free of the hermeneutical traits of later tradents—can be viewed with confidence as authentic words of Jesus. They speak directly to the heart of the concerns bearing down on the crowds coming to him in the Galilean countryside. Within those crowds would have been peasant farmers and day laborers reduced to poverty by the repressive patronage and onerous taxes of the Romans. Widows with their children in tow would have been present as well, desperately living from week to week without assurance of daily bread.

Swirling as a dark cloud would have been the starkly contradictory collective memories of, on the one hand, a proud and independent Jewish nation under its Davidic king and, on the other, Rachel's weeping over her lost children and exiles cut off from their beloved Jerusalem and intoning laments by the waters of Babylon. Broken of pride, reduced to powerlessness, and spurned by both affluent, complicit compatriots and ruthless occupation forces, it was an audience yearning for a new chapter in their nation's story. What word of hope and comfort, what good news capable of affirming the loving care of the one proclaimed by the ancestral faith as the king of the universe or—in terms of the genres provided within the framework of traditional Jewish covenantal thought—what beatitudes could Jesus offer to the poor, the hungry, the sorrowful, and the pariahs of the land?

The lead weight on the backs of the people was constituted not solely by the cruelty of their oppressors. A major tradition flowed through their own religious lore that interpreted poverty, hunger, bereavement, and persecution as the just deserts of sinners who had violated the stipulations of the Mosaic covenant. Little wonder that fiery insurgents summoning the people to bloody conflict against the Romans gained considerable traction among the people of the land. Again, what words of hope, what beatitudes could Jesus offer such a crowd?

The answer given by Jesus was succinct and, in the minds of many, including the pragmatic activists of his time like the Zealots, woefully inadequate, or even derelict and scandalous: "Blessed are you who are poor, you that hunger now, you that weep now, for yours is the kingdom of God!" So they were down on luck and lacking daily bread; in the kingdom they would be satisfied. So they were filled with sadness now; in the kingdom they would be filled with laughter. Is this not an outrageously feckless response to human need?

Well-intentioned modern interpreters have displayed considerable creativity in their efforts to explain away what offends modern liberal sensitivities: The otherworldly emphasis on the coming kingdom of God was not part of the historical Jesus' message, they claim, but rather was related by confounded followers after Jesus' death. In stripping away eschatological accretions it is possible to get back to the original teachings of the itinerant Galilean teacher, a practical-minded sage offering sound advice in the Greek tradition of the peripatetic Cynic philosophers.

As argued above, we believe that the cultural context within which Jesus grew up and in which his religious views were formed, while not untouched by the widespread influence of Hellenism, was primarily imbued with the beliefs and values of the ancestral Jewish faith. Once the question of the historical Jesus is pursued within that context, more specifically, within the prophetic tradition that viewed all of creation from the perspective of God's plan for God's people and the nations of the world, the rush to purge Jesus' message of all traces of eschatology in the pursuit of a Jesus more compatible with contemporary views on social reform will be rejected as an indefensible tour de force.

In seeking to recover a reliable historical perspective from which to understand Jesus and his teaching, one does well to remember the incisiveness with which Albert Schweitzer exposed the spurious nature of the popular nineteenth-century portraits of the historical Jesus, portraits resembling in many ways recent historical-Jesus reconstructions. The first step toward genuine understanding is taken when one recognizes that themes deriving from Jewish eschatology lie at the heart of Jesus' perception of the world and form the central thrust of his message. To be sure, once that conclusion has been drawn, it can be taken in a number of different directions. In the case of Schweitzer, honest reckoning with the apocalyptic heart of Jesus' worldview led him to reject that view as untenable within the modern world. While rejection will not be the path we shall follow, we will have to be as honest as Schweitzer in admitting that Jesus' response to the human needs of poverty, hunger, and deep sorrow with the promise of reversal in the kingdom of God raises for the contemporary reader a tough hermeneutical challenge.

The first step in meeting that challenge is an unabashed acknowledgment of the centrality in Jesus' view of reality of the prophetic eschatological tradition of God's promise to restore Israel, and through Israel the entire world, to the wholeness that reflects the loving nature of the Creator. Recourse to a Kantian Jesus, or to the updated neo-Kantianism of John Rawls, solves a raft of hermeneutical problems by offering a direct delivery service from the New Testament to a reform program promulgated by liberal political rationalism, but the price theologically and politically is intolerable, for it is Jesus' eschatological message of the kingdom of God that offers the key to an understanding of the ills of this world's political and economic structures that is distinctive, deeper than the conceptual field of secular systems of thought, and resistant to co-optation by worldly powers and nationalistic ideologies. Tempting as it may be for the church to "adjust" the vision of a realm in which all those who hunger are filled, all who weep laugh with joy, all who are poor are given the kingdom of God, so that it comes into alignment with the harsh realities of this world, the centrality in Jesus' message of God's promise of a thorough transformation of a fallen world must not be sacrificed.

To revise the Beatitudes in the effort to claim Jesus as the architect of a realistic social reform program would be to wreck the foundation upon which the church must insist lasting reform can alone be accomplished. The reason is simple: the church claims that the only agent capable of accomplishing lasting change is God. Christian social ethics, Christian political theory, Christian economic reform can be safeguarded from modulating into yet another secular effort at human engineering, only if the theological basis of its message to society and world remains firm.

Front and center in our approach to understanding the significance of the theme of the kingdom of God in Jesus' message, we must place this stark fact: to the poor, the hungry, and the persecuted, Jesus offers as the priceless basis for hope the promise of the kingdom of God. Negatively, this means that Jesus rejects as inadequate *all* human models of governance. Included in this rejection were the gilded icons of his nation's past, the Davidic monarchy and the Jerusalem temple. Jesus' critique of all human institutions is consistent and radical in nature. This stunning denunciation is the move not of an anarchist or nihilist, but rather of one who sees as the only alternative to the endless cycles of human conflict and tragedy an entirely different starting point, a radically different basis for hope. That basis is the kingdom of God.

People of faith dare not remain silent when modern culture stridently proclaims that basing hope for justice and peace on a transcendent reality is escapist and utopian. The only honest position, according to this view, is to accept that humans, as the product of an arbitrary natural process, stand alone in the vast universe. Viewed materialistically, from the perspective of Karl Marx or Richard Dawkins, invocation of a transcendent notion like the kingdom of God as a political strategy invites not discourse but derision.

From the side of faith, not derision but engagement with other perspectives is called for. As an aid to such discourse, four interpretive steps can be helpful: (1) clearly depicting the roots of Jesus' eschatology in his ancestral monotheistic faith; (2) demonstrating how the manner in which his confidence in the final victory of God's kingdom over all the forces of evil infuses the entirety of his teachings and acts and comes to expression in the lives of his followers; (3) explicating the function of that key metaphor in his manner of responding to both the oppressive Roman rule of his time and the alternative strategies of competing Jewish parties; (4) within the concrete setting of our contemporary world, parsing the way in which the notion of the kingdom of God provides a solid foundation for constructing political strategies that can both contribute to discussions addressing the myriad crises facing modern humanity and motivate those of "clean heart" and "right spirit" to redouble their efforts on behalf of a peaceable kingdom embracing all peoples and all creation. Within a diverse culture, in which the elusive but critically important task of cooperative alliances dedicated to the common good increases in direct proportion to the magnitude of the threats to peace and shared prosperity posed by self-serving agents of violent conquest, it is to be hoped that this four-stage intellectual pilgrimage will be taken seriously, not only by members of explicitly defined communities of faith, but also by honest inquirers of all persuasions. A giant step forward will be accomplished, for example, when a believer's commitment to seeing our threatened planet through the eyes of an astrophysicist will be reciprocated by the latter's willingness to take a second look at the politics of the ancient rabbis, including Hillel and Jesus. I sincerely believe that such a reclaiming of the disputational style of dialogue developed by the Pharisees and practiced by Jesus can disarm old animosities and create an openness to the political implications of Jesus' kingdom-based theocratic view of reality.

THE PARABLES OF THE KINGDOM

The parables of Jesus in the New Testament Gospels have as their central theme the kingdom of God. Add to this the high degree of reliability accorded to them by critical scholars,[51] and it becomes obvious that they are entitled to a position of honor in any study seeking to fathom the meaning and significance of the kingdom of God in Jesus' teaching and its bearing on his theo-political thought.

Among the genres utilized by the teachers and prophets of antiquity, the parable is perhaps the best suited to transmit the meaning intended by Jesus in his use of the metaphor of kingdom. The order of righteousness, mercy, peace, and shared prosperity that Jesus associated with God's reign was not a vacuous concept, but one characterized by specific qualities and demands. The objects, characters, and actions that we find in the parables vividly depict those features. At the same time, they point the imagination beyond themselves to a reality that transcends what humans associate with prevailing institutions and social relations, a phenomenon possible because there is more than a one-to-one correspondence between the elements of a parable and their referents.

In his poem "Gedichte sind gemalte Fensterscheiben" ("Poems are painted windowpanes"), Goethe invoked an image that elucidates the way the metaphor of kingdom functions in the parables, namely, the image of a cathedral's stained-glass windows. He contrasts two kinds of vision. To the philistine—by which he signifies one blind to the mystery and wonder lying beyond the obvious—all that is seen is the surface of a pane of glass. How different the encounter of the one possessing the sensitivity to peer *through* the window to the numinous luminosity within the sanctum! Of course, images do not need to exclude scholarly definitions, and this one offered by Klyne Snodgrass concisely captures the central point: "In most cases . . . a parable is an expanded analogy used to convince and persuade."[52]

Important lessons have been learned over the history of the scholarly study of the parables of Jesus. Favored among the teachers of the early and medieval church was an allegorical method that assigned a deeper, hidden meaning to

---

51. "[V]irtually everyone grants that they are the surest bedrock we have of Jesus' teaching. . . . I am convinced . . . that the parables are indeed the surest place where we have access to Jesus' teaching. . . . As far as we can tell, the early church hardly ever told parables. Parables fit Jesus' prophetic stance, and the teaching in the parables can be corroborated in non-parabolic material" (Klyne Snodgrass, *Stories with Intent: A Comprehensive Guide to the Parables of Jesus* [Grand Rapids: Eerdmans, 2008], 31).

52. Ibid., 9.

every detail, for example, the foolish maidens represented the synagogue, the wise maidens the church. A major shift was introduced in the last quarter of the nineteenth century by Adolf Jülicher[53] and subsequently popularized in the middle of the twentieth century by Joachim Jeremias.[54] It attributed allegorizing tendencies in the New Testament texts (e.g., the parable of the Sower) and the elaborate allegorizing interpretations in subsequent postbiblical commentaries to a misunderstanding of the essential character of parables, namely, focus on a single central point. While sensitivity to the unique character of each parable is to be preferred to the procrustean bed of any particular methodology, it is generally the case that each of Jesus' parables seeks to teach a central truth, most commonly having to do with an aspect of the kingdom of God.

Before turning to the parables themselves, a further cautionary word is in order, in this case having to do with the application of the meaning of New Testament parables to contemporary realities. Earlier in this chapter we referred in general terms to the danger of imposing on the words of Jesus modern political ideologies and agendas. Given the metaphorical and accordingly opaque nature of the parables, they are particularly vulnerable to modern Rorschach-type readings that are reflective more of the contemporary interpreter's perspective than of the original intent of the prophet of Nazareth.[55] While eschewing as well the opposite danger of the false historical certainties of positivism, we shall seek as an initial move in understanding the parables of Jesus the attempt to explain their intent and significance within the context of their location in history. The goal of explicating their political meaning for the contemporary world can be pursued only after the historical task has been completed, which goal we consider a self-conscious second stage of hermeneutical reflection that must be chastened by the limits provided by historical research.

Through his parables, Jesus instructed his disciples regarding four dimensions of the kingdom that he experienced as both present and yet to come in its fullness: (1) the nature of the kingdom's God, (2) the qualities that will characterize the lives of those who heed the kingdom's call, (3) the significance that attentive waiting for the kingdom's coming in fullness has for his followers, and (4) God's

---

53. Adolf Jülicher, *Die Gleichnisreden Jesu*, 2 vols. (Tübingen: Mohr [Siebeck], 1888).

54. Joachim Jeremias, *The Parables of Jesus*, trans. S. H. Hooke, 2nd ed. (New York: Scribner & Sons, 1954).

55. To cite one example: Though I learned much from Luise Schottroff's *The Parables of Jesus*, trans. Linda M. Maloney (Minneapolis: Fortress Press, 2006), and ultimately derive from Jesus' parables similar compelling mandates for social-political action, I find myself proceeding through a hermeneutical step missing in her analysis: While she finds what I would characterize as modern feminist and social-justice themes in the parables attributable to Jesus, I find teachings relating, for example, to the kingdom of God, that first must be contextualized within their ancient setting in Roman-occupied Galilee and Judea, and only then, in a critical hermeneutical move, translated into appropriate/analogous contemporary realities. In this regard, I find myself in agreement with Klyne Snodgrass: "I do not seek the intent of the church, a psychologist, a sociologist, a feminist, or any other such rewritings common as they are. I seek to hear the intent of Jesus to his contemporaries— his disciples and his fellow Jews" (*Stories*, 3, cf. n. 95). Ever lurking in this position, however, is another danger, the false assurance of positivism, the most effective safeguard against which is ongoing interdisciplinary dialogue.

renewed initiative to restore God's covenant people, Israel. Though the sheer number and complexity of the parables preclude a systematic treatment of these four themes, we shall draw upon representative parables in describing each.

The greatest mystery of all, and at the same time the most important window opened by the parables, is the *nature of the kingdom's God*. All that is awry in the world, as well as every hope for creation's healing, can be answered by reference to one reality alone, and that is the creator and redeemer of the universe. With tenderness as well as shocking honesty, Jesus reveals the heart of his heavenly Father, a God both tireless in seeking to reclaim the lost and incisive in rendering judgment against the enemies of the peaceable kingdom.

We begin with the parable of the Lost Sheep (Matt.18:12–14; Luke 15:3–7), which invokes a bucolic metaphor deeply rooted in Hebrew prophetic tradition. The history of wicked shepherds who neglected, abused, and consumed their sheep[56] only deepened the longing in Israel for the Good Shepherd, whom only God could provide to heal and restore his scattered flock.[57] For many in Jesus' time, that Shepherd was expected to arise from the royal house of David, in keeping with the messianic hope expressed in *Psalm of Solomon* 17. Jesus refrained from tying the prophetic yearning for the Good Shepherd sent by God to the Davidic dynasty, and we associate this with his chastened view of the historical institution of Judean monarchy. This does not diminish the audacity of his affirmation that the people Israel would not be forsaken, for their true Shepherd was *God*, and God's care for the safety of every last member of his flock was so unconditional that he would set out from the sheepfold in search of the one that had strayed. Such was the quality of God's love for his people—unequivocal and audacious beyond all reckoning!

Many of the parables that illustrate aspects of God's nature modulate explicitly into the *qualities* that Jesus' disciples were to incorporate in their daily lives. In their versions of the Good Shepherd, both Matthew and Luke shape the parable into a lesson on how the leaders of the nascent church were to follow the Shepherd's example in looking after the lost. But there are other parables in which such paraenesis clearly came to expression in the original telling of the story by Jesus.

The parable of the Prodigal Son (Luke 15:11–32), for example, elaborates on the picture of the extravagantly loving heavenly Father whose outreach heeds no bounds. It goes on to show how the love emanating from the kingdom is to infuse the relationships of humans in their everyday lives. After the younger son took the inheritance he had requested, squandered it on a profligate lifestyle, then out of the depths of his depravity repented and returned to the security of the home and the parent he had renounced, he is welcomed by his father with a lavish feast! This is extravagant love indeed, and good news for those mired in self-perceived hopelessness, but the story has a second panel, a tougher

---

56. Ezek. 34:1–10; Zech. 10:2–3; 11:4–17.
57. Isa. 40:11; Jer. 31:10; Ezek. 34:11–16, 23–24; 37:24.

lesson conveyed through the response of the faithful, diligent, responsible elder brother. He is exasperated, and the listener could add, justifiably so!

Alas, the father, while giving the elder brother reassuring words ("Son, you are always with me, and all that is mine is yours" [Luke 15:31]), does not join in defaming the younger brother, but rather responds with festive celebration over the one who was lost, as good as dead, and had returned home. Here the audience is subjected to one of the most difficult lessons of the kingdom, for it flies in the face of the natural inclination to grumble over the odiousness of having one who is deemed inferior to oneself become the focus of special attention and favor. How thorough a transformation of human nature is required to feel a spontaneous surge of joy over the rescue of a tramp from the brink of ruin!

Conventional human sensibilities are destabilized again in the parable of the Vineyard Workers (Matt. 20:1–16). How patently unfair of the boss to pay those who worked the entire day no more than those brought in at day's end! We sympathize with their grumbling, and together with them are put in our place, on the basis of a concept we grasp only with great difficulty: God's generosity is not regulated by human reckoning! Begrudging the good fortune of others, feeling the heat of jealousy build up when an undeserved boon falls into the lap of a fellow human—these are be purged from the mind-set of the one who has accepted the call to the new order of the kingdom. "Or are you envious because I am generous?" invades our consciousness, seeking to replace our instinctive way of viewing the world with the perspective of the kingdom, a perspective that decenters self and sees others with eyes radiating God's love for all God's children.

Human concepts of status are contrasted with God's perception of worth in the parable of the Pharisee and the Tax Collector (Luke 18:9–17). The conventional barrier that humans construct between meritorious members of a community and social outcasts is delineated by the distance separating the Pharisee and the tax collector in the temple. In the kingdom of God, a great reversal of human ranking occurs; unlike Santa Claus, God does not keep a list, but searches the heart. From his heart the Pharisee boasted of self-worth, while the tax collector could only utter a confession of sin and a plea for mercy. It was the heart of the latter that was open to God's free gift of forgiveness.

The transformation heralded by the kingdom was not a matter of small adjustments in habits and tastes. It called for undivided attention, an active kind of hearing that followed through in producing results analogous to that arising out of the good soil in the parable of the Sower (Matt. 13:3–9). It meant acknowledging the fundamental inadequacy of a "normal" state of being, repenting of the hollowness of a life centered on self, and accepting as a gift a new and clean heart open to God's love, and thereby opened in love to all of God's children.

The anthropology reflected in Jesus' invitation to the way of the kingdom would have been familiar to anyone in his audience acquainted with the prophetic tradition. Jeremiah had spoken of the human heart as devious and perverse and comprehensible to God alone (Jer. 17:9–10). Ezekiel peered deeply only to find the heart to be an object of stone that God alone could remedy by replacing it with a heart of flesh (Ezek. 36:26). The psalmist pleaded with God, "Create in me a clean heart, O God, and put a new and right spirit within me" (Ps. 51:10). The latter-day prophet John the Baptist called for the about-face of repentance.

Jesus extended to his hearers the call to a new manner of being as members of God's kingdom. As was the case of the individual who discovered treasure hidden in a field (Matt. 13:44) and the merchant who found a precious pearl (Matt. 13:45–6), those who heard aright Jesus' message of the kingdom would experience the devaluation of all earthly currencies as they took possession of the only object whose value was eternal. All else that life could offer represented distractions that must vanish in the joyous embrace of that which alone is price-less and capable of redefining life and remaking identity in the image of God.

Alas, distractions were everywhere! As if to warn their readers of the deadly danger of distractions, Matthew and Luke place the story of the temptation of Jesus at the beginning of his public ministry.[58] Jesus in effect had to defang the source of all fatal attractions before he himself could instruct his followers. Luke adds to the concluding scene of the devil's departing from Jesus the ominous words "until an opportune time" (Luke 4:13). For the one accepting the ines-timable worth of the kingdom into their lives, the devil would ever be awaiting an opportune time. In a number of parables, Jesus warned his disciples of the many ways in which the devil could distract those being offered the kingdom from embracing the prize.

Among distractions, none receives more attention in Jesus' parables than wealth and possessions. In the parable of the Rich Man and Lazarus (Luke 16:19–31) the rich man cuts himself off from God by viewing his wealth not out of a sense of solidarity with his fellows but as wherewithal to construct walls that remove the sight of human misery from his comfortable surroundings. Not to be missed in the story is a sharp warning directed at those complacently com-fortable in their traditional religiosity. In calling out to Abraham, the rich man names him "father," and Abraham in turn calls him "child"; but such religious familiarity is no substitute for the basic act of generosity that is expected of everyone with sufficient means to alleviate the misery of a fellow human who is hungry, homeless, or in harm's way.

To locate security in the abundance of possessions is to be seduced into the illusory investment strategy of the rich fool (Luke 12:16–21). God does not mask his scorn in pointing out the lethal miscalculation: "You fool! This very night your life is being demanded of you!" Here was a man with enviable opportunity to make a lasting contribution to life, and he blew it! "So it is with those who store up treasures for themselves but are not rich toward God" (Luke 12:21).

The effectiveness with which a parable can explore spiritual mysteries that even the most meticulous application of traditional methods of Torah exposition

---

58. Matt. 4:1–11; Luke 4:1–13. Mark mentions the temptation without elaboration (1:12–13).

cannot match comes to light in Luke 10:25–37. The opening scene describes a learned discussion between Jesus and a lawyer who inquires what he must do "to inherit eternal life." Jesus draws upon his religious education in providing his interlocutor with an answer that summarizes the essence of Jewish faith, love of God and love of neighbor as self. But the discussion swiftly moves beyond traditional exegesis to a more penetrating level, when the lawyer asks, "And who is my neighbor?" and Jesus responds with a parable.

The story of the Good Samaritan is perhaps the best known of all of the New Testament parables. It captures in one poignant vignette the central characteristic of the one whose life conforms to the ethos of the kingdom of God. Unfortunately, interpretation both ancient and modern frequently has become mired down in parsing the moral flaws of the priest and the Levite, creating a wide-open door for anti-Judaic diatribes that devour the central point of the parable. The clue to what is central and what is peripheral is provided by the language of the narrative itself, according to which it was "by chance a priest was going down that road," "so likewise a Levite." As supporting members of the cast, they are present to illuminate the main point, namely, that the life of the kingdom of God is open to anyone, regardless of pedigree. Indeed in this case the third passerby, who happens to be a Samaritan, that is, an outcast, provides an unforgettable picture of the one who incorporates into his daily life the meaning of true religion.

Entirely in the spirit of the Hebrew prophets, Jesus focuses on the quality Søren Kierkegaard later described as "the purity of heart."[59] When he saw a human in need, the Samaritan was moved "to will one thing," the alleviation of suffering and the restoration to health of a fellow human being. That the person in need happened to be a total stranger was inconsequential. Self/other distinctions do not pertain to the kingdom, and the Samaritan and the beaten man form a cast of two to drive home that central point. For many, notions of religious purity had marginalized the Samaritan; for others, a person in need who fell outside the bonds of kinship imposed no obligations. But the marginalized Samaritan, spontaneously and from the heart treating the marginalized stranger as his dear brother, unequivocally answered the lawyer's question, "Who is my neighbor?" Yet, from the age of Cain and Abel to the days of Rwanda, Darfur, and Haiti, equivocation stands as a sturdy wall against the sister- and brotherhood that could bring humanity nearer to the peaceable kingdom—or should we rather say, that could make present among humans the justice, peace, and shared prosperity of the kingdom of God.

Exercising caution not to blunt the central point of the parable of the Good Samaritan by overemphasizing the element of polemic between Jesus and his coreligionists, however, should not be carried so far as to encourage attempts, however well intentioned, to expurgate as a matter of principle the element of

---

59. Søren Kierkegaard, *Purity of Heart Is to Will One Thing: Spiritual Preparation for the Feast of Confession,* trans. Douglas V. Steere (New York: Harper & Bros., 1938).

inner-Jewish disputation from the parables. We can illustrate this point with scenes described by Luke.

In the opening verses of chapter 14 of his Gospel, Luke takes note of "one occasion when Jesus was going to the house of a leader of the Pharisees to eat a meal on the sabbath." He records this event as if it belonged to the common-place rather than the unusual. The modern reader who is acquainted with the social and religious conventions of well-educated Jews during the Roman period will recognize a familiar setting, a gathering of the ḥābûrā (i.e., "table fellow-ship") of a prominent Pharisee. So what did the participants at such an event do? Of course they shared bread and wine, but those basic gifts of the vine and field were invitations to more serious business, namely, rigorous debate over differing interpretations of Torah, such as laws regulating Sabbath (Luke 14:3–5).[60]

Luke finds the Pharisee's table a suitable setting for another topic, namely, the proper seating arrangements at the heavenly banquet (Luke 14:7–14). Jesus demonstrated his familiarity with the format of such a "symposium" by asking a question and then giving a provocative answer: "Where should you sit in enter-ing the banquet hall?" "Take the lowest place." "And whom should you expect to see sitting beside you? Your friends, relatives, rich neighbors? No, rather the poor, the crippled, the lame, and the blind!" Here we find Jesus again using a story to present a point with clarity and poignancy that more conceptual modes of formulation would be incapable of matching, and in this case it is a point with an unmistakable polemical edge. The new order to which he felt called and which he believed was unfolding in the lives of his followers was oblivious of the distinctions in status that played such a deleterious role in shredding human communities. Where humans are united in the love of God, the emptiness that requires boasting and an arrogant sense of superiority vis-à-vis others is filled with a sense of mutual caring and support. In a kingdom that embraces all with-out exception, the self/other distinction evaporates.

We turn next to a group of parables that trouble many commentators by appearing to commend character traits that contradict the ethos embodied in other parables, such as the Good Samaritan and the Good Shepherd, and in the Beatitudes. For there is nothing meek or merciful about either the harsh master

60. Two blind spots in modern understandings of Jesus' relation to his Jewish coreligionists have unnecessarily encumbered efforts to understand the polemical elements in the Gospel narratives and led instead to contorted efforts to explain them away: (1) a failure to situate Jesus' debates with groups identified as scribes or Pharisees within a historical setting where lively disputation defined the vocation of the teachers of the Jewish community; (2) a failure to distinguish between the differ-ent Jewish parties and groups with whom Jesus interacted. In his meticulous study of the historical Jesus, John Meier has provided the most reliable basis to date for redressing this twofold failure. First, in relation to the latter point above, he makes this important observation pertaining to both the Synoptic Gospels and John: "While Jesus can at times engage in civilized debate or even friendly dialogue with Pharisees, scribes, or 'rulers,' the priests are never presented in such a positive light." Secondly, in relation to the former point above, he argues that supporting the historicity of civil debates between Jesus and the Pharisees is the fact that such accounts would not have arisen later in the first century when the Pharisees and their heirs, the rabbis, became the major opponents of the emerging Christian movement (Meier, *A Marginal Jew*, 1:349).

or the clever investor of the five talents entrusted to him (Matt. 25:14–30; cf. Luke 19:11–27). We find quite despicable the conniving unjust steward who feathers his nest before being fired (Luke 16:1–13). In the case of these enigmatic parables, the lesson taught by Adolf Jülicher and Joachim Jeremias should be kept in mind: parables should not be reduced to morality plays in which each actor serves as an exemplum of one of the seven virtues or vices. In the case of the clever investor and the unjust steward, points are made that are at home in one of the most tried and tested traditions in antiquity, namely, wisdom.

A saying of Jesus found in his instructions to the Twelve as they embark upon a mission journey can clarify our point. When he instructs them to be "wise as serpents and innocent as doves" (Matt. 10:16), he is commending neither serpentine nor dovish behavior as an alternative to the authentic compassion and mercy that are to shape the essential being of the righteous. Rather, he is giving practical advice for the survival of the righteous in a world inhabited by "wolves." To simply bare their throats to the attacks of the ungodly would achieve nothing for the kingdom. Rather, they are to marshal the gifts with which they have been endowed *for the sake* of the gospel; when confronted by those seeking to ensnare them, they are to keep their wits about them, lest their efforts on behalf of truth and justice be undone.

We have already noted how this application of worldly-wise wisdom to the goals of the kingdom led Jesus to distance himself from both the violent tactics of the Zealots and Sicarii and the withdrawal from political engagement of the Essenes and the protognostics. We can summarize the relation between kingdom-centeredness and the application of worldly wisdom to specific situations thus: once persons of faith are committed unconditionally to the kingdom and its righteousness, they are free to apply common sense in such ways as to maximize their effectiveness for the sake of the well-being of all God's children.

Three short parables, straightforward rather than perplexing in nature, also fit what can be considered words of practical advice to would-be disciples. In the case of the builder planning to construct a house (Matt. 7:24–27), the man intending to build a tower (Luke 14:28–30), and the king setting out to battle (Luke 7:31–32), the exercise of common sense was commended by Jesus. One can well imagine that some enthusiastically joining the ranks of the disciples would have been tempted to forsake all human considerations, out of trust in God's ability to achieve his purpose without human forethought or reasoning. Such heedlessness, Jesus taught, was as stupid as building a house on sand, only to see it swept away by the first flash flood or mudslide, or equivalent to running short of building materials with only the foundation of the tower laid, or as suicidal as marching out to battle without having estimated the firepower of the enemy.

The ethos of the kingdom does not exclude a healthy dose of pragmatism. Of course, such practical advice would immediately be perverted if an earthly tactic or temporal objective compromised the core allegiance of the disciples to the kingdom and its righteousness. The rich fool on the one hand and the wise tower builder on the other teach distinct lessons bearing on the reign of God, and we merge or confuse them at the peril of our misunderstanding Jesus' multifaceted teachings regarding the kingdom of God.

Wisdom is applied by Jesus not solely in teaching his disciples survival tactics in a dangerous world. Wisdom is also commended as an attribute to be exercised in relation to a profoundly serious aspect of the life of discipleship, namely, patient preparedness as the faithful await the coming of the kingdom in fullness. In the parable of the Wise and Foolish Bridesmaids (Matt. 25:1–13), the foolish maidens were not villains; they were simply fallible humans who faltered in maintaining the purity of heart to will one thing. Medieval paintings and cathedral sculptures excel in describing the lurid sins to which the foolish maidens had fallen. In Jesus' telling of this parable, such moralizing embellishments are missing, and undivided focus is on the unrivaled preeminence of commitment to God's kingdom in the life of the disciple. Kingdom-consciousness will imbue every aspect of life. Whether awake or asleep (n.b.: both the foolish and the wise maidens fell asleep!), at work or at play, seeking the kingdom and its righteousness will guide the lives of the faithful, for kingdom and righteousness have been inscribed on the heart by God. Totality of commitment to God's kingdom and preparedness for its coming in fullness is brilliantly conveyed also in the parable of the Faithful and the Wicked Slaves (Matt. 24:45–51; Luke 12:42–48).

A group of parables shaped by an eschatological perspective addresses the nagging question when, or how long until. The narratives of the Gospels and of Acts are filled with fierce opposition, defeats, and disappointments that undoubtedly created a sense of conflict between the disciples' hearing Jesus' announcement of the kingdom in parables and sayings, experiencing the presence of the kingdom in acts of compassion and healing, and then slamming against powerful forces seemingly poised to bring all of their efforts to naught. The parables of the Scattered Seeds (Mark 4:26–29) and the Mustard Seed (Mark 4:30–32; Matt. 13:31–32) focus on simple observations of nature to encourage patience based on unwavering trust that, even when tangible signs are lacking, growth that is fostered by powers beyond the influence or control of humans is taking place and will culminate in abundance.

Another agrarian parable introduces a more sinister dimension, namely, the presence of invasive, nocuous growth among the wheat, stemming from the stealthful work of an enemy (Matt. 13:24–30). The allegorizing interpretation that follows in verses 36–43 identifies the enemy with the devil, but this is a reference that would have been transparent to anyone in Jesus' original audience. The frustration addressed by the parable is the experience of the infiltration of the circles of Jesus' followers by false believers. The human impulse would be to expunge them by some manner of force. Not so, says the Teacher. Judgment belongs to God. In the meantime, the disciples are to persevere out of trust that God's kingdom ultimately will prevail over the assaults of every enemy. Essentially the same lesson is taught in the parable of the Fishing Net (Matt. 13:47–50).

Of all of the eschatological parables, the most poignant one depicts the judging of the sheep and the goats (Matt. 25:31–46). To this day I remember a conversation in Marburg, Germany, with a doctoral student of Rudolf Bultmann, in which he passionately commended this parable to me as *the* quintessential formulation of the gospel of Jesus. I still accord with the preeminent status that he ascribed to this parable—though I had then and still have difficulty accepting his accompanying dismissal of all subsequent church teaching as a betrayal of that original, pure kernel!

As in the parable of the Good Samaritan, the final judgment scene in Matthew 25 depicts compassion as the criterion for inclusion in the kingdom. But it is not a pampering compassion, for it preserves the purity of divine compassion by upholding its inseparable bond with divine justice. Those who renounce mercy introduce a chaotic element that must be purged, in order to restore harmony within the human family, in which the merciful reach out to the hungry, the lonely, the sick, and imprisoned, without calculation or pursuit of reward, but out of the love of their heart. They are the ones who through the ages have taught us the meaning of the biblical concept of the *miṣwāh,* the act of loving-kindness.

What then is the essential nature of the *miṣwāh* that shapes the meaning of this parable? I share this experience of a contemporary enactment of a *miṣwāh.* Walking one chilly night through Harvard Square in the company of the late George Wald, a Nobel Prize winner in biology, I saw him hand money to a beggar. In the style of the freewheeling Jewish/Christian discourse with which we both felt comfortable, I expressed my Protestant point of view. "George, he's going to go directly to the corner liquor store and with one gulp, your charity will be wasted." "Not wasted," George replied with a beneficent smile. "He will feel the warmth we take for granted for a moment or two."

Turning back to the biblical parable, we find a remarkable turn. In caring for the needy and the destitute, the caregivers learn that they were not simply showing their compassion for strangers; in attending to those strangers, they were extending their love to the Son of Man, the heavenly judge. Thus they were enacting the fundamental truth upon which the moral universe is constructed: as humans we inhabit an order built upon compassion, a compassion that is blind to all distinctions, that does not know the language of self and other. When we choose the path of love for neighbor, we find ourselves in the company of the source of all that is loving, our Lord, the one sent by the king of the universe to restore creation to its intended wholeness.

We turn now to the last cluster of parables that we shall consider. In them the general theme of the crisis invoked by the preaching of John the Baptist and Jesus is applied to the leaders of the Jewish community. Their history has reached a decisive turning point. In the events around them are to be seen signs of *God's acting to restore his covenant people, Israel.* However, this is an occasion not only of great rejoicing, but of dread, for restoration is accomplished not only by ingathering, but also by exclusion of the wicked and unfaithful. This double-edged message continues the centuries-long proclamation of the Hebrew prophets.

In order to grasp the political thrust of these parables as told by Jesus, one must recognize the fact that they have been subjected to a torturous history of reinterpretation, through which they have been forced into the service of a vitriolic supersessionist polemic. We must be clear that the situation addressed by Jesus was not the *interreligious* conflict emerging in the Pauline letters and coming to full expression in Justin Martyr's *Dialogue with Trypho*, but rather the kind of *inner-community* struggle engaged earlier by the prophets Isaiah, Jeremiah, and Ezekiel. As we observed above, even in the case of the parable of the Good Samaritan, the prophetic message of Jesus was obscured by interpreters' clothing groups like priest, Levite, and Samaritan with connotations arising out of later anti-Judaic polemic. The ugly history of anti-Judaic interpretation of the parables must be faced openly and dealt with. Different strategies have emerged in recent scholarship regarding how that can be accomplished.

At an earlier point in our discussion we expressed our disagreement with a revisionist approach that copes with noxious interpretations by a sweeping dismissal of historical-critical research. Especially in relation to the parables in which Jesus addressed what he clearly viewed as an imminent eschatological crisis, the problematical nature of some radical methodological interventions becomes apparent. I have in mind especially approaches in which a contemporary meaning of the text is forced open with a key provided by socioeconomic theory. As a result, traditional readings of a parable like the Wicked Tenants, with their attribution to God of acts of harsh judgment, are replaced with interpretations in which the agent of punishment is the Roman occupation, whose economic exploitation of the land pitted Jew against Jew in a class struggle for survival.

While it is emphatically true that the Bible as a whole and the teachings of Jesus in particular present a solid line of defense against all forms of exploitation and oppression, interpretations that abandon historical understanding, in favor of a hermeneutic functioning in support of modern political theories, ultimately undercut the credibility of the Bible as a source for political reflection. The reason is this: a sturdy foundation for reclaiming the Bible as a resource for combating exploitation and restoring universal human integrity and equality cannot be constructed out of revisionist reconstructions that ignore historical setting and meaning, but only through careful analysis of the texts dedicated to regaining historical understanding, even in cases where such interpretations are not immediately compatible with modern sensitivities.

What is the alternative to radical expository revision based on modern social-scientific theory? The history of poisonous anti-Judaic interpretation cannot be denied. What I hope to demonstrate is that the approach to the parables that seeks to understand their original setting, meaning, and function is the most reliable path to a new level of interreligious understanding.

Here we are simply applying to a specific group of texts the approach outlined earlier. We need to understand the religious and political background of the parables and the prophetic tradition to which Jesus belonged as the basis upon which to interpret the parables themselves. Rather than repeat what we described earlier about the Jews in Galilee and Judea during the Roman period and about Jesus' identity as one standing in the long line of prophets of Israel, we shall engage in a mental exercise aimed at sharpening our understanding of the historical situation. We imagine Jesus calling to mind Jeremiah's sermon at the temple gate (Jer. 7:1–15), as he intoned his own lament over the city of Jerusalem, a city tragically persisting in its rebellion against God (Matt. 23:37–38//Luke 13:34–35). Perhaps he was impelled by Zephaniah's indictment of a "soiled, defiled, oppressing city," ruled by ravenous judges, reckless prophets, and profane priests. What is regained by recalling the messages of earlier prophets is a historical sense of the situation Jesus faced and a perspective to understand the intended message of the disturbing parables of the Barren Fig Tree, the Two Sons, and the Wicked Tenants.

The parable of the Barren Tree (Luke 13:6–9) adapts the agrarian imagery of Isaiah's song of the vineyard (Isa. 5:1–7), though Jesus adds to the woeful warning of impending judgment issued by Isaiah to "the house of Israel and the people of Judah" (Isa. 5:7) a significant codicil: there will be a limited reprieve allowing for an eleventh-hour repentance. In an economy of words that is characteristic of many of Jesus' shorter parables, valuable insight into the nature and intended function of prophetic pronouncements of judgment (e.g., the baffling words of Isa. 6:9–13) is gained. For a God who wills not the death of his people, but that they return to him and live (Ezek. 18:32), pronouncements of judgment ultimately are in the service of God's merciful outreach to restore his people: "Sir, let it alone for one more year, until I dig around it and put manure on it. If it bears fruit next year, well and good; but if not, you can cut it down" (Luke 13:8–9).

The parable of the Two Sons (Matt. 21:28–32) describes with dazzling clarity the nature of the obedience that God demands. *Words* of willingness alone carry no weight. *Action*, including action that reverses earlier words of *un*willingness, counts. Jesus applies the parable to those who are particularly vulnerable to the lure of status and prestige, with shocking words that reflect a passionate disdain for pretentiousness and hypocrisy: "the tax collectors and the prostitutes are going into the kingdom of God ahead of you" (Matt. 21:31).

We conclude with the parable of the Wicked Tenants (Matt. 21:33–46; Mark 12:1–12; Luke 20:9–19), a parable whose polemical thrust is so harsh and seemingly conducive to anti-Judaic applications as to lead many well-intentioned commentators into contorted interpretations that transform a stinging invective against religious leaders into a progressive agenda of socioeconomic reform. To take one example, Luise Schottroff, in applying her method of "social-historical analysis" to the parable, concludes that the vineyard owner acts in such a cruel manner as to exclude the possibility that his action could refer to God: "The owner of the vineyard acts like an opponent of God; he does the opposite of what the God of the Torah and the Lord's Prayer desires and does."[61] One might ask, how can a thoroughly trained scholar like Schottroff, who recognizes the roots of this parable in Isaiah's song of the vineyard, draw such a conclusion? After all, the connection in Isaiah is explicit: "For the vineyard of the LORD of hosts is the house of Israel" (Isa. 5:7). God *destroys his vineyard!*

What we encounter in Schottroff's interpretation is an anomaly: while she draws from the Isaiah text certain socioeconomic details, its central theological content is ignored. In appealing to the Torah and the Lord's Prayer, she maintains that the God who expects of the faithful that they will forgive as they have been forgiven could not be portrayed as punishing derelict servants. Such a conclusion produces an unbiblical view of God, a God whose demand for justice is ignored and whose mercy thereby is degraded to that of an indulgent parent.

More specifically, what is to be said about Schottroff's unexplicated appeal to the Torah and the Lord's Prayer in support of her picture of Jesus' understanding of God's attributes? The foundation upon which the entire edifice of the Torah is built is the moral universe in which obedience brings life and disobedience death (e.g., Deut. 30:15–20). The one who maintains the integrity of that moral universe is the one who alone has authority to judge the heart, God. As for the Lord's Prayer, the petition "thy will be done, on earth as it is in heaven" does not mean "how nice when humans choose to obey." Rather, it carries with it the entire weight of a religious tradition that takes with utter seriousness the tragic consequences of disobedience.

The exegetical blindness that leads to distortion of the meaning of the parable of the Wicked Tenants can be remedied only by situating Jesus within the tradition to which he belongs, the tradition of the Hebrew prophets, a tradition dedicated to preserving the meaning and intention of the Torah as the only way to preserve the life of the people Israel amid this world's myriad threats. Jesus, like the prophets before him, felt called to struggle for the heart of his people. The struggle was not casual. It was critical, for the period of God's forbearance was running short. The nation was facing a crisis, and the message to be proclaimed began with a dire warning of impending punishment and a call for repentance. Regarding the weight of iniquity that was placing the nation in such a perilous spot vis-à-vis God's scale of righteousness, the leaders of the nation bore particular responsibility. Involved was not a romanticizing of the peasant and servant classes, but simply the insight that was cultivated throughout the prophetic period and was well summarized by Chaucer's simple itinerant clerk:

> And this figure he added eek therto,
> That if gold ruste, what shal yren do?
> For if a preest be foul, on whom we truste,
> No wonder is a lewed man to ruste.[62]

---

61. E.g., Schottroff, *Parables*, 15–28.
62. Geoffrey Chaucer, *The Canterbury Tales*, Prologue, lines 499–502.

Jeremiah, in a stinging invective against the leaders of his own time, serves as worthy representative of the whole chain of Hebrew prophets acting as the conscience of the nation:

> The priests did not say, "Where is the LORD?"
>   Those who handle the law did not know me;
> the rulers transgressed against me,
>   the prophets prophesied by Baal,
>   and went after things that do not profit.
>   (Jer. 2:8)

While the core of the nation was rotting, it would have been most unmerciful not to stand up to shock its leaders into recognition that judgment was at hand. Isaiah did, as did Jeremiah and Ezekiel, and it is within that tradition that we can understand Jesus' indictment of the religious leaders of his time.

The Gospel writers were aware that some of Jesus' parables, including the Wicked Tenants, arose out of his disputes with leaders of the Jewish community. Matthew names "the chief priests and the Pharisees" (Matt. 21:45); Luke identifies them as "the scribes and chief priests" (Luke 20:19). Specifically in the case of the parable of the Wicked Tenants, their post-Easter faith led them, in light of Psalm 118:22, to interpret the "beloved Son" in christological terms. Nonetheless, the parable as Jesus narrated it remains essentially intact. Tragically though, leaders of the early church appropriated the parable for use in its vitriolic campaign against "unrepentant" Judaism, thereby degrading a classic inner-community disputation directed at specific leaders within the Jewish community into a blunt weapon directed at defamation of those who did not share the tenets of their Christology.

Before we situate this parable within Jesus' prophetic ministry, we add one further note relating to the criticism made above of using socioeconomic analysis to redirect the polemic away from Jewish leaders to the exploitative Roman administration of the land. It is patently clear that Jesus decried the flagrant social and economic mistreatment of the peasants and day laborers who constituted the vast majority of his followers. He was well aware of the lethal blend of exploitation and cruelty that the Romans used to subjugate the Jews. He tirelessly sought to restore their full humanity, integrity, and well-being, through acts of feeding, healing, advocacy, and consoling. But he did not allow himself to be so consumed by the endless day-to-day efforts on behalf of the poor ("the poor will be with you forever" [Matt. 26:11; Mark 14:7; John 12:8]) as to lose sight of a major systemic obstacle to the healing of a broken society and world, namely, derelict, self-serving leaders.

Supreme political authority, to be sure, resided in the Roman chain of command, but complicit in the strategies of foreign aggressors were figures closer to his religious home, and they included members of the temple hierocracy, who, in their valuing worldly status and wealth above the well-being of their flock, were perceived by Jesus to be enemies of God's reign. The central message of the parable of the Wicked Tenants is lost at the point where its indictment of derelict indigenous leaders is surgically removed, out of discomfort with messy inner-Jewish community political disputes during the Roman period.

As we struggle to understand this and other parables serving an invective function, we do well to remind ourselves that Jesus stood solidly in the tradition of the Hebrew prophets when he engaged in disputes with coreligionists. Like the prophets before him, he viewed his mission in the first instance as that of calling his people back to their covenant with God. That they seemed intent on resisting that call and persisting in rebellion against God was leading to a double calamity, the ruin of their nation and the nullification of its sacred vocation of mediating divine blessing to all nations. In the parable of the Wicked Tenants, we find Jesus adding his witness to the crisis facing his nation with shocking clarity.[63]

Was he aware that the role of the son of the householder was one that he would soon assume? That is within the realm of possibility, given the fact that suffering and rejection and the threat of death run like a steady current through the history of the prophets. We have already suggested that in an especially poignant way, the figure of the Suffering Servant in the book of Isaiah shaped Jesus' understanding of what lay ahead of him. We have also seen how he found in the words and acts of Jeremiah patterns fitting his own life. Finally, he may well have viewed the hostile response to his message by the leaders of his day in light of Ezra's lament: "Nevertheless they were disobedient and rebelled against you and cast your law behind their backs and killed your prophets, who had warned them in order to turn them back to you, and they committed great blasphemies" (Neh. 9:26; cf. 2 Chr. 24:19).

Against that background, we can understand the message Jesus expressed in the drama of the parable of the Wicked Tenants. With remarkable persistence and restraint, God had sent his prophets with an appeal to the leaders charged with the well-being of his people Israel, and in each case the response was an act of heinous rejection. Consequently, the nation had reached a point of unprecedented crisis. It stood at a crossroads with an invitation to participate in the unfolding of God's redemptive plan, or to persist in stubborn rebellion and forfeit its birthright.

If we find it difficult to accept the description of the judgment inflicted on the tenants as applicable to the God of Israel, we must ask whether there existed a viable alternative. To allow the wickedness of the tenants to go unpunished would be tantamount to conceding control of the universe to evil. But the consequence of destroying the incorrigible nation was also dreadful and had to be addressed: "He will put those wretches to a miserable death, and lease the vineyard to other tenants." As cataclysmic as was the sentence of destruction on the very people God had chosen as his redemptive agent, it was not the end of God's

---

63. Though there is considerable variation in details among the three Synoptic versions of the parable of the Wicked Tenants, the plot and denouement are essentially the same in all three.

purpose for his creation. Others would be found who, as Matthew adds, "will give him the produce at the harvest time" (Matt. 21:41).

When distorted into a prediction for an apocalyptic timetable, this parable becomes fertile ground for futuristic speculation: because of Israel's sin, God will call another people to represent him in the world. The result of this line of thought is *supersessionism*. Because Israel rejected God's covenant, God will select an obedient community for his new covenant, which translates into the related concept of *replacement theology*. In such interpretations, the setting and purpose of the parable become twisted into a monster whose appetite to scapegoat and consume rivals has been insatiable through the ages.

If the well-intentioned attempts to break the anti-Judaic expository history of the parable through a radical revision of its plain meaning cannot be justified, what alternative approach can be taken? Its starting point is the realization that Jesus' aim was not to present a comprehensive blueprint for the rise and fall of nations and religions. His focus was much more concrete. Candidly and urgently he appealed one more time to the hearts of the people he loved. In the manner of Isaiah's hyperbole, Jeremiah's jeremiad, and Ezekiel's shocking metaphors, Jesus sought to get the attention of his kin and jolt them into repentance and recommitment to God's will. The response from leading members of the community was no different than that experienced by the prophets before him. But real life is different in one major respect from the drama of a parable: it goes on, and God's call to prophets to speak to the hearts of his people would go on, in keeping with the astonishing tenacity of the divine judge.

In the case of the prophetic ministry of Jesus, however, another development would complicate God's plan: Though not resolving itself as certain Christian leaders would have wished through supersession or replacement, the conflict between Jesus and the Pharisees would eventuate in separation into two religious communities. This posed a question of utmost importance: what would be the nature of the relationship between Judaism and Christianity? Sadly, the dominant responses have ranged from tension to conflict to persecution. Only in the post-Holocaust era has a different paradigm begun to cultivate a constructive and mutually enriching discourse, one that acknowledges as part of God's redemptive plan the parallel existence of two covenants, both living, both inviting humans to accept citizenship in God's kingdom as the only allegiance that carries ultimate significance, both entailing the ongoing struggle between sinful human hearts and the loving heart of God, both unfolding in the lives of those dedicated to God's kingdom and yearning for its coming in fullness. This new paradigm represents a development within the sister faiths growing out of biblical tradition that is of signal importance for an adequate contemporary understanding of the politics of the Bible

We conclude our discussion of the parables of Jesus by summarizing what they reveal about his politics. At the center is a picture of God's nature as a loving Father who is indefatigable in seeking to restore all of his children to a blessed and harmonious community. The response of the faithful to the call to that community, traditionally named the kingdom of God, is a wholehearted embrace of that which alone has ultimate value. Running against the grain of conventional notions of membership, the community that Jesus describes banishes categories of pedigree, social prominence, and ostentatious religiosity, while fostering qualities of the heart such as meekness, compassion, and a lavish generosity reaching out to all people.

It should come as no surprise, therefore, that in the history of interpretation of the parables much effort has been made to massage their lessons into ones more in alignment with modern notions of social propriety and decorum. The parables have proven stubbornly uncooperative vis-à-vis such revisionary efforts. For they, in concert with other sayings traceable to the historical Jesus, arise from his sense that the world was at a critical turning point and that the purpose of his life was to awaken his people to the inescapable choice between life-restoring repentance and stubborn resistance to the gospel, leading to death. Far from being a time for business as usual, it was a time of crisis, demanding a radical change both in the human heart and in human behavior.

SAYINGS OF JESUS AND NARRATIVES

Sayings attributable to Jesus develop the same themes as the parables, beginning with the inaugural words of Jesus recorded by Mark, "The time is fulfilled, and the kingdom of God has come near; repent, and believe in the good news" (Mark 1:15). Among Jesus' sayings are ones that stress the unavoidable choice that the kingdom presented to his audience: "No slave can serve two masters; for a slave will either hate the one and love the other, or be devoted to the one and despise the other. You cannot serve God and wealth [Gk. *mammon*]" (Luke 16:13; Matt. 6:24). The lesson presented graphically in the parable of the Rich Fool and the parable of the Rich Man and Lazarus he reformulated in this saying: "Sell your possessions, and give alms. Make purses for yourselves that do not wear out, an unfailing treasure in heaven, where no thief comes near and no moth destroys. For where your treasure is, there your heart will be also" (Luke 12:33–34; Matt. 6:19–21). To the theme of the supernal worth of the kingdom he added, by reference to the birds of the air and the lilies of the field, this promise: "Strive first for the kingdom of God and his righteousness, and all these things will be given to you as well" (Matt. 6:33; Luke 12:31).

He cautioned the disciples that their commitment to God's order of justice and compassion would frequently place them in conflict with those who govern human affairs in the present order: "Blessed are you when people revile you and persecute you and utter all kinds of evil against you falsely on my account" (Matt. 5:11; Luke 6:22). To the parables like the Unrighteous Steward and the Money Entrusted by a Master to Three Servants, he adds lessons on surviving as "sheep among wolves": "When you go with your accuser before a magistrate, on the way make an effort to settle the case, or you may be dragged before the judge, and the judge hand you over to the officer, and the officer throw you in prison. I tell you, you will never get out until you have paid the very last penny" (Luke 12:57–59; Matt. 5:25–26).

The narratives into which the parables and other sayings of Jesus are embedded in the Gospels describe how Jesus incorporated his understanding of the new order of the kingdom into his daily life. Eschewing accolades, he embodied a deep compassion and respect for the marginal and the poor that challenged conventional stereotypes. We are informed of his eating and drinking with "tax collectors and sinners" at Levi's banquet (Luke 5:27–32; Matt. 9:9–13; Mark 2:13–17) and his acquiring, in certain circles, the unenviable reputation of being "a glutton and a drunkard, a friend of tax collectors and sinners" (Luke 7:34; Matt. 11:19). The Gospel of John poignantly captures Jesus' acceptance of all classes of people in the story of his defense of the woman accused of adultery (John 8:1–11).

Exemplary for the qualities that he associated with knowledge of the kingdom were not those with advanced education, but children: "I thank you, Father, Lord of heaven and earth, because you have hidden these things from the wise and the intelligent and have revealed them to infants; yes, Father, for such was your gracious will" (Luke 10:21; Matt. 11:25–26). The fact that Jesus can be counted among "the wise and the intelligent" of his society assures us that he was not extolling ignorance or mental sloth. Rather, his words arose from his conviction that entrance into God's kingdom depended not on personal status and achievement, but on openness to God's grace and trust in God's promises. There is no reasonable basis to deny the historical veracity of the consistent picture given in the Gospels of one seeking not to impress others through the company he kept, but rather seeking to shock his compatriots through his words and actions into encountering a God who peers beneath every outward trait to examine the heart.

Out of Jesus' love and devotion to his Father arose his compassion for the diverse needs of all those he encountered in his travels through the hills of Galilee. He sought through his example to tutor his followers in the same translation of love for God to love for fellow humans. Accordingly, he offered simple metaphors for how the love of the kingdom was to radiate from the circle of disciples into the wider world. They had been recipients of a light that was not to be hidden under a bushel (Luke 11:33; Matt. 5:15; Mark 4:21). They were to be like salt that retains its saltiness (Luke 14:34–35; Matt. 5:13). They were to bear witness to the good news entrusted to them, not through pomp and arrogance, but as servants aware of the rules of the kingdom: "Love your enemies." "Do to others as you would have them do to you." "Do not judge."

What is conspicuously lacking in this rudimentary theo-politics is the stridency that so often characterizes religious crusades and movements, from biblical times to the present. Not belligerent assertiveness in promoting a definitive truth, but patient dedication to the well-being of all humans, including those who would inflict harm. A lamp shedding light on all inhabitants in a dark universe; salt offered to all, free of conditions or credentials; turning the other cheek, rather than perpetuating the spiral of violence through acts of revenge; mercy extended to the prisoner or the beggar regarded as equal to proffering hospitality to the king of the universe: such are the ingredients prescribed by the Gospel for a polity that pulsates with the loving heart of the Creator.

To underline the essential point: in such a polity, the individual protagonist of this religious position or that partisan policy is repositioned from assertive lordship to faithful servanthood. One of the joyous discoveries of the gospel is that the perspective of the kingdom can lead normal people to a world-changing transmutation of conventional structures. Life's supernal purpose is redirected from the selfish heart to giving God alone the glory. Out of praise of the Creator arises compassion for all fellow humans and advocacy for the "least of these."

Alas, such a political theory has little marketing power in the agoras of the world, whether then or now. To announce meekness as the key to the polity of a new kingdom at first must have appeared bizarre in the imperial world of Jesus' time. To declare love as the transformative power of a kingdom that was to prevail over all the kingdoms of the earth no doubt was dismissed by those wielding worldly power as the product of the grandiose illusions of yet another self-proclaimed messiah, until, that is, that declaration began to attract sufficiently large audiences to raise concerns among the officers of the occupation for the maintenance of order over a volatile Jewish people.

The imperial response to that challenge is ensconced in the legend of the slaughter of the innocents. Herod was going to take no chances! More revealing, however, and historically closer to the conflict precipitated by the introduction into Galilee and Judea of an alternative to the rule enforced by Rome with the assistance of Jewish collaborators, are the reports that run like a leitmotif throughout the Gospels: Jesus' ministry, like that of John the Baptist, evoked hostility among virtually all leaders of the prevailing regime and culminated in a Roman trial producing a guilty verdict for treason, with the penalty of death.

Jesus' execution by crucifixion under the Romans is the last datum in a historical account of his political career. The coercive/violent tactics of this world's mightiest power achieved its goal and maintained its dominance over the Jewish populace. It would maintain that control through two Jewish revolts. But the account of the politics of the Bible ends neither with the execution of Jesus nor with the suppression of two Jewish revolts. The postexecution and postrevolt era holds the key to the alternative power of the two religions that survived and outlived the world's most powerful kingdom, Eternal Rome. That power was patient and, when necessary, suffering love, not coercion and violence. Such was the way that Jesus followed and to which he invited those who would hear his message (Luke 6:27–35; Matt. 5:38–47). It was categorically different from the business-as-usual ways of this world, for it derived its sense of direction and goals from the example of the heavenly Father: "Be merciful, just as your Father is merciful" (Luke 6:36).

The polity that Jesus sought to inculcate within his circle of followers arose directly from his understanding of his own prophetic vocation as a servant of God, called to serve God's people. As we suggested above in describing the religious background of Jesus' sense of calling, the tradition with which he identified included suffering as an inevitable consequence of faithfulness. A climactic point of that prophetic tradition was reached in Isaiah 53, where was seen, in the slaughter of an innocent victim, the mysterious will of God, a merciful God reaching out in this shocking display of persistent mercy to forgive his people, declare their righteousness, and restore with them the covenant of blessing for themselves and through them for the nations. Jesus' lecture to his disciples on the servant consciousness that was to determine the polity of their community amounts to a parsing of his Servant identity into the identity he sought to transmit to his disciples. It is a polity that is unmistakably contrarian in relation to the political conventions of his time (and ours!): "The kings of the Gentiles lord it over them; and those in authority over them are called benefactors. But not so with you; rather the greatest among you must become like the youngest, and the leader like one who serves. For who is greater, the one who is at the table or the one who serves? Is it not the one at the table? But I am among you as one who serves" (Luke 22:25–27).

In no uncertain terms, Jesus sets before his disciples a notion of community that turns the table on conventional political theory. It was a lesson their days in his company had taught them, for they had witnessed in their teacher the enactment of leadership that found its model not in fearsome warriors but in children, of planning for the future not in amassing wealth but in following the example of the birds of the air and the lilies of the field, of an invitation to discipleship accompanied not by the promise of comfort but by the prospect of nowhere to lay one's head. The calculus of the kingdoms of this world would be incapable of issuing a visa for entry into such a community. Disciples of the teacher of an alternative way were enfranchised solely by their trust in their Master and dedication to the redemptive plan of his heavenly Father.

THE MIRACLES: SIGNS OF THE KINGDOM

As with the parables and sayings, the significance of the miracles ascribed to Jesus comes to special clarity in relation to his central message concerning the kingdom of God, a reign of peace that extends its healing powers to all of creation. Every particular case of alleviation of hunger, release from bondage, and restoration to health was an episode in the wider drama of the healing of the cosmos or, in the words of the Hebrew prophets, a "new creation." What Jesus and the disciples witnessed in the lives of the recipients of their caring was a dethroning of the great imposter and the restoration of the legitimate king of the universe.

Understood thus, the miracles of Jesus were enactments of the lessons he had taught about God's nature and the manner of life that those who lived in gratitude to God would live. God intended that the bounty of the earth be shared so as to end hoarding by some at the cost of the impoverishment of others. Jesus demonstrated the table fellowship of God's kingdom in breaking bread with his disciples, as well as in feeding loaves and fishes to the crowds that followed him. God intended soundness of health throughout his creation, so the faithful Son reached out to heal sickness wherever he encountered it, sickness of body as well as sickness of the mind. Modern readers of the Gospels can still recognize in the activities of Jesus the effects of the kingdom, a transformation manifested in the lives of individuals and families, from the brokenness of a fallen order to the wholeness of life in the presence of God.

THE COST OF DISCIPLESHIP

Participating in the kingdom's coming was not a blithe activity, for the same dark powers that had frustrated God's creative purposes from the beginning and had led to repeated tragedy in the history of the people with whom God had covenanted were present in force during Jesus' lifetime (Matt. 11:12). The profound significance of the parables is lost if the transcendent dimension that frames them in Scripture is expurgated through a misdirected program of demythologizing. To picture Jesus as a wandering healer offering bandages and ointments to ease the pain of suffering humans and pumping up the self-confidence of those plagued by mental stress is to degrade a cosmic drama to a muddling, anemic vignette.

When tempted to dismiss as naively premodern Jesus' jubilant response that he saw Satan falling from heaven when his disciples' reported the success of their healing mission (Luke 10:18), we may remember that the rigorously trained intellectual Dietrich Bonhoeffer saw in Hitler's ruthless campaign into France evidence of the antichrist's assault on humanity. He witnessed more than misguided human intentions, more than one man's *Kampf*, more than the paying back of old nationalistic animosities, much more! Bonhoeffer, like Jesus, recognized a spiritual battle, an attack on the moral order that held the cosmos together, a battle calling for nothing less than a wholehearted response guided and empowered by the Spirit of God and entailing "the cost of discipleship."

The theme of struggle, suffering, and death is thus at the heart of Jesus' ministry, and it is clear that he understood the miracles he performed to be part of God's struggle to save humanity and the universe it coinhabited from *chaos*: "if it is by the Spirit of God that I cast out demons, then the kingdom of God has come to you" (Matt. 12:28; Luke 11:20). But the drama is not a solo performance, with humans as passive bystanders. The conflict between God's righteous reign and the dark dominion of evil placed upon every individual the crucial choice between God and Satan, between Jesus and all those in league against him: "No one can serve two masters" (Matt. 6:24; Luke 16:13). "Whoever is not with me is against me, and whoever who does not gather with me scatters" (Matt. 12:30; Luke 11:23).

Jesus seemed intent on pointing out to his disciples that following him be made with awareness that they were choosing a life of risk and struggle. It was his own experience that the coming of God's reign in its fullness did not occur during his lifetime; rather, he lived within the tension of already/not yet by witnessing the presence of God in miracles of healing alongside the counteroffensive of the forces of evil in the ferociousness with which his enemies attacked and slandered him. With audacity, however, he expressed his confidence in God's ultimate victory by proleptically reconstituting Israel under twelve disciples representing the twelve tribes and reaffirming God's covenant with them on the occasion of his last Passover meal with this inchoate Israel.

No clearer expression could have been given to Jesus' confidence in the trustworthiness of God's commitment to the people he had chosen as agents of God's redemptive activity on behalf of all creation than that Last Supper. The most basic of all the fruits of the earth, wine and bread, became signs of the communion between creator and creation that ultimately would triumph over all adversity. The bearer of those signs was Jesus himself, who would continue to be present with his disciples as they gathered for their common meal in remembrance of his inestimable gift and in anticipation of their joyous reunion in the blessed Kingdom (Matt. 26:26–29; Mark 14:22–25).

What is most important of all to note in Jesus' celebration of that last meal with his disciples is that his attention remained clearly focused on the reality to which he had been called and to which he had devoted his entire life: "Truly I tell you, I will never again drink of the fruit of the vine until that day when I drink it new [or with you] in the kingdom of God" (Mark 14:25, Matt. 26:29). With these words he bequeathed a lasting reminder that his followers were not being sent out into the world to practice politics in the conventional sense of the word, but to be witnesses to the transcendent order of God's kingdom as the basis for a movement dedicated to the restoration of *shalom* encompassing all peoples.

While Jesus' trust in the final victory of his Father's kingdom endured the tests of persecution and death, it is clear that he regarded as misdirected all human efforts aimed at hastening the day when God's will would be done "on earth as it is in heaven," as were attempts to predict the day of fulfillment. We can restate Jesus' message thus: While the kingdom and its righteousness are the most treasured realities in the entire universe for the person of faith, they are not possessions already grasped, but rather goals toward which the faithful long with single focus, deep passion, and abiding trust. While awareness of the "not yet" dimension of God's final purpose safeguards against human inclinations to reduce the kingdom to human standards, its "now" dimension inspires a life embodying the qualities of the peaceable kingdom in the present imperfect world, the qualities of compassion, fairness, honesty, and dedication to justice and equality for all God's children as well as preservation of the integrity of God's creation. Jesus made this point suc-cinctly in reply to a question regarding the time of the kingdom's coming: "The kingdom of God is not coming with things that can be observed; nor will they say, 'Look, here it is!' or 'There it is!' For, in fact, the kingdom of God is among you" (Luke 17:20–21; cf. Matt. 24:23).

While resisting accommodation to or co-option by the kingdoms of this world, the kingdom-based politics of Jesus was not utopian but realistic in its relation to existing institutions and structures. Earlier we contrasted Jesus' political strategy vis-à-vis the Romans with that of absolutists like the Zealots and Sicarii. The vignette in Luke, according to which Jesus rebukes the good intentions of one of his followers who sought to defend his master against those seeking to arrest him by wielding his sword, poignantly captures that contrast (Luke 22:47–53; cf. John 18:10–11). "No more of this!" he shouted. To oppose violence with violence was to lose the distinction between the power of the kingdom and the dark forces of worldly power. Even if an uprising against the Romans and their Jewish collaborators were to succeed (an unlikely prospect!), it would have signaled a defeat of all that Jesus' politics stood for by merely replac-ing one regime built upon violence with another. And the spiral of violence would accelerate.

To teach that there was an alternative to rule by coercion and violence was not an easy assignment. Indeed, the results were ruthless reprisal by the Roman and temple authorities, misunderstanding even by those within Jesus' innermost circle, and finally the ironic denouement of the one heralded as the long-awaited redeemer of Israel falling victim to the ignominy and curse of crucifixion.

THE POLITICS OF THE KINGDOM AMID THE AMBIGUITIES OF THIS WORLD

Two narratives provide insight into Jesus' manner of relating God's reign to the jurisdiction of earthly institutions and regimes. The former portrays Jesus' dealing with the most powerful Jewish institution within the domain of Roman rule, the Jerusalem temple. The latter relates his exclusive allegiance to God's kingdom to the emperor's assertion of unqualified authority.

In Matthew 17:24–27 the claims laid by the Jerusalem temple on the Jewish people have posed a dilemma, claims deriving their sting from the function of the temple as the indigenous arm of the Roman occupation. The annual temple tax required of each adult male was a half-shekel, a tax reflecting a hierocratic polity according to which revenue was exacted from the subjects for the purpose of maintaining imperial structures of order and control. For Zealots, such a tax represented a refutation of God's sole authority and called for a declaration of holy war against those regarded as apostates and traitors.

Jesus' response was much more complex and was introduced with a cryptic question: "From whom do kings of the earth take toll or tribute? From their children or from others?" The answer is clear: "From others." The injustice of the tax levied by priests in the name of God is thus exposed, for it allies God's rule with the oppressive ways of earthly kings. Jesus' stinging critique is akin to his dramatic demonstration against profanation of the sacred by overturning the money changers' tables in the temple. Turning God into an entrepreneur profiteering at the expense of the people was an idolatrous tactic repugnant to the Holy One and hostile to true religion.

The question raised is theo-political in nature: how did the person of faith who acknowledged no ultimate authority save that of God respond to idolatrous encroachments upon true worship? To adopt the violent tactics of the revolutionaries, such as assassination, blood vengeance, and conspiracy, was to confuse the way of the kingdom with the worldly strategies of brute force. But surrender to the authority of ruthless tyrants amounted to a validation of the principalities and powers of this world. Jesus responded to the conundrum with a tactic that charted a course that avoided both the Scylla of suicidal insurrection and the Charybdis of repudiating the theocratic principle of God's sole sovereignty through collaboration.

He did so in a manner rife with irony and humor: The disciples were saved from the either/or of rebellion or submission by a fish that provided the coin for payment. Deftly, Jesus avoided the trap set for him by the tax collectors at the same time that he provided the disciples with an escape from the offense of contributing from their own assets to an oppressive regime. To be sure, the episode did not provide a permanent, fail-safe rule for negotiating the hazardous terrain of citizenship. Rather, the disciples as well as the generations of faithful that would follow were equipped with an unforgettable example of living "wise as serpents and innocent as doves" (Matt. 10:16) within the tension between ultimate and penultimate loyalties.

Alongside the indigenous authority of the temple, the Jews of Galilee and Judea had to contend with an even more imperious authority, the Roman Empire. A source of particular resentment was the tax levied by the Romans on the Jews, for not only did it place a strain on the finances of families struggling against the ever-present threat of poverty; it also was a reminder that the national autonomy for which they longed was kept from them by the iron grip of the foreign occupier. The palpable reminder of that bitter fact was the image of the "divine" Caesar stamped upon their coinage.

All three Synoptic Gospels contain the story of the test to which Jesus was subjected revolving around the question of whether or not religious Jews should feel duty-bound to pay the despised imperial tax (Matt. 22:15–22; Mark 12:13–17; Luke 20:20–26). Jesus' reply is well known and enjoys a place of preeminence among his authentic words: "Render therefore to Caesar the things that are Caesar's, and to God the things that are God's" (Matt. 22:21 RSV). The political subtlety of his reply is remarkable. The issue at hand was of critical importance for the Jews of that time, and the question of what they owed to Caesar and what to God demanded an answer. Underlying Jesus' reply was his belief in the sovereignty of God over all that is: ultimately, all things belong to God, and God alone. But a clear lesson taught to Jews by their history was that on this earth God delegated limited, temporal authority to human rulers, even foreign human rulers like Nebuchadnezzar and Cyrus. In that limited role, Caesar was exercising authority over the provinces of the Mediterranean world, including Judea. So Jesus asks, "Whose likeness and inscription is this?" "Caesar's," they reply. That provided the key to his lesson. Caesar minted it, placed his name and image on it, and so if he wanted it back, they were to give him what was his. But in doing so, they were to remember that there was something that belonged alone to God, their ultimate devotion; and that was something that no earthly ruler could claim, regardless of how many divine epithets he displayed.

Alongside the misinterpretation that would construe Jesus' response as submission to Roman authority is another, namely, reading it as reflecting a strategy of withdrawing from engagement with all matters political. This interpretation is refuted both by frequent reports of Jesus' arguing with rulers of the community over issues of leadership and, above all, by the fact that both the Romans and the Herodians determined that he was such a major threat to their regime as to deserve the penalty of death. Jesus stood consistently in opposition to anything that called into question the theocratic principle of God's ultimate authority. The priests, in demanding tax in God's name, were making God a captive to their hierocratic ideology. So too were the Zealots, in demanding that their fellow Jews offer their lives sacrificially for a revolutionary nationalistic ideology. Both removed God as the sole reality determining the actions of the person of faith in every setting by elevating *penultimate* powers to the level of *ultimate* authority over the human conscience.

These two episodes revolving around the question of taxation contribute substantially to the discussion of the relation between faith and politics. They clarify the major premise for the citizenship of people of faith and for the nature and extent of the loyalty they owe to earthly governments. It is a premise that countless Jewish and Christian theologians and philosophers over the centuries would revisit, refine, and elaborate on. In discussing the politics of the apostle Paul, we shall look at Romans 13 as one concrete example of the ongoing effort to define the kind of citizenship required of those who acknowledge the ultimate authority of God alone.

While we have drawn attention to the adroitness with which Jesus addressed the questions raised by taxation and civil responsibility, many readers of Scripture prefer to find clear rules, rather than dynamic, situation-focused, inspired reflection. Taken as a whole, however, the Gospel narratives do not present Jesus as the author of an immutable political philosophy or a timeless set of policies. Rather, they offer modern readers examples of Jesus as the practitioner of kingdom politics who diligently teaches his disciples how to translate their faith in the only universal sovereign into the transitory structures and institutions of this world.

The picture we receive of those disciples is far from heroic. While the popular appeal of later legends of saints and martyrs is undeniable, it is the ragged picture of the disciples in the four Gospels that is one of the most important marks of historical veracity. It is also the picture that enables modern readers, amid their struggles with ambiguous political issues, to find inspiration and guidance as they identify with followers who eagerly gathered to their teacher in the heyday of his popularity, but when opposition mounted and their own safety was cast into jeopardy, frequently chose the option of scattering or denying affiliation with their persecuted Master. Even in relation to Jesus' earlier promises in the Beatitudes to those who embraced the kingdom, one would have to conclude that their experiences were a mixture of blessing and curse—not only theirs, but Jesus' experiences as well: "Cursed is everyone who hangs on a tree," the apostle pointed out a generation later (Gal. 3:13 < Deut. 21:23).

The political journey traveled by Jesus of Nazareth in the Gospels of the New Testament thus remains a very bumpy road. Modern renditions that recast the portrait of Jesus as the key to worldly success and prosperity are historically inaccurate and theologically misleading. No more emphatic repudiation of a triumphalist interpretation of the politics of Jesus could be imagined than the fact that his career was cut short by a death sentence.

THE IRONY OF THE CROSS

In reading the account of Jesus' trial and execution, one is forced to ask, "Which kingdom emerged as victor in the struggle between Jesus and those who plotted against him? God's kingdom or imperial Rome?" To the witnesses peering at one hanging from a cross and crying out to a silent heaven, the answer must have seemed clear: Rome had reasserted its sovereignty and its local collaborators had been vindicated. To modern readers, the brutal death suffered by Jesus may seem like an overly harsh lesson against the common tendency of religious communities to make worldly success a part of their self-legitimation. But the cross through the ages has stood stubbornly against the lure of Constantine's sword. It remains true that those following Jesus' teaching can grasp aright the kingdom to which he invites them and the nature of political engagement it demands of them only in the shadow of one surrendering his own life as a sign of a reign that, while present in the world of empires, is not of that world. Indeed, it is a reign that stands resolutely as an alternative to worldly power. And the testimonies to the resurrection of Jesus on the third day undergird the dialectical message of a victory that arises from surrender to the sole ruler of the universe, even when that surrender entails what against worldly standards appears to be humiliating defeat.

Chapter 27

The Politics
of the Apostle Paul

THE APOSTLE PAUL'S WORLD

Paul of Tarsus played a crucial role in transitioning the movement initiated by Jesus of Nazareth from a Jewish phenomenon located in Galilee and Judea to a missionary endeavor that reached out across the Mediterranean and drew into its ranks adherents of diverse ethnic and religious backgrounds. Inevitably, this transition was accompanied by change in the formulation of the beliefs of the fledgling church, as well as in the strategies developed for relating to the regnant political power of the time, the Roman Empire, and the religious cults and philosophical schools that vied for influence under its aegis. As is typical of a vibrant religious tradition, however, such change occurred within the parameters of a faith that resiliently preserved a core of central confessions and a view of reality that defined itself in opposition to prevailing worldviews.

The resiliency of the early church was based neither on a systematic formulation of its doctrines nor on an authoritative centralized organization (both of which would develop centuries later), but rather on reliance on Jewish Scripture as its source of identity and purpose and on preservation of the words and recitation of the narratives of the one they confessed to be the Anointed One sent by God to fulfill the long-awaited promises to Israel and the nations conveyed through the prophets.

Helmut Koester has drawn together the relevant textual and archaeological evidence into a vivid picture of the church into which Paul was baptized and within which he was introduced to the kerygma of the crucified and risen Christ.[1] The congregation in Antioch that welcomed Paul after his conversion was already flourishing in 35 CE, just five years after Jesus' death. Its spiritual life revolved around readings from Scripture (especially passages from the Psalms and the Prophets that shed light on the meaning of Jesus' life, death, and resurrection), collective memory of the words and deeds of Jesus, and reenactment of the meal in which they celebrated the presence of the risen Christ in anticipation of the heavenly banquet in which the divine plan for which he had given his life would be fulfilled.

The transition from a circle of Jewish disciples following the Nazarene teacher through the Galilean countryside to a collection of Greek-speaking congregations along the eastern Mediterranean and Aegean confessing faith in Jesus as Messiah was a dynamic process in which faithfulness to the received tradition was accompanied by adaptations to a complex hellenized world. While some scholars depict that transition in terms of categorical change or even the distortion of an original collection of Jesus' teachings, we discern the dialectical relationship between continuity and adaptation that is the mark of vibrant religious traditions of every age.[2]

From Paul comes the earliest evidence of the growth of concise formulations of the faith that manifest the tensive interplay between continuity and adaptation. In 1 Corinthians 15 he cites one such formulation, likely stemming from the Antioch congregation, which he had handed on to his brothers and sisters in Corinth "as of first importance," noting that it was not his free composition but "what I in turn had received" (1 Cor. 15:3). The term he uses in this chapter for this early credo is "gospel" (*euangelion*). It reads: "that Christ died for our sins in accordance with the scriptures, and that he was buried, and that he was raised on the third day in accordance with the scriptures" (1 Cor. 15:3–4). It concludes with a list of those to whom the risen Christ had appeared, at the end of which list he names himself. We will return below to the noteworthy juxtaposition of acknowledged indebtedness to a received tradition and the audacious claim to having experienced, like the disciples preceding him, an appearance of the risen Christ. Indebtedness to tradition and audacious adaptation thus describe the modus operandi of Paul of Tarsus. Little wonder that he has been such a controversial figure in the history of Christianity, a distinction he retains down to the present.

1. Helmut Koester, *Introduction to the New Testament: History and Literature of Early Christianity* (Philadelphia: Fortress Press, 1982), 2:91–93. In this chapter, we shall draw only on the epistles that have a solid claim to Pauline authorship, namely, 1 Thessalonians, Galatians, 1 and 2 Corinthians, Philippians, Philemon, and Romans.

2. See above page 507 for our critique of interpretations that accentuate discontinuity and fracture in the move from the Jesus movement to the early church.

As in the case of the reception history of the Gospel formulae, so too in relation to the central rite of the early church, we find Paul emphasizing his linkage with the first generation of disciples. In introducing the words of Jesus that constituted the eucharistic meal, he again acknowledges his indebtedness: "For I received from the Lord what I also handed on to you" (1 Cor. 11:23). Shared memory handed down from the Lord to disciples to subsequent generations of the faithful: such is the chain that connected Paul to the generation that preceded him.

Continuity does not imply a static relation to what has been handed down. The time period from Jesus' Galilean ministry to the time of Paul's membership in the church in Antioch was anything but a static period, for it was marked by the event that Paul announced had reshaped human existence from the core: God had vindicated the Servant Jesus whom the powers of this world had tried to eliminate. In the resurrection, which became personal for Paul in his encounter with the risen Christ on the road to Damascus, he found the key that opened up for him the reality-transforming meaning of his Jewish faith. The era promised by the prophets, in which the dispersion of Israel, the brokenness of humanity, and the decay of the entire created order would be restored to integrity and health, had dawned. In accepting Christ's death as one's own death to sin and Christ's resurrection as one's own entry into grace and freedom, the believer became a member of the new creation through which was being manifest to the world the fulfillment of God's eternal purpose.

But the victory was not complete, for the powers of this world, if anything, had grown more belligerent than ever. The life of faith was therefore defined as a life of sharing in the patient, suffering love of the Lord. Living "in Christ" became the vocation of the one accepting God's gracious gift of redemption. Later we shall probe more deeply the foundational role played in Paul's thought by the gospel of God's redemptive act in Christ, and the way in which the concept of the new creation shaped his understanding of the church and the responsibilities to the wider society carried by those living "in Christ." First, note that Paul's efforts on behalf of the gospel did not occur within the tranquility of a scholar's study or the serenity of a united church, but amid bitter struggle with competing construals of the concept *gospel*.

The most serious challenge to Paul's proclamation of the inauguration of God's reign of universal peace and justice was presented by the cult of the divine emperor. Since the assassination of Julius Caesar and the promulgation of the *divus Julius* cult by Caesar Augustus, the Julio-Claudian emperors had disseminated (through persuasion of the client-elite and fear-driven coercion of the lower classes of society) their utopian gospel (*euangelion*) of the arrival of a golden age bestowed on the human race by the almighty and all-wise divine savior emperors.

Thanks to recent scholarly studies, we now have a clearer picture of the context within which the rhetoric of Paul's letters becomes intelligible, namely, a political arena in which the two rival gospels were locked in deadly conflict.

Both made use of apocalyptic terminology enjoying widespread currency in both Jewish and Hellenistic worlds to describe the advent of an era of unprecedented, all-embracing peace and prosperity. Confrontation was inevitable, for by definition, there could be but one *universal* Savior and Lord. The claims of Paul's Christ and Calpurnius Siculus's Caesar were mutually exclusive. The backdrop of Paul's ministry was thus the increasingly bitter conflict between opposing claims to the titles of Savior and Lord.

In the words of Neil Elliott, who draws on observations of John I. White and Karl P. Donfried, "Paul's proclamation of Jesus as *kyrios,* the 'lord of God's empire,' relied heavily on Roman political concepts, and 'could easily be understood as violating the *decrees of Caesar* in the most blatant manner.'"[3] The net result is that terms such as "righteousness of God," "Christ as Lord," and "*euangelion,*" which in traditional New Testament scholarship were understood as relating narrowly to justification of the individual, have been revised to embrace wide-ranging social and political connotations. Neil Elliott's conclusion may be overstated, but his central point provides an important corrective to personalistic interpretations: "[T]he letter Paul directed to Rome is not a theological brief. It is a defiant indictment of the rampant injustice and impiety of the Roman 'golden age.'"[4]

While the Romans were tolerant of a broad range of cults and philosophies, their tolerance did not extend to acknowledgment of political saviors besides Caesar. The plethora of temples and shrines in Rome and in the provincial capitals must not be construed as compromising the imperial doctrine that acceptance of a *heavenly* realm populated by a host of deities did not jeopardize the imperial decree (enforced by capital punishment) that in the *earthly* realm there could be but one divine ruler.

Within the Roman Empire, Jews and Christians accordingly lived in constant danger, for they held the opposite position. While tolerating different earthly regimes and rulers, they held defiantly to their ancestral theocratic confession that in *heaven*, one God alone reigned. For them, the emperor cult accordingly was idolatrous, ethically repugnant, and an abomination to their God. Their uncompromising witness resulted in a history of persecution recorded with the blood of the martyrs.

Though Paul's generation was spared the sweeping persecutions that marked the latter years of Nero and the reign of Vespasian, the grave threat to the gospel of Jesus Christ posed by an idolatrous regime was clear to the apostle to the Gentiles. To those reading his letters, there could have been no doubt that he had the cult of the divine emperor in mind when he denounced the "rulers" and "powers" opposed to God's reign (Rom. 8:38), warned the Thessalonians to be aware of the realized eschatology of "peace and security" touted by the

3. Neil Elliott, "Paul and the Politics of Empire," in *Paul and Politics: Ekklesia, Israel, Imperium, Interpretation: Essays in Honor of Krister Stendahl,* ed. Richard A. Horsley (Harrisburg, PA: Trinity Press, 2000), 25.

4. Ibid., 36.

headstrong empire (1 Thess. 5:3), and ridiculed those whose "god is the belly" (Phil. 3:19). It is likely that the opposition in congregations in Corinth and Philippi to Paul's gospel, of a kingdom inaugurated by Christ but still suffering patiently as it awaited the final victory in which all knees would bow to the one true Lord, arose in part out of fear that the gauntlet that he was throwing down before the emperor would disrupt the fragile peace under which the Jews and Christians of the time were obliged to live.

Later we shall discuss how discord between the harsh indictments raised by Paul against the imperial cult in the above citations (usually in code language, to be sure) and the more measured formulation in Romans 13 can be explained in terms of the precarious course he had to chart between repudiation of idolatry, on the one hand, and a policy of coexistence aimed at averting futile bloodshed, on the other. For now, it is sufficient to suggest that the tensions between what on the surface appear to be contradictions reflect the range of political strategies he could devise in an ever-changing political climate, due to his being heir to both the theocratic principle of sole devotion to the one God of the universe and the political strategy of accommodation utilized by Ezra and his latter-day spiritual descendants, the Pharisees.

More exasperating to Paul on a day-to-day basis than the pagans and their idolatrous ways were the opponents he encountered within his own congregations. In Corinth and Philippi he encountered a gnosticizing version of the gospel whose strident proponents claimed special knowledge (*gnosis*) not shared by "ordinary" Christians and a personal status glorified by full possession of the divine spirit that enabled them to perform extraordinary acts. For Paul, these "strong people" fractured the one body of Christ and smuggled in a divisive elitism that was contrary to the humility, patience, and loving care for all members, including the weak and vulnerable, that lay at the heart of the gospel (1 Cor. 8:9–13). Rather than following the way of Christ, they were conforming to the prevailing protocols of the Greek *polis*, the professional guilds, and the judicial courts in which "there was one law for the rich and another for the poor."[5] Later we shall elaborate on Paul's communal ideal of humility and loving care in imitation of Christ.

A third "false gospel" that Paul found it necessary to refute was one that distorted, into license for obeying one's passions, his teaching that salvation was a free gift and not the reward for obedience to the law (Rom. 6). In waging his battle against the antinominians, Paul drew upon the history of Israel for examples of the consequences of idolatry and sexual promiscuity (1 Cor. 10:6–13). In similar manner, the author of the letter of Jude (who quite possibly was the brother of James and Jesus) enlisted typological exegesis in expositing passages from the Hebrew Bible and Jewish apocalyptic writings like *1 Enoch* to combat

5. G. E. M. de Ste. Croix, *The Class Struggle in the Ancient Greek World, from the Archaic Age to the Arab Conquests* (Ithaca, NY: Cornell University Press, 1918), 330. The two-tiered structure of ancient law sheds light on Paul's admonition, "When any of you has a grievance against another, do you dare to take it to court before the unrighteous, instead of taking it before the saints?" (1 Cor. 6:1).

the licentiousness of itinerant charismatic teachers who were infiltrating circles of Jewish Christians.[6]

A fourth threat that Paul encountered took the form of sectarianism, according to which the church became split between groups claiming Apollos or Cephas or Paul as their leader, thereby denying the oneness of all those belonging to Christ. Paul's appeal was earnest: "Now I appeal to you, brothers and sisters, by the name of our Lord Jesus Christ, that all of you be in agreement and that there be no divisions among you, but that you be united in the same mind and the same purpose" (1 Cor. 1:10). The "same mind" that Paul refers to is of course "the mind of Christ" (1 Cor. 2:16).

Paul's most personal struggle was with a number of his fellow Jewish Christian leaders in Jerusalem who insisted that the ritual laws of the Torah remained binding on all Christians. Paul's resolute position that Gentile Christians were not subject to the dietary laws and ritual circumcision revolved around his understanding of the radical nature of God's grace in Christ and the release from bondage thereby accomplished. Any custom or law that encouraged the believer to regard his obedience as a contributing factor in salvation became an enemy of the gospel by undermining the liberty that accompanies, but is not achieved by, faith.

A historical event described by Paul in Galatians 2:1–10 that occurred in 48 CE in Jerusalem provides a clear picture of the apostle's position regarding the Torah. In response to dispersions being cast on his Gentile mission by those he accused of seeking to deny non-Jewish converts "the freedom we have in Christ" (Gal. 2:4), Paul traveled to Jerusalem to explain to the leaders of the local congregation, James, Cephas (Peter), and John, the gospel he was proclaiming among the Gentiles. The result was an agreement according to which Paul's and Barnabas's gospel to the uncircumcised (i.e., Gentiles) would continue alongside Cephas's and James's gospel to the circumcised (i.e., Jewish Christians).

The account that immediately follows in Galatians 2:11–14 indicates that the Jerusalem Council decision did not end the controversy. Paul reports that Cephas, on a visit to Antioch, capitulated to the Judaizing faction by refusing to eat with Gentiles. Paul's outrage flows into one of his most concise formulations of the relation between Torah and faith: "we know that a person is justified not by the works of the law but through faith in Jesus Christ" (Gal. 2:16). Within the vast freedom safeguarded by faith, Jewish Christians could continue to remain true to their ancestral practices like circumcision and dietary laws, but that same freedom was violated by any attempt to impose those practices on Gentile converts.

---

6. See Richard J. Bauckham, *Jude, 2 Peter*, Word Biblical Commentary, vol. 50 (Waco, TX: Word, 1983), 12–13.

THE FOUNDATION OF THE APOSTLE PAUL'S POLITICS

The battle that Paul waged against opponents on several fronts was in defense of what he regarded to be one essential truth, the gospel of God's gracious saving act in Jesus Christ that the believer accepts as an act of faith, with no claim to worthiness or merit. We turn now to the task of describing the nature of that gospel truth, as understood by Paul, and the bearing it had on the lives of those living in this world as members of a community reconciled with God and obedient to God's will.

Of utmost importance for Paul was the primacy of grace, for unclarity regarding the utter dependence of the human on God was tantamount with remaining captive to sin and death. Only within the framework provided by faith in the all-sufficiency of God's grace, in turn, could the role of ethics and civic responsibility in the life of the believer be understood. Paul frequently contrasted the "ungodliness and wickedness of those who by their wickedness suppress the truth" with the virtues that uphold the health and integrity of the community of faith (e.g., Rom. 1:29–31; 1 Cor. 13:4–7). But he was emphatic in insisting that true virtue comes as the fruit of faith, not as an achievement of well-intentioned humans.

The reason is this: according to the gospel, in Jesus Christ God entered human history in a way that cast in a whole new light the age-old questions of deliverance from sin, liberation from political tyranny, and the cultivation of a human community defined by compassion, justice, and mutual caring. The epoch-making newness of God's initiative demanded more than a reform of existing social structures or the introduction of a stricter code of ethics in the public sphere, though those inevitably would follow. What the gospel announced was an event, in fulfillment of Hebrew prophecy, through which God contended with the tragic condition that plagued the human race since Adam, rebellion against God's will, which leads to estrangement from the source of all goodness and bondage to sin, from which no human effort, however heroic, was able to achieve release.

As one thoroughly trained in the traditions of his ancestral religion, Paul was aware that God's struggle for the heart of his creation was not new. God had appeared to Abraham with a promise that from him would arise a great nation through which blessing would flow to all the families of the earth. Through Moses God gave that nation a law to safeguard its well-being within the covenant. However, according to Paul God's people had jeopardized the promise to Abraham by conforming to—rather than being a blessing to—the nations and distorting the law from being a gift nurturing obedience into serving as an instrument for self-achieved righteousness. Like Jesus, Paul grieved over a people that rejected the prophets God had sent to call them back to the covenant through repentance.

At the same time he drew specifically upon the prophetic tradition to explain God's initiative in Christ: The fatal curse could be broken only through the unprecedented and the humanly unthinkable, an event so raw, so visceral, as to startle nations and shock kings (Isa. 52:14–15). The gospel that shaped the heart of Paul's thought announced that in Christ, God's unfathomable love had expressed itself in the ultimate act of compassion, the sending of his Son into a fallen world to expose the bogus nature of its self-designated "divine" rulers, the futility of human efforts to achieve redemption from sin, and the impotency of all earthly institutions to establish lasting peace and justice. According to the irony residing in the core of the gospel, the sole power that was able to save humanity from bondage and the world from corruption could manifest itself only by first succumbing to the powers of this world, so as to expose their emptiness through the victory of the one in whose weakness was hidden God's saving strength.

Karl Barth described Paul's understanding of that victory with these words: "God's revelation in Jesus Christ is God's apocalyptic triumph over all the enslaving powers and gods of this world, a triumph that in turn delivers idolaters [for Barth, this means all of humankind] from their imprisonment to these other, finally immanent and impotent powers and gods."[7] From the pre-Pauline churches in Judea and Asia Minor, on to Paul and the teachers who elaborated on his message and the tradents who shaped the Gospels, and then finally to the churches scattered throughout the Roman world, the "good news" was transmitted that Christ is risen, Christ has triumphed.

However, like any audaciously new message, the proclamation of God's victory in Christ over all foes became the object of competing interpretations. Two of those competing interpretations persisted with such tenacity as to shape much of the subsequent history of Western Christendom. One was the narrowing of the universal vision of redemption into the promise of release of the individual soul from the prison of flesh. First thriving among gnostic communities, it morphed within the mainstream church into an "introspective consciousness" that fostered an individualistic understanding of Paul's proclamation of justification by faith.[8]

A second rival gospel arose through the transmutation of the gospel of Christ's triumph into a strident "triumphalism" within Christendom. The gospel of God's victory over the ruthless powers of this world through Christ's divesting himself of divine glory was supplanted by the church's claiming that victory as its license to conquer all rivals through the exercise of its newly acquired *earthly* power. The denouement of this distorted gospel was the transformation of the church into yet one more regime in the chain of worldly empires—Ashurbanipal's Assyria, Nebuchadnezzar's Babylon, Cyrus's Persia, Alexander's Greece, Augustus's Rome—and now, Constantine's Roman Empire.[9]

7. As quoted in Douglas Harink, *Paul among the Post-Liberals: Pauline Theology beyond Christendom and Modernity* (Grand Rapids: Brazos Press, 2003), 47–48.

8. Krister Stendahl, "Paul and the Introspective Consciousness of the West," in *Paul among Jews and Gentiles, and Other Essays* (Philadelphia: Fortress Press, 1976).

9. See James Carroll, *Constantine's Sword: The Church and the Jews: A History* (Boston: Houghton Mifflin, 2001).

In combating superapostles and triumphalists, Paul enlisted the only warrant that in his mind held any validity, the example of Christ himself; for he was convinced that the central aim of the faithful was to

> let the same mind be in you that was in Christ Jesus,
> who, though he was in the form of God,
>> did not regard equality with God
>> as something to be exploited,
> but emptied himself,
>> taking the form of a slave. . . .
>> [H]e humbled himself
>> and became obedient to the point of death—
>> even death on a cross.
>
> (Phil. 2:5–8)

In this hymn, stemming from wisdom tradition and modified so as to reach beyond a conventional individualistic understanding to a vision of the all-inclusive body of Christ, Paul reveals two central truths that shape a Christian theo-politics based on the gospel. The first truth describes the power with which the community of faith is endowed and the inner-community life that it fosters. The second clarifies the manner of engagement with the broader society and its structures of governance that is consistent with commitment to the one true God revealed in Jesus Christ.

What was the nature of the power with which God's people were equipped? According to Paul, the power manifested on the cross and destined to triumph over all foes differed categorically from conventional understandings of power: "[T]he message about the cross is foolishness to those who are perishing, but to us who are being saved it is the power of God" (1 Cor. 1:18). The lesson was given a very personal twist when, in response to his supplication regarding his own bodily affliction, the answer he received from the Lord was, "My grace is sufficient for you, for [my] power is made perfect in weakness" (2 Cor. 12:9). As regards the myriad other afflictions suffered by the faithful, Paul gives as the reason "that it may be made clear that this extraordinary power belongs to God and does not come from us" (2 Cor. 4:7). Paul thus draws a categorical distinction between his understanding of charisma and that touted by his opponents, the "super-apostles" (2 Cor. 11:5; 12:11).

As astonishing as it must have seemed to those suffering under the iron fist of the Romans, even eternal Rome would one day yield to the "extraordinary power" mysteriously revealed in the one who had been slain by this world's most powerful leaders, tyrants who were confident that they had thereby secured absolute dominion over the earth. According to the hymn in Philippians 2, the path to victory came not through brute force, but through self-emptying, through servanthood, through humbling of self and willingness to die for others. Through God's alternative power the mighty of the earth would be stripped of the weapon of terror with which they held their subjects in bondage. The universal reign of peace touted by the *divine* Caesars had been exposed by the crucified and risen one to be based on hubris, presumptiveness, and deceit.

The true reign of universal peace and justice would soon be established—in the most miraculous of all ironies—by the very one they had executed alongside common criminals. The result would be a reordering of political realities reminiscent of the song of Hannah and the Magnificat of Mary:

> Therefore God also highly exalted him
>   and gave him a name
>   that is above every name,
> so that at the name of Jesus
>   every knee should bend,
>   in heaven and on earth and under the earth,
> and every tongue should confess
>   that Jesus Christ is Lord,
>   to the glory of God the Father.
>   (Phil. 2:9–11)

Such is the sentence handed down by the judicial court of the true ruler of the universe and sealed by the blood of his Son. Its language gives expression to what in the Roman world would have amounted to the most egregious form of seditious insubordination imaginable: "every name . . . every knee . . . every tongue." Was not such submission precisely what was demanded of every subject by the divine lord and savior Nero and reserved for him alone? Little wonder that the setting within which Paul penned these words was a Roman prison! What is more, the apostle's repeated references to the likelihood of his sharing in Christ's death at the hands of the Romans takes on a vivid existential dimension.

For Paul, the cross of Christ marked a crucial turning point in world history. The event anticipated by the royal psalms and promised by the prophets was shaping an entirely new reality.[10] He turned to prophetic and apocalyptic literature for language straining to describe the new order that God had inaugurated in Christ, language like "new creation" (2 Cor. 5:17; Gal. 6:15) and "new covenant" (2 Cor. 3:6). From those same traditional sources, he drew polarities that pointed to the categorical distinction between the age that was passing and the one that was dawning: "first Adam/last Adam" (1 Cor. 15:45), "children of darkness/children of light" (1 Thess. 5:5), "flesh/Spirit" (Gal. 5:16–26), "bondage/freedom" (Rom. 8:21), "Esau/Jacob" (Rom. 9:13), "present Jerusalem/Jerusalem above" (Gal. 4:25–26), "Hagar/Sarah" (Gal. 4:24–31). It is no accident that one manifesting admirable pragmatic instincts in building and preserving a vast network of new churches and a high level of skill in resolving tensions and controversies would turn to the brash polarities of apocalypticism when seeking to convey what God was accomplishing in the world and the entire cosmos in Christ.

---

10. Pss. 72:8; 80:11; 89:25–27.

Only thus could he point out the sharp contrast between the public projects of Athenian philosopher-kings and Roman emperor-saviors, that is, "the wisdom of the world," and the message of the cross, that is, "God's foolishness" (1 Cor. 1:18–25). For God, the creator of all that is, had entered human experience in an act so revolutionary as to be understood as a new reality, comparable only negatively to the ephemeral monuments of this world's potentates, the reality of a peaceable kingdom inhabited by new creatures endowed with compassionate hearts and living in harmony with their Creator and with one another within the protective shelter of a renewed covenant.

On the basis of the new order initiated by Christ, Paul explains the quality of the community believers would foster and the manner in which they would engage in public life. In the new era, those who received God's gift in faith were a new creation, called to be the body of Christ and to bear witness to God's reign of peace (Gal. 6:15). Regarding their relation to the broader society he admonished them, "[P]resent your bodies as a living sacrifice, holy and acceptable to God, which is your spiritual worship. Do not be conformed to this world, but be transformed by the renewing of your minds, so that you may discern what is the will of God—what is good and acceptable and perfect" (Rom. 12:1–2).

The transformation Paul described was not an exercise in self-improvement, but the result of a fundamental change in being. In baptism the believer had shared in Christ's death, "so that, just as Christ was raised from the dead by the glory of the Father, so we too might walk in newness of life" (Rom. 6:4). Paul argued that even the hardships endured by the believer had a purpose, "always carrying in the body the death of Jesus, so that the life of Jesus may also be made visible in our bodies" (2 Cor. 4:10).

Paul's references to his own physical ailments and afflictions functioned as part of his polemic against rivals who were claiming that with Christ's resurrection the Parousia, the blessed age, had come in its fullness: "the day of the Lord is already here," they exulted (2 Thess. 2:2). Combating that interpretation raised for Paul a particularly vexing problem. How could he claim that Jesus was the Christ (i.e., Messiah) and yet insist that those following Christ still lived in a world afflicted by the forces opposed to God? His argument was predicated on a distinction between God's initiation of the kingdom in Christ's life, death, and resurrection and the future "day of Jesus Christ," when all enemies of righteousness would be defeated and the kingdom would be fulfilled (Phil. 1:6). While his present generation was immeasurably blessed by bearing witness to the former, its members remained pilgrims in this world, awaiting the world to come. Although Paul himself lived in the expectation of Christ's return during his own lifetime, he warned those exalting in their superior knowledge that the day could not be predicted; indeed, it would come "like a thief in the night" (1 Thess. 5:2).

This tension between "already" and "not yet" provides a key to Paul's description of the life lived by members of the body of Christ. They were to live as a community not luxuriating like gnostics and superapostles in heavenly bliss, but as a community both modeling itself after their suffering Master as they awaited "the revealing of our Lord Jesus Christ" and trusting in God to strengthen them "to the end" (1 Cor. 1:7–8). It was in such terms that Paul understood his own life, a life in which he had not yet "reached the goal," but, as he expressed his situation, "I press on to make it my own, because Christ Jesus has made me his own" (Phil. 3:12).

The perspective on life in this world of those called into communion with Christ (the *ekklesia*) comes to vivid expression in the contrast Paul makes in Philippians 3:19–20 between two mind-sets. On the one hand are those whose "minds are set on earthly things," on the other those living in expectation of the Lord and knowing that their "citizenship is in heaven." With the latter phrase, Paul gave expression to the theocratic principle affirming the sole sovereignty of God, which constitutes the core of biblical political thought, and to its corollary, namely, that the regimes and institutions of this world hold no *ultimate* significance for people of faith.

To be sure, as is characteristic of his plainspoken rhetorical style, Paul used an earthier phrase to describe all things worldly, namely, "rubbish," or more literally, "excrement." Yet unlike the gnostics and ascetics who were moved by their vision of the heavenly realm to denounce this world and abdicate all responsibility for society, Paul admonished those who would be faithful to Christ to "live your life in a manner worthy of the gospel of Christ" (Phil. 1:27), insisting that there was only one way in which they could do that, namely, through imitation of Christ (Phil. 2:5). Unlike the superapostles, with their triumphal boasting and claims to special privilege, true disciples were to share patiently and lovingly in Christ's suffering, with confidence that on the day of Christ's return God would gather his faithful into their eternal home.

The Greek word translated in Philippians 1:27 in the NRSV as "live your life" is *politeuesthai*. A more literal translation of the verse would be "conduct your life as a citizen in a manner worthy of Christ." The conduct Paul was urging was not aimed merely at gaining respect from non-Christian members of the society or avoiding conflict. Indeed, in the next sentences he described opposition, struggle, and suffering as intrinsic to life in imitation of the suffering Christ. No, Paul was consistent in grounding all aspects of the life of faith in the *gospel*. So the reason he gave for good conduct in the public realm was that believers be found "worthy of the gospel of Christ." Good citizenship *in this world* for those whose ultimate citizenship was *in heaven* was mandated by the gospel itself!

We shall return to a fuller exploration of this understanding of Christian political engagement, but first we need to describe more specifically the qualities Paul claimed believers were to embody within their *own* community, since in his understanding the effectiveness of the political dimension of the Christian vocation was inextricably tied to and dependent upon the quality of its inner-community life.

We need look no further than the paragraph immediately following Paul's admonition to good citizenship to find a description of the life worthy of the gospel of Christ. The intimate connection between moral conduct and the gospel of Christ is evident in the envelope structure (aba) of this section of Philippians: (a) "live your life in a manner worthy of the gospel of Christ" (1:27), (b) the qualities of community life that reflect the gospel (2:1–4), (a) a dramatic snapshot of the heart of the gospel in the hymn praising the Servant Jesus who was obedient unto death and the heavenly Father who exalted him (2:5–11).

Here then is Paul's description of the community modeling itself after the one who gathered it together as one family ("let the same mind be in you that was in Christ Jesus" [2:5]): "[B]e of the same mind, having the same love, being in full accord and of one mind. Do nothing from selfish ambition or conceit, but in humility regard others as better than yourselves. Let each of you look not to your own interests, but to the interests of others" (2:2–4).

As already noted, Paul penned these words as he was being held prisoner by a regime that was intolerant of challenges to its self-acclaimed divine status and maintained its authority through the application of ruthless power. It was a regime that sponsored many *ekklesiae,* that is, affinity groups reserved exclusively for elite members of society. Paul wrote in the name of a Lord who challenged the "divine power" of the Roman emperor, a Lord whose alternative power was manifested not through ruthless oppression of all who refused to submit, but through the willingness to die for the oppressed. Through the crucified and exalted one, power was redefined as meekness, humility, and love for others that placed their interests above one's own. This Lord called into being not exclusive affinity groups for the privileged members of society, but one *ekklesia* to which *all* were welcomed, without regard to status, religious background, or gender, for they were all "one in Christ" (Gal. 3:28).

The simplicity and lucidity with which Paul described the fellowship of believers is remarkable. It calls to my mind the Shaker hymn that we sang before the evening meal when our children were young and that still arises spontaneously when we gather at a larger table now including seven grandchildren: "'Tis a gift to be simple, 'tis a gift to be free, 'tis a gift to come down where we ought to be."

Against the background of the sublime example in Christ of humility and loving care for the neighbor that Paul held up before the eyes of the churches with which he corresponded, the bitter polemical tone of many other parts of his letters seems rudely discordant. Why did those who heard and accepted the good news of God's gift so readily refuse to live in harmony with Christ's example? Paul responded by pointing to various obstacles to the life of faith. Clearly, the lure of the blandishments offered by the dominant society was unrelenting, and Paul repeatedly had to warn, "Do not be conformed . . . , but be transformed . . ." (Rom. 12:2). The tentacles of evil relentlessly reached deeply into the churches themselves. Paul, like Jeremiah and Ezekiel before him, anguished over the perversity of the human heart. Within the congregations, he contended with false teachers whose twisted gospel fostered elitism, conceit, and callousness toward anyone they regarded as weak or inferior. He denounced as "contempt for the church" the conduct of those who, in the sacred meal celebration defining the heart of the faith, behaved like carousing pagans: "When you come together, it is not really to eat the Lord's supper. For when the time comes to eat, each of you goes ahead with your own supper, and one goes hungry and another becomes drunk" (1 Cor. 11:20–21).

Rather than living in a manner worthy of the gospel of Christ, they were conforming to the ways of those whose "god is the belly" (Phil. 3:19). In the wake of conflicting loyalties, there followed all of the heinous acts that assaulted the kingdom of God. Hence, Paul's battle for the purity of the church was ongoing, sometimes taking the form of long lists of evil acts (1 Cor. 6:9–10), sometimes expressed with the poignancy of a short proverb: "Bad company ruins good morals" (1 Cor. 15:33), but most often formulated with loving passion: "Let us then pursue what makes for peace and for mutual upbuilding" (Rom. 14:19).

On the deepest level, the most adequate explanation of the incorrigibility with which Paul was forced to contend likely is that the new manner of life commended by the gospel ran just as directly against the grain of conventional worldly ways as did the manner of leadership practiced by Jesus himself. Let us illustrate this by reference to the concept of liberation or freedom.

In a world suffering diverse forms of bondage—poverty, political persecution, religious, ethnic, and gender discrimination—the theme of freedom resonated with the peasant population, making them vulnerable to self-proclaimed savior-messiahs. But the nature of the freedom arising from Christ's example was more subtle and difficult to grasp. Popularly understood, freedom provides the opportunity to retaliate and to seize for oneself what previously had been denied (naturally at the expense of someone else, in a zero-sum game). Paul argued that such "freedom" only leads to a deeper bondage. Instead, he described an alternative understanding of freedom residing in the heart of the Torah and reaffirmed by the gospel: "For you were called to freedom, brothers and sisters; only do not use your freedom as an opportunity for self-indulgence, but through love become slaves to one another. For the whole law is summed up in a single commandment, 'You shall love your neighbor as yourself'" (Gal. 5:13–14).

"'Tis a gift to be simple, 'tis a gift to be free": to be simple and free seems like a wonderful way to live in community, but the apostle hit a roadblock: "I do not do what I want, but I do the very thing I hate" (Rom. 7:15). Authentic liberation could not be achieved by simple human resolve and action. Apart from divine involvement in the plight of humans, the situation was hopeless. The personal reflections Paul shared in his letters indicate that his discovery of the radical nature of God's liberating act in Christ was not the fruit of abstract reflection, but arose from his own experience of helplessness and despair: "Wretched man that I am! Who will rescue me from this body of death?" (Rom. 7:24). In his zeal to be perfect, he became conscious of the dark abyss that Jeremiah had described: "The heart is devious above all else; it is perverse—who can understand it?" (Jer. 17:9). Like Jeremiah, he discovered that God alone was capable of breaking the bondage of sin and death.

The gauntlet thus thrown down to conventional notions of community building was stark. Efforts to construct a world of peace and shared prosperity on the basis of inherent human potential were utopian, since they ignored the incorrigibility of the selfish and deceitful human heart. Humans could live in harmony only by relocating the center of existence from sinful selves to the one God in whom all mortals "live and move and have [their] being" (Acts 17:28). The peaceable community and, finally, the good society were achievable not by human contractors under the hire of this world's financiers, but only by servants committed to the alternative power of Christ and the alternative community of mutual caring to which God has invited all humanity. Paul identified the alternative power as *love* and the alternative community as the *body of Christ*.

The life of the church as life in imitation of Christ could not be expressed more vividly than in the image of the body of Christ animated by love. Here was a community without borders, without distinctions regarding vocation or status. It was not a segmented society, after the style of the Hellenistic *polis* or Roman guild. What in worldly ideologies were lowly vocations were just as important as those normally ascribed an exalted status. In the body of Christ, a profound solidarity among all members was to exist, for the self/other distinction was replaced by a loving inclusivity where "there may be no dissension within the body, but the members may have the same care for one another. If one member suffers, all suffer together with it; if one member is honored, all rejoice together with it" (1 Cor. 12:25–26).

Once the essential nature of the church had been clarified, practical matters such as delegation of responsibilities and fiscal obligations could be worked out. In chapter 12 of Romans, Paul returned to the metaphor of the body of Christ to stress the unity and equal worth of each member that stripped differences in talent or vocation of any ultimate significance: "so we, who are many, are one body in Christ, and individually we are members one of another" (Rom. 12:5). This, however, did not preclude attention to organizational detail, but provided for such practical matters as appropriate assignments and funding. Hence, Paul moved from the unity of all in Christ to designation of diverse offices (Rom. 12:6–8) and to the financial obligation he insisted the Gentile churches held in relation to the Jewish mother church in Jerusalem and toward strangers (Rom. 12:13).

This practical side of community life came to expression in relation to other issues: Those practicing religiously motivated dietary disciplines or moved by the Spirit to speak in tongues were to take care not to offend others (1 Cor. 8:7–13; 14:26–33). In formulating the rules of the community, Paul did not overlook the important role played by common sense: "Let all things be done for building up" (1 Cor. 14:26); "all things should be done decently and in order" (1 Cor. 14:40). While the gift of the Spirit was of great importance for the vitality of the body of Christ, it did not exclude clear-headed reason: "I will pray with the spirit, but I will pray with the mind also; I will sing praise with the spirit, but I will sing praise with the mind also" (1 Cor. 14:15).

Finally, however, the most important source of community life traced back to what Victor Furnish has called "the uncommon love" of God known in Christ.[11] As stated by Paul, "Let love be genuine; . . . love one another with mutual affection" (Rom. 12:9–10). Paul reminds his readers of the source of their knowledge of that love: "Now I would remind you, brothers and sisters, of the good news" (1 Cor. 15:1).

PAUL'S STRATEGIES FOR ENGAGEMENT OF THE CHURCH WITH THE WIDER SOCIETY

As Christ had lived and died not for himself but the entire world (2 Cor. 5:19), those belonging to the community called together to continue his loving care were to extend that care not only to fellow members, but to all in need: "always seek to do good to one another and *to all*" (1 Thess. 5:15, emphasis added).[12] Realistically, a struggling and often persecuted minority scattered across the provinces of the Roman world was limited in the extent to which it could "do good to all." But even when suffering adversity, even when all it could do was "bless those who persecute you" (Rom. 12:14), those following in the path of Jesus were not to lose sight of their godly vocation: "so that you may be blameless and innocent, children of God without blemish in the midst of a crooked and perverse generation, in which you shine like stars in the world" (Phil. 2:15). Paul never lost sight of the ultimate motivation behind their good deeds: "you glorify God by your obedience" (2 Cor. 9:13).

Some scholars have argued that Paul could not have taken seriously a civic dimension to the Christian life, given his expectation of Christ's imminent return to establish God's universal kingdom.[13] How an apocalyptic worldview could be compatible with a sense of responsibility for the wider world is a question requiring explanation. Could Paul have been serious in his admonition that those awaiting their Lord exercise in their cities and towns virtues normally associated with Hellenistic virtues or the ideals of an honorable Roman citizen (e.g., Phil. 4:8–9)?

In truth, it was precisely in light of, not in spite of, their ultimate citizenship being in heaven and their living in expectation of their Lord Jesus Christ (Phil. 3:20) that the faithful were to "let their gentleness be known to everyone"

11. "The love that Paul regarded as definitive of God's self-disclosure in Christ is 'uncommon' in the sense that it is uniquely an expression of God's own being and saving power, and is therefore present for humankind always and only as a 'gift.'" (Victor Paul Furnish, "Uncommon Love and the Common Good: Christians as Citizens in the Letters of Paul," in *In Search of the Common Good,* ed. Dennis McCann and Patrick D. Miller [New York: T. & T. Clark, 2005], 58–90).

12. Cf. 1 Thess. 3:12; 4:12 and Gal. 6:10.

13. Considerable scholarly attention has been given to the tension between Paul's apocalyptic vision of a new creation and the responsibilities of Christians to the realm of politics. See E. P. Sanders, *Paul and Palestinian Judaism* (Philadelphia: Fortress Press, 1977), and Richard A. Horsley, ed., *Paul and the Roman Imperial Order* (New York: Trinity Press, 2004).

by being good citizens. They were to engage in civil society not by abdicating moral critique and blithely affirming all Roman practices, but by exercising their prophetic responsibility as a community representing and foreshadowing in the present world a righteous order that in God's time would come in its fullness. Paul in Romans 8:23 depicted those responding to Christ's call as "the first fruits of the Spirit" in a redemptive drama that ultimately would encompass the entire cosmos.

There is another side to Paul's understanding of the relation of "citizens of heaven" to the political and social institutions of this world. The example of law-abiding citizens that followers of Christ were to hold up before nonbelievers was not to be viewed as a futile act, for "when Gentiles, who do not possess the law, do instinctively what the law requires, these, though not having the law, are a law to themselves. They show that what the law requires is written on their hearts" (Rom. 2:14–15). In other words, Paul's understanding of what in modern philosophy would be designated "natural law" lent support to cooperation between believers and pagans in the struggle for civic justice and integrity or, again in a more contemporary idiom, for "the good society." To be sure, Paul did not flesh out this idea, for his primary reason for appealing to natural law was to argue that no human could escape God's judgment for his or her acts. This does not detract from the major contribution made by Paul to an understanding of the part believers can play to building public virtue on the basis of an inference they draw from their theocratic worldview, namely, as a part of the sovereign's rule, moral principles are built into the very fabric of being.

In 2 Corinthians 5:14–21, Paul gave his most eloquent expression to the earthly vocation of those who through their communal life bore witness to the new creation or, in other words, who having received God's gift of reconciliation through Christ become ambassadors of that good news to others:

> For the love of Christ urges us on, because we are convinced that one has died for all; therefore all have died. And he died for all, so that those who live might live no longer for themselves, but for him who died and was raised for them.
>
> From now on, therefore, we regard no one from a human point of view; even though we once knew Christ from a human point of view, we know him no longer in that way. So if anyone is in Christ, there is a new creation: everything old has passed away; see, everything has become new! All this is from God, who reconciled us to himself through Christ, and has given us the ministry of reconciliation; that is, in Christ God was reconciling the world to himself, not counting their trespasses against them, and entrusting the message of reconciliation to us. So we are ambassadors for Christ, since God is making his appeal through us; we entreat you on behalf of Christ, be reconciled to God. For our sake he made him to be sin who knew no sin, so that in him we might become the righteousness of God.

The priority of the gospel in Paul's understanding of the Christian life could not have been expressed more clearly than in this passage. Those who were "in

Christ"' constituted a new creation, viewing life from the perspective of the world to come. Living as responsible citizens in word and deed was one of the ways in which they were to "become the righteousness of God."

To become God's righteousness in the world was the apostle Paul's passion. That most of his kin did not share his understanding of Christ's role in God's plan was the source of his deepest anguish. Today it is the source of a deep misunderstanding of Paul's position vis-à-vis his fellow Jews, a misunderstanding arising from an exclusive focus on texts in which Paul rails against those who seek to establish their righteousness before God through obedience to the law. However, in Romans 9–11, after reiterating his distinction between faith and works, Paul proceeded to a profound description of the role played by the Jews in God's plan of salvation. Their present "stumbling" provided opportunity for salvation to be extended to the Gentiles.

But he cautioned against boasting on the part of the Gentiles, for they were latecomers grafted onto the original olive tree. Above all, they were to draw from their own experience of God's mercy and forgiveness this lesson about God's elect, the people of Israel: "all Israel will be saved," for "the gifts and the calling of God are irrevocable" (Rom. 11:26, 29). Paul ends his reflection on the relation between God's outreach to the Gentiles and God's ongoing faithfulness to his covenant with Israel with acknowledgment of the inscrutable ways of God. Appropriately he ends not with a summary formulation, but with a hymn to the transcendent mystery of God (Rom. 11:33–36).

In Romans 13:1–7, Paul sketched what among his writings most closely approximates a formal statement of the responsibilities of the Christian as citizen. For some, his words sound like those of a royalist urging uncritical submission to ruling authorities. Had the apostle who earlier had served jail time under the Romans lost nerve and relented in his old age?

A proper understanding of Romans 13:1–7 is impossible without an awareness that Paul did not adhere to a political theory that he had formulated immediately after his conversion and then spent the rest of his life applying to every situation he encountered. Rather, as he traveled from city to city and province to province, he responded with remarkable alacrity to the ever-changing circumstances he faced. For example, when in the provincial capital of Philippi he encountered an official cult that was alluring church members away from sole worship of their God, he denounced the notion of the divine emperor and ended up in chains. In his letter "to all God's beloved in Rome," however, we find the reflections of one hoping to fulfill a dream to visit his fellow Christians in the capital of the empire, and it should come as no surprise that he formulates his understanding of the role of human government in a manner that will not provoke unnecessary tension with the authorities on the eve of his visit. After all, he had a farther destination planned in his itinerary, namely, a visit to Spain. In other words, Romans 13 is Paul's reflection on a specific situation at a particular time in his life.

The importance of sensitivity to the specific historical context within which Paul formulated Romans 13:1–7 is matched by the need to be attentive to the literary context, especially the envelope function played by Romans 12 and 13:8–14. Chapter 12 describes a community of believers not conforming to the retaliatory ways of this world, but manifesting what is "good and acceptable and perfect," namely, love for one another, patience in suffering, harmony within the family of faith, and living peaceably with all others. Romans 13:8–14 picks up anew the central theme of neighborly love. Clearly, the political advice Paul offers in 13:1–7 is cradled in the qualities forming the heart of the life of faith and should be interpreted in relation to those qualities.

His opening injunction to "be subject to the governing authorities" accordingly can be seen as an application of his plea in 12:18: "If it is possible, so far as it depends on you, live peaceably with all." But being subject to a political power is not an unqualified, ideological commitment; indeed, it entails a double qualification. If subjection entails worshiping Caesar, for example, it is *not* possible for those who reserve worship for one God. If the condition for living peaceably with neighbors entails participation in their debaucheries, refusal is the only option, come what may. But Paul adds a third, even weightier qualification that locates his advice squarely under the theocratic principle of the Hebrew Bible: "for there is no authority except from God, and those authorities that exist have been instituted by God" (Rom. 13:1). The authority of this world's rulers, judges, and magistrates is penultimate, mediated, and derivative. Its validity reaches to the extent that it conforms to God's order of righteousness and mercy, and no further.

The distinction between the qualified authority of this world's rulers and God's ultimate authority ("there is no authority except from God") expressed by Paul in the first verse of Romans 13 places him within the central stream of the theo-politics of the Bible. However, subsequent verses lead one to ask whether Paul had not gone so far in his accommodation with the Romans as to compromise the classical theocratic position of his ancestral faith: "whoever resists authority resists what God has appointed, and those who resist will incur judgment. For rulers are not a terror to good conduct, but to bad. . . . [T]he authority does not bear the sword in vain! It is the servant of God to execute wrath on the wrongdoer" (Rom. 13:2–4).

The simplest solution would be to claim that these words are inauthentic, added by a post-Pauline writer trying to prove the ultrapatriotism of Christians to the Roman regime. Unfortunately, and in contrast to the injunction that women remain silent in the churches (1 Cor. 14:33b–34a), no credible argument can be made for deleting these words from the corpus of authentic Pauline words. But to grant them unqualified authority in relation to the politics of the Bible is to dishonor the cry of millions who have fallen to the swords of medieval Crusaders, Nazi-sympathizing bishops, and other self-appointed enforcers of God's fear. Romans 13:1–7, as a "text of terror" for countless victims of

Christian triumphalism, behooves us to seek God's truth amid the muddled reflections of his fallible witnesses.

Ironically, the apostle Paul provides a tool equal to this daunting task: we are to interpret not only with "the spirit," but with "the mind also" (1 Cor. 14:15). Additionally, it is helpful to recall that while Paul handed on words "received from the Lord," he could also admit, in relation to his advice concerning virgins, "I have no command of the Lord, but I give my opinion as one who by the Lord's mercy is trustworthy" (1 Cor. 7:25). In seeking to create a temperate political atmosphere for his long-anticipated visit to the capital of the mighty Roman Empire, Paul wrote words that require hermeneutical scrutiny both critically astute and spiritually faithful in nature.

In other words, following the example of the scribe in Matthew 13:52, we need to sift through truths that lie at the heart of biblical tradition and applications that relate to a specific historical political setting. Appropriately, Paul reaffirms in the first verse the principle that constitutes the very heart of the politics of the Bible: "there is no authority except from God." Since, as he continues, the authority that human rulers exercise derives from the one ultimate authority, those whose true citizenship is in heaven must in each historical situation discern the civic behavior that is consistent with the First Commandment and facilitate an appropriate mediation of God's authoritative rule within the context of fallible human institutions.

Paul's own discernment of the situation in Rome led him to commend strict adherence to Roman civil law regarding taxes and revenue, motivated both by fear of punishment for noncompliance and an attitude of honor and respect for civil authorities. In contrast to the normative monotheistic principle with which he begins, his specific advice on matters like taxation must be understood as adaptations to the situation in Rome during the first half of Nero's rule, in anticipation of his upcoming visit. It is also helpful to contrast the bluntness of his admonition to "pay all that is due them" with the exquisite irony woven into Jesus' words about what should be rendered to Caesar and what to God, all the while keeping in mind the provisionality of Paul's own advice in the previous chapter (Rom. 12:18).

Finally, the contemporary interpreter cannot ignore the history of interpretation of this text through the centuries and the connotations that have become attached to certain of its images, for example, "for the authority does not bear the sword in vain." Especially in light of the Holocaust, modern Christians are behooved to move beyond mechanical proof-texting to a theological struggle with the text that takes into account its mixed legacy of interpretation and misinterpretation, faithful application and abhorrent abuse.

If Paul projected his most submissive civic position in Romans 13, in Romans 8:18–36 he composed an audacious vision of cosmic transformation, charged with political implications and defiant with regard to worldly powers. If he pragmatically grasped the realpolitik of the political microcosm in the former, he envisioned the vastness of the creator God's macrocosm in the latter. In that envisioning process, he sketched a theo-political perspective capable of reaching from the exuberant praise of the Hebrew psalmists to the awe of the contemporary believer glimpsing an ever-expanding universe through the lens of the Hubble telescope.

That his apocalyptic perspective played a midwifery role in the fashioning of the bold vision in Romans 8 is obvious. The world was not being eased gently toward an ever-brighter future. Rather, creation was in crisis, on the brink of disaster, "subjected to futility." As we read these verses, the stage seems set for a motif popular in modern cinema: impending disaster on a cosmic scale. But the cosmos Paul sees is not one destined by blind fate. It "was subjected to futility, not of its own will but by the will of one who subjected it, in the hope that the creation itself will be set free from its bondage to decay and will obtain the freedom of the glory of the children of God" (Rom. 8:20–21).

Two bold themes distinguish this drama from a film like the Vietnam-era *Apocalypse Now*: "subjected to futility . . . in hope" and "creation itself will be set free from its bondage to decay and will obtain the freedom of the glory of the children of God." This is not the rhetoric of naturalism, nor is it the view of humanism. Paul's eschatological/apocalyptic faith introduced a daring alternative to anthropocentric cosmologies. God himself initiated the dreadful crisis when God sent his Son to confront in a final assize the dark principalities and powers that were corrupting creation. What is remarkable is the cosmic scope of God's liberating act, *creation itself*! The new creation inaugurated by Christ's reconciling act reached beyond the human community to embrace an entire cosmos that has been yearning alongside humanity for the redemption and wholeness intended by God.

Paul ended his vision of cosmic redemption with an exuberant celebration of the gospel message, "the love of God in Christ Jesus our Lord" (Rom. 8:39), from which nothing was capable of separating God's elect. Although, in contrast to his practical advice in Roman 13, his vision in chapter 8 did not delve into the minutiae of political affairs, its implications for a robust theo-politics are profound: Among the threats included by Paul among the evil forces are "rulers" and "powers." In chapter 13 of Romans Paul may have tiptoed his way toward avoiding conflict with Nero as he planned his trip to Rome, but in the same letter he did not fail to restate the bold message of his Letter to the Philippians, thereby clarifying the issue of political authority by relating it to the only power that is ultimate and eternal:

> so that at the name of Jesus
>   every knee should bend,
>   in heaven and on earth and under the earth,
> and every tongue should confess
>   that Jesus Christ is Lord,
>   to the glory of God the Father.
>   (Phil. 2:10–11)

At key points in his writings Paul expressed the heart of his message, and thus the heart of his theo-politics, by adopting the elevated style of the hymn. In

Romans 8 he celebrated "the love of God in Christ Jesus our Lord," even as in Philippians 2 the drama of Christ's obedience to death and exaltation reached its final goal in the phrase "to the glory of God the Father." In 1 Corinthians 15:28, Paul linked his Christ-centered soteriology to the theocratic principle ensconced in the heart of his Jewish faith: "When all things are subjected to him, then the Son himself will also be subjected to the one who put all things in subjection under him, so that God may be all in all." The blessing of the new creation and the harmony that will embrace all of God's creatures in Paul's thinking had as its ultimate source the oneness of God the Father.

What would be a fitting conclusion to a discussion of the politics of the apostle Paul? To end with a hymnic celebration of the God who is "all in all" would be to end on a lofty, indeed ethereal, note. While Paul understood his life as directed by God's cosmos-embracing purpose, however, he spent most of his days struggling with the difficult task of integrating God's plan into the day-to-day lives of sinful humans and a fallen social order. We choose, therefore to conclude this chapter with a glimpse of the pastoral Paul as he spells out in a specific case what he meant when he wrote: "There is no longer Jew or Greek, there is no longer slave or free, there is no longer male and female; for all of you are one in Christ Jesus" (Gal. 3:28).

While in prison, Paul brought the good news of God's grace in Christ to a fellow prisoner named Onesimus, who was the slave of Paul's "dear friend and co-worker," Philemon. The short letter that he addresses to Philemon demonstrates the subtlety with which Paul applies his understanding of freedom and equality in Christ to a sensitive situation. The problem is this: as a result of his conversion, Onesimus is now a brother, a member in the household of faith. But is his freedom limited to the spiritual realm? Within the Roman legal system, he is also the property of his owner, Philemon. Paul is dealing with a genuine dilemma: "though I am bold enough in Christ to command you to do your duty, yet I would rather appeal to you on the basis of love" (Phlm. 8–9).

Though Paul did not hesitate on other occasions to appeal to his apostolic authority in the attempt to bring individuals and congregations in line with his understanding of the gospel, in this case he takes another approach, one that balances the clear gospel message of equality of all brothers and sisters in Christ with Philemon's freedom in Christ. In effect, Paul is being guided by words he had addressed to the Galatians: "For you were called to freedom, brothers and sisters; only do not use your freedom as an opportunity for self-indulgence, but through love become slaves to one another" (Gal. 5:13). How would Philemon use his freedom in this case? Receive him back, "no longer as a slave but more than a slave, a beloved brother" (Phlm. 16). Paul concludes his appeal by giving expression to his profound confidence in Philemon's faith: "Confident of your obedience, I am writing to you, knowing that you will do even more than I say" (Phlm. 21).

Clearly, Paul has tried his utmost to respect the freedom and integrity of a fellow worker, but this does not prevent him from indicating clearly his stand on the question of Christians holding fellow Christians as slaves! His intention goes beyond counseling one individual. He addresses the letter not to Philemon alone, but to Apphia, Archippus, and "to the church in your house" (Phlm. 2). The lesson Paul thereby bequeaths to the church through this concrete example is enormously important for successive generations, including the generation immediately following Paul, as they retreat into the slave-holding conventions of the culture with which they were striving to ingratiate themselves.

Chapter 28

The Church Accommodates Itself to a World Not About to End

An important lesson regarding the relation between faith community and state emerged in the previous chapter: Even over the course of the life of one individual, different strategies for dealing with those in high office may be exercised. Flexibility, rather than reflecting a lack of religious conviction and moral principle, can function as an expression of a profound faith, sensitive to the responsibility of believers to mediate God's sovereign rule within the flux of fallible human institutions. Accordingly, an apostle preparing the way for a visit to the imperial capital formulated a rationale for accommodating to the authority of the state that differed from earlier harsher words, written while he was being detained as a political prisoner. This having been said, one principle remained constant throughout Paul's career as missionary to the Gentiles and provocateur in dialogue with his fellow Jews: "there is no authority except from God" (Rom. 13:1). Over the course of the various strategies Paul adopted in response to changing political circumstances, he struggled to uphold (albeit at times imperfectly) the central theocratic principle of biblical faith, namely, acknowledgment of one ultimate sovereign, and insistence that the provisional authority of all human regimes retains its legitimacy solely to the degree that it conforms to and promotes the justice and mercy defined by God's universal reign.

We turn now to a period that confronted the fledgling Christian church with enormous challenges, a period in which a span of merely a decade could transform a world from one tolerant of those confessing Christ as Lord to one persecuting those whose identity was tied to the one under whose authority they claimed God had placed all nations. That it was a period in which the manner of relating to the ruling powers of this earth ranged from docile accommodation to bitter denunciation and resistance becomes comprehensible to the extent that the political and religious environment that each writing addressed can be brought to light. While reconstruction of context is complicated by the anonymity and pseudonymity of the letters and tractates that we shall examine, anyone interested in ferreting out the diverse approaches to politics in the Bible has no alternative to the time-tested historical exercise of seeking to glimpse the audiences being addressed and the circumstances in which they were living.

Since even the dates of composition of the writings we shall study in the following pages are uncertain, our order of studying them cannot claim to follow a precise chronological sequence. However, adoption of an atemporal approach—be it canonical, thematic, or typological—cuts the investigation off from a dimension of politics in the Bible that is essential, its grounding in the concreteness of human existence and the chain of events that shape historical communities. What we shall try to trace, therefore, is the general trajectory of a young church responding to changing circumstances and adopting diverse theo-political strategies deemed appropriate for a people acknowledging the ultimate authority of one universal sovereign and seeking to translate that allegiance into life in a world governed by worldly powers ranging from tolerant and benign to hostile and pernicious.

In tracing that trajectory, we shall not be exhaustive in our approach. For example, after discussing 1 and 2 John, little will be sacrificed if we pass over the beautiful but largely repetitious contents of 3 John. Moreover, since trajectory is a more flexible category than chronology, we shall exercise a certain degree of freedom in the order in which we discuss the various writings. Since several post-Pauline writings not only bear the apostle's signature, but also elaborate on central Pauline themes, we shall begin our discussion in this chapter with Colossians, Ephesians, 1 and 2 Timothy, and Titus. Then we shall examine books that lie outside of the Pauline tradition but belong roughly to the same time frame, namely, 1 and 2 Peter, Hebrews, James, and 1 and 2 John. In the chapter that follows, we shall analyze the book of Revelation, followed in chapter 30 with a description of the political positions coming to expression in the final redaction of Mark, Matthew, Luke–Acts, and John.

THE POLITICS OF COLOSSIANS AND EPHESIANS

Most critical scholars attribute Colossians to a disciple of Paul who writes in defense of the apostle's version of the gospel (Col. 1:23) against two imminent threats. First, there is the temptation to despair in the face of persecution: "may you be prepared to endure everything with patience" (Col. 1:11, 24). Secondly, he mounts a bitter attack against "philosophy and empty deceit, according to human tradition, according to the elemental spirits of the universe, and not according to Christ" (Col. 2:8). Making inroads into the church at Colossae was apparently a syncretistic cult that mixed elements common to the mystery religions popular at the time with ascetic practices promoting rigorous moral demands without theological grounding in God's grace revealed in Christ's life, death, and resurrection. He pronounces judgment against what he regards a hollow piety in no uncertain terms: "These have indeed an appearance of wisdom in promoting self-imposed piety, humility, and severe treatment of the body, but they are of no value in checking self-indulgence" (Col. 2:23). We see here the familiar pattern that plagued ascetic movements in medieval times as well, namely, the swing from severe denial of the flesh to libertine indulgence.

When the author turns to the inferences that he draws from faith in Christ for living in this world, we find the conventional ethics of a generation of believers striving to conduct their lives in a manner above reproach in the eyes of their pagan neighbors. The genre adopted is one common among the moral philosophers of the time, namely, household rules (Ger. *Haustafeln*). Against the background of a list of the cardinal vices (Col. 3:5–9), a summary of the virtues with which Christians are to be clothed is given: "As God's chosen ones, holy and beloved, clothe yourselves with compassion, kindness, humility, meekness, and patience. Bear with one another and, if anyone has a complaint against another, forgive each other; just as the Lord has forgiven you, so you also must forgive. Above all, clothe yourselves with love, which binds everything together in perfect harmony" (Col. 3:12–14).

The author then proceeds to elaborate on two specific instances of godly behavior, relations between wives, husbands, and their children, and the conduct required of slaves and masters. While both conform to the conventions of Hellenistic-Roman culture, they receive a specific christological motivation: "Wives, be subject to your husbands, as is fitting in the Lord. . . . Slaves, obey your earthly masters in everything . . . fearing the Lord . . . as done for the Lord and not for your masters, since you know that from the Lord you will receive the inheritance as your reward; you serve the Lord Christ" (Col. 3:18, 22–23). To be sure, husbands are to love their wives and refrain from harsh treatment (Col. 3:19) and masters are to treat their slaves "justly and fairly." Yet, in spite of inclusion of the apostle Paul's formula of "neither Greek/Jew, slave/free" (Col. 3:11), the sensitivity with which Paul addressed the relationship between Philemon and his slave Onesimus ("no longer as a slave but more than a slave, a beloved brother" [Phlm. 16]) has yielded to an uncritical endorsement of the master/slave protocol that was conventional in Greco-Roman society.

Belonging to the same stage of the church's development as Colossians is the Letter to the Ephesians. Its literary style resembles the epideictic genre common in the Hellenistic world, though the christological adaptation is once again emphatic: not an earthly ruler or institution receives the praise, not even a local deity or saint, but rather the triumphant Christ, whom God has placed "far above all rule and authority and power and dominion, and above every name that is named, not only in this age but also in the age to come" (Eph. 1:21).

The writer then proceeds to summon his audience back to the basic truths of Paul's teaching, back to affirming that they are saved by God's grace through faith in Christ and constitute together with their Jewish brethren "a holy temple in the Lord," built upon "the foundation of the apostles and prophets" (Eph. 2:21, 20).

Having clarified the foundation of their spiritual identity, he goes on to two matters that reflect the life of a church accommodating itself to a world not about to end soon, namely, the organization of the church into various functions and offices (Eph. 4:11–16), and the promulgation of rules for everyday life conducted in a manner honorable and exemplary in the eyes of nonbelieving neighbors. Both betray roots in Pauline teaching. The latter (Eph. 4:25–6:9)—comprised of vices and their corresponding virtues, and again taking the form of the conventional household code—bear close resemblance to the rules set down for wives and husbands, slaves and masters in Colossians. Civility and demonstration of public respectability has become a distinguishing characteristic of the post-Pauline church in Asia Minor.

1 AND 2 TIMOTHY AND TITUS

The writer of 1 and 2 Timothy eloquently applies the Pauline version of the gospel to a community no longer expecting the imminent return of its Lord and struggling with the growing influence of a gnosticizing inversion of the gospel (1 Tim. 1:4; 4:1–5; 2 Tim. 2:18). Arising from that situation were two practical issues: the need to develop more permanent institutional structures and the challenge to define a manner of citizenship suitable for a minority religious community located within a vast and powerful pagan empire and often suffering persecution on account of their faith (2 Tim. 3:12).

Though likely writing two or three decades after the martyrdom of Paul, the writer has managed in certain passages to capture the message and tenor of the apostle with such effectiveness that some scholars believe they can identify fragments that were written by Paul and integrated into the text (e.g., Titus 3:4–7). In this way the spirit of Paul continued to be present among the believers in Ephesus to whom Timothy was being sent to "instruct certain people not to teach any different doctrine, and not to occupy themselves with myths and endless genealogies that promote speculations rather than the divine training that is known by faith" (1 Tim. 1:3–4; cf. 1 Tim. 4:11–16).

At stake in the defense of "sound teaching" (1 Tim. 1:10; 2 Tim. 1:13; Titus 2:1) was not an abstract theological formulation, but rather an integrated understanding of the relation of genuine faith to the kind of life that reflects the love of God in Christ: "the aim of such instruction is love that comes from a pure heart, a good conscience, and sincere faith" (1 Tim. 1:5). With this précis, the writer secures a sound theological framework for the lives of those seeking to live in imitation of their Lord as sojourners in an often-hostile world.

It is understandable that the practical challenges facing congregations as they settled down for the long haul would lead to the cultivation of a detailed pedagogy of the Christian life. Though the apostle Paul had not hesitated to admonish and instruct members of the fledgling churches he had founded, the post-Pauline church became more deliberate in enumerating the civic virtues such as purity, righteousness, godliness, faith, love, endurance, gentleness, temperance, seriousness, prudence, self-control, chastity, and kindness (1 Tim. 4:12; 6:11; Titus 2:2) that would establish its members as respected members of society and in contrasting them with the vices of the godless (1 Tim. 1:8–11; 6:3–10; 2 Tim. 3:2–5), even identifying by name certain notorious reprobates (1 Tim. 1:20; 2 Tim. 2:17). Though there is no indication that the congregants being addressed were experiencing the vicious persecutions that were soon to break out in the latter years of Domitian's reign,[1] they clearly were a minority that felt vulnerable to victimization and exercised extreme caution so as to be found above reproach: "Show yourself in all respects a model of good works, and in your teaching show integrity, gravity, and sound speech that cannot be censured; then any opponent will be put to shame, having nothing evil to say of us" (Titus 2:7–8).

The Pastoral Epistles are thus well named. They are the product of loving pastoral concern. They present in vivid detail the dilemma facing a confessional community seeking to work out a modus vivendi with a culture whose worldview, on the deepest level, differs radically from its own and whose religious beliefs and practices fall under the category of blasphemy. But the precariousness of their existential dilemma exacts a stinging toll: as in the case of Ephesians and Colossians, so too in 1 and 2 Timothy, we find the pursuit of public acceptance leading to a blunting of the radically egalitarian ethic manifested in Jesus' teaching and in Paul's proclamation of a love ethic that transcended distinctions of race, class, and gender. For example, while the instructions given to men revolve around self-control, good works, integrity, gravity and sound speech (Titus 2:6–8), the behavior expected of women extends to the clothing they are allowed to wear, the hairstyle that is permissible, and the mandate of "silence with full submission" (1 Tim. 2:9–11). What is more, the authoritative voice of Paul is invoked to decree: "I permit no woman to teach or to have authority over a man; she is to keep silent. For Adam was formed first, then Eve; and Adam was not deceived, but the woman was deceived and became a transgressor. Yet

---

1. The imperial policy of persecution of Christians qua Christians that was instituted by Domitian around 90 CE likely was the historical context within which the book of Revelation was written. The slightly earlier Pastoral Epistles, on the other hand, reflect a community living in anxious anticipation of the possibility of an officially instigated assault on their congregations and cautiously ordering their public life in the hopes of avoiding the wrath of the arrogant imposter god, the Roman emperor.

she will be saved through childbearing, provided they continue in faith and love and holiness, with modesty" (1 Tim. 2:12–15).

Particularly strict guidelines were imposed as well upon widows, with "real widows," namely, those sixty and older, enjoying privileges denied "younger widows," whose "sensual desires alienate them from Christ" and who "learn to be idle, gadding about from house to house [as] gossips and busybodies." The rule applying to younger widows, which again reflects concern for public image, is this: "marry, bear children, and manage their households, so as to give the adversary no occasion to revile us" (1 Tim. 5:9–16).

As for "all who are under the yoke of slavery," they are to "regard their masters as worthy of all honor." The motive clause enforcing this rule is particularly shocking, inasmuch as it equates the withholding of slavish reverence for the master with blasphemy against God (1 Tim. 6:1)! In a codicil striking one as a direct refutation of the apostle Paul's advocacy for the slave Onesimus in his letter to Philemon, the author decrees that the master-slave relationship must not be compromised in the case of "believing masters, . . . rather, they must serve them all the more" (1 Tim. 6:2).

While playing an important role, ethical instruction in the form of circulating letters and the admonitions of itinerant teachers proved insufficient in quelling heresy and maintaining high ethical standards within congregations scattered over increasingly vast and ethnographically diverse regions. The result was what Max Weber described as the "routinization of charisma," that is, the transformation of a church shaped by an intimate spiritual experience of the risen Lord into one deriving its cohesion from creedal statements and the formation of institutional structures. Elaborating on the rudimentary stage of church leadership found in Paul's letters, 1 Timothy sketches job descriptions for the offices of bishop (1 Tim. 3:1–7) and deacon (1 Tim. 3:8–13). Regarding the bishop, we find a list of virtues profiling the quintessential Christian, "temperate, sensible, respectable, hospitable, an apt teacher, not a drunkard, not violent but gentle, not quarrelsome, and not a lover of money" (1 Tim. 3:2–3; cf. Titus 1:7–9). Sensitivity to public image is manifest: "he must be well thought of by outsiders, so that he may not fall into disgrace" (1 Tim. 3:7). Here, in agreement with the apostle Paul's insistence that civic responsibility began with inner-community harmony, the distinction between personal life and public image dissolves: "for if someone does not know how to manage his own household, how can he take care of God's church?" (1 Tim. 3:5). As with bishops, so with deacons: "if they prove themselves blameless, let them serve as deacons" (1 Tim. 3:10). To assure that only impeccable appointments were made, thoroughness in the vetting process was stipulated: "Do not ordain anyone hastily" (1 Tim. 5:22). A verse in the Letter to Titus clarifies the purpose underlying sound appointments within an evolving church hierarchy: "so that you should put in order what remained to be done" (Titus 1:5). Fittingly included in the maintenance of order was a system of disciplining the incompliant and protecting the innocent from false accusations (1 Tim. 5:19–21).

Finally, we turn to the question of policy regarding the way Christians are to relate to governing authorities in these three Pastoral Epistles. Here we find that, in continuity with the accommodationist strategy outlined by the apostle Paul in Romans 13 and practiced until 70 CE by the Jewish community in the form of the temple prayer for the emperor, the author of 1 Timothy prescribes a manner of deferring to imperial powers in a situation that is delicate and fraught with danger for religious minorities: "First of all, then, I urge that supplications, prayers, intercessions, and thanksgivings be made for everyone, for kings and all who are in high positions, so that they may lead a quiet and peaceable life in all godliness and dignity" (1 Tim. 2:1–2). The strategy of deference and respect in relation to a pagan ruling power was a time-tested model within Judaism.[2]

Tragically, in the case of Christians living in the final decades of the first century CE, the political model of accommodation led not to its intended goal of a "quiet and peaceable life in all godliness and dignity," but to a period of horrific persecution, sanctioned by official imperial policy. One of the results would be the reappearance of another of the theo-political models that had emerged over the centuries of biblical history, the apocalyptical model, which in the New Testament finds its parade expression in the book of Revelation. It is important to note, however, that in this case, as in earlier attempts to appease foreign powers, accommodation stopped short of compromise of the central theocratic principle of biblical faith, namely, the sole lordship of the one true God.

That principle is reaffirmed in its Christian version in the verse immediately following the admonition to pray for all who are in high positions: "For there is one God; there is also one mediator between God and humankind, Christ Jesus, himself human, who gave himself a ransom for all" (1 Tim. 2:5). Rather than being in conflict with the political strategy of accommodation, this confession points to a vital link between faith and politics. While the king of the universe requires the intercessory prayers of no mortal, human rulers depend on the spiritual nurturance of their subjects. So long as it does not entail compromising their unequivocal allegiance to the one God, Christians, as exemplary citizens, are encouraged to pray for those who exercise authority over their lives and the lives of all citizens on this earth. In supporting the mediation of God's normative rule within the provisional structures of human government, they benefited from the role model of God's own choosing, his beloved, faithful Son.

1 AND 2 PETER

From the opening verse of the First Letter of Peter we learn that the author is writing to fellow Christians in Asia Minor. The salutation with which the letter concludes informs us that he is writing from "Babylon," that is, Rome.

---

2. Compare the Jewish community's policy of accommodation to the Persian Empire at the time of Ezra and Nehemiah as described in chapter 20.

The situation is similar to the one reflected by 1 and 2 Timothy, namely, those who bear the name of Christ are being subjected to abuse and persecution, which, they are reminded, is an inevitable part of those who are "aliens and exiles" in this world (1 Pet. 2:11). Moreover, precisely in their suffering they experience their solidarity with their Lord and fulfill their calling of bearing witness to unbelievers: "Keep your conscience clear, so that, when you are maligned, those who abuse you for your good conduct in Christ may be put to shame" (1 Pet. 3:16). The instruction in that same verse that they are to bear testimony to their faith "with gentleness and reverence" reflects a delicate situation in which anything other than exemplary conduct can become the pretense for persecution.

An admonition close to the end of 1 Peter incorporates language that calls to mind the imagery of apocalyptic writings and may indicate that the author senses that his generation stands on the brink of a period of end-time tribulation. It is possible that Diocletian had begun his violent campaign against Christians: "Discipline yourselves, keep alert. Like a roaring lion your adversary the devil prowls around, looking for someone to devour. Resist him, steadfast in your faith, for you know that your brothers and sisters in all the world are undergoing the same kinds of suffering" (1 Pet. 5:8–9).

Though the writer does not identify the adversary, the fact that five verses later he designates Rome as Babylon suggests that his view of the Roman Empire and its self-designated divine rulers is taking on the bleak tones of later apocalyptic works like the book of Revelation.

The volatility and precariousness of the situation within which the Christians addressed by this author are living offers a plausible explanation for the cautious, conventional nature of his lessons on civility: "Conduct yourselves honorably among the Gentiles, so that, though they malign you as evildoers, they may see your honorable deeds and glorify God when he comes to judge" (1 Pet. 2:12). "Honorable conduct" in the case of slaves entailed submission to their masters out of the knowledge that they enjoyed God's approval, not when enduring punishment for wrongdoing, but for suffering patiently when beaten for no wrongdoing at all. The warrant given for this code of conduct is the example of the innocent suffering of Christ (1 Pet. 2:18–25)! In the eyes of twenty-first-century Christians, the fact that the author's detailed description of the gospel of the cross functions in defense of slavery is an occasion for deep sadness and community-wide self-examination.

The conventional code of conduct applied to women in 1 Peter 3 does not require comment, being essentially the same as we found in the letters to Timothy. The same applies to the enumeration of civic virtues and the vices with which they are contrasted. We also note in passing that the author addresses the importance of proper structures and offices within a community seeking to establish itself within a volatile world (1 Pet. 5:1–5).

Finally, we turn our attention to the deportment required of Christians in relation to the governing authorities. Here we find reapplication of the strategy of accommodation articulated in 1 Timothy and Romans 13:[3] "For the Lord's sake accept the authority of every human institution, whether of the emperor as supreme, or of governors, as sent by him to punish those who do wrong and to praise those who do right. . . . Honor everyone. Love the family of believers. Fear God. Honor the emperor" (1 Pet. 2:13–17).

Embedded in this admonition for exemplary citizenship are two elaborations. The first identifies the motivation underlying this policy of proper civic deference: "For it is God's will that by doing right you should silence the ignorance of the foolish" (1 Pet. 2:15). The second adds an explanatory qualification to a principle central to Pauline theology, namely, Christian liberty: "As servants of God, live as free people, yet do not use your freedom as a pretext for evil" (1 Pet. 2:16).

First and Second Peter are books that reflect the strains experienced by members of a community living as a religious minority within a threatening world. As that community attended to the contradictions of living as aliens and exiles awaiting the end of this world and the inauguration of a heavenly order, while striving to develop a code of conduct befitting citizens of a powerful world empire, and as it sought to reconcile the radical gospel message of freedom and equality with the conventions of a corrupt autocratic regime, it handed on to future generations less an ideal political model than an example of endurance and perseverance. One need only read the words of 2 Peter 3:8–13 to admire the profound faith of this struggling ancestral community. The question it poses remains as relevant today as in its own time: "Since all these things are to be dissolved in this way, what sort of persons ought you to be in leading lives of holiness and godliness?" (2 Pet. 3:11).

HEBREWS

Like 1 and 2 Timothy, Titus, and 1 and 2 Peter, Hebrews belongs to the corpus of writings arising from the period following the death of the apostle Paul but predating the outbreak of persecutions late in the reign of Domitian (81–96 CE). The preponderance of quotations from and allusions to Hebrew Scripture has led scholars to surmise that both author and audience are Hellenistic Jewish Christians who are struggling to live peaceably with pagan neighbors who have shown little restraint in abusing those who follow the way of Jesus Christ (Heb. 10:32–36; 13:3). Neither capitulation nor insurrection is commended, but rather an understanding of suffering as "the discipline of the Lord, . . . for the Lord disciplines those whom he loves, and chastises every child whom he accepts" (12:5–6). Within the host of witnesses upon whose examples they can draw, they are to look with praise and thanks especially to the "pioneer and perfecter" of their

---

3. It is worthy of note that the rule governing submission of slaves to their masters in 1 Pet. 2:18–21 follows directly on instructions regulating deference to ruling authorities and that the verb used is *hypotassein* (usually translated as "be subject to"), the same verb used by Paul in Rom. 13:1 and by the pastoral author in Titus 3:1.

faith. It is out of this focus on the suffering Jesus that the author develops a "theology of the cross" that is poignantly relevant to a threatened religious minority and uniquely imprinted with a sacerdotal interpretation of the incarnation and atoning sacrifice of Christ: "Therefore he had to become like his brothers and sisters in every respect, so that he might be a merciful and faithful high priest in the service of God, to make a sacrifice of atonement for the sins of the people. Because he himself was tested by what he suffered, he is able to help those who are being tested" (2:17–18).

To what then might the life of these first-century Christians be compared? They are "strangers and foreigners on the earth, . . . [who] desire a better country, that is, a heavenly one" (11:13–16). Does that mean that they are to live in isolation from the dominant society, cultivating—as did the apocalyptic conventicle of Qumran—a "perfect hatred" for those falling outside of the bounds of their circle? One might expect such monastic withdrawal of a community living with a faith defined as "the assurance of things hoped for, the conviction of things not seen" (11:1) and conducting their day-to-day affairs in light of "the Day approaching" (10:25). World-disdaining isolation is not what the author of Hebrews urges, for what he draws from the examples of the long line of biblical heroes of faith culminating with the high priest Jesus is an ethic of patient, suffering love: "Pursue peace with everyone, and the holiness without which no one will see the Lord. See to it that no one fails to obtain the grace of God; that no root of bitterness springs up and causes trouble, and through it many become defiled" (12:14–15).

By following the example of Christ and the other martyrs, one prepares for life in the heavenly city by living a life of holiness and righteousness and compassion in this world: "Let mutual love continue. Do not neglect to show hospitality to strangers, for by doing that some have entertained angels without knowing it. Remember those who are in prison. . . . Let marriage be held in honor by all. . . . Keep your lives free from the love of money" (13:1–5). "Do not neglect to do good and to share what you have, for such sacrifices are pleasing to God" (13:16).

The book of Hebrews has less to say with regard to political strategies than Paul or the post-Pauline letters we have already considered. But there are hints at concern for proper institutional structure: "Remember your leaders, those who spoke the word of God to you; consider the outcome of their way of life, and imitate their faith" (13:7). "Obey your leaders and submit to them, for they are keeping watch over your souls and will give an account" (13:17). Heresy must be repudiated: "Do not be carried away by all kinds of strange teachings," with explicit reference being made to "regulations about food, which have not benefited those who observe them" (13:9). Right teaching is defined in Pauline terms: "my righteous one will live by faith" (10:38).

Regarding the author's strategy toward the Roman authorities, we are limited largely to inferences drawn from his survey of past heroes. We read that Moses was unafraid of the Pharaoh's anger and thereby delivered the "firstborn of Israel" from the "destroyer" (11:23–28), that the Maccabean martyrs endured faithfully unimaginable suffering (11:35–38), and that Jesus "endured the cross, disregarding its shame" (12:2). Past history would seem to instill little confidence in earthly rulers. Nevertheless, a strategy of retreat from the world does not follow. Again, the example leading to this seemingly incongruous conclusion is the mysterious, divinely impelled life of the high priest Jesus: "Therefore Jesus also suffered outside the city gate in order to sanctify the people by his own blood. Let us then go to him outside the camp and bear the abuse he endured" (13:12–13).

Suffering in the world for the sake of the world is a vocational imperative in the lives of those living by the example of their Lord. The day is coming when this world will yield to the world to come, and the orders maintained by earthly rulers will submit to the order instituted from the beginning by God and patiently awaiting the time of its fulfillment through the sacrificial offering of the high priest Jesus Christ. In anticipation of "the city of the living God, the heavenly Jerusalem," pioneers and aliens naming themselves after the one who willingly sacrificed himself for the redemption of humanity engage as agents of their high priest in that redemption drama.

JAMES

For most students of the Bible, the theme in the Letter of James that first comes to mind is this: "So faith by itself, if it has no works, is dead" (Jas. 2:17). There is no reason to doubt that this polemic is directed against Christians who were perverting the Pauline version of the gospel into an abuse of liberty expressing itself in discrimination against and even cruelty toward poor members of the community. That interpretation is valid as far as it goes. But it can lead to setting Paul's letters over against the Letter of James in a way that leads to a misleadingly harsh contradiction. More to be preferred is a historical account that situates the Letter of James within the same tense setting that gave rise to the Letters of Timothy, Peter, and Hebrews, a setting in which rigorous scrutiny is being given to the image Christians are projecting to the wider world by their conduct. The author looks around him and observes behavior that he believes contradicts the heart of the Christian faith:

> My brothers and sisters, do you with your acts of favoritism really believe in our glorious Lord Jesus Christ? For if a person with gold rings and in fine clothes comes into your assembly, and if a poor person in dirty clothes also comes in, and if you take notice of the one wearing the fine clothes and say, "Have a seat here, please," while to the one who is poor you say, "Stand there," or, "Sit at my feet," have you not made distinctions among yourselves and become judges with evil thoughts? (2:1–4)

It is true that some of the words directed at the rich are harsh: "the rich will disappear like a flower in the field" (1:10). "Come now, you rich people, weep and wail for the miseries that are coming to you" (5:1). But what might appear to be vindictive class outrage takes on a different meaning when one takes note that the rich who are being threatened with judgment are not merely opulent, but out of hardness of heart they have accumulated their riches through cruel exploitation of the poor: "The wages of the laborers who mowed your fields, which you kept back by fraud, cry out, and the cries of the harvesters have reached the ears of the Lord of hosts" (5:4).

The author of James stands in the tradition of Amos, Isaiah, Jeremiah, and Nehemiah, defending the rights of the humble poor against the arrogant rich. Within the context of the Roman Empire, he is renewing the theme found in Jesus' parable of the Rich Man and Lazarus and in Paul's attack on those who turn the *agape* meal into a private feast of the rich to the exclusion of the poor. Clarity with regard to the prophetic background of his message liberates the faith/works contrast in James from the realm of abstract theological controversy and restores its real-life setting: "If a brother or sister is naked and lacks daily food, and one of you says to them, 'Go in peace; keep warm and eat your fill,' and yet you do not supply their bodily needs, what is the good of that? So faith by itself, if it has no works, is dead" (2:15–17).

We have noted above that the second generation of the church was sensitive to its public image. The author of the Letter of James also is wary of the discrediting effects of "conflicts and disputes among you" (4:1). He was intent on cultivating a communal style that would not invite censure that in turn could lead to persecution: "the wisdom from above is first pure, then peaceable, gentle, willing to yield, full of mercy and good fruits, without a trace of partiality or hypocrisy" (3:17). To limit the development of its communal ethic to the desire to appear respectable in the wider world would be to overlook the roots of that ethic in the central confessions of the ancestral faith. That source is summarized in these noble words: "Religion that is pure and undefiled before God, the Father, is this: to care for orphans and widows in their distress, and to keep oneself unstained by the world" (1:27).

THE JOHANNINE EPISTLES

Reflected in 1, 2, and 3 John is a community that finds itself staring into the face of the beast: "Children, it is the last hour! As you have heard that antichrist is coming, so now many antichrists have come. From this we know that it is the last hour" (1 John 2:18). The evidence cited for this conclusion is the widespread phenomenon of false teaching in the form of denial of the full humanity of Christ (1 John 4:2–3; 2 John 7). Here we see an early stage of the teaching the church would come to denounce as heretical, namely, Docetism. We also witness the response adopted by the nascent church, namely, an appeal to the ancestral tradition: "Let what you heard from the beginning abide in you. If what you heard from the beginning abides in you, then you will abide in the Son and in the Father" (1 John 2:24).

A pattern found in the post-Pauline epistles that we have already discussed is repeated here. The struggle for faithfulness to the received tradition is waged not on an abstract level but in the form of a struggle for a communal way that is true to its core beliefs. Thus the emphatic theme of the Johannine tradition is this: "God is love" (1 John 4:16). The corollary drawn for everyday life is just as straightforward: "those who love God must love their brothers and sisters also" (1 John 4:21).

The application of this classic phenomenon of extrapolation of ethics from core beliefs is complicated, however, by the intervention of real life. In this case, that real life involves the increasing hostility of the world to the community of faith: "Do not love the world or the things in the world" (1 John 2:15), "the world hates you" (1 John 3:13). With these words it becomes clear that a community is moving closer to an apocalyptic consciousness of its situation. Light and darkness describe its relationship to its neighbors (1 John 1:5–7; 2:8–11). The division between God's children and the rest of the world takes on a dualistic tone: "We know that we are God's children, and that the whole world lies under the power of the evil one" (1 John 5:19).

In jeopardy is communal commitment to civility and participation in the broader culture. A sectarian response begins to emerge out of the perception of the hostility of non-Christian neighbors: "Do not receive into the house or welcome anyone who comes to you and does not bring this teaching; for to welcome is to participate in the evil deeds of such a person" (2 John 10–11).

The desire to be accepted as cocitizens in a world governed by the Romans was yielding to an ethic of wariness, withdrawal, and accepting no support from nonbelievers. Striving to be honorable and respected citizens in a pagan society was surrendering to the defensiveness of a community facing persecution. One senses the gathering of the storm clouds that would darken the tumultuous sky of the book of Revelation. Accommodation had ceased to be a viable strategy in a world demanding as a condition for participation worship of the dragon. Another political strategy was being forced upon a martyr community as the only viable option available to those refusing apostasy: the strategy of resistance shaped by a bleak apocalyptic outlook.

Chapter 29

The Book of Revelation

A Persecuted Community Seeks Shelter
in an Apocalyptic Vision

HISTORICAL BACKGROUND

In the previous chapter we witnessed fledgling communities struggling to gain acceptance and respect within a powerful imperial culture disposed to repress any minority religious community that challenged its political ideology. In the case of the status of Jews and Christians, the major stumbling block to toleration was the fundamental difference between their theocratic principle, according to which no earthly authority or regime could claim the right to absolute authority over its citizens, and the political ideology of the Romans, which affirmed the divinity of its emperor and derived support from a vast network of cults whose gods, goddesses, priests, and priestesses channeled the devotion of a scattered populace into the maintenance of strict public order. That the politics of accommodation practiced in the post-Pauline generation would ultimately break down under the overbearing hegemony of the Romans was foreshadowed by the occasional appearance of apocalyptic themes in letters otherwise characterized by the

587

cultivation of impeccable civic virtues intended as proof that Christians were outstanding, trustworthy contributors to harmony within the empire.[1]

The prelude to an age of repression and persecution came during the final years of Nero's reign (64–68 CE). Though the criminalization of Christian belief did not become official Roman policy until nearly two centuries later, the years of Domitian's reign (81–96 CE) were marked by an atmosphere of increased hostility against those professing belief in Christ. In the nineties this erupted into sporadic persecution and martyrdom.

HISTORICAL SETTING

The book of Revelation was likely written during the turbulent final years of Domitian's reign. It was addressed to seven churches in Anatolia, a region in which the regional governors displayed considerable zeal in defending their "Lord and God," the Roman emperor, and in professing their devotion to the matron goddess of the capital city, *Dea Roma*.

Ironically, the case against Christians revolved around accusations of atheism. In denying the divinity of the Roman emperor and in refusing to sacrifice to the deities to whom the numerous local cults were dedicated, Christians were exercising a form of treasonous unbelief that in the mind of the Romans threatened the harmony between humans and the gods, thereby placing in jeopardy the much touted *Pax Romana*. By raising the specter of social discord, they became denounced as enemies of the state, and all that was necessary for an outbreak of violence against them was an informer reporting to a regional governor who in turn was eager to display his loyalty to Rome by cleansing his territory of traitors.

Under the increased belligerence and mounting tension of the final years of the first century, the guise of patriotism displayed by those reserving worship for their one God could no longer be maintained in the manner of the previous generation, that is, through the cultivation of sterling personal character and public virtue. The theocratic principle affirming the sole sovereignty of one God, which to those addressed by the book of Revelation constituted the heart of their faith, became the basis for the twin charges of impiety and treason. Conflict was inevitable. The outlook for the Christian communities scattered across the empire grew dim. Pessimism regarding the prospect of accommodation achieving peaceful coexistence with pagan neighbors increased. John of Patmos, turning to God for answers, witnessed the opening up of heaven and the unfolding of a cosmic drama, centering on Jesus Christ, in which God would overcome the present evil order and establish his eternal reign of righteousness and peace. The announcement to messenger and audience was urgent: "Blessed

---

1. E.g., 1 Pet. 5:8–9; 1 John 2:18.

is the one who reads aloud the words of the prophecy, and blessed are those who hear and keep what is written in it; for the time is near" (Rev. 1:3).

LETTERS TO THE SEVEN CHURCHES

The letters to the seven churches in the first three chapters of Revelation indicate that many were wavering, due to the blandishments of false teachers and the likelihood of persecution that awaited those who remained faithful. As a warning to those backsliders, the judgment scenes that follow in subsequent chapters describe in lurid detail the torment that awaited apostates. But outright apostasy was not the only threat to the survival of the Christian churches in Anatolia. The letter to the church in Laodicea in Revelation 3:14–22 takes the form of reproof and a plea for repentance, directed at a church that had slipped into religious complacency and complicity with the mores prevailing in Roman society. The recurrent call to repent in the letters to the seven churches demonstrates clearly that one of the central aims of the book is the prophetic aim of calling a straying people back to their faith (Rev. 2:5, 16, 21, 22; 3:3, 19). It therefore would be a mistake to exaggerate the differences in function between prophetic and apocalyptic messages (cf. Rev. 19:10). In the book of Revelation, the prophetic call to repentance and the apocalyptic message of hope to those who suffer persecution for their faithfulness are complementary themes.

Lamentably, in the eyes of many, the benefits of the noncommittal position of being "lukewarm . . . neither cold nor hot," were irresistible: "I am rich, I have prospered, and I need nothing," they boasted (Rev. 3:17a). But in their boasting, they were proving that their values had become twisted. They had traded the "gold refined by fire" for earthly riches and their moral purity for shame. The resulting indictment is harsh: "You do not realize that you are wretched, pitiable, poor, blind, and naked" (Rev. 3:17b).

The pattern of moral laxity rebuked in the letter to the Laodiceans is an all-too-familiar one in the history of civilization. Whether occupying the position of high priest or village elder, wealthy merchant or tenant farmer, Roman Catholic pope or incarcerated Jew, complicity with the Seleucids, the Romans, or the Nazis was rewarded with momentary exemption from the cruel fate awaiting those who remained true to their ancestral faith and values.

In Revelation 18 a triad of taunts patterned after Ezekiel 26–28 enables us to peer beyond generalities and archetypal patterns of behavior to the specific nature of the vast economic monopoly imposed by the Romans. It consisted of three layers: (1) regional dynasts who provided both resources and markets for a cartel built on avarice and cruelty (Rev. 18:9–10); (2) global merchants trading both in commodities like gold, silver, jewels, and pearls and in processed goods like fine linen, purple, silk, and scarlet, as well as scented wood, articles of ivory, costly wood, bronze, iron and marble, in addition to cinnamon, spice, incense, myrrh, flour and wheat, cattle and sheep, horses and chariots, and slaves (Rev.

18:11–17); (3) shipping companies comprising a merchant marine capable of linking commodities and products to their processors and retail markets (Rev. 18:17–19). The enormity of wealth generated by this three-tiered economic cartel was sufficient to reward all who conformed to its rules in the form of luxury for the ruling class, vast profits for the merchants, lucrative lading accounts for the shippers, and steady wages for the working class. From the perspective of earthly standards, only fools would refuse to join the system by including the emperor in their divine pantheon.

The choice facing those addressed by the book of Revelation was stark: is your commitment to your Lord sufficiently deep to lead you to renounce all of the riches that accompany bending your knee before the emperor, or do you prefer the popular path of joining in the festivities and reaping the harvest of the normative culture and its civil religion? The benefits accompanying the latter option were immediate and tangible. The only benefit that was immediate and tangible for those in the path of faithfulness to God and the Lamb was sharing in the suffering of the Lamb and in the likelihood of death. To be sure, an audacious promissory note accompanied the description of persecution by this world's powers. The reign of terror was transitory. The economic empire would crumble. All the riches of the local dynasts, the global merchants, and the shippers would go up like smoke, and you, though persecuted and perhaps beheaded for your religious confession, would live forever in the glorious presence of the only true universal king. The catch was this: that promise was to be accepted on faith, in the face of the imperious counterclaim of the blasphemous rival to God's reign, a regime purporting to underwrite a universal order of peace and prosperity that would endure forever.

THE RHETORIC OF MYTH

What form of human discourse was capable of making a credible argument for the validity of God's universal reign against the tangible display of Rome's military might and economic hegemony? The nature of the contrast between a spiritual realm not yet visible to eyes of flesh and a world empire dominating every facet of daily existence called for an extraordinary rhetoric, the rhetoric of myth that already had been incorporated into Jewish sacred tradition in the form of apocalyptic eschatology. It was a rhetoric suited for unmasking the delusory nature of pretentious worldly powers and revealing the eternal validity of the order that, though not yet visible, had set the course of human destiny from the beginning of time. Other forms of discourse were inadequate, for they by nature were designed to describe what was transient and foundered when attempting to describe the transcendent and eternal.

The linguistic challenge in question was not limited to antiquity. It has been experienced also in modern times both in practice and in theory. As already noted, Dietrich Bonhoeffer, in struggling to unmask the true nature of Hitler and the Nazi regime, reached beyond normal political discourse when he invoked the category of antichrist. The phenomenon he and his fellow believers were experiencing reached more deeply into the abyss than conventional war reporting could convey. Larger than one human agent, more pernicious by far than any military campaign, was the evil he sought to depict. Not unlike those experiencing the wrath of Antiochus IV Epiphanes during the Maccabean period, Bonhoeffer recognized an assault of Satan and his sons of darkness against Christ and his faithful martyrs.

Thanks to the revival of apocalyptic imagery in contemporary literature and film, many contemporary readers have regained the ability to appreciate the bizarre language of the book of Revelation. In addition to sensitivity to mythic motifs and images, however, interpretation requires knowledge of the historical setting, which we have sketched above. Especially in the case of enigmatic books like Daniel and Revelation, an approach combining thorough linguistic understanding with appreciation of setting is essential, for the history of interpretation is rife with examples of capricious explanations of apocalyptic beasts and omens and heavenly warriors that can abet persecution of still more innocent victims and exacerbate tensions among world powers.

THE DRAMATIC STRUCTURE OF THE BOOK

The curtain rises on the central drama of the book of Revelation with an announcement in 12:7: "And war broke out in heaven." The catalyst for conflict was the birth of a child to a woman, who immediately came under attack by "a great red dragon, with seven heads and ten horns, and seven diadems on his heads." The reason for the aggressive action taken by the dragon would have been clear to ancient readers familiar with a similar monstrous assault on heaven in Daniel 7. The dragon represents a pagan emperor who threatens to obliterate the religion of God's people and force them into acknowledgment of his own purported divinity and participation in his idolatrous cult. In the case of the book of Daniel, the emperor can be identified as Antiochus IV Epiphanes. In the case of the book of Revelation, we suggested above that the most likely historical background of the book was the latter years of Domitian's reign, but we shall also see that the imagery was interpreted so as to include the entire succession of emperors from Nero through all three members of the Flavian dynasty.

The reason why rulers and military figures from different periods and empires could be identified with the same cast of nether-worldly monsters stems from the worldview of myth, according to which happenings on earth were reflections of conflicts occurring within a superterrestrial realm. The assumption that God's faithful followers repeatedly would be assaulted by such miscreants reflects the political pessimism of apocalyptic communities. World governments were viewed as agencies adhering to an order hostile to God. The kingdoms of this world and the kingdom of heaven were incompatible. It is no accident that the catalyst for the violent attack of the red dragon in Revelation 12 was the birth of a child to a "woman clothed with the sun, with the moon under her feet," on whose head was "a crown of twelve stars" (Rev. 12:1). Even in his infancy, the child was recognizable to the dragon as a grave threat to his dominion. Though formulated by the Gospel writer in historical prose rather than in the mythic drama of the book of Revelation, the vicious and ultimately ill-fated assault by King Herod against the baby sought out by the star-guided wise men from the east described in the second chapter of Matthew conveys essentially the same message: the ruler chosen by God to be king was destined to become locked in a deadly conflict with the self-designated rulers of this world, a conflict in which only one of them could prevail.[2]

The stylistic differences between the Gospel of Matthew and the book of Revelation are also significant. The narrative that follows the Herod episode in Matthew unfolds in a sequential manner that is easily followed by the reader. God, by warning Jesus' parents, provides an escape from the evil king. The child grows to manhood, spends his short career teaching the way of God's kingdom and demonstrating its saving nature through his acts of healing the sick and feeding the hungry. In a final attack on their dreaded rival, the lords of this world unite in plotting his death. But their victory is pyrrhic, for God raises him from the dead and validates the legitimacy of his reign.

In relation to the Gospel of Matthew the book of Revelation blends thematic similarity with a stark contrast in staging and rhetoric. The theme in both is one of conflict, with the faithful experiencing initial defeat followed by final vindication. But in the book of Revelation the stage has been moved from earth to heaven, Pilate's regional court having been supplanted by the supreme court of the Almighty. The iron grip of imperial Rome was loosening. The ambiguity of human experience was yielding to the more certain verities of the heavenly realm. Historical vignettes characterized by soft pastels were yielding to the severe black-and-white contrast of William Blake's *Last Judgment*. In addition, a shift in structure has occurred, which going unrecognized leads inevitably to confusion: The straightforward order of the Gospels yields to a mythopoeic rhetoric flouting linear development in favor of repetition, flashbacks, and the melding and reconfiguring of grotesque images.

These rhetorical traits are evident in the scenes that follow the birth of the child who was "to rule all the nations" (Rev. 12:5). As noted, this nativity led to the outbreak of a celestial war. Swiftly, however, Michael and his angels defeated and cast down from heaven the dragon, "that ancient serpent, who is called the Devil and Satan, the deceiver of the whole world" (Rev. 12:9). It might appear as though the drama were moving swiftly to its denouement with the pronouncement from heaven, "Now have come the salvation and the power and the kingdom of our God and the authority of his Messiah" (Rev. 12:10). But the conflict was far from ended. Though the child had been taken up into the security of the throne room of God (Rev. 12:5), the dragon, in spite of being cast down from his heavenly

2. Matt. 2:1–18.

habitation, renewed his pursuit of the woman and "the rest of her children, those who keep the commandments of God and hold the testimony of Jesus" (Rev. 12:17). The message thereby conveyed to the persecuted minority was of the "good news/bad news" variety: The fate of the dragon had been sealed, for he had been dethroned. To be sure, the community of the faithful would continue to suffer for their faith, but they could be comforted that the dragon's continued violence against them amounted to the thrashings of one in the throes of death.

The next chapter is sobering. Satan may have been cast down, but his ability to unleash the powers of darkness against the children of light remained daunting. Daniel 7 supplies the imagery for the first of two beasts authorized by the dragon to carry on his evil work (Rev. 13:1–10). The result was the spread of worship of both dragon and beast across the nations of the earth, with the only exception being those whose names were entered into "the book of life of the Lamb that was slaughtered" (Rev. 13:8). The message underlying this dreadful picture of apostasy, war, and violence against the elect is stated explicitly at the end of the passage describing the beast from the sea: "Here is a call for the endurance and faith of the saints."

Mimicking the depiction of Leviathan and Behemoth in the contemporaneous apocryphal book of *4 Ezra*, the author of Revelation pairs the beast of the sea with a beast rising out of the earth, a miscreant equally committed to spreading apostasy in the form of image worship enforced by the threat of death to the noncompliant. Its role in reinforcing the economic stranglehold of the evil empire on the earth's inhabitants is also noted: Only those bearing its number 666 will be permitted "to buy or sell." The discrimination suffered by those reserving their worship for the one true God is not only religious in nature, but economic and social as well.

Who is this beast? "Anyone with understanding" will be able to identify him, the reader is informed, the meaning of which likely was transparent to the original audience. Commentators of subsequent generations, however, lacking direct knowledge of the historical background of the book, have allowed imagination to fill in where facts were lacking, resulting in a repertoire of beast candidates ranging from various popes to Adolf Hitler and Mikhail Gorbachev. Later in our discussion of Revelation 17 we shall return to the riddle of beast identification.

The "call for the endurance of the saints" is renewed in succeeding chapters by alternating depictions of the dreadful punishments awaiting the followers of the beast with celestial visions of the worship of God and the Lamb. Included are hymnic reaffirmations of the central ancestral confession of the faithful, their belief in the one true God. The "song of Moses" in 15:3–4 reaffirms the theocratic principle that we have traced throughout the Bible as the foundational theme undergirding the diverse political models arising in response to changing historical circumstances:

> Great and amazing are your deeds,
>   Lord God the Almighty!

> Just and true are your ways,
>   King of the nations!
> Lord, who will not fear
>   and glorify your name?
> For you alone are holy.
>   All nations will come
>   and worship before you,
> for your judgments have been revealed.

Sublimely, majestically the chord is sounded that holds together in symphonic richness the diverse strategies for relating the ancestral faith to changing political regimes and socioeconomic conditions. What defines the identity of the faithful and what upholds them through hardship and calamity is faith in the one holy God who is the ruler and judge of all nations.[3] In the case of persecuted communities staring into the maw of the dragon and his deputies, the insatiable beasts of sea and land, that ancestral confession was put to its most severe test. It stands boldly in Scripture as a testimony to the perseverance of faith even in the most calamitous circumstances humans can experience or even imagine.

Sadly, rather than being reserved for those in later generations facing similar diabolical circumstances, whether in their private lives or in public, the rich and often enigmatic apocalyptic writings of the Bible repeatedly have fallen victim to one or another misappropriation. Either the message is distorted into an instrument of inhumane vitriol by false prophets hijacking religion to undergird their death wish for all peoples refusing to subscribe to their illusions of grandeur; or those enjoying the comforts of economic prosperity and national security dismiss or denounce the imagery of the apocalyptic biblical writings as crude, violent, and grotesque. Unfortunately, these two misguided responses to the apocalyptic texts of the Bible reinforce each other: Jim Jones and David Koresh absorb the ridicule of mainstream society into their wounded souls and massage it into their growing paranoia, while those choosing to identify biblical religion in general with the fanaticism of such fringe figures draw freely on Daniel and the book of Revelation in support of their strident crusades.

In a modern cultural environment mimicking Laodicea, where the dark evils of hunger and impoverishment of both human and natural resources are airbrushed, in which inequalities in educational and vocational opportunities are dismissed as inevitable results of a complex global economy, and in which corruption and scandal in high places evoke little more than a salacious wink, an urgent challenge is thrust upon conscientious interpreters of the Bible to explain the significance of writings in which victims of the exploitation of blatant malefactors dare to describe the true character and magnitude of the abuse of power and insensitivity of humans to fellow humans.

Returning to the drama of the book of Revelation, we find chapter 16 circling back to the theme of the judgment awaiting those who worship the beast.

---

3. Hymns in praise of the Lord God run as a golden thread through the book of Revelation: 4:11; 5:11–14; 7:12; 14:7; 15:3–4; 19:1–8.

In imagery that again strikes many modern readers as repulsively violent, it describes "seven bowls of the wrath of God," bowls containing punishments reminiscent of the plagues Moses released at God's command against the Egyptian pharaoh. True to the pattern of the other septets in the book of Revelation, the seventh bowl is climactic. Indeed, it brings to a climax the entire chain of seals, trumpets, portents, and bowls that John of Patmos had witnessed. Resembling a nuclear warhead in devastating power, it is aimed at Babylon, the archetype of evil power, incarnated in the author's time by Rome, which like Babylon before had committed the heinous crime of destroying the Holy City of Jerusalem. Demonic spirits assemble "the kings of the whole world" to Harmagedon, where they let loose the fury of "the great day of God Almighty" (Rev. 16:14). With an image drawn from Jeremiah 25, God serves this Babylon "the wine-cup of the fury of his wrath" (Rev. 16:19). This ghastly seventh bowl and the havoc that it wreaks provide the segue leading to chapters 17 and 18.

Chapter 17 portrays "the great whore," *Dea Roma*, "sitting on a scarlet beast" filled with "blasphemous names" and sporting "seven heads and ten horns." This is the beast of the sea earlier encountered in chapter 13. The source of the seer's vitriol toward this "mother of whores" is then revealed: "the woman was drunk with the blood of the saints and the blood of the witnesses to Jesus" (Rev. 17:6).

The details of this lurid scene reflect images found on Roman coins of the time: The seven heads of the goddess's monstrous steed represent simultaneously the seven hills of Rome and "seven kings, of whom five have fallen, one is living, and the other has not yet come" (Rev. 17:9–10). Though the speculations of scholars, ancient and modern, have not resolved the riddle of the identity of these kings, the last mentioned likely refers to Nero, who, in keeping with the popular legend of the time, is here cryptically anticipated as one day returning to reconquer Rome and reestablish his reign, thereby also becoming the eighth king. The ten horns, in turn, are described as ten other (i.e., lesser, regional) kings.

More important than perpetuating the dubitable efforts to identify the Roman kings and regional rulers, however, is discerning the significance of the event in preparation for which they unite, namely, an attack coordinated by the beast (Nero redivivus?) against the whore Rome. The mighty empire, variously feared and revered by its subjects far and wide as the self-proclaimed instrument of universal peace and affluence, was showing signs of fragmentation. The countdown to the end had begun with an attack on the eternal city that was the penultimate event preparing for the culminating end-time battle.

In chapter 18 heavenly messengers intone verses mocking the once-defiant city. In our earlier discussion of the Roman monopoly on the commerce of the greater Mediterranean region, we discussed the taunts, summons to flight, and dirges directed against Rome found in Revelation 18.[4] They reapply ancient prophetic

---

4. Cf. Isa. 21:9; Jer. 51:6–10; and Ezek. 26–28. Refer above to pp. 589–90 for a description of the economic organization of the Roman Empire reflected in the taunts of Rev. 18.

genres to vilify and mock the archetypal enemy of God's people. In the overall structure of the book, they provide a momentary reprieve before the final assize.

We move now to discuss the climactic events toward which the drama of the entire book of Revelation—often in sweeping circular or swinging pendular motions—has been moving. A resounding hallelujah intoned by a heavenly chorus announces the dawn of a new era (Rev. 19:1). Thrice more the hallelujah sounds forth, and we witness the multitudes of the righteous joining in their most sublime acts, worship of the Almighty and preparation for the marriage of the Lamb and his bride. On the advent of the holy war that will end all wars, worship is the appropriate preparation, for on the field of battle holy angels and mortals sanctified by the blood of the Lamb will stand cheek by jowl against the beast and his minions:

> Hallelujah!
> For the Lord our God
>   the Almighty reigns.
> Let us rejoice and exult
>   and give him the glory,
> for the marriage of the Lamb has come
>   and his bride has made herself ready.
>   (Rev. 19:6–7)

The heavenly battle scene unfolds with a flurry of images. A warrior mounted on a white horse identified as "The Word of God" leads the armies of heaven in the attack against the nations allied with the beast. In a manner recalling Ezekiel 39, an angel invites "the birds that fly in midheaven" to a banquet consisting of the flesh of the fallen kings, their horses, and their warriors. Like Tiamat rising up against Marduk in Babylonian myth, the beast itself attacks the messianic warrior, is captured, and is cast into a lake of fire, along with the prophet who was instrumental in promoting worship of the beast and its image. Leaderless, the remaining wicked warriors fall by the sword of the Holy One to become carrion for the swooping birds.

Though at this point the reader may well be ready for the stillness of eternal peace, divine war breaks out anew in chapter 20, for the father of all wickedness, the dragon (aka the devil and Satan) proves to be a dogged foe. He is thrown by an angel into "the bottomless pit," where he will remain bound for a thousand years, thereby beginning the millennium reign of Christ and the martyrs raised in the first resurrection. After that thousand-year interim, Satan will gather his forces in one last assault against the saints and Jerusalem (a battle alluding to both Zech. 14 and the Gog of Magog prophecy in Ezek. 38–39), only to be defeated by fire from heaven and cast into the eternal torment of the fiery lake, already inhabited by the beast and the false prophet. Chapter 20 concludes with a final court scene in which the heavenly judge consults the books in which are recorded the names of those destined for eternal torment and of those who, in a second resurrection, will join the saints of the first resurrection.[5]

5. Cf. Dan. 7:9–10.

The modern reader, having been taken on the long, tumultuous pilgrimage through chapters 1–20, is prepared to welcome the unspeakable joy elicited by the opening verses of chapter 21:

> Then I saw a new heaven and a new earth, for the first heaven and the first earth had passed away, and the sea was no more.[6] And I saw the holy city, the new Jerusalem, coming down out of heaven from God, prepared as a bride adorned for her husband. And I heard a loud voice from the throne saying,
>
> > "See, the home of God is among mortals.
> > He will dwell with them as their God,
> > they will be his peoples,
> > and God himself will be with them;
> > he will wipe every tear from their eyes,
> > Death will be no more;
> > mourning and crying and pain will be no more;
> > for the first things have passed away."
> > (Rev. 21:1–4)

This vision of the blessed era of God's reign, of creation restored to the peace and blessing intended by God from the beginning, draws on the traditional repertory of apocalyptic imagery found in canonical and apocryphal writings, while simultaneously reshaping them. Traditional are the contrast between the new heaven/earth and the heaven/earth that has passed away, the covenant formula of God and people, the banishment of tears, mourning and pain, and the vanquishing of death. The new element, so radical in nature as to lead some scholars to describe the book of Revelation as antiapocalyptic,[7] is the *location* of the new creation and the habitation prepared for the faithful who have been raised from the dead. Unlike, for example, the vision in chapter 12 of Daniel, where those raised to life will join the stars, or the judgment scene of *1 Enoch* 62, where the blessed will be lifted up to heaven to join the Lord of spirits and the Son of Man, here the Holy City, the new Jerusalem, comes *down* from heaven to be established *on earth*! "See, the home of God is among mortals" (Rev. 21:3). To be sure, its characteristics surpass in splendor the temples of Solomon or Herod, drawing on Edenic motifs like its adornment with precious gems and metals, its illumination by the light of God that banishes the darkness of night, and its being the wellspring of the river of life (a topos as ancient as the visions of Gudea, king of the Third Dynasty of Ur, and found in the creation story of Gen. 2 as well as in late prophecy [Ezek. 47] and full-blown apocalyptic [*4 Ezra*]). What is notable is that these motifs are redirected from a celestial setting and integrated into a temple situated amid the political structures of this world: "The nations will walk by its light, and the kings of the earth will bring their glory into it. . . . People will bring into it the glory and honor of the nations" (Rev. 21:24, 26).[8]

---

6. The sea referred to is the primordial sea from which arose the Beast (Rev. 13:1–4; cf. Dan. 7:1–8).

7. Dieter Georgi, b-greek-digest V1 #767 – Ibiblio, cited by Pat Tiller in a note dated June 28, 1995.

8. Cf. Isa. 60:1–3; Zech. 8:20–23.

The picture thus painted is one of restoration of God's creation to its intended integrity and purity (*shalom*). As in the eschatological vision of Isaiah 51:9–11, "nothing unclean will enter it," and true to the prophecy of Isaiah 2, Isaiah 60, and Zechariah 8, it will be the destination not only for the twelve tribes of Israel (Rev. 21:12), but pilgrims from all nations (Rev. 21:24). It is quite astonishing that a book that has been the most frequently cited source of otherworldly visions of spiritual destiny unfolds for the careful reader an outline of a world order in which the monstrous beasts of imperial power and economic exploitation would be replaced by the universal harmony and righteousness that arises when God renews God's covenant with mortals and dwells with them as their God. The sorrow and pain of persecution would be replaced with rejoicing over the marriage of the Lamb and his bride, the Holy City, Jerusalem. It was the day celebrated by the psalmists and glimpsed by the prophets. It was the inauguration of the era Jesus described in his parables and prayed for when he addressed his Father, "Thy kingdom come, thy will be done, on earth as it is in heaven." It remains the day that people of faith still long for and that their prophets still hold before them when they grow weary and discouraged. "I have a dream," one of those prophets proclaimed. Martin Luther King's words lead to the question of contemporary relevance.

THE CONTEMPORARY SIGNIFICANCE OF THE BOOK OF REVELATION'S APOCALYPTIC POLITICAL MODEL

For nearly two millennia, the book of Revelation has evoked extreme responses. It has provided the impetus for uprisings against ruling authorities. It has led sectarian enclaves to divest themselves of all earthly goods, in anticipation of God's destruction of the present order and creation of "a new heaven and a new earth." It has evoked cautionary comment from reformers like Martin Luther and denunciation from Enlightenment philosophers like Immanuel Kant. But the same book also has provided an oasis of refuge and support for modern pastors and martyrs like Hanns Lilje and Dietrich Bonhoeffer. If ever there were a situation in which the biblical exegete felt the need for guidance from the angel who originally opened up the heavens for John of Patmos, it would be in the struggle to understand the riddles of the book of Revelation!

Above we have noted dangers inherent in interpretations that fail to follow hermeneutical guidelines appropriate for such a cryptic work, guidelines such as situating the book in its original setting, exercising care in grasping the nature and function of its mythical symbols and images, and following the steps necessary for discerning the contemporary meaning of a work remotely situated in historical time and cognitive space.

Sufficient scholarship has already been devoted to deconstructing the bizarre apocalyptic world-conflagration scenarios of Hal Lindsey and Tim LaHaye and the tragic paranoid actions of Jim Jones and David Koresh to obviate the need for further critique. More productive for our purposes is the effort to locate within the book of Revelation itself the foundation stones for an interpretation that is faithful to the overarching biblical story and responsible in relation to the wider world of politics within which people of faith live and on behalf of which they are called to serve.

As was the case with each of the other biblical writings we have studied, it is important to begin with an understanding of historical setting and original message. The reason for this starting point stems from the intrinsic nature of Jewish and Christian Scripture. Each writing reflects a particular historical situation and articulates the message of a person or community inspired to communicate its understanding of God's word and will for the audience.

This historical understanding exercises a restraining effect on the interpreter's imagination. The words of Scripture are crafted by humans within the linguistic and ideational settings of their time; that is, they are neither timeless nor applicable without attention to the complex hermeneutical process involved in the transfer of meaning from the world of the Bible to the world of the interpreter.[9]

Specifically with regard to political strategies, the vast range of circumstances addressed within the writings of the Bible itself precludes the possibility of a single biblical model (e.g., accommodation) applying to all contemporary political settings. Stated more theoretically, there is no one normative archetypal human condition for which a political strategy could be devised and then made available for all subsequent generations. History is marked by change, and even at one given point in time, human circumstances vary greatly, for example, the circumstances of a patrician senator in Rome and a Jewish tent maker in Smyrna in 198 CE, or of a peasant farmer in North Korea and a cattle rancher in North Dakota in the year 2014.

Adding to the interpretive challenge is another disjunction, that involving comprehensive conceptions or worldviews. In antiquity, the boundary religious people perceived between their human habitation and the transcendent realm was more porous than it is for most religious people today. The language the former used to describe the relations between earth and heaven derived largely from myth, a world filled with pernicious beasts and dragons as well as beneficent patrons and their hosts. Granted, there are people today who view the universe in a similar way, and among them one finds individuals who ensconce themselves within a communal compound and await superterrestrial beings to spirit them away in a flying saucer or to intervene on their behalf by fending off federal authorities and initiating an end-time battle between a government perceived to be evil and God's chosen branch. In other words, we must acknowledge that a literal interpretation of the mythical images of Revelation and Daniel still comports with the worldview of some people. But on moral grounds we feel obliged to refute such literal interpretation when it functions to incite wanton violence

---

9. In Martin Luther's terminology, the words of the Bible are *verba* that become *scriptura* in the sermon, through the inspiration of the Holy Spirit.

and inhumane abuse that contradict moral principles central to biblical teaching and values shared by fair-minded humans of every race and creed.

We turn then to inquire into the contemporary significance of the book of Revelation for readers who approach the biblical text with a hermeneutical sensitivity to historical setting and meaning, to the mythological origin of many of its symbols, to its location within the larger context of the biblical canon, and to the highly diverse recipient audience in today's world.

The setting within which the ancient writer (John of Patmos) and audience (the churches of Asia Minor) were situated can be described with two key words: the experience of horrendous physical and emotional *affliction,* and *powerlessness* in relation to the structures of oppression that bound them. Though it is likely that the people witnessing the slaughter of their own family members and living with the daily possibility of persecution were not essentially different in their basic beliefs from those we encountered in 1 Peter, the political implications drawn by their respective leaders were vastly different. In 1 Peter we found this advice: "For the Lord's sake accept the authority of every human institution, whether of the emperor as supreme, or of governors, as sent by him to punish those who do wrong and to praise those who do right" (1 Pet. 2:13–14). Within that earlier context Christians perceived opportunities to participate in the civil task of advancing the common good. Their partners in that task were the Roman authorities, from the emperor on down to the local magistrate.

In the book of Revelation, however, the institutions and authorities of state have assumed an adversarial stance: Rome has become the mother of all whores who wantonly slaughters those refusing to worship her and becomes drunk with the blood of her victims; the empire has emerged as the new Babylon, and the ruling authorities, far from being God's appointed agents for the good, have become incarnations of Satan's rapacious beasts!

A situation casting believers into the abyss of unspeakable terror proved to be the catalyst for the rediscovery of a discourse well suited for describing phenomena that cannot be grasped by normal human language, namely, the discourse of myth. In that discourse, Diocletian bore the marks of something far more sinister than a human being of humble origin who rose to be emperor. His application to himself of the titles of divinity was self-incriminating. In the sardonic mythical recasting of his character, he retains his titles of Lord and God, but his subjects no longer are the peoples of a vast Mediterranean empire, but the malevolent miscreants of hell. Similarly, descriptions of Rome as a dazzling capital city or an economic hub of international commerce failed to capture its true character. The coins she herself minted testified against her: She was a whore lewdly sprawling out over its seven hills and enjoying luxury purchased with the lives of its subjects.

As was the case with antecedent Jewish apocalyptic writings like Daniel and *1 Enoch*, the book of Revelation poses an urgent existential question: what power was capable of breaking the dominion of monstrous evil? Certainly nothing within the grasp of the powerless victims of the beast! Even within the orbit of world powers, no army was capable of challenging the ruthless hegemony of Rome. If no earthly power was conceivable, was the situation hopeless? Yes, if it were not for a truth hidden from the eyes of world potentates, but revealed to the humble followers of God's chosen emissary: the saving truth that in Christ's resurrection from the dead God had secured their ultimate vindication through the intervention of a power superior in might to that of the combined forces of the dragon and the beast!

The characters and episodes constituting the archetypal conflict between the primordial antagonists were as well known to those living in the first century as are the characters and exploits of Darth Vader and Luke Skywalker to a generation growing up with *Star Wars*. Whether the conflict myth depicted the deadly conflict between Tiamat and Marduk, Yam and Baal, Hedammu and Teshub, or the Titans and Zeus, the underlying drama was essentially the same, namely, the struggle between contending forces of the cosmos, each determined to rule a universe in which there is room for the dominion of only one of them. Here was a story that was capable of functioning as the etiology of every panoptic conflict.

For those possessing no human explanation for their ineluctable earthly misfortune, the conflict myth offered the most satisfactory source of hope. The human turmoil that was engulfing them reflected a much more encompassing conflict, one of cosmic dimensions. Here was the hopeful part: if a prophet or seer arose who could peer into heaven and witness the unfolding of the phases of that conflict, the outcome could be foreseen. Since the climax of all versions of the conflict myth featured the victory of the side that from the vantage point of the protagonist group was the good side over the powers of evil, its relevance and applicability to the plight of those viewing themselves as innocent victims of infernal powers is not difficult to comprehend.[10]

Equally important to understanding the symbolic nature of the images in the book of Revelation is being sensitive to tone. One fact cannot be denied: the tone is shrill, violent, disturbing, and often excessive to the modern ear. Indignant dismissal is as understandable as in the case of the outrage expressed in Psalm 137 against a previous transgressor of the Holy City: "Happy shall they be who take your little ones and dash them against the rock!" How does the student of Hebrew Scripture reconcile such an inverted beatitude with the God remembered for his love and compassion on behalf of helpless mothers and their children? How can the Beatitudes, "blessed are the poor, hungry, sorrowful," proclaimed by the one anointed by God to redeem Israel and inaugurate the kingdom of *shalom* embracing all nations, be reconciled with the violence of a Messiah slaughtering his enemies and casting the victims into a lake of eternal sulfur and fire? Without an understanding of the physical pain and mental anguish of those contending with unbearable and, in human terms, incomprehensible suffering, in other words, without a situation-specific sensitivity to the

10. The dualism implicit in the conflict myth comes to expression in various polarities, e.g., light/darkness, order/chaos, fertility/sterility, life/death, sweet water/salt water.

particularity of each apocalyptic text, an adequate answer seems impossible, for the two alternative "solutions" are invidious: either hate-filled vendettas, based on a literal reading of apocalyptic imagery; or, conversely, an indignant dismissal of a three-millennium-long tradition in favor of the purported superior knowledge of the new age.

Even for those finding those alternatives unsatisfactory, the book of Revelation raises serious, if not intractable, problems. Especially given the many violent movements over the centuries that have derived their inspiration from this cryptic book, its graphic pictures are disturbing: pictures of a banquet offering the flesh of world rulers, a fiery lake in which evildoers suffer eternally, and the wine press of God's wrath in which the blood of those being trampled rises to the height of a horse's bridle. But not only disturbing! Do they not stand in irresolvable conflict with the Prince of Peace, who does not allow his disciples to raise the sword in self-defense, but rather surrenders to those plotting to take his life?

As with many other violent sections of Scripture, it is insufficient to ascribe such images to the crude mentality of a bygone age and dismiss them from further reflection. Humanly comprehensible, given the extremity of the suffering of the helpless victims, yes! But more must be said in response to conscientious readers who are baffled with the question of the contemporary relevance of many troubling parts of the Bible.

An important clue that emerges from a close reading of the text is this: the genre of the conflict myth that furnishes the narrative structure, as well as the violent characters and images of the book, is not preserved intact, but is infiltrated by a countertheme that ruptures the mythic scenario. While the conflict scenes often depict dragon slayer and evil opponents in deadly conflict, another character emerges as the more significant instrument of God's saving activity. This is the Lamb, the nature of whose power is quite the opposite of that of the hero wielding his sword from a white steed. The power of the Lamb resides in perseverance and a willingness to suffer and die for those in solidarity with whom he has entered the world. Complementing the image of the Lamb is the child born of a woman clothed with the sun, both of them pursued by the dragon intent on devouring them and all those who remain faithful to God's commandments. Stalked, hunted, and slain, the one anointed by God to deliver the righteous victims of the devil's fury does not respond in kind, but with an alternative power derived from the one true God. The primary venue for this deliverer's activity is not the field of military conflict, but the company of those who refuse to worship the beast. For them, the Lamb surrenders to the enemy, only to be vindicated by God in the resurrection.

A tensive dimension thus enters the drama through the intertwining of two stage settings, the heavenly battlefield and the heavenly throne room. The book pays attention to each, and each addresses aspects of the plight of persecuted believers. The throne room emerges as the master image, for it is in the throne room that the martyrs join the angels gathered around the Almighty to sing their Hallelujahs, affirming their central confession in God's unrivaled sovereignty:

"The kingdom of the world has become the kingdom of our Lord and of his Messiah, and he will reign forever and ever" (Rev. 11:15). It is in the throne room that preparation is made for the renewal of the covenant through the wedding of the Lamb and the bride (Rev. 19:5–8). Finally, it is from the throne room that the bride, the New Jerusalem, descends to earth to become God's dwelling place with his people (Rev. 21:2).

It would not be possible to speak as we have of a master image, apart from the religious tradition that shaped the understanding of author and audience alike, namely, the centuries-long, identity-shaping story of the relationship between a loving Father and his oft-straying children: God's deliverance of slaves from the wrath of the pharaoh, God's restoration of exiles from their Babylonian bondage, and God's victory over this world's rulers through the saving irony of the cross. The prism provided by the central biblical stories is consistent. Not through human force, but through the gracious saving activity of God, have God's oppressed children been delivered from the oppressor. The scholarly view is thus correct that the book of Revelation commends not violent resistance, but nonviolent perseverance and trust. Above all, it is an interpretation that stands the test of the biblical canon and the central event of the Christian gospel, God's redemption of a fallen world through the gift of his Son.

This understanding of the message of the book of Revelation and its continuity with the gospel tradition sets the parameters for contemporary interpretation. We can identify six guidelines for an interpretation that is both sensitive to the book's original message and responsible within its present-day setting:

1. The book reaffirms the theocratic principle of the sole sovereignty of God as the foundation and starting point for all authentic biblically based political reflection.
2. It proclaims that in spite of the ascendency of evil in the world, the plan that has guided human destiny since the creation continues to do so, thereby assuring those suffering oppression that in the final denouement God's eternal reign of peace and righteousness will be established.
3. The kingdom of God does not nullify the world God created in the beginning, but redeems and fulfills it.
4. While God's upholding the moral foundation of creation necessitates cleansing the earth of evil, the path to the eternal kingdom ultimately is the path of the Lamb and involves suffering and sacrifice.
5. Those confessing the one true God and accepting his call to discipleship will cherish worship as their quintessential act and Scripture as their source of identity.
6. In community with all believers, the faithful will devote their energy to the compassion, peace, justice, and universal human dignity that are the marks of God's reign and the foundation for a harmony embracing nature as well as all living beings.

Chapter 30

The Politics
of the Four Gospels
and Acts of the Apostles

THE RELATION OF THE FOUR GOSPELS
TO THE HISTORICAL JESUS

In chapter 26 we applied historical criticism to identify within the narratives of the New Testament Gospels the words spoken by Jesus of Nazareth and the actions attributable to him. On that basis we sought to delineate his politics. That task having been finished, however, did not mark the completion of our political analysis of those four books. Like the other sections of the Bible, the Gospels are not lapidary in character, but rather reflect a history of growth, extending from the gathering together of Jesus' own words and narratives describing his activities to the reapplication of those historical materials by followers of Jesus to later settings. That phenomenon of decades of growth of the Gospel narratives has enabled scholars to study the four New Testament Gospels with an eye to discovering the unique emphases and themes of each.

It is not amiss to see in the interpretive strategies of the authors of the Gospels helpful guidelines for our own efforts to discover the significance of the Gospels for our own times. Indeed, we are led to admire the audacity with which they went about their task, for the world they inhabited was one significantly different from the one in which Jesus had lived. It was a world shaken by the revolt of the Jewish people against the Roman occupation, which culminated in the destruction of their temple in Jerusalem and harsh new restrictions on their way of life. And it was a much wider world, for the message Jesus had proclaimed had been carried to lands far beyond the borders of Judea and Galilee. Most significant of all, it was a world changed from within, for they were no longer in the company of Jesus as the original disciples had been. Rather, they faced the challenge of integrating into their understanding of God's saving activity the testimony of those who had experienced a risen Christ and the presence of the Holy Spirit in their community.

In their canonical form, all four Gospels reflect a post-Easter setting. The historical figure with whom the original disciples had trod the paths of Galilee that finally led to Jerusalem, and whose death on the cross they had witnessed, had come to be acknowledged by the generation producing the final form of the Gospels as the Messiah promised by the prophets. How they understood the relation of that Messiah to their own time, however, varied in accordance with circumstances they were experiencing, as well as the particular theological lens that shaped their understanding. While sharing the central confessions of Jesus' role in God's plan for the redemption of Israel, of the commission they had received to proclaim the good news of salvation to all those willing to hear and respond in faith, and of the abiding presence of their Lord in their daily lives and in the meal he had instituted in his memory, the specific shaping each gave to that shared legacy contributes a richness reflective of the creativity, audacity, and dynamism we have noted throughout the Bible.

THE POLITICS OF THE GOSPEL OF MARK

There is wide (though not unanimous) agreement among scholars that the Gospel of Mark was the first of the four canonical Gospels to be written. It reflects a community reeling from the trauma of the destruction of the Jerusalem temple in 70 CE by the Roman general Titus. In Mark, Jesus is presented as God's Messiah, who endures horrific suffering for the sake of a people straying from their ancestral faith. The world in which he faithfully carries out the will of his Father by calling for repentance is a world filled with peril. For this reason Jesus admonishes his disciples to hold steadfastly to the truth that has been revealed to them, namely, the identity of their Lord as the suffering Messiah, but to keep it to themselves, which proves to be difficult from the onset of his public ministry, given the palpability of the events signaling the dawning of God's kingdom, such as the public testimony of the demonically possessed and the physically afflicted whom Jesus healed (Mark 1:34, 43–44; 3:12; 5:43).

Though all three Synoptic Gospels (Matthew, Mark, and Luke) incorporate sayings about the signs of the end time, the so-called Markan apocalypse (Mark 13) stands out in its expression of imminent crisis and in the severity of its indictment of the Romans. For the author of Mark, the key to the trials engulfing those remaining faithful to Christ was found in Daniel 11:31: "Forces sent by him shall occupy and profane the temple and fortress. They shall abolish the regular burnt offering and set up the abomination that makes desolate." Important lessons were to be found in the suffering and persecution endured two centuries earlier by the Jewish community under Antiochus IV Epiphanes, the archenemy of God's people who desecrated the Jerusalem temple and sought through violence to coerce the defeated people to renounce their faith in the God of Israel and to worship pagan deities.

Like that generation, the community addressed by Mark was to be prepared for brutal attempts by a foreign ruler to lead them to denounce their Lord, which would result in beatings, betrayals by family members, and the seductions of false messiahs. They were to endure all of this, solely on the basis of the assurance that all such personal trials and the turmoil of the nations around them were signs of the imminence of their Lord's return to gather and deliver them.

Politically speaking, the Gospel of Mark reflects the perspective of an apocalyptic worldview. Through the messianic mission of Christ, a secret, known at present only by those whom God has chosen as his witnesses in a world overrun by evil, is about to be revealed. The tone is one common to apocalyptic writings of all times: the tone of confidentiality, of the sharing of esoteric knowledge with the elect ("let the reader understand" [13:14]). And the division of the world between God's people and the evil empire represented by Vespasian and Titus, which was about to be destroyed by the Son of Man and his heavenly hosts in preparation for the blessed kingdom, reflect an apocalyptic model of politics. Implicit in this model is a blunt strategy leaving no room for accommodation or compromise with the world powers. Rome and its agents are doomed. The end is near. Nothing can reverse the divine plan that has been set in motion by the birth of the Messiah. The affinities with the book of Revelation are unmistakable.

Reflected is a political situation that reverses both the pre–70 CE custom of daily temple prayers for the emperor, accompanied by sacrifices offered up for the peace and prosperity of the empire, and the cautious approach taken by the historical Jesus to the leading civil authorities of his time. The sense of imminent ending of the normal course of world events leaves its imprint on another feature of Mark's Gospel. Whereas, as we shall see below, Matthew and Luke address the issue of church organization, Mark leaves out of his account attention to the institutional concerns that arise routinely within communities preparing for the long term.

THE POLITICS OF MATTHEW

The author of the Gospel of Matthew shares Mark's central message: Jesus is the Messiah promised by God through the prophets and now commissioned to judge Israel and redeem all who repent of their sins. But instead of receiving a public welcome, the long-awaited Immanuel encounters widespread opposition and increasing abuse. The particular tone that Matthew gives to the ensuing interreligious polemics between Jesus and his interlocutors is harsh. The leading interpreters of the Torah, the scribes and the Pharisees, are portrayed as seeking opportunities to prove Jesus to be a false teacher (Matt. 23), even as the leading representatives of the Jewish establishment, the high priest and the members of the Sanhedrin, are presented as antagonists determined to see Jesus brought to trial and executed on both religious (blasphemy) and political (insurrection) grounds (26:3–5, 47–68).

Matthew aims to prove that Jesus, far from corrupting the ancestral faith, is the servant sent by God to fulfill the ancient prophetic promises. Many of the specific themes woven into the narrative by Matthew reflect a Jewish Christian audience facing a particularly challenging situation. We can begin explicating that situation by contrasting Matthew's redactionary approach to that of Mark.

Whereas Mark launched his Gospel directly with the appearance of John the Baptist preaching repentance and announcing the imminent arrival of the Messiah promised by the prophet Malachi, Matthew first develops a rich narrative background to the core gospel message. Initially, the reader is presented with a genealogy tracing Jesus' kinship all the way back to Abraham and including ancestors as sociologically varied as Tamar and Ruth, on the one hand, and David and Solomon, on the other. The genealogy comes to a conclusion with a stunning revelation: "and Jacob the father of Joseph the husband of Mary, of whom Jesus was born, who is called the Messiah" (1:16).

That conclusion leads seamlessly to an account of the miraculous circumstances of Jesus' birth and the angel's instructions regarding the naming of the child: "and you are to name him Jesus, for he will save his people from their sins" (1:21).[1] Matthew's sensitivity to his Jewish Christian audience is obvious. This is a version of the Gospel that relates to the deepest longings and concerns of a people awaiting their Messiah deliverer. The precariousness of their situation is also obvious. God's initiative to restore Israel runs counter to the grandiose ambitions of the local ruler deputized by the Romans to safeguard their interests in the region. The inevitable conflict leaps to the fore in the episode following upon the birth narrative, the arrival of the magi searching for the king of the Jews. Hearing of this turn of events, Herod is hurled into blind paranoiac rage at the prospect of a rival to his throne. His final solution consists of the merciless purge of all infant males in the vicinity of Bethlehem. The reader would be heartless indeed not to sense in the reference to Rachel's weeping for her children and her refusal to be consoled the dread with which Matthew's generation lived under the Romans (2:18).[2]

---

1. Matt. 1:21. Jesus in Hebrew is *yešuʿa*, which according to this verse is derived from the verb *yšʿ*, to save.

2. Walter Pilgrim described Matthew's world with poignant accuracy as "the historical reality of occupied people, subject to mass terror, innocent victims, harsh taxation, and long-suffering exploitation. It is the reality of a priestly hierarchy clinging to power and privilege, currying favor with

Matthew takes care to point out to his readers that all of these events are in accordance with their Hebrew Scriptures, for example, Bethlehem as the birthplace of Messiah (Mic. 5:2) and Rachel weeping for her children (Jer. 31:15). Moreover, the hasty flight to Egypt and the sojourn there roots the child's story firmly in the Epic of the Jewish people; one could even say that Matthew depicts Jesus' life right from its humble beginning as a recapitulation of the salvation history of Israel.

The typological trajectory that Matthew follows continues beyond his introductory narratives and on into his organization of the received corpora of Jesus sayings. For example, in chapter 5 he depicts Jesus as a second Moses, from a mountain revealing the commandments of God and the new righteousness that is constitutive of the kingdom this Messiah had come to establish.

In light of the controversies that had arisen between Jesus and the Pharisees over differing interpretations of Mosaic law, it is important to observe how Matthew treats this issue, which no doubt was of deep concern to his Jewish Christian audience. Jesus, according to Matthew's account, had come not to abolish the law, but to fulfill it. He did not seek to nullify the commandments but, in the spirit of Jeremiah and Ezekiel, sought to plant them securely in the human heart (5:17–48). For those drawn into the community acknowledging the lordship of Jesus, teaching of and obedience to the true meaning of the law were to be regarded as essential aspects of discipleship. It seems likely that Matthew has his audience in mind when he appends to his collection of Jesus' parables the following saying: "Therefore every scribe who has been trained for the kingdom of heaven is like the master of a household who brings out of his treasure what is new and what is old" (13:52). As Matthew himself assembled a poignant version of the gospel by drawing from the oral and written traditions handed down to him, so too he expected his generation of readers to continue to hand on the treasure they had received in preparation for the return of their Master.

Matthew's emphasis on the teaching function of those constituting the nascent church can be understood as arising out of his profound sense of indebtedness to the Torah tradition of his ancestors. It also reflects another concern. Unlike Mark, who viewed world events from the perspective of a vivid sense of the imminent return of the Son of Man, Matthew envisioned a community that was to be prepared for a delay in the second coming.[3] What is more, diligent training in the rules of the kingdom "on earth" implied the responsibility to develop community structures and institutions that would provide political stability for Christ's followers in the precarious years ahead.[4] Accordingly, Mat-

---

bribes and collaboration with the oppressor" (Walter Pilgrim, *Uneasy Neighbors: Church and State in the New Testament* [Minneapolis: Fortress Press, 1999], 76).

3. The contrast between Mark's emphasis on the imminence of the Parousia and Matthew's sense of delay comes to expression at various points in their respective narratives. For Mark, the end will come within the lifetime of the disciples gathered around Jesus (Mark 13:28–30), whereas Matthew places emphasis on the need for patience (Matt. 24:48; 25:5–19).

4. This didactic aspect of the Matthean Gospel resembles the rules of organization and conduct found in the early Christian treatise, the *Didache*, which was composed roughly a generation after Matthew.

thew expands the compact disciplinary rule in the Q source (Matt. 18:15//Luke 17:3) into a detailed multistage legal procedure to be followed by the church in dealing with wayward members (Matt. 18:16–20). To Simon Peter's confession, found in all three Synoptic Gospels (Matt. 16:15; Mark 8:29; Luke 9:20), that Jesus is the Christ, Matthew adds words that were to have more significance in the development of the hierarchy of the Western church than any other portion of Scripture: "And Jesus answered him, 'Blessed are you, Simon son of Jonah. For flesh and blood has not revealed this to you, but my Father in heaven. And I tell you, you are Peter, and on this rock I will build my church, and the gates of Hades will not prevail against it. I will give you the keys of the kingdom of heaven, and whatever you bind on earth will be bound in heaven, and whatever you loose on earth will be loosed in heaven'" (Matt. 16:17–19).

Permeating the structure of Matthew's Gospel from introductory narratives to conclusion is a theme that is of signal importance for understanding his politics: The kingdom introduced by God's messianic messenger has repercussions that extend far beyond the inner-religious controversies of what in the broader context of Mediterranean civilization was a rather minor religious community. It set in opposition two irreconcilable imperia, the reign of justice, mercy, and peace that the God of Israel had entrusted to his anointed one and the reign of violence, persecution, and terror of the Roman emperor and his local collaborators, Herod and the sons who succeed him, Archelaus and Herod Antipas, together with Jewish religious leaders willing to resort to conspiracy, bribery, and violence to maintain the benefits they could reap from the Roman hegemony.

In Matthew's narrative introduction, the story of the slaughter of the innocents casts a dark shadow over subsequent chapters, and the account of the beheading of the forerunner to Jesus, John the Baptist, who dared to censure the potentate who considered himself above the law that was binding on normal subjects, adds grim testimony to the fact that the wickedness and cruelty of Herod the Great persisted relentlessly under the rule of his son and successor Antipas. The leitmotif of the abuse of power by evildoers and the innocent suffering of the weak supplies a narrative thread that leads ineluctably to the death of the story's hero. Whether that outcome was determined by fate or divine purpose is a question Matthew presses on the consciousness of his readers, for nothing less was at stake in the unfolding conflict than the foundational theocratic principle of the ancestral faith: was the God of Abraham in truth the sole universal sovereign, all the blustering claims and acts of the Roman emperor notwithstanding?

As for Matthew himself, it is clear that he possessed a keen sense of the political implications of the conflict, a sense informed and refined by his having inherited the long line of political theory and practice that had been cultivated over the centuries of Israelite history that we have traced in earlier chapters. In his perception, a profound irony lies at the heart of the gospel story: the struggle between the regnant world empires and the kingdom of heaven will culminate historically in the ignominious scene of the Messiah of the Jews dying on a

Roman cross. Precisely in that tragedy the secret of the alternative to rule by violence and ruthlessness begins to emerge. Though all the legions of heaven stood at his command (26:47–56), the Messiah did not respond in kind to the deadly brute force of this world's rulers, but accepted obedience to God's kingdom and the resulting death on a cross as the path that would lead to the advent of a reign of justice, peace, and prosperity open to all people.[5]

The cross accordingly stood audaciously as a symbol not of defeat, but of the victory of the one chosen by the sovereign of all nations. Lest the central criterion for membership in "the kingdom prepared for you from the foundation of the world" be missed by his readers, Matthew included the dramatic scene in which the Son of Man presided over the final judgment of "all the nations" (25:31–46). That criterion was loving compassion for those considered by worldly standards to be "the least," such as the hungry, the thirsty, the stranger, the naked, and the sick. In the eyes of the heavenly judge, those basic acts of mercy to the humble of the earth were acts done on behalf of none other than the sovereign of all nations. No clearer expression could be given to the oneness of all creation in the new order that had been inaugurated in the life, death, and resurrection of Christ. It was the exquisite secret of the gospel that the apostle Paul expressed in his own way, "If one member suffers, all suffer together with it; if one member is honored, all rejoice together with it" (1 Cor. 12:26).

At the end of the passion story, in which the child king ruthlessly has been hunted and finally killed by the defenders of the purportedly eternal *Pax Romana,* Matthew concludes his Gospel with an audacious claim. The risen Christ assures his disciples: "All authority in heaven and on earth has been given to me" (28:18). On the basis of that authority, he commissions them to bring the good news to all nations. Matthew thus records the initiation of a movement bringing hope to a world grown weary through grinding hardship and calamity, a gentle alternative movement in which the meek of the earth are called to be agents of a peaceable kingdom. The reign of terror of those claiming divine privilege is ended, and the worth and dignity of every individual is affirmed by the obedient Son of Man and his heavenly Father.

THE POLITICS OF LUKE

In his eloquently written account of the life of Jesus and, in the book of Acts, of the activities of the first generation of the church, Luke has constructed what could be called a primer on the politics of the nascent Christian church. It is thus understandable that John Yoder could write a popular book based on Luke's version of the Jesus story and simply entitle it *The Politics of Jesus.*

5. Though Matthew, in 21:1–9, includes the story of Jesus' "triumphal" entry into Jerusalem as well as his messianic title, Son of David, in quoting Zech. 9:9 to present the event as the fulfillment of prophecy, he deletes the phrase "triumphant and victorious," thus placing emphasis on Jesus' meekness ("humble, and mounted on an ass").

When applied to Luke's thought, politics must be conceived of in the deep sense that is appropriate when describing the engagement with the world of any vital religious community, ancient or modern: It is based on the premise—already applied by Paul to the congregations he counseled—that the political strategies guiding a community of faith in its engagement with the broader society and world must arise organically from the attributes and values that characterize its internal life. Those inner values and attributes, in turn, are the fruits of its core beliefs.

Constituting the heart of Luke's core beliefs is his belief that Jesus is the long-awaited Servant Messiah sent by God to restore Israel, a people held captive in bonds that are political, economic, physical, and spiritual in nature. That central confession will infuse every chapter of Luke–Acts, beginning with his introduction to the words, life experiences, and mission of Jesus of Nazareth found in the first two chapters of his Gospel.

In his opening words, Luke informs his patron Theophilus (and by implication his wider audience) that he aims to describe the historical events constituting the life of Jesus as those events had been transmitted by eyewitnesses. In other words, it was within the realm of human history and at a specific point in that history, namely, the reign of Herod, that the meaning and significance of the life of Jesus were revealed.

But to uncover that meaning and significance, his history reporting could not be conducted in the manner of a detached observer appearing on the scene to record the breaking news in Galilee and Judea. What he aimed to produce was not the ancient equivalent to a modern newsreel. Already in the book's first episode it becomes clear that he viewed the material he had gathered from a historiographic perspective capable of revealing the *salvatory* significance of otherwise ordinary happenings.[6]

The first character we meet in his narrative is Zechariah, a priest serving in the Jerusalem temple, whose wife Elizabeth was a descendant of Aaron. While going about his assigned duties, the wizened priest faltered in reacting to an angelic herald's announcement that he and his aged wife were to become parents to a son whom they were to name John. The consequence of his disbelief was muteness. Thus a story dealing with one of the most basic of all life experiences, conception and birth, begins to disclose a transcendent dimension. The appearance of Gabriel indicates that the child born to Elizabeth has a divine calling, namely, "to make ready a people prepared for the Lord" (Luke 1:17). The story is infused with details that tie the birth of John to the history of God's covenant relationship with Israel. Not only is Zechariah a temple priest; he also bears the name of one of the Hebrew prophets. As for his wife Elizabeth, she is a descendant of Aaron. The dumbness with which Zechariah is struck after doubting Gabriel's announcement flashes back to Ezekiel's similar affliction. Most

---

6. *Heilsgeschichte* ("salvation history"), a term used by prominent German biblical theologians like Gerhard von Rad, is well suited as a description of Luke's style of history writing.

important of all, John will be imbued with the "the spirit and power of Elijah" (1:17) as he prepares the way for the Messiah. The climactic turning point in history prophesied by Malachi has arrived (Mal. 4:5–6 [Heb. 3:23–24])!

It is helpful to compare Luke's introductory words with those of the other Gospel writers. It will be recalled that Mark's Gospel opened abruptly with the fire-and-brimstone call to repentance by John the Baptist. On the other hand, the objective achieved by Luke resembles in function what Matthew accomplished by opening his chronicle with an extended genealogy locating Jesus in the long story of God's covenant relationship with Israel. At the same time, however, the inimitable skill of a master storytelling interpreter of the origins of the Jesus movement is evident in the homey details animating Luke's account of Zechariah and Elizabeth. This in turn is quite distinct from the Johannine Gospel's magisterial prelude celebrating Jesus as eternal *logos,* an introduction in harmony with that writer's lofty Christology.

At a later point Luke will return to the life of Zechariah, but true to his aim of an "orderly account," he first records a second birth announcement, focusing on the figure whose superiority over John is already expected by the reader on the basis of the Elijah-Messiah topos. The story develops the mystery of the incarnation (hymnically celebrated by the apostle Paul in Phil. 2:5–11) in the style of another lovely narrative. The incomparable significance of the life of this child is signaled by an extraordinary detail: the expectant mother is a virgin! As for messenger Gabriel, he pulls out all stops when he describes the one to be named *Jesus* (i.e., "YHWH delivers"): "He will be great, and will be called the Son of the Most High, and the Lord will give to him the throne of his ancestor David. He will reign over the house of Jacob forever, and of his kingdom there will be no end" (1:32–33). Here are politically loaded words akin to those that had fomented insurrections among the Jews of the time, for the political environment was of such a volatile nature as to incite zealous nationalists to rally around their respective messiahs in what inevitably proved to be suicidal revolts against Rome.[7] But the narrative hastens to inject a profound irony, lest readers confuse the kingdom Jesus was sent to inaugurate with kingdoms build upon worldly might. It is an irony that emanates through the drafty walls of this "king's" birthplace, emphatically not a palace befitting the splendor of Solomon or Herod, but a stable! As for the attendants ministering to this king, they are not royal heralds and courtiers, but peasants accompanied by their lowing cattle![8]

Mary blends the announcement of Gabriel and the symbolism of the stable into a beautiful vision of the new order to be initiated by the manger king, a vision indebted to the song of her ancestral soul mate, Hannah (1 Sam. 2:1–10). In one deft move she weaves into a seamless fabric the history of God's imbedded action to restore to health and dignity the poor and oppressed of the earth.

---

7. Regarding the appearance of self-proclaimed messiahs during the period of the Roman occupation, see above pages 445–46 and 456.

8. William Chatterton Dix's carol captures the exquisite irony of the birth of this king: "Why lies he in such mean estate / Where ox and ass are feeding?"

The picture given is not of a smooth transition within existing institutions, but of a turning of the tables from which the rich and powerful dined at the expense of their impoverished subjects. The audacity of the vision of the reordering of social and economic structures glimpsed by the lowly handmaidens Hannah and Mary is stunning: "[the Lord] has scattered the proud in the thoughts of their hearts. He has brought down the powerful from their thrones, and lifted up the lowly; he has filled the hungry with good things, and sent the rich away empty" (1:51–53). Mary, as she grows large with the Messiah being sent by God in accordance with a promise reaching back to Abraham, reaffirms the steadfast goal of God's redemptive program. Luke will spend the rest of his Gospel spelling out the specific mandates of that program.

In the meantime, old priest Zechariah has gotten back his voice, which he uses to join Mary in celebrating the advent of the Messiah whom God had sent to redeem Israel (1:68–79). In his iteration of the theme of salvation, he highlights the birth of the child Jesus as fulfillment of the words of the prophets and of the covenant oath that God had sworn to Abraham. He ends with a theme that points to the program that Luke will unfold in the chapters to follow, the theme of Jesus being the guide blazing the path of forgiveness and salvation that the disciples were to take up as their own life mission.

Continuing his pattern of interlarding hymns praising the Messiah with folk narratives locating the newborn within the sociopolitical structures of the time, Luke moves next to the story of the birth of Jesus in Bethlehem and the arrival of the shepherds (2:1–20).

Once again, he builds tension into the story by a jarring juxtaposition: The opening verse of chapter 2 describes Augustus Caesar, the Roman *Divi filius* ("son of God"), issuing a decree that all subjects were legally bound to obey. The registration referred to was the census of 6 CE, which provided the demographic basis for the deeply resented tax system with which Rome financed its sprawling empire and a military force capable of mercilessly suppressing any revolt. In the case of Judea, the regional Roman representative in charge of enforcement was Quirinius, governor of Syria.[9] Encoded in the story is the stinging reality that the parents of the child born as the legitimate heir to the royal title "Son of God" are not exempt from obeying the orders of an imposter who has seized for himself that very title. For readers familiar with their religious Epic, an exquisite truth emerges. By refusing to join the widespread rebellions that broke out in Galilee and Judea

---

9. The account in 2:1–7 offers a vivid example of Luke's sensitivity to the essential importance of human history in the redemptive drama that unfolded in Jesus' life. His reference to the census ordered by Emperor Augustus and administered by his Syrian governor Quirinius may at first blush appear to be a trivial detail recorded by a dilettante amateur historian. Not so! The census was Rome's lethal instrument for securing its stranglehold on restive Jewish subjects (compare the signal importance of ID cards in apartheid South Africa). And it exploded in a full-scale revolt that was ruthlessly repressed by the Romans through a major military initiative, a fact recorded by Rome's historians that held profound significance for Luke, inasmuch as he recognized in the familiar pattern of hegemonic repression of dissidence by a world power the clash between contending *cosmic* powers.

in response to the census, Joseph and Mary in their civil compliance contribute to the undermining of the authority of the spurious "son of God" and to the unfolding of the redemptive plan of the one true God, according to which plan the legitimate heir to the throne of David was to be born in Bethlehem (Mic. 5:2).

The staging is in place for the next story, in which Luke—in contrast to Matthew, who told of the deranged hubris of Herod—tells us of a group of simple shepherds, that is, members of a class consigned to the bottom of the social pyramid, due to their being bound to a work schedule that did not allow them to obey the ancestral ritual laws and observances. The story brilliantly reveals the social structure of the manger-child's kingdom. Shepherds, smelling of the herds they keep, no doubt wearing garb patched with repairs, plain spoken: to the likes of these common folk *angels* appear! Their every response is exemplary of the manner in which humans are to receive the gospel: initial fright, followed by ingenuous enthusiasm, with which they hasten to see the babe announced by the heavenly messengers (the story's implied detail of sheep left bleating on the hillside as their guardians scamper off toward Bethlehem is not to be missed), then discovery of parents and child in the manger, and finally dispersing to spread the good news to the amazement of all who heard.

The concluding stories in Luke's introduction revolve around the circumcision of Jesus and then his temple visit as a twelve-year-old. We are introduced to righteous Simeon, who sings a hymn of gratitude at seeing the Lord's Messiah before his own death and then shares ominous words concerning the destiny of this child: "for the falling and the rising of many in Israel" (2:34). He ends with a shocking salutation to the parents: "and a sword will pierce your own soul too" (2:35). Though brief, Simeon's appearance in the story adds in effect a warning to the reader that the newborn's life will be filled with trials and tribulations. Simeon is followed by one of "great age," Anna, who is described as something of a forerunner to the disciples: "she came and began to praise God and to speak about the child to all who were looking for the redemption of Jerusalem" (2:38). Finally, in 2:41–51, Jesus' Passover visit to the Jerusalem temple allows Luke to prepare the reader for the life of one imbued with knowledge and love of his religious heritage and dedicated to searching its riches in the company of his followers, as well as in disputation with teachers holding views differing from his own.

It will be helpful to ask at this point what the introductory section of Luke's Gospel reveals about his approach to politics. Initially, we suggested that his understanding of the strategies that were to guide the church in its dealing with the wider society arose from the inner life of the community of believers. In other words, politics was to be the public expression of those shaped by commitment to the one they believed was the Messiah sent by God to redeem Israel and to establish the peaceable kingdom. What have we learned from the first two chapters of Luke about his interpretive approach?[10]

---

10. In the technical lingo of scholarship, we are inquiring into Luke's *historiography, hermeneutics*, and *theo-political theory*.

First, it is clear that Luke took with utter seriousness human history as the context for understanding God's redemptive initiative in the life of Messiah Jesus. This he stated clearly in his opening words to his patron Theophilus (1:1–4). For Luke the stories relevant to his account were not inventions or the fictive imaginations of a mythopoeic consciousness. They were based on materials that were "handed on to us by those who from the beginning were eyewitnesses." But Luke also guards against a misunderstanding that stands as the opposite pole to fantasy, namely, positivism, the (illusory) claim that the historian's responsibility is to record naked, objective facts, untainted by interpretation. Therefore he adds to "eyewitnesses" an important qualifying phrase, "eyewitnesses *and servants of the word.*" Luke's nuanced formulation calls to mind the distinction the German language preserves between two aspects or dimensions of history, *Historie* and *Geschichte.* While utilizing all he can gather concerning the happenings occurring in Jesus' lifetime (*Historie*), Luke is not willing to have his *understanding* of those happenings limited to naked facts. He is looking deeper, in search of the patterns of purpose uncovered by *Geschichte.* This said, it is important to repeat that what distinguishes that deeper understanding from fiction is its firm grounding in events transpiring in the realm of human history.

The historical references provided by Luke attest to the firm anchoring of his narrative in the political realities of Jesus' time: "I too decided . . . to write an orderly account for you, most excellent Theophilus" (1:3), "in the days of King Herod of Judea" (1:5), "in those days a decree went out from Emperor Augustus . . . while Quirinius was governor of Syria" (2:1–2). Finally, the most detailed reference introduces Luke's account of John the Baptist: "In the fifteenth year of the reign of Emperor Tiberius, when Pontius Pilate was governor of Judea, and Herod was ruler of Galilee, and his brother Philip ruler of the region of Ituraea and Trachonitis, and Lysanias ruler of Abilene, during the high priesthood of Annas and Caiaphas" (3:1–2). At the same time, the stories thus framed reveal Luke's theo-political perspective. Historical events are to be understood on the deepest level as parts of a drama in which God's purposes, anticipated by biblical prophecy, are being fulfilled. Already in his introduction, Luke has made clear the centrality of Jesus' role in that drama.

With the appearance of John the Baptist, Luke's Gospel begins the pattern of interweaving quotations, narratives, and editorial comments characteristic of all three Synoptic Gospels (similarities with the Gospel of John are less evident). In what follows we shall focus on texts not found in the other Gospels, inasmuch as they give insight into Luke's specific emphases.

After detailing the political situation in the Mediterranean world at the time of John the Baptist's arrival at the Jordan River, Luke follows the general line of tradition concerning John found in all four Gospels. Then to John's call to repentance and the audience reaction he adds a question raised by the crowds, "What then should we do?" (3:10) and a response by John that gives a unique glimpse into Luke's understanding of the social obligations of members of society. John enjoined his audience to share with those in need what they possessed

in excess of their own life's necessities. He admonished tax collectors to practice honesty, exacting no more than the prescribed rate. Solders were to refrain
from using the power of office to exploit others. If one were to extrapolate from
these specific stipulations, one could elaborate a social contract that assumed the
legitimacy of the institutions of human government, emphasized the necessity
of personal generosity among the citizenry as well as adherence to the law, and
finally expected honesty and integrity among the ranks of civil servants and the
military. Even the specific detail about soldiers being satisfied with their wages
is indicative of a broader social phenomenon: dissatisfaction with wages is commonly an abetting force behind public larceny and fraud!

In chapter 4, Luke follows the narrative thread of the other two Synoptic
writers, according to which Jesus travels to Nazareth only to be repudiated by
those familiar with his common family background. Into the framework provided by this narrative he inserts a story that provides a deep insight into his
understanding of the politics of Jesus. Asked to read at the Sabbath service in
the Nazareth synagogue, Jesus opened the scroll of the prophet Isaiah and read:

> The Spirit of the Lord is upon me,
>   because he has anointed me
>   to bring good news to the poor.
> He has sent me to proclaim release to the captives
>   and recovery of sight to the blind,
>   to let the oppressed go free,
> to proclaim the year of the Lord's favor.
>   (Luke 4:18–19; from Isa. 61:1–2)

With all eyes riveted on him, he proceeded to announce: "Today this scripture
has been fulfilled in your hearing" (Luke 4:21).

Luke in these verses introduced to his readers the one anointed by God as
the long-awaited deliver and endowed with God's Spirit to inaugurate the year
of the Lord's favor, that is, the jubilee. Receiving its classical formulation in
Leviticus 25, the jubilee year was the year culminating a cycle of seven sabbatical
years (i.e., the forty-ninth [or according to an alternative calculation the fiftieth]
year) in which the land was to be restored to its divinely ordained wholeness.
After centuries witnessing the violation of the provisions of the jubilee and the
consequent impoverishment of the weak and vulnerable, God's Messiah had
arrived proclaiming "good news to the poor." The Jewish people living under
the deprivations inflicted by the Romans were keenly aware of the social, political, and economic abuses that cried out for redress, but previous self-proclaimed
messiahs and deliverers had only created greater hardship and unrest.

Luke would have the reader imagine the question passing through the audience in Nazareth: "What was the program of restoration that this wandering
preacher had in mind?" Reaching back to his prophetic forerunners, Jesus revived
a vivid poetic picture of the transformative healing that he was anointed by God
to inaugurate in fulfillment of the long awaited year of the Lord's favor: release

of captives, recovery of sight to the blind, freedom for the oppressed, expressed in the language of Hebrew Scripture as *šālôm* or in rabbinical Hebrew as *tiqqûn 'ôlām* ("healing of the universe"). Such a restoration of all aspects of the created order could be accomplished only by God's Messiah, that is, the one commissioned by the Holy One who in the beginning created the heavens and the earth and declared that what he had accomplished was very good. The apostle Paul in Romans 8 had struggled to find words to express the *cosmic* dimensions of the envisioned new creation. As we shall see in the unfolding of his narrative, Luke chose to focus on the *political* aspects of the jubilee in terms of social justice, distribution of wealth, appropriate forms of governance, physical healing, and coping with the persistent humanly contrived obstructions to the fulfillment of God's plan. At the center of his account stands the one endowed with God's spirit and anointed "to bring good news to the poor."

A thematic thread runs from Jesus' reading from the prophet Isaiah in the Nazareth synagogue to his version of the Beatitudes in 6:20–23. In discussing the words attributable to the historical Jesus, we contrasted the "spiritualizing" tendency of Matthew's iteration of the Beatitudes with the concrete social grounding found in Luke. In Luke, the Lord promises the kingdom, not to the "poor *in spirit*," but simply to the *poor!* Relief is promised not to those who hunger *for righteousness*, but to those *who are hungry now!* The interpretive task is not to privilege one reading over the other. The Lord's blessings as formulated in Matthew have served as an inspiration throughout the centuries. Within the context of discussing Luke's politics, however, it is important to hear the clear message of the Anointed One who insists that where God is obeyed, the poor are blessed with all the amenities of the kingdom, the hungry are fed, and the sorrowful rejoice with gladness of heart. But the promise is accompanied by a solemn warning: where selfishness and gluttony rule, divine wrath will enter to safeguard the world from imploding into moral chaos.

At this point we take exception to our method of focusing on passages unique to Luke's Gospel, by citing one that he shares with Matthew, the passage describing the conveyance of the imprisoned John the Baptist's question to Jesus, "Are you the one who is to come?"[11] (7:19). By way of explaining this exception, we suggest that inclusion of a saying found as well in another Gospel can shed valuable light on the theological emphases of an author or redactor. In this case we find an account that extends the Lukan thread reaching from the Nazareth synagogue reading and his version of the Beatitudes to the reply Jesus now gives to his former teacher, John: "[T]he blind receive their sight, the lame walk, the dead are raised, the poor have good news brought to them" (7:22).

Facing death for condemning the adulterous behavior of King Antipas, John in his prison cell likely was pondering, "In a world of impairment, brokenness, hunger, and despair, where is God? Where is there evidence of rule other than that of thugs and tyrants like Antipas? Can anyone point to signs of hope for

---

11. Matt. 11:7–19//Luke 7:24–35.

creation's healing?" Luke was well aware of the propensity of professional sages to search the heavens for signs of the new age; but words that he included elsewhere in his narration, which fittingly follow upon Jesus' healing ten lepers, direct the reader's attention back to earth, that is, to everyday human experience: "The kingdom of God is not coming with things that can be observed [e.g., astral portents]; nor will they say, 'Look, here it is!' or 'There it is!' For, in fact, the kingdom of God is among you" (17:20–21). "Among you" for Jesus meant among the blind, the deaf, the poor, and the dying. The kingdom was found not by searching the heavens, but by paying attention to what was going on across town from you, in the back row of your place of worship, in the homeless shelter or prison compound. This is the blunt truth that people do not like to hear—then or now. No wonder Jesus concluded his reply to John with, "And blessed is anyone who takes no offense at me" (7:23).

Luke shares Jesus' awareness of the resistance welling up in humans to a gospel that identifies God's presence with the suffering and the impoverished. Like Jesus, he does not tame the truth of the gospel. For those who hear the word and follow it, the gates of heaven are opened, but for the many who insist on pursuing the rewards of this world, the glittering signposts they follow will lead to perdition. No genre serves better Luke's purpose of stressing this categorical choice than Jesus' parables, dozens of which he includes, many of them attested only in his Gospel.

A large collection of parables is found in chapters 15–16. The lessons taught by Jesus in that popular literary form function as vivid commentaries on the contrast between the spiritual and moral attributes adhering to God's kingdom and the sinful habits of those living according to worldly standards.

The core of Luke's Gospel that comes poignantly to expression in the parables is in harmony with the other two Synoptic Gospels: the keystone identifying the gate leading to God's kingdom is faith in the one true God, Jesus' heavenly Father. The heart of discipleship is undistracted commitment to the kingdom, as exemplified by the parable of the Lost Coin (15:8–10). As the parable of the Prodigal Son (15:11–32) indicates, the nature of the kingdom is determined by the nature of the king, who is a loving, forgiving father who seeks above all to rescue those of his children who are lost in sin.

However, the love of the Father is not pandering, for it would be the height of parental neglect to wink at the obstacles with which humans block their paths to the kingdom. Chief among those obstacles is a love of riches that becomes so overweening as both to harden their hearts toward their neighbor and to estrange them from their God.

When discussing Luke's understanding of wealth and poverty, it is well to begin with this caveat: Luke neither condemns the former nor valorizes the latter. He peers more deeply and uncovers the most dependable gauge to an individual's ultimate devotion, namely, the disposition of the heart. He records the results of his research in the form of narratives from the life of Jesus and parables that reveal a man who has a remarkable openness to people of diverse back-grounds and who rejects conventional divisions dictated by wealth and class.

In one short narrative vignette, Luke portrays Jesus approaching the wealthy tax collector Levi (5:27–28), enlisting him as one of his twelve disciples, and then socializing with "tax collectors and others" at a great banquet thrown by Levi in his honor, in spite of the criticism this provokes from the scribes and Pharisees. Later he encounters Zacchaeus, described as "a chief tax collector and . . . rich." In spite of renewed criticism from those viewing a sinner like Zac-chaeus as unsuitable company for righteous people, Jesus invites himself to be a houseguest and expresses his admiration for Zacchaeus's honesty and generosity to the poor (19:1–10). The warmth of friendship that Jesus enjoyed at the home of Mary and Martha adds another dimension to our understanding of the ease with which he mingled with people of means: In a society in which comradery was reserved for gentlemen, with women confined to the role of unobtrusive food preparation and table service, Jesus defends Mary's full participation in the circle gathered at his feet and listening to his words (10:38–42). In more than one way it seems that the Jesus portrayed by Luke took aim at the social and religious conventions that divided humans into discrete classes.

While Luke gave a clear picture of the ease with which Jesus mixed with people of means, and the delight he took in their acts of hospitality and generos-ity, he also included parables in which Jesus issued a harsh warning against the spiritually lethal practice of amassing wealth for its own sake. The prosperous farmer, in ever adding to the capacity of his granary, proves his folly by not real-izing the ultimate uselessness of wealth (12:16–21). The man living in luxury who denied the beggar at his gate scraps from his table is graphically pictured suffering eternal torment (16:19–31) and being denied his plea for Abraham's intervention to warn his brothers. Sufficient, he was bluntly informed, were the witnesses to God's righteous kingdom publicly available to all, namely, Moses and the prophets! When it comes down to the rules of God's kingdom, there are no excuses. God's faithful messengers have given clear witness, often with uncanny conciseness:

> He has told you, O mortal, what is good;
> and what does the LORD require of you
> but to do justice, and to love kindness,
> and to walk humbly with your God?
> (Mic. 6:8)

Walk humbly! In Luke's understanding of the attributes of God's people, *humility*, born of the awareness that there is only one entity in the universe wor-thy of unqualified worship and praise, ranks alongside justice and mercy. While Luke includes snapshots of Jesus socializing with individuals of rank like Levi, Zacchaeus, Mary and Martha, more often his companions are folks disdained as outcasts by refined citizens.

"[W]hat is prized by human beings is an abomination in the sight of God" (16:15): strong words attributed by Luke to Jesus! But they are words he has seen fit to include in his version of the Gospel, words supported by parables drawn from his sources. "When you are invited by someone to a wedding banquet, do not sit down at the place of honor. . . . For all who exalt themselves will be humbled, and those who humble themselves will be exalted" (14:7–11). Then of course there is the contrast between the boastful prayer of the Pharisee and the breast-beating plea of the publican (18:9–14).

Luke earns a blue ribbon for preserving Jesus' parable of the Good Samaritan (10:29–37). In one unforgettable figure justice, mercy, and humility merge into a paradigm of godliness. It is not absurd to imagine the good Samaritan leading the ranks of those invited into the kingdom in the final judgment scene depicted in Matthew 25, for he stands as a parade example of the mortal living on earth as a citizen of heaven. What is more, it seems entirely consistent with Luke's politics that he reports Jesus' response to the success of the seventy with the image of Satan falling from heaven (10:17–18). We have seen repeatedly that evidence for the victory of the peaceable kingdom of God that Messiah Jesus was sent to inaugurate was discerned preeminently in the healing of the impaired, release of the imprisoned, feeding of the poor, and the dethroning of ruthless oppressors.

If Luke's understanding of the Christian community's relation to the political realities of this world had concluded with the image of Satan's fall and a claim of final victory of God's kingdom over all opposition, he would have taken his place in the history of early Christianity with the gnostics and other enthusiasts, a position upholding a triumphalistic worldview at the cost of stripping mortal flesh and human political institutions of any religious significance. However, a pivotal text in Luke stands in staunch denial of any translation of the gospel into an esoteric, world-denying cult. Having entered Jerusalem, where in a few days he would be put to a cruel and untimely death, Jesus wept over the city: "If you . . . had only recognized on this day the things that make for peace!" (19:42). Every day of his life had been directed by his sense of having been called by God for one purpose: "Your kingdom come." But rather than instituting the compassion, justice, and harmony of the peaceable kingdom, his life had stirred up the hatred of those clinging to the exploitive political order upon which their lives of privilege and luxury depended. In their judgment, Jesus, the one who denied the legitimacy of unjust regimes, religious as well as civil, had to die!

By bringing his gospel to its high point with the passion narrative, Luke, in harmony with the other Gospel writers, preserved the tensive enigma that pulsates at the heart of the politics of early Christianity. Though not detached from the world in the manner of Gnosticism or the Roman mystery cults, the kingdom of God does not belong to this world, for the lofty institutions of this world are structures, like the tower of Babel, built by humans to assert their reliance on and commitment to no power or dominion but their own. Denounced and condemned by those in authority, Jesus and the alternative order to which he was called could carry on the righteous struggle only by way of death and resurrection, death so as to give proof positive that the kingdoms of this world and the kingdom of God can never merge, and resurrection as God's assurance that compassionate justice would ultimately prevail.

An unusual phrase captures the historiographical perspective that arises from Luke's theology of the cross: "the times of the Gentiles" (21:24).[12] It appears in his version of the description of the end time, when the inimical powers of this world and the destruction they cause would be defeated and supplanted by God's reign of peace. It serves the critical function of setting the time frame for the second half of the "orderly account" Luke wrote for Theophilus, the chronicle of the life of the early church, as it carried on Christ's work in this world while awaiting his return. Luke's understanding of the eschatological location of the church compactly formulated as "the times of the Gentiles" is amplified by Peter in the sermon he preached in Solomon's portico: "Repent therefore, and turn to God so that your sins may be wiped out, so that times of refreshing may come from the presence of the Lord, and that he may send the Messiah appointed for you, that is, Jesus, who must remain in heaven until the time of universal restoration that God announced long ago through his holy prophets."[13]

The church that Luke will describe in Acts lives between the "already" of Jesus' life and the "not yet" of God's completion of God's plan for creation.

Before launching into book two, Luke concludes his first book with a beautiful vignette that reminds the reader that the Jesus story is not an isolated tragedy, but a pivotal moment in the ongoing drama of God's redemptive acts for his creation: "Then [Jesus] opened their minds to understand the scriptures, and he said to them, 'Thus it is written, that the Messiah is to suffer and to rise from the dead on the third day, and that repentance and forgiveness of sins is to be proclaimed in his name to all nations, beginning from Jerusalem'" (24:45–47).

One authorial challenge remained for Luke, the construction of a literary bridge to carry the reader from the story of Jesus and the twelve disciples to the story of the subsequent period in which the apostles continued the work of their Master. He constructed that bridge on two pylons. On one side is Jesus' parting instruction: "And see, I am sending upon you what my Father promised; so stay here in the city until you have been clothed with power from on high" (Luke 24:49). On the other side the instruction is reiterated: "While staying with them, he ordered them not to leave Jerusalem, but to wait there for the promise of the Father" (Acts 1:4).

The plot that unfolds in the book of Acts revolves around the proclamation of the gospel into the wider reaches of the Roman world and the harsh opposition the apostles encountered from both Jewish leaders and the Romans. But before Luke embarks on his description of the politics of the church in its relation to the outside world, he focuses on the politics internal to the fledgling

---

12. This phrase is comparable to words spoken by Jesus in the account of his arrest (Luke 22:53): "this is your hour, and the power of darkness."
13. Acts 3:19–21.

movement and its need to move from being a loosely structured group of devotees, following an itinerant teacher, to being an organized community, capable
of existing within the context of a complicated and threatening world. The dominant models available in Greco-Roman society, such as emperor cult, mystery
cult, symposium, guild, or club, were inadequate for the followers of the Way.
They were to be an *ekklesia,* called together by God to be a light to the world. Its
organizational structure was to embody and amplify to the world the qualities of
the kingdom taught by Jesus.

Luke's commitment to a community organization that was consistent with
the gospel came to expression already in his version of the call of the disciples:
"he called his disciples and chose twelve of them, *whom he also named apostles*" (Luke 6:12–16).[14] The first order of business in this episode was one that
seems very natural for an organizational meeting, namely, appointment of a
new apostle to fill the vacancy created by the death of Judas (Acts 1:21–26).
That item of practical business completed, the scene shifts to high drama, the
enactment of "what my Father promised . . . clothed with power from on high."
In chapter 2, the birthday of the church as a creation of the Father is described
with the theophanic pyrotechnics of Pentecost introducing the promised one,
the Holy Spirit, who would unify and empower the fledgling movement as it
carried the redemptive work of God into the wider world. Peter, taking on the
role of primus inter pares, interprets for those gathered from the wide reaches
of the empire how the extraordinary phenomenon they had experienced was
in fulfillment of Scripture.[15] The assembly is animated with intimations of the
long-awaited new age when Peter concludes: "Therefore let the entire house of
Israel know with certainty that God has made him both Lord and Messiah, this
Jesus whom you crucified" (Acts 2:36).

Following Peter's sermon and in the ingenuous enthusiasm of the awesome
charism they had shared, those gathered moved promptly to enact policies that
translated the heart of Jesus' teachings into community organization: "All who
believed were together and had all things in common; they would sell their possessions and goods and distribute the proceeds to all, as any had need. Day by
day, as they spent much time together in the temple, they broke bread at home
and ate their food with glad and generous hearts, praising God and having the
goodwill of all the people" (Acts 2:43–47).

Up to this point, Luke has described an idealistic community life that could
raise hopes that Jesus' prayer to his Father was finding fulfillment, "Your kingdom come" (Luke 11:2). But that jubilant note soon is disrupted by the arrest
of Peter and John (Acts 4); growing discord within the community of believers, involving the theft by Ananias and Sapphira of what was to be common
property (Acts 5:1–11); imprisonment of other apostles (Acts 5:17–18); and

14. Italics added. Luke's placing "disciples" and "apostles" in apposition signals the importance
he attached to the historical roots of the office of apostle in Jesus' original appointment of the twelve
disciples. Cf. Luke 6:13 with Mark 3:14 and Matt. 10:1–2.

15. Joel 2:28–32; Pss. 16:8–11; 110:1.

dissension within the community between Hellenistic and Hebrew members, leading to a restructuring of leadership into the twelve apostles dedicated to prayer and proclamation and seven deacons serving as manual servants (Acts 6:1–6). Such rapid decline of community life into the gritty stuff sooner associated with worldly associations might well have called to mind the words of Peter in 3:19–20: "Repent therefore, and turn to God so that your sins may be wiped out, so that times of refreshing may come from the presence of the Lord."

Luke the historian, who already in his Gospel had demonstrated the profound complexity and frequent irony of his historiography, again unveils his unflinching honesty and explanatory deftness. What began in Acts 1–2 as a dazzling display of divine power, unifying a linguistically and geographically diverse body and awakening hopes for the final restoration of Israel foretold by the prophets, modulates in the following chapters into the ponderous uncertainty of the in-between times in which the followers of the Way were obliged—at least for now—to live. Troubling, yes, unfamiliar, no; for it was the world of embodied faith in which Luke already had located Jesus.

Another point of contention revolved around the extent to which Gentile male converts were to be required to undergo circumcision. A council held in Jerusalem in 49 CE adopted the flexible policy of exempting Gentile converts from that requirement, thereby removing an obstacle to the spread of the church into the wider world and illustrating that, while muddling through an imperfect world, the early leaders of the church strove to keep their eyes on the moral compass provided by the gospel.

It thus seems apparent that leaders like Peter, Paul, and Barnabas, though faced with what was proving itself to be an flawed embodiment of the kingdom, did not lose sight of its raison d'etre, namely, to be faithful to Christ's mandate "that repentance and forgiveness of sins is to be proclaimed in his name to all nations" (Luke 24:47; cf. Acts 1:8). That mandate brings our discussion from inner-community politics to the second precarious orbit in which the politics of the early church evolved, since "all nations" at that time meant peoples unified under the iron fist of Roman rule and required to submit to the cult of the divine emperor. To proclaim the exclusive authority of a rival king, and to refuse any compromise or accommodation to this world's religious and imperial rulers, was a sure formula for bitter contention. The cause of contention was the same one that distinguished the children of God from other peoples in all ages: "We must obey God rather than any human authority" (Acts 5:29). Throughout all stages of biblical history, the theocratic principle expressed in the First Commandment remained constant as the guide to the faithful community's political engagement and policy. It also remained constant as the source of tension and conflict with the idolatrous leaders of this world and their worshipful minions.

As if in testimony to the eagerness of the enemies of the church to get on with the battle, we read already in the fourth chapter of Acts that the apostles Peter and John were summoned by the Sanhedrin and ordered to desist from proclaiming the story about Jesus. Their reply was unequivocal: "Whether it is right in God's sight to listen to you rather than to God, you must judge; for we cannot keep from speaking about what we have seen and heard" (4:19–20, cf. 5:17–42). They insist that their position was not an ad hoc strategy, but one informed by their deep understanding of Scripture. Through the drama of Psalm 2, they paint a world in which the oppressive kingdoms of the earth and the righteous kingdom of God's Messiah were locked in violent conflict. Though they could have confidence in God's ultimate victory, they must be prepared to live a life of patient endurance in suffering (e.g., Acts 14:22; 20:19, 23).

As followers of a Messiah who had been charged by religious authorities as a blasphemer and executed under Roman law as a criminal, the early followers of Christ needed to be prepared not only for persecution, but for suffering unto death. Among those actively preaching the gospel to their fellow Jews in Jerusalem was Stephen. The charge raised against him echoes the one that had been raised against Jesus: "We have heard him speak blasphemous words against Moses and God" (6:11). Brought before the high priest and council, he refused to recant, but rehearsed for them the great acts of God on Israel's behalf and then accused them of "forever opposing the Holy Spirit" by breaking the law, persecuting the prophets, and slaying "those who foretold the coming of the Righteous One" (7:51–52). He was stoned, "and Saul approved of their killing him" (8:1).

A story about Herod Agrippa in chapter 12 graphically displays the conflict between the wicked powers of this world and the righteous rule of the one true God. After engaging in a series of executions of church leaders, he dons his royal regalia and gives a public address, to which the audience responds, "The voice of a god, and not of a mortal" (12:22). "And immediately, because he had not given the glory to God, an angel of the Lord struck him down, and he was eaten by worms and died" (12:23).[16]

In the meantime the one who zealously had persecuted followers of the Way experienced a call to follow Christ that led to an about-face, from a life as persecutor to a life of suffering and finally dying in imitation of his new Master (cf. Luke 18:31–33 with Acts 16:19–23). Paul thus enacts Jesus' description of the end-time trials found in Luke's Gospel: "But before all this occurs, they will arrest you and persecute you; they will hand you over to synagogues and prisons, and you will be brought before kings and governors because of my name" (Luke 21:12).

A distinct political drama shapes the narrative of the second half of the book of Acts: Paul's proclamation of the messiahship of Jesus incurs the wrath of Jewish leaders, who urge the Roman authorities to have him killed. He is summoned to appear before Herod Agrippa and the Roman governors Festus and Felix, whose personal investment in a case they regard as bothersome religious infighting revolves around their desire to extort bribes. Experiencing the futility of the judicial process on the regional level, Paul audaciously appeals to Caesar

16. Cf. Josephus, *Ant.* 19.343–52.

himself. The hazardous journey on the raging sea simply prolonged the pointless struggle for justice. Roman law on all its levels failed to defend the rights of its courageous, outspoken citizen from Tarsus. As presented by Luke, the composite picture of Paul's experience with the political institutions of his time is thus decidedly negative: futile petition on the basis of his Roman citizenship, beatings, judicial hearings marred by confusion and pettifoggery, years of imprisonment, and ultimately, a total miscarriage of justice.[17]

The picture of Paul in Acts, however, presents more than the biography of one person; it described for the early church the ominous uncertainties engulfing all followers of the Way. Their commitment to the biblical theme of outreach to the Gentiles kindled the ire of Jewish religious leaders, who in turn looked to the support of the Roman courts. The Romans, sensing no imminent danger of insurrection from the rather docile Jesus movement, were reluctant to hand down and enforce harsh sentences. At the same time, however, the gauntlet Jesus' followers threw down, by their insistence on worshiping only their ancestral God, raised doubts about their dependability as subjects in an empire whose cohesiveness was preserved by worship of Caesar. This suspicion was reinforced by the unconventional nature of many of their social and economic practices (Acts 2:43–47) and their unhierarchical concept of community organization (Luke 22:24–27). Though not conducting themselves as belligerently as the Zealots or as nationalistically as self-proclaimed Jewish messiahs like Judas of Galilee or Menahem ben Judah, in a more subtle sense the accusation could be substantiated: "These people who have been turning the world upside down have come here also" (Acts 17:6). The most remarkable thing about Luke's formulation is that it resonated in a certain sense with the outlook of both sides. To the Romans, the followers of Christ were worrisome; after all, they worshiped a king other than Caesar. To the Christians, the kingdom they proclaimed had entered the world precisely to overturn the conventional way of viewing reality. Exacerbating the tension was the fact that the Romans failed to recognize the categorical distinction between their worldly kingdom and the kingdom of heaven announced by Christ's followers.

Summary of Luke's politics

More thoroughly than the other three Gospel writers, and arguably more profoundly than any of the other New Testament writers (Paul included!), Luke, a patron-sponsored historian known only through his literary legacy of Luke–Acts, compiled a priceless compendium of theo-political reflection. His sources

---

17. For a fuller description of what we have condensed into one sentence, see 21:27–26:32. I do not agree with scholars who argue that Luke seeks to give a positive portrait of the Romans, whether directed to a Roman audience (Hans Conzelmann, *The Theology of St. Luke* [New York: Harper & Row, 1960]) or to his fellow Christians (John Riches, *The Purpose of Luke–Acts* [Edinburgh: T. & T. Clark, 1982]). To me the evidence makes clear an authorial position highly critical of both the Jewish and the Roman authorities. See Richard J. Cassidy, *Society and Politics in the Acts of the Apostles* (Maryknoll, NY: Orbis, 1987) and Pilgrim, *Neighbors*.

included the words spoken and the deeds enacted by Jesus of Nazareth, the oral traditions of the first disciples, legends with which followers had filled in details of the life of the one they had come to acknowledge as the Messiah, and, finally, his own editorial organization and literary interventions in the service of constructing an authentic living picture of the one he believed God had chosen to redeem wayward Israel and free the wider world from imposter god-kings.

As is typical of those endowed with uncommon humaneness, Luke inserted no self-adulating accolades into his writing. Though it is impossible to know whether he identified personally with the servant in the short Jesus parable found only in his Gospel, its description of the faithful servant gives an apt description of Luke: "We have done only what we ought to have done!" (Luke 17:10). Luke clearly understood his work as a historian as a task that had fallen to him in service of the truth (Luke 1:4).

Of first importance in grasping the politics of Luke is recognition that he continues to apply to the changing circumstances of history the time-tested theocratic principle affirming sole sovereignty and authority of God. Specifically, in the Roman environment in which Luke wrote, that principle mandated that no earthly power could bind the conscience of the believer. In this, Jesus served as Luke's primary example. Jesus courageously spoke out against the abuse of authority by figures like Pilate (the wanton slayer of Galileans who had come to Jerusalem to sacrifice, Luke 13:1–5) and Antipas ("the fox," Luke 13:32). Even in his trial he deferred neither to the chief priest nor to the Romans. He instructed his disciples to pattern their community structure not after the high-handed style of the kings of Gentiles, but in imitation of their Lord "as one who serves" (Luke 22:24–27). Yet the circle led by Jesus was not a community disdaining the world and avoiding involvement, but finding their priority in care for the sick, oppressed, and hungry, which brought them into conflict with authorities defending the status quo out of self-interest and fear of disturbing the delicate modus vivendi with Rome.

How does Luke's politics line up with the six political models we have discussed in previous chapters? Clearly, the prophetic dialectic model offers the closest match. Luke pictures both Jesus and the apostles of the earliest church engaged with both religious and civic leaders, but in a way consistent with their faith and trust in the God they worship. They neither plot for the overthrow of Rome (the option of the Zealots) nor withdraw categorically from engagement with the institutions of this world in anticipation of the grand assize (the apocalyptic option). Emphatically they reject collaboration with the Romans, as practiced by the Jerusalem temple leadership and many of the members of the Sanhedrin.

The political strategy that thus emerges in the canonical books of Luke and Acts is prophetic engagement guided by the beliefs and values of an alternative order to the customary practices of earthly regimes, an order eschewing force ("it is enough," Luke 22:38), shaping community in a manner consistent with and in the faithful service of the kingdom of God, and amid suffering, persecution, and martyrdom patiently trusting that God's righteous reign ultimately would prevail over all earthly kingdoms.

THE POLITICS OF THE GOSPEL OF JOHN

No comparison illustrates more vividly the theological and political richness that results from the significant differences among the four Gospels than the comparison between Luke and John. Though they share the central Christian confession that Messiah Christ is God's agent for the restoration of Israel and the redemption of the world, they are quite distinct from one another in the way they depict the challenge facing those called to continue Christ's work.

We described the politics of Luke in terms of the theocratic principle as mediated by the prophetic-dialectical model. Human institutions and social structures possessed no intrinsic, ultimate value or permanence, but Jesus, the disciples, and the apostles engaged with them and their leaders by holding them responsible for implementing the mercy and justice of God's universal rule in their structures of government on behalf of their subjects. Guiding them was a clear paradigm of proper governance and lasting peace, namely, God's universal rule as revealed in Hebrew Scripture and renewed in Jesus' life and teachings. To be sure, Luke shared with Jesus and the apostle Paul the conviction that in God's time the transitory kingdoms of this world would be replaced by the eternal reign of the only authentic ruler, but in the meantime, in "the time of the Gentiles," the followers of the Way were to work lovingly and patiently for the healing and well-being of all God's children.

In comparison to Luke, the lofty perspective from which the Gospel of John was written is unveiled in its prologue. Whereas Luke introduced Jesus through a series of stories depicting one of humble birth, John begins with the revelation of the *Logos,* the preexistent Word, through whom creation came into being. To be sure, John safeguards his high Christology against the gnostic (and later docetic) denial of Jesus' humanity by picking up in 1:19–51 the Gospel tradition about John the Baptist and the call of the disciples. But a metaphor introduced in the prologue continues to shape the discourse throughout the book, namely, light and darkness. Known from its dualistic function in the determinism of the Dead Sea Scrolls,[18] it plays a similar role in John, dividing between those who accept Christ and become children of God and those who reject him and incur "the wrath of God" (John 3:36): "And this is the judgment, that the light has come into the world, and people loved darkness rather than light because their deeds were evil. For all who do evil hate the light and do not come to the light, so that their deeds may not be exposed. But those who do what is true come to

---

18. See especially the Dead Sea scroll entitled *The Battle between the Sons of Light and the Sons of Darkness.*

the light, so that it may be clearly seen that their deeds have been done in God" (3:19–21).

The categorical nature of the division brought about by the Word become flesh is explained by Jesus in a dispute with "the Jews." Jesus sets the theme: "I am the light of the world. Whoever follows me will never walk in darkness but will have the light of life" (8:12). His adversaries accuse him of false testimony. Jesus goes on to explain the source of the conflict: "I came from God. . . . You are from your father the devil" (8:42, 44).

What explains the metaphysical coloring with which the theme of conflict has been infused in John? The most plausible explanation is that the division between synagogue and an increasingly Gentile church has grown so deep that the tone of inner-religious polemic seems to have been supplanted by dualistic caricature and categorical vilification of the opponent. John's Jesus claims equality with God; the opponents (no longer Pharisees, scribes, or Sadducees, but summarily "the Jews") accuse him of blasphemy, and the dispute spills over into the political tug-of-war between high priest, Roman governor, and an incited public, with the result that the Son of God, light of the world, falls victim to the hatred of the sons of darkness. But those chosen to be children of God are in possession of the knowledge that the death of the Son was an essential part of God's salvific plan.

What political model is reflected by John's theology? Revealing is Pilate's interrogation of Jesus in 18:33–38, in the course of which Jesus does not deny his royal status, but carefully distinguishes it from conventional categories: "My kingdom is not from this world. If my kingdom were from this world, my followers would be fighting to keep me from being handed over to the Jews. But as it is, my kingdom is not from here" (18:36). Like the Master are his followers: "They do not belong to the world, just as I do not belong to the world" (17:16). That world was doomed to destruction and could be saved no more than Judas, "the one destined to be lost" (17:12). All Jesus could do regarding the remaining time, during which his followers would be subject to the hatred of this world, was to petition his heavenly Father: "protect them in your name that you have given me, so that they may be one, as we are one" (17:11). The life of persevering in this world was merely provisional, a preparation for their final home: "Father, I desire that those also, whom you have given me, may be with me where I am, to see my glory" (17:24).

Since the political climate within which the Gospel of John was written was one of seething bitterness against Rome, often erupting in acts of resistance and even full-scale revolt, it is proper to ask whether the Jesus he portrayed was a Zealot. The precariousness of the situation of the Jews living under a foreign occupation that had a proven record of using the slightest pretense to repress dissidence sheds light on a comment attributed to the Sanhedrin concerning the political liability Jesus represented: "If we let him go on like this, everyone will believe in him, and the Romans will come and destroy both our holy place and our nation" (11:48). To this the high priest Caiaphas responds, "You do not understand that it is better for you to have one man die for the people than to have the whole nation destroyed" (11:50). What on the surface appears to be an assessment guided by realpolitik is interpreted by John as a prophecy of Jesus' vicarious sacrifice.

With regard to Jesus' strategy vis-à-vis the Romans, however, this text comports with the Johannine narrative as a whole in offering no evidence for identifying Jesus as a political revolutionary. He neither resorts personally to violence nor organizes his followers to revolt against the Roman occupation. Those who sought to build a case for treason against him, and on that basis demanded that he be executed, were testifying to their failure to understand the nature of his kingship. But from John's perspective, misunderstanding was inevitable among those belonging to the dark side and was a sign of their damnation.

Looking at the opposite side of the political continuum, is it possible to place John's Jesus under the rubric of collaborator or accommodationist? This is clearly unthinkable for one who viewed the world and its leaders as hostile to himself and his disciples and who was under judgment (9:39; 12:31; 17:9).

Is he then a prophet? Lacking in John's portrait of Jesus is the effort to reform the social and economic institutions of this world or to alter the unjust practices of its religious and political leaders, in other words, the portrait of an Amos or an Isaiah.

Finally, does he fit into the mold of an apocalyptic visionary? This option bears further scrutiny.

In a broad sense, one can distinguish between two types of apocalyptic strategies. On one side is the violent approach of the Sicarii and Zealots in Roman times and suicide bombers (Christian, Muslim, Hindu, etc.) in the contemporary world. They consider themselves called into the holy war of the Almighty to hasten the final battle through which all the enemies of true religion would be destroyed and the faithful martyrs would be transported to eternal paradise. On the other side is the apocalypticism with which students of the Bible are familiar, inasmuch as it shapes the worldview of Daniel and the book of Revelation. Those viewing events from this perspective live with a sense of imminent ending, but what they feel called to is not violence, aimed at destruction of the evil empire, but faithful witness to the sole sovereignty of the God of compassionate justice and patient endurance in the face of persecution.

Considerable evidence in the Gospel of John points toward the nonviolent variety of apocalypticism. It stems from the understanding of the kingdom of God that Jesus tried to explain to Pilate (18:33–38). It is also exemplified by the Johannine version of the feeding of the five thousand (6:1–15). Having been miraculously fed, the people respond in astonishment, "This is indeed the prophet who is to come into the world" (6:14). The concluding comment added by John is revealing: "When Jesus realized that they were about to come and take him by force to make him king, he withdrew again to the mountain by himself" (6:15). In so doing, he made it clear that the yearning of the captive nation for a political Messiah was not going to be fulfilled by him.[19] However, he does

---

19. John thereby distances Jesus from the political messianic ideology of *Psalm of Solomon* 17.

not use his withdrawal as a final strategy, but uses the puzzlement of the people over the distinctions between his kingdom and the kingdoms of this world as a learning moment. Taking bread as his theme, he explains: "Do not work for the food that perishes, but for the food that endures for eternal life, which the Son of Man will give you" (6:27). Then the mystery of his identity is unveiled: "I am the living bread that came down from heaven. Whoever eats of this bread will live forever; and the bread I will give for the life of the world is my flesh" (6:51).

The theo-politics of the Gospel of John does not offer a comprehensive primer for Christians conscientiously trying to live as faithful witnesses to the qualities of the kingdom of God within the broken and finite structures of their society. Neither does it invite followers of the Word to escape into the gnostic's world-denying realm of pure spirit. Though the historical entity of imperial Rome is portrayed through an apocalyptic lens inattentive to concrete details, its reality as a power inimical to God's rule is acknowledged in the crucifixion of Jesus and the persecution faced by his followers. Furthermore, the cause for Jesus' death is traced in John's version of the passion narrative to the acts of actual Jewish and Roman authorities.

We conclude then that the Gospel of John, in its particular way, does enrich our understanding of the life of persons of faith in the world of human governments and religious institutions. It does not place in their hands, in the manner of Luke–Acts, a guide to everyday strategies for feeding the hungry, more equitably distributing wealth, caring for those broken in mind and body, and advocating for those suffering from injustice. Instead, it presents a rich and comprehensive picture of the cosmos-transforming act of God in sending the Word, Jesus the king, who even amid the sufferings and deprivations of this broken world was drawing his followers into the blessings of the world to come.

Epilogue

What Is the Bible's Message for Today?

Our survey in part 1 of the relation between biblical tradition and political process in the history of the United States demonstrated how deeply religion has influenced both domestic and international policy and contributed to the nation's sense of identity and purpose. In spite of the secularizing trends accompanying modernity, the role of religion in political debate and in the wider public arena remains strong. The results are no less mixed now than in previous centuries.

On the positive side is the fact that the passion for justice and equality at home and concern for the health and security of the masses of the poor and suffering in other parts of the world run deeply in the American soul and help shape the country's policies and actions. On the negative side, there persists a sense of entitlement and destiny that often translates on the international level into self-serving intrusion into the affairs of other sovereign states and, closer to home, into a growing gap between rich and poor and legislative hardening along party lines resistant to compromise and vulnerable to procedural gridlock.

Since it also has become clear that the religious arguments advanced in support of political positions frequently enlisted biblical texts for support, the question we need to address in this conclusion is apparent: can the Bible that frequently has been enlisted in defense of unjust and even inhumane practices and has fomented bitter inner-religious conflict be reengaged on the basis of a more trustworthy hermeneutic that provides safeguards against arbitrariness and guidelines for appropriate application? We shall organize our affirmative answer under two rubrics that have threaded like warp and weft through parts 1 and 2 of our study, namely, *story* and *theocratic principle*; we will then conclude with a description of our proposed *theo-political hermeneutic.*

STORY (WARP)

As pointed out in the introduction, *story* as a metaphor captures the Bible's dynamic understanding of the manner in which God reaches out in covenant to humans. Like the dry bones in Ezekiel's vision, divine spirit is breathed into the pages of the Bible when they are read not as timeless, inerrant laws mixed with sundry cosmological, numerological, calendrical, and teleological data, but as chapters of a story recounting the identity-shaping relationship between a loving God and all that God has created. For many, to be sure, a chiseled-in-stone method has a greater appeal than a narrative approach, for it generates an authoritative handbook providing definitive answers to all questions, rather than opening up a living drama that invites readers to lifelong engagement. However, the deity encountered in the Bible is not a pulpited lecturer dictating timeless verities, but a living Lord who enters into the thickness and concreteness of human life and discloses himself as one who delivers slaves from bondage, not as a one-time episode, but as the inaugural event of a lasting relationship, the unfolding of which is recorded in the stories of the Bible.

Authentic biblical interpretation therefore begins not with broad generalities or abstract concepts, but individual stories, for each narrative pulsates with meaning, even revelatory meaning. However, the auspicious dynamic of encounter is lost if impatience to seize a final, immutable truth spurns the caressing intimacy of the *mysterium*, a lesson learned long ago by Jacob: "Surely the LORD is in this place—and I did not know it" (Gen. 28:16).

At the same time it is important to realize that attentiveness to the distinctive meaning of each story does not lead to the atomization of Scripture into a disjointed anthology, but opens up a vast drama. Standing out with particular luminosity in that drama are certain episodes we have designated as paradigms, that is, stories opening a window through which we can discern an ongoing divine purpose amid the flux of human experience. The Passover story in Exodus will serve as an example of a paradigmatic story.

The stage is set in the land of pharaohs with a description of an oppressed, enslaved people. Out of their misery they cry to a God they know only vaguely through their ancestral stories. The compassionate reply that reaches them from heaven inaugurates a new age and a new reality, an age of freedom and the reality of living in a covenant relationship with a God preveniently gracious.

The unfolding of the exodus story reveals the heart of the Bible's historical view of reality. God's reaching into human life to deliver slaves from their bondage reveals the divine nature and attributes:

> The LORD, the LORD,
> a God merciful and gracious,
> slow to anger,
> and abounding in steadfast love and faithfulness,
> keeping steadfast love for the thousandth generation,
> forgiving iniquity and transgression and sin,
> yet by no means clearing the guilty.
> (Exod. 34:6–7a)

To be noted is the manner in which the historicist perspective of the Bible arises out of narrative detail. Beginning in the raw stuff of human existence, the story is moved forward by the divine deliverer reaching into a perilous situation, disclosing his personal identity, and manifesting justice and loving-kindness in saving an enslaved people.

Since every authentic relationship depends on reciprocity, we now turn to the human side of the covenant, beginning with the hymn of praise performed by Miriam and her maidens on behalf of the community (Exod. 15:20–21) as they respond to the saving acts of the one now recognized as the only true God. In this phase of the story we witness how recitation and commitment to memory of the story of God's beneficent acts, and celebration of the divine nature and attributes manifested in those acts, shape Israel's identity as a people. This shaping of character through immersion in the story accounts for the inseparable bond between Israel's Epic and its Torah, the latter consisting of the inferences for daily living drawn by the faithful from the ongoing experience of God in their midst. This organic connection between story and behavior can be illustrated by a poignant example: "You shall not oppress a resident alien; you know the heart of an alien, for you were aliens in the land of Egypt" (Exod. 23:9). To oppress a migrant is not only heartless; it is the *obliteration* of your heart, of what makes you authentically human.

We can conclude our description of the felicitousness of the metaphor of *story* to convey the dynamics of the biblical understanding of reality as follows: each episode arising out of the experiences of a people struggling to shape its common life in relation to its God amid the concreteness of human existence has a particular lesson to teach. But as the chapters of an individual's life disclose threads of meaning that emerge into an identity-shaping whole, so too the chapters of the Bible allow the attentive reader to discern the warp of a purposeful drama from a promise-filled beginning, through stages replete with the tragedy and comedy of human existence, and on toward fulfillment in God's time of the peaceable kingdom.

THEOCRATIC PRINCIPLE (WEFT)

Appreciation of the dynamic function of story in shaping the identity of a covenant people provides the conceptual framework for summarizing the insights gained from our study regarding the Bible's contribution to *political thought*. As in the realm of biblical theology generally, so too in the more circumscribed area of biblical politics, the Bible does not transmit logical formulations lending themselves to a system, in this case a *political philosophy of the Bible*. What we find instead are narratives, speeches, prayers, admonitions, and guidelines arising within a nation seeking to organize its public life in a manner that will enable it to survive within the concrete circumstances of its world, while it remains faithful to its identity as a people called into being by a loving God. Once again careful attention to individual texts leads to recognition of a unifying strand, a *theocratic principle,* the weft in our homespun metaphor. It affirms that there is but one ruler of the universe, whose attributes and commensurate standards of governance are known through his self-disclosure in the events of history. These attributes and standards constitute the ideal that a faithful nation will seek to implement in its ongoing historical task of forging viable political institutions and social structures.

The texts that we studied in part 2 amount to a running commentary on the covenant community's ongoing task of formulating and then implementing the qualities of God's universal rule within the sphere of human history. From the divine imperative to adhere to the theocratic principle arises the Bible's rich body of texts dealing with judges, kings, landowners, peasants, prophets, and scribes. Every lesson reverberating through these texts adheres to a pattern inherent in the theocratic principle itself: since all human institutions are subject to the ultimate authority of the sovereign of all nations, it is the responsibility not only of the nation called to be God's people but of all nations to implement the normative standards of divine governance within the particularities of their time and setting. To this is added a solemn warning: the provisional legitimacy of any government extends only to the extent that it conforms to the governing standards of the heavenly sovereign.

What is created by this melding of theocratic principle and mandate to adapt the eternal qualities of divine rule to the ever-changing circumstances of human history is a dynamic set of paradoxes. The authority of all human regimes is relativized by the only authority that is absolute, yet all such regimes are held responsible for implementing the qualities of the heavenly sovereign's rule. What is more, while human servants of the sovereign one are responsible for counseling and judging their leaders against the normative standard of divine governance, that standard by definition transcends the limits of mortal understanding, giving rise to the unremitting conundrum of discerning between true and false prophecy. There is ample evidence in the Bible of an acute awareness of these paradoxes, for example, in Deuteronomy 18:18–22 the warning against illegitimate forms of prophecy and in Deuteronomy 4:7–8 the emphasis on the only possible source of human knowledge of *torah* residing in God's gracious drawing near to humans.

An understanding of politics in the Bible in terms of an ongoing task of implementing God's eternal rule within the temporal sphere of human history explains the structure of our investigation in part 2, namely, a period-by-period examination of relevant texts. This historical approach was called for by the nature of the object of our research, the relationship between God and the people God called into a living covenant. Because that object is not static, but dynamically moving through time, we were challenged to trace the strategies, policies, and structures of governance as they developed over time, identifying lines of continuity as well as disjunctures. What prevented the unceasing movement from devolving into conceptual anomie was the communal vocation inherent in the divine-human covenant, that is, the injunction from deity to people to conform their governing structures to God's universal order of compassionate justice as it was disclosed to them in the events of their history and preserved in the collective memory of their story.

Not to be attributed to coincidence is the fact that the chronological framework structuring our study of biblical politics in part 2 mirrors the one ordering our survey in part 1 of the interplay between biblical tradition and political process in US history. While the theological uniqueness of the Bible is not thereby questioned, the setting of both narratives in human history enables people of faith to discern the presence of God in the events of the contemporary world as vividly as in the biblical past. The result is that the applicability of the Bible to current events is not mechanical in nature but covenantal.

We are connected to the victims of genocide in central Africa within the same covenant of compassion that bound the Hebrews to the homeless of their time. We know that the cries arising from the homes demolished by a supertyphoon in the Philippines are heard in heaven as urgently as were the cries of Hebrew slaves in the land of the pharaoh. Disturbingly unbiblical, on the other hand, is the rupturing of the tie between our world and the world of the Bible by the myopia of ascribing an order of creation to the world of the Bible categorically different from the one visible to the modern mind. Inherent instead in the biblical understanding of God's universal sovereignty is that it extends seamlessly over all space *and* time.

THE DYNAMIC EFFECT OF THE THEOCRATIC PRINCIPLE: A BRIEF REVIEW

Not to be captured in a blueprint, definitive formulation, or even list of six prototypical models, the politics of the Bible can be glimpsed most vividly as the phenomenon that it is by describing episodes in the historically rooted process of generations of the covenant community implementing their developing understanding of God's universal rule within their ever-changing world.

Respecting the brevity befitting a conclusion, we limit ourselves to six paradigmatic accounts that, as a representative section of the weft of God's abiding presence, will serve as the staging for our final task of outlining a suitable
theo-political hermeneutic.

Already in the period of the tribal confederacy, the identity-shaping power
of reciting stories of God's involvement in a people's history became an essential dimension of Israel's worldview. From recital and ritual enactment arose
the audacious claim that one God alone created and forever will reign over the
cosmos. Thus it was that a unique political perspective emerged that defined a
people in covenant with its God and distinct from neighboring nations and their
purported gods.

A major crisis was precipitated by the introduction of monarchy, for it set
alongside the sole sovereign a potential rival, a human tempted by the luster
of royal ideology to go beyond mediating the qualities of divine rule by claiming divine status and special entitlements. Crisis proved to be the mother of
an important adaptation of the theocratic principle to the new model of government. The threat of an idolatrous distortion of God's exclusive sovereignty
gave birth to a new office filled by an unco-opted representative of the heavenly
king, the office of prophet. In part 1 we noted the perduring importance of this
adaptation of the theocratic principle to a new environment, given the perpetual
conflict between the Yahwistic ideal of God's universal standard of impartial justice and equality and the idolatry of claiming special entitlements for privileged
classes, nations, or races.

Like all else political in the Bible, the office of prophet defies a precise job
profile. Compare Isaiah and Jeremiah, one an aristocrat and the other a political outcast. Prophets, like the stories they tell, are spokespersons of the eternal
embedded in the temporal. One quality alone is shared by all true prophets:
they acknowledge only one absolute authority, the sovereign of all creation,
whom they served in a struggle to preserve the heart of a people that was
endangered by hostile empires, to be sure, but even more by themselves and
their leaders.

For our next example of embedded politics, we jump to the community
struggling to adapt its core theo-political principle of God's universal sovereignty to a series of calamities with the potential to annihilate its identity as
a nation: destruction of temple and royal capital by a pagan empire, exile of
its nobility and upper classes to a foreign land, and finally return to a ravaged
homeland, only to be made subject to another foreign king. Israel, now obliged
to honor a king who attributed his authority to a deity other than YHWH, was
facing a challenge unprecedented in its history, the challenge of reserving ultimate allegiance for its sole sovereign in the face of a rival.

That a viable solution was found is attributable to the contributions of the
prophets to a deepened understanding of the theocratic principle, illustrated by
the following examples. In renunciation of King Jeroboam's idolatrous attempt
to nationalize the cult and silence the prophets, Amos depicted YHWH as the

sovereign of *all* nations who not only delivered Israel from Egypt but "the Philistines from Caphtor and the Arameans from Kir" (Amos 9:7). In Isaiah 44:24–45:7 we meet YHWH the creator and redeemer whose unrestricted authority enables him to appoint the mighty Persian emperor, Cyrus, as the "messiah" who will fulfill his plan for the nations. Within such an expansive vision of YHWH's universal dominion, accommodation to a political arrangement in which a foreign king maintained civil order, while Israel was free to worship and obey its exclusive Lord, was a viable form of implementing YHWH's reign. Here again we witness a changed historical setting prompting an enrichment of Israel's theo-political understanding through adaptation of the theocratic principle in such a way as to enable the covenant community to preserve its unique identity even in Diaspora or as a population colonized by a foreign power. As John Yoder has pointed out, the example of a sojourn people stands even to the present time as a witness against the hubris and triumphalism of imperial religion.

Since our limited purpose here is to illustrate the adaptability to change that was inherent in biblical political reflection and practice, we can skip over two forms of mediation examined in part 2, the "natural law" model coming to expression in Wisdom writings like Proverbs and Sirach and the apocalyptic model of Daniel and the book of Revelation. We turn then to Jesus and the apostle Paul.

In shaping his theo-politics under the master image of the kingdom of God, Jesus located himself in the tradition of the Hebrew prophets. He adapted that image in such a manner as to heighten the tensive relationship between a vision of the fulfillment of God's universal reign ("on earth as it is in heaven") and the provisional nature of God's imminence ("among you"). This balancing of the "already/not yet" provided a robust defense against the idolatrous utopias of false messiahs, even as it spurred the disciples to embody the qualities of God's reign in a world in transition. Specifically regarding the foreign occupation, it allowed him to follow a path of limited accommodation, balancing acceptance of the provisional governance of the Romans in civil affairs with uncompromising acknowledgment of God's universal sovereignty ("unto Caesar . . . unto God").

The apostle Paul's politics was forged within an eschatological tension similar to the one visible in the authentic sayings and parables of Jesus. He introduced a political classification that defines in a poignant way the identity of one who affirms the theocratic principle of God's sole sovereignty, namely, those whose "citizenship is in heaven" (Phil. 3:20). What guides the political engagement of such citizens is the belief that this world and its ruling powers are ephemeral, while the world to come, in which God alone reigns, is authentic and eternal. The result was a political realism that enabled him to adapt his political strategies in relation to the Romans with a flexibility ranging from denunciation leading to imprisonment (Phil. 3:19) to accommodation bordering on appeasement (Rom. 13:1–7).

A THEO-POLITICAL HERMENEUTIC

One task remains: to describe a method of interpretation capable of transmitting the meaning of the Bible for contemporary political thought and action in a manner both sensitive to the intrinsic nature of the Bible itself and suitable for the particular setting of a religiously/philosophically diverse constitutional democracy.[1]

Given the chaotic nature of much that conscientious citizens hear from the halls of Congress, it is not surprising to witness a widespread desire to discover in the Bible the source of an unequivocal, unchanging political truth. Drawing on the imagery of our age of information technology, this would enable us to send through the Internet a search request: *Bible: God's plan for government.* With our cursor we drag the plan and paste it onto a document that then serves us as an e-manual covering all matters of political policy and action and including links offering definitive answers to specific issues like abortion, sexual orientation, immigration.

For better or for worse (depending on one's theological perspective), our study of the Bible reveals not timeless answers but a lively discussion on issues relating to being authentically human and fashioning a common life that envelops all members in loving-kindness, equality, and peace.

Contemporary communities that look to the Bible for guidance and insight are heirs to that discussion, not as passive beneficiaries, but as active participants mediating the wisdom and virtue of our spiritual ancestors to the present world and the world of future generations. The meeting place in which we gather is filled with sacred stories, all of which we are to treat with respect combined with audacity, for the one convening the symposium is the Creator whose loving care for his children enlists them in his plan for universal justice and peace.

Given the living, open-ended nature of our scriptural inheritance, the passive e-manual analogy is inadequate as a medium for depicting our method of interpreting the Bible. We turn instead to an action-filled image borrowed from the world of sailing. Guided by this image, our theo-political hermeneutic will lead us through a five-stage venture involving *a compass, a chart room, a rudder, a convoy,* and *a home port.*

COMPASS (STEP 1)

A ship without a reliable compass is likely to founder. The individual citizen or party engaging in politics without a reliable moral compass will more likely promote social decline than enhancement of the common good. So who in a modern society is the keeper of the compass?

---

1. See "A Five-Step Hermeneutic for a Biblical Based Political Theology," in Paul D. Hanson, *Political Engagement as Prophetic Mandate* (Eugene, OR: Cascade Books, 2010; and Cambridge, UK: James Clark and Co., 2010), 35–41.

The first part of the answer we offer may appear to be complicit in abetting social decline, for it argues that in a constitutional democracy, a claim to the right to calibrate the society's moral compass by any one group, be it religiously, philosophically, or ethically defined, is illicit. However, have we not seen deeply ingrained in the American moral consciousness the conviction that the virtues requisite for the integrity and strength of a nation do not arise spontaneously from human nature, but require cultivation? In replying in the affirmative, we may seem to be introducing a contradiction, or at least a conundrum, for our question takes on an added dimension of complexity, "Is *anyone* in the society qualified to serve as keeper of the moral compass?"

Our reply that *all* of the constituent religious/philosophical/ethical groups in the society are responsible may seem to address the constitutional issue, but confound the moral dimension of the discussion by raising the specter of ethical relativism, that is, a compass spinning endlessly in all directions at once.

The caveat is serious and calls for a credible answer, and while the lively debate between neo-Kantian, communitarian, and pragmatist philosophers offers assurance that pluralism does not lead inevitably to moral paralysis,[2] the biblical heritage we have studied adds an important insight. The invitation to inclusive participation in discourse concerning the sources of public virtue is based not merely on civility or social etiquette, but more fundamentally on a categorical imperative inherent in the theocratic affirmation of God's sole sovereignty: God's reign alone is absolute, all human governments and political philosophies are provisional; therefore no mortal individual or group can claim more than *partial* understanding of the attributes of God's universal rule that human regimes are to mediate. From this faith perspective, inclusiveness in the debate over public virtue is not the blight of secular relativism but the rediscovery of the political implication of the First Commandment's injunction against idolatry, that is, the confusion of what is human with the divine. Or back to our analogy, since no human is capable of precise calibration of the compass, the input of the captains of all vessels in the convoy is important.

Though conceptually clear, the above description of the theological case for an inclusive form of moral discourse lacks the passion and power requisite to the cultivation of public virtue that we have described through the analogy of *story*: divine and human examples of compassionate justice embedded in life experiences shape a strong sense of identity infused with virtue. The process of character formation arises not out of abstract rational thinking, but from the beliefs and practices of flesh-and-blood communities. So we need to add a living dimension to our description of the moral compass, and in the case of a Christian community this would embrace the sacred stories comprising the Bible, the

2. Though in our case the five steps describing the process of transition from a particular community of discourse to the public forum draw on Christian tradition, the structure of our *theo*-political hermeneutic can be recast in terms drawn from any other religion or restated as a *philosophical*-political hermeneutic. To cite one example of the latter, the function of "biblical tradition" in our hermeneutic would be exercised in the neo-Kantian philosophy of John Rawls by his "theory of justice."

inspired reliving of those stories in sermons, and eucharistic fellowship with the Lord who has called humans into a servant community. This leads as well to an enrichment of our metaphor. The compass modulates in our imagination into the form of a cross. Imagine, further, worship becoming the holy space in which the faith community can calibrate its moral direction in the world more clearly and with a more profound sense of commitment than in any other place.

CHART ROOM (STEP 2)

Important as the transformation of the heart through story and practice is for an individual's or group's sense of moral direction, the process of reshaping embraces the mind as well. Again we cite as our example one of the constituent communities in a diverse society: a Christian congregation, which, having renewed its bond with its source in worship, gathers for study in the fellowship hall or, let us imagine, the *chart room.*

Here the beliefs and values of the faith community are exposed to the enormous complexity and confounding urgency of the needs of society and world. The ensuing discussion is rigorous, drawing on a critical understanding of Scripture and the history of biblical interpretation as well as the church's creeds and confessions. The global horizon of its focus is secured to the extent of its racial, geographic, and socioeconomic embrace. Participants seek to bring to bear on their deliberations the specialized knowledge requisite to intelligent discussion, and to that end they both consult relevant study documents of their own denomination and other agencies and invite into their midst reliable experts. Throughout the process of inquiry and study they dispel any pretense of superior knowledge with humility born of honesty.

The goal of the chart room is preparatory in nature: Drawing on the resources it has inherited, those gathered strive to formulate positions and strategies that will alleviate world hunger, advance the crusade against disease, promote justice and equality, foster peace among the nations, and hasten the ultimate goal of *tiqqûn ʿôlām.*

The last mentioned goal stands as culminating objective and is written in the language of the portion of Scripture the Christian community shares with Judaism for both substantive and heuristic reasons. Translated "healing of the world," it conveys the heart of the Bible's understanding of God's plan for creation. By being written in Hebrew, it reminds us that "chart room" talk is parochial and draws on the intimately communal language of its particular understanding of life's deepest mysteries that is alone capable of nurturing the passion essential to authentic selfhood but is fragile when exposed to the clamor of Babel. Yet the temptation to remain in the warmth of the chart room would be to indulge in a manner denied Peter, James, and John on the mountain (Matt. 17:1–8). For God calls together a people not for personal comfort, but for engagement in a plan for all creation. Prepared with a clearer understanding of the tasks at hand, we thus leave the private discourse of the chart room and make our way to the rudder.

RUDDER (STEP 3)

In the endeavor to contribute from one's own field of study to the growth of a good society and more peaceable world, the benefits gained by the student of the Bible from theologians, philosophers, and political scientists are enormous. To take one example, the writings of communitarian savants like Alasdair MacIntyre and Stanley Hauerwas can kindle one's sensitivity to the profound significance of a community's intimate familiarity with its traditions and practices for its self-understanding, as manifested in steps 1 and 2. However, the challenge presented to a community by step 3, and correspondingly the nature of the help it seeks from philosophy, is directed not toward further enhancement of self-understanding, but toward the desire to share what it can from its own legacy for the benefit of the wider society and world.

This involves translating ideals and strategies from the comfort zone of our own communal traditions and practices into a language comprehensible to the other communities populating a diverse society. Expressed within the frame of our metaphor, the question reads, what philosophical perspective will enable us to trim the rudder in such a manner as to carry our cargo from home port into less familiar waters and hopefully into constructive contact with the other vessels encountered? Though the clear beacon of John Rawls's goal of defining a universal theory of justice as the foundation of civil harmony serves to urge communities of all persuasions to persevere in the search for truth, the more down-to-earth pragmatism of Jeffrey Stout offers a practical program for uniting a cacophony of world visions into a productive plan of action. What it calls for in a world in which widespread agreement in the areas of metaphysics and meta-ethics is impossible to reach is a more modest agenda, which can be described thus: (1) It invites participants of all persuasions to contribute to public discourse views, drawn from their deepest convictions and values, with the only condition that they be as attentive and respectful of the views of others as they desire others to be of theirs. (2) The participants commit themselves to defining reasonable goals and then working together to achieve them.

CONVOY (STEP 4)

Our ship has joined a convoy comprising ships from different ports of origin, each guided by a compass calibrated and a chart drawn by the wisest of their officers and a rudder trimmed for progress toward the final destination. The ensuing interaction between the ships is not predetermined. Different scenarios are possible. Since each crew deems its cargo of great value and perhaps more precious than that borne by any other ship, one option is to view the other vessels as likely hostile and justifying preemptive fire. Another option is to seek to establish contact aimed at clarifying their origins, cargoes, and destinations. The outcomes of the two strategies are diametric, the former leading to widespread destruction benefiting none, the latter to discovery that all are trying to reach the same distant and elusive harbor and that the likelihood of success is greatly enhanced by the free flow of communication and the sharing of information regarding the most favorable winds, the location of dangerous shoals, and the hideaway coves of pirates.

We concluded our historical survey in part 1 with the deplorable picture of a nation following the former option of lack of genuine communication and hostility, leading to great damage to political process and ultimately to the health of the nation. Accompanying the mood of cynicism and partisan warfare is a cry from the broader public for a restoration of healthy political process. This is the aim of step 4.

The prerequisite for constructive public discourse is not the exclusion of values and beliefs rooted deeply in the identity-shaping traditions and practices of the diverse communities constituting a modern society. Contrariwise, the wide array of such values and beliefs is celebrated as an irreplaceable asset in the kind of robust discussion that can forge long-range solutions to the most intransigent domestic and international problems. But such discussion is not for the pettyminded or faint-hearted. It requires leaders and a supporting public that can clarify goals and then subsume lesser objectives, like party ideological supremacy and victory in the next election, to the give-and-take (yes, compromise) that gets the res publica back on a course of rebuilding the commonwealth.

At this point we cannot ignore the role religion has played in the realm of public discourse. In any period of the nation's history it would be difficult to determine whether the influence of religious leaders and groups has weighed in more heavily in support of option one or option two. Within the guidelines of our theo-political hermeneutic, the case has been made that the Bible's central theo-political principle of God's sovereign rule nullifies as idolatrous any group's claim to absolute truth and authority. From the First Commandment then we derive the theological argument for the inclusive approach to public debate as the one most consonant with biblical faith. This is not to deny the importance of the arguments for such debate deriving from other philosophies or religions, for example, practical reasoning, civil decorum, and humanistic sensitivities. As stated in the introduction, the tent is wide that welcomes fair-minded citizens of all persuasion to goal-oriented political discourse, and written into the historical identity of the Christian community is the mandate to join the common cause.

HOME PORT (STEP 5)

Step 5 functions to restrain the common inclination of social reformers to confuse their achievements with the final goal of human history, the reign of universal peace and justice. Such human utopian dreams inevitably collapse amid the ruins of war, economic depression, or urban decay. Inordinate trust in the ability of humans to build the perfect society and world order commonly yields to cynicism and despair.

We have found that the biblical antidote to political hubris again arises out of its core theo-political principle: humans are incapable of building or even predicting the advent of the perfect society. To them is assigned the provisional work of living in an imperfect order as citizens of heaven who embody the qualities of the kingdom to come. It is a work they can carry on courageously even in the face of failure, for "faith is the assurance of things hoped for, the conviction of things not seen" (Heb. 11:1). "For now we see in a mirror, dimly, but then we will see face to face" (1 Cor. 13:12).

With confidence then in the plan God has been enacting since creation, we sail on, grateful for belonging to a diverse convoy of fellow mariners and benefiting from calibrating the readings of our compass against theirs, comparing charts, trimming rudders, and peering together through clouded lenses in the hope of finally bringing our convoy into the safety of home port.

Index of Scripture
and Other Ancient Sources

Index of Subjects

659